New York Real Estate

Second Edition

New York State Association of REALTORS®, Inc.
Charles J. Jacobus
T. Melissa Martin

Prentice Hall
Upper Saddle River, New Jersey 07458

Library of Congress Cataloging-in-Publication Data

New York real estate / New York State Association of Realtors, Charles
  J. Jacobus, T. Melissa Martin.—2nd ed.
    p. cm.
    Rev. ed. of: New York real estate / New York State Association of
  Realtors, Inc. & Bruce Harwood. c 1981.
    Includes bibliographical references and index.
    ISBN 0-13-226796-9
    1. Real estate business—New York (State) 2. Real estate
  business—Law and legislation—New York (State)   3. Real estate
  business—Licenses—New York (State) I. Jacobus, Charles J.
  II. Martin, Melissa. III. Harwood, Bruce M., 1941- New York real
  estate. IV. New York State Association of Realtors.
  HD266.N7H37 1997
  333.33'09747—dc21   96-6717
                                                               CIP

Acquisitions Editor: *Elizabeth Sugg*
Director of Production and Manufacturing: *Bruce Johnson*
Managing Editor: *Mary Carnis*
Editorial/production supervision: *Inkwell Publishing Services*
Manufacturing buyer: *Marc Bove*
Marketing Manager: *Danny Hoyt*

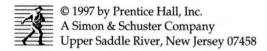

© 1997 by Prentice Hall, Inc.
A Simon & Schuster Company
Upper Saddle River, New Jersey 07458

Printed in the United States of America

10 9 8 7 6 5 4 3 2 1

ISBN 0-13-226796-9

Prentice-Hall International (UK) Limited, *London*
Prentice-Hall of Australia Pty. Limited, *Sydney*
Prentice-Hall Canada Inc., *Toronto*
Prentice-Hall Hispanoamericana, S.A., *Mexico*
Prentice-Hall of India Private Limited, *New Delhi*
Prentice-Hall of Japan, Inc., *Tokyo*
Simon & Schuster Asia Pte. Ltd., *Singapore*
Editors Prentice-Hall do Brasil, Ltda., *Rio de Janeiro*

New York Real Estate is dedicated to my son, Marty Ryan,
whose sweet dreams allowed me time to work on this second edition
and to his Dad, who took over when the Sandman failed me.

Contents

Preface

Under all is the land. This most basic tenet of the REALTOR®
philosophy seems to take on an even more cogent meaning in
New York.

From its sandy and seemingly endless beaches on Long
Island, to the concrete and glass caverns of Manhattan, to the
majestic beauty of its Adirondack mountains, and to its great
falls at Niagara, New York real estate can only be considered
unique. Nowhere in the United States, or in the world, does one
state boast of such a diverse and unparalleled natural treasure.

This treasure has, in turn, been the motivating force behind
an equally impressive genesis of development to meet man-
kind's needs. From farms to skyscrapers and from country
cabins to suburban estates, New York boasts an endless array of
properties to match its natural endowments.

The members of the New York State Association of REAL-
TORS® stand dedicated to meeting the challenges generated by
the land on which we live and work. As a membership organization of over 23,000 strong with representatives from throughout our great state, we take an active interest in its development
and preservation.

To aid our membership and all others who have chosen real
estate as a career, an investment, or an educational study, we are
proud to have co-authored this book. In it the reader will become
acquainted, in a readable manner, with not only the qualities of
New York real estate itself, but also with the laws and methods
of doing business which guide its transaction.

We're certain that you'll find this book informative and we
extend our best wishes that you'll find your experience in reading it a profitable one.

NEW YORK STATE ASSOCIATION OF REALTORS®, INC.

Note to Readers

The authors anticipate that as many women will read this book as men. However, it would make the sentences in this book harder to read if "he and she" and "his and her" were used on every possible occasion. Therefore, when you read, "he," "his," or "him" in this book, please note that they are being used in their grammatical sense and refer to women as well as men.

*　*　*

The forms in this text are for information only and are not intended for use as legal documents. In such matters, an attorney should be consulted.

1

Introduction to Real Estate

Real estate is a unique subject and, because it is unique, real estate has spawned complex legal theories and very unusual fact situations. No two situations are ever exactly alike and the subject never ceases to be intellectually stimulating. Everyone has a favorite story about real estate; it has remained a fascinating topic for centuries. This fascination is what makes real estate such a fun, interesting business.

As a new real estate student, one must be prepared to learn a lot of new concepts, and be willing to commit the time and effort to that end. There are some who say that the only way to learn real estate is by experience. Many years ago this was the traditional concept. Real estate was then considered to be a "marketing" or "salesmanship" business, and experience was the best teacher. Recent years, however, have seen the development of extensive academic applications in real estate education. Real estate has come to the academic forefront—undergraduate degrees in real estate are becoming more common and graduate-level degree programs are proliferating. This trend results in an emphasis on the professionalism and ethics of the new real estate professionals. Unlike many other academic subjects, however, real estate continues to emphasize experience in the "people oriented" aspects of the business. Experience has a high correlation with success in the real estate business.

With these combinations in mind, this book has been written to provide you with an understanding of the basic principles and business fundamentals of real estate. Emphasis is placed on an easily readable presentation that combines explanations of the basic principles of the subject with the "why" things are done and "how" these principles apply to everyday activities.

HOW TO READ THIS BOOK

At the beginning of each chapter (2 through 26) there is a list of the new Key Terms that you will learn, along with brief definitions. Read these before starting the chapter. In the body of the chapter these terms, as well as other terms important to real estate, are set in **boldface type** and are given more in-depth discussion. At the end of each chapter is a vocabulary review plus questions and problems. These are designed to help you test yourself on your comprehension of the material in the chapter you've just read. The answers are given in Appendix H in the back of the book.

Also at the back of this book is a combined index and glossary, meant to reinforce your familiarity with the language of real estate. Terms in this index and glossary receive a short definition, followed by a page reference for more detailed discussion.

Another feature of this book is its simplified documents. Deeds, mortgages, and title policies, for example, are sometimes written in legal language that may be confusing to anyone except a lawyer. In the chapters ahead, you will find simplified versions of these documents, written in plain English and set in standard size type. The intention is to give you a clearer understanding of these important real estate documents.

This book also features a wide margin on each page. Besides its eye appeal, the margin is helpful for locating subject headings and provides handy space for your study notes.

TRANSACTION OVERVIEW

Figure 1.1 provides a visual summary of the real estate transaction cycle. It is included here to give you an overview of the different steps involved in the sale of real property and to show how these steps are related to one another. The chapter where

Figure 1.1. An overview of a real estate transaction.

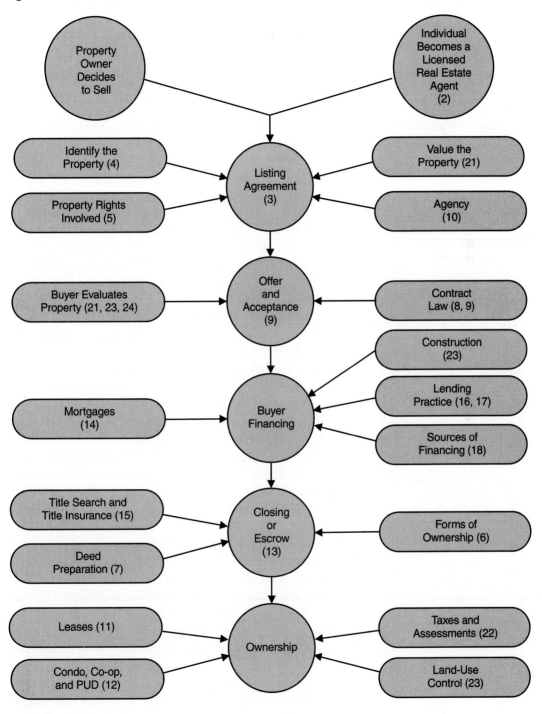

NOTE: Numbers in parentheses refer to chapter numbers.

each step is discussed is shown in parentheses. Whether your point of view is that of a real estate agent, owner, buyer, or seller, you will find the chapters that follow to be informative and valuable.

Chapter Organization

Great care has been taken to organize this text in a manner that will build your knowledge of real estate. For example, land description methods and rights and interests in land are necessary to sales contracts, abstracts, deeds, mortgages, and listings and therefore are discussed early in the text.

Chapter 2 deals with New York license law requirements, how a salesperson chooses a broker, and professional ethics. Chapter 3 examines agreements between real estate agents and buyers and sellers. Special emphasis is placed on the duties and obligations of brokers, and the New York Agency Disclosure requirements are discussed.

In Chapter 4 you will find such topics as metes and bounds and tract maps. You will also find a discussion of what is real estate and what is not, and how land is physically and economically different from other commodities. Having described real estate, the next logical step is to look at the various rights and interests that exist in a given parcel of land. In Chapter 5 you will see that there is much more to ownership of land than meets the eye! In Chapter 6 we look at how a given right or interest in land can be held by an individual, by two or more persons, or by a business entity. Included in this chapter are discussions of joint tenancy, tenancy in common, and equitable distribution. Chapter 7 discusses how property is transferred through deeds and wills.

In Chapters 8 and 9 we turn to contract law and its application to offers and acceptances. Because so much of what takes place in real estate is in the form of contracts, you need to have a solid understanding of what makes a contract legally binding and what doesn't. Chapter 10 concentrates on the law of agency.

Chapter 11 deals with leasing real estate and includes a sample lease document with discussion. Chapter 12 explores the condominium, cooperative, and planned unit development forms of real estate ownership—including timesharing. The chapter examines how these forms are created and the various rights and interests in land that are created by them.

Chapter 13 explains title closing and Chapter 14 explains mortgages and the laws regarding their use. Chapter 15 deals with how a person gives evidence to the world that he or she possesses a given right or interest in land. Abstracts and title insurance are among the topics included. Chapter 16 deals with amortized loans, points, FHA and VA programs, loan application, and mortgage insurance. Consumer issues are discussed in Chapter 17. Mortgage lenders, the secondary mortgage market, and due-on-sale clauses are explained in Chapter 18. Adjustable rate mortgages and financing alternatives are covered in Chapter 19. Chapter 20 talks about state and federal laws that prohibit discrimination in housing and credit.

Chapter 21 explores the language, principles, and techniques of real estate appraisal, and Chapter 22 discusses how property taxes and assessments are calculated.

Chapter 23 attempts to convey a basic understanding of the principles of construction and acquaints you with the builder's basic terminology. It also discusses the New York State Uniform Fire and Building Code and the State Energy Conservation Code. Chapter 24 deals with zoning, land-use planning, and deed restrictions. These are important topics because any limitation on a landowner's right to develop and use land can have a substantial effect on its value. This area has been subject to many changes in New York law in the last few years.

Chapter 25 takes a look at environmental and public health issues, which are increasingly important for buyers, sellers, and licensees to understand.

The final chapter, Chapter 26, explores several pertinent and timely relationships between the value of real estate and the condition of the economy.

Following the final chapter are several useful appendices. These include reproductions of the New York State real estate licensing law and licensing regulations. Following these is a review of real estate mathematics, with explanations and answers. Also available in the appendices are compound interest, present value, and measurement conversion tables. Answers to the end-of-chapter Vocabulary Reviews and Questions and Problems (Chapters 2–26) are found in the final appendix. The Index and Glossary on page 681 may be used as a study aid and as a reference to more detailed discussions in the text. Additionally, you will find a short real estate math review section plus the answers to the quizzes and problems found following Chapters 2 through 26.

The contents and organization of this book are designed for people who are interested in real estate because they now own or plan to own real estate, and for people who are interested in real estate as a career. It is to those who are considering real estate as a profession that the balance of this chapter is devoted.

Most people who are considering a career in real estate think of becoming a real estate agent who specializes in selling homes. This is quite natural because home selling is the most visible segment of the real estate industry. It is the area of the business most people enter, and the one in which most practicing real estate licensees make their living. Selling residential property is a good experience. Entry level positions are more available, and it can help you to decide whether or not real estate sales appeals to you.

Residential Brokerage

Residential brokerage requires a broad knowledge of the community and its neighborhoods; an understanding of real estate principles, law, and practice; and an ability to work well with people. Working hours often include nights and weekends as these times are usually most convenient for buyers and sellers. A residential agent must also supply an automobile that is suitable for taking clients to see property.

In only a few real estate offices are new residential salespersons given a minimum guaranteed salary or a draw against future commissions. Therefore, a newcomer should have enough capital to survive until the first commissions are earned—and that can take four to six months. Additionally, the salesperson must be capable of developing and handling a personal budget that will withstand the feast-and-famine cycles that can occur in real estate selling.

A person who is adept at interpersonal relations, who can identify clients' buying motives and find the property to fit, will probably be quite successful in this business.

Commercial Brokerage

Commercial brokers, also called income property brokers, specialize in income-producing properties such as apartment and office buildings, retail stores, and warehouses. In this specialty, the salesperson is primarily selling monetary benefits. These benefits are the income, appreciation, mortgage reduction, and tax shelter that a property can reasonably be expected to produce.

To be successful in income property brokerage, one must be very competent in mathematics, know how to finance transactions, and keep abreast of current tax laws. One must also have a sense for what makes a good investment, what makes an investment salable, and what the growth possibilities are in the neighborhood where a property is located.

Commission income from commercial brokerage is likely to be less frequent, but in larger amounts than from residential brokerage. The time required to break into the business is longer but, once in the business, agent turnover is low. The working hours of a commercial broker are much closer to regular business hours than are those in residential selling.

Industrial Brokerage

Industrial brokers specialize in finding suitable land and buildings for industrial concerns. This includes leasing and developing industrial property, as well as listing and selling it. An industrial broker must be familiar with industry requirements such as proximity to raw materials, water and power, labor supplies, and transportation. An industrial broker must also know about local building, zoning, and tax laws as they pertain to possible sites, and about the schools, housing, cultural, and recreational facilities that would be used by future employees of the plant.

Commissions are irregular, but usually substantial. Working hours are regular business hours, and sales efforts are primarily aimed at locating facts and figures and presenting them to clients in an orderly fashion. Industrial clients are usually sophisticated business people. Gaining entry to industrial brokerage and acquiring a client list can be slow.

Farm Brokerage

With the rapid disappearance of the family farm, the farm broker's role is changing. Today a farm broker must be equally capable of handling the 160-acre spread of farmer Jones and the 10,000-acre operation owned by an agribusiness corporation. College training in agriculture is an advantage and on-the-job training is a must. Knowledge of soils, seeds, plants, fertilizers, production methods, new machinery, government subsidies, and tax laws is vital to success. Farm brokerage offers as many opportunities to earn commissions and fees from leasing and property management as from listing and selling property.

Property Management

For an investment property, the property manager's job is to supervise every aspect of a property's operation so as to produce the highest possible financial return over the longest period of time. The manager's tasks include renting, tenant relations, building repair and maintenance, accounting, advertising, and supervision of personnel and tradespeople.

The current boom in condominiums has resulted in a growing demand for property managers to maintain them. In addition, large businesses that own property for their own use hire property managers. Property managers are usually paid a salary and, if the property is a rental, a bonus for keeping the building fully occupied. To be successful, a property manager should be not only a public relations expert and a good book-keeper, but also at ease with tenants, handy with tools, and knowledgeable about laws applicable to rental units.

Rental Listing Services

In some cities rental listing services help tenants find rental units and landlords find tenants. Most compile lists of available rent-als and sell this information to persons looking for rentals. A few also charge the landlord for listing the property. The objective is to save a person time and gasoline by providing pertinent information on a large number of rentals. Each property on the list is accompanied by information regarding location, size, rent, security deposit, pet policy, etc.

Especially popular in cities with substantial numbers of single persons are roommate listing services. These maintain files on persons with space to share (such as the second bedroom in a two-bedroom apartment) and those looking for space. The files contain such information as location, rent, gender, smoking preference, etc. Most roommate and rental listing services have been started by individual entrepreneurs and are not affiliated with real estate offices. Depending on the state, a real estate license may or may not be required.

Real Estate Appraising

The job of the real estate appraiser is to gather and evaluate all available facts affecting a property's value. Appraisal is a real estate career opportunity that does not require property selling;

however, it does demand a special set of skills of its own. The job requires practical experience, technical education, and good judgment. If you have an analytical mind and like to collect and interpret data, you might consider becoming a real estate appraiser. The job combines office work and field work, and the income of an expert appraiser can match that of a top real estate salesperson. One can be an independent appraiser, or there are numerous opportunities to work as a salaried appraiser for local tax authorities or lending institutions. The appraisal process is now becoming more complex, however. Most lenders and taxing authorities require that their appraisers have some advanced credential designation to assure an adequate level of competence.

Government Service

Approximately one-third of the land in the United States is government owned. This includes vacant and forested lands, office buildings, museums, parks, zoos, schools, hospitals, public housing, libraries, fire and police stations, roads and highways, subways, airports, and courthouses. All of these are real estate and all of these require government employees who can negotiate purchases and sales, appraise, finance, manage, plan, and develop. Cities, counties, and state governments all have extensive real estate holdings. At the federal level, the Forest Service, Park Service, Department of Agriculture, Army Corps of Engineers, Bureau of Land Management, and General Services Administration are all major landholders. In addition to outright real estate ownership, government agencies such as the Federal Housing Administration, VA, and Federal Home Loan Bank employ thousands of real estate specialists to operate their real estate lending programs.

Land Development

Most new homes in the United States are built by developers who in turn sell them to homeowners and investors. Some homes are built by small-scale developers who produce only a few a year. Others are part of 400-home subdivisions and 40-story condominiums that are developed and constructed by large corporations that have their own planning, appraising, financing, construction, and marketing personnel. There is equal opportunity for success in development whether you build 4 houses a year or work for a firm that builds 400 a year.

Urban Planning	Urban planners work with local governments and civic groups for the purpose of anticipating future growth and land-use changes. The urban planner makes recommendations for new streets, highways, sewer and water lines, schools, parks, and libraries. Emphasis on environmental protection and controlled growth has made urban planning one of real estate's most rapidly expanding specialties. An urban planning job is usually a salaried position and does not emphasize sales ability.
Mortgage Financing	Specialists in mortgage financing have a dual role: (1) to find economically sound properties for lenders, and (2) to locate money for borrowers. A mortgage specialist can work independently, receiving a fee from the borrower for locating a lender, or as a salaried employee of a lending institution. The ease with which mortgages can be bought and sold has encouraged many individuals to open their own mortgage companies in competition with established lending institutions. Some mortgage specialists also offer real estate loan consulting for a fee. They help a borrower choose from among the numerous mortgage loan formats available today, find the best loan for the client, and assist in filling out and processing the loan application.
Securities and Syndications	Limited partnerships and other forms of real estate syndications that combine the investment capital of a number of investors to buy large properties number in the thousands. The investment opportunities and professional management offered by syndications are eagerly sought after by people with money to invest in real estate. As a result, job opportunities are available in creating, promoting, and managing real estate syndications.
Consulting	Real estate consulting involves giving others advice about real estate for a fee. A consultant must have a very broad knowledge about real estate, including financing, appraising, brokerage, management, development, construction, investing, leasing, zoning, taxes, title, economics, and law. To remain in business as a consultant, one must develop a good track record of successful suggestions and advice.
Research and Education	A person interested in real estate research can concentrate on such matters as improved construction materials and management methods or on finding answers to economic questions

such as "What is the demand for homes going to be next year in this community (state, country)?"

Opportunities abound in real estate education. Nearly all states require the completion of specified real estate courses before a real estate license can be issued. A growing number of states also require continued education for license renewal. As a result, persons with experience in the industry and an ability to teach the subject effectively are much sought after as instructors.

One of the advantages of the free enterprise system is that you can choose to become a full-time investor solely for yourself. A substantial number of people have quit their jobs to work full-time with their investment properties and have done quite well at it. A popular and successful route for many has been to purchase, inexpensively and with a low down payment, a small apartment building that has not been maintained but is in a good neighborhood. The property is then thoroughly reconditioned and rents are raised. This process increases the value of the property. The increase is parlayed into a larger building—often through a tax-deferred exchange—and the process is repeated. Alternatively, investors can increase the mortgage loan on the building and take the cash received as a "salary" for themselves or use it as a down payment on another not-too-well-maintained apartment building in a good neighborhood. This can also be done with single-family houses. It is not unusual for investors to acquire several dozen rental houses over a period of years.

Full-Time Investor

Other individual investors have done well financially by searching newspaper ads and regularly visiting real estate brokerage offices looking for underpriced properties that can be sold at a markup. A variation of this practice is to write to out-of-town property owners in a given neighborhood to see if any wish to sell at a bargain price. Another approach is to become a small-scale developer and contractor. (No license is needed if you work with your own property.) Through your own personal efforts you create value in your projects and then hold them as investments.

Property owners who deal only with their own property are not required to hold a real estate license. New York requires any person who, for compensation or the promise of compensation,

LICENSE REQUIREMENTS

lists or offers to list, sells or offers to sell, buys or offers to buy, negotiates or offers to negotiate either directly or indirectly for the purpose of bringing about a sale, purchase, or option to purchase, exchange, auction, lease, or rent real estate, or any interest in real estate, hold a valid real estate license. New York also requires people who manage rental property, or negotiate a loan secured by a mortgage (other than a mortgage banker or broker) and tenant relocators (as defined in Article 12-A) to hold a real estate license.

If your real estate plans are such that you may need a license, pay special attention to Chapter 2 and the material there regarding real estate licensing.

ADDITIONAL READINGS

At the end of each chapter you will find a list of additional readings. These are included to give you a cross section of written materials you may find valuable in furthering your real estate education. Due to space limitations, not all real estate books, booklets, and periodicals currently available are listed in the additional readings. A visit to your local library and bookstores will undoubtedly produce additional real estate material not listed here, and each year brings new titles.

Real Estate: A Case Study Approach, by **William Poorvu** (Regents/ Prentice Hall, 1992, 350 pages). A collection of cases dealing with different aspects of developing, owning, and operating real estate.

In Search of Excellence, by **Thomas Peters** and **Robert Waterman, Jr.** (Harper and Row, 1982, 360 pages). Timeless, valuable, and interesting reading for anyone planning to go into business, including real estate, and be successful.

Principles of Real Estate for License Preparation, 4th Ed., by **Dennis Tosh** and **Nicholas Ordway** (Prentice Hall, 1990, 432 pages). Excellent resource text containing over 1,100 practice questions involving material tested on license examinations.

Handbook of Real Estate Terms, by **Dennis S. Tosh** (Regents/ Prentice Hall, 1992). Contains over 2,400 up-to-date terms and definitions with cross references.

The Language of Real Estate, 3rd Ed., by **John W. Reilly** (Real Estate Education Co., 1989, 630 pages). This single-volume reference book contains over 2,200 of the most frequently encountered real estate terms. Includes basic definitions, examples, and cross references.

2

Licensing Laws and Professional Affiliation

KEY • TERMS

Article 12-A: the section of New York Real Property Law that governs the regulation of brokers and salespersons

Associate broker: a person who holds a broker's license and chooses to work as a sales associate under the supervision of a principal broker

Broker: a person or legal entity licensed to act independently in conducting a real estate brokerage business

Department of State: a state agency that advises and sets policies regarding real estate licensees and transaction procedures

Division of Licensing Services: the division within the Department of State that oversees the licensing process and enforces the licensing laws

Independent contractor: one who contracts to do work according to his own methods and is responsible to his employer only for the results of that work

License revocation: to recall and make void a license

License suspension: the act of temporarily making a license ineffective

Licensee: one who holds a license

Principal broker: the broker in charge of a real estate office

Realtor: a registered trademark owned by the National Association of Realtors for use by its members

Recovery fund: a state-operated fund that can be tapped to pay for uncollectible judgments against real estate licensees

Salesperson: a person employed by a broker to list, negotiate, sell, or lease real property for others

For most owners of real estate the decision to sell means hiring a broker to find a buyer. Although some owners choose to market their properties themselves, most find it advantageous to turn the job over to a real estate broker and pay a commission for the service of finding a buyer and carrying the deal through closing. The next two chapters are for the owner who plans to use a broker and for the person who plans to be a real estate salesperson or broker. We begin with a simplified real estate listing contract. Next we take a close look at the agency responsibilities a broker has toward a seller, together with the seller's obligations toward the broker. Then we discuss seller and broker responsibilities toward persons who are interested in purchasing the listed property. This chapter discusses examination and licensing requirements and gives an overview of how states regulate the real estate profession, including sections on how to choose a broker with whom to affiliate and professional real estate associations, in particular the National Association of REALTORS®.

RATIONALE FOR LICENSING

Does the public have a vested interest in seeing that real estate salespersons and brokers have the qualifications of honesty, truthfulness, good reputation, and real estate knowledge before they are allowed to negotiate real estate transactions on behalf of others? This concern brought about real estate licensing laws as we know them today. Until 1917, no state required real estate agents to be licensed. Anyone who wanted to be an agent could simply hang up a sign. In larger cities persons and firms specialized in bringing buyers and sellers together. In smaller towns, a local banker, attorney, or barber would know who had what for sale and be the person a buyer would ask for property information.

The first attempt to require that persons acting as real estate agents be licensed was made by the California legislature in 1917. That law was declared unconstitutional, with the main opposition being that the state was unreasonably interfering with the right of every citizen to engage in a useful and legitimate occupation. Two years later, in 1919, the California legislature passed a second real estate licensing act. This time it was upheld by the Supreme Court. That same year Michigan, Oregon, and Tennessee also passed real estate licensing acts. Today, all 50 states and the District of Columbia require that persons who offer their services as real estate agents be licensed.

The first license laws did not require examinations for competency nor did they require real estate education. Those provisions came later. The first laws were aimed at weeding out persons who placed loyalty to themselves above loyalty to those they were representing. By requiring persons to be licensed, the state had the power to refuse to issue a license to someone with a past record of dishonesty and untruthfulness. Additionally, the state could temporarily or permanently take away a license once it had been issued. To help make licensing laws work, the state refused to allow its courts to enforce claims for commissions by unlicensed persons. That a real estate license applicant has a good reputation for honesty and truthfulness is still a very important part of real estate licensing today. The New York Division of Licensing Services requires applicants to have a thumbprint taken at the testing site.

Loyalty, Honesty, and Truthfulness

    In the 1930s and 1940s states began adding the requirement of a license examination in an attempt to determine whether or not the license applicant also had some level of technical ability in real estate. Beginning in the 1950s, states began adding the requirement that a person take a certain number of hours of real estate education before being licensed. Today a person who plans to be a real estate agent must qualify both ethically and technically before being issued a license.

In what situations does a person need a real estate license? A person who, for compensation or the promise of compensation, lists or offers to list, sells or offers to sell, buys or offers to buy, negotiates or offers to negotiate either directly or indirectly for the purpose of bringing about a sale, purchase, or option to purchase, exchange, auction, lease, or rent real estate, or any interest in real estate, is required to hold a valid real estate license. Some states also require persons offering their services as real estate appraisers, property managers, mortgage bankers, or rent collectors to hold real estate licenses.

PERSONS REQUIRED TO BE LICENSED

    Property owners dealing with their own property and licensed attorneys conducting a real estate transaction as an incidental part of their duties as an attorney for a client are exempt from holding a license. Also exempt are trustees and receivers in bankruptcy, legal guardians, administrators and executors handling a deceased's estate, officers and employees of a government agency dealing in real estate, and persons holding power of attorney from an owner. However, the law does not permit a person to use the exemptions as a means of conducting a brokerage business without the proper license; that is, an unlicensed person cannot take a listing under the guise of a power of attorney and then act as a real estate broker.

BROKER

Before the advent of licensing laws, there was no differentiation between real estate brokers and real estate salespersons. People who brought about transactions were simply called real estate agents or whatever else they wanted to be called. With licensing laws came two classes of **licensee:** real estate broker and real estate salesperson (for many years called real estate salesman). A **real estate broker** is a person licensed to act independently in conducting a real estate brokerage business. A broker brings together those with real estate to be marketed and those seeking real estate and negotiates a transaction. For those services the broker receives a fee, usually in the form of a commission based on the selling price or lease rent. The broker may represent the buyer or the seller or, upon full disclosure, both at the same time. The role is more than that of a middleman who puts two interested parties in contact with each other, for the broker usually takes an active role in negotiating price and terms acceptable to both the buyer and seller. A broker can be an actual person or a legal entity, i.e., a business firm. If the entity is a business firm, the person in charge must be a broker. The laws of all states permit a real estate broker to hire others for the purpose of bringing about real estate transactions. These persons may be other licensed real estate brokers or they may be licensed real estate salespersons.

ASSOCIATE BROKER

The New York License Law now defines an **associate broker** as someone who has the same training as a broker and has passed the broker's examination, but who chooses not to work as a principal broker, often because they do not want the responsibility of supervising other sales associates and managing the office. The associate broker affiliates with a principal broker and has the same agency relationship with the principal broker as the salespeople.

A **real estate salesperson,** within the meaning of the license laws, is a person employed by a real estate broker to list and negotiate the sale, exchange, lease, or rental of real property for others for compensation under the direction, guidance, and responsibility of the employing broker. Only an actual person can be licensed as a salesperson (a business firm cannot be licensed as a salesperson), and a salesperson must be employed by a broker (a salesperson cannot operate independently). Thus, a salesperson who takes a listing on a property does so in the name of the broker, and in some states the broker must sign along with the salesperson for the listing to be valid. In the event of a legal dispute caused by a salesperson, the dispute would be between the principal and the broker. Therefore, some brokers take considerable care to oversee the documents that their salespeople prepare and sign. Other brokers do not, relying instead on the knowledge and sensibility of their salespeople and accepting a certain amount of risk in the process.

Employing salespeople is a means by which brokers can expand their sales forces. Presumably, the more salespeople a broker employs, the more listings and sales are generated, and thus more commissions are earned by the broker. In turn, the broker must pay enough to keep the sales force from leaving, provide sales facilities and personnel management, and take ultimate responsibility for any mistakes the salespersons make.

SALESPERSON

Of the two license levels, the salesperson's license is regarded as the entry-level license and as such requires no previous real estate sales experience. In New York, an applicant for a real estate broker's license must be a U.S. citizen, be at least 19 years old, and have at least one year of experience as a salesperson or two years of "equivalent experience" as set out in the Department of State regulations.

QUALIFICATIONS FOR LICENSING

Examination of the license applicant's knowledge of real estate law and practices, mathematics, valuation, finance, and the like, is required for license granting in all states. Salesperson exams in New York typically contain 50 multiple-choice questions. Usually 1 hour is allowed to complete the exam. Salesperson exams cover the basic aspects of state license law, contracts and agency, real property ownership, transfer and use, subdivision map reading, fair housing laws, and the ability

Examination

to follow written instructions. Broker exams cover the same topics in more depth and test the applicant's ability to prepare listings, offer and acceptance contracts, leasing contracts, and closing statements. The applicant's knowledge of real estate finance, appraisal, and office management are also tested.

Education Requirements

Nearly all states require that license applicants take real estate education courses at private real estate schools, colleges, or through adult education programs at high schools. Table 2.1 shows the education and experience requirements in the United States at the time this book was written. The table is included to give you an overview of the emphasis currently being placed on education and experience by the various states. For up-to-the-minute information on education and experience requirements, you should contact the New York State Department of State, Division of Licensing Services at 84 Holland Avenue, Albany, NY 12208.

Continuing Education

Licensing authorities in a growing number of states require additional course work each time a license is renewed. This is called **continuing education,** and its purpose is to force licensees to stay up to date in their field as a prerequisite to license renewal. States with continuing education requirements are also shown in Table 2.1.

LICENSING PROCEDURE

An application for a real estate salesperson or broker license can be obtained either in person or by mail from the New York State Department of State, Division of Licensing Services in Albany or by calling the department's voice mail response system at (518) 474-4429. Applications are also available from the department's District Licensing Offices in Manhattan, Hauppauge, Binghamton, Utica, Syracuse, Rochester, and Buffalo. The application is completed and returned to the department with the required fee.

Aspects of the applicant's character are checked and, if approved, an examination date is scheduled. (Some states reverse this and give the exam first and check the references second.) Most states offer their real estate exams monthly. A few offer testing bimonthly or quarterly. Five states offer exams at least once a week.

Table 2.1. Real Estate Education and Experience Requirements

STATE	SALESPERSON LICENSE Education Requirement	Continuing Education	BROKER LICENSE Education Requirement	Experience Requirement	Continuing Education
Alabama	45 hours	Yes	60 hours	2 years	Yes
Alaska	20 hours	Yes	35 hours	2 years	Yes
Arizona	90 hours	Yes	180 hours	3 years	Yes
Arkansas	60 hours	Yes	None	2 years	Yes
California	135 hours	Yes	360 hours	2 years	Yes
Colorado	72 hours	Yes	120 hours	2 years	Yes
Connecticut	30 hours	Yes	90 hours	2 years	Yes
Delaware	93 hours	Yes	168 hours	5 years	Yes
Dist. of Col.	45 hours	Yes	135 hours	2 years	Yes
Florida	63 hours	Yes	135 hours	1 year	Yes
Georgia	75 hours	Yes	135 hours	3 years	Yes
Hawaii	45 hours	Yes	91 hours	2 years	Yes
Idaho	90 hours	Yes	180 hours	2 years	Yes
Illinois	30 hours	Yes	90 hours	1 year	Yes
Indiana	54 hours	Yes	108 hours	1 year	Yes
Iowa	60 hours	Yes	120 hours	2 years	Yes
Kansas	30 hours	Yes	54 hours	2 years	Yes
Kentucky	96 hours	Yes	336 hours	2 years	Yes
Louisiana	90 hours	Yes	240 hours	2 years	Yes
Maine	39 hours	Yes	168 hours	1 year	Yes
Maryland	45 hours	Yes	135 hours	2 years	Yes
Massachusetts	24 hours	No	54 hours	1 year	No
Michigan	40 hours	Yes	130 hours	3 years	Yes
Minnesota	90 hours	Yes	30 hours	2 years	Yes
Mississippi	60 hours	Yes	150 hours	1 year	Yes

Explanation: Hours are clock-hours in the classroom; experience requirement is experience as a licensed real estate salesperson; continuing education refers to education required for license renewal. Some states credit completed salesperson education toward the broker education requirement.

The applicant is notified of the results in approximately 4 to 6 weeks. In New York, a salesperson or broker who has passed the examination must apply to the Department of State for a license. Each license is effective for 2 years. Also, salesperson applicants must name the broker they will be working for. This information is usually provided on a form signed by the employing broker. Broker applicants must give the address where they plan to operate their brokerage businesses. These forms are processed by the department and a license is mailed to the applicant in

Table 2.1. **Real Estate Education and Experience Requirements** (continued)

STATE	SALESPERSON LICENSE		BROKER LICENSE		
	Education Requirement	Continuing Education	Education Requirement	Experience Requirement	Continuing Education
Missouri	60 hours	Yes	108 hours	1 year	Yes
Montana	60 hours	Yes	120 hours	2 years	Yes
Nebraska	60 hours	Yes	240 hours	2 years	Yes
Nevada	90 hours	Yes	1,050 hours	8 years	Yes
New Hampshire	None	Yes	None	1 year	Yes
New Jersey	75 hours	No	225 hours	3 years	No
New Mexico	60 hours	Yes	180 hours	2 years	Yes
New York	45 hours	Yes	90 hours	1 year	Yes
North Carolina	30 hours	Yes	120 hours	2 years	Yes
North Dakota	30 hours	Yes	90 hours	2 years	Yes
Ohio	120 hours	Yes	240 hours	2 years	Yes
Oklahoma	90 hours	Yes	165 hours	2 years	Yes
Oregon	90 hours	Yes	150 hours	3 years	Yes
Pennsylvania	60 hours	Yes	300 hours	3 years	Yes
Rhode Island	None	Yes	90 hours	1 year	Yes
South Carolina	30 hours	Yes	90 hours	3–5 years	Yes
South Dakota	40 hours	Yes	100 hours	2 years	Yes
Tennessee	60 hours	Yes	120 hours	3 years	No
Texas	180 hours	Yes	900 hours	2 years	Yes
Utah	90 hours	Yes	120 hours	3 years	Yes
Vermont	None	Yes	8 hours	1 year	Yes
Virginia	60 hours	Yes	240 hours	3 years	Yes
Washington	60 hours	Yes	180 hours	2 years	Yes
West Virginia	90 hours	Yes	180 hours	2 years	Yes
Wisconsin	72 hours	Yes	108 hours	None	Yes
Wyoming	30 hours	Yes	60 hours	2 years	Yes

Source: National Association of Real Estate License Law Officials (1996 Digest), 563 West 500 South, Bountiful, Utah 84010. These requirements and credit for prior course work change regularly. Check with your state for any subsequent changes.

the case of a broker, or to the employing broker in the case of a salesperson.

If the applicant fails the written examination, the usual procedure is to allow the applicant to repeat it until it is passed. A fee is charged to retake the exam and the applicant must wait until the next testing date.

License and Pocket Card   The Department of State issues successful applicants a license showing the licensee's place of business. The broker's license must be conspicuously displayed at the broker's principal place of business at all times.

Each broker and salesperson is also issued a pocket card by the department showing the licensee's place of business and, in the case of a salesperson, the name of the broker with whom he or she is associated. The card must be produced on demand. If a salesperson resigns, the broker must file a termination of the association with the Department of State. If the sales agent is going to work for a new broker, the salesperson's license may be endorsed to a new broker and the Department of State will issue another pocket card showing the new affiliation.

Once licensed, as long as a person remains active in real estate and meets any continuing education requirements, the license can be renewed by paying the required renewal fee. If a license is not renewed before it expires, New York allows a 2-year grace period, and charges a late renewal fee. Once the grace period has passed, all license rights lapse and the individual must meet current application requirements and take the current written exam.

Renewal

The general rule regarding license requirements is that a person must be licensed in the state within which he or she negotiates. Thus, if a broker or one of the broker's sales associates sells an out-of-state property, but conducts the negotiations entirely within the borders of his or her own state, a license is not needed in the state where the land is located. State laws also permit a broker in one state to split a commission with a broker in another state provided each conducts negotiations only within the state where he or she is licensed. Therefore, if Broker B, licensed in State B, takes a listing at her office on a parcel of land located in State B, and Broker C in State C sells it conducting the sale negotiations within State C, then Brokers B and C can split the commission. If, however, Broker C comes to State B to negotiate a contract, then a license in State B is necessary.

NONRESIDENT LICENSING

Many states issue a **nonresident license** to out-of-state brokers. This is particularly helpful if a broker is located near a state border. In issuing a nonresident license, a state usually requires substantially the same examination and experience requirements as demanded of resident brokers. Some states give the out-of-state broker credit for the uniform part of a license test already taken, requiring only passage of a test on local law, custom, and practice. Others require a complete examination. A few require no examination.

Notice of Consent

When brokers operate outside their home states, they may be required to file a **notice of consent**, usually with the secretary of state, in each state in which they intend to operate. This permits the secretary of state to receive legal summonses on behalf of the nonresident broker and provides a state resident an avenue for bringing a lawsuit against a broker who is a resident of another state.

Moving to Another State

When a broker or salesperson moves his place of business from one state to another, a license is required in the new state. Many states will give credit for experience and part or all of the examination that was passed in the previous state. This can be particularly helpful for two-income families when one spouse is transferred to another state. Details of what a state will allow as credit are too complex and too changeable to include here. If negotiating across state lines or moving to another state as a real estate agent is of interest to you, you should contact that state's real estate licensing authority.

LICENSING THE BUSINESS FIRM

When a real estate broker wishes to establish a brokerage, the simplest method is a sole proprietorship under the broker's own name, such as David Lee, Real Estate Broker. Some states permit a broker to operate out of his residence. However, operating a business in a residential neighborhood can be bothersome to neighbors, and most states require brokers to maintain a place of business in a location that is zoned for businesses.

Fictitious Business Name

A real estate broker can operate as a sole proprietorship either under the broker's own name or a fictitious name. When a person operates under a name other than his own, he must register that name by filing a **fictitious business name statement** with the county clerk and the state real estate licensing authority. This statement must also be published in a local newspaper. Thus, if David Lee wishes to call his brokerage business Great Lakes Realty, his business certificate would show "David Lee, doing business as Great Lakes Realty." (Sometimes *doing business as* is shortened to dba or d/b/a.)

A broker can also operate in partnership with other brokers or as a corporation. Since a corporation is an artificial being (not an actual person), it cannot take a real estate examination. Therefore, its chief executive officer (usually the president) or some designated officer must be a licensed real estate broker and be responsible for the management of the firm. Other officers and stockholders may include brokers and salespersons and nonlicensed persons. However, only those actually licensed can represent the corporation in activities requiring a real estate license.

If a broker expands by establishing branch offices that are geographically separate from the main or home office, each branch must have a branch office license and a licensed broker in charge. Often referred to as a **principal broker,** this person can be a partner, a corporate owner who is a broker, or a sales associate who has a broker's license. A few states allow a salesperson licensee to be in charge.

Branch Offices

The legislature of each state has established a government agency for the purpose of regulating real estate licensing procedures and real estate practices with the state. These regulatory agencies are variously known as real estate commissions or departments or divisions of real estate, or they may be a part of the state's business and vocational licensing and regulation. In New York, the responsibility falls on the **Department of State.**
    In New York, Article 12-A of the **Real Property Law** is the principal section of law governing the regulation of real estate brokers and salespersons.

REAL ESTATE
REGULATION

The day-to-day responsibility of real estate regulation in New York rests with the **Division of Licensing Services** within the Department of State. Staffed by full-time civil service employees, the Division answers correspondence, sends out application forms, arranges for examinations, collects fees, issues licenses, and so forth. The Division is responsible for investigating complaints against licensees, non-licensees, regulating subdivisions, real estate syndicates, and for auditing broker trust fund accounts. Additionally, the Department publishes information about New York laws that pertain to real estate ownership, licensing, and subdivisions. In short, it is the Division of Licensing Services with which licensees have the most contact, but it

Division of Licensing
Services

is the Department of State and the legislature that set the license requirements.

Advisory Board

New York law also provides for a real estate board within the Department of State to advise and assist the Secretary of State with the administration of the licensing laws. The Board consists of the Secretary of State, the Executive Director of the State Consumer Protection Board, and 13 additional members who are appointed to 2-year terms by the governor and legislative leaders. Five of these must be licensed real estate brokers and the others must also be real estate licensees. The Board advises the Secretary on matters pertaining to the approval of schools offering real estate licensing courses and the examination of applicants. It also makes recommendations concerning the revision of laws and regulations affecting the industry and the enforcement of the licensing laws. In addition, the Board is required to hold public hearings each year in Buffalo, New York City, and Albany to solicit public comments about New York real estate practice.

LICENSE SUSPENSION AND REVOCATION

The most important control mechanism a state has over its real estate salespersons and brokers is that it can **suspend** (temporarily make ineffective) or **revoke** (recall and make void) a real estate license. Without a license, a person may not lawfully engage in real estate activities for the purpose of earning a commission or fee. Unless an agent has a valid license, a court of law will not uphold a claim for a commission from a client.

Reasons for license suspension and revocation include any violation of the state's real estate laws, misrepresentation or false promises, undisclosed dual agency, commingling, and acting as an undisclosed principal. Licenses can also be revoked or suspended for false advertising, obtaining a license by fraud, negligence or incompetence, failure to supervise salespersons, failure to properly account for clients' funds, practicing law without a license, paying commissions to unlicensed persons, conviction of a felony or certain types of misdemeanors, dishonest conduct in general, and, in many states, failure to have a fixed termination date on an exclusive listing.

When the Department of State receives a complaint from someone who feels he was wronged by a licensee, an investigation is conducted by the Division of Licensing Services staff. Statements are received from witnesses. Title company records, public records, and the licensee's bank records are checked as necessary. The investigator may call an informal conference and invite all parties involved to attend. If it appears that the complaint is serious and that a violation of the law has occurred, a formal hearing is held in the presence of the full commission. The licensee, the party bringing the complaint, and any necessary witnesses appear. Testimony is taken under oath and a written record is made of the proceedings. If the Division decides to suspend or revoke the respondent's license, the respondent has the right of appeal to the courts.

The potential of license loss for a wrongdoing strongly encourages licensees to operate within the law. However, suspension or revocation of a license does nothing to provide financial compensation for any losses suffered by a wronged party. This must be recovered from the broker either through a mutually agreed-on monetary settlement or a court judgment resulting from a civil lawsuit brought by the wronged party. But all too often court judgments turn out to be uncollectible because the defendant has no money.

BONDS AND RECOVERY FUNDS

There are two common solutions to the uncollectible judgment problem. Six states (Alabama, Alaska, Massachusetts, Montana, Tennessee, and West Virginia) require that a person post a bond with the state before a license will be issued. In the event of an otherwise uncollectible court judgment against a licensee, the bond money is used to provide payment. Bond requirements vary from $1,000 to $100,000, with $5,000 to $10,000 being the most popular range. Licensees can obtain these bonds from bonding companies for an annual fee or post the required amount of cash or securities with the state.

The second method of protecting the public is through a state-sponsored **recovery fund.** A portion of the money that each licensee pays for a real estate license is set aside in a fund that is made available for the payment of otherwise uncollectible judgments. Recovery funds offer coverage ranging from $2,000 to $100,000 per licensee, with most states in the $25,000 to $50,000 range. The District of Columbia and 34 states use recovery funds. These states are Alabama, Alaska, Arizona, Arkansas, California, Colorado, Connecticut, Delaware, Florida, Georgia,

Hawaii, Idaho, Illinois, Kansas, Kentucky, Louisiana, Maryland, Minnesota, Montana, Nevada, New Jersey, New Mexico, North Carolina, North Dakota, Ohio, Oklahoma, Pennsylvania, Rhode Island, South Dakota, Tennessee, Texas, Utah, Virginia, and Wyoming.

The requirement for bonds and the establishment of recovery funds are not perfect solutions to the problem of uncollectible judgments because wronged parties must expend considerable effort to recover their losses, and it is quite possible that the maximum amount available per transaction or licensee will not fully compensate for the losses suffered. As of this writing, New York requires neither a bond nor the establishment of a recovery fund.

SECURITIES LICENSE

Be aware that sometimes a real estate salesperson or broker also needs a securities license. This occurs when the property being sold is an investment contract in real estate rather than real estate itself. Such an investment contract is classified as a **security.** Examples of securities include real estate limited partnerships, rental pools in which condominium owners put their units into a pool for a percentage of the pool's income, and some timeshares. Securities licenses are issued by the National Association of Securities Dealers based on successful completion of their examination. Legal counsel is advised if there is the possibility you may be selling securities. Counsel will also advise on state and federal laws requiring the registration of real estate securities before they are sold.

AFFILIATING WITH A BROKER

If you plan to enter real estate sales, selecting a broker to work for is one of the most important decisions you must make. The best way to approach it is to consider carefully what you have to offer the real estate business and what you expect in return. And look at it in that order! It is easy to become captivated by the big commission income you visualize coming your way. But if that is your only perspective, you will meet with disappointment. The reason people will pay you money is to receive some product or service in return. Your clients are not concerned with your income goal; it is only incidental to their goals. If you help them attain their goals, you will reach yours.

Before applying for a real estate license, ask yourself whether the working hours and conditions of a real estate agent are suitable to you. Specifically, are you prepared to work on a commission-only basis? Evenings and weekends? On your own? With people you've never met before? If you can comfortably answer yes to these questions, then start looking for a broker to sponsor you. (Salesperson license educational requirements can be completed and the examination taken without broker sponsorship, but a salesperson must have a broker to work for before the actual license is issued.)

Training

Your next step is to look for those features and qualities in a broker that will complement, enhance, and encourage your personal development in real estate. If you are new to the industry, training and education will most likely be at the top of your list. Therefore, in looking for a broker you want to find one that will offer you some on-the-job training. (What you have learned to date from books, classes, and license examination preparation will be helpful, but you will need additional specific training.) Real estate franchise operations and large brokerage offices usually offer extensive training. In smaller offices, the broker in charge is usually responsible for seeing that newcomers receive training. An office that offers no training to a newcomer should be avoided.

Compensation

Another question high on your list will be compensation. Very few offices provide a newcomer with a guaranteed minimum wage or even a draw against future commissions. Most brokers feel that one must produce to be paid and the hungrier the salesperson, the quicker the production. A broker who pays salespersons regardless of sales produced simply siphons the money from those who are producing. The old saying, "There's no such thing as a free lunch," applies to sales commissions.

Compensation for salespersons is usually a percentage of the commissions they earn for the broker. How much each receives is open to negotiation between the broker and each salesperson employed. A broker who provides office space, extensive secretarial help, a large advertising budget, a mailing program, and generous long-distance telephone privileges might take 40% to 50% of each incoming commission dollar for office overhead. A broker who provides fewer services might take 25% or 30%.

Salespersons with proven sales records can usually reduce the portion of each commission dollar that must go to the broker. Brokers know that with an outstanding sales performer, a high volume of sales will offset a smaller percentage for overhead. Conversely, a new and untried salesperson or one with a mediocre past sales record may have to give up a larger portion of each dollar for the broker's overhead.

When one brokerage agency lists a property and another locates the buyer, the commission is split according to any agreement the two brokers wish to make. The most common arrangement is a fifty-fifty split. After splitting, each broker pays a portion of the money received to the salesperson involved in accordance with their commission agreement.

While investigating commission arrangements, one should also inquire about incentive and bonus plans, automobile expense reimbursement, health insurance, life insurance, errors and omission insurance, and retirement plans.

An alternative commission arrangement is the **100% commission** wherein the salesperson does not share the commission with the broker. Instead the salesperson is charged a fee for office space, advertising, telephone, multiple listing, and any other expenses the broker incurs on behalf of the salesperson. Generally speaking, 100% arrangements are more popular with proven performers than with newcomers.

Broker Support

Broker support has an impact on success. Some specific questions to consider include: Does each salesperson have a desk to work from? Are office facilities efficient and modern? Does the broker provide secretarial services? What is the broker's advertising policy and who pays for ads? Who pays for signs, business cards, franchise fees, and realty board dues? Does the broker have sources of financing for clients? Does the broker allow salespersons to invest in real estate? Does the broker have a good reputation in the community?

Finding a Broker

Many licensees associate with a particular broker as a result of friendship or word-of-mouth information. However, there are other ways to find a suitable position. An excellent way to start your search is to decide what geographical area you want to work in. If you choose the same community or neighborhood in which you live, you will already possess a valuable sense and feel for that area.

Having selected a geographical area, look in the Sunday newspaper real estate advertisements section and the telephone book Yellow Pages for names of brokers. Hold interviews with several brokers and, as you do, remember that you are interviewing them just as intensively as they are interviewing you. During your visits with brokers be particularly alert to your feelings. Intuition can be as valuable a guide to a sound working relationship as a list of questions and answers regarding the job.

As you narrow your choices, revisit the offices of brokers who particularly impressed you. Talk with some of the salespersons who have worked or are working there. They can be very candid and valuable sources of information. Be wary of individuals who are extreme in their opinions: rely instead on the consensus of opinion. Locate clients who have used the firm's services and ask them their opinions of the firm. You might also talk to local appraisers, lenders, and escrow agents for candid opinions. If you do all this advance work, the benefits to you will be greater enjoyment of your work, more money in your pocket, and less likelihood of wanting to quit or move to another office.

Having selected a broker with whom to associate, your next step is to make an employment contract. An **employment contract** formalizes the working arrangement between the broker and the salespersons. An oral contract may be satisfactory, but a written one is preferred because it sets forth the relationship with a higher degree of precision and is a written record of the agreement. This greatly reduces the potential for future controversy and litigation.

Employment Contract

The employment contract will cover such matters as compensation (how much and under what circumstances); training (how often and if required); hours of work (including assigned office hours and open houses); company identification (distinctive articles of clothing and name tags); fees and dues (license and realty board); expenses (automobile, advertising, telephone); fringe benefits (health and life insurance, pension, and profit-sharing plans); withholding (income taxes and social security);

territory (assigned area of the community); termination of employment (quitting and firing); and general office policies and procedures (office manual).

INDEPENDENT CONTRACTOR STATUS

Is the real estate sales associate an employee of the broker or an independent contractor? The answer is both. On one hand, the sales associate acts like an **employee** because the associate works for the broker, usually at the broker's place of business; prepares listings and sales documents on forms specified by the broker; and upon closing, receives payment from the broker. On the other hand, the sales associate acts like an **independent contractor** because the associate is paid only if the associate brings about a sale that produces a commission. An important distinction between the two is whether or not the broker must withhold income taxes and social security from the associate's commission checks. If the sales associate is considered by the Internal Revenue Service (IRS) to be an employee for tax purposes, the broker must withhold. If classed as an independent contractor for tax purposes, the sales associate is responsible for his own income taxes and social security. The IRS prefers employee status because it is easier to collect taxes from an employer than from an employee.

The IRS treats real estate sales associates as independent contractors if they meet the following three requirements. First, the associate must be a licensed real estate agent. Second, a large percentage of the associate's payment for services as a real estate agent must be directly related to sales—not to hours worked. Third, a written agreement must exist between the associate and the broker stating that the associate will be treated as an independent contractor for tax purposes. If an agent and the sponsoring broker do not comply with this statute, they run the risk of losing their independent contractor status. If this occurs the sponsoring broker becomes subject to the same filing requirements as any other employer in the normal course of business.

New York's Labor and Worker's Compensation Laws also specifically exclude a real estate agent from the definition of employee. This exclusion allows the real estate broker to avoid paying for unemployment insurance, worker's compensation, and disability benefits for sales agents.

These are highlights of the issue. If you plan to work for a broker, you may find it valuable to have this matter, as well as your entire employment contract, reviewed by an attorney before you sign it.

Prior to the early 1970s, real estate brokerage was a small business industry. Most brokerages were one-office firms. A large brokerage was one having four or five offices and selling 200 properties a year. Then real estate franchise organizations entered the real estate business in a big way. **Franchisers** such as Century 21, Red Carpet, REMAX, and Gallery of Homes offered brokerage firms national identification, large-scale advertising, sales staff training programs, management advice, customer referrals, financing help for buyers, and guaranteed sales plans. In return, the brokerage firm (the franchisee) paid a fee of from 3% to 8% of gross commission income. The idea became popular and by the mid-1980s approximately half of the real estate licensees affiliated with the National Association of REALTORS® were working in franchised offices, and their numbers continued to grow through the 1990s. Meanwhile, the number of franchisers grew to over 60 including such names as Realty World, ERA, International Real Estate Network, Better Homes and Gardens Realty, and Mayflower Realty.

Statistics show that franchising appeals mostly to firms with 10 to 50 sales associates. Larger firms are more capable of providing the advantages of a franchise for themselves. Smaller firms tend to occupy market niches and often consist of one or two licensees who do not bring in additional sales associates. For a newly licensed salesperson wishing to affiliate with a firm, a franchised firm offers immediate public recognition, extensive training opportunities, established office routines, regular sales meetings, and access to a nationwide referral system. Franchise affiliation is not magic however; success still depends on the individual to make sales calls, value property, get listings, advertise, show property, qualify, negotiate, and close transactions.

FRANCHISED OFFICES

During the late 1970s a large real estate firm in California—Coldwell Banker—began an expansion program by purchasing multibranch real estate firms in other states. Merrill Lynch, the

National Real Estate Firms

Wall Street stock brokerage firm, has also entered the real estate brokerage business. To accomplish this, Merrill Lynch bought existing real estate brokerage firms. Other Wall Street firms are looking into the real estate brokerage business, as are several large corporations. Other large national and regional firms include Cushman and Wakefield, REMAX, Grubb & Ellis, Long and Foster, Shannon and Luchs, Marcus and Millichap, and Rubloff, Inc. Recently the ultimate in expansion occurred when Century 21, Coldwell Banker, and ERA (three large franchise firms) were acquired by the same company, although they still remain competitors. What could be next?

For a newcomer, affiliating with a national or regional real estate firm offers benefits like those of a franchised firm (recognition, training, routines, etc.). The main difference is who owns the firm. A franchised firm is locally owned and managed, i.e., an independent firm. Regional and national firms are locally managed, but the sales associate only occasionally, if ever, meets the owner(s).

PROFESSIONAL REAL ESTATE ASSOCIATIONS

Professional real estate organizations existed even before laws required real estate agents to have licenses. Called real estate boards, they joined together agents within a city or county on a voluntary basis. The push to organize came from real estate people who saw the need for some sort of controlling organization that could supervise the activities of individual agents and elevate the profession's status in the public's mind. Gradually, local boards grouped themselves into state associations, and finally in 1908 the National Association of Real Estate Boards (NAREB) was formed. In 1914, NAREB developed a model license law that became the basis for real estate license laws in many states.

Today the local boards are still the fundamental units of the National Association of REALTORS® (NAR; the name was changed from NAREB in 1974). Local board membership is open to anyone holding a real estate license. Called boards of REALTORS®, real estate boards, realty boards, or Associations of REALTORS®, they promote fair dealing among their members and with the public and protect members from dishonest and irresponsible licensees. They also promote legislation that protects property rights, offer short seminars to keep members up to date with current laws and practices, and in general do whatever is necessary to build the dignity, stability, and professionalization of the industry. Local boards often operate the local multiple listing service, although in some communities multiple listing is a privately owned and operated business.

State associations are composed of the members of local boards plus sales associates and brokers who live in areas where no local board exists. The purposes of the state associations are to unite members statewide, to encourage legislation that benefits and protects the real estate industry and safeguards the public in their real estate transactions, and to promote economic growth and development in the state. Also, state associations hold conventions to educate members and foster contacts among them. The New York State Association of REALTORS® is located at 130 Washington Avenue, Albany, New York 12210.

Realtor

The NAR is made up of local boards and state associations in the United States. The term **REALTOR**® is a registered trade name that belongs to NAR. REALTOR® is not synonymous with real estate agent. It is reserved for the exclusive use of members of the National Association of REALTORS,® who as part of their membership pledge themselves to abide by the association's Code of Ethics. The term REALTOR® cannot be used by nonmembers, and in some states the unauthorized use of the term is a violation of the real estate law. Prior to 1974, the use of the term REALTOR® was reserved primarily for principal brokers. Then, by a national membership vote, the decision was made to create an additional membership class, the **REALTOR-ASSOCIATE,**® for salespersons and broker licensees working for members.

One of the most important features of the National Association of REALTORS® is its **Code of Ethics.** First adopted in 1913, the REALTOR® Code of Ethics has since been revised several times and now contains 23 articles that pertain to REALTORS'® relations to their clients, to other real estate agents, and to the public as a whole. The full code is reproduced in Figure 2.1.

Although a complete review of each article is beyond the scope of this chapter, it can be seen that some articles parallel existing laws. For example, Article 10 speaks against racial

Code of Ethics

discrimination and Article 12 speaks for full disclosure. However, the bulk of the code addresses itself to the obligations of a REALTOR® that are beyond the written law. For example, in Article 2, the REALTOR® agrees to stay informed regarding laws and regulations, proposed legislation, and current market conditions in order to advise clients properly. In Article 5, the REALTOR® agrees to share willingly with other REALTORS® the lessons of experience. In other words, to be recognized as a REALTOR®, one must not only comply with the letter of the law, but also observe the ethical standards by which the industry operates.

In some states, ethical standards such as those in the NAR Code of Ethics have been legislated into law. Called **canons** or **standards of conduct,** their intent is to promote ethical practices by all real estate licensees, not just by those who join the National Association of REALTORS®. Additionally, the National Association of REALTORS® publishes 34 **Standards of Practice.** These interpret various articles in the Code of Ethics.

In addition to its emphasis on real estate brokerage, the National Association of REALTORS® also contains a number of specialized professional groups within itself. These include the American Institute of Real Estate Appraisers, the Farm and Land Institute, the Institute of Real Estate Management, the Realtors National Marketing Institute, the Society of Industrial Realtors, the Real Estate Securities and Syndication Institute, the American Society of Real Estate Counselors, the American Chapter of the International Real Estate Federation, and the Women's Council of Realtors. Membership is open to REALTORS® interested in these specialties.

To help encourage and recognize professionalism in the real estate industry, state Boards of REALTORS® sponsor education courses leading to the GRI designation. Course offerings typically include real estate law, finance, appraisal, investments, office management, and salesmanship. Upon completion of the prescribed curriculum, the designation Graduate Realtor's Institute is awarded.

Realtist   The National Association of Real Estate Brokers (NAREB) is a national trade association representing minority real estate professionals actively engaged in the industry. Founded in 1947, its 5,000 members use the trade name **Realtist.** The organization

Code of Ethics and Standards of Practice

of the

NATIONAL ASSOCIATION OF REALTORS®

Effective January 1, 1995

Where the word REALTORS® is used in this Code and Preamble, it shall be deemed to include REALTOR-ASSOCIATE®s.

While the Code of Ethics establishes obligations that may be higher than those mandated by law, in any instance where the Code of Ethics and the law conflict, the obligations of the law must take precedence.

Preamble...

Under all is the land. Upon its wise utilization and widely allocated ownership depend the survival and growth of free institutions and of our civilization. REALTORS® should recognize that the interests of the nation and its citizens require the highest and best use of the land and the widest distribution of land ownership. They require the creation of adequate housing, the building of functioning cities, the development of productive industries and farms, and the preservation of a healthful environment.

Such interests impose obligations beyond those of ordinary commerce. They impose grave social responsibility and a patriotic duty to which REALTORS® should dedicate themselves, and for which they should be diligent in preparing themselves. REALTORS®, therefore, are zealous to maintain and improve the standards of their calling and share with their fellow REALTORS® a common responsibility for its integrity and honor.

In recognition and appreciation of their obligations to clients, customers, the public, and each other, REALTORS® continuously strive to become and remain informed on issues affecting real estate and, as knowledgeable professionals, they willingly share the fruit of their experience and study with others. They identify and take steps, through enforcement of this Code of Ethics and by assisting appropriate regulatory bodies, to eliminate practices which may damage the public or which might discredit or bring dishonor to the real estate profession.

Realizing that cooperation with other real estate professionals promotes the best interests of those who utilize their services, REALTORS® urge exclusive representation of clients; do not attempt to gain any unfair advantage over their competitors; and they refrain from making unsolicited comments about other practitioners. In instances where their opinion is sought, or where REALTORS® believe that comment is necessary, their opinion is offered in an objective, professional manner, uninfluenced by any personal motivation or potential advantage or gain.

NATIONAL ASSOCIATION OF REALTORS®
430 North Michigan Avenue
Chicago, Illinois 60611-4087

Figure 2.1. Code of Ethics.

The term REALTOR® has come to connote competency, fairness, and high integrity resulting from adherence to a lofty ideal of moral conduct in business relations. No inducement of profit and no instruction from clients ever can justify departure from this ideal.

In the interpretation of this obligation, REALTORS® can take no safer guide than that which has been handed down through the centuries, embodied in the Golden Rule, "Whatsoever ye would that others should do to you, do ye even so to them."

Accepting this standard as their own, REALTORS® pledge to observe its spirit in all of their activities and to conduct their business in accordance with the tenets set forth below.

Duties to Clients and Customers

Article 1

When representing a buyer, seller, landlord, tenant, or other client as an agent, REALTORS® pledge themselves to protect and promote the interests of their client. This obligation of absolute fidelity to the client's interests is primary, but it does not relieve REALTORS® of their obligation to treat all parties honestly. When serving a buyer, seller, landlord, tenant or other party in a non-agency capacity, REALTORS® remain obligated to treat all parties honestly. *(Amended 1/93)*

- **Standard of Practice 1-1**
  REALTORS®, when acting as principals in a real estate transaction, remain obligated by the duties imposed by the Code of Ethics. *(Amended 1/93)*

- **Standard of Practice 1-2**
  The duties the Code of Ethics imposes on agents/representatives are applicable to REALTORS® acting as agents, transaction brokers, facilitators, or in any other recognized capacity except for any duty specifically exempted by law or regulation. *(Adopted 1/95)*

- **Standard of Practice 1-3**
  REALTORS®, in attempting to secure a listing, shall not deliberately mislead the owner as to market value.

- **Standard of Practice 1-4**
  REALTORS®, when seeking to become a buyer/tenant representative, shall not mislead buyers or tenants as to savings or other benefits that might be realized through use of the REALTOR®'s services. *(Amended 1/93)*

- **Standard of Practice 1-5**
  REALTORS® may represent the seller/landlord and buyer/tenant in the same transaction only after full disclosure to and with informed consent of both parties. *(Adopted 1/93)*

- **Standard of Practice 1-6**
  REALTORS® shall submit offers and counter-offers objectively and as quickly as possible. *(Adopted 1/93, Amended 1/95)*

- **Standard of Practice 1-7**
  When acting as listing brokers, REALTORS® shall continue to submit to the seller/landlord all offers and counter-offers until closing or execution of a lease unless the seller/landlord has waived this obligation in writing. REALTORS® shall not be obligated to continue to market the property after an offer

Figure 2.1. (continued)

has been accepted by the seller/landlord. REALTORS® shall recommend that sellers/landlords obtain the advice of legal counsel prior to acceptance of a subsequent offer except where the acceptance is contingent on the termination of the pre-existing purchase contract or lease. *(Amended 1/93)*

• Standard of Practice 1-8

REALTORS® acting as agents of buyers/tenants shall submit to buyers/tenants all offers and counter-offers until acceptance but have no obligation to continue to show properties to their clients after an offer has been accepted unless otherwise agreed in writing. REALTORS® acting as agents of buyers/tenants shall recommend that buyers/tenants obtain the advice of legal counsel if there is a question as to whether a pre-existing contract has been terminated. *(Adopted 1/93)*

• Standard of Practice 1-9

The obligation of REALTORS® to preserve confidential information provided by their clients continues after the termination of the agency relationship. REALTORS® shall not knowingly, during or following the termination of a professional relationship with their client:
1) reveal confidential information of the client; or
2) use confidential information of the client to the disadvantage of the client; or
3) use confidential information of the client for the REALTOR®'s advantage or the advantage of a third party unless the client consents after full disclosure except where the REALTOR® is:
   a) required by court order; or
   b) it is the intention of the client to commit a crime and the information is necessary to prevent the crime; or
   c) necessary to defend the REALTOR® or the REALTOR®'s employees or associates against an accusation of wrongful conduct. *(Adopted 1/93, Amended 1/95)*

• Standard of Practice 1-10

REALTORS® shall, consistent with the terms and conditions of their property management agreement, competently manage the property of clients with due regard for the rights, responsibilities, benefits, safety and health of tenants and others lawfully on the premises. *(Adopted 1/95)*

• Standard of Practice 1-11

REALTORS® who are employed to maintain or manage a client's property shall exercise due diligence and make reasonable efforts to protect it against reasonably foreseeable contingencies and losses. *(Adopted 1/95)*

Article 2

REALTORS® shall avoid exaggeration, misrepresentation, or concealment of pertinent facts relating to the property or the transaction. REALTORS® shall not, however, be obligated to discover latent defects in the property, to advise on matters outside the scope of their real estate license, or to disclose facts which are confidential under the scope of agency duties owed to their clients. *(Amended 1/93)*

• Standard of Practice 2-1

REALTORS® shall be obligated to discover and disclose adverse factors reasonably apparent to someone with expertise in only those areas required by their real estate licensing authority.

Article 2 does not impose upon the REALTOR® the obligation of expertise in other professional or technical disciplines. *(Amended 11/86)*

• Standard of Practice 2-2

When entering into listing contracts, REALTORS® must advise sellers/landlords of:
1) the REALTOR®'s general company policies regarding cooperation with subagents, buyer/tenant agents, or both;
2) the fact that buyer/tenant agents, even if compensated by the listing broker, or by the seller/landlord will represent the interests of buyers/tenants; and
3) any potential for the listing broker to act as a disclosed dual agent, e.g. buyer/tenant agent. *(Adopted 1/93)*

• Standard of Practice 2-3

When entering into contracts to represent buyers/tenants, REALTORS® must advise potential clients of:
1) the REALTOR®'s general company policies regarding cooperation with other firms; and
2) any potential for the buyer/tenant representative to act as a disclosed dual agent, e.g. listing broker, subagent, landlord's agent, etc. *(Adopted 1/93)*

• Standard of Practice 2-4

REALTORS® shall not be parties to the naming of a false consideration in any document, unless it be the naming of an obviously nominal consideration.

• Standard of Practice 2-5

Factors defined as "non-material" by law or regulation or which are expressly referenced in law or regulation as not being subject to disclosure are considered not "pertinent" for purposes of Article 2. *(Adopted 1/93)*

Article 3

REALTORS® shall cooperate with other brokers except when cooperation is not in the client's best interest. The obligation to cooperate does not include the obligation to share commissions, fees, or to otherwise compensate another broker. *(Amended 1/95)*

• Standard of Practice 3-1

REALTORS®, acting as exclusive agents of sellers/landlords, establish the terms and conditions of offers to cooperate. Unless expressly indicated in offers to cooperate, cooperating brokers may not assume that the offer of cooperation includes an offer of compensation. Terms of compensation, if any, shall be ascertained by cooperating brokers before beginning efforts to accept the offer of cooperation. *(Amended 1/94)*

• Standard of Practice 3-2

REALTORS® shall, with respect to offers of compensation to another REALTOR®, timely communicate any change of compensation for cooperative services to the other REALTOR® prior to the time such REALTOR® produces an offer to purchase/lease the property. *(Amended 1/94)*

• Standard of Practice 3-3

Standard of Practice 3-2 does not preclude the listing broker and cooperating broker from entering into an agreement to change cooperative compensation. *(Adopted 1/94)*

Figure 2.1. (continued)

Standard of Practice 3-4

REALTORS®, acting as listing brokers, have an affirmative obligation to disclose the existence of dual or variable rate commission arrangements (i.e., listings where one amount of commission is payable if the listing broker's firm is the procuring cause of sale/lease and a different amount of commission is payable if the sale/lease results through the efforts of the seller/landlord or a cooperating broker). The listing broker shall, as soon as practical, disclose the existence of such arrangements to potential cooperating brokers and shall, in response to inquiries from cooperating brokers, disclose the differential that would result in a cooperative transaction or in a sale/lease that results through the efforts of the seller/landlord. If the cooperating broker is a buyer/tenant representative, the buyer/tenant representative must disclose such information to their client. *(Amended 1/94)*

Standard of Practice 3-5

It is the obligation of subagents to promptly disclose all pertinent facts to the principal's agent prior to as well as after a purchase or lease agreement is executed. *(Amended 1/93)*

Standard of Practice 3-6

REALTORS® shall disclose the existence of an accepted offer to any broker seeking cooperation. *(Adopted 5/86)*

Standard of Practice 3-7

When seeking information from another REALTOR® concerning property under a management or listing agreement, REALTORS® shall disclose their REALTOR® status and whether their interest is personal or on behalf of a client and, if on behalf of a client, their representational status. *(Amended 1/95)*

Standard of Practice 3-8

REALTORS® shall not misrepresent the availability of access to show or inspect a listed property. *(Amended 11/87)*

Article 4

REALTORS® shall not acquire an interest in or buy or present offers from themselves, any member of their immediate families, their firms or any member thereof, or any entities in which they have any ownership interest, any real property without making their true position known to the owner or the owner's agent. In selling property they own, or in which they have any interest, REALTORS® shall reveal their ownership or interest in writing to the purchaser or the purchaser's representative. *(Amended 1/91)*

Standard of Practice 4-1

For the protection of all parties, the disclosures required by Article 4 shall be in writing and provided by REALTORS® prior to the signing of any contract. *(Adopted 2/86)*

Article 5

REALTORS® shall not undertake to provide professional services concerning a property or its value where they have a present or contemplated interest unless such interest is specifically disclosed to all affected parties.

Article 6

When acting as agents, REALTORS® shall not accept any commission, rebate, or profit on expenditures made for their principal, without the principal's knowledge and consent. *(Amended 1/92)*

Standard of Practice 6-1

REALTORS® shall not recommend or suggest to a client or a customer the use of services of another organization or business entity in which they have a direct interest without disclosing such interest at the time of the recommendation or suggestion. *(Amended 5/88)*

Standard of Practice 6-2

When acting as agents or subagents, REALTORS® shall disclose to a client or customer if there is any financial benefit or fee the REALTOR® or the REALTOR®'s firm may receive as a direct result of having recommended real estate products or services (e.g., homeowner's insurance, warranty programs, mortgage financing, title insurance, etc.) other than real estate referral fees. *(Adopted 5/88)*

Article 7

In a transaction, REALTORS® shall not accept compensation from more than one party, even if permitted by law, without disclosure to all parties and the informed consent of the REALTOR®'s client or clients. *(Amended 1/93)*

Article 8

REALTORS® shall keep in a special account in an appropriate financial institution, separated from their own funds, monies coming into their possession in trust for other persons, such as escrows, trust funds, clients' monies, and other like items.

Article 9

REALTORS®, for the protection of all parties, shall assure whenever possible that agreements shall be in writing, and shall be in clear and understandable language expressing the specific terms, conditions, obligations and commitments of the parties. A copy of each agreement shall be furnished to each party upon their signing or initialing. *(Amended 1/95)*

Standard of Practice 9-1

For the protection of all parties, REALTORS® shall use reasonable care to ensure that documents pertaining to the purchase, sale, or lease of real estate are kept current through the use of written extensions or amendments. *(Amended 1/93)*

Duties to the Public

Article 10

REALTORS® shall not deny equal professional services to any person for reasons of race, color, religion, sex, handicap, familial status, or national origin. REALTORS® shall not be parties to any plan or agreement to discriminate against a person or persons on the basis of race, color, religion, sex, handicap, familial status, or national origin. *(Amended 1/90)*

Standard of Practice 10-1

REALTORS® shall not volunteer information regarding the racial, religious or ethnic composition of any neighborhood and shall not engage in any activity which may result in panic selling. REALTORS® shall not print, display or circulate any statement or advertisement with respect to the selling or renting of a property that indicates any preference, limitations or discrimination based on race, color, religion, sex, handicap, familial status or national origin. *(Adopted 1/94)*

Figure 2.1. (continued)

Article 11

The services which REALTORS® provide to their clients and customers shall conform to the standards of practice and competence which are reasonably expected in the specific real estate disciplines in which they engage; specifically, residential real estate brokerage, real property management, commercial and industrial real estate brokerage, real estate appraisal, real estate counseling, real estate syndication, real estate auction, and international real estate.

REALTORS® shall not undertake to provide specialized professional services concerning a type of property or service that is outside their field of competence unless they engage the assistance of one who is competent on such types of property or service, or unless the facts are fully disclosed to the client. Any persons engaged to provide such assistance shall be so identified to the client and their contribution to the assignment should be set forth. *(Amended 1/95)*

- **Standard of Practice 11-1**

  The obligations of the Code of Ethics shall be supplemented by and construed in a manner consistent with the Uniform Standards of Professional Appraisal Practice (USPAP) promulgated by the Appraisal Standards Board of the Appraisal Foundation. *(Adopted 1/95)*

- **Standard of Practice 11-2**

  The obligations of the Code of Ethics in respect of real estate disciplines other than appraisal shall be interpreted and applied in accordance with the standards of competence and practice which clients and the public reasonably require to protect their rights and interests considering the complexity of the transaction, the availability of expert assistance, and, where the REALTOR® is an agent or subagent, the obligations of a fiduciary. *(Adopted 1/95)*

Article 12

REALTORS® shall be careful at all times to present a true picture in their advertising and representations to the public. REALTORS® shall also ensure that their professional status (e.g., broker, appraiser, property manager, etc.) or status as REALTORS® is clearly identifiable in any such advertising. *(Amended 1/93)*

- **Standard of Practice 12-1**

  REALTORS® shall not offer a service described as "free of charge" when the rendering of a service is contingent on the obtaining of a benefit such as a listing or commission.

- **Standard of Practice 12-2**

  REALTORS® shall not represent that their services are free or without cost if they expect to receive compensation from any source other than their client. *(Adopted 1/95)*

- **Standard of Practice 12-3**

  The offering of premiums, prizes, merchandise discounts or other inducements to list, sell, purchase, or lease is not, in itself, unethical even if receipt of the benefit is contingent on listing, selling, purchasing, or leasing through the REALTOR® making the offer. However, REALTORS® must exercise care and candor in any such advertising or other public or private representations so that any party interested in receiving or otherwise benefiting from the REALTOR®'s offer will have clear, thorough, advance understanding of all the terms and conditions of the offer. The offering of any inducements to do business is subject to the limitations and restrictions of state law and the ethical obligations established by any applicable Standard of Practice. *(Amended 1/95)*

- **Standard of Practice 12-4**

  REALTORS® shall not offer for sale/lease or advertise property without authority. When acting as listing brokers or as subagents, REALTORS® shall not quote a price different from that agreed upon with the seller/landlord. *(Amended 1/93)*

- **Standard of Practice 12-5**

  REALTORS® shall not advertise nor permit any person employed by or affiliated with them to advertise listed property without disclosing the name of the firm. *(Adopted 11/86)*

- **Standard of Practice 12-6**

  REALTORS®, when advertising unlisted real property for sale/lease in which they have an ownership interest, shall disclose their status as both owners/landlords and as REALTORS® or real estate licensees. *(Amended 1/93)*

- **Standard of Practice 12-7**

  Only REALTORS® as listing brokers, may claim to have "sold" the property, even when the sale resulted through the cooperative efforts of another broker. However, after transactions have closed, listing brokers may not prohibit successful cooperating brokers from advertising their "cooperation," "participation," or "assistance" in the transaction, or from making similar representations.

  Only listing brokers are entitled to use the term "sold" on signs, in advertisements, and in other public representations. *(Amended 1/90)*

Article 13

REALTORS® shall not engage in activities that constitute the unauthorized practice of law and shall recommend that legal counsel be obtained when the interest of any party to the transaction requires it.

Article 14

If charged with unethical practice or asked to present evidence or to cooperate in any other way, in any disciplinary proceeding or investigation, REALTORS® shall place all pertinent facts before the proper tribunals of the Member Board or affiliated institute, society, or council in which membership is held and shall take no action to disrupt or obstruct such processes. *(Amended 1/90)*

- **Standard of Practice 14-1**

  REALTORS® shall not be subject to disciplinary proceedings in more than one Board of REALTORS® or affiliated institute, society or council in which they hold membership with respect to alleged violations of the Code of Ethics relating to the same transaction or event. *(Amended 1/95)*

- **Standard of Practice 14-2**

  REALTORS® shall not make any unauthorized disclosure or dissemination of the allegations, findings, or decision developed in connection with an ethics hearing or appeal or in connection with an arbitration hearing or procedural review. *(Amended 1/92)*

Figure 2.1. (continued)

- **Standard of Practice 14-3**

  REALTORS® shall not obstruct the Board's investigative or disciplinary proceedings by instituting or threatening to institute actions for libel, slander or defamation against any party to a professional standards proceeding or their witnesses. *(Adopted 11/87)*

- **Standard of Practice 14-4**

  REALTORS® shall not intentionally impede the Board's investigative or disciplinary proceedings by filing multiple ethics complaints based on the same event or transaction. *(Adopted 11/88)*

Duties to REALTORS®

Article 15

REALTORS® shall not knowingly or recklessly make false or misleading statements about competitors, their businesses, or their business practices. *(Amended 1/92)*

Article 16

REALTORS® shall not engage in any practice or take any action inconsistent with the agency of other REALTORS®.

- **Standard of Practice 16-1**

  Article 16 is not intended to prohibit aggressive or innovative business practices which are otherwise ethical and does not prohibit disagreements with other REALTORS® involving commission, fees, compensation or other forms of payment or expenses. *(Adopted 1/93, Amended 1/95)*

- **Standard of Practice 16-2**

  Article 16 does not preclude REALTORS® from making general announcements to prospective clients describing their services and the terms of their availability even though some recipients may have entered into agency agreements with another REALTOR®. A general telephone canvass, general mailing or distribution addressed to all prospective clients in a given geographical area or in a given profession, business, club, or organization, or other classification or group is deemed "general" for purposes of this standard.

  Article 16 is intended to recognize as unethical two basic types of solicitations:

  First, telephone or personal solicitations of property owners who have been identified by a real estate sign, multiple listing compilation, or other information service as having exclusively listed their property with another REALTOR®; and

  Second, mail or other forms of written solicitations of prospective clients whose properties are exclusively listed with another REALTOR® when such solicitations are not part of a general mailing but are directed specifically to property owners identified through compilations of current listings, "for sale" or "for rent" signs, or other sources of information required by Article 3 and Multiple Listing Service rules to be made available to other REALTORS® under offers of subagency or cooperation. *(Amended 1/93)*

- **Standard of Practice 16-3**

  Article 16 does not preclude REALTORS® from contacting the

client of another broker for the purpose of offering to provide, or entering into a contract to provide, a different type of real estate service unrelated to the type of service currently being provided (e.g., property management as opposed to brokerage). However, information received through a Multiple Listing Service or any other offer of cooperation may not be used to target clients of other REALTORS® to whom such offers to provide services may be made. *(Amended 1/93)*

- **Standard of Practice 16-4**

  REALTORS® shall not solicit a listing which is currently listed exclusively with another broker. However, if the listing broker, when asked by the REALTOR®, refuses to disclose the expiration date and nature of such listing; i.e., an exclusive right to sell, an exclusive agency, open listing, or other form of contractual agreement between the listing broker and the client, the REALTOR® may contact the owner to secure such information and may discuss the terms upon which the REALTOR® might take a future listing or, alternatively, may take a listing to become effective upon expiration of any existing exclusive listing. *(Amended 1/94)*

- **Standard of Practice 16-5**

  REALTORS® shall not solicit buyer/tenant agency agreements from buyers/tenants who are subject to exclusive buyer/tenant agency agreements. However, if a buyer/tenant agent, when asked by a REALTOR®, refuses to disclose the expiration date of the exclusive buyer/tenant agency agreement, the REALTOR® may contact the buyer/tenant to secure such information and may discuss the terms upon which the REALTOR® might enter into a future buyer/tenant agency agreement or, alternatively, may enter into a buyer/tenant agency agreement to become effective upon the expiration of any existing exclusive buyer/tenant agency agreement. *(Adopted 1/94)*

- **Standard of Practice 16-6**

  When REALTORS® are contacted by the client of another REALTOR® regarding the creation of an agency relationship to provide the same type of service, and REALTORS® have not directly or indirectly initiated such discussions, they may discuss the terms upon which they might enter into a future agency agreement or, alternatively, may enter into an agency agreement which becomes effective upon expiration of any existing exclusive agreement. *(Amended 1/93)*

- **Standard of Practice 16-7**

  The fact that a client has retained a REALTOR® as an agent in one or more past transactions does not preclude other REALTORS® from seeking such former client's future business. *(Amended 1/93)*

- **Standard of Practice 16-8**

  The fact that an agency agreement has been entered into with a REALTOR® shall not preclude or inhibit any other REALTOR® from entering into a similar agreement after the expiration of the prior agreement. *(Amended 1/93)*

- **Standard of Practice 16-9**

  REALTORS®, prior to entering into an agency agreement, have an affirmative obligation to make reasonable efforts to determine whether the client is subject to a current, valid exclusive agreement to provide the same type of real estate service. *(Amended 1/93)*

Figure 2.1. (continued)

- **Standard of Practice 16-10**

  REALTORS®, acting as agents of buyers or tenants, shall disclose that relationship to the seller/landlord's agent at first contact and shall provide written confirmation of that disclosure to the seller/landlord's agent not later than execution of a purchase agreement or lease. *(Amended 1/93)*

- **Standard of Practice 16-11**

  On unlisted property, REALTORS® acting as buyer/tenant agents shall disclose that relationship to the seller/landlord at first contact for that client and shall provide written confirmation of such disclosure to the seller/landlord not later than execution of any purchase or lease agreement.

  REALTORS® shall make any request for anticipated compensation from the seller/landlord at first contact. *(Amended 1/93)*

- **Standard of Practice 16-12**

  REALTORS®, acting as agents of sellers/landlords or as subagents of listing brokers, shall disclose that relationship to buyers/tenants as soon as practicable and shall provide written confirmation of such disclosure to buyers/tenants not later than execution of any purchase or lease agreement. *(Amended 1/93)*

- **Standard of Practice 16-13**

  All dealings concerning property exclusively listed, or with buyer/tenants who are exclusively represented shall be carried on with the client's agent, and not with the client, except with the consent of the client's agent. *(Adopted 1/93)*

- **Standard of Practice 16-14**

  REALTORS® are free to enter into contractual relationships or to negotiate with sellers/landlords, buyers/tenants or others who are not represented by an exclusive agent but shall not knowingly obligate them to pay more than one commission except with their informed consent. *(Amended 1/94)*

- **Standard of Practice 16-15**

  In cooperative transactions REALTORS® shall compensate cooperating REALTORS® (principal brokers) and shall not compensate nor offer to compensate, directly or indirectly, any of the sales licensees employed by or affiliated with other REALTORS® without the prior express knowledge and consent of the cooperating broker.

- **Standard of Practice 16-16**

  REALTORS®, acting as subagents or buyer/tenant agents, shall not use the terms of an offer to purchase/lease to attempt to modify the listing broker's offer of compensation to subagents or buyer's agents nor make the submission of an executed offer to purchase/lease contingent on the listing broker's agreement to modify the offer of compensation. *(Amended 1/93)*

- **Standard of Practice 16-17**

  REALTORS® acting as subagents or as buyer/tenant agents, shall not attempt to extend a listing broker's offer of cooperation and/or compensation to other brokers without the consent of the listing broker. *(Amended 1/93)*

- **Standard of Practice 16-18**

  REALTORS® shall not use information obtained by them from the listing broker, through offers to cooperate received through Multiple Listing Services or other sources authorized by the listing broker, for the purpose of creating a referral prospect to a third broker, or for creating a buyer/tenant prospect unless such use is authorized by the listing broker. *(Amended 1/93)*

- **Standard of Practice 16-19**

  Signs giving notice of property for sale, rent, lease, or exchange shall not be placed on property without consent of the seller/landlord. *(Amended 1/93)*

Article 17

In the event of a contractual dispute between REALTORS® associated with different firms, arising out of their relationship as REALTORS®, the REALTORS® shall submit the dispute to arbitration in accordance with the regulations of their Board or Boards rather than litigate the matter.

In the event clients of REALTORS® wish to arbitrate contractual disputes arising out of real estate transactions, REALTORS® shall arbitrate those disputes in accordance with the regulations of their Board, provided the clients agree to be bound by the decision. *(Amended 1/94)*

- **Standard of Practice 17-1**

  The filing of litigation and refusal to withdraw from it by REALTORS® in an arbitrable matter constitutes a refusal to arbitrate. *(Adopted 2/86)*

- **Standard of Practice 17-2**

  Article 17 does not require REALTORS® to arbitrate in those circumstances when all parties to the dispute advise the Board in writing that they choose not to arbitrate before the Board. *(Amended 1/93)*

The Code of Ethics was adopted in 1913. Amended at the Annual Convention in 1924, 1928, 1950, 1951, 1952, 1955, 1956, 1961, 1962, 1974, 1982, 1986, 1987, 1989, 1990, 1991, 1992, 1993 and 1994.

EXPLANATORY NOTES

The reader should be aware of the following policies which have been approved by the Board of Directors of the National Association:

In filing a charge of an alleged violation of the Code of Ethics by a REALTOR®, the charge must read as an alleged violation of one or more Articles of the Code. Standards of Practice may be cited in support of the charge.

The Standards of Practice serve to clarify the ethical obligations imposed by the various Articles and supplement, and do not substitute for, the Case Interpretations in **Interpretations of the Code of Ethics**.

Modifications to existing Standards of Practice and additional new Standards of Practice are approved from time to time. Readers are cautioned to ensure that the most recent publications are utilized.

NATIONAL ASSOCIATION
OF REALTORS®
430 North Michigan Avenue
Chicago, Illinois 60611-4087

EQUAL HOUSING
OPPORTUNITY

extends through 14 regions across the country with more than 60 active local boards. NAREB education and certification programs include the Real Estate Management Brokers Institute, National Society of Real Estate Appraisers, Real Estate Brokerage Institute, and United Developers Council. The organization's purposes are to promote high standards of service and conduct and to protect the public against unethical, improper, or fraudulent real estate practices.

Match terms **a–x** *with statements* **1–23.**

VOCABULARY REVIEW

a. *Broker*
b. *Code of Ethics*
c. *Continuing education*
d. *Employment contract*
e. *Fictitious business name*
f. *Franchisee*
g. *GRI*
h. *Independent contractor*
i. *Licensee*
j. *Nonresident license*
k. *Notice of consent*
l. *Principal broker*

m. *Division of Licensing Services*
n. *Real estate salesperson*
o. *Realtist*
p. *REALTOR®*
q. *REALTOR-ASSOCIATE®*
r. *Realty board*
s. *Revoke*
t. *Associate broker*
u. *Securities license*
v. *Standards of practice*
w. *Suspend*

1. One who holds a license.
2. A person who is licensed to bring about real estate transactions for a fee, but who must do so only in the employment of a real estate broker.
3. A registered trademark owned by the National Association of REALTORS® for exclusive use by its members.
4. Broker in charge of an office.
5. A business operated under any name other than the owner's name.
6. An independent agent who negotiates transactions for a fee.
7. To temporarily make ineffective.
8. To recall and make void.
9. A local trade organization for real estate licensees and other persons allied with the real estate industry.
10. A broker employed by a principal broker.
11. A state agency that advises and sets policies regarding real estate licensees and real estate transaction procedures.
12. One who uses his or her own methods and is responsible only as to the results.
13. A requirement for license renewal in many states, its purpose is to help licensees keep up to date in real estate.

14. Required of a real estate broker in order to conduct negotiations within another state.
15. Permits the secretary of state to receive legal summonses on behalf of a nonresident broker.
16. Required when selling an investment contract.
17. Formalizes the working arrangement between the broker and salespersons.
18. The party holding a franchise such as a franchised brokerage office.
19. Membership designation for salespersons and broker licensees working for REALTORS®.
20. Standards by which members of the National Association of REALTORS® agree to abide.
21. Interpretations of various articles of the REALTORS® Code of Ethics.
22. A registered trademark for use by members of the National Association of Real Estate Brokers.
23. A designation awarded for completion of real estate courses sponsored by Boards of REALTORS®.

QUESTIONS AND PROBLEMS

1. What factors do brokers consider when deciding what percentage of commissions should be paid to the salespersons in their offices?
2. When is a person required to hold a real estate license?
3. What was the purpose of early real estate license law?
4. Does your state subscribe to the AMP or ASI exam service or does it write all its own questions? How often are the exams given?
5. What trends are apparent in your state with regard to real estate education requirements?
6. What is the name of the person currently in charge of real estate regulation for your state? What are his or her duties and responsibilities?
7. Under what circumstances are real estate licenses suspended or revoked in your state?
8. What is the purpose of a bond or recovery fund? What does your state require?
9. What is the purpose of the National Association of REALTORS®?
10. What items would be covered by an employment contract between a broker and a salesperson?
11. If you were seeking employment as a salesperson for a brokerage firm, how would you decide which firm to associate with?

ADDITIONAL READINGS

Real Estate Brokerage: A Success Guide, 3rd Ed., by **Cyr, Sobeck,** and **Mayfield** (Real Estate Education Co., 1992, 472 pages). Focuses on the nuts and bolts of starting and managing a brokerage business.

Digest of Real Estate License Laws (National Association of Real Estate License Law Officials, 1996, 265 pages). Contains summaries of real estate license laws for each of the United States and the Canadian provinces. Published annually.

Real Estate Principles for License Preparation for the ASI® Exam, 4th Ed. (Regents/Prentice Hall, 1990, 432 pages). A complete overview of information needed for exam success.

* * *

The following periodicals may also be of interest to you: *Affirmative Action Register, Civil Rights Update, Real Estate Business, Real Estate Perspectives, Real Estate Selling, Real Estate Success Secrets, Real Estate Today,* and *Realtor News.*

3

The Principal-Broker Relationship—Employment

KEY • TERMS

Advance fee listing: listing in which a broker gets paid in advance and charges an hourly rate

Broker: one who, for a fee, acts as an agent for others in negotiating contracts or sales

Exclusive authority to purchase: listing utilized by buyer's brokers

Exclusive right to sell: listing that gives the broker the right to collect a commission no matter who sells the property during the listing period

Multiple listing service (MLS): organization of member brokers agreeing to share listing information and commissions

Net listing: a listing agreement that pays the broker an uncertain amount of commission, generating net proceeds from the sale to the principal

Ready, willing, and able buyer: a buyer who is ready to buy at the seller's price and terms and who has the financial capability to do so

Real estate listing: a contract in which a broker is employed to find a buyer or tenant

Chapter 2 discussed licensure requirements and professional affiliations. Chapter 3 expands into theories of agency relationships and duties of care that result from the laws of agency. This chapter discusses the principal-broker relationship as it relates to employment, listing agreements, and compensation of real estate brokers. Note that the formalities of employment are not necessarily required to establish an agency relationship, so the licensee may be responsible as an agent without the benefits of formal employment! In addition, a broker may be hired by a seller/landlord, a buyer/tenant, or both. Let's discuss how this occurs.

A **real estate listing** is an *employment contract* between a property owner and a real estate broker. Through it the property owner appoints the broker as the owner's agent for the specific purpose of finding a buyer or tenant who is willing to meet the conditions set forth in the listing. It does not authorize the broker to sell or convey title to the property or to sign contracts.

LISTING AGREEMENT

Although persons licensed as real estate salespersons perform listing and sales functions, they are actually extensions of the broker. A seller may conduct all aspects of a listing and sale through a salesperson licensee or an associate broker, but it is the broker behind the salesperson with whom the seller has the listing contract and who is legally liable for its proper execution. If you plan to be a salesperson for a broker, be aware of what is legally and ethically required of a broker because you are the broker's eyes, ears, hands, and mouth. If your interest is in listing your property with a broker, know that it is the broker with whom you have the listing contract even though your day-to-day contact is with the broker's sales associates. Sales associates are the licensed salespersons or brokers who work for a broker.

When a property owner signs a listing, all the essential elements of a valid contract must be present. The owner and broker must be legally capable of contracting, there must be mutual assent, and the agreement must be for a lawful purpose. Nearly all states require that a listing be in writing and signed to be valid and thereby enforceable in a court of law.

Figure 3.1 illustrates a simplified **exclusive right to sell** listing agreement. Actual listing contracts tend to be longer and

Figure 3.1.

EXCLUSIVE RIGHT TO SELL
LISTING CONTRACT

[1] *Property Description:*   A single-family house at 2424 E. Main Street, City, State. Legally described as Lot 17, Tract 191, County, State.

Price: $105,000

Terms: Cash

[2] *In consideration of the services of ABC Realty Company (herein called the "Broker"), to be rendered to Roger Leeving and Mary Leeving (herein called the "Owner"), and the promise of said Broker to make reasonable efforts to obtain a purchaser, therefore, the Owner hereby grants to the Broker*

[3] *for the period of time from noon on April 1, 19xx to noon on July 1, 19xx (herein called the "listing period")*

[4] *the exclusive and irrevocable right to advertise and find a purchaser for the above described property at the price and terms shown*

[5] *or for such sum and terms or exchange as the owner later agrees to accept.*

[6] *The Owner hereby agrees to pay Broker a cash fee of 6% of the selling or exchange price:*

[7] *(A) in case of any sale or exchange of the above property within the listing period either by the Broker, the Owner, or any other person, or*

[8] *(B) upon the Broker finding a purchaser who is ready, willing, and able to complete the purchase as proposed by the owner, or*

[9] *(C) in the event of a sale or exchange within 60 days of the expiration of the listing period to any party shown the above property during the listing period by the Broker or his/her representative and where the name was disclosed to the Owner.*

[10] *The Owner agrees to give the Broker access to the buildings on the property for the purposes of showing them at reasonable hours, and allows the Broker to post a "For Sale" sign on the premises.*

Figure 3.1. (continued)

[11] *The Owner agrees to allow the Broker to place this listing information in any multiple listing organization of which he/she is a member and to engage the cooperation of other brokers as subagents to bring about a sale.*

[12] *The Owner agrees to refer to the Broker all inquiries regarding this property during the listing period.*

[13] *Accepted:*

  ABC Realty Company
  By: Kurt Kwiklister   *Owner:* Roger Leeving
                                      Owner: Mary Leeving

  Date: April 1, 19xx

more complex and vary in detail from one contract to the next. The listing in Figure 3.1 is an educational introduction to listings that provides in plain English commonly found listing contract provisions. Beginning at **[1]** is a description of the property plus the price and terms at which the broker is instructed to find a buyer. At **[2]** the broker promises to make a reasonable effort to find a buyer. The period of time that the listing is to be in effect is shown at **[3]**. It is usually to the broker's advantage to make the listing period for as long as possible as this provides more time to find a buyer. Sometimes even an overpriced property will become saleable if the listing period is long enough and prices rise fast enough. However, most owners want a balance between their flexibility and the amount of time necessary for a broker to conduct a sales campaign. In residential sales, 3 to 4 months is a popular compromise; farm, ranch, commercial, and industrial listings are usually made for 6 months to 1 year.

At **[4]** the owner agrees not to list the property with any other brokers, permit other brokers to have a sign on the property, or advertise it during the listing period. Also, the owner agrees not to revoke the broker's exclusive right to find a buyer as set forth by this contract.

The broker recognizes that the owner may later accept price and terms that are different from those in the listing. The wording at **[5]** states that the broker will earn a commission no matter what price and terms the owner ultimately accepts.

Brokerage Commission

At [6] the amount of compensation the owner agrees to pay the broker is established. The usual arrangement is to express the amount as a percentage of the sale or exchange price, although a stated dollar amount could be used if the owner and broker agreed. In any event, the amount of the fee is negotiable between the owner and the broker. An owner who feels the fee is too high can list with someone who charges less or sell the property himself. The broker recognizes that if the fee is too low it will not be worthwhile spending time and effort finding a buyer. The typical commission fee in the United States at present is 5% to 7% of the selling price for houses, condominiums, and small apartment buildings, and 6% to 10% on farms, ranches, and vacant land. On multimillion-dollar improved properties, commissions usually drop to the 1% to 4% range. Brokerage commissions are not set by a state regulatory agency or by local real estate associations. In fact, any effort by brokers to set commission rates among themselves is a violation of federal and state antitrust laws. The penalty can be as much as triple damages and criminal liability.

The conditions under which a commission must be paid by the owner to the broker appear next. At [7] a commission is deemed to be earned if the owner agrees to a sale or exchange of the property regardless of who finds the buyer. (Recall that this is an "exclusive right to sell" listing agreement.) In other words, even if the owner finds a buyer, or a friend of the owner finds a buyer, the broker is entitled to a full commission fee. If the owner disregards the promise at [4] and lists with another broker who then sells the property, the owner is liable for two full commissions.

Protecting the Broker

The wording at [8] is included to protect the broker against the possibility that the owner may refuse to sell after the broker has expended time and effort to find a buyer at the price and terms of the listing contract. The listing itself is not an offer to sell property. It is strictly a contract whereby the owner employs the broker to find a buyer. Thus, even though a buyer offers to pay the exact price and terms shown in the listing, the buyer does not have a binding sales contract until the offer is accepted in writing by the owner. However, if the owner refuses to sell at the listed price and terms, the broker is still entitled to a commission. If the owner does not pay the broker voluntarily, the broker can file a lawsuit against the owner to collect.

At **[9]** the broker is protected against the possibility that the listing period will expire while still working with a prospective purchaser. In fairness to the owner, however, two limitations are placed on the broker. First, a sales contract must be concluded within a reasonable time after the listing expires, and second, the name of the purchaser must have been given to the owner before the listing period expires.

Protecting the Owner

Continuing at **[10]**, the owner agrees to let the broker enter the property at reasonable hours to show it and put a "For Sale" sign on the property. At **[11]** the property owner gives the broker specific permission to enter the property into a multiple listing service and to engage the cooperation of other brokers as sub-agents to bring about a sale.

At **[12]** the owner agrees to refer all inquiries regarding the availability of the property to the broker. The purpose is to discourage the owner from thinking that he might be able to save a commission by personally selling it during the listing period, and to provide sales leads for the broker. Finally, at **[13]** the owner and the broker (or the broker's sales associate if authorized to do so) sign and date the agreement.

The listing illustrated in Figure 3.1 is called an **exclusive right to sell** or **exclusive authorization to sell** listing. Its distinguishing characteristic is that no matter who sells the property during the listing period, the listing broker is entitled to a commission. This is the most widely used type of listing in the United States. Once signed by the owner and accepted by the broker, the primary advantage to the broker is that the money and effort the broker expends on advertising and showing the property will be to the broker's benefit. The advantage to the owner is that the broker will usually put more effort into selling a property if the broker holds an exclusive right to sell than if the broker has an exclusive agency or an open listing.

EXCLUSIVE RIGHT TO SELL LISTING

The **exclusive agency listing** is similar to the listing shown in Figure 3.1, except that the owner may sell the property himself during the listing period and not owe a commission to the broker. The broker, however, is the only broker who can act as

EXCLUSIVE AGENCY LISTING

an agent during the listing period; hence the term exclusive agency. For an owner, this type of listing may seem like the best of two worlds: the owner has a broker looking for a buyer, but if the owner finds a buyer first, the owner can save a commission fee. The broker is less enthusiastic because the broker's efforts can be undermined too easily by the owner. Consequently, the broker may not expend as much effort on advertising and showing the property as with an exclusive right to sell.

OPEN LISTING

Open listings carry no exclusive rights. An owner can give an open listing to any number of brokers at the same time, and the owner can still find a buyer and avoid a commission. This gives the owner the greatest freedom of any listing form, but there is little incentive for the broker to expend time and money showing the property since the broker has little control over who will be compensated if the property is sold. The broker's only protection is that if the broker does find a buyer at the listing price and terms, the broker is entitled to a commission. This reluctance to develop a sales effort usually means that few, if any, offers will be received and the result may be no sale or a sale below market price. Yet, if a broker does find a buyer, the commission earned may be the same as with an exclusive right to sell.

NET LISTING

A **net listing** is created when an owner states the price he wants for his property and then agrees to pay the broker anything above that price as the commission. It can be written in the form of an exclusive right to sell, an exclusive agency, or an open listing. If a homeowner asks for a "net $60,000" and the broker sells the home for $65,000, the commission would be $5,000. By using the net listing method, many owners feel that they are forcing the broker to look to the buyer for the commission by marking up the price of the property. In reality though, would a buyer pay $65,000 for a home that is worth $60,000? Because of widespread misunderstanding regarding net listings, some states, including New York, prohibit them outright, and most brokers strenuously avoid them even when requested by property owners. There is no law that says a broker must accept a listing; a broker is free to accept only those listings for which the broker can perform a valuable service and earn an honest profit.

Traditionally, real estate brokers charge a fee for their services based on a percentage of the sales price. Out of this percentage, the broker (1) pays all out-of-pocket costs of marketing the property such as advertising and office overhead, (2) pays those who negotiate the transaction, and (3) earns a profit for the firm. If a buyer is not found, the broker receives no money. This means commissions earned from sold properties must also pay for costs incurred by nonsales. Sellers who have marketable property that is priced to sell subsidize sellers whose property is either unattractive or overpriced. As a solution to this inequity, attention is now being given by the real estate industry to the concept of advance fee listings and advance cost listings.

ADVANCE FEE LISTING

An **advance fee listing** is a listing in which a broker charges a seller much like an attorney charges a client. In other words, the broker asks for an advance deposit from the seller. Against this the broker charges an hourly fee for time spent selling the property plus out-of-pocket expenses. With the seller paying for services as consumed, the seller becomes much more realistic about marketability and listed price. There is less inclination to price above market in hopes that if the broker works long enough, a buyer might be found who will pay above market or that the market will eventually rise to the asking price.

An **advance cost listing** covers only out-of-pocket costs incurred by the broker such as advertising, multiple listing fees, flyers, mailings, toll calls, survey, soil report, title report, travel expenses, and food served during open houses. With either the advance fee or advance cost arrangement the broker can still charge a commission based on sales price. In this case, costs and hourly fees are deducted from the commission at the closing. With the broker receiving payment for costs (and effort) up front, the sales commission can be lowered.

Advance Cost Listing

The mechanics of advance fee and advance cost listings must be very clearly explained to the seller before the listing is signed. There must be an accurate accounting of where the seller's money is being spent. (This is an ideal task for a computer.) Moreover, state real estate regulators may have specific rules and prohibitions that must be followed. Watch the advance fee trend. If it takes hold, it will be an important factor in changing real estate agents from commissioned salespeople to professionals who can command an hourly fee for their time.

*EXCLUSIVE
AUTHORITY
TO PURCHASE*

Previous portions of this chapter have presumed the general rule that the real estate broker represents the seller. Historically, it has been the seller who has hired brokers to assist in marketing property. There are circumstances, however, in which a buyer may want to employ a broker's services to help them to locate property, or to assist them in negotiating the acquisition of a specified property. In such cases, the broker's primary responsibility is to the purchaser rather than to the seller. In this circumstance, the purchaser can reveal confidential information to the broker and rely on the broker's expertise and competence. This may be particularly helpful in situations where a real estate transaction is complex, or there are peculiar concerns unique to certain regions of the country (termites in Houston, radon in Maine, soil conditions in California) about which a buyer wants to be adequately advised before buying real estate in that area. In some cases, a purchaser simply feels he needs expert advice on making real estate acquisitions anywhere.

In these situations, the principal needs to be assured as to the scope of employment of the broker (i.e., locating the property) and, similar to a listing contract, the broker needs to be assured that he is protected, and that the buyer does not "go around" the broker and cut the broker out of a commission once the property has been identified. Figure 3.2 shows a simplified version of an **exclusive authority to purchase** contract. Note at [1] the parties are named. The real difference in this contract, versus the Listing Agreement, occurs at [2], designating the property to be acquired in general terms, so that the broker has guidance as to what type of property to be looking for. Compensation is different also. Most buyer's brokers would anticipate being able to access commission splits through the traditional MLS system. If, however, a seller or listing broker refuses to split a commission, there must be an alternative for compensation at [3] for that buyer's broker. Note at [4] that there is an expiration date for the term of the agreement; at [5], a requirement by the owner to refer all inquiries to the broker; and at [6], a signature provision for both the buyer's broker and the purchaser.

*MULTIPLE LISTING
SERVICE*

Multiple listing service (MLS) organizations enable a broker with a listing to make a blanket offering of subagency and/or compensation to other member brokers, thus broadening the market exposure for a given property. Member brokers are author-

Figure 3.2. Exclusive authority to purchase.

[1] This Agreement is made in _____ on this _____ day of _____ , 19 _____ , whereby _____ (hereinafter referred to as "Buyer") hereby appoints Buyer's Broker (hereinafter referred to as "Broker") as Buyer's exclusive agent for the purposes set forth in Section 2 hereof and under the terms specified herein.

[5] Section 1. Buyer agrees to conduct all negotiations for property of the type described in Section 2 hereof through Broker, and to refer to Broker all inquiries received in any form from real estate brokers, salespersons, prospective sellers, or any other source, during the time this Agreement is in effect.

[2] Section 2. Buyer desires to purchase or lease real property (which may include items of personal property) described as follows:

Type: (_) Residential   (_) Residential Income   (_) Other
        (_) Commercial   (_) Industrial   (_) Vacant Land

General Description: _____

Approximate price range: $ _____ to $_____ , or any other amount which Buyer ultimately decides to spend.

Preferred Terms: _____

[4] Section 3. Broker's authority as Buyer's exclusive agent shall begin upon Buyer's signing this Agreement, and shall continue until _____ , 19 _____ , unless sooner terminated or by completion of the purpose(s) of the agency as set forth in Section 2 hereof.

Section 4. Broker represents that Broker is duly licensed as a real estate broker, and agrees that Broker will use Broker's best efforts as Buyer's agent to locate property as described in Section 2 hereof, and to negotiate acceptance of any offer to purchase or lease such property. Broker shall submit to Buyer for the Buyer's consideration, properties appearing to Broker to substantially meet the criteria set forth in Section 2.

[3] Section 5. In consideration of the services to be performed by Broker, Buyer agrees to pay Broker an amount equal to the greater of:

(a)   (_) Retainer Fee. Buyer will pay Broker a nonrefundable retainer fee of $ _____ due and payable upon signing of this Agreement. (_) Retainer Fee shall be credited against commission, IF ANY, as set forth in Subsection 5(c) herein or Retainer Fee shall be retained by Broker in addition to commission; or

(b)   (_) Hourly Fee. Buyer will pay Broker at the rate of $ _____ per hour for the time spent by Broker pursuant to this Agreement, to be paid to Broker when billed to Buyer.   (_) Fee shall be credited against commission, IF ANY, or   (_) Fee shall be considered full payment of Broker's compensation; or

(c)   (_) Commission. Parties hereby agree that Broker shall first seek compensation out of the transaction. Should the fee so obtained be greater than that listed in Subsection (c) (1) or (2) below, Broker shall pay Buyer the difference at closing. Should the fee so obtained be less than that listed in Subsection (1) or (2) hereof, Buyer shall pay Broker the difference at closing.

Section 6. If a seller in an agreement made on behalf of Buyer fails to close such agreement, with no fault on the part of Buyer, the commission provided in Section 5, Subsection (c), shall be waived. If such transaction fails to close because of any fault on the part of Buyer, such commission will not be waived, but will be due and payable immediately in an amount no less than that referred to in Section 5, said amount to be agreed upon by the parties to be liquidated damages. In no case shall Broker be obligated to advance funds for the benefit of Buyer in order to complete a closing.

Section 7. (_) Broker does (_) does not have Buyer's permission to disclose Buyer's identity to third parties without prior written consent of Buyer.

Section 8. Buyer understands that other potential buyers may consider, make offers on, or purchase through, Broker the same or similar properties as Buyer is seeking to acquire. Buyer consents to Broker's representation of such other potential buyers before, during, and after the expiration of this Agreement.

Section 9. The parties agree not to discriminate against any prospective seller or lessor because of the race, creed, color, sex, marital status, national origin, familial, or handicapped status of such person.

Accepted:

[6] _____   _____
(Buyer's Broker)   (Buyer)

By: _____   _____
        (Title)   (Buyer)

ized to show each other's properties to their prospects. If a sale results, the commission is divided between the broker who found the buyer and the broker who obtained the listing, less a small deduction for the cost of operating the multiple listing service.

Market Exposure   A property listed with a broker who is a multiple listing service member receives the advantage of greater sales exposure which, in turn, means a better price and a quicker sale. For the buyer it means learning about what is for sale at many offices without having to visit each individually. For a broker or salesperson with a prospect, but not a suitable property listed in that office, the opportunity to make a sale is not lost because the prospect can be shown the listings of other brokers.

To give a property the widest possible market exposure and to maintain fairness among its members, most multiple listing organizations obligate each member broker to provide information to the organization on each new listing within 3 to 7 days after the listing is taken. To facilitate the exchange of information, multiple listing organizations have developed customized listing forms. These forms are a combination of an exclusive right to sell listing agreement (with authority to place the listing into multiple) plus a data sheet on the property. The data sheet, which describes all the physical and financial characteristics of the property, and a photograph of the property are published weekly in a multiple listing book that is distributed to MLS members. Then, if Broker B has a prospect interested in a property listed by Broker A, Broker B telephones Broker A and arranges to show the property. If Broker B's prospect makes an offer on the property, Broker B contacts Broker A and together they call on the seller with the offer.

MLS has recently amended their by-laws to allow for buyer brokerage. The MLS profile sheets provide the listing broker the opportunity to make an offer to compensate the buyers' brokers. They allow the buyer's broker, who is a member of MLS, to access all the benefits of MLS, but to reject the automatic offer of subagency. In effect, the buyer's broker can access the commission split, but maintain a fiduciary duty to the purchaser, rather than to the seller of the property.

MLS organizations have been challenged in court for being open only to members of local real estate associations. The courts have also tested the idea that an MLS should be open to anyone who wants to list a property, broker or owner. It is generally held, though, that the MLS membership criterion is valid and important to the system's function. Owners lacking real estate sophistication would place much inaccurate information in the MLS and this would do considerable harm to MLS members who must rely on that information when describing and showing properties. It is important to note that the sharing of MLS information with nonmembers violates federal copyright laws.

In addition to publishing MLS books, a number of multiple listing services store their listing information in computers. A salesperson with a briefcase-sized MLS terminal can use any telephone, dial the MLS computer, place the handpiece on the terminal, and request up-to-the-minute information for any property in the computer. This system is popular with salespeople who are constantly in the field showing property or in their cars (where they can link up by cellular telephone). It is also quicker than waiting for updated printed MLS information.

Computerized MLS

Electronic advances now make it possible to give a prospective buyer a visual tour through a neighborhood without leaving the broker's office. A single videodisc can store over 100,000 still photographs of individual properties, neighborhoods, schools, shopping centers, recreation facilities, and so on. The discs are professionally shot and duplicated and made available to real estate offices for a fee. The storage capacity of a disc is so large that every property in a community can be photographed and placed on the disc. In the real estate office a salesperson can play back any image from the disc onto a television screen. With an MLS book in hand, the salesperson can show a prospect a color picture of each property for sale, along with pictures of the street, neighborhood, nearby schools, and shopping facilities. Realty offices with computerized access to MLS files can interface the videodisc with the MLS computer.

Videodisc

A broker earns a commission at whatever point in the transaction broker and owner have agreed on. In nearly all listing contracts, this point occurs when the broker produces a **"ready, willing, and able buyer"** at price and terms acceptable to the owner. (See **[8]** in Figure 3.1.) "Ready and willing" means

BROKER COMPENSATION

a buyer who is ready to buy at the seller's price and terms. "Able" means financially capable of completing the transaction. An alternative arrangement is for the broker and owner to agree to a "no sale, no commission" arrangement whereby the broker is not entitled to a commission until the transaction is closed.

The difference between the two arrangements becomes important when a buyer is found at price and terms acceptable to the owner, but no sale results. The "ready, willing, and able" contract provides more protection for the broker since the commission does not depend on the deal reaching settlement. The "no sale, no commission" approach is to the owner's advantage, because commission payment is not required unless the sale is completed. Court decisions have tended to blur the clear-cut distinction between the two. For example, with a "no sale, no commission" agreement, it would appear that if the broker found a ready, willing, and able buyer at the listing price and terms and the owner refused to sell, the owner would owe no commission because no sale was completed. However, a court of law would find in favor of the broker for the full amount of the commission if the refusal to sell was arbitrary and without reasonable cause or in bad faith.

Another change taking place is that traditionally the owner determined whether the buyer was, in fact, financially able to buy. The legal thinking today is that brokers should be responsible for this determination because they are in a much better position to analyze the buyer's financial ability than are owners.

Procuring Cause   Under an open listing or an exclusive agency listing a broker is entitled to a commission if the broker was the procuring cause of the sale and can prove it. **Procuring cause** means that broker's efforts originated the sale. Suppose that a broker shows an open-listed property to a prospective buyer and during the listing period or an extension the prospect goes directly to the owner and concludes a deal. Even though the owner negotiates his or her own transaction and prepares the sales contract, the broker is entitled to a full commission for finding the buyer. This would also be true if the owner and the buyer used subterfuge or a straw man to purchase the property to avoid paying a commission. State laws protect the broker who, in good faith, has produced a buyer at the request of an owner.

When an open listing is given to two or more brokers, the first one who produces a buyer is entitled to the commission. For example, Broker 1 shows a property to Prospect P, but no sale is made. Later P goes to Broker 2 and makes an offer that is accepted by the owner. Although two brokers have attempted to sell the property, only Broker 2 has succeeded, and so Broker 2 is entitled to the commission. The fact that Broker 1 receives nothing, even though considerable effort may have been expended, is an important reason why brokers dislike open listings.

Buyer's brokers present different issues with respect to procuring cause. Buyer's representation agreements typically do not have a legal description of the specific property to be acquired; it is described in general terms as to type and price range. In effect, a buyer's broker has the right to pursue a commission against the buyer when the designated property has been located, but the buyer refuses to purchase. Similar problems may occur if the buyer locates another property without the buyer's broker's assistance, then refuses to compensate the broker. The buyer's broker has the right to pursue compensation, but proving the "designated product" may be difficult.

In a listing contract the usual situation is that the broker finds a buyer acceptable to the owner. Thus, in most listing contracts the agency terminates because the objective of the contract has been completed. In the bulk of the listings for which a buyer is not found, the agency is terminated because the listing period expires. If no listing period is specified, the listing is considered to be effective for a "reasonable" length of time. A court might consider 3 months to be reasonable for a listing for a home and 6 months reasonable for an apartment building or commercial property. Listing contracts without termination dates are revocable by the principal at any time, provided the purpose of the revocation is not to deprive the broker of an earned commission. A major disadvantage of listings without termination dates is that all too often they evolve into expensive and time-consuming legal hassles.

Even when a listing has a specific termination date, the owner may still tell the broker to stop showing the property and stop bringing offers. However, liability for breach of the employment aspect of the contract remains, and the broker can demand

TERMINATING
THE EMPLOYMENT
CONTRACT

compensation for effort expended on behalf of the owner to that point. This can be as much as a full commission if the broker has already found a ready, willing, and able buyer at the owner's price and terms.

Mutual Agreement

A listing can be terminated by mutual agreement of both the owner and broker without money damages. Because listings are the stock in trade of the brokerage business, brokers do not like to lose listings, but sometimes this is the only logical alternative available since the time and effort spent setting and collecting damages can be very expensive. Suppose, however, that a broker has an exclusive right to sell listing and suspects that the owner is requesting cancellation because he or she has found a buyer and wants to avoid paying a commission. The broker can stop showing the property, but the owner is still obligated to pay a commission if the property is sold before the listing period expires. Whatever the broker and seller decide should be put in writing and signed by both parties.

With an open listing, once the property is sold by anyone, broker or owner, all listing agreements pertaining to the property automatically terminate. Similarly, with an exclusive agency listing, if the owner sells the property the broker's listing automatically terminates.

Abandonment

A listing can be terminated by improper performance or abandonment by the broker. Thus, if a broker acts counter to the owner's best financial interests, the listing is terminated, no commission is payable, and the broker may be subject to a lawsuit for any damages suffered by the owner. If a broker takes a listing and then does nothing to promote it, the owner can assume that the broker abandoned it and thereby has grounds for revocation. The owner should keep written documentation in the event the matter ever goes to court.

A listing is automatically terminated by the death of either the owner or the broker, or if either is judged legally incompetent by virtue of insanity.

BARGAIN BROKERS

The full-service real estate broker who takes a listing and places it in the multiple listing service, places and pays for advertising, holds open houses, qualifies prospects, shows property, obtains offers, negotiates, opens escrow, and follows through until closing is the mainstay of the real estate selling industry. The vast majority of open-market sales are handled that way. The remainder are sold by owners, some handling everything themselves and some using flat-fee brokers who oversee the transaction but do not do the actual showing and selling.

For a fee that typically ranges from $400 to $1,500, a **flat-fee broker** will list a property, suggest a market price, write advertising, assist with negotiations, draw up a sales contract, and turn the signed papers over to an escrow company for closing. The homeowner is responsible for paying for advertising, answering inquiries, setting appointments with prospects, showing the property, and applying whatever salesmanship is necessary to induce the prospect to make an offer. Under the flat-fee arrangement, also called self-help brokerage, the homeowner is effectively buying real estate services on an a la carte basis. Some brokerage firms have been very successful offering sellers a choice between a la carte and full service.

Flat-Fee Broker

A **discount broker** is a full-service broker who charges less than the prevailing commission rates in the community. The discount broker attracts sellers by offering to do the job for less money, for example, 3% to 4% instead of 5% to 7%. Charging less means a discount broker must sell more properties to be successful. Consequently, most discount brokers are careful to take listings only on property that will sell quickly.

Discount Broker

Before leaving the topic of listings, it is valuable to spend a moment discussing the perceived value of real estate sales services. Several studies have shown that sellers of homes feel the fee charged by brokers is too high in relation to time spent selling the property. Those in the real estate business know that the amount of time and effort required to market a property is extensive and often all for nothing if the property does not sell. However, the public does not see this and believes that very little effort is involved, especially if the home sells at market value in 2 or 3 weeks after being shown only a handful of times. Ironically, a market value sale within a month and without the inconvenience of dozens of showings is what the seller is actually seeking. Once it is achieved, however, the fee seems too expensive for the time involved. This leads some sellers to think

PERCEIVED VALUE

in terms of selling their property themselves, perhaps with the aid of a self-help brokerage service. For example, if a person is selling a $100,000 house with an $80,000 loan against it, there is but $20,000 in equity to work with. If the broker's commission is 6% of the sales price ($6,000), the seller is actually paying 30% of his equity to the broker.

What stops more people from do-it-yourself selling is that they need a broker to evaluate the property, describe current market and financing conditions, estimate the most probable selling price, write the sales contract, and handle the closing. To a considerable degree, a real estate licensee's success comes from providing the services homeowners feel they need, listing property at or near market, emphasizing the value of services rendered, and operating in a professional manner to bring about a smooth and speedy sale.

VOCABULARY REVIEW

Match terms **a–i** *with statements* **1–9.**

a. *Advance fee listing*
b. *Agent*
c. *Exclusive agency listing*
d. *Exclusive right to sell*
e. *Flat-fee broker*
f. *Multiple listing service (MLS)*
g. *Net listing*
h. *Open listing*
i. *Procuring cause*

1. A listing that gives a broker a nonexclusive right to find a purchaser.
2. A listing that gives the broker the right to collect a commission no matter who sells the property during the listing period.
3. A listing wherein the owner reserves the right to sell the property himself, but agrees to list with no other broker during the listing period.
4. Person empowered to act by and on behalf of the principal.
5. A listing for which the commission is the difference between the sales price and a minimum price set by the seller.
6. An organization of real estate brokers that exists for the purpose of exchanging listing information.
7. The broker who is the primary cause of a transaction.
8. A listing wherein the broker charges for time by the hour and for out-of-pocket expenses to market a property.
9. A broker who charges a preset brokerage fee that is collected whether or not the property sells.

QUESTIONS AND PROBLEMS

1. Why do brokers strongly prefer to take exclusive right to sell listings rather than exclusive agency or open listings?
2. What does the phrase *ready, willing, and able buyer* mean in a real estate contract?

3. How are listings terminated?
4. What are the primary differences between a broker employed by a seller and a broker employed by the buyer?

ADDITIONAL READINGS

"Multiple Listing Service, Q & A" (*Real Estate News,* Jan. 1994, pp. 7–8). Written by the National Association of Realtors®, this article discusses the MLS and its operation.

Real Estate Brokerage Law, by **Arthur Gaudio** (West Publishing, updated annually). This current book is one of the most complete studies of agency law available.

Real Estate Brokerage Law and Practice, by **Rohan, Goldstein,** and **Bobis** (Matthew Bender, updated annually). See Chapter 2 on brokerage practice.

4

Nature and Description of Real Estate

KEY • TERMS

Fixture: an object that has been attached to land so as to become real estate

Improvement: any form of land development, such as buildings, roads, fences, pipelines, and so on

Meridians: imaginary lines running north and south, used as references in mapping land

Metes and bounds: a detailed method of land description that identifies a parcel by specifying its shape and boundaries

Monument: an iron pipe, stone, tree, or other fixed point used in making a survey

Personal property: a right or interest in things of a temporary or movable nature; anything not classified as real property

Real estate: land and improvements in a physical sense as well as the rights to own or use them; see also **real property**

Recorded plat: a subdivision map filed in the county recorder's office that shows the location and boundaries of individual parcels of land

Riparian right: the right of a landowner whose land borders a river or stream to use and enjoy that water

What is real estate? **Real estate,** or **real property,** is land and the improvements made to land, and the rights to use them. Let us begin this chapter by looking more closely at what is meant by land and improvements. Then in the next chapter we focus our attention on the various rights one may possess in land and improvements.

LAND

Often we think of land as only the surface of the earth, but it is substantially more than that. As Figure 4.1 illustrates, land starts at the center of the earth, passes through the earth's surface, and continues on into space. An understanding of this concept is important because, given a particular parcel of land, it is possible for one person to own the rights to use its surface **(surface rights)**, another to own the rights to drill or dig below its surface **(subsurface rights)**, and still another to own the rights to use the airspace above it **(air rights)**.

Figure 4.1.

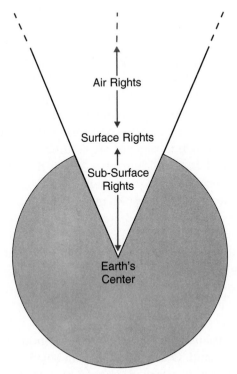

Land includes the surface of the earth and the sky above and everything to the center of the earth.

IMPROVEMENTS

Anything affixed to land with the intent of being permanent is considered to be part of the land and therefore real estate. Thus houses, schools, factories, barns, fences, roads, pipelines, and landscaping are real estate. As a group, these structures are referred to as **improvements** because they improve or develop land.

Being able to identify what is real estate and what is not is important. For example, in conveying ownership to a house, only the lot is described in the deed. It is not necessary to describe the dwelling unit itself or the landscaping, driveways, sidewalks, wiring, or plumbing. Items that are not a part of the land, such as tables, chairs, beds, desks, automobiles, farm machinery, and the like, are classified as **personal property**; if the right to use them is to be transferred to the buyer, a separate **bill of sale** must be drawn, in addition to the deed. Broadly speaking, personal property is everything that is not real property and vice versa.

FIXTURES

When an object that was once personal property is attached to land (or a building thereon) so as to become part of the real estate, it is called a **fixture**. As a rule, a fixture is the property of the landowner and when the land is conveyed to a new owner, it is automatically included with the land. The question of whether an item is a fixture also arises with regard to property taxes, mortgages, lease terminations, and hazard insurance policies. Specifically, real estate taxes are based on real property valuation. Real estate mortgages are secured by real property. Objects attached to a building by a tenant may become real property and hence belong to the building's owner. Hazard insurance policies treat real property differently from personal property.

Whether or not an object becomes real estate depends on whether the object was affixed or installed with the *intention* of permanently improving the land. Intention is evidenced by four tests: (1) the manner of attachment, (2) the adaptation of the object, (3) the existence of an agreement, and (4) the relationship of the parties involved.

Manner of Attachment

The first test, *manner of attachment,* refers to how the object is attached to the land. Ordinarily, when an object that was once personal property is attached to land by virtue of its being imbedded in the land or affixed to the land by means of cement, nails, bolts, and so on, it becomes a fixture. To illustrate, when asphalt and concrete for driveways and sidewalks are still on the delivery truck, they are movable and therefore personal property. But once they are poured into place, the asphalt and concrete become part of the land. Similarly, lumber, wiring, pipes, doors, toilets, sinks, water heaters, furnaces, and other construction materials change from personal property to real estate when they become part of a building. Items brought into the house that do not become permanently affixed to the land remain personal property; for example, furniture, clothing, cooking utensils, radios, and television sets.

Adaptation of the Object

Historically, the manner of attachment was the only method of classifying an object as personal property or real estate, but as time progressed this test alone was no longer adequate. For example, how would you classify custom-made drapes, made for an unusual window? For the answer, we must apply a second test: *How is the article adapted* to the building? If the drapes are specifically made for the window, they are automatically included in the purchase or rental of the building. Another example is the key to a house. Although it spends most of its useful life in a pocket or purse, it is nonetheless quite specifically adapted to the house and therefore a part of it.

Existence of an Agreement

The third test is the *existence of an agreement* between the parties involved. For example, a seller can clarify in advance and in writing to the broker what he considers personal property and thus will be removed and what he does not consider personal property and thus will transfer to the buyer. Likewise, a tenant may obtain an agreement from his landlord stating that items installed by the tenant will not be considered fixtures by the landlord. When it is not readily clear if an item is real or personal property, the use of a well-written agreement can minimize or avoid a subsequent controversy.

Relationship of the Parties

The fourth test in determining whether an item of personal property has become a fixture is to look at the *relationship of the parties*. For example, a supermarket moves into a rented building, then buys and bolts to the floor various **trade fixtures** such as display shelves, meat and dairy coolers, frozen food counters, and checkout stands. When the supermarket later moves out, do these items, by virtue of their attachment, become the property of the building owner? Modern courts rule that tenant-owned trade fixtures do not become the property of the landlord. However, they must be removed before the expiration of the lease and without seriously damaging the building.

Ownership of Plants, Trees, and Crops

Trees, cultivated perennial plants, and uncultivated vegetation of any sort are considered part of the land. For example, landscaping is included in the sale or rental of a house. If a tenant plants a tree or plant in the ground while renting, the tree or plant stays when the lease expires unless both landlord and tenant agree otherwise. Plants and trees in movable pots are personal property and are not generally included in a sale or lease.

Annual cultivated crops are called **emblements,** and most courts of law regard them as personal property even though they are attached to the soil. For example, a tenant farmer is entitled to the fruits of his labor even though the landlord terminates the lease part way through the growing season. When property with harvestable plants, trees, or crops is offered for sale or lease, it is good practice to make clear in any listing, sale, or lease agreement who will have the right to harvest the crop that season. This is particularly true of farm property, where the value of the crop can be quite substantial.

APPURTENANCES

The conveyance of land carries with it any appurtenances to the land. An **appurtenance** is a right or privilege or improvement that belongs to and passes with land but is not necessarily a part of the land. Examples of appurtenances are easements and rights of way (discussed in Chapter 5), condominium parking stalls, and shares of stock in a mutual water company that services the land.

WATER RIGHTS

The ownership of land that borders on a river or stream carries with it the right to use that water in common with the other landowners whose lands border the same watercourse. This is known as a **riparian right**. The landowner does not have absolute ownership of the water that flows past his land but may use it in a reasonable manner. This is the law in New York. In some states, riparian rights have been modified by the **doctrine of prior appropriation**: the first owner to divert water for his or her own use may continue to do so, even though it is not equitable to the other landowners along the watercourse. Where land borders on a lake or sea, it is said to carry **littoral rights** rather than riparian rights. Littoral rights allow landowners to use and enjoy the water touching their land provided they do not alter the water's position by artificial means. Littoral rights would apply to a lakefront lot owner, for example.

Ownership of land normally includes the right to drill for and remove water found below the surface. Where water is not confined to a defined underground waterway, it is known as **percolating water**. In some states, a landowner has the right, in conjunction with neighboring owners, to draw a share of percolating water. Other states subscribe to the doctrine of prior appropriation. When speaking of underground water, the term **water table** refers to the upper limit of percolating water below the earth's surface, also called the **groundwater level**. This level may be only a few feet below the surface or hundreds of feet down.

In 1969, New York voters approved an amendment to the State Constitution declaring the protection of water resources and the abatement of pollution to be the policy of the state. In the years that followed, several new provisions of the state's Environmental Conservation Law have been enacted in keeping with this policy.

LAND DESCRIPTIONS

There are six commonly used methods of describing the location of land: (1) informal reference, (2) metes and bounds, (3) rectangular survey system, (4) recorded plat, (5) assessor's parcel number, and (6) reference to documents other than maps. We shall look at each in detail.

Informal References

Street numbers and place names are informal references: the house located at 7216 Maple Street; the apartment identified as Apartment 101, 875 First Street; the office identified as Suite 222, 3570 Oakview Boulevard; or the ranch known as the Rocking K Ranch—in each case followed by the city (or county) and state where it is located. The advantage of an informal reference is that it is easily understood. The disadvantage from a real estate standpoint is that this method of land description is not precise: a street number or place name does not provide the boundaries of the land at that location, and these numbers and names change over the years. Consequently, in real estate the use of informal references is limited to situations in which convenience is more important than precision. Thus, in a rental contract, Apartment 101, 875 First Street, city and state, is sufficient for a tenant to find the apartment unit. However, if you were buying the apartment building, you would want a more precise land description.

Metes and Bounds　　Early land descriptions in America depended heavily on convenient natural or man-made objects called **monuments**. A stream might serve to mark one side of a parcel, an old oak tree to mark a corner, a road another side, a pile of rocks a second corner, a fence another side, and so forth. This survey method was handy, but it had two major drawbacks: there might not be a convenient corner or boundary marker where one was needed, and, over time, oak trees died, stone heaps were moved, streams and rivers changed course, stumps rotted, fences were removed, and unused roads became overgrown with vegetation. The following description excerpted from the Hartford, Connecticut, probate court records for 1812 illustrates just how difficult it can be to try to locate a parcel's boundaries precisely using only convenient natural or man-made objects:

> Commencing at a heap of stone about a stone's throw from a certain small clump of alders, near a brook running down off from a rather high part of said ridge; thence, by a straight line to a certain marked white birch tree, about two or three times as far from a jog in a fence going around a ledge nearby; thence by another straight line in a different direction, around said ledge, and the Great Swamp, so called; thence . . . to the "Horn," so called, and passing around the same as aforesaid, as far as the "Great Bend," so called, and . . . to a stake and stone not far off from the old Indian trail; thence, by another straight line . . . to the stump of the big hemlock tree where Philo Blake killed the bear; thence, to the corner begun at by two straight lines of about equal length, which are to be run by some skilled and competent surveyor, so as to include the area and acreage as herein before set forth.[*]

---

[*] F. H. Moffit and Harry Bouchard, *Surveying*, 6th Ed. (New York: Harper & Row, 1975). By permission.

The drawbacks of the above outmoded method of land description are resolved by setting a permanent man-made **monument** at one corner of the parcel. This monument is typically an iron pin or pipe 1 to 2 inches in diameter driven several feet into the ground. Sometimes concrete or stone monuments are used. To guard against the possibility that the monument might later be destroyed or removed, it is referenced by means of a connection line to a nearby permanent reference mark established by a government survey agency. Other parcels in the vicinity will also be referenced to the same permanent reference mark.

The surveyor then describes the parcel in terms of distance and direction from that point. This is called **metes and bounds** surveying, which means distance (metes) and direction (bounds). From the monument, the surveyor runs the parcel's outside lines by compass and distance so as to take in the land area being described. Distances are measured in feet, usually to the nearest one-tenth or one-hundredth of a foot. Direction is shown in degrees, minutes, and seconds. There are 360 degrees (°) in a circle, 60 minutes (') in each degree, and 60 seconds (") in each minute. The abbreviation 29°14'52" would be read as 29 degrees, 14 minutes, and 52 seconds. Figure 4.2 illustrates a simple modern metes and bounds land description. Note that at

Permanent Monuments

Figure 4.2. Describing land by metes and bounds.

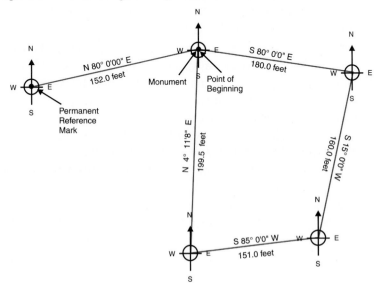

each corner there is superimposed a coordinate system. This may help you better understand how the bounds are set from each point.

Note in Figure 4.2 that with a metes and bounds description, you start from a permanent reference mark and travel to the nearest corner of the property. This is where the parcel survey begins and is called the **point of beginning** or **point of commencement**. From this point in Figure 4.2, we travel clockwise along the parcel's perimeter, reaching the next corner by going in the direction 80° east of south for a distance of 180 feet. We then travel in a direction 15° west of south for 160 feet, thence 85° west of south for 151 feet, and thence 4°, 11', and 8" east of north for 199.5 feet back to the point of beginning. In mapping shorthand, this parcel would be described by first identifying the monument, then the county and state within which it lies, and "thence S80°0'0"E, 180.0'; thence S15°0'0"W, 160.0'; thence S85°0'0"W, 151.0'; thence N4°11'8"E, 199.5' back to the p.o.b." Although one can successfully describe a parcel by traveling around it either clockwise or counterclockwise, it is customary to travel clockwise.

The job of taking a written land description (such as the one in the foregoing example) and locating it on the ground is done by a two-person survey team. The survey team drives a wooden or metal stake into the ground at each corner of the parcel. If a corner lies on a sidewalk, a nail through a brass disc about one-half inch wide is used. (Look closely for these next time you are out walking. At construction sites you will see that corner stakes often have colored streamers on them.) The basic equipment of a survey team includes a compass, a transit, a sight pole or rod, a steel tape, and a computation book. A transit consists of a very accurate compass plus a telescope with cross hairs that can be rotated horizontally and vertically. A transit measures angles accurately to one second of a degree. The sight pole is about 8 feet high and held by the rodman, the second member of the survey team. The surveyor aligns marks on the sight pole with the cross hairs in the telescope. A 100-foot steel tape, made of a special alloy that resists expansion on hot days, is used to measure distances. For longer distances and especially distances across water, canyons, heavy brush, etc., surveyors use laser beam equipment. The beam is aimed at a mirror on the sight pole, bounced back, and electronically converted to a digital readout that shows the distance to the pole. Handheld computers now perform many of the angle and distance computations necessary to a survey.

The compass illustrated in Figure 4.3A shows how the direction of travel along each side of the parcel in Figure 4.2 is determined. Note that the same line can be labeled two ways, depending on which direction you are traveling. To illustrate, look at the line from P to Q. If you are traveling toward P on the line, you are going N 45°W. But, if you are traveling toward point Q on the line, you are going S 45°E.

Curved boundary lines are produced by using arcs of a circle. The length of the arc is labeled L or A; the radius of the circle producing the arc is labeled R. The symbol δ (delta) indicates the angle used to produce the arc (see Figure 4.3B). Where an arc connects to a straight boundary or another arc, the

Compass Directions

Figure 4.3. Metes and bounds mapping.

(A) Naming Directions for a Metes and Bounds Survey

(B) Mapping a Curve

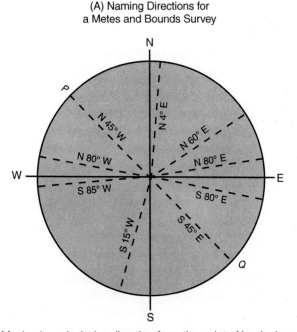

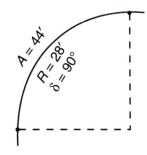

A = Length of the arc. (Some maps use the letter L)
R = Radius of the circle necessary to make the required arc (shown here by the broken lines)
δ = Angle necessary to make the arc, i.e., the angle between the broken lines

Moving in a clockwise direction from the point of beginning, set the center of a circle compass (like the one shown above) on each corner of the parcel to find the direction of travel to the next corner.

connection is indicated by a small circle or by a dot, as shown in Figure 4.3B.

Bench marks are commonly used as permanent reference marks. A bench mark is a fixed mark of known location and elevation. It may be as simple as an iron post or as elaborate as an engraved 3¾" brass disc set into concrete. The mark is usually set in place by a government survey team from the United States Geological Survey (USGS) or the United States Coast and Geodetic Survey (USCGS). Bench marks are referenced to each other by distance and direction. The advantages of this type of reference point, compared with stumps, trees, rocks, and the like, are permanence and accuracy to within a fraction of an inch. Additionally, even though a reference point or monument can be destroyed, it can be replaced in its exact former position because the location of each is related to other reference points. In states using the rectangular survey system or a grid system (discussed shortly), a section corner or a grid intersection is often used as a permanent reference mark. As a convenience to surveyors, it is physically marked with an iron post or a brass disc set in concrete.

Rectangular Survey
System

The **rectangular survey system** was authorized by Congress in May 1785. It was designed to provide a faster and simpler method than metes and bounds for describing land in newly annexed territories and states. New York does not use the rectangular survey system, but one should be familiar with it, since many states do. Rather than using available physical monuments, the rectangular survey system, also known as the **government survey** or **U.S. public land survey system**, is based on imaginary lines. These lines are the east-west **latitude lines** and the north-south **longitude lines** that encircle the earth, as illustrated in Figure 4.4. A helpful way to remember this is that longitude lines **(meridians)** run the long way around the earth.

Certain longitude lines were selected as **principal meridians**. For each of these an intercepting latitude line was selected as a **base line**. Every 24 miles north and south of a base line, **correction lines** or **standard parallels** were established. Every 24 miles east and west of a principal meridian, **guide meridians** were established to run from one standard parallel to the next. These are needed because the earth is a sphere, not a flat surface. As

Figure 4.4. Selected latitude and longitude lines serve as base lines and meridians.

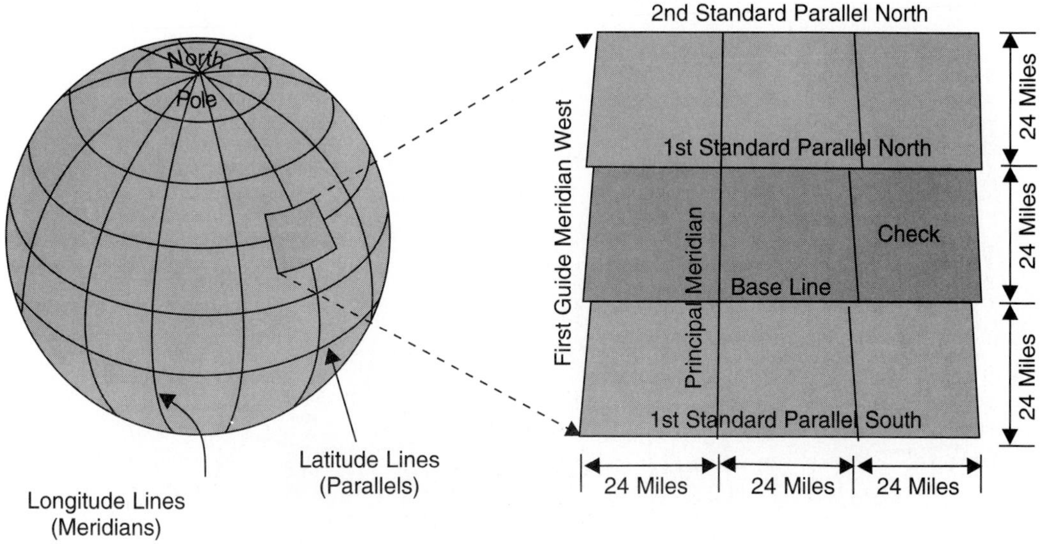

one travels north in the United States, longitude (meridian) lines come closer together—that is, they converge. Figure 4.4 shows how guide meridians and correction lines adjust for this problem. Each 24-by-24-mile area created by the guide meridians and correction lines is called a **check** or **quadrangle**.

There are 36 principal meridians with their intersecting base lines in the U.S. public land survey system. Figure 4.5 shows the states in which this system is used and the land area for which each principal meridian and base line act as a reference. For example, the 6th Principal Meridian is the reference point for land surveys in Kansas, Nebraska, and portions of Colorado, Wyoming, and South Dakota. In addition to the U.S. public land survey system, a portion of western Kentucky was surveyed into townships by a special state survey. Also, the state of Ohio contains eight public land surveys that are rectangular in design, but use state boundaries and major rivers rather than latitude and longitude as reference lines.

Figure 4.6 shows how land is referenced to a principal meridian and a base line. Every 6 miles east and west of each principal meridian, parallel imaginary lines are drawn. The resulting 6-mile-wide columns are called **ranges** and are numbered consecutively east and west of the principal meridian. For example, the first range west is called Range 1 West and

Range

Figure 4.5. The public land survey systems of the United States.

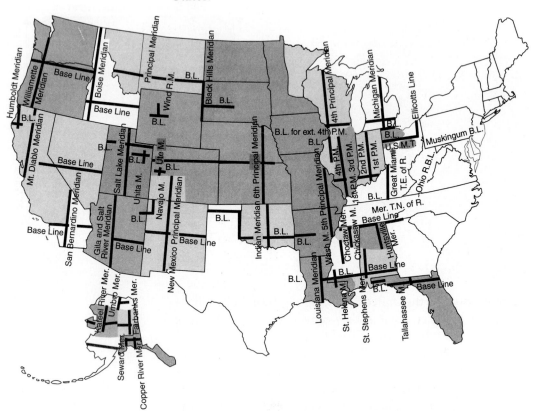

abbreviated R1W. The next range west is R2W, and so forth. The fourth range east is R4E.

Township   Every 6 miles north and south of a base line, township lines are drawn. They intersect with the range lines and produce 6-by-6-mile imaginary squares called **townships** (not to be confused with the word *township* as applied to political subdivisions). Each tier or row of townships thus created is numbered with respect to the base line. Townships lying in the first tier north of a base line all carry the designation Township 1 North, abbreviated T1N. Townships lying in the first tier south of the base line are all designated T1S, and in the second tier south, T2S. By adding a range reference, an individual township can be identified. Thus, T2S, R2W would identify the township lying in the second tier south of the base line and the second range west of the principal meridian. T14N, R52W would be a township 14 tiers north of the base line and 52 ranges west of the principal meridian.

Each 36-square-mile township is divided into 36 one-square-mile units called **sections**. When one flies over farming areas, particularly in the Midwest, the checkerboard pattern of farms and roads that follow section boundaries can be seen. Sections are numbered 1 through 36, starting in the upper right corner of the township. With this numbering system, any two sections with consecutive numbers share a common boundary. The section numbering system is illustrated in the right half of Figure 4.6 where the shaded section is described as Section 32, T2N, R3E, 6th Principal Meridian (P.M.).

Section

Each square-mile section contains 640 acres, and each **acre** contains 43,560 square feet. Any parcel of land smaller than a full 640-acre section is identified by its position in the section. This is done by dividing the section into quarters and halves as

Acre

Figure 4.6. Identifying townships and sections.

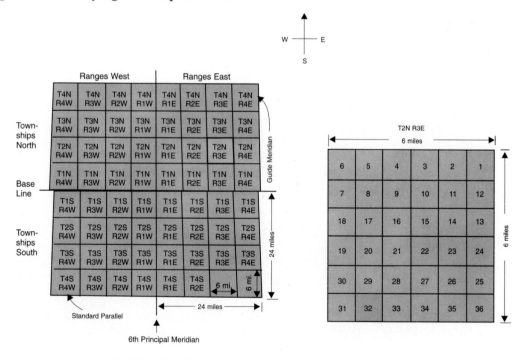

Identifying Townships

Township Divided into Sections

shown in Figure 4.7. For example, the shaded parcel shown at
(A) is described as the NW¼ of the SW¼ of Section 32, T2N, R3E,
6th P.M. Additionally, it is customary to name the county and
state in which the land lies. How much land does the NW¼ of
the SW¼ of a section contain? A section contains 640 acres;
therefore, a **quarter-section** contains 160 acres. Dividing a
quarter-section again into quarters results in four 40-acre parcels.
Thus, the northwest quarter of the southwest quarter contains
40 acres.

The rectangular survey system is not limited to parcels of
40 or more acres. To demonstrate this point, the SE¼ of Section
32 is exploded in the right half of Figure 4.7. Parcel (B) is described as the SE¼ of the SE¼ of the SE¼ of the SE¼ of Section
32 and contains 2½ acres. Parcel (C) is described as the west 15
acres of the NW¼ of the SE¼ of Section 32. Parcel (D) would
be described in metes and bounds using the northeast corner of
the SE¼ of Section 32 as the starting point. When locating or
sketching a rectangular survey on paper, many people find it

Figure 4.7. Subdividing a section.

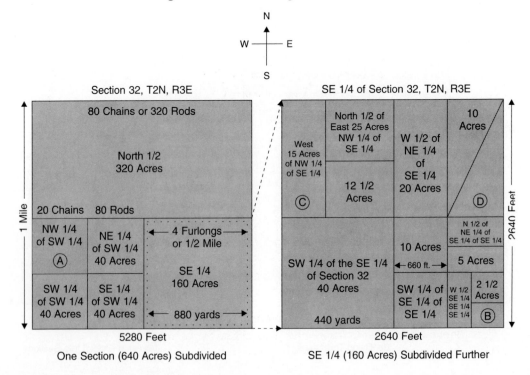

helpful to start at the end of the description and work to the beginning, i.e., to work backwards. Try it.

Not all sections contain exactly 640 acres. Some are smaller because the earth's longitude lines converge toward the North Pole. Also, a section may be larger or smaller than 640 acres due to historical accommodations or survey errors dating back a hundred years or more. For the same reason, not all townships contain exactly 36 square miles. Between 1785 and 1910, the U.S. government paid independent surveyors by the mile. The job was often accomplished by tying a rag to one spoke of the wheel of a buckboard wagon. A team of horses was hitched to the wagon and the surveyor, compass in hand, headed out across the prairie. Distance was measured by counting the number of wheel turns and multiplying by the circumference of the wheel. Today, large area surveys are made with the aid of aerial photographs, sophisticated electronic equipment, and earth satellites.

In terms of surface area, more land in the United States is described by the rectangular survey system than by any other survey method. But in terms of number of properties, the recorded plat is the most important survey method.

Recorded Plat

When a tract of land is ready for subdividing into lots for homes and businesses, reference by **recorded plat** provides the simplest and most convenient method of land description. A **plat** is a map that shows the location and boundaries of individual properties. Also known as the **lot-block-tract system, recorded map**, or **recorded survey**, this method of land description is based on the filing of a surveyor's plat in the public recorder's office of the county where the land is located. Figure 4.8 illustrates a plat. Notice that a metes and bounds survey has been made and a map prepared to show in detail the boundaries of each parcel of land. Each parcel is then assigned a lot number. Each block in the tract is given a block number, and the tract itself is given a name or number. A plat showing all the blocks in the tract is delivered to the county recorder's office, where it is placed in **map books** or **survey books**, along with plats of other subdivisions in the county.

Each plat is given a book and page reference number, and all map books are available for public inspection. From that point on, lengthy metes and bounds descriptions of parcels are

Figure 4.8. Land description by recorded plat.

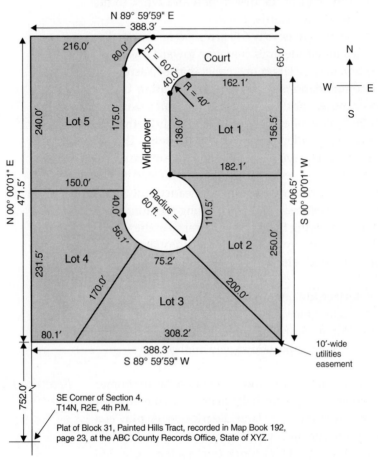

no longer necessary. Instead, one need only provide the lot and block number, tract name, map book reference, county, and state. To find the location and dimensions of a recorded lot, one simply looks in the map book at the county recorder's office.

Note that the plat in Figure 4.8 combines both the land descriptions just discussed. The boundaries of the numbered lots are in metes and bounds. These, in turn, are referenced to a section corner in the rectangular survey system.

Assessor's Parcel Numbers

In many counties in the United States, the tax assessor assigns an **assessor's parcel number** to each parcel of land in the county. The primary purpose is to aid in the assessment of property for tax-collection purposes. However, these parcel numbers are public information and real estate brokers, appraisers, and investors can and do use them extensively to assist in identifying real properties.

A commonly used system is to divide the county into map books. Each book is given a number and covers a given portion of the county. On every page of the map book are parcel maps, each with its own number. For subdivided lots, these maps are based on the plats submitted by the subdivider to the county records office when the subdivision was made. For unsubdivided land, the assessor's office prepares its own maps.

Each parcel of land on the map is assigned a parcel number by the assessor. The assessor's parcel number may or may not be the same as the lot number assigned by the subdivider. To reduce confusion, the assessor's parcel number is either circled or underlined. Figure 4.9 illustrates a page out of an assessor's map book. The assessor also produces an assessment roll that lists every parcel in the county by its assessor's parcel number. Stored and printed by computer now, this roll shows the current owner's name and address and the assessed value of the land and buildings.

The assessor's maps are open to viewing by the public at the assessor's office. In many counties, private firms reproduce the maps and the accompanying list of property owners and make them available to real estate brokers, appraisers, and lenders for a fee.

Before leaving the topic of assessor's maps, a word of caution is in order. These maps should not be relied on as the final authority for the legal description of a parcel. That can come only from a title search that includes looking at the current deed to the property and the recorded copy of the subdivider's plat. Note also that an assessor's parcel number is never used as a legal description in a deed.

Reference to Documents Other Than Maps

Land can also be described by referring to another publicly recorded document, such as a deed or a mortgage, that contains a full legal description of the parcel in question. For example, suppose that several years ago Baker received from Adams a deed that contained a long and complicated metes and bounds description. Baker recorded the deed in the public records office, where a photocopy was placed in Book 1089, page 456. If Baker later wants to deed the same land to Cooper, Baker can describe the parcel in the deed to Cooper by saying, "all the land described in the deed from Adams to Baker recorded in Book 1089, page 456, county of ABC, state of XYZ, at the public recorder's office for said county and state." Because these books are open to the public, Cooper (or anyone else) could go to Book 1089, page 456 and find a detailed description of the parcel's boundaries.

The key test of a land description is: "Can another person, reading what I have written or drawn, understand my description and go out and locate the boundaries of the parcel?"

GRID SYSTEMS   Several states, such as North Carolina and Connecticut, have developed their own statewide systems of reference points for land surveying. The North Carolina system, for example, divides that state into a grid of 84 blocks, each side of which

Figure 4.9. Assessor's map.

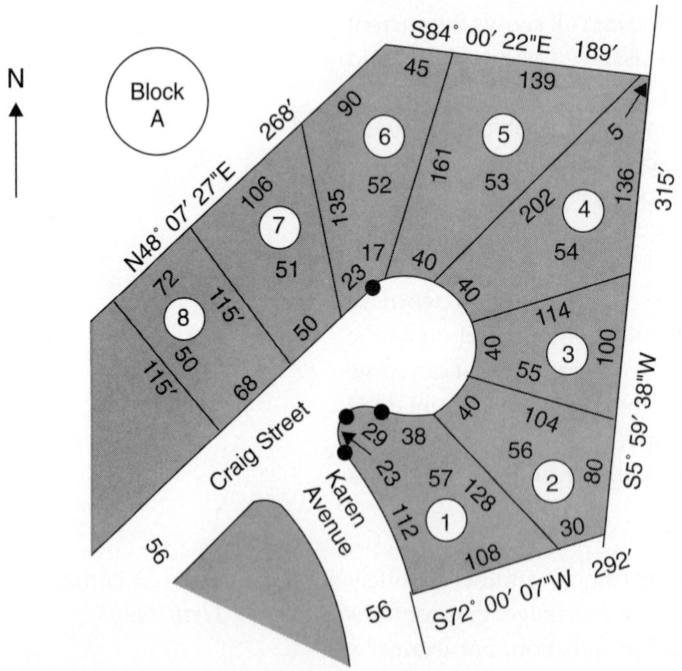

Assessor's Map
Book 34
Page 18

Assessor Parcel Numbers shown in circles

Lots 50 through 57 of Tract 2118, filed in Recorded Maps, Book 63, page 39.

The tax assessor assigns every parcel of land in the county its own parcel number. For example, the westernmost parcel (Lot 50) in the map would carry the number 34-18-8, meaning Book 34, Page 18, Parcel 8.

corresponds to 30 minutes (one-half of one degree) of latitude or longitude. This establishes a **grid system** of intersecting points throughout the state to which metes and bounds surveys can be referenced. State-sponsored grid systems (also called coordinate systems) are especially helpful for surveying large parcels of remote-area land.

In addition to surface land descriptions, land may also be described in terms of vertical measurements. This type of measurement is necessary when air rights or subsurface rights need to be described—as for multistory condominiums or oil and mineral rights.

VERTICAL LAND
DESCRIPTION

A point, line, or surface from which a vertical height or depth is measured is called a **datum**. The most commonly used datum plane in the United States is mean sea level, although a number of cities have established other data surfaces for use in local surveys. Starting from a datum, bench marks are set at calculated intervals by government survey teams; thus, a surveyor need not travel to the original datum to determine an elevation. These same bench marks are used as reference points for metes and bounds surveys.

In selling or leasing subsurface drilling or mineral rights, the chosen datum is often the surface of the parcel. For example, an oil lease may permit the extraction of oil and gas from a depth greater than 500 feet beneath the surface of a parcel of land. (Subsurface rights are discussed in Chapter 5.)

An **air lot** (a space over a given parcel of land) is described by identifying both the parcel of land beneath the air lot and the elevation of the air lot above the parcel (see Figure 4.10A). Multistory condominiums use this system of land description.

Contour maps (topographic maps) indicate elevations. On these maps, **contour lines** connect all points having the same elevation. The purpose is to show hills and valleys, slopes, and water runoff. If the land is to be developed, the map shows where soil will have to be moved to provide level building lots. Figure 4.10B illustrates how vertical distances are shown using contour lines.

In talking about subdivisions you should be familiar with several terms. All of these are illustrated in Figure 4.11. A **cul de sac** is a street that is closed at one end with a circular

LOT TYPES

Figure 4.10. Air lot and contour lines.

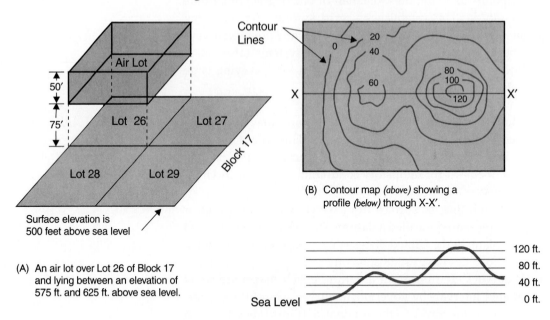

(A) An air lot over Lot 26 of Block 17 and lying between an elevation of 575 ft. and 625 ft. above sea level.

(B) Contour map *(above)* showing a profile *(below)* through X-X'.

turnaround. The pie-shaped lots fronting on the turnaround are called **cul de sac lots**. A **flag lot** is a lot shaped like a flag on a flagpole. This method is popular for creating a buildable lot from the land at the back of a larger lot. A **corner lot** is a lot that fronts on two or more streets. Because of added light and access, a corner lot is usually worth more than an **inside lot**, i.e., a lot with only one side on a street. A **key lot** is a lot that adjoins the side or rear property line of a corner lot. The key lot has added value if it is needed by the corner lot for expansion. A **T lot** is a lot at the end of a **T intersection** as shown in Figure 4.11.

PHYSICAL CHARACTERISTICS OF LAND

The physical characteristics of land are immobility, indestructibility, and nonhomogeneity. This combination of characteristics makes land different from other commodities and directly and indirectly influences man's use of it.

Immobility

A parcel of land cannot be moved. It is true that soil, sand, gravel, and minerals can be moved by the action of nature (erosion) or man (digging); however, the parcel itself still retains its same geographical position on the globe. Because land is *immobile*, a person must go to the land; it cannot be brought to him. When

Figure 4.11. Lot types.

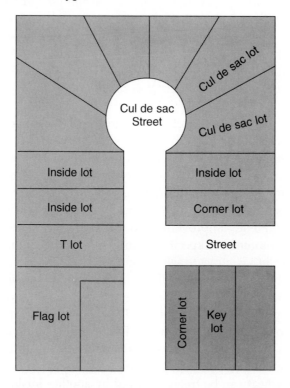

land is sold, the seller cannot physically deliver his land to the buyer. Instead, the seller gives the buyer a document called a deed that transfers to the buyer the right to go onto that land and use it. Because land is immobile, real estate offices nearly always limit their sales activities to nearby properties. Even so, a great deal of a salesperson's effort is used in traveling to show properties to clients. Immobility also creates a need for property management firms because, unless an owner of rental property lives on it or nearby, neither land nor buildings can be effectively managed.

Land is **indestructible**, that is, durable. Today one can travel to the Middle East and walk on the same land that was walked on in Biblical days. Most of the land that we use in the United States today is the same land used by Native Americans a thousand years ago.

Indestructibility

The characteristic of physical durability encourages many people to buy land as an investment because they feel that stocks and bonds and paper money may come and go, but land will always be here. Although this is true in a physical sense, whether a given parcel has and will have economic value depends on one's ability to protect that ownership and on subsequent demand for that land by others. Physical durability, then, must not be confused with economic durability.

Nonhomogeneity The fact that no two parcels of land are exactly alike because no two parcels can occupy the same position on the globe is known as **nonhomogeneity** (heterogeneity). Courts of law recognize this characteristic of land and consequently treat land as a **nonfungible** (pronounced non•fun′je′ble) commodity; that is, nonsubstitutable. Thus, in a contract involving the sale or rental of land (and any improvement to that land), the courts can be called on to enforce specific performance of the contract. For example, in a contract to sell a home, if the buyer carries out his or her obligations and the seller fails to convey ownership to the buyer, a court of law will force the seller to convey ownership of *that* specific home to the buyer. The court will not require the buyer to accept a substitute home. This is different from a homogeneous or **fungible** commodity that is freely substitutable in carrying out a contract. For example, one bushel of no. 1 grade winter wheat can be freely replaced by another bushel of the same grade, and one share of General Motors common stock can be substituted for another, as all are identical.

Although land is nonhomogeneous, there can still be a high degree of physical and economic similarity. For example, in a city block containing 20 house lots of identical size and shape, lots will have a high degree of similarity even though they are still nonhomogeneous. Finding similar properties is, in fact, the basis for the market-comparison approach to appraising real estate.

ECONOMIC *CHARACTERISTICS* *OF LAND* The dividing line between the physical and economic characteristics of land is sometimes difficult to define. This is because the physical aspects of land greatly influence man's economic behavior toward land. However, four economic characteristics are generally recognized: scarcity, modification, permanence of investment (fixity), and area preference (situs, pronounced sī′tus).

The shortage of land in a given geographical area where there is great demand for land is referred to as **scarcity**. It is a man-made characteristic. For example, land is scarce in Miami Beach, Florida, because a relatively large number of people want to use a relatively small area of land. Another well-known example is 2-mile-wide, 13-mile-long Manhattan Island in New York City, where more than a million people live and twice that number work. Yet one need travel only 25 miles west of Miami Beach or into central New York State to find plenty of uncrowded land available for purchase at very reasonable prices. The sheer quantity of undeveloped land in the United States as seen from an airplane on a cross-country flight is staggering.

Scarcity

Land scarcity is also influenced by man's ability to use land more efficiently. To illustrate, in agricultural areas, production per acre of land has more than doubled for many crops since 1940. This is not due to any change in the land, but is the result of improved fertilizers and irrigation systems, better seeds, and modern crop management. Likewise, in urban areas, an acre of land that once provided space for five houses can be converted to high-rise apartments to provide homes for 100 or more families.

Thus, although the physical amount of land on the earth's surface is limited, scarcity is chiefly a function of demand for land in a given geographical area and the ability of man to make land more productive. The persistent notion that all land is scarce has led to periodic land sale booms in undeveloped areas, followed by a collapse in land prices when it becomes apparent that that particular land is not economically scarce.

Land use and value are greatly influenced by **modification**— that is, improvements made by man to surrounding parcels of land. For example, the construction of an airport increases the usefulness and value of land parallel to runways but has a negative effect on the use and value of land at the ends of runways because of noise from landings and takeoffs. Similarly, land subject to flooding becomes more useful and valuable if government-sponsored flood control dams are built upriver.

Modification

One of the most widely publicized cases of land modification occurred near Orlando, Florida, when Disney World was constructed. Nearby land previously used for agricultural purposes suddenly became useful as motel, gas station, restaurant, house, and apartment sites and increased rapidly in value.

Fixity   The fact that land and buildings and other improvements to land require long periods of time to pay for themselves is referred to as **fixity** or **investment permanence**. For example, it may take 20 or 30 years for the income generated by an apartment or office building to repay the cost of the land and building plus interest on the money borrowed to make the purchase. Consequently, real estate investment and land-use decisions must involve consideration of not only how the land will be used next month or next year, but also the usefulness of the improvements 20 years from now. There is no economic logic in spending money to purchase land and improvements that will require 20 to 30 years to pay for themselves if their usefulness is expected to last only 5 years.

Fixity also reflects the fact that land cannot be moved from its present location to another location where it will be more valuable. With very few exceptions, improvements to land are also fixed. Even with a house, the cost of moving it, plus building a foundation at the new site, can easily exceed the value of the house after the move. Thus, when an investment is made in real estate, it is regarded as a **fixed** or **sunk cost**.

Situs   **Situs** or **location preference** refers to location from an economic rather than a geographic standpoint. It has often been said that the single most important word in real estate is *location*. This maxim refers to people's preference for a given area. For a residential area, such preferences are the result of *natural* factors, such as weather, air quality, scenic views, and closeness to natural recreation areas, and of *human* factors, such as job opportunities, transportation facilities, shopping, and schools. For an industrial area, situs depends on such things as an available labor market, adequate supplies of water and electricity, nearby rail lines, and highway access. In farming areas, situs depends on soil and weather conditions, water and labor availability, and transportation facilities.

Situs is the reason that house lots on street corners sell for more than identical-sized lots not on corners. This price differential reflects a preference for open space. The same is true in apartments; corner units usually rent for more than similar-sized noncorner units. In a high-rise apartment building, units on the top floors, if they offer a view, command higher prices than identical units on lower floors. On a street lined with stores, the side of the street that is shaded in the afternoon attracts more shoppers than the unshaded side. Consequently, buildings on the shaded side generate more sales and, as a result, are worth more.

It is important to realize that, since situs is a function of people's preferences and preferences can change with time, situs can also change. For example, the freeway and expressway construction boom that started in the 1950s and accelerated during the 1960s increased the preference for suburban areas, resulting in declining property values in inner city areas and increasing land values in the suburbs. Today, historic rehabilitation and a desire to live closer to work are drawing people back to downtown areas.

Match terms **a–v** *with statements* **1–22.**

VOCABULARY REVIEW

a. *Acre*	**l.** *Government survey*
b. *Appurtenance*	**m.** *Lot-block-tract*
c. *Assessor's parcel number*	**n.** *Meridian*
d. *Base line*	**o.** *Metes and bounds*
e. *Bill of sale*	**p.** *Monument*
f. *Contour line*	**q.** *Quarter-section*
g. *Cul de sac*	**r.** *Riparian right*
h. *Datum*	**s.** *Section*
i. *Emblement*	**t.** *Subsurface right*
j. *Fixture*	**u.** *Township*
k. *Flag lot*	**v.** *Water table*

1. An object that has been attached to land so as to become real estate.
2. Contains 36 sections of land.
3. The depth below the surface at which water-saturated soil can be found.
4. A survey line running east and west from which townships are established.
5. Contains 640 acres of land.
6. The right of landowners to use water flowing past their land.
7. An iron pipe or other object set in the ground to establish land boundaries.
8. A survey line that runs north and south in the rectangular survey system.
9. Annual crops produced by people.
10. A horizontal plane from which height and depth are measured.
11. A numbering system to aid in the assessment of property for tax-collection purposes.

12. A system of land description that identifies a parcel by specifying its shape and boundaries.
13. A land survey system based on imaginary latitude and longitude lines.
14. Includes the right to mine minerals and drill for oil.
15. Lines on a map that connect points having the same elevation.
16. Land description by reference to a recorded map.
17. 43,560 square feet.
18. Contains 160 acres of land.
19. A right or privilege or improvement that passes with land.
20. A document that transfers title to personal property.
21. A street that is closed at one end with a circular turnaround.
22. A lot shaped like a flag on a pole.

QUESTIONS AND PROBLEMS

1. Is the land on which you make your residence described by metes and bounds, lot-block-tract, or the rectangular survey system?
2. On a sheet of paper sketch the following parcels of land in Section 6, T1N, R3E: (a) the NW¼; (b) the SW¼ of the SW¼; (c) the W½ of the SE¼; (d) the N17 acres of the E½ of the NE¼; (e) the SE¼ of the SE¼ of the SE¼ of the NE¼.
3. How many acres are there in each parcel described in number 2?
4. Describe the parcels labeled A, B, C, D, and E in the section shown in the margin.
5. Using an ordinary compass and ruler, sketch the following parcel of land: "Beginning at monument M, thence due east for 40 feet, thence south 45° east for 14.1 feet, thence due south for 40 feet, thence north 45° west for 70.7 feet back to the point of beginning."
6. If a landowner owns from the center of the earth to the limits of the sky, are aircraft that pass overhead trespassers?
7. Would you classify the key to the door of a building as personal property or real property?
8. With regard to your own residence, itemize what you consider to be real property and what you consider to be personal property.
9. With regard to riparian rights, does your state follow the doctrine of prior appropriation or the right to a reasonable share?
10. What effects do you think changes in the location of the magnetic north pole would have on surveys over a long period of time? How would earthquakes affect bench marks?

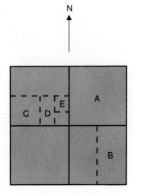

N

ADDITIONAL READINGS

"Deeds: Resolving an Ambiguity in a Land Description" (*Real Estate Law Report,* Nov. 1993, p. 8). Article discusses legal descriptions, boundaries, and contracts.

"Land for All: A History of U.S. Real Estate to 1900," by **John McMahan** (*Real Estate Review*, Winter 76, p. 78). A fascinating four-part history of American real estate speculation and development before the year 1900.

MAP Seminar #1: History of Real Estate, a video by **John Tuccillo** (National Association of Realtors, Dec. 1994). An hour-long video discusses the evolution of real estate and the real estate professional.

Real Estate Law, 10th Ed., by **Robert Kratovil** and **Raymond Werner** (Prentice Hall, 1993, 673 pages). Chapter 2 discusses land and its elements, Chapter 3 is on fixtures, and Chapter 5 deals with land descriptions.

5

Rights and Interests in Land

KEY • TERMS

Chattel: an article of personal property

Easement: the right or privilege one party has to use land belonging to another for a special purpose not inconsistent with the owner's use of the land

Eminent domain: the right of government to take privately held land for public use, provided fair compensation is paid

Encroachment: the unauthorized intrusion of a building or other improvement onto another person's land

Encumbrance: any impediment to a clear title, such as a lien, lease, or easement

Estate: one's legal interest or rights in land

Fee simple: the largest, most complete bundle of rights one can hold in land; land ownership

Lien: a hold or claim which one person has on the property of another to secure payment of a debt or other obligation

Title: the right to or ownership of something; also the evidence of ownership, such as a deed or bill of sale

Early man was nomadic and had no concept of real estate. Roaming bands followed game and the seasons and did not claim the exclusive right to use a given area. When man began to cultivate crops and domesticate animals, the concept of an exclusive right to the use of land became important. This right was claimed for the tribe as a whole, and each family in the tribe was given the right to the exclusive use of a portion of the tribe's land. In turn, each family was obligated to aid in defending the tribe's claim against other tribes.

FEUDAL AND ALLODIAL SYSTEMS

As time passed, individual tribes allied with each other for mutual protection; eventually these alliances resulted in political states. In the process, land ownership went to the head of the state, usually a king. The king, in turn, gave to select individuals, called lords, the right (called a feud) to use large tracts of land. The lords did not receive ownership. They were tenants of the king and were required to serve and pay duties to the king and to help fight the king's wars. It was customary for the lords to remain tenants for life, subject, of course, to the defeat of their king by another king. This system, whereby all land ownership rested in the name of the king, became known as the **feudal system.**

Feudal System

   The lords gave their subjects the right to use small tracts of land. For this, the subjects owed their lord a share of their crops and their allegiance in time of war. The subjects (vassals) were, in effect, tenants of the lord and subtenants of the king. Like the lord, the vassal could not sell his rights nor pass them to his heirs.

The first major change in the feudal system occurred in 1285 when King Edward I of England gave his lords the right to pass their tenancy rights to their heirs. Subsequently, tenant vassals were permitted to convey their tenancy rights to others. By the year 1650, the feudal system had come to an end in England; in France, it ended with the French Revolution in 1789. In its place arose the **allodial system** of land ownership under which individuals were given the right to own land. Initially, lords became owners and peasants remained tenants of the lords. As time passed, the peasants became landowners either by purchase or by gift from the lords.

Allodial System

When the first European explorers reached North American shores, they claimed the land in the name of the king or queen whom they represented. Later, when the first settlers came to America from England, they claimed the land in the name of their mother country. However, since the feudal system had been abolished in the meantime, the king of England granted the settlers private ownership of the land on which they settled, while retaining the claim of ownership to the unsettled lands.

Claims by the king of England to land in the 13 colonies ended with the American Revolution. Subsequently, the U.S. government acquired the ownership right to additional lands by treaty, wars, and purchase, resulting in the borders of the United States as we know them today. The United States adopted the allodial system of ownership, and not only permits but encourages its citizens to own land within its borders.

GOVERNMENT RIGHTS IN LAND

Under the feudal system, the king was responsible for organizing defense against invaders, making decisions on land use, providing services such as roads and bridges, and generally carrying out the administration of the land and his subjects. An important aspect of the transition from feudal to allodial ownership was that the need for these services did not end. Consequently, even though ownership could now be held by private citizens, the government necessarily retained the rights of taxation, eminent domain, police power, and escheat. Let us look at each of these more closely.

Property Taxes

Under the feudal system, governments financed themselves by requiring lords and vassals to share a portion of the benefits they received from the use of the king's lands. With the change to private ownership, the need to finance governments did not end. Thus, the government retained the right to collect **property taxes** from landowners. Before the advent of income taxes, the taxes levied against land were the main source of government revenues. Taxing land was a logical method of raising revenue for two reasons: (1) until the Industrial Revolution, which started in the mid-eighteenth century, land and agriculture were the primary sources of income—the more land one owned, the wealthier one was considered to be and therefore the better able to pay taxes to support the government; (2) land is impossible to hide, making it easily identifiable for taxation. This is not true of other valuables such as gold or money.

The real property tax has endured over the centuries, and today it is still a major source of government revenue. The major change in real estate taxation is that initially it was used to support all levels of government, including defense. Today, defense is supported by the income tax, and real estate taxes are sources of city, county, and, in some places, state revenues. At state and local government levels, the real property tax provides money for such things as schools, fire and police protection, parks, and libraries. To encourage property owners to pay their taxes in full and on time, the right of taxation also enables the government to seize ownership of real estate for which taxes are delinquent and to sell the property to recover the unpaid taxes.

The right of government to take ownership of privately held real estate regardless of the owner's wishes is called **eminent domain.** Land for schools, freeways, streets, parks, urban renewal, public housing, public parking, and other social and public purposes is obtained in this way. Quasi-public organizations such as utility companies and railroads are also permitted by state law to obtain land needed for utility lines, pipes, and tracks. The legal proceeding involved in eminent domain is a **condemnation proceeding,** and property owners must be paid the fair market value of the properties taken from them. The actual condemnation is usually preceded by negotiations between the property owner and an agent of the public body wanting to acquire ownership. If the agent and the property owner can arrive at a mutually acceptable price, the property is purchased outright. If an agreement cannot be reached, a formal proceeding in eminent domain is filed against the property owner in a court of law. The court hears expert opinions from appraisers brought by both parties, and then sets the price the property owner must accept in return for the loss of ownership.

Eminent Domain

When only a portion of a parcel of land is being taken, **severance damages** may be awarded in addition to payment for land actually being taken. For example, if a new highway requires a 40-acre strip of land through the middle of a 160-acre farm, the farm owner will not only be paid for the 40 acres, but will also receive severance damages to compensate for the fact that the farm will be more difficult to work because it is no longer in one piece.

An **inverse condemnation** is a proceeding brought about by a property owner demanding that his land be purchased from him. In a number of cities, homeowners at the end of airport runways have forced airport authorities to buy their homes because of the deafening noise of jet aircraft during takeoffs. Damage awards may also be made when land itself is not taken but its usefulness is reduced because of a nearby condemnation. These are **consequential damages,** and might be awarded, for instance, when land is taken for a sewage treatment plant, and privately owned land downwind from the plant suffers a loss in value owing to foul odors.

Police Power   The right of government to enact laws and enforce them for the order, safety, health, morals, and general welfare of the public is called **police power.** Examples of police power applied to real estate are zoning laws; planning laws; building, health, and fire codes; and rent control. A key difference between police power and eminent domain is that, although police power restricts how real estate may be used, police power involves no legally recognized "taking" of property. Consequently, no payment is made to an owner who suffers a loss of value through the exercise of police power. A government may not utilize police power in an offhand or capricious manner; to be valid, any law that restricts how an owner may use his or her real estate must be deemed in the public interest and applied evenhandedly. The breaking of a law based upon police power results in either a civil or criminal penalty rather than in the seizing of real estate, as in the case of unpaid property taxes. Of the various rights government holds in land, police power has the most impact on land value.

Escheat   When a person dies and leaves no heirs and no instructions as to how to dispose of his real and personal property, or when property is abandoned, the ownership of that property reverts to the state. This reversion to the state is called **escheat** from the Anglo-French word meaning to *fall back.* Escheat solves the problem of property becoming ownerless.

It cannot be overemphasized that, to have real estate, there must be a system or means of protecting rightful claims to the use of land and the improvements thereon. In the United States, the federal government is given the task of organizing a defense system to prevent confiscation of those rights by a foreign power. The federal government, in combination with state and local governments, also establishes laws and courts within the country to protect the ownership rights of one citizen in relation to another citizen. Whereas the armed forces protect against a foreign takeover, within a country deeds, public records, contracts, and other documents have replaced the need for brute force to prove and protect ownership of real estate.

PROTECTING OWNERSHIP

The concept of real estate ownership can be more easily understood when viewed as a collection or bundle of rights. Under the allodial system, the rights of taxation, eminent domain, police power, and escheat are retained by the government. The remaining bundle of rights, called **fee simple,** is available for private ownership. The fee simple bundle of rights can be held by a person and his heirs forever, or until his government can no longer protect those rights. Figure 5.1 illustrates the fee simple bundle of rights concept.

FEE SIMPLE

The word **estate** is synonymous with bundle of rights. Stated another way, *estate* refers to one's legal interest or rights in land, not the physical quantity of land as shown on a map. A fee simple is

Figure 5.1. The fee simple bundle of rights.

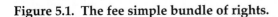
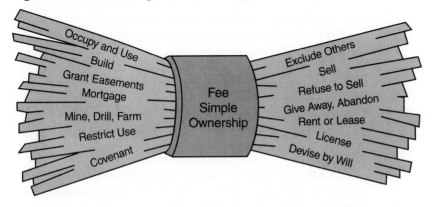

Real estate ownership is, in actuality, the ownership of rights to land. The largest bundle available for private ownership is called "fee simple."

the largest estate one can hold in land. Most real estate sales are for the fee simple estate. When people say they "own" or have "title" to real estate, it is usually the fee simple estate that is being discussed. The word *title* refers to the ownership of something. All other lesser estates in land, such as life estates and leaseholds, are created from the fee estate.

Real estate is concerned with the "sticks" in the bundle: how many there are, how useful they are, and who possesses the sticks not in the bundle. With that in mind, let us describe what happens when sticks are removed from the bundle.

ENCUMBRANCES

Whenever a stick is removed from the fee simple bundle, it creates an impediment to the free and clear ownership and use of that property. These impediments to title are called encumbrances. An **encumbrance** is defined as any claim, right, lien, estate, or liability that limits the fee simple title to property. An encumbrance is, in effect, a stick that has been removed from the bundle. Commonly found encumbrances are easements, encroachments, deed restrictions, liens, leases, and air and subsurface rights. In addition, qualified fee estates are encumbered estates, as are life estates.

The party holding a stick from someone else's fee simple bundle is said to hold a claim to or a right or interest in that land. In other words, what is one person's encumbrance is another person's right or interest or claim. For example, a lease is an encumbrance from the standpoint of the fee simple owner. But from the tenant's standpoint, it is an interest in land that gives the tenant the right to the exclusive use of land and buildings. A mortgage is an encumbrance from the fee owner's viewpoint but a right to foreclose from the lender's viewpoint. A property that is encumbered with a lease and a mortgage is called "a fee simple subject to a lease and a mortgage." Figure 5.2 illustrates how a fee simple bundle shrinks as rights are removed from it. Meanwhile, let us turn our attention to a discussion of individual sticks found in the fee simple bundle.

Easements

An **easement** is a right or privilege one party has to the use of the land of another for a special purpose consistent with the general use of the land. The landowner is not dispossessed from the land but rather coexists side by side with the holder of the easement. Examples of easements are those given to telephone

Figure 5.2. Removing sticks from the fee simple bundle.

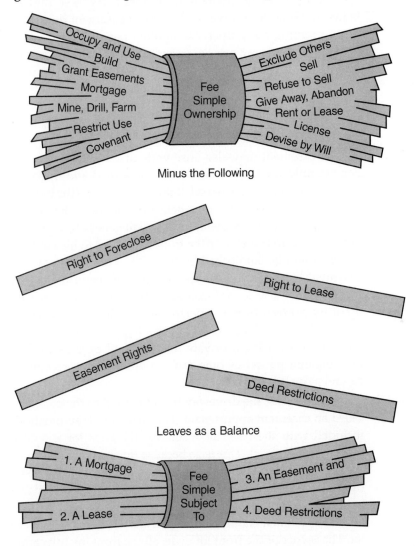

Note that the fee simple bundle shrinks as an owner voluntarily removes rights from it.

and electric companies to erect poles and run lines over private property, easements given to people to drive or walk across someone else's land, and easements given to gas and water companies to run pipelines to serve their customers. Figure 5.3 illustrates several examples of easements.

Easements can come into being in several different ways. One way is for the landowner to use a written document to specifically grant an easement to another party. A second way is for an owner to reserve (withhold) an easement in the deed when granting the property to another party. For example, a land developer may reserve easements for utility lines when selling the lots and then grant the easements to the utility companies that will service the lots. Another way for an easement to be created is by government condemnation, such as when a government flood control district purchases an easement to run a drainage pipe under someone's land.

An easement may also arise without a written document. For example, a parcel of land fronts on a road and the owner sells the back half of the parcel. If the only access to the back half is by crossing over the front half, even if the seller did not expressly grant an easement, the law will generally protect the buyer's right to travel over the front half to get to his land. The buyer cannot be landlocked by the seller. This is known as an **easement by necessity.** Another method of acquiring an easement without a written document is by constant use, or **easement by prescription:** if a person acts as though he owns an easement long enough, he will have a legally recognized easement. Persons using a private road without permission for a long enough period of time can acquire a legally recognized easement by this method.

Easement Appurtenant

In Figure 5.3, the driveway from the road to the back lot is called an **easement appurtenant.** This driveway is automatically included with the back lot whenever the back lot is sold or otherwise conveyed. This is so because this easement is legally connected (appurtenant) to the back lot. Please note that just as the back lot benefits from this easement, the front lot is burdened by it. Whenever the front lot is sold or otherwise conveyed, the new owners must continue to respect the easement to the back lot. The owner of the front lot owns all the front lot, but cannot put a fence across the easement, or plant trees on it, or grow a garden on it, or otherwise hamper access to the back lot. Because the front lot serves the back lot, the front lot is called the **servient estate** and the back lot is called the **dominant estate.** When one party has the right or privilege, by usage or contract, to travel over a designated portion of another person's land, it is called a **right of way.**

Although the law generally protects the first purchaser through the doctrine of easement by necessity, it is nonetheless

Figure 5.3. Commonly found easements.

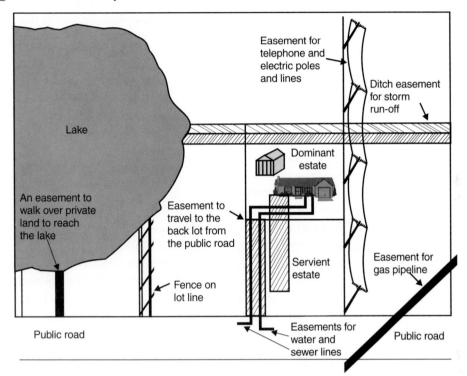

critical that any subsequent purchaser of back lots and back acreage carefully inspect the public records and the property to make certain there is both legal and actual means of access from a public road to the parcel. It is also important for anyone purchasing land to inspect the public records and the property for evidence of the rights of others to pass over that land, for example, a driveway or private road to a back lot or a pathway used by the public to get from a road to a beach.

An **easement in gross** differs from an easement appurtenant because there is a servient estate but no dominant estate. Some examples will illustrate this: telephone, electricity, and gas line easements are all easements in gross. These easements belong to the telephone, electric, and gas companies, respectively, not to a parcel of land. The servient estate is the parcel on which the telephone, electric, and gas companies have the right to run their lines. All future owners of the parcel are bound by these easements.

Easement in Gross

Although utility easements are the most common examples of easements in gross, the ditch easement for storm runoff in Figure 5.3 is also an easement in gross. It will most likely be owned by a flood control district. Note that utility and drainage easements, although legally a burden on a parcel, are consistent with the use of a parcel if the purpose of the easement is to provide utility service or flood control for the parcel. In fact, without these services, a parcel would be less useful and hence less valuable.

It is also possible to grant an easement to an individual for personal use. In Figure 5.3, a landowner has given a friend a personal easement in gross to walk over the land to reach a choice fishing area on the lakeshore. An easement in gross for personal use is not transferable and terminates with the death of the person holding the easement. In contrast, the holder of a commercial easement, such as a utility or flood control easement, usually has the right to sell, assign, or devise that easement.

Party Wall Easement

Party wall easements exist when a single wall is located on the lot line that separates two parcels of land. The wall may be either a fence or the wall of a building. In either case, each lot owner owns that portion of the wall on his or her land, plus an easement in the other half of the wall for physical support. Party walls are common where stores and office buildings are built right up to the lot line. Such a wall can present an interesting problem when the owner of one lot wants to demolish the building. Since the wall provides support for the building next door, the owner must leave the wall and provide special supports for the adjacent building during demolition and until another building is constructed on the lot. A party wall is an easement appurtenant.

Easement Termination

Easements may be terminated when the necessity for the easement no longer exists (for example, a public road is built adjacent to the back half of the lot mentioned earlier), or when the dominant and servient estates are combined (merged) with the intent of extinguishing the easement, or by release from the easement holder to the servient estate, or by lack of use (abandonment).

Encroachments

The unauthorized intrusion of a building or other form of real property onto another person's land is called an **encroachment.** A tree that overhangs into a neighbor's yard, or a building or eave of a roof that crosses a property line are examples of encroachments. The owner of the property being encroached on has the right to force the removal of the encroachment. Failure to do so may adversely affect the property owner's title and make the land less saleable. Ultimately, inaction on the property owner's part may result in the encroaching neighbor claiming a legal right to continue the use. Figure 5.4 illustrates several commonly found encroachments.

Private agreements that govern the use of land are known as **deed restrictions** or **deed covenants.** For example, a land subdivider can require that persons who purchase lots from him build only single-family homes containing 1,200 square feet or more. The purpose of such a restriction would be to protect those who have already built houses from an erosion in property value due to the construction of nearby buildings not compatible with the neighborhood. Where scenic views are important, deed restrictions may limit the height of buildings and trees to 15 feet. Buyers would still obtain fee simple ownership, but at the same time would voluntarily give up some of their rights to do as they please. Buyers would be said to receive a fee simple title subject to deed restrictions. The right to enforce the restrictions is usually given by the developer to the subdivision's homeowner association. Violation of a deed restriction can result in a civil

Deed Restrictions

Figure 5.4. Commonly found encroachments.

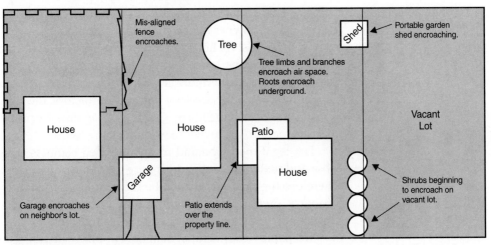

Most commonly found encroachments are not intentional but are due to poor or nonexistent planning. For example, a weekend garden shed, fence, or patio project is built without surveying to find the lot line, or a tree or bush grows so large it encroaches upon a neighbor's land.

court action brought by other property owners who are bound by the same deed restriction.

Liens

A hold or claim that one person has on the property of another to secure payment of a debt or other obligation is called a **lien.** Common examples are property tax liens, mechanic's liens, judgment liens, and mortgage liens. From the standpoint of property owners, a lien is an encumbrance on the title. Note that a lien does not transfer title to property. In most states, the debtor retains title unless the lien is foreclosed. When more than one lien is held against a property, the lien that was recorded first usually has the highest priority in the event of foreclosure. Property tax liens are, however, always superior to other liens.

Property Tax Liens

Property tax liens result from the right of government to collect taxes from property owners. At the beginning of each tax year, a tax lien is placed on taxable property. It is removed when the property taxes are paid. If they are not paid, the lien gives the government the right to force the sale of the property in order to collect the unpaid taxes.

Mechanic's Lien

Mechanic's lien laws give anyone who has furnished labor or materials for the improvement of land the right to place a lien against those improvements and the land if payment has not been received. A sale of the property can then be forced to recover the money owed. To be entitled to a mechanic's lien, the work or materials must have been provided pursuant to contract with the landowner or the landowner's representative. For example, if a landowner hires a contractor to build a house or add a room to an existing house and then fails to pay the contractor, the contractor may file a mechanic's lien against the land and its improvements. Furthermore, if the landowner pays the contractor but the contractor does not pay subcontractors, the subcontractors are entitled to file a mechanic's lien against the property. In this situation, the owner may have to pay twice.

The legal theory behind mechanic's lien rights is that the labor and materials supplied enhance the value of the property. Therefore the property should be security for payment. If the property owner does not pay voluntarily, the lien can be enforced with a court-supervised foreclosure sale.

Mechanics (contractors), material suppliers, architects, surveyors, and engineers are among those who may be entitled to the protection of mechanic's lien laws. All mechanic's liens attach and take effect at the time the first item of labor or material is furnished, even though no document has been filed with the county recorder. To preserve the lien, a lien statement must be filed in the county where the property is located and within 20 to 120 days (depending on the state) after labor or material has been furnished. This is called **perfecting the lien.**

Whenever improvements are made to the land, all persons (including sellers under a contract for deed and landlords) may be held to have authorized the improvements. As protection, an owner can serve or post notice that the improvements are being made without the owner's authority.

A lender planning to finance a property will be particularly alert for the possibility of mechanic's liens. If work has commenced or material has been delivered before the mortgage is recorded, the mechanic's lien may be superior to the mortgage in the event of foreclosure.

Judgment liens arise from lawsuits for which money damages are awarded. The law permits a hold to be placed against the real and personal property of the debtor until the judgment is paid. Usually the lien created by the judgment covers only property in the county where the judgment was awarded. However, the creditor can extend the lien to property in other counties by filing a **notice of lien** in each of those counties. If the debtor does not repay the lien voluntarily, the creditor can (although this can change from state to state) ask the court to issue a **writ of execution** that directs the county sheriff to seize and sell a sufficient amount of the debtor's property to pay the debt and expenses of the sale.

Judgment Lien

A **mortgage lien** is created when property is offered by its owner as security for the repayment of a debt. If the debt secured by the mortgage lien is not repaid, the creditor can foreclose and sell the property. If this is insufficient to repay the debt, some states allow the creditor to petition the court for a judgment lien for the balance due. (Mortgage law is covered in more detail in Chapter 14.)

Mortgage Lien

A **voluntary lien** is a lien created by the property owner. A mortgage lien is an example of a voluntary lien; the owner voluntarily creates a lien against his or her property in order to borrow money. An **involuntary lien** is created by operation of law. Examples are property tax liens, judgment liens, and mechanic's liens.

Voluntary and Involuntary Liens

Special and General Liens

A **special lien** is a lien on a specific property. A property tax lien is a special lien because it is a lien against a specific property and no other. Thus, if a person owns five parcels of land scattered throughout a given county and fails to pay the taxes on one of those parcels, the county can force the sale of just that one parcel; the others cannot be touched. Mortgages and mechanic's liens are also special liens in that they apply to only the property receiving the materials or labor. In contrast, a **general lien** is a lien on all the property of a person in a given jurisdiction. For example, a judgment lien is a lien on all the debtor's property in the county or counties where the judgment has been filed. Federal and state tax liens are also general liens.

Lienor, Lienee

The party holding the lien is called the **lienor.** Examples of lienors are mortgage lenders, judgment holders, and tax authorities. The party whose property is subject to the lien is called a **lienee.** The terms *lienor* and *lienee* apply whether the lien is voluntary or involuntary, specific or general.

QUALIFIED FEE ESTATES

A **qualified fee estate** is a fee estate that is subject to certain limitations imposed by the person creating the estate. Qualified fee estates fall into three categories: determinable, condition subsequent, and condition precedent. They will be discussed only briefly as they are rather uncommon.

A **fee simple determinable estate** indicates that the duration of the estate can be determined from the deed itself. For example, Mr. Smith donates a parcel of land to a church so long as the land is used for religious purposes. The key words are *so long as*. So long as the land is used for religious purposes, the church has all the rights of fee simple ownership. But if some other use is made of the land it reverts back to the grantor (Mr. Smith) or someone else named by Mr. Smith (called a **remainderman**). Note that the termination of the estate is automatic if the land is used contrary to the limitation stated in the deed.

A **fee simple subject to condition subsequent** gives the grantor the *right* to terminate the estate. Continuing the above example, Mr. Smith would have the right to reenter the property and take it back if it were no longer being used for religious purposes.

With a **fee simple upon condition precedent,** title will not take effect until a condition is performed. For example, Mr.

Smith could deed his land to a church with the condition that the deed will not take effect until a religious sanctuary is built.

Occasionally, qualified fees have been used by land developers in lieu of deed restrictions or zoning. For example, buyers have fee title so long as they use the land for single-family residences. In another example, a land developer might use a condition precedent to encourage lot purchasers to build promptly. This would enhance the value of the unsold lots. From the standpoint of the property owner, a qualification is an encumbrance to the title.

A **life estate** conveys an estate for the duration of someone's life. The duration of the estate can be tied to the life of the **life tenant** (the person holding the life estate) or to a third party. In addition, someone must be named to acquire the estate upon its termination. The following example illustrates the life estate concept. Suppose you have an aunt who needs financial assistance and you have decided to grant her, for the rest of her life, a house to live in. When you create the life estate, she becomes the life tenant. Additionally, you must decide who gets the house upon her death. If you want it back, you would want a **reversion** for yourself. This way the house reverts back to you or, if you predecease her, to your heirs. If you want the house to go to someone else, your son or daughter for example, you could name him or her as the remainderman. Alternatively, you could name a friend, relative, or charity as the remainderman. Sometimes a life estate is used to avoid the time and expense of probating a will and to reduce estate taxes. For example, an aging father could deed his real estate to his children but retain a life estate for himself.

LIFE ESTATES

Since a life estate arrangement is temporary, the life tenant must not commit **waste** by destroying or harming the property. Furthermore, the life tenant is required to keep the property in reasonable repair and to pay any property taxes, assessments, and interest on debt secured by the property. The life tenant is entitled to income generated by the property and may sell, lease, rent, or mortgage his or her interest.

Although the life estate concept offers intriguing gift and estate planning possibilities, the uncertainty of the duration of the estate makes it rather unmarketable. Thus, you will rarely

Prohibition of Waste

see a life estate advertised for sale in a newspaper or listed for sale at a real estate brokerage office.

STATUTORY ESTATES   Statutory estates are created by state law. They include dower, which gives a wife rights in her husband's real property; curtesy, which gives a husband rights in his wife's real property; and community property, which gives each spouse a one-half interest in marital property. Additionally there is homestead protection, which is designed to protect the family's home from certain debts and, upon the death of one spouse, provide the other with a home for life.

Dower   Historically, **dower** came from old English common law in which the marriage ceremony was viewed as merging the wife's legal existence into that of her husband's. From this viewpoint, property bought during marriage belongs to the husband, with both husband and wife sharing the use of it. As a counterbalance, the dower right recognizes the wife's efforts in marriage and grants her legal ownership to one-third (in some states one-half) of the family's real property for the rest of her life. This prevents the husband from conveying ownership of the family's real estate without the wife's permission and protects her even if she is left out of her husband's will. New York abolished the right of dower in all marriages taking place after August 31, 1930. A woman married prior to September 1, 1930 is entitled, upon the death of her husband, to a life interest in one-third of all real property owned by her husband during their marriage.

In real estate sales, the effect of dower laws is such that when a husband and wife sell their property, the wife must relinquish her dower rights. This is usually accomplished by the wife signing the deed with her husband or by signing a separate quitclaim deed. If she does not relinquish her dower rights, the buyer (or even a future buyer) may find that, upon the husband's death, the wife may return to legally claim an undivided ownership in the property. This is important if you buy real estate. Have the property's ownership researched by an abstracter and the title insured by a title insurance company.

Curtesy   Roughly the opposite of dower, **curtesy** gives the husband benefits in his deceased wife's property as long as he lives. In New York, in order for curtesy to apply, the couple must have had a child. Like most states, New York has abolished the right of curtesy. It does not apply in New York to any marriages which took place after August 31, 1930.

Because dower and curtesy rights originally were unequal, some states interpret dower and curtesy so as to give equal rights, while other states have enacted additional legislation to protect spousal rights. To summarize, the basic purpose of dower and curtesy (and community property laws) is to require both spouses to sign any deed or mortgage or other document affecting title to their lands, and to provide legal protection for the property rights of a surviving spouse.

Community Property

Eight states (Arizona, California, Idaho, Louisiana, Nevada, New Mexico, Texas, and Washington) subscribe to the legal theory that each spouse has an equal interest in all property acquired by their joint efforts during the marriage. This jointly produced property is called **community property.** Upon the death of one spouse, one-half of the community property passes to the heirs. The other one-half is retained by the surviving spouse. When community property is sold or mortgaged, both spouses must sign the document. Community property rights arise upon marriage (either formal or common law) and terminate upon divorce or death. Community property is discussed at greater length in Chapter 6.

Homestead Protection

Nearly all states have passed **homestead protection** laws, usually with two purposes in mind: (1) to provide some legal protection for the homestead claimants from debts and judgments against them that might result in the forced sale and loss of the home, and (2) to provide a home for a widow, and sometimes a widower, for life. Homestead laws also restrict one spouse from acting without the other when conveying the homestead or using it as collateral for a loan. In New York, the homestead of a person is exempt from levy and sale under a writ of execution up to a value of $10,000. Although dower, curtesy, and community property rights are automatic in those states that have them, the homestead right may require that a written declaration be recorded in the public records. As referred to here, homestead is not the acquiring of title to state or federally owned lands by filing and establishing a residence (see Chapter 7). Additionally, *homestead protection* should not be confused with the *homestead exemption* some states grant to homeowners in order to reduce their property taxes (see Chapter 21).

A homeowner is also protected by the Federal Bankruptcy Reform Act of 1979. A person who seeks protection under this act is entitled to an exemption of up to $7,500 of the equity in his or her residence. Also exempt is any household item that does not exceed $200 in value.

FREEHOLD ESTATES

In a carryover from the old English court system, estates in land are classified as either **freehold estates** or **leasehold estates.** The main difference is that freehold estate cases are tried under real property laws whereas leasehold (also called nonfreehold or less-than-freehold) estates are tried under personal property laws.

The two distinguishing features of a freehold estate are: (1) there must be actual ownership of the land, and (2) the estate must be of unpredictable duration. Fee estates, life estates, and estates created by statute are freehold estates. The distinguishing features of a leasehold estate are: (1) although there is possession of the land, there is no ownership, and (2) the estate is of definite duration. Stated another way, freehold means ownership and less-than-freehold means rental.

LEASEHOLD ESTATES

As previously noted, the user of a property need not be its owner. Under a leasehold estate, the user is called the **lessee** or **tenant,** and the person from whom the property is leased is the **lessor** or **landlord.** As long as the tenant has a valid lease, abides by it, and pays the rent on time, the owner, even though he or she owns the property, cannot occupy it until the lease has expired. During the lease period, the freehold estate owner is said to hold a *reversion,* i.e., the right to recover possession at the end of the lease period. Meanwhile, the lease is an encumbrance against the property.

Leasehold estates are of four categories: estate for years, periodic estate, estate at will, and tenancy at sufferance. Note that in this chapter we examine leases primarily from the standpoint of estates in land. Leases as financing tools are discussed in Chapter 19 and lease contracts are covered in Chapter 11.

Estate for Years

Also called a tenancy for years, the **estate for years** is somewhat misleadingly named as it implies that a lease for a number of years has been created. Actually, the key criterion is that the lease have a specific starting time and a specific ending time. It can be for any length of time, ranging from less than a day to many years. An estate for years does not automatically renew itself. Neither the landlord nor the tenant must act to terminate it, as the lease agreement itself specifies a termination date.

Usually the lessor is the freehold estate owner. However, the lessor could also be a lessee. To illustrate, a fee owner leases to a lessee who in turn leases to another person. By doing this, this first lessee has become a **sublessor.** The person who leases from this sublessor is a **sublessee.** It is important to realize that in no case can a sublessee acquire from the lessee any more rights than the lessee has. Thus, a lessee who has a 5-year lease with 3 years remaining, can assign to a sublessee only the remaining 3 years or a portion of it.

Also called an estate from year-to-year or a periodic tenancy, a **periodic estate** has an original lease period with fixed length; when it runs out, unless the tenant or the landlord act to terminate it, renewal is automatic for another like period of time. A month-to-month apartment rental is an example of this arrangement. To avoid last-minute confusion, rental agreements usually require that advance notice be given if either the landlord or the tenant wishes to terminate the tenancy.

Periodic Estate

Also called a tenancy at will, an **estate at will** is a landlord-tenant relationship with all the normal rights and duties of a lessor-lessee relationship, except that the estate may be terminated by either the lessor or the lessee at any time. However, most states recognize the inconvenience a literal interpretation of *any time* can cause, and require that reasonable advance notice be given. What is considered "reasonable" notice is often specified by state law.

Estate at Will

A **tenancy at sufferance** occurs when a tenant stays beyond the legal tenancy without the consent of the landlord. In other words, the tenant wrongfully holds the property against the owner's wishes. In a tenancy at sufferance, the tenant is commonly called a **holdover tenant,** although once the stay exceeds the terms of the lease or rental agreement, he or she is not actually a tenant in the normal landlord-tenant sense. The landlord is entitled to evict the tenant and recover possession of the

Tenancy at Sufferance

property, provided the landlord does so in a timely manner. A tenant at sufferance differs from a trespasser only in that the original entry was rightful. If during the holdover period the tenant pays and the landlord accepts rent, the tenancy at sufferance changes to a periodic estate.

OVERVIEW   Figure 5.5 provides an overview of the various rights and interests in land that are discussed in this chapter and the previous chapter. This chart is designed to give you an overall perspective of what real estate includes.

License   A **license** is not a right or an estate in land but a personal privilege given to someone to use land (the *license*). It is nonassignable and can be canceled by the person who issues it. A license to park is typically what an automobile parking lot operator provides for persons parking in the lot. The contract creating the license is usually written on the stub that the lot attendant gives the driver, or it is posted on a sign on the lot. Tickets to theaters and sporting events also fall into this category. Because it is a personal privilege, a license is not an encumbrance against land.

Chattels   A **chattel** is an article of personal property. The word comes from the Old English word for cattle, which, of course, were (and still are) personal property. Chattel is a word more often heard in a law office than in a real estate office. Occasionally you will see it used in legal documents, such as in the case of a **chattel mortgage,** which is a mortgage against personal property.

Law Sources   You will better understand real estate law when you understand its roots. Most American law originally came from early English law through English colonization of America. Additionally, Spanish law, via Spain's colonization of Mexico, can be found in Arizona, California, Idaho, Nevada, New Mexico, Texas, and Washington. Lastly, old French civil law, by way of the French ownership of Louisiana, is the basis for that state's law. In all three of these, the law that took root in America originated in predominantly agricultural economies. Consequently, there has been a great deal of legal modification over the years by legislatures and courts.

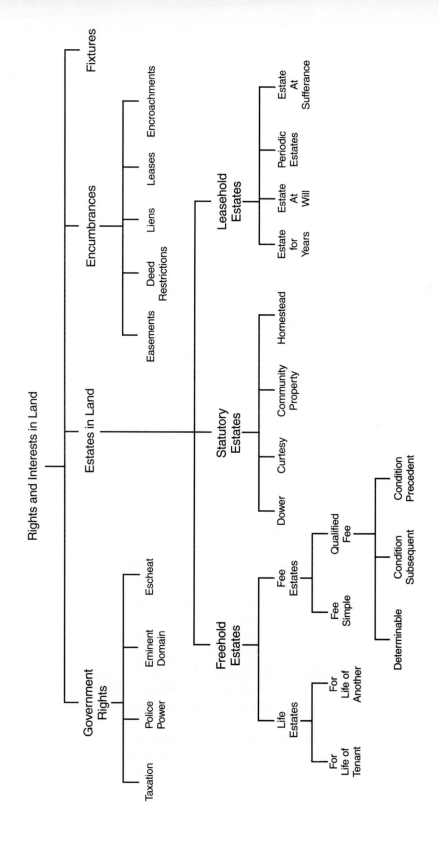

Figure 5.5. Rights and interests in land.

Common Law   You will also find it helpful to understand the difference between common law and statutory law. **Common law** derives its authority from usage and custom over long periods of time. Thus the concepts of fee simple estates, qualified fee estates, life estates, leasehold estates, mortgages, air rights, and subsurface rights, for example, grew out of usage over hundreds of years. Individual court decisions (called **case law**) also contributed to the development of common law in England and the United States.

Statutory Law   **Statutory law** is created by the enactment of legislation. Examples of statutory laws are laws enacted by state legislatures that require the licensing of real estate agents. Zoning laws and building codes are also statutory laws as they have their source in legislative enactment. Federal and state income tax and local property tax laws are statutory laws.

Sometimes common law concepts are enacted into statutory law. For example, many statutory laws pertaining to leasehold estates and the rights and obligations of landlords and tenants have come directly from common law. Additionally, statutory laws have been passed where common law was held to be unclear or unreasonable. For example, Old English law did not provide equality in property rights for both spouses. Modern statutory laws do provide equality.

Pictorial Summary   Let us conclude this chapter by combining what has been discussed in Chapter 4 regarding the physical nature of land with what has been covered in this chapter regarding estates and rights in land. The results, diagrammed in Figures 5.6a and 5.6b, show why real estate is both complicated and exciting. A single parcel of land can be divided into subsurface, surface, and airspace components. Each of these carries its own fee simple bundle of rights, which, in turn, can be divided into the various estates and rights discussed in this chapter.

To more clearly convey this idea, let us turn our attention to Figure 5.6. In parcel A, the fee landowner has leased to a farmer the bulk of the surface and air rights, plus the right to draw water from the wells, for the production of crops and livestock. This leaves the fee owner with the right to lease or sell subterranean rights for mineral, oil, and gas extraction. With a single parcel of land, the fee owner has created two estates, one for farming and

Figure 5.6a. Cross section of estates and rights in land.

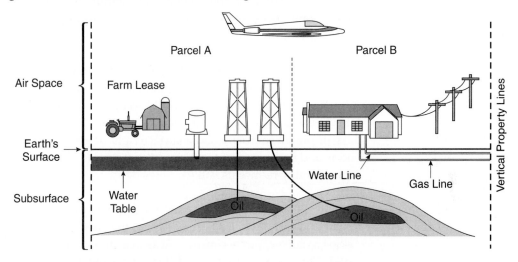

another for oil and gas production. With the minor exception of
the placement of the well platforms, pumps, and pipes, neither
use interferes with the other and both bring income to the
landowner. The farmer, in turn, can personally utilize the leasehold estate he or she possesses or can sublease it to another
farmer. The oil company, if it has leased its rights, can sublease
them; if it has purchased them, it can sell or lease them. A
variation would be for an oil company to buy the land in fee,
conduct its drilling operations, and lease the surface to a farmer.
In the public interest, the government has claimed the right to
allow aircraft to fly over the land. Although a landowner technically owns from the center of the earth out to the heavens, the
right given aircraft to fly overhead creates a practical limit on
that ownership.

In parcel B, the fee simple landowner has leased or sold the right   *Surface Right of Entry*
to extract oil and gas from beneath the land. However, no surface
right for the purpose of entering and drilling has been leased or
sold. Thus, the oil company must slant drill from a nearby
property where it does have a **surface right of entry.** The remaining rights amount to a full fee estate in the surface and
airspace. However, use of those rights is subject to zoning laws
and building codes that restrict what can be built. Deed restrictions may include additional limitations on the type of structure
that can be built. Also, the government claims airspace rights for

passing aircraft, as it does over all land within its borders. Just above and beneath the surface, easement rights have been granted to utility companies for electric, telephone, water, and gas lines.

Despite the fact that this homeowner's bundle of rights is not complete, the remaining rights are quite suitable for a home site. Recognizing this, lenders would accept the owner's offer of this house and lot as collateral for a loan. This might not be the case if the oil company had a surface right of entry. The noise, odor, and fire hazard of a working oil well next to a house would considerably reduce its value as a residence.

Land Lease   In parcel C shown in Figure 5.6b, the fee owner has created an estate for years by a long-term lease of the land to an investor, who has subsequently constructed an apartment building on the land. This estate gives the building owner the right to occupy and use the land for a fixed period of time, most often between 55 and 99 years. In turn, the building owner rents out apartment units on a monthly or yearly basis. The rights to any mineral, oil, or gas deposits can either be included in the lease or reserved by the landowner. At the end of the lease period, the reversion held by the owner of the fee estate entitles the owner to retake

Figure 5.6b. Cross section of estates and rights in land (continued)

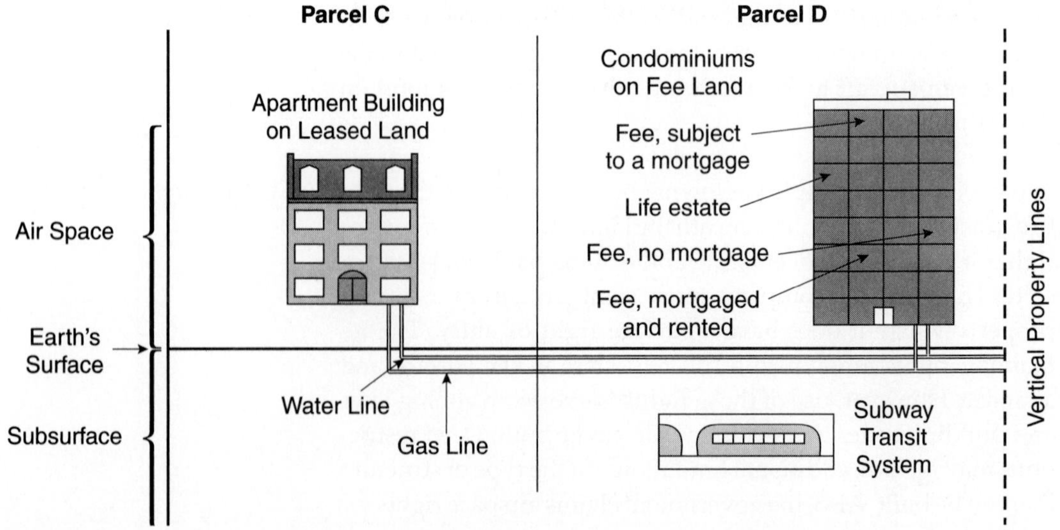

possession of the land, including the buildings and other improvements thereon.

In parcel D, fee simple air lots have been sold to individual apartment owners in a condominium apartment building. The owner of each air lot has a fee simple bundle of rights and is free to mortgage it by taking the foreclosure "stick" out of the bundle and giving it to a lender in exchange for a loan. Also, the owner can lease the unit to a tenant, thereby creating a leasehold estate and a reversion.

Condominium Lots

Condominium owners as a group usually own the surface of the land upon which the building rests, any airspace not used as air lots, and the subsurface. In parcel D, the owners have either sold, leased, or granted to a transit authority the right to build a subway line under this parcel. Underground rights of this type are very important in cities with subsurface transportation networks and will continue to be so as more cities open underground mass transit systems.

An alternative to fee owners granting a subsurface right for underground transportation lines is for the line owner to own the fee interest in the entire parcel, use the subsurface portion for its tracks, and sell or lease the use of the surface and airspace above. In Chicago and New York City, for instance, railroads have sold or leased surface and air rights above their downtown tracks for the purpose of constructing office buildings and convention halls. Passenger trains run just below the surface, while new buildings occupy the space above.

Match terms **a–x** *with statements* **1–24.**

VOCABULARY REVIEW

a. *Allodial*
b. *Chattel*
c. *Common law*
d. *Dominant estate*
e. *Easement*
f. *Easement appurtenant*
g. *Eminent domain*
h. *Encroachment*
i. *Encumbrance*
j. *Escheat*
k. *Estate*
l. *Estate for years*

m. *Freehold estate*
n. *Inverse condemnation*
o. *Lessor*
p. *Lien*
q. *Life estate*
r. *Mechanic's lien*
s. *Party wall*
t. *Periodic tenancy*
u. *Right-of-way*
v. *Specific lien*
w. *Statutory law*
x. *Voluntary lien*

1. A lease with a specific starting and ending date and no automatic renewal provision.
2. A charge or hold against property to use it as debt security.
3. A leasehold estate that automatically renews itself unless canceled.
4. An article of personal property.
5. The unauthorized intrusion of a building or other improvement on the land of another.
6. Any impediment to clear title.
7. The right of government to take property from private owners, who in turn must be compensated.
8. A real property ownership system that allows land to be owned by individuals.
9. One's legal interest or rights in land.
10. A lawsuit by a property owner demanding that a public agency purchase his or her property.
11. The reversion of property to the state when the owner dies without leaving a will or heirs.
12. One who holds title and leases out property; the landlord.
13. A right or privilege one party has in the use of land belonging to another.
14. Law based on custom and court decisions.
15. Law created by the enactment of legislation.
16. A lien purposely created by a property owner.
17. A lien on a specific property.
18. Lien rights for suppliers of labor or materials.
19. The parcel that benefits from an easement across another person's land.
20. An easement attached to a parcel of land and included with that parcel whenever it is conveyed.
21. An estate indicating actual ownership of land.
22. An estate for the duration of someone's life.
23. A wall located on a property boundary line.
24. The right to travel over a portion of another's land.

QUESTIONS AND PROBLEMS

1. Distinguish between freehold estates and leasehold estates in land.
2. Under what conditions may an easement be created without there being specific mention of it in writing?
3. What steps have been taken by your state legislature to recognize the legal equality of married women in real estate ownership?
4. What three European countries provided the basis for real estate law in the United States?
5. From the standpoint of possession, what is the key difference between an easement and a lease?
6. What is an encumbrance? Give three examples.
7. In your community, name specific examples of the application of police power to the rights of landowners.

8. If your state has a homestead protection law, how much protection does it offer and what must a person do to qualify?

"Adverse possession and access easements," by **Wisconsin Realtors Association** (*Legal Update* 93.07, July 1993, pp.1–7). Discusses the legal aspects of access rights, land titles, and land ownership.

"Considering the Many Options Can Save Money and Avoid Unnecessary Ownership Hassles in the Future; What's in a Home Title? Plenty of Choices," by **Robert J. Bruss** (*Chicago Tribune*, March 2, 1995, p. 5).

How to Survive While Realestating by **Marvin Myers** and **Alison Myers** (M&M Productions, 1985, 63 pages). Contains 55 humorous cartoons about real estate that both teach and entertain.

The Law of Easements and Licenses in Land, by **Jon W. Bruce** and **James Ely** (Warren, Gorham & Lamont, 1992). Entire book provides information on measurements, land utilization, land ownership, and real estate law.

The Smart Investors' Guide to Real Estate, 3rd Ed., by **Robert Bruss** (Crown, 1984, 270 pages). Emphasis is on the do-it-yourself investor with a small amount to invest. Author is a nationally syndicated real estate columnist.

ADDITIONAL READINGS

6

Forms of Ownership

KEY • TERMS

Board of Directors: individuals elected by the shareholders to oversee the operation of a company

Community property: ownership whereby spouses are treated as equal partners with each owning a one-half interest

Concurrent ownership: ownership by two or more persons at the same time

Estate in severalty: estate owned by one person; sole ownership

Joint tenancy: a form of property co-ownership that features the right of survivorship

Limited Liability Company: organization of members or managers with little formal organization and limited liability

Limited partnership: a form of organization composed of general partners who mainly organize and operate the partnership and limited partners who provide the capital

Right of survivorship: a feature of joint tenancy whereby the surviving joint tenants automatically acquire all the rights, title, and interest of the deceased joint tenant

Tenancy by the entirety: a form of joint ownership reserved for married persons; right of survivorship exists and neither spouse has a disposable interest during the lifetime of the other

Tenants in common: shared ownership of a single property among two or more persons; interests need not be equal and no right of survivorship exists

Undivided interest: ownership by two or more persons that gives each the right to use the entire property

In Chapter 4 we looked at land from a physical standpoint: the size and shape of a parcel, where it is located, and what was affixed to it. In Chapter 5 we explored various legal rights and interests that can be held in land. In this chapter we look at how a given right or interest in land can be held by one or more individuals.

When title to property is held by one person, it is called an **estate in severalty** or **sole ownership.** Although the word *severalty* seems to imply that several persons own a single property, the correct meaning can be easily remembered by thinking of "severed" ownership. Sole ownership is available to single and married persons, although the nature of ownership can vary, depending on an individual state's marital property laws. Businesses usually hold title to property in severalty. It is from the estate in severalty that all other tenancies are created.

The major advantage of sole ownership for an individual is flexibility. As a sole owner you can make all the decisions regarding a property without having to get the agreement of co-owners. You can decide what property or properties to buy, when to buy, and how much to offer. You can decide whether to pay all cash or to seek a loan by using the property as collateral. Once you have bought the property, you control (within the bounds of the law) how the property will be used, how much will be charged if it is rented, and how it will be managed. If you decide to sell, you alone decide when to offer the property for sale and at what price and terms.

But freedom and responsibility go together. For example, if you purchase a rental property, you must determine the prevailing rents, find tenants, prepare contracts, collect the rent, and keep the property in repair; or you must hire and pay someone else to manage the property. Another deterrent to sole ownership is the high entry cost. This form of real estate ownership is usually not possible for someone with only a few hundred dollars to invest.

Let us now turn to methods of **concurrent ownership**—that is, ownership by two or more persons at the same time.

When two or more persons wish to share the ownership of a single property, they may do so as **tenants in common.** As tenants in common, each owns an **undivided interest** in the

SOLE OWNERSHIP

TENANTS IN COMMON

whole property. This means that each owner has a right to possession of the entire property. None can exclude the others nor claim any specific portion. In a tenancy in common, these interests need not be the same size, and each owner can independently sell, mortgage, give away, or devise his individual interest. This independence is possible because each tenant in common has a separate legal title to an undivided interest.

Suppose that you invest $20,000, along with two of your friends who invest $30,000 and $50,000, respectively; together you buy 100 acres of land as tenants in common. Presuming that everyone's ownership interest is proportional to his or her cash investment, you will hold a 20% interest in the entire 100 acres and your two friends will hold 30% and 50%. You cannot pick out 20 acres and exclude the other co-owners from them, nor can you pick out 20 acres and say, "These are mine and I'm going to sell them"; nor can they do that to you. You do, however, have the legal right to sell or otherwise dispose of your 20% interest (or a portion of it) without the permission of your two friends. Your friends have the same right. If one of you sells, the purchaser becomes a new tenant in common with the remaining co-owners.

Wording of Conveyance

As a rule, a tenancy in common is indicated by naming the co-owners in the conveyance and adding the words *as tenants in common*. For example, a deed might read, "Samuel Smith, John Jones, and Robert Miller, as tenants in common." If nothing is said regarding the size of each co-owner's interest in the property, the law presumes that all interests are equal. Therefore, if the co-owners intend their interests to be unequal, the size of each co-owner's undivided interest must be stated as a percent or a fraction, such as 60% and 40% or one-third and two-thirds.

In nearly all states, including New York, if two or more persons are named as owners, and there is no specific indication as to how they are taking title, they are presumed to be tenants in common. Thus, if a deed is made out to "Donna Adams and Barbara Kelly," the law would consider them to be tenants in common, each holding an undivided one-half interest in the property. An important exception to this presumption is when the co-owners are married to each other. In this case, the presumption in New York is that they are taking ownership as tenants by the entirety.

No Right of Survivorship

When a tenancy in common exists, if a co-owner dies, his interest passes to his heirs or devisees, who then become tenants in common with the remaining co-owners. There is no **right of survivorship;** that is, the remaining co-owners do not acquire the deceased's interest unless they are named in the deceased's last will and testament to do so. When a creditor has a claim on a co-owner's interest and forces its sale to satisfy the debt, the new buyer becomes a tenant in common with the remaining co-owners. If one co-owner wants to sell (or give away) only a portion of his undivided interest, he may; the new owner becomes a tenant in common with the other co-owners.

Co-Owner Responsibilities

Any income generated by the property belongs to the tenants in common in proportion to the size of their interests. Similarly, each co-owner is responsible for paying his proportionate share of property taxes, repairs, upkeep, and so on, plus interest and debt repayment, if any. If any co-owner fails to contribute his proportionate share, the other co-owners can pay on his behalf and then sue him for that amount. If co-owners find that they cannot agree as to how the property is to be run and cannot agree on a plan for dividing or selling it, it is possible to request a court-ordered partition. A **partition** divides the property into distinct portions so that each person can hold his proportionate interest in severalty. If this is physically impossible, such as when three co-owners each have a one-third interest in a house, the court will order the property sold and the proceeds divided among the co-owners.

"What Ifs"

The major advantage of tenancy in common is that it allows two or more persons to achieve goals that one person could not accomplish alone. However, prospective co-owners should give advance thought to what they will do (short of going to court) (1) if a co-owner fails to pay his share of ownership expenses, (2) if differences arise regarding how the property is to be operated, (3) if agreement cannot be reached as to when to sell, for how much, and on what terms, and (4) if a co-owner dies and those who inherit his interest have little in common with the surviving co-owners. The counsel of an attorney experienced in property ownership can be very helpful when considering the co-ownership of property.

JOINT TENANCY

Another form of concurrent ownership is **joint tenancy.** The most distinguishing characteristic of joint tenancy is the right of survivorship. Upon the death of a joint tenant, his or her interest does not descend to the heirs or pass by a will. Rather, the entire ownership remains in the surviving joint tenant(s). In other words, on the death of a joint tenant, there is simply one less owner.

Four Unities

To create a joint tenancy, **four unities** must be present. They are the unities of time, title, interest, and possession.

Unity of time means that each joint tenant must acquire an ownership interest at the same moment. Once a joint tenancy is formed, it is not possible to add new joint tenants later unless an entirely new joint tenancy is formed among the existing co-owners and the new co-owner. To illustrate, suppose that A, B, and C own a parcel of land as joint tenants. If *A* sells his interest to *D,* then *B, C,* and *D* must sign documents to create a new joint tenancy among them. If this is not done, *D* automatically becomes a tenant in common with *B* and *C* who, between themselves, remain joint tenants. *D* will then own an undivided one-third interest in common with *B* and *C* who will own an undivided two-thirds interest as joint tenants.

Unity of title means that the joint tenants acquire their interests from the same source, i.e., the same deed or will. (Some states allow a property owner to create a valid joint tenancy by conveying to him- or herself and another without going through a third party.)

Unity of interest means that the joint tenants own one interest together and each joint tenant has exactly the same right in that interest. (This, by the way, is the foundation on which the survivorship feature rests.) If the joint tenants list individual interests, they lack unity of interest and will be treated as tenants in common. Unity of interest also means that, if one joint tenant holds a fee simple interest in the property, the others cannot hold anything but a fee simple interest.

Unity of possession means that the joint tenants must enjoy the same undivided possession of the whole property. All joint tenants have the use of the entire property, and no individual owns a particular portion of it. By way of contrast, unity of possession is the only unity essential to a tenancy in common.

The feature of joint tenancy ownership that is most widely recognized is its **right of survivorship.** Upon the death of a joint tenant, that interest in the property is extinguished. In a two-person joint tenancy, when one person dies, the other immediately becomes the sole owner. With more than two persons as joint tenants, when one dies, the remaining joint tenants are automatically left as owners. Ultimately, the last survivor becomes the sole owner. The legal philosophy is that the joint tenants constitute a single owning unit. The death of one joint tenant does not destroy that unit—it only reduces the number of persons owning the unit. For the public record, a copy of the death certificate and an affidavit of death of the joint tenant is recorded in the county where the property is located. The property must also be released from any estate tax liens.

Right of Survivorship

It is the right of survivorship that has made joint tenancy a popular form of ownership among married couples. Married couples often want the surviving spouse to have sole ownership of the marital property. Any property held in joint tenancy goes to the surviving spouse without the delay of probate and usually with less legal expense.

Because of the survivorship feature, joint tenancy has loosely been labeled a "poor man's will." However, it cannot replace a properly drawn will as it affects only that property held in joint tenancy. Moreover, a will can be changed if the persons named therein are no longer in one's favor. But once a joint tenancy is formed, title is permanently conveyed and there is no further opportunity for change. As a joint tenant, you cannot will your joint tenancy interest to someone because your interest ends upon your death. Also, be aware that ownership in joint tenancy may result in additional estate taxes.

"Poor Man's Will"

Another important aspect of joint tenancy ownership is that it can be used to defeat dower or curtesy rights. If a married man forms a joint tenancy with someone other than his wife (such as a business partner) and then dies, his wife has no dower rights in that joint tenancy. As a result, courts have begun to look with disfavor on the right of survivorship. Louisiana, Ohio, and Oregon either do not recognize joint tenancy or have abolished it.* Of the remaining states that recognize joint tenancy ownership (see Table 6.1), 14 have abolished the automatic presumption of survivorship. In these states, if the right of survivorship is desired in a joint tenancy, it must be clearly stated in the conveyance. For example, a deed might read, "Karen Carson and Judith Johnson, as joint tenants with the right of survivorship and not as tenants in common." Even in those states not requiring it, this wording is often used to ensure that the right of survivorship is intended. In community property states, one spouse cannot take community funds and establish a valid joint tenancy with a third party.

The Estates, Powers and Trusts Law of New York provides that every transfer of real property to two or more unmarried persons is a tenancy in common unless a joint tenancy is specified. (An exception is made for estates held by executors or trustees.)

There is a popular misconception that a debtor can protect himself from creditors' claims by taking title to property as a joint tenant. It is generally true that in a joint tenancy the surviving joint tenant(s) acquire(s) the property free and clear of any liens against the deceased. However, this can happen only if the debtor dies before the creditor seizes the debtor's interest.

Only a human being can be a joint tenant. A corporation cannot be a joint tenant. This is because a corporation is an artificial legal being and can exist in perpetuity—that is, never die. Joint tenancy ownership is not limited to the ownership of land; any estate in land and any chattel interest may be held in joint tenancy.

TENANCY BY THE ENTIRETY

Tenancy by the entirety (also called *tenancy by the entireties*) is a form of joint tenancy specifically for married persons. To the four unities of a joint tenancy is added a fifth: **unity of person.** The basis for this is the legal premise that a husband and wife are an indivisible legal unit. Two key characteristics of a tenancy by the entirety are: (1) the surviving spouse becomes

---

* In Ohio and Oregon, other means are available to achieve rights of survivorship between nonmarried persons. When two or more persons own property together in Louisiana, it is termed an *ownership in indivision* or a *joint ownership.* Louisiana law is based on old French civil law.

Table 6.1. Concurrent Ownership by States

State	L.L.P.	L.L.C.	Tenancy in Common	Joint Tenancy	Tenancy by the Entirety	Community Property
Alabama	X	X	X	X		
Alaska		X	X	X	X	
Arizona	X	X	X	X		X
Arkansas		X	X	X	X	
California			X	X		X
Colorado		X	X	X		
Connecticut		X	X	X		
Delaware	X	X	X	X	X	
District of Columbia	X		X	X	X	
Florida		X	X	X	X	
Georgia	X	X	X	X		
Hawaii		X	X	X		
Idaho		X	X	X		X
Illinois		X	X	X		
Indiana		X	X	X	X	
Iowa	X	X	X	X		
Kansas	X	X	X	X		
Kentucky		X	X	X	X	
Louisiana	X	X				X
Maine		X	X	X		
Maryland	X	X	X	X	X	
Massachusetts		X	X	X	X	
Michigan	X	X	X	X	X	
Minnesota	X	X	X	X		
Mississippi	X	X	X	X	X	
Missouri		X	X	X	X	
Montana		X	X	X		
Nebraska		X	X	X		
Nevada		X	X	X		X
New Hampshire		X	X	X		
New Jersey	X	X	X	X	X	
New Mexico		X	X	X		X
New York		X	X	X	X	
North Carolina	X	X	X	X	X	
North Dakota		X	X	X		
Ohio	X	X	X		X	
Oklahoma		X	X	X	X	
Oregon		X	X		X	
Pennsylvania			X	X	X	
Rhode Island		X	X	X	X	
South Carolina		X	X	X		
South Dakota		X	X	X		
Tennessee		X	X	X	X	
Texas	X	X	X	X		X
Utah	X	X	X	X	X	
Vermont			X	X	X	
Virginia	X	X	X	X	X	
Washington		X	X	X		X
West Virginia		X	X	X	X	
Wisconsin		X	X	X		X
Wyoming		X	X	X	X	

L.L.P.: Limited Liability Partnership
L.L.C.: Limited Liability Company

the sole owner of the property upon the death of the other, and (2) neither spouse has a disposable interest in the property during the lifetime of the other. Thus, while both are alive and married to each other, both signatures are necessary to convey title to the property. With respect to the first characteristic, tenancy by the entirety is similar to joint tenancy because both feature the right of survivorship. They are quite different, however, with respect to the second characteristic. Whereas a joint tenant can convey to another party without approval of the other joint tenant(s), a tenancy by the entirety can be terminated only by joint action of (or joint judgment against) husband and wife.

States that recognize tenancy by the entirety are listed in Table 6.1. Some of these states, including New York, automatically assume that a tenancy by the entirety is created when married persons buy real estate. However, it is best to use a phrase such as "John and Mary Smith, husband and wife as tenants by the entirety with the right of survivorship" on deeds and other conveyances. This avoids later questions as to whether their intention might have been to create a joint tenancy or a tenancy in common.

Advantages and Disadvantages

Tenancy by the entirety ownership has several important advantages: (1) it protects against one spouse conveying or mortgaging the couple's property without the consent of the other, (2) in many states it provides some protection from the forced sale of jointly held property to satisfy a debt judgment against one of the spouses, and (3) it features automatic survivorship. Disadvantages are that tenancy by the entirety: (1) provides for no one except the surviving spouse, (2) may create estate tax problems, and (3) does not replace the need for a will to direct how a couple's personal property shall be disposed of.

Effect of Divorce

In the event of divorce, the parting spouses become tenants in common. This change is automatic, as tenancy by the entirety can exist only when the co-owners are husband and wife. If the ex-spouses do not wish to continue co-ownership, either can sell his or her individual interest. If a buyer cannot be found for a partial interest nor an amicable agreement reached for selling the interests of both ex-spouses simultaneously, either may seek a court action to partition the property.

Note that severalty, tenancy in common, joint tenancy, and tenancy by the entirety are called English common law estates because of their historical roots in English common law.

Laws and customs acquired from Spain and France when vast areas of the United States were under their control are the basis for the **community property** system of ownership for married persons. Table 6.1 identifies the eight community property states. The laws of each community property state vary slightly, but the underlying concept is that the husband and wife contribute jointly and equally to their marriage and thus should share equally in any property purchased during marriage. Whereas English law is based on the merging of husband and wife upon marriage, community property law treats husband and wife as equal partners, with each owning a one-half interest.

COMMUNITY PROPERTY

Property owned before marriage and property acquired after marriage by gift, inheritance, or purchase with separate funds, can be exempted from the couple's community property. Such property is called **separate property** and can be conveyed or mortgaged without the signature of the owner's spouse. The owner of a separate property also has full control over naming someone in his or her will to receive the property. All other property acquired by the husband or wife during marriage is considered community property and requires the signature of both spouses before it can be conveyed or mortgaged. Each spouse can name in his or her will the person to receive his or her one-half interest. It does not have to go to the surviving spouse. If death occurs without a will, in six states (California, Idaho, Nevada, New Mexico, Texas, and Washington) the deceased spouse's interest goes to the surviving spouse. In Arizona and Louisiana, the descendants of the deceased spouse are the prime recipients. Texas also allows community property to be held with a right of survivorship. Neither dower nor curtesy exists in community property states.

Separate Property

The major advantage of the community property system is found in its philosophy: it treats the spouses as equal partners in property acquired through their mutual efforts during marriage. Even if the wife elects to be a full-time homemaker and all the money brought into the household is the result of her husband's job (or vice versa), the law treats them as equal co-owners in any property bought with that money. This is true even if only one spouse is named as the owner.

Philosophy

In New York, property owned before marriage or separately acquired after marriage is treated in the same way as in a community property state. All other property is termed *marital property*. New York's **equitable distribution law** directs the judge in a divorce proceeding to divide marital property "equitably" rather than "equally." The statute lists a number of factors the court must consider in determining what is equitable, including the duration of the marriage, the tax consequences for each party, and the contribution of each partner to the marriage.

In the event of divorce, if the parting couple cannot amicably decide how to divide their community property, the courts will do so. If the courts do not, the ex-spouses become tenants in common with each other. Either can file suit for partition, if it should become necessary later.

Caveat to Agents

Often, while preparing a real estate purchase contract, the buyers ask the real estate agent how to take title. This question is especially common from married couples purchasing a home. If the agent attempts to answer with a specific recommendation, the agent is practicing law, and that requires a license to practice law. The agent can describe the ownership methods available in the state, but should then refer the buyers to their lawyer for a specific recommendation. This is important because the choice of ownership method cannot be made in the vacuum of a single purchase: the choice must be made in light of the buyers' total financial picture and estate plans, by someone well versed in federal and state estate and tax laws. Meanwhile, on the purchase contract the agent can enter the names of the purchasers and add the words, *vesting to be supplied before closing*. This gives the buyers time to decide how to hold title without delaying preparation of the purchase contract. The buyers can then seek legal counsel and advise the closing agent how they want to take title on the deed.

PARTNERSHIP

A **partnership** exists when two or more persons, as partners, unite their property, labor, and skill as a business to share the profits and losses created by it. The agreement between the partners need not be formal and may be oral or written. The partners may hold the partnership property either in their own names or in the name of the partnership (which would hold title in severalty). For convenience, especially in a large partnership,

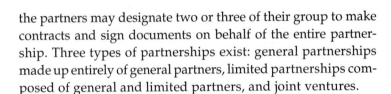

the partners may designate two or three of their group to make contracts and sign documents on behalf of the entire partnership. Three types of partnerships exist: general partnerships made up entirely of general partners, limited partnerships composed of general and limited partners, and joint ventures.

The **general partnership** is an outgrowth of common law. However, to introduce clarity and uniformity into general partnership laws across the United States, 49 states and the District of Columbia have adopted the **Uniform Partnership Act** either in total or with local modifications. (The exception is Louisiana.) Briefly, the highlights of the act are: (1) title to partnership property may be held in the partnership's name, (2) each partner has an equal right of possession of partnership property—but only for partnership purposes, (3) upon the death of one partner his or her rights in the partnership property go to the surviving partners—but the deceased's estate must be reimbursed for the value of the interest in the partnership, (4) a partner's right to specific partnership property is not subject to dower or curtesy, and (5) partnership property can be attached by creditors only for debts of the partnership, not for debts of a partner.

General Partnership

As a form of property ownership, the partnership is a method of combining the capital and expertise of two or more persons. It is equally important to note that the profits and losses of the partnership are taxable directly to each individual partner in proportion to his or her interest in the partnership. Although the partnership files a tax return, it is for informational purposes only. The partnership itself does not pay taxes. Negative aspects of this form of ownership center around financial liability, illiquidity, and, in some cases, management.

Financial liability means that each partner is personally responsible for all the debts of the partnership. Thus, each general partner can lose not only what was invested in the partnership, but more, up to the full extent of his or her personal financial worth. If one partner makes a commitment on behalf of the partnership, all partners are responsible for making good on that commitment. If the partnership is sued, each partner is fully responsible, although many states have now enacted **limited liability partnerships**—usually referred to as L.L.P.s—which prohibit unlimited liability for nonresponsible partners. **Illiquidity** refers to the possibility that it may be very difficult to sell one's partnership interest on short notice in order to raise cash. **Management** means that each general partner is expected to take an active part in the operation of the partnership.

Limited Partnership

Because partners bear management responsibility and the potential for unlimited financial liability, another partnership form, the **limited partnership,** has developed. Forty-nine states, plus the District of Columbia, have adopted the **Revised Uniform Limited Partnership Act.** The only exception is Louisiana, which has its own general and limited partnership laws. The limited partnership acts recognize the legality of limited partnerships and require that a limited partnership be formed by a written document.

A limited partnership is composed of general and limited partners. The **general partners** organize and operate the partnership, contribute some capital, and agree to accept the full financial liability of the partnership. The **limited partners** provide the bulk of the investment capital, have little say in the day-to-day management of the partnership, share in the profits and losses, and contract with their general partners to limit the financial liability of each limited partner to the amount he or she invests. Additionally, a well-written partnership agreement allows for the continuity of the partnership in the event of the death of a general or limited partner.

The advantages of limited liability, minimum management responsibility, and direct pass-through of profits and losses for taxation purposes have made this form of ownership popular. However, being free of management responsibility is only advantageous to the investors if the general partners are capable and honest. If they are not, the only control open to the limited partners is to vote to replace the general partners. A limited partner should be cautioned, however, not to get too involved in the management of a limited partnership. A limited partner who does become so sufficiently involved may become a general partner by operation of law, and have more liability than was bargained for!

Before investing in a limited partnership, one should investigate the past record of the general partners, for this is usually a good indication of how the new partnership will be managed. The investigation should include the partners' previous investments, checking court records for any legal complaints brought against them, and talking to past investors. Additionally, the prospective partner should be prepared to stay in for the duration of the partnership as the resale market for limited partnership interests is small.

Limited partnerships are a popular method of investing in real estate. The general partners find property, organize and promote the partnership, and invite people to invest money to become limited partners. Such a partnership can be as small as a dozen or so investors or as large as the multimillion-dollar partnerships marketed nationally by major stock brokerage firms. If a limited partnership consists of more than a few close friends, registration with state and federal securities agencies is required before partnerships can be sold to investors.

A **joint venture** is a partnership to carry out a single business project. A joint venture is treated as a partnership for tax purposes. Examples of joint ventures in real estate are the purchase of land by two or more persons with the intent of grading it and selling it as lots, the association of a landowner and builder to build and sell, and the association of a lender and builder to purchase land and develop buildings on it to sell to investors. Each member of the joint venture makes a contribution in the form of capital or talent, and all have a strong incentive to make the joint venture succeed. If more than one project is undertaken, the relationship becomes more like a general partnership than a joint venture.

Joint Venture

Each state has passed laws to permit groups of people to create **corporations** that can buy, sell, own, and operate in the name of the corporation. The corporation, in turn, is owned by stockholders who possess shares of stock as evidence of their ownership.

CORPORATIONS

Because the corporation is an entity (or legal being) in the eyes of the law, the corporation must pay income taxes on its profits. What remains after taxes can be used to pay dividends to the stockholders, who in turn pay personal income taxes on their dividend income. This double taxation of profits is the most important negative factor in the corporate form of ownership. On the positive side, the entity aspect shields the investor from unlimited liability. Even if the corporation falls on the hardest of financial times and owes more than it owns, the worst that can happen to the stockholder is that the value of the stock will drop to zero. Another advantage of corporations is that shares of stock are much more liquid than any previously discussed form of real estate ownership, even sole ownership. Stockbrokers who specialize in the purchase and sale of corporate stock usually complete a sale in a week or less. Furthermore, shares of stock in most corporations sell for less than $100, thus enabling an investor to operate with small amounts of capital. In a corporation, the stockholders elect a board of directors, who in turn hire the management needed to run the day-to-day operations of the company. As a practical matter, however, unless people are major shareholders in the corporation, they have little control over management. The solution is to buy stock in firms where one likes the management and sell where one does not.

S Corporations

Several large real estate corporations are traded on the New York Stock Exchange, and the corporation is a popular method of organization for real estate brokers and developers. Nevertheless, most real estate investors shun corporations to avoid the double taxation feature and because the tax benefits of owning real estate are trapped inside the corporation.

In 1958, the Internal Revenue Code first allowed **Subchapter S** corporations that provided the liability protection of a corporation with the profit-and-loss pass-through of a partnership. Although the original 10-stockholder maximum was a drawback, the real problem for real estate investors was that no more than 20% of a Subchapter S's gross receipts could come from passive income. And rent is passive income. In October 1982, Congress revised the rules and eliminated the passive income restriction, increased the maximum number of shareholders to 35, and changed the name to **S corporations.** (Regular corporations are now called C corporations.)

Caveat

A caution should be noted in utilizing the corporate entity. Although the foregoing discussion generally presumes a typical publicly held corporation, the laws in various states have enabled certain creditors to pierce corporate veils (find individual liability for owners, directors, and shareholders) when the corporation has been fraudulently created, was undercapitalized, or has been involved in dishonest activities. Simply incorporating, by itself, does not insulate from all forms of liability and counsel should be consulted.

In all states, the trust form of ownership can be used to provide for the well-being of another person. Basically, this arrangement enables title to real and/or personal property to be transferred by its owner (the **trustor**) to a trustee. The **trustee** holds title and manages the property for the benefit of another (the **beneficiary**) in accordance with instructions given by the trustor. Trust forms include the inter vivos trust (also called a living trust), the testamentary trust, land trusts, and real estate investment trusts.

TRUSTS

An **inter vivos trust** takes effect during the life of its creator. For example, you can transfer property to a trustee with instructions that it be managed and that income from the trust assets be paid to your children, spouse, relatives, or a charity.

   A **testamentary trust** takes effect after death. For example, you could place instructions in your will that upon your death, your property is to be placed into a trust. You can name whomever you want as trustee (a bank or trust company or friend, for example) and whomever you want as beneficiaries. You can also give instructions as to how the assets are to be managed and how much (and how often) to pay the beneficiaries. Because trusts provide property management and financial control as well as a number of tax and estate planning advantages, this form of property ownership is growing in popularity.

*Inter Vivos
and Testamentary Trusts*

In New York and several other states, owners of real estate may create a trust, called a **land trust,** wherein they are both the trustor and the beneficiary. The landowner conveys real property to a trustee, who in turn manages the property according to the beneficiary's (owner's) instructions. Because the beneficial interest created by the trust is considered personal property, the land trust effectively converts real property to personal property. Originally, the land trust gained popularity because true ownership could be cloaked in secrecy behind the name of a bank's trust department. Today, however, New York law prohibits the creator of a land trust from using the trust to hide from creditors. Nevertheless, its popularity continues, due to the

Land Trusts

Figure 6.1. Holding title.

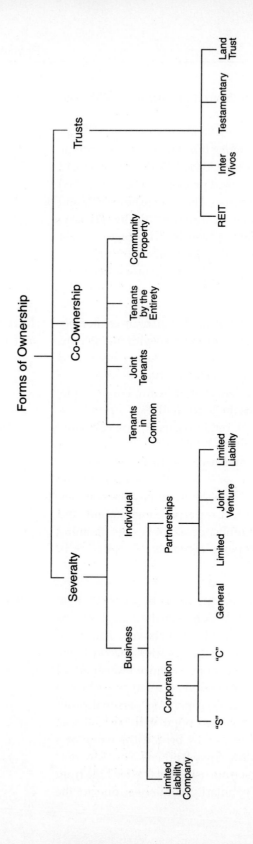

simplified probate procedures available to a person who lives in one state and owns land in another. The land trust is also a useful vehicle for group ownership and is not subject to legal attachment as is real property. Figure 6.1 provides a visual summary of the various forms of ownership described in this chapter.

The idea of creating a trust that in turn carries out the investment objectives of its investors is not new. What has changed is that in 1961 Congress passed a law allowing trusts that specialize in real estate investments to avoid double taxation by following strict rules. These **real estate investment trusts (REITs)** pool the money of many investors for the purchase of real estate, much as mutual funds do with stocks and bonds. Investors in a REIT are called **beneficiaries** and they purchase **beneficial interests** somewhat similar to shares of corporate stock. The trust officers, with the aid of paid advisors, buy, sell, mortgage, and operate real estate investments on behalf of the beneficiaries. If a REIT confines its activities to real estate investments, and if the REIT has at least 100 beneficiaries and distributes at least 95% of its net income every year, the Internal Revenue Service will collect tax on the distributed income only once—at the beneficiaries' level. Failure to follow the rules results in double taxation.

Real Estate Investment Trusts

The REIT is an attempt to combine the advantages of the corporate form of ownership with single taxation status. Like stock, the beneficial interests are freely transferable and usually sell for $100 each or less, a distinct advantage for the investor with a small amount of money to invest in real estate. Beneficial interests in the larger REITs are sold on a national basis, thus enabling a REIT to have thousands of beneficiaries and millions of dollars of capital for real estate purchases.

There has been legitimate, and probably justified, concern over liabilities of defendants in a business environment. One understands that if a person is harmed, there should be an ability to recover from the wrongdoer, yet many juries are awarding significant sums of money, and attempting to pursue personal liability for officers and directors of corporations because of their duties of care in the business entity (including real estate brokers!). At this time, at least 40 states have adopted legislation of historical significance by passing laws providing for the exist-

LIMITED LIABILITY COMPANIES

ence of a limited liability company. There will be a lot of case law and perhaps amendments to the statutes forthcoming in the next few years.

Any natural person of 18 years of age or older can act as organizer of a limited liability company by signing the articles of organization of such limited liability company and giving the original copy of the articles to the department of the state responsible for company registrations. The state then issues a certificate of organization, and the existence of the limited liability company begins.

The limited liability company name must include the word *Limited* or the abbreviation *Ltd., L.L.C.,* or *L.C.* It must maintain a registered office and registered agent (similar to a corporation); and all real or personal property owned or purchased by the limited liability company shall be held and owned, and the conveyance shall be made, in the name of the limited liability company. All instruments and documents providing for the acquisition, mortgage, or disposition of the limited liability company shall be valid and binding upon the company if they are executed by one or more persons acting as manager or member (if the management of the limited liability company is retained by the members).

In general terms, a member or manager of a limited liability company is not liable for debts, obligations, or liabilities of a limited liability company. A membership interest is considered personal property and the member has no interest in specific limited liability company property. Please note that limited liability companies are not corporations, nor partnerships, nor limited partnerships. They are a totally new theory of ownership (New York passed legislation authorizing limited liability companies in 1994) and, as stated previously, a lot of law is yet to be made in this area.

SYNDICATION   Although you often hear the word **syndication** used in such a way as to imply that it is a form of ownership, it is not. There is no such thing as "tenancy by syndication"; rather, syndication is a broad term that simply refers to two or more individuals who have combined to pursue an investment enterprise too large for any of them to undertake individually. The form of ownership might be a tenancy in common, joint tenancy, general or limited partnership, joint venture, or a corporation. When people talk about a syndication in the context of real estate investing, it most likely refers to the real estate limited partnership.

The purpose of this chapter has been to acquaint you with the fundamental aspects of the most commonly used forms of real estate ownership in the United States. You undoubtedly saw instances where you could apply these concepts. Unfortunately, it is not possible in a real estate principles book to discuss each detail of each state's law (many of which change frequently) nor to take into consideration the specific characteristics of a particular transaction. In applying the principles in this book to a particular transaction, you should obtain competent legal advice regarding your state's legal interpretation of these principles.

CAUTION

Match terms **a–q** *with statements* **1–17.**

VOCABULARY REVIEW

a. *Community property*
b. *Estate in severalty*
c. *Financial liability*
d. *General partnership*
e. *Joint tenancy*
f. *Joint venture*
g. *Limited partnership*
h. *Partition*
i. *Real estate investment trust (REIT)*

j. *Right of survivorship*
k. *Separate property*
l. *Syndication*
m. *Tenancy by the entirety*
n. *Tenants in common*
o. *Undivided interest*
p. *Unity of interest*
q. *Unity of time*

1. Owned by one person only; sole ownership.
2. Each owner has a right to use the entire property.
3. Undivided ownership by two or more persons without right of survivorship; interests need not be equal.
4. The remaining co-owners automatically acquire the deceased's undivided interest.
5. A form of co-ownership in which the most widely recognized feature is the right of survivorship.
6. All co-owners have an identical interest in the property; a requirement for joint tenancy.
7. All co-owners acquired their ownership interests at the same time; a requirement for joint tenancy.
8. Spouses are treated as equal partners with each owning a one-half interest; French and Spanish law origin.

9. An English-law form of ownership reserved for married persons. Right of survivorship exists and neither spouse has a disposable interest during the lifetime of the other.

10. Each partner is fully liable for all the debts and obligations of the partnership.

11. A member of a limited partnership whose financial liability is limited to the amount invested.

12. Two or more persons joining together on a single project as partners.

13. Property acquired before marriage in a community property state.

14. A type of mutual fund for real estate investment and ownership wherein a trustee holds property for the benefit of the beneficiaries.

15. A general term that refers to a group of persons who organize to pool their money.

16. Refers to the amount of money a person can lose.

17. To divide jointly held property so that each owner can hold a sole ownership.

QUESTIONS AND PROBLEMS

1. What is the key advantage of sole ownership? What is the major disadvantage?

2. Explain what is meant by the term *undivided interest* as it applies to joint ownership of real estate.

3. Name the four unities of a joint tenancy. What requirements do they impose on the joint tenants?

4. What does the term *right of survivorship* mean in real estate ownership?

5. Suppose that a deed was made out to "John and Mary Smith, husband and wife" with no mention as to how they were taking title. Which would your state assume: joint tenancy, tenancy in common, tenancy by the entirety, or community property?

6. Does your state permit the right of survivorship among persons who are not married?

7. If a deed is made out to three women as follows, "Susan Miller, Rhoda Wells, and Angela Lincoln," with no mention as to the form of ownership or the interest held by each, what can we presume regarding the form of ownership and the size of each woman's ownership interest?

8. In a community property state, if a deed names only the husband (or the wife) as the owner, can we assume that only that person's signature is necessary to convey title? Why or why not?

9. List two ways in which a general partnership differs from a limited partnership.

10. What advantages does a real estate investment trust offer a person who wants to invest in real estate?

ADDITIONAL READINGS

"Ins and Outs of Ownership: For Today's First Time Investor, Here's a Guide to the Many Forms of Land Ownership," by **John Simon** (*Farm and Land Realtor,* July/Aug. 1985, pp. 27–30).

Martindale-Hubble Law Dictionary (Martindale-Hubble, published annually). Contains summaries of law, including real estate, for each state and several foreign countries. Excellent reference material.

Origins of the Common Law, by **Arthur Hogue** (Indiana University Press, 1966, 276 pages). Provides a fascinating historical review of the origins of common law in England and how it was transplanted to the United States.

Real Estate Limited Partnership, 3rd Ed., by **Theodore S. Lynn, Harry F. Goldberg,** and **Michael Hirshfeld** (Wiley, 1991, 552 pages). Text covers areas of real estate transactions that involve partnerships and syndicates.

7

Transferring Title

Adverse possession: acquisition of land through prolonged and unauthorized occupation

Bargain and sale deed: a deed that contains no covenants, but does imply that the grantor owns the property being conveyed

Cloud on the title: any claim, lien, or encumbrance that impairs title to property

Color of title: some plausible, but not completely clear-cut indication of ownership rights

Consideration: anything of value given to induce another to enter into a contract

Covenant: a written agreement or promise

Deed: a written document that when properly executed and delivered conveys title to land.

Grantee: the person named in a deed who acquires ownership

Grantor: the person named in a deed who conveys ownership

Quitclaim deed: a legal instrument used to convey whatever title the grantor has; it contains no covenants, warranties, nor implication of the grantor's ownership

Special warranty deed: grantor warrants title only against defects occurring during the grantor's ownership

Warranty: an assurance or guarantee that something is true as stated

The previous three chapters emphasized how real estate is described, the rights and interests available for ownership, and how title can be held. In this chapter we discuss how ownership of real estate is conveyed from one owner to another. We begin with the voluntary conveyance of real estate by deed, and then continue with conveyance after death and conveyance by occupancy, accession, public grant, dedication, and forfeiture.

A **deed** is a written legal document by which ownership of real property is conveyed from one party to another. Deeds were not always used to transfer real estate. In early England, when land was sold, its title was conveyed by inviting the purchaser onto the land. In the presence of witnesses, the seller picked up a clod of earth and handed it to the purchaser. Simultaneously, the seller stated that he was delivering ownership of the land to the purchaser. In times when land sales were rare, because ownership usually passed from generation to generation, and when witnesses seldom moved from the towns or farms where they were born, this method worked well. However, as transactions became more common and people more mobile, this method of title transfer became less reliable. Furthermore, it was susceptible to fraud if enough people could be bribed or forced to make false statements. In 1677, England passed a law known as the **Statute of Frauds.** This law, subsequently adopted by each of the American states, requires that transfers of real estate ownership be in writing and signed in order to be enforceable in a court of law. Thus, the need for a deed was created.

DEEDS

What makes a written document a deed? What special phrases, statements, and actions are necessary to convey the ownership rights one has in land and buildings? First, a deed must identify the **grantor,** who is the person giving up ownership, and the **grantee,** the person who is acquiring that ownership. To be legally enforceable, the grantor must be of legal age (18 years in most states) and of sound mind.

Essential Elements of a Deed

Second, the deed must state that **consideration** was given by the grantee to the grantor. In New York, although it is not mandatory that the actual amount of consideration be recited in a deed, prudent practice dictates that some evidence of value received should be noted. This not only provides for the making of a better marketable title, but also insulates the transfer from allegations of fraud. It is common in New York to see the phrase, *For one dollar ($1.00) and other good and valuable consideration.* The phrase, *For valuable consideration* is also sufficient. These meet the legal requirement that consideration be shown, but retain privacy regarding the exact amount paid.

If the conveyance is a gift, the phrase *For natural love and affection* may be used, provided the gift is not for the purpose of defrauding the grantor's creditors. In these situations, consideration is not required in a deed, and the conveyance is still valid.

Words of Conveyance

Third, the deed must contain **words of conveyance.** With these words the grantor (1) clearly states that he is making a grant of real property to the grantee, and (2) identifies the quantity of the estate being granted. Usually the estate is fee simple, but it may also be a lesser estate (such as a life estate) or an easement.

A **land description** that cannot possibly be misunderstood is the fourth requirement. In New York, the general rule regarding the sufficiency of a description is that the land shall be identified with reasonable certainty. Metes and bounds, recorded plat, and reference to another recorded document are acceptable legal descriptions and should be used. However, the courts in New York have held words of general description to be sufficient as well. Thus, words such as "all of the grantor's property," or the name of a particular estate, or the use of street numbers are not void for uncertainty, but they are not recommended. It must also be remembered that in cases where discrepancies between land descriptions are found to exist, the description with the highest degree of certainty prevails. If the deed conveys only an easement or air right, the deed states that fact along with the legal description of the land. The key point is that a deed must clearly specify what the grantor is granting to the grantee.

Signature

Fifth, the grantor executes the deed by signing it. If the grantor is unable to write his name, he may make a mark, usually an *X*, in the presence of witnesses. They in turn print his name next to the *X* and sign as witnesses. If the grantor is a corporation, the corporation's seal is affixed to the deed and two of the corporation's officers sign it.

Figure 7.1.

Witnesseth, _John Stanley_ *, grantor, for valuable consideration given by* _Robert Brenner_ *, grantee, does hereby grant and release unto the grantee, his/her heirs and assigns to have and to hold forever, the following described land: [insert legal description here].*

John Stanley
Grantor's signature

Figure 7.1 illustrates the essential elements that combine to form a deed. Notice that the example includes an identification of the grantor and grantee, fulfills the requirement for consideration, has words of conveyance, a legal description of the land involved, and the grantor's signature. The words of conveyance are *grant and release* and the phrase *to have and to hold forever* says that the grantor is conveying all future benefits, not just a life estate or a tenancy for years. Ordinarily, the grantee does not sign the deed.

Delivery and Acceptance

For a deed to convey ownership, there must also be **delivery and acceptance.** Although a deed may be completed and signed, it does not transfer title to the grantee until the grantor voluntarily delivers it to the grantee and the grantee willingly accepts it. At that moment title passes. As a practical matter, the grantee is presumed to have accepted the deed if the grantee retains the deed, records the deed, encumbers the title, or performs any other act of ownership. This includes the grantee's appointment of someone else to accept and/or record the deed on the grantee's behalf. Once delivery and acceptance have occurred, the deed is evidence that the title transfer has taken place.

Covenants and Warranties

Although legally adequate, a deed meeting the preceding requirements can still leave a very important question unanswered in the grantee's mind: "Does the grantor possess all the right, title, and interest he or she is purporting to convey by this deed?" As a protective measure, the grantee can ask the grantor to include certain covenants and warranties in the deed. These are written promises by the grantor that the condition of title is as stated in the deed together with the grantor's guarantee that if title is not as stated the grantee will be compensated for any loss suffered. Five covenants and warranties have evolved over the centuries for use in deeds, and a deed may contain none, some, or all of them, in addition to the essential elements already discussed. They are seizin, quiet enjoyment, against encumbrances, further assurance, and warranty forever.

Under the **covenant of seizin** (sometimes spelled seisin), the grantor warrants (guarantees) that he is the owner and possessor of the property being conveyed and that he has the right to convey it. Under the **covenant of quiet enjoyment,** the grantor warrants to the grantee that the grantee will not be disturbed, after he takes possession, by someone else claiming an interest in the property.

In the **covenant against encumbrances,** the grantor guarantees to the grantee that the title is not encumbered with any easements, restrictions, unpaid property taxes, assessments, mortgages, judgments, etc., except as stated in the deed. If the grantee later discovers an undisclosed encumbrance, the grantor can be sued for the cost of removing it. The **covenant of further assurance** requires the grantor to procure and deliver to the grantee any subsequent documents that might be necessary to make good the grantee's title. **Warranty forever** is a guarantee to the grantee that the grantor will bear the expense of defending the grantee's title. If at any time in the future someone else can prove that he is the rightful owner, the grantee can sue the grantor for damages up to the value of the property at the time of the sale. Because these warranties and covenants are a formidable set of promises, grantors often back them up with title insurance (see Chapter 15). The grantee is also more comfortable if the deed is backed by title insurance.

Date and Acknowledgment

Although it is customary to show on the deed the **date** of execution by the grantor, it is not essential to the deed's validity. Remember that title passes upon **delivery** of the deed to the grantee, and this may not necessarily occur on the date it is signed.

Standard practice is to have the grantor appear before a notary public or other public officer and formally declare that he or she signed the deed as a voluntary act. This is known as an **acknowledgment.** Most states, including New York, consider a deed to be valid even though it is not witnessed or acknowledged, but very few states will allow such a deed to be recorded in the public records. Acknowledgments and the importance of recording deeds are covered in more detail in

Chapter 15. Meanwhile, let's turn our attention to examples of the most commonly used deeds in the United States.

The **full covenant and warranty deed,** also known as the **general warranty deed** or **warranty deed,** contains all five covenants and warranties. It is thus considered to be the best deed a grantee can receive, and is used extensively in New York and most other states.

Full Covenant and Warranty Deed

Figure 7.2 illustrates in plain language the essential parts of a warranty deed. Beginning at **[1]** , it is customary to identify at the top of the document that it is a warranty deed. At **[2]** the wording begins with *This deed ....* These words are introductory in purpose. The fact that this is a deed depends on what it contains, not on what it is labeled. A commonly found variation starts with *This indenture* (meaning this agreement or contract) and is equally acceptable. The place the deed was made **[3]** and the date it was signed **[4]** are customarily included, but are not necessary to make the deed valid.

At **[5]** and **[6]** the grantor is identified by name and, to avoid confusion with other persons having the same name, by address. Marital status is also stated: husband and wife, single man, single woman, widow, widower, divorced and not remarried. To avoid the inconvenience of repeating the grantor's name each time it is needed, the wording at **[7]** states that in the balance of the deed the word *Grantor* will be used instead. A common variation of this is to call the first party named *the party of the first part.* Next appears the name and marital status of the *Grantee* **[8]** and the method by which title is being taken (severalty, tenants in common, joint tenants, etc.). The grantee's address appears at **[9]**, and the wording at **[10]** states that the word *Grantee* will now be used instead of the grantee's name. The alternative method is to call the grantee *the party of the second part.*

The legal requirement that consideration be shown is fulfilled at **[11]**. Next we come to the **granting clause** at **[12]**. Here the grantor states that the intent of this document is to pass ownership to the grantee; and at **[13]** the grantor describes the extent of the estate being granted. The phrase *The grantee's heirs and assigns forever* indicates a fee simple estate. The word **assigns** refers to anyone the grantee may later convey the property to, such as by sale or gift.

Granting Clause

Figure 7.2.

WARRANTY DEED [1]

[2] *THIS DEED, made in the city of* [3] Exeter *, state of* XY *on the* [4] 4th *day of* April *, 19* xx *, between* [5] Henry Odom, a single man *, residing at* [6] 1234 Pleasant Rd., Exeter, XY *, herein called the GRANTOR,* [7] *and* [8] Peter Letz and Julie Letz, husband and wife as tenants by the entirety *, residing at* [9] 567 Friendly Lane, Exeter, XY, *herein called the GRANTEE.* [10]

WITNESSETH that in consideration [11] *of ten dollars ($10.00) and other valuable consideration, paid by the Grantee to the Grantor, the Grantor does hereby grant* [12] *and convey unto the Grantee, the Grantee's* [13] *heirs and assigns forever, the following described parcel of land:*

[legal description of land] [14]

together with the buildings [15] *and improvements thereon and all the estate* [16] *and rights pertaining thereto,*

[17] *TO HAVE AND TO HOLD the premises herein granted unto the Grantee, the Grantee's heirs* [18] *and assigns forever.*

The premises are free from encumbrances except as stated herein: [19]

[note exceptions here]

The Grantee shall not: [20]

[list restrictions imposed by Grantor on the Grantee]

The Grantor is lawfully seized [21] *of a good, absolute, and indefeasible estate in fee simple and has good right, full power, and lawful authority to convey the same by this deed.*

The Grantee, the Grantee's heirs and assigns, shall peaceably [22] *and quietly have, hold, use, occupy, possess, and enjoy the said premises.*

Figure 7.2. (continued)

The Grantor shall execute or procure any further **[23]** necessary assurance of the title to said premises, and the Grantor will forever **[24]** warrant and defend the title to said premises.

IN WITNESS WHEREOF, the Grantor has duly executed this deed the day and year first written above. **[25]**

[location of the
acknowledgment:
see Chapter 15] **[28]**

[26] Henry Odom
(Grantor's signature)

[27] (SEAL)

The legal description of the land involved is then shown at **[14]**. A grantor who is unable or does not wish to convey certain rights of ownership can list the exceptions here. For example, a grantor either not having or wishing to hold back oil and gas rights may convey to the grantee the land described, "except for the right to explore and recover oil and gas at a depth below 500 feet beneath the surface." The separate mention at numbers **[15]** and **[16]** of buildings, estate, and rights is not an essential requirement as the definition of land already includes these items. Some deed forms add the word **appurtenances** at **[16]**. Again, this is not essential wording as appurtenances by definition belong to and pass with the conveyance of the land unless specifically withheld by the grantor. Examples of real estate appurtenances are rights of way and other easements, water rights, condominium parking stalls, and improvements to land.

The **habendum clause,** sometimes called the "To have and to hold clause," begins at **[17]** and continues through **[18]**. This clause, together with the statements at **[12]** and **[13]**, forms the deed's words of conveyance. For this reason, the words at **[18]** must match those at **[13]**. Number **[19]** identifies the covenant against encumbrances. The grantor warrants that there are no encumbrances on the property except as listed here. The most common exceptions are property taxes, mortgages, and assessment (improvement district) bonds. For instance, a deed may recite, "Subject to an existing mortgage ...," and name the mortgage holder and the original amount of the loan, or "Subject to a city sewer improvement district bond in the amount of $1,500."

Habendum Clause

At [20] the grantor may impose restrictions as to how the grantee may use the property. For example, "The grantee shall not build upon this land a home with less than 1,500 square feet of living space."

Special Wording

The covenants of seizin and quiet enjoyment are located at [21] and [22], respectively. Number [23] identifies the covenant of further assurance, and at [24] the grantor agrees to warrant and defend forever the title he is granting. The order of grouping of the five covenants is not critical, and in some states laws permit the use of two or three special words to imply the presence of all five covenants. For example, in Alaska, Illinois, Kansas, Michigan, Minnesota, and Wisconsin, if the grantor uses the words *convey and warrant*, the five covenants are implied even though they are not listed in the deed. The words *warrant generally* accomplish the same purpose in Pennsylvania, Vermont, Virginia, and West Virginia, as do *grant, bargain, and sell* in the states of Arkansas, Florida, Idaho, Missouri, and Nevada. No such shortcut wording is used in New York.

At [25] the grantor states that he signed this deed on the date noted at [4]. This is the **testimony clause;** although customarily included in deeds, it is redundant and could be left out as long as the grantor signs the deed at [26]. Historically, a seal made with hot wax was essential to the validity of a deed. New York no longer requires a seal. Those few states that do require a seal [27] accept a hot wax seal, a glued paper seal, an embossed seal, the word *seal* or *L.S.* The letters *L.S.* are an abbreviation for the Latin words *locus sigilli* (place of the seal). The acknowledgment is placed at [28], the full wording of which is given in Chapter 15. If an acknowledgment is not used, this space is used for the signatures of witnesses to the grantor's signature. Their names would be preceded by the words *"In the presence of, ..."*

Deed Preparation

The exact style or form of a deed is not critical as long as it contains all the essentials clearly stated and in conformity with state law. For example, one commonly used warranty deed format begins with the words *Know all men by these presents*, is written in the first person, and has the date at the end. The New York Real Property Law includes fill-in-the-blank deed forms, although the writing of deeds should be left to experts in the field. In fact, some states permit only attorneys to write deeds for other persons. Even the preparation of preprinted deeds from stationery stores and title companies should be left to knowledgeable persons. Preprinted deeds contain several pitfalls for the unwary. First, the form may have been prepared and printed in another state and, as a result, may not meet the laws of your state. Second, if the blanks are incorrectly filled in, the deed may not accomplish its intended purpose. This is a particularly difficult problem when neither the grantor nor grantee realizes it until several years after the deed's delivery. Third, the use of a form deed presumes that the grantor's situation can be fitted to the form and that the grantor will be knowledgeable enough to select the correct form.

Some states, notably California, Idaho, and North Dakota, use a grant deed instead of a warranty deed. In a **grant deed** the grantor covenants and warrants that (1) he has not previously conveyed the estate being granted to another party, (2) he has not encumbered the property except as noted in the deed, and (3) he will convey to the grantee any title to the property he may later acquire. These covenants are fewer in number and narrower in coverage than those found in a warranty deed, particularly the covenant regarding encumbrances. In the warranty deed, the grantor makes himself responsible for the encumbrances of prior owners as well as his own. The grant deed limits the grantor's responsibility to the period of time he owned the property.

Grant Deed

    Why have grantees, in states with more than one-tenth of the total U.S. population, been willing to accept a deed with fewer covenants than a warranty deed? The primary reason is the early development and extensive use of title insurance in these states, whereby the grantor and grantee acquire an insurance policy to protect themselves if a flaw in ownership is later discovered. Title insurance is now available in all parts of the United States and is explained in Chapter 15.

In a **special warranty deed,** the grantor warrants the property's title only against defects occurring during the grantor's ownership and not against defects existing before that time. The special warranty deed is typically used by executors and trustees who convey on behalf of an estate or principal because the executor or trustee has no authority to warrant and defend the acts of previous holders of title. The grantee can protect against this gap in warranty by purchasing title insurance. The special warranty

Special Warranty Deed

deed is also known in New York as a bargain and sale deed with a covenant against only the grantor's acts.

Bargain and Sale Deed

The basic **bargain and sale deed** contains no covenants and only the minimum essentials of a deed (see Figure 7.3). It has a date, identifies the grantor and grantee, recites consideration, describes the property, contains words of conveyance, and has the grantor's signature. But lacking covenants, what assurance does the grantee have that he or she is acquiring title to anything? Actually, none. In this deed the grantor only *implies* that he owns the property described in the deed and is granting it to the

Figure 7.3

BARGAIN AND SALE DEED

THIS DEED made _____ , *between* _____
                         (date)

residing at _____ , *herein called the Grantor, and* _____ *residing at* _____ , *herein called the Grantee.*
     WITNESSETH, that the Grantor, in consideration of _____ , *does hereby grant and release unto the Grantee, the Grantee's heirs, successors, and assigns forever, all that parcel of land described as*

[legal description of land]

     TOGETHER WITH the appurtenances and all the estate and rights of the Grantor in and to said property.
     TO HAVE AND TO HOLD the premises herein granted together with the appurtenances unto the Grantee. This conveyance is made however, without any warranties, express, implied, or statutory.
     IN WITNESS WHEREOF, the Grantor sets his/her hand and seal the day and year first written above.

_____ *L.S.*
                  (Grantor)

[location of the acknowledgment]

grantee. Logically, then, a grantee will much prefer a warranty deed over a bargain and sale deed, or will require title insurance.

A **quitclaim deed** has no covenants or warranties (see Figure 7.4). Moreover, the grantor makes no statement, nor even implies that he owns the property quitclaimed to the grantee. Whatever rights the grantor possesses at the time the deed is delivered are conveyed to the grantee. If the grantor has no interest, right, or title to the property described in the deed, none is conveyed to the grantee. However, if the grantor possesses fee simple title,

Quitclaim Deed

Figure 7.4

QUITCLAIM DEED

THIS DEED, made the _____ day of ____ , 19 ____ , BETWEEN _____ of _____ , party of the first part, and _____ of _____ , party of the second part.

WITNESSETH, that the party of the first part, in consideration of ten dollars ($10.00) and other valuable consideration, paid by the party of the second part, does hereby remise, release, and quitclaim unto the party of the second part, the heirs, successors, and assigns of the party of the second part forever.

ALL that certain parcel of land, with the buildings and improvements thereon, described as follows,
                    [legal description of land]
TOGETHER WITH the appurtenances and all the estate and rights of the Grantor in and to said property.

TO HAVE AND TO HOLD the premises herein granted unto the party of the second part, the heirs or successors and assigns of the party of the second part, forever.

IN WITNESS WHEREOF, the party of the first part has duly executed this deed the day and year first above written.

_____
                    (Grantor)

[location of the acknowledgment]

fee simple title will be conveyed to the grantee. The quitclaim deed is a common form of conveyance in New York.

The critical wording in a quitclaim deed is the grantor's statement that he or she *does hereby remise, release, and quitclaim forever.* **Quitclaim** means to renounce all possession, right, or interest. **Remise** means to give up any existing claim one may have, as does the word **release** in this usage. A grantor who subsequently acquires any right or interest in the property is not obligated to convey it to the grantee.

At first glance it may seem strange that such a deed should even exist, but it does serve a very useful purpose. Situations often arise in real estate transactions when a person claims to have a partial or incomplete right or interest in a parcel of land. Such a right or interest, known as a **title defect** or **cloud on the title,** may have been due to an inheritance, a dower, curtesy, or community property right, or to a mortgage or right of redemption due to a court-ordered foreclosure sale. By releasing that claim to the fee simple owner through the use of a quitclaim deed, the cloud on the fee owner's title is removed. A quitclaim deed can be used to create an easement, as well as release (extinguish) an easement. It can also be used to release remainder and reversion interests. It cannot be used to perpetuate a fraud, however.

Other Types of Deeds
A **gift deed** is created simply by replacing the recitation of money and other valuable consideration with the statement, *in consideration of his [her, their] natural love and affection.* This phrase may be used in a warranty, special warranty, or grant deed. However, it is most often used in quitclaim or bargain and sale deeds, as these permit the grantor to avoid being committed to any warranties regarding the property.

A **guardian's deed** is used to convey a minor's interest in real property. It contains only one covenant, that the guardian and minor have not encumbered the property. The deed must state the legal authority (usually a court order) that permits the guardian to convey the minor's property.

Sheriff's deeds and **referee's deeds in foreclosure** are issued to the new buyer when a person's real estate is sold as the result of a mortgage or other court-ordered foreclosure sale. The deed should state the source of the sheriff's or referee's authority and the amount of consideration paid. Such a deed conveys only the foreclosed party's title, and at most carries only one covenant: that the sheriff or referee has not damaged the property's title.

A **correction deed,** also called a deed of confirmation, is used to correct an error in a previously executed and delivered deed. For example, a name may have been misspelled or an error found in the property description. A quitclaim deed containing a statement regarding the error is used for this purpose. A **cession deed** is a form of quitclaim deed wherein a property owner conveys street rights to a county or municipality. An **interspousal deed** is used in some states to transfer real property between spouses. A **tax deed** is used to convey title to real estate that has been sold by the government because of the nonpayment of taxes. A **deed of trust** may be used to convey real estate to a third party as security for a loan, and is discussed in Chapter 14.

A person who dies without leaving a last will and testament (or leaves one that is subsequently ruled void by the courts because it was improperly prepared) is said to have died **intestate,** which means without a testament. When this happens, state law directs how the deceased's assets shall be distributed. This is known as a **title by descent** or **intestate succession.** The surviving spouse and children are the dominant recipients of the deceased's assets. The deceased's grandchildren receive the next largest share, followed by the deceased's parents, brothers and sisters, and their children. These are known as the deceased's **heirs** or, in some states, **distributees.** The amount each heir receives, if anything, depends on individual state law. New York's Estates, Powers, and Trusts Law provides the rules for distribution of the estate of an intestate decedent. If no heirs can be found, the deceased's property escheats (reverts) to the state.

CONVEYANCE AFTER DEATH

A person who dies and leaves a valid will is said to have died **testate,** which means that a testament with instructions for property disposal was left behind. The person who made the will is the **testator** (masculine) or **testatrix** (feminine). In the will, the testator names the persons or organizations who are to receive the testator's real and personal property. Real property that is willed is known as a **devise** and the recipient, a **devisee.** Personal property that is willed is known as a **bequest** or **legacy,** and the recipient, a **legatee.** In the will, the testator usually names an **executor**

Testate, Intestate

(masculine) or **executrix** (feminine) to carry out the instructions. If one is not named, the court appoints an **administrator.** In some states, including New York, the person named in the will or appointed by the court to settle the estate is called a **personal representative.**

Notice an important difference between the transfer of real estate ownership by deed and by will: once a deed is made and delivered, the ownership transfer is permanent, the grantor cannot have a change of mind and take back the property. With respect to a will, the devisees, although named, have no rights to the testator's property until the testator dies. Until that time the testator is free to have a change of mind, revoke the old will, and write a new one.

Probate or Surrogate Court

Upon death, New York requires that the deceased's will must be filed with a court having power to admit and certify wills, called the **surrogate court** of the decedent's residence. This court determines whether or not the will meets all the requirements of law: in particular, that it is genuine, properly signed and witnessed, and that the testator was of sound mind when the will was made. At this time anyone may step forward and contest the validity of the will. If the court finds the will to be valid, the executor is permitted to carry out its terms. If the testator owned real property, its ownership is conveyed using an **executor's deed** prepared and signed by the executor. The executor's deed is used both to transfer title to a devisee and to sell real property to raise cash. It contains only one covenant, a covenant that the executor has not encumbered the property. An executor's deed is a special warranty deed.

Protecting the Deceased's Intentions

Because the deceased is not present, state laws attempt to ensure that fair market value is received for the deceased's real estate by requiring court approval of proposed sales and, in some cases, by sponsoring open bidding in the courtroom. As protection, a purchaser should ascertain that the executor has the authority to convey title.

For a will to be valid it must meet specific legal requirements. All states recognize the **formal** or **witnessed** will, a written document prepared in most cases by an attorney. In New York, the testator must sign the will at the end. He must also declare it to be his will and sign it or acknowledge the signature to two attesting witnesses. The second witness must attest to the will within 30 days of the first witness' signature. A formal will prepared by an attorney is the preferred method, as the will then conforms explicitly to the law. This greatly reduces the likelihood of its being contested after the individual's death. Additionally, an attorney may offer valuable advice on how to word the will to reduce estate and inheritance taxes.

A **holographic will** is a will that is entirely handwritten, with no typed or preprinted words. The will is dated and signed by the testator, but there are no witnesses. New York is one of 19 states that recognize holographic wills as legally binding. In New York, holographic wills are recognized only in very limited circumstances: (1) if made by a member of the armed forces of the United States while in actual service during a war or other armed conflict; (2) if made by a person accompanying or serving with a U.S. military force at war or in an armed conflict; and (3) if made by a mariner at sea. Holographic wills executed in circumstances other than the foregoing are invalid. Furthermore, the holographic will remains valid only for one year from military discharge for a member of the service, one year from cessation of service by someone accompanying the military, and three years from the date of execution for a mariner at sea. The will must be proven to be in the handwriting of the testator.

Holographic Will

    Besides the fact that holographic wills are considered to have no effect in 31 states, they often result in much legal argument in states that do accept them. This can occur when the testator is not fully aware of the law as it pertains to the making of wills. Many otherwise happy families have been torn apart by dissension when a relative dies and they read the will, only to find a question as to whether or not it was properly prepared and hence valid. Unfortunately, what follows is not what the deceased intended; those who would receive more from intestate succession will request that the will be declared void and of no effect. Those with more to gain if the will stands as written will muster legal forces to argue for its acceptance by the probate court.

Oral wills, also known as nuncupative wills, are also valid in New York; however, they are subject to the same rules of validity and termination as holographic wills. In order to be valid, an oral will must be clearly established by at least two witnesses.

Oral Will

Codicil   A **codicil** is a written supplement or amendment made to a previously existing will. It is used to change some aspect of the will or to add a new instruction, without the work of rewriting the entire will. The codicil must be dated, signed, and witnessed in the same manner as the original will. The only way to change a will is with a codicil or by writing a completely new will. The law will not recognize cross-outs, notations, or other alterations made on the will itself.

ADVERSE POSSESSION   Through the unauthorized occupation of another person's land for a long enough period of time, it is possible under certain conditions to acquire ownership by **adverse possession.** The historical roots of adverse possession go back many centuries to a time before written deeds were used as evidence of ownership. At that time, in the absence of any claims to the contrary, a person who occupied a parcel of land was presumed to be its owner. Today, adverse possession is, in effect, a statute of limitations that bars a legal owner from claiming title to land when he has done nothing to oust an adverse occupant during the statutory period. From the adverse occupant's standpoint, adverse possession is a method of acquiring title by possessing land for a specified period of time under certain conditions.

Courts of law are quite demanding of proof before they will issue a decree in favor of a person claiming title by virtue of adverse possession. The claimant must have maintained actual, visible, continuous, hostile, exclusive, and notorious possession and be publicly claiming ownership to the property. These requirements mean that the claimant's use must have been visible and obvious to the legal owner, continuous and not just occasional, and exclusive enough to give notice of the claimant's individual claim. Furthermore, the use must have been without permission (hostile), and the claimant must have acted as though he were the owner, even in the presence of the actual owner. Finally, the adverse claimant must be able to prove that he has met these requirements for a period of 10 years. Other states require that property be adversely possessed for a period of 3–30 years, as shown in Table 7.1.

Color of Title   The required occupancy period is shortened and the claimant's chances of obtaining legal ownership are enhanced in many states if the claimant has been paying the property taxes and the pos-

Table 7.1. Adverse Possession: Number of Years of Occupancy Required to Claim Title*

	Adverse Occupant Lacks Color of Title & Does Not Pay the Property Taxes	Adverse Occupant Has Color of Title &/or Pays the Property Taxes		Adverse Occupant Lacks Color of Title & Does Not Pay the Property Taxes	Adverse Occupant Has Color of Title &/or Pays the Property Taxes
Alabama	20	3-10	Missouri	10	10
Alaska	10	7	Montana		5
Arizona	10	3	Nebraska	10	10
Arkansas	15	2-7	Nevada		5
California		5	New Hampshire	20	20
Colorado	18	7	New Jersey	30-60	20-30
Connecticut	15	15	New Mexico	10	10
Delaware	20	20	New York	10	10
District of Columbia	15	15	North Carolina	20-30	7-21
			North Dakota	20	10
Florida		7	Ohio	21	21
Georgia	20	7	Oklahoma	15	15
Hawaii	20	20	Oregon	10	10
Idaho	5	5	Pennsylvania	21	21
Illinois	20	7	Rhode Island	10	10
Indiana		10	South Carolina	10-20	10
Iowa	10	10	South Dakota	20	10
Kansas	15	15	Tennessee	20	7
Kentucky	15	7	Texas	10-25	3-5
Louisiana	30	10	Utah		7
Maine	20	20	Vermont	15	15
Maryland	20	20	Virginia	15	15
Massachusetts	20	20	Washington	10	7
Michigan	15	5-10	West Virginia	10	10
Minnesota	15	15	Wisconsin	20	10
Mississippi	10	10	Wyoming	10	10

*As may be seen, in a substantial number of states, the waiting period for title by adverse possession is shortened if the adverse occupant has color of title and/or pays the property taxes. In California, Florida, Indiana, Montana, Nevada, and Utah, the property taxes must be paid to obtain the title. Generally speaking, adverse possession does not work against minors and other legal incompetents. However, when the owner becomes legally competent, the adverse possession must be broken within the time limit set by each state's law (the range is 1–10 years). In the states of Louisiana, Oklahoma, and Tennessee, adverse possession is referred to as title by prescription.

session has been under "color of title." **Color of title** suggests some plausible appearance of ownership interest, such as an improperly prepared deed that purports to transfer title to the claimant or a claim of ownership by inheritance. In accumulating the required number of years, an adverse claimant may **tack on** his or her period of possession to that of a prior adverse occupant. This could be done through the purchase of that right. The current adverse occupant could in turn sell his or her claim to a still later adverse occupant until enough years were accumulated to present a claim in court.

Although the concept of adverse possession often creates the mental picture of a trespasser moving onto someone else's land and living there long enough to acquire title in fee, this is not the usual application. More often, adverse possession is used to extinguish weak or questionable claims to title. For example, if a person buys property at a tax sale, takes possession, and pays the property taxes each year afterward, adverse possession laws act to cut off claims to title by the previous owner. Another source of successful adverse possession claims arises from encroachments. If a building extends over a property line and nothing is said about it for a long enough period of time, the building will be permitted to stay.

EASEMENT BY PRESCRIPTION

An easement can also be acquired by prolonged adverse use. This is known as acquiring an **easement by prescription.** As with adverse possession, the laws are strict: the usage must be openly visible, continuous and exclusive, as well as hostile and adverse to the owner. Additionally, the use must have occurred over a period of 5–20 years, depending on the state. All these facts must be proved in a court of law before the court will issue the claimant a document legally recognizing his or her ownership of the easement. As an easement is a right to use land for a specific purpose, and not ownership of the land itself, courts rarely require the payment of property taxes to acquire a prescriptive easement.

As may be seen from the foregoing discussion, a landowner must be given obvious notification *at the location* of his or her land that someone is attempting to claim ownership or an easement. Since an adverse claim must be continuous and hostile, an owner can break it by ejecting the trespassers or by preventing them from trespassing, or simply by giving them permission to be there. Any of these actions would demonstrate the landowner's superior title. Owners of stores and office buildings with private sidewalks or streets used by the public can take action to break claims to a public easement either by periodically barricading the sidewalk or street or by posting signs giving permission to pass. These signs are often seen in the form of brass plaques embedded in the sidewalk or street. In certain states, a landowner may record with the public records office a **notice of consent.** This is evidence that subsequent uses of his or her land for the purposes stated in the notice are permissive and not adverse. The notice may later be revoked by recording a **notice of revocation.** Federal, state, and local governments protect themselves against adverse claims to their lands by passing laws making themselves immune.

OWNERSHIP BY ACCESSION

The extent of one's ownership of land can be altered by **accession.** This can result from natural or human causes. With regard to natural causes, the owner of land fronting on a lake, river, or ocean may acquire additional land because of the gradual accumulation of rock, sand, and soil. This process is called **accretion** and the results are referred to as *alluvion* and *reliction*. **Alluvion** is the increase of land that results when waterborne soil is gradually deposited to produce firm dry ground. **Reliction** (or dereliction) results when a lake, sea, or river permanently recedes, exposing dry land. When land is rapidly washed away by the action of water, it is known as **avulsion.** Humanly produced accession occurs through **annexation** of personal property to real estate. For example, when lumber, nails, and cement are used to build a house, they alter the extent of one's land ownership.

PUBLIC GRANT

A transfer of land by a government body to a private party is called a **public grant.** Since 1776, the federal government has granted millions of acres of land to settlers, land companies, railroads, state colleges, mining and logging promoters, and any war veteran from the American Revolution through the Mexican War. Most famous was the Homestead Act passed by the U.S. Congress in 1862. That act permitted persons wishing to settle on otherwise unappropriated federal land to acquire fee simple ownership by paying a small filing charge and occupying and cultivating the land for 5 years. Similarly, for only a few dollars, a person may file a mining claim to public land for the purpose of extracting whatever valuable minerals can be found. To retain the claim, a certain amount of work must be performed on the land each year. Otherwise, the government will consider the claim abandoned and another person may claim it. If the claim is worked long enough, a public grant can be sought and fee simple title obtained. In the case of both the homestead settler and the mining claim, the conveyance document that passes fee title from the government to the grantee is known as a **land patent.** In 1976, the U.S. government ended the homesteading program in all states except Alaska.

DEDICATION   When an owner makes a voluntary gift of land to the public, it is known as **dedication.** To illustrate, a land developer buys a large parcel of vacant land and develops it into streets and lots. The lots are sold to private buyers, but what about the streets? In all probability they will be dedicated to the town, city, or county. By doing this, the developer, and later the lot buyers, will not have to pay taxes on the streets, and the public will be responsible for maintaining them. The fastest way to accomplish the transfer is by either statutory dedication or dedication by deed. In **statutory dedication** the developer prepares a map showing the streets, has the map approved by local government officials, and then records it as a public document. In **dedication by deed** the developer prepares a deed that identifies the streets and grants them to the city.

Common law dedication takes place when a landowner, by his acts or words, shows that he intends part of his land to be dedicated even though he has never officially made a written dedication. For example, a landowner may encourage the public to travel on his roads in an attempt to convince a local road department to take over maintenance. In most situations, this does not transfer title (there is not clear intent to convey). It merely grants to the public the right to use.

FORFEITURE   **Forfeiture** can occur when a deed contains a condition or limitation. For example, a grantor states in the deed that the land conveyed may be used for residential purposes only. If the grantee constructs commercial buildings, the grantor can reacquire title on the grounds that the grantee did not use the land for the required purpose.

A change in ownership of any kind is known as an **alienation.** In addition to the forms of alienation discussed in this chapter, alienation can result from court action in connection with escheat, eminent domain, partition, foreclosure, execution sales, quiet title suits, and marriage. These topics are discussed in other chapters.

ALIENATION

*Match terms **a–z** with statements **1–26.***

VOCABULARY REVIEW

a. *Accretion*
b. *Adverse possession*
c. *Alienation*
d. *Alluvion*
e. *Bargain and sale deed*
f. *Cloud on the title*
g. *Codicil*
h. *Color of title*
i. *Consideration*
j. *Correction deed*
k. *Covenant and warranties*
l. *Dedication*
m. *Deed*

n. *Easement by prescription*
o. *Executor*
p. *Grant*
q. *Grantor*
r. *Holographic will*
s. *Intestate*
t. *Land patent*
u. *Probate*
v. *Quitclaim deed*
w. *Special warranty deed*
x. *Statute of Frauds*
y. *Warranty deed*
z. *Will*

1. A written document that, when properly executed and delivered, conveys title to land.
2. Requires that transfers of real estate be in writing to be enforceable.
3. Person named in a deed who conveys ownership.
4. The act of conveying ownership.
5. Anything of value given to produce a contract.
6. Promises and guarantees found in a deed.
7. Any claim, lien, or encumbrance that impairs title to property.
8. A deed that contains the covenants of seizin, quiet enjoyment, encumbrances, further assurance, and warranty forever.
9. A deed that contains no covenants; it only implies that the grantor owns the property described in the deed.
10. A deed with no covenants and no implication that the grantor owns the property being deeded to the grantee.
11. To die without a will.
12. A will written entirely in one's own handwriting and signed but not witnessed.
13. The process of verifying the legality of a will and carrying out its instructions.
14. A supplement or amendment to a previous will.
15. Acquisition of real property through prolonged and unauthorized occupation.

16. Some plausible but not completely clear-cut indication of ownership rights.
17. Acquisition of an easement by prolonged use.
18. Waterborne soil deposited to produce firm, dry ground.
19. A document for conveying government land in fee to settlers and miners.
20. Private land voluntarily conveyed to the government.
21. The process of land buildup due to the gradual accumulation of rock, sand, and soil.
22. A change in ownership of any kind.
23. Used to correct an error in a previously executed and delivered deed.
24. A person named in a will to carry out its instructions.
25. Grantor warrants title only against defects occurring during the grantor's ownership.
26. Instructions stating how a person wants his or her property disposed of after death.

QUESTIONS AND PROBLEMS

1. Is it possible for a document to convey fee title to land even though it does not contain the word deed? If so, why?
2. In the process of conveying real property from one person to another, at what instant in time does title actually pass from the grantor to the grantee?
3. What legal protections does a full covenant and warranty deed offer a grantee?
4. As a real estate purchaser, which deed would you prefer to receive: warranty, special warranty, or bargain and sale? Why?
5. What are the hazards of preparing your own deeds?
6. Name five examples of title clouds.
7. What is meant by the term intestate succession?
8. With regard to probate, what is the key difference between an executor and an administrator?
9. Does your state consider holographic wills to be legal? How many witnesses are required by your state for a formal will?
10. Can a person who has rented the same building for 30 years claim ownership by virtue of adverse possession? Why or why not?
11. Cite examples from your own community or state where land ownership has been altered by alluvion, reliction, or avulsion.

ADDITIONAL READINGS

New Encyclopedia of Real Estate Forms, by **Jerome Gross** (Prentice Hall, 1983, 701 pages). Chapter 10 contains examples of deeds, including warranty deed, grant deed, special warranty deed, quitclaim deed, executor's deed, life estate deed, correction deed, cession deed, and referee deed.

Mastering Real Estate Mathematics, 4th Ed., by **William Ventolo, Jr.** and **Wellington Allaway** (Real Estate Education Co., 1984, 368 pages). A self-instruction book for percentages, fractions, and decimals as they apply to commissions, interest, appraisal, leases, loan points, taxes, proration, and price problems.

Plan Your Estate, 4th Ed., by **Denis Clifford.** (Nolo Press, 1986, 242 pages). Explains wills, probate avoidance, trusts, and taxes. Most bookstores carry a variety of books on this subject.

Real Estate Law, by **Charles Jacobus** (Reston, 1986, 550 pages). Chapter 8 discusses conveyancing and Chapter 9 the recording of interests in real estate.

8

Contract Law

KEY • TERMS

Breach of contract: failure, without legal excuse, to perform as required by a contract

Competent party: persons considered legally capable of entering into a binding contract

Consideration: an act or promise given in exchange for something

Contract: a legally enforceable agreement to do (or not to do) a particular thing

Counteroffer: any response to an offer that varies the terms of the original offer

Duress: the application of force to obtain an agreement

Forbearance: refraining from acting when one has a legal right to act

Fraud: an act intended to deceive for the purpose of inducing another to give up something of value

Liquidated damages: an amount of money specified in a contract as compensation to be paid if the contract is not satisfactorily completed

Novation: substitution of a new contract for an existing one by agreement of the parties

Offer and acceptance: essential elements of contract formation

Power of attorney: a document by which one person authorizes another to act on his or her behalf

Specific performance: contract performance according to the precise terms agreed on

Void contract: a contract that has no binding effect on the parties who made it

Voidable contract: a contract that is able to be voided by one of its parties

A **contract** is a legally enforceable agreement to do (or not to do) a specific thing. In this chapter we see how a contract is created and what makes it legally binding. Topics covered include offer and acceptance, fraud, mistake, lawful objective, consideration, performance, and breach of contract. In Chapter 9 we will turn our attention to the purchase contract, installment contract, lease with option to buy, right of first refusal, and trade agreement.

HOW A CONTRACT IS CREATED

A contract may be either expressed or implied. An **expressed contract** occurs when the parties to the contract declare their intentions either orally or in writing. [The word **party** (plural, **parties**) is a legal term that refers to a person or group involved in a legal proceeding.] A lease or rental agreement, for example, is an expressed contract. The lessor (landlord) expresses the intent to permit the lessee (tenant) to use the premises, and the lessee agrees to pay rent in return. A contract to purchase real estate is also an expressed contract.

An **implied contract** is created by neither words nor writing but rather by actions of the parties indicating that they intend to create a contract. For example, when you step into a taxicab, you imply that you will pay the fare. The cab driver, by allowing you in the cab, implies that you will be taken where you want to go. The same thing occurs at a restaurant. The presence of tables, silverware, menus, waiters, and waitresses implies that you will be served food. When you order, you imply that you are going to pay when the bill is presented.

Bilateral Contract

A contract may be either bilateral or unilateral. A **bilateral contract** results when a promise is exchanged for a promise. For example, in a typical real estate sale, the buyer promises to pay the agreed price, and the seller promises to deliver title to the buyer. In a lease contract the lessor promises the use of the premises to the lessee, and the lessee promises to pay rent in return. A bilateral contract is basically an "I will do this *and* you will do that" arrangement. Depending on its wording, a listing can be a bilateral contract with the broker promising his or her best efforts to locate a buyer and the seller promising to pay a commission when a buyer is found. On the other hand, a listing can be a unilateral contract, discussed next.

Unilateral Contract

A **unilateral contract** results when a promise is exchanged for performance. For instance, during a campaign to get more listings, a real estate office manager announces to the firm's sales staff that an extra $100 bonus will be paid for each saleable new listing. No promises or agreements are necessary from the salespersons. However, each time a salesperson performs by bringing in a saleable listing, he or she is entitled to the promised $100 bonus. An option to purchase is a unilateral contract until it is exercised, at which time it becomes a bilateral contract. A listing can be structured as a unilateral contract wherein the seller agrees to pay a commission if the broker finds a buyer. When the broker produces a buyer for the property the contract becomes bilateral. A unilateral contract is basically an "I will do this *if* you will do that" arrangement.

Forbearance

Most contract agreements are based on promises by the parties involved to act in some manner (pay money, provide services, or deliver title). However, a contract can contain a promise to **forbear** (not to act) by one or more of its parties. For example, a lender may agree not to foreclose on a delinquent mortgage loan if the borrower agrees to a new payment schedule.

Valid, Void, Voidable

A **valid contract** is one that meets all the requirements of law. It is binding on its parties and legally enforceable in a court of law. A **void contract** has no legal effect and, in fact, is not a contract at all. Even though the parties may have gone through the motions of attempting to make a contract, no legal rights are created and any party thereto may ignore it at his or her pleasure. A **voidable contract** is a contract that is able to be voided by one of its parties. In effect, it is a contract that is not binding on one of its parties. Examples of valid, void, and voidable contracts are included throughout this chapter. Let us turn our attention to the requirements of a valid contract.

ESSENTIALS OF A VALID CONTRACT

For a contract to be legally valid, and hence binding and enforceable, the following five requirements must be met:

1. Legally competent parties
2. Mutual agreement
3. Lawful objective
4. Consideration or cause
5. Contract in writing when required by law

If these conditions are met, any party to the contract may, if the need arises, call on a court of law either to enforce the contract as written or to award money damages for nonperformance. In reality, a properly written contract seldom ends up in court because each party knows it will be enforced as written. It is the poorly written contract or the contract that borders between enforceable and unenforceable that ends up in court. A judge must then decide if a contract actually exists and determines the obligations of each party. Using the courts, however, is an expensive and time-consuming method of interpreting an agreement. It is much better to have a correctly prepared contract in the first place. Let's look more closely at the five requirements of an enforceable contract.

For a contract to be legally enforceable, all parties entering into it must be legally **competent.** In deciding competency, the law provides a mixture of objective and subjective standards. The most objective standard is that of age. A person must reach the age of majority to be legally capable of entering into a contract. **Minors** do not have contractual capability. In New York and most other states, the age for entering into legally binding contracts is 18 years. The purpose of majority laws is to protect minors (also known as "infants" in legal terminology) from entering into contracts that they may not be old enough to understand. Most contracts made with minors, except those for necessities such as food and clothing, are voidable by the minor at the minor's option. For example, a deed by a minor is voidable, although a minor can be a grantee. A minor wishing to disaffirm a contract must do so while still a minor or within a reasonable time after reaching majority. If not, the contract becomes valid. In some cases, a contract with a minor is void. For example, a minor does not have the capacity to appoint someone to sell his property. Any contract to do so (called a power of attorney) is void from the outset. If a contract with a minor is required, it is still possible to obtain a binding contract by working through the minor's legal guardian.

Competent Parties

If a deliberate attempt was made to intoxicate a person for the purpose of approving a contract, the intoxicated person, upon sobering up, can call on the courts to cancel the contract. A contracting party who was voluntarily drunk to the point of incompetence may ratify or deny the contract if he does so promptly. However, some courts look at the matter strictly from the standpoint of whether or not the intoxicated person had the capability of formulating the intent to enter into a contract. Obviously, there are some fine and subjective distinctions here, and a judge may interpret them differently than the parties to the contract. The points made in this paragraph also apply to a person who contracts while under the influence of other legal or illegal drugs.

Persons of unsound mind who have been declared incompetent by a judge may not make a valid contract, and any attempt to do so results in a void contract. The solution is to contract through the person appointed to act on behalf of the incompetent. A person who has not been judged legally incompetent but nonetheless appears incapable of understanding the transaction in question has no legal power to contract. Illegal aliens also lack legal competency. In some states persons convicted of felonies may not enter into valid contracts without the prior approval of the parole board.

Power of Attorney

An individual can give another person the power to act on his behalf: for example, to buy or sell land or sign a lease. The document that accomplishes this is called a **power of attorney.** The person holding the power of attorney is called an **attorney-in-fact.** With regard to real estate, a power of attorney must be in writing because the real estate documents to be signed must be in writing. In order to be legally binding any document signed with a power of attorney should be executed as follows: "Paul Jones, principal, by Samuel Smith, agent, his attorney-in-fact." If the attorney-in-fact is to convey title to land, then the power of attorney must be acknowledged by the principal and recorded. The attorney-in-fact is legally competent to the extent of the powers granted by the principal as long as the principal remains legally competent, and as long as both of them are alive. The power of attorney can, of course, be terminated by the principal at any time. A recorded notice of revocation is needed to revoke a recorded power of attorney.

Corporations, etc.

Corporations are considered legally competent parties. However, the individual contracting on behalf of the corporation must have authority from the board of directors. Some states also require that the corporate seal be affixed to contracts. A partnership can contract either in the name of the partnership or in the name of any of its general partners. Executors and administrators with court authorization can contract on behalf of estates, and trustees on behalf of trusts.

The requirement of **mutual agreement** (also called **mutual consent** or **mutual assent** or **meeting of the minds**) means that there must be agreement to the provisions of the contract by the parties involved. In other words, there must be a mutual willingness to enter into a contract. The existence of mutual agreement is evidenced by the words and acts of the parties indicating that there is a valid offer and an unqualified acceptance. In addition, there must be no fraud, misrepresentation, or mistake, and the agreement must be genuine and freely given. Let us consider each of these points in more detail.

Mutual Agreement

Offer and acceptance requires that one party (the **offeror**) makes an offer to another party (the **offeree**). If the offer is acceptable, the offeree must then communicate the acceptance to the offeror. The means of communication may be spoken or written or an action that implies acceptance. To illustrate, suppose that you own a house and want to sell it. You tell your listing broker that you will accept $100,000 and that you would deliver a general warranty deed and pay the normal closing costs for the area. Within a few days, the broker submits a signed document from a prospective buyer. This constitutes an offer, and the buyer (the offeror) has just communicated it to you (the offeree). One requirement of a valid offer is that the offer be specific in its terms. Mutual agreement cannot exist if the terms of the offer are vague or undisclosed and/or the offer does not clearly state the obligations of each party involved. If the seller were to say to a prospective purchaser "Do you want to buy this house?" without stating the price, and the prospective purchaser said yes, the law would not consider this to be a valid offer.

Offer and Acceptance

Upon receiving the offer, the offeree has three options: to agree to it, to reject it, or to make a **counteroffer.** If the offeree agrees, he or she must agree to every item of the offer. An offer is considered by law to be rejected, not only if the offeree rejects it outright, but also if any change is made in the terms. *Any* change in the terms is considered a **counteroffer.** Although it may appear that the offeree is only amending the offer before accepting it, the offeree has actually rejected it, and is making a new offer. This now makes the seller the offeror. To illustrate,

Counteroffer

suppose the prospective purchaser submits an offer to the listing broker to purchase the property for $95,000, but instead of accepting the $95,000 offer, the seller amends the contract to reflect a selling price of $100,000. This is a rejection of the original offer and creates a counteroffer to the purchaser. The purchaser now has the right to accept or reject this counteroffer. If, however, the original $95,000 offer is agreeable to the offeree (seller) he or she must communicate the acceptance to the purchaser. While a spoken "Yes, I'll take it," would be legally adequate, prudent real estate brokers should obtain the signature of the seller on a contract, without any further changes.

It should also be pointed out that an offer can be revoked by the offeror at any time prior to the offeror hearing of its acceptance. For example, if you tell prospective tenants that they can rent the property for $495 per month and, while waiting for their response you find another prospective tenant who is willing to pay more, you can revoke your first offer at any time prior to hearing of its acceptance, then make your contract with the second prospective tenant. An offeror should be strongly advised, however, not to initiate more than one offer at a time, since considerable confusion can be caused by multiple offers, revocations, and acceptances in one transaction.

Fraud Mutual agreement requires that there be no fraud, misrepresentation, or mistake in the contract if it is to be valid. A **fraud** is an act intended to deceive for the purpose of inducing another to part with something of value. It can be as blatant as knowingly telling a lie or making a promise with no intention of performance. For example, you are showing your apartment and a prospective tenant asks if there is frequent bus service nearby. There isn't, but you say yes as you sense this is important and want to rent the apartment. The prospective tenant rents the apartment, relying on this information from you, and moves in. The next day your tenant calls saying there is no public transportation, and wanting to break the rental agreement immediately. Because mutual agreement was lacking, the tenant can **rescind** (cancel) the contract and get his money back.

Fraud can also result from failing to disclose important information, thereby inducing someone to accept an offer. For example, the day you show your apartment to a prospective tenant the weather is dry. But you know that during every rainstorm the tenant's automobile parking stall becomes a lake of water 6 inches deep. This would qualify as a fraud if the prospective tenant was not made aware of the problem before agreeing to the rental contract. Once again, the law permits the aggrieved party to rescind the contract. However, the tenant does not have to rescind the contract. If other features of the apartment are desirable enough, the tenant may elect to live with the flooded parking stall.

If a real estate agent commits a fraud to make a sale and the deceived party later rescinds the sales contract, not only is the commission lost, but explanations will be required by the other parties to the contract. Moreover, state license laws provide for suspension or revocation of a real estate license for fraudulent acts.

Innocent misrepresentation differs from fraud (intentional misrepresentation) in that the party providing the wrong information is not doing so to deceive another for the purpose of reaching an agreement. To illustrate, suppose that over the past year you have observed that city buses stop near your apartment building. If you tell a prospective tenant that there is bus service, only to learn the day after the tenant moves in that service stopped last week, this is innocent misrepresentation. Although there was no dishonesty involved, the tenant still has the right to rescind the contract. If performance has not begun on the contract (in this case the tenant has not moved in), the injured party may give notice that he **disaffirms** (revokes) the contract. However, if the tenant wants to break the contract, he must do so in a timely manner; otherwise the law will presume that the situation is satisfactory to the tenant.

Innocent Misrepresentation

Mistake as applied in contract law has a very narrow meaning. It does not include innocent misrepresentation nor does it include ignorance, inability, or poor judgment. If a person enters into a contract and later regrets it because he did not investigate it thoroughly enough, or because it did not turn out to be beneficial, the law will not grant relief to him on the grounds of mistake, even though he may now consider it was a "mistake" to have made the contract in the first place. Mistake as used in contract law arises from ambiguity in negotiations and mistake of material fact. For example, you offer to sell your mountain cabin to an acquaintance. He has never seen your cabin, and you give him instructions on how to get there to look at it. He returns and accepts your offer. However, he made a wrong turn and the

Mistake

cabin he looked at was not your cabin. A week later he discovers his error. The law considers this ambiguity in negotiations. In this case the buyer, in his mind, was purchasing a different cabin from the one the seller was selling; therefore, there is no mutual agreement and any contract signed is void.

To illustrate a mistake of fact, suppose that you show your apartment to a prospective tenant and tell him that he must let you know by tomorrow if he wants to rent it. The next day he visits you and together you enter into a rental contract. Although neither of you is aware of it, there has just been a serious fire in the apartment. Since a fire-gutted apartment is not what the two of you had in mind when the rental contract was signed, there is no mutual agreement.

Occasionally, "mistake of law" will be claimed as grounds for relief from a contract. However, mistake as to one's legal rights in a contract is not generally accepted by courts of law unless it is coupled with a mistake of fact. Ignorance of the law is not considered a mistake.

Contractual Intent

Mutual agreement also requires that the parties express **contractual intent.** This means that their intention is to be bound by the agreement, thus precluding jokes or jests from becoming valid contracts.

Duress

The last requirement of mutual agreement is that the offer and acceptance be genuine and freely given. **Duress** (use of force), **menace** (threat of violence), or **undue influence** (unfair advantage) cannot be used to obtain agreement. The law permits a contract made under any of these conditions to be revoked by the aggrieved party.

Lawful Objective

To be enforceable, a contract cannot call for the breaking of laws. This is because a court of law cannot be called upon to enforce a contract that requires a law to be broken. Such a contract is void, or if already in operation, is unenforceable in a court of law. For example, a debt contract requiring an interest rate in excess of that allowed by state law may be void. If the borrower had started repaying the debt and then later stopped, the lender would not be able to look to the courts to enforce collection of the balance. Contracts contrary to good morals and general public policy are also unenforceable.

For an agreement to be enforceable it must be supported by **consideration.** The purpose of requiring consideration is to demonstrate that a bargain has been struck between the parties to the contract. The size, quantity, nature, or amount of what is being exchanged is irrelevant as long as it is present. Consideration is usually something of value such as a promise to do something, money, property, or personal services. For example, there can be an exchange of a promise for a promise, money for a promise, money for property, goods for services, and so on. Forbearance also qualifies as consideration.

Consideration

In a typical offer to purchase a home, the consideration is the mutual exchange of promises by the buyer and seller to obligate themselves to do something they were not previously required to do. In other words, the seller agrees to sell on the terms agreed on and the buyer agrees to buy the property on those same terms. The earnest money the buyer may put down is not the consideration necessary to make the contract valid. Rather, earnest money is a tangible indication of the buyer's intent and may become a source of compensation (damages) to the seller in the event the buyer does not carry out his or her promises.

Exchange of Promises

In a deed the consideration requirement is usually met with a statement such as "For ten dollars and other good and valuable consideration." Also, the purchase contract is part of the consideration and is legally merged into the deed. In a lease, the periodic payment of rent is the consideration for use of the premises.

A contract fails to be legally binding if consideration is lacking from any party to the contract. The legal philosophy is that a person cannot promise to do something of value for someone else without receiving in turn some form of consideration. Stated another way, each party must give up something—that is, each must suffer a detriment. For example, if I promise to give you my car, the consideration requirement is not met since you promise nothing in return. But if I promise to give you my car when you take me to Hawaii, the consideration requirement is met. As a group, money, plus promises, property, legal rights, services, and forbearance, if they are worth money, are classified as **valuable consideration.**

Valuable Consideration

What about outright gifts such as the gift of real property from a parent to a child based solely on love and affection? Although this is not valuable consideration, it is nonetheless **good consideration** and as such fulfills the legal requirement

Good Consideration

that consideration be present. The law generally will not inquire as to the adequacy of the consideration unless there is evidence of fraud, mistake, duress, threat, or undue influence. For instance, if a person gave away property or sold it very cheaply to keep it from creditors, the creditors could ask the courts to set aside those transfers.

Multiple Meanings of the
Word *Consideration*

If the word consideration continues to be confusing to you, it is because the word has three meanings in real estate. The first is consideration from the standpoint of a legal requirement for a valid contract. You may wish to think of this form of consideration as **legal consideration** or **cause.** The second meaning is money. For example, the consideration on which conveyance taxes are charged is the amount of money exchanged in the transaction. The third meaning is acknowledgment. Thus the phrase "in consideration of ten dollars" means "in acknowledgment of" or "in receipt of."

Contract in Writing

Each state has a law commonly known as a **statute of frauds.** The New York statute can be found in General Obligations Law S.5-703(2). Its purpose is to prevent frauds by requiring that all contracts for the sale of land, or an interest in land, be in writing and signed to be enforceable in a court of law. This includes such things as offers, acceptances, binders, land contracts, deeds, escrows, and options to purchase. Mortgages and trust deeds (and their accompanying bonds and notes) and leases for more than one year must also be in writing to be enforceable. In addition, most states have adopted the **Uniform Commercial Code** that requires, among other things, that the sale of personal property with value in excess of $500 be in writing.

Purpose

The purpose of requiring that a contract be written and signed is to prevent perjury and fraudulent attempts to seek legal enforcement of a contract that never existed. It is not necessary that a contract be a single formal document. It can consist of a series of signed letters or memoranda as long as the essentials of a valid contract are present. Note that the requirement for a written contract relates only to the enforceability of the contract. Thus if Mr. Colby orally agrees to sell land to Mr. Conan and they carry out the deal, neither can come back after the contract was performed and ask a court to rescind the deal because the agreement to sell was oral.

The most common real estate contract that does not need to be in writing to be enforceable is a month-to-month rental agreement that can be terminated by either landlord or tenant on one month's notice. Nonetheless, most are in writing because people tend to forget oral promises. Although the unhappy party can go to court, the judge may have a difficult time determining what oral promises were made, particularly if there were no witnesses other than the parties to the agreement. Hence, it is advisable to put all important contracts in writing and for each party to recognize the agreement by signing it. If a party is a corporation, most states require the signatures of two corporate officers plus the corporate seal. It is also customary to date written contracts, although most can be enforced without showing the date the agreement was reached.

A written contract supersedes an oral one. Thus, if two parties orally promise one thing and then write and sign something else, the written contract will prevail. This has been the basis for many complaints against overzealous real estate agents who make oral promises that do not appear anywhere in the written sales contract.

Under certain circumstances the **parol evidence rule** permits oral evidence to complete an otherwise incomplete or ambiguous written contract. However, the application of this rule is quite narrow. If a contract is complete and clear in its intent, the courts presume that what the parties put into writing is what they agreed on.

Parol Evidence Rule

A contract that is in the process of being carried out is said to be **executory**—that is, in the process of being performed. Once completed, it is said to be **executed**—that is, performance has taken place. This may refer to the signing of the contract or to its completed performance depending on what the contract requires. The word **execute,** a much more frequently used term, refers to the process of completing, performing, or carrying out something. Thus, you execute a document when you sign it, and this is the most common use of the term. Once signed, you execute the contract by carrying out its terms.

Executory, Executed, Execute

Most contracts are discharged by being fully performed by the contracting parties in accordance with the contract terms. However, alternatives are open to the parties to the contract. One is

PERFORMANCE AND DISCHARGE OF CONTRACTS

to sell or otherwise **assign** the contract to another party. Unless prohibited by the contract, rights, benefits, and obligations under a contract can be assigned to someone else. The original party to the contract, however, still remains ultimately liable for its performance. Note, too, that an assignment is a contract in itself and must meet all the essential contract requirements to be enforceable. A common example of an assignment occurs when a lessee wants to move out and sells his lease to another party. When a contract creates a personal obligation, such as a listing agreement with a broker, an assignment may not be made.

Novation   A contract can also be performed by **novation.** Novation is the substitution of a new contract between the same or new parties. For example, novation occurs when a buyer assumes a seller's loan, *and* the lender releases the seller from the loan contract. With novation the departing party is released from the obligation to complete the contract.

If the objective of a contract becomes legally impossible to accomplish, the law will consider the contract discharged. For example, a new legislative statute may forbid what the contract originally intended. If the parties mutually agree to cancel their contract before it is executed, this too is a form of discharge. For instance, you sign a 5-year lease to pay $900 per month for an office. Three years later you find a better location and want to move. Meanwhile, rents for similar offices in your building have increased to $1,000 per month. Under these conditions, the landlord might be happy to agree to cancel your lease.

Deceased Party   If one of the contracting parties dies, a contract is considered discharged if it calls for some specific act that only the dead person could have performed. For example, if you hired a freelance gardener to tend your landscaping and he died, the contract would be discharged. However, if your contract is with a firm that employs other gardeners who can do the job, the contract would still be valid.

If there is a valid purchase contract and one party dies, the contract is usually enforceable against the estate because the estate has the authority to carry out the deceased's affairs. Similarly, if a person mortgages his or her property and dies, the estate must continue the payments or lose the property.

Under the **Uniform Vendor and Purchaser Risk Act,** if neither possession nor title has passed and there is material destruction to the property, the seller cannot enforce the contract and the purchaser is entitled to his money back. If damage is minor and promptly repaired by the seller, the contract would still be enforceable. If either title or possession has passed and destruction occurs, the purchaser is not relieved of his duty to pay the price, nor is he entitled to a refund of money already paid.

Property Damage

When one party fails to perform as required by a contract and the law does not recognize the reason for failure to be a valid excuse, a **breach of contract** occurs. The wronged or innocent party has six alternatives: (1) to accept partial performance, (2) to rescind the contract unilaterally, (3) to sue for specific perform- ance, (4) to sue for money damages, (5) to accept liquidated money damages, or (6) to mutually rescind the contract. Let us consider each of these.

BREACH OF CONTRACT

Partial performance may be acceptable to the innocent party because there may not be a great deal at stake or because the innocent party feels that the time and effort to sue would not be worth the rewards. Suppose that you contracted with a roofer to fix your roof for $400. When the worker was finished, you paid the bill. A week later, you discover a spot that the worker had agreed to fix but missed. After many futile phone calls, you accept the breach and consider the contract discharged because it is easier to fix the spot yourself than to keep pursuing the roofer.

Partial Performance

Under certain circumstances, the innocent party can **unilaterally rescind** a contract, i.e., the innocent party can take the position that if the other party is not going to perform his obligations, then the innocent party will not either. An example would be a rent strike in retaliation to a landlord who fails to keep the premises habitable. Unilateral rescission should be resorted to only after consulting an attorney.

Unilateral Rescission

If the damages to the innocent party can be reasonably expressed in terms of money, the innocent party can sue for **money damages.** For example, you rent an apartment to a tenant. As part of the rental contract, you furnish the refrigerator

Lawsuit for Money Damages

and freezer unit. While the tenant is on vacation, the unit breaks down, and $200 worth of frozen meat and other perishables spoil. Since your obligation under the contract is to provide the tenant with a working refrigerator-freezer, the tenant can sue you for $200 in money damages and can also recover interest on the money awarded from the day of the loss to the day the loss is reimbursed.

Lawsuit for Specific Performance

A lawsuit for **specific performance** is an action in court by the innocent party to force the breaching party to carry out the remainder of the contract according to the precise terms, price, and conditions agreed on. For example, you make an offer to purchase a parcel of land and the seller accepts. A written contract is prepared and signed by both of you. If you carry out all your obligations under the contract, but the seller has a change of mind and refuses to deliver title to you, you may bring a lawsuit against the seller for specific performance. In reviewing your suit, the court will determine whether or not the contract is valid and legal, whether or not you have carried out your duties under the contract, and whether or not the contract is just and reasonable. If you win your lawsuit, the court will force the seller to deliver title to you as specified in the contract.

Comparison

Note the difference between suing for money damages and suing for specific performance. When money can be used to restore one's position (as in the case of the tenant who can buy $200 worth of fresh food), a suit for money damages is appropriate. In situations in which money cannot provide an adequate remedy, and this is often the case in real estate because no two properties are exactly alike, specific performance is appropriate. Notice, too, that the mere existence of the legal rights of the wronged party is often enough to gain cooperation. In the case of the spoiled food, you would give the tenant the value of the lost food before spending time and money in court to hear a judge tell you to do the same thing. A threat of a lawsuit will often bring the desired results if the defendant knows that the law will side with the wronged party. The cases that do go to court are usually those in which the identity of the wronged party and/or the extent of the damages is not clear.

The parties to a contract may decide in advance the amount of damages to be paid in the event either party breaches the contract. An example is an offer to purchase real estate that includes a statement to the effect that, once the seller accepts the offer, if the buyer fails to complete the purchase, the seller may keep the buyer's deposit (the earnest money) as **liquidated damages.** If a broker is involved, seller and broker usually agree to divide the damages, thus compensating the seller for damages and the broker for time and effort. Another case of liquidated damages occurs when a builder promises to finish a building by a certain date or pay the party that hired him a certain number of dollars per day until it is completed. This impresses on the builder the need for prompt completion and compensates the property owner for losses due to the delay.

Liquidated Damages

Specific performance, money damages, and liquidated damages are all designed to aid the innocent party in the event of a breach of contract. However, as a practical matter, the time and cost of pursuing a remedy in a court of law may sometimes exceed the benefits to be derived. Moreover, there is the possibility the judge for your case may not agree with your point of view. Therefore, even though you are the innocent party and you feel you have a legitimate case that can be pursued in the courts, you may find it more practical to agree with the other party (or parties) to simply rescind (i.e., cancel or annul) the contract. To properly protect everyone involved, the agreement to cancel must be in writing and signed by the parties to the original contract. Properly executed, **mutual rescission** relieves the parties to the contract from their obligations to each other.

Mutual Rescission

    An alternative to mutual rescission is novation. As noted earlier, this is the substitution of a new contract for an existing one. Novation provides a middle ground between suing and rescinding. Thus the breaching party may be willing to complete the contract provided the innocent party will voluntarily make certain changes in it. If this is acceptable, the changes should be put into writing (or the contract redrafted) and then signed by the parties involved.

The **statute of limitations** limits by law the amount of time a wronged party has to seek the aid of a court in obtaining justice. Aggrieved parties must start legal proceedings within a certain

STATUTE
OF LIMITATIONS

period of time or the courts will not help them. The amount of time varies from state to state and by type of legal action involved. However, time limits of 3 to 7 years are typical for breach of contract. In New York, the limit is 6 years.

IMPLIED
OBLIGATIONS

As was pointed out at the beginning of this chapter, one can incur contractual obligations by implication as well as by oral or written contracts. Home builders and real estate agents provide two timely examples. For many years, if homeowners discovered poor design or workmanship after they had bought a new home, it was their problem. The philosophy was *caveat emptor*—let the buyer beware *before* buying. Today, courts of law find that in building a home and offering it for sale, the builder simultaneously implies that it is fit for living. Thus, if a builder installs a toilet in a bathroom, the implication is that it will work. In fact, New York and many other states have now passed legislation that makes builders liable for their work for one year.

Similarly, real estate agent trade organizations, such as the National Association of REALTORS® and state and local realtor associations, are constantly working to elevate in the public mind the status of real estate brokers and salespersons to that of competent professional. But professional status is accompanied by an implied obligation to dispense professional-quality service. Thus, an individual agent is responsible not only for acting in accordance with written laws, but also for being competent and knowledgeable. Once recognized as a professional by the public, the real estate agent will not be able to plead ignorance.

In view of the present trend toward consumer protection, the concept of "Let the buyer beware" is being replaced with "Let the seller beware" and "Let the agent beware."

VOCABULARY
REVIEW

Match terms **a–z** *with statements* **1–26.**

a. *Assign*
b. *Attorney-in-fact*
c. *Breach of contract*
d. *Competent party*
e. *Consideration*
f. *Contract*
g. *Counteroffer*
h. *Disaffirm*
i. *Duress*

j. *Execute*
k. *Forbear*
l. *Fraud*
m. *Liquidated damages*
n. *Minor*
o. *Money damages*
p. *Mutual agreement*
q. *Novation*
r. *Offeror*

s. *Party*	**w.** *Statute of limitations*
t. *Rescind*	**x.** *Unilateral contract*
u. *Specific performance*	**y.** *Void contract*
v. *Statute of frauds*	**z.** *Voidable contract*

1. A legally enforceable agreement to do (or not to do) something.
2. A contract in which one party makes a promise or begins performance without first receiving any promise to perform from the other.
3. An act intended to deceive for the purpose of inducing another to part with something of value.
4. A person who is considered legally capable of entering into a contract.
5. A person who is not old enough to enter into legally binding contracts.
6. A contract that is not legally binding on any of the parties who made it.
7. The party who makes an offer.
8. An offer made in response to an offer.
9. To cancel a contract and restore the parties involved to their respective positions before the contract was made.
10. Use of force to obtain contract agreement.
11. Not to act.
12. To transfer one's rights in a contract to another person.
13. Damages that can be measured in and compensated by money.
14. Failure, without legal excuse, to perform any promise called for in a contract.
15. Contract performance according to the precise terms agreed on.
16. A sum of money called for in a contract that is to be paid if the contract is breached.
17. Laws that set forth the period of time within which a lawsuit must be filed.
18. A person or group involved in a legal proceeding.
19. A contract that is able to be voided by one of its parties.
20. The person holding a power of attorney on behalf of another.
21. A meeting of the minds.
22. To revoke.
23. An act or promise given in exchange for something.
24. Requires all contracts for the sale of land to be in writing to be enforceable in a court of law.
25. To complete, perform, or carry out something.
26. The substitution of a new contract for an existing one.

QUESTIONS AND PROBLEMS

1. What is the difference between an expressed contract and an implied contract? Give an example of each.
2. Name the five requirements of a legally valid contract.

3. What is the difference between a void contract and a voidable contract?

4. Give four examples of persons not considered legally competent to enter into contracts.

5. How can an offer be terminated prior to its acceptance?

6. What does the word *mistake* mean when applied to contract law?

7. Why must consideration be present for a legally binding contract to exist? Give examples of three types of consideration.

8. If a contract is legally unenforceable, are the parties to the contract stopped from performing it? Why or why not?

9. If a breach of contract occurs, what alternatives are open to the parties to the contract?

10. Assume that a breach of contract has occurred and the wronged party intends to file a lawsuit over the matter. What factors would be considered in deciding whether to sue for money damages or for specific performance?

ADDITIONAL READINGS

Real Estate, 12th Ed., by **Alfred Ring**, **James Shilling,** and **Jerome Dasso** (Prentice Hall, 1995, 638 pages). A decision-making and analysis approach to real estate from the point of view of the investor. Book covers ownership rights, conveying those rights, financing, markets, investment, ownership, and management.

Real Estate Law, by **Charles Jacobus** (Reston, 1986, 387 pages). A guide to the legal aspects of sales, mortgages, conveyances, exchanges, and leasing. Examines broker-lawyer relationship and identifies various legal entanglements and methods to avoid them.

9

Real Estate Sales Contracts

KEY • TERMS

Binder: a short purchase contract used to secure a real estate transaction until a more formal contract can be signed

Counteroffer: any response to an offer that varies the terms of the original offer

Default: failure to perform a legal duty, such as failure to carry out the terms of a contract

Earnest money deposit: money that accompanies an offer to purchase as evidence of good faith

Equitable title: the right to demand that title be conveyed on payment of the purchase price

Installment contract: a method of selling and financing property whereby the seller retains title but the buyer takes possession while making the payments

Lease-option: allows the tenant to buy the property at preset price and terms for a given period of time

Qualified intermediary: the third-party escrow agent used in tax-deferred exchange

Rider: addition to a document, also referred to as an addendum or attachment

Right of first refusal: the right to match or better an offer before the property is sold to someone else

Tax-deferred exchange: a sale of real property in exchange for another parcel of real estate, to effect a nontaxable gain

"Time is of the essence": a phrase meaning that the time limits of a contract must be faithfully observed or the contract is voidable

Trading up: acquiring a property of greater value by exchanging a property of lesser value plus cash

This chapter focuses on contracts used to initiate the sale of real estate. Chiefly we look at the purchase contract, the installment contract, and the lease with option to buy. Also included are brief discussions of real estate binder, letter of intent, right of first refusal, and real estate exchange.

PURPOSE OF SALES CONTRACTS

What is the purpose of a real estate sales contract? If a buyer and a seller agree on a price, why can't the buyer hand the seller the necessary money and the seller simultaneously hand the buyer a deed? The main reason is that the buyer needs time to ascertain that the seller is, in fact, legally capable of conveying title. For protection, the buyer enters into a written and signed contract with the seller, promising that the purchase price will be paid only after title has been searched and found to be in satisfactory condition. The seller, in turn, promises to deliver a deed to the buyer when the buyer has paid the purchase price. This exchange of promises forms the legal consideration of the contract. A contract also gives the buyer time to arrange financing and to specify how such matters as taxes, existing debts, leases, and property inspections will be handled.

A properly prepared contract commits each party to its terms. Once a sales contract is in writing and signed, the seller cannot have a change of mind and sell to another person. The seller is obligated to convey title to the buyer when the buyer has performed as required by the contract. Likewise, the buyer must carry out his or her promises, including paying for the property, provided the seller has done everything required by the contract.

PURCHASE CONTRACTS

Variously known as a **purchase contract,** deposit receipt, offer and acceptance, purchase offer, or purchase and sales agreement, these preprinted forms contain four key parts: (1) provision for the buyer's earnest money deposit, (2) the buyer's offer to purchase, (3) the acceptance of the offer by the seller, and (4) provisions for the payment of a brokerage commission.

Figure 9.1 illustrates in simplified language the highlights of a real estate purchase contract.* The purchase contract begins

---

* This illustration has been prepared for discussion purposes only and not as a form to copy and use in a real estate sale. For that purpose, you must use a contract specifically legal in your state.

Figure 9.1.

REAL ESTATE PURCHASE CONTRACT

[1] *City of* __Riverdale__ , *State of New York,* __October 10,__ 19 xx [2].

[3] Samson Byers *(herein called the Buyer) agrees to purchase and* [4] William Ohner and Sarah Ohner *(herein called the Seller) agree to sell the following described real property located in the City of* [5] Riverdale *, County of* Lakeside, *State of New York,* a single-family dwelling commonly known as 1704 Main Street *, and legally described as* Lot 21, Block C of Madison's Subdivision as per map in Survey Book 10, page 51, in the Office of the County Recorder of said County .

[6] *The total purchase price is* ninety thousand *dollars* ($90,000.00), *payable as follows:* Three thousand dollars ($3,000.00) is given today as an earnest money deposit, receipt of which is hereby acknowledged. An additional $15,000.00 is to be placed into escrow by the Buyer before the closing date. The remaining $72,000.00 is to be by way of a new mortgage on said property .

[7] *Seller will deliver to the Buyer a* warranty *deed to said property. Seller will furnish to the Buyer at the* Seller's *expense a standard American Land Title Association title insurance policy issued by* First Security Title Company *showing marketable title vested in the Buyer and that the Seller is conveying title free of liens, encumbrances, easements, rights, and conditions except as follows:* People's Gas and Electric Company utility easement along eastern five feet of said lot .

[8] *The closing will take place at the office of* [the lender] *on or about* [date] .

[9] *Property taxes, property insurance, mortgage interest, income and expense items shall be prorated as of* the close of escrow .

[10] *Any outstanding bonds or assessments on the property shall be* paid by the Seller .

[11] *Any existing mortgage indebtedness against the property is to be* paid by the Seller .

Figure 9.1. (continued)

[12] *Seller will provide Buyer with a report from a licensed pest control inspector that the property is free of termites and wood rot. The cost of the report and any corrective work deemed necessary by the report are to be paid for by the* __Seller__ .

[13] *Possession of the property is to be delivered to the Buyer* at transfer of title .

[14] *Escrow expenses shall be* shared equally by the Buyer and Seller .

[15] *Conveyance tax to be paid by* __Seller__ .

[16] *The earnest money deposit to be held* in escrow *by* _____ *in* _____ *Bank.*

[17] *All attached floor coverings, attached television antenna, window screens, screen doors, storm windows, storm doors, plumbing and lighting fixtures (except floor, standing, and swag lamp), curtain rods, shades, venetian blinds, bathroom fixtures, trees, plants, shrubbery, water heaters, awnings, built-in heating, ventilating, and cooling systems, built-in stoves and ranges, and fences now on the premises shall be included unless otherwise noted. Any leased fixtures on the premises are not included unless specifically stated.*

[18] *Other provisions:* the purchase of this property is contingent upon the Buyer obtaining a mortgage loan on this property in the amount of $72,000.00 or more, with a maturity date of at least 25 years, at an interest rate no higher than $11\frac{1}{2}\%$ per year and loan fees not to exceed two points. Purchase price to include the refrigerator currently on the premises. Purchase is subject to buyer's approval of a qualified building inspector's report. Said report to be obtained within 7 days at Buyer's expense .

[19] *If the improvements on the property are destroyed or materially damaged prior to the close of escrow, or if the Buyer is unable to obtain financing as stated herein, or if the Seller is unable to deliver title as promised, then the Buyer, at his/her option, may terminate this agreement and the deposit made by him/her shall be returned to him in full. If the Seller fails to fulfill any of the other agreements made herein, the Buyer may*

Figure 9.1. (continued)

terminate this agreement with full refund of deposit, accept lesser performance, or sue for specific performance.

[20] If this purchase is not completed by reason of the Buyer's default, the Seller is released from his/her obligation to sell to the Buyer and shall retain the deposit money as his/her sole right to damages.

[21] Upon the signature of the Buyer, this document becomes an offer to the Seller to purchase the property described herein. The Seller has until 11:00 P.M., October 13, 19xx to indicate acceptance of this offer by signing and delivering it to the Buyer. If acceptance is not received by that time, this offer shall be deemed revoked and the deposit shall be returned in full to the Buyer.

[22] Time is of the essence in this contract.

Real Estate Broker   Riverdale Realty Company .

By [23] Shirley Newhouse .

Address   1234 Riverdale Blvd. Telephone 333-1234 .

[24] The undersigned offers and agrees to buy the above described property on the terms and conditions stated herein and acknowledges receipt of a copy hereof.

> Buyer   Samson Byers
> Address   2323 Cedar Ave., Riverdale
> Telephone   666-2468

Acceptance

[25] The undersigned accepts the foregoing offer and agrees to sell the property described above on the terms and conditions set forth.

[26] The undersigned has employed   Lakeside Realty Company   as Broker and for Broker's services agrees to pay said Broker as set forth in the listing agreement.

[27] The undersigned acknowledges receipt of a copy hereof.

> Seller   Sarah Ohner
> Seller   William Ohner
> Address   1704 Tenth St., Riverdale
> Telephone   333-3579   Date 10/10/xx

Figure 9.1. (continued)

> **Notification of Acceptance**
> **[28]***Receipt of a copy of the foregoing agreement is hereby acknowledged.*
>
> *Buyer* __Samson Byers__   *Date* __10/10/xx__

at **[1]** and **[2]** by identifying the location and date of the deposit and offer. At **[3]** the name of the buyer is written, and at **[4]** the name of the property owners (sellers). At **[5]** the property for which the buyer is making his offer is described. Although the street address and type of property (in this case a house) are not necessary to the validity of the contract, this information is often included for convenience in locating the property. The legal description that follows is crucial. Care must be taken to make certain that it is correct.

Earnest Money Deposit

The price that the buyer is willing to pay, along with the manner in which he proposes to pay it, is inserted at **[6]**. Of particular importance in this paragraph is the **earnest money deposit** that the buyer submits with his offer. With the exception of court-ordered sales, no laws govern the size of the deposit or even the need for one. Generally speaking though, the sellers and their agent want a reasonably substantial deposit to show the buyer's earnest intentions and to have something for their trouble if the sellers accept and the buyer fails to follow through. The buyer prefers to make as small a deposit as possible, as a deposit ties up his capital and there is the possibility of losing it. However, the buyer also recognizes that the sellers may refuse even to consider the offer unless accompanied by a reasonable deposit. In most parts of the country, a deposit of $2,000 to $5,000 on a $90,000 offer would be considered acceptable. In court-ordered sales, the required deposit set by the court is usually 10% of the offering price.

Deed and Condition of Title

At **[7]** the buyer requests that the sellers convey title by means of a warranty deed and provide and pay for a policy of title insurance showing the condition of title to be as described here. Before the offer is made, the broker and sellers will have told the buyer about the condition of title. However, the buyer has no way of verifying that information until the title is actually searched. To protect himself, the buyer states at [7] the condition of title that he is willing to accept. If title to the property is not presently in this condition, the sellers are required by the contract to take whatever steps are necessary to place title in this condition before title is conveyed. If, for example, there is an existing mortgage or judgment lien against the property, the sellers must have it removed. If there are other owners, their interests must be extinguished. If anyone has a right to use the property (such as a tenant under a lease), or controls the use of the property (such as a deed restriction), or has an easement, other than what is specifically mentioned, the sellers must remove these before conveying title to the buyer.

Closing Agent

At [8] the contract names the attorney, broker, or other person responsible for carrying out the paperwork and details of the purchase agreement and sets the date and location of the closing. On that date that the sellers will receive their money and the buyer his deed. The selection of a closing date is based on the estimated length of time necessary to carry out the conditions of the purchase contract. Normally, the most time-consuming item is finding a lender to make the necessary mortgage loan. Typically, this takes from 30 to 60 days, depending on the lender and the availability of loan money. The other conditions of the contract, such as the title search and arrangements to pay off any existing liens, take less time and can be done while arranging for a new mortgage loan. Once a satisfactory loan source is found, the lender makes a commitment to the buyer that the needed loan money will be placed into escrow on the closing date.

Prorating

Number [9] deals with the question of how certain ongoing expenses, such as property taxes, insurance, and mortgage interest, will be divided between the buyer and the sellers. For example, if the sellers pay $220 in advance for a 1-year fire insurance policy and then sell their house halfway through the policy year, what happens to the remaining 6 months of coverage that the sellers paid for but will not use? One solution is to transfer the remaining 6 months of coverage to the buyer for $110. Income items are also prorated. Suppose that the sellers have been renting the basement of their house to a college student for $90 per month. The student pays the $90 rent in advance on the first of each month. If the property is sold part way through the month, the buyer is entitled to the portion of the month's rent that is earned while he owns the property. This process of dividing ongoing expenses and income items is known as **prorating.** More information and examples regarding the prorating process are included in Chapter 13.

At [10] the buyer states that, if there are any unpaid assessments or bonds currently against the property, the sellers shall pay them as a condition of the sale. Alternatively, the buyer could agree to assume responsibility for paying them off. Since the buyer wants the property free of mortgages so that he can arrange for his own loan, at [11] he asks the sellers to remove any existing indebtedness. On the closing date, part of the money received from the buyer is used to clear the sellers' debts against the property. Alternatively, the buyer could agree to assume responsibility for paying off the existing debt against the property as part of the purchase price.

Termite Inspection

At [12] the buyer asks that the property be inspected at the sellers' expense for signs of termites and rotted wood (**dry rot**), and that the sellers pay for extermination and repairs. If the property is offered for sale as being in sound condition, a termite and wood rot clause is reasonable. If the property is being offered for sale on an **"as-is"** basis in its present condition with no guarantee or warranty of quality and if it has a price to match, then the clause is not reasonable. If the seller is quite sure that there are no termites or wood rot, this condition would not be a major negotiating point, as the cost of an inspection without corrective work is a minor cost in a real estate transaction.

Possession

The day on which possession of the property will be turned over to the buyer is inserted at [13]. As a rule, this is the same day as the closing date. If the buyer needs possession sooner or the sellers want possession after the closing date, the usual procedure is to arrange for a separate rental agreement between the buyer and sellers. Such an agreement produces fewer problems if the closing date is later changed or if the transaction falls through and the closing never occurs.

At [14] the purchase contract calls for the buyer and sellers to share escrow expenses equally. The buyer and sellers could divide them differently if they mutually agreed. Most states, including New York, charge a conveyance or transfer tax when a deed is recorded. At [15] the sellers agree to pay this tax. This is in addition to the fee the buyer pays to have the deed recorded in the public records. At [16] the buyer and sellers agree as to where the buyer's deposit money is to be held pending the close of the transaction. It could be held by the broker, the seller, or an attorney.

The paragraph at [17] is not absolutely essential to a valid real estate purchase contract, since what is considered real estate (and is therefore included in the price) and what is personal property (and is not included in the price) is a matter of law. However, because the buyer and seller may not be familiar with the differences between real property and personal property, this statement is often included to avoid misunderstandings. Moreover, such a statement can clarify whether or not an item such as a storm window or trash compactor, which may or may not be real property depending on its design, is included in the purchase price. If the buyer and seller intend that an item mentioned here not be included, that item is crossed out and initialed by all of them.

At [18] space is left to add conditions and agreements not pro-vided for elsewhere in the preprinted contract. To complete his purchase of this property, the buyer must obtain a $72,000 loan. However, what if he agrees to the purchase but cannot get a loan? Rather than risk losing his deposit money, the buyer makes his offer subject to obtaining a $72,000 loan on the property. To further protect himself against having to accept a loan "at any price," he states the terms on which he must be able to borrow. The sellers, of course, take certain risks in accepting an offer subject to obtaining financing. If the buyer is unable to obtain financing on these terms, the sellers will have to return the buyer's deposit and begin searching for another buyer. Meanwhile, the sellers may have lost anywhere from a few days to a few weeks of selling time. But without such a condition, a buyer may hesitate to make an offer at all. The solution is for the sellers to accept only those loan conditions that are reasonable in the light of current loan availability. For example, if lenders

Loan Conditions

are currently quoting 9% interest for loans on similar properties, the sellers would not want to accept an offer subject to the buyer obtaining a 7% loan. The possibility is too remote. If the buyer's offer is subject to obtaining a loan at current interest rates, the probability of the transaction collapsing on this condition is greatly reduced. The same principle applies to the amount of loan needed, the number of years to maturity, and loan fees: they must be reasonable in light of current market conditions.

Additional Conditions In the paragraph at [18] we also find that the buyer is asking the sellers to include an item of personal property in the selling price. While technically a bill of sale is used for the sale of personal property, such items are often included in the real estate purchase contract if the list is not long. If the refrigerator were real property rather than personal, no mention would be required, as all real property falling within the descriptions at [5] and [17] is automatically included in the price. The third item in the paragraph at [18] gives the buyer an opportunity to have the property inspected by a professional building inspector. Most home buyers do not know what to look for in the way of structural deterioration or defects that may soon require expensive repairs. Consequently, in the past several years, property inspection clauses in purchase contracts have become more common. The cost of this inspection is borne by the buyer. The inspector's report should be completed as soon as possible so that the property can be returned to the market if the buyer does not approve of the findings.

Property Damage The paragraph at [19] sets forth conditions under which the buyer can free himself of his obligations under this contract and recover his deposit in full. It begins by addressing the question of property destruction between the contract signing and the closing date. Fire, wind, rain, earthquake, or other damage does occasionally occur during that period of time. Whose responsibility would it be to repair the damage, and could the buyer point to the damage as a legitimate reason for breaking the contract? It is reasonable for the buyer to expect that the property will be delivered to him in as good a condition as when he offered to buy it. Consequently, if there is major damage or destruction, the wording here gives the buyer the option of rescinding the contract and recovering his deposit in full. Note, however, that this clause does not prevent the buyer from accepting the damaged property or the sellers from negotiating with the buyer to repair any damage in order to preserve the transaction.

Paragraph [19] also states that, if the buyer is unable to obtain financing as outlined at [18] or the sellers are unable to convey title as stated at [7], the buyer can rescind the contract and have his deposit refunded. However, if the buyer is ready to close the transaction and the sellers decide they do not want to sell, perhaps because the value of the property has increased between the signing of the contract and the closing date, the buyer can force the sellers to convey title through use of a lawsuit for specific performance.

Buyer Default

Once the contract is signed by all parties involved, if the buyer fails to carry out his obligations, the standard choices for the sellers are: (1) release the buyer and return his deposit in full, (2) sue the buyer for specific performance, or (3) sue the buyer for damages suffered. Returning the deposit does not compensate for the time and effort the sellers and their broker spent with the buyer, nor for the possibility that, while the sellers were committed to the buyer, the real estate market turned sour. Yet the time, effort, and cost of suing for specific performance or damages may be uneconomical. Consequently, it has become common practice in many parts of the country to insert a clause in the purchase contract whereby the buyer agrees in advance to forfeit his deposit if he defaults on the contract, and the sellers agree to accept the deposit as their sole right to damages. Thus, the sellers give up the right to sue the buyer and accept instead the buyer's deposit. The buyer knows in advance how much it will cost if he defaults, and the cost of default is limited to that amount. This is the purpose of paragraph [20].

Time Limits

At [21] the buyer clearly states that he is making an offer to buy and gives the sellers a certain amount of time to accept. If the sellers do not accept the offer within the time allotted, the offer is void. This feature is automatic: the buyer does not have to contact the sellers to tell them that the offer is no longer open. The offer must be open long enough for the sellers to physically receive it, make a decision, sign it, and return it to the buyer. If the sellers live nearby, the transaction is not complicated, and the offer can be delivered in person, 3 days is reasonable. If the offer must be mailed to an out-of-town seller, 7 to 10 days is appropriate.

If the buyer wants to offer on another property should the first offer not be accepted, the offer can be made valid for only a day, or even a few hours. A short offer life also limits the amount of time the sellers have to hold out for a better offer. If a property is highly marketable, a buyer will want the offer accepted before someone else makes a better offer. Some experienced real estate buyers argue that a purposely short offer life has a psychological value. It motivates the seller to accept before the offer expires. Note, too, a buyer can withdraw and cancel an offer at any time before the seller has accepted and the buyer is aware of that acceptance.

"Time Is of the Essence"

Time is of the essence at [22] means that the time limits set by the contract must be faithfully observed or the contract is voidable by the nondefaulting party. Moreover, lateness may give cause for an action for damages. Neither buyer nor sellers should expect extensions of time to complete their obligations. This clause does not prohibit the buyer or sellers from voluntarily giving the other an extension. But extensions are neither automatic nor mandatory.

Time is of the essence is a very difficult issue to litigate in court, and courts interpret it inconsistently. Generally speaking, courts disfavor automatic cancellation and forfeiture of valuable contract rights after "slight" or "reasonable" delays in performance. This is because unexpected delays are commonplace, and buyers and sellers customarily overlook delays in order to allow a deal to close. As a practical matter, the phrase, when used without additional supporting language, seems to be a firm reminder to all parties to keep things moving toward completion. If time is truly an important issue (as in an option contract, for example), the parties must be very explicit in the contract regarding their intentions.

Signatures

The real estate agency and salesperson responsible for producing this offer to buy are identified at [23]. At [24] the buyer clearly states that this is an offer to purchase. If the buyer has any doubts or questions regarding the legal effect of the offer, he should take it to an attorney for counsel before signing it. After he signs, the buyer retains one copy and the rest are delivered to the sellers for their decision. By retaining one copy, the buyer has a written record to remind him of his obligations under the offer. Equally important, the sellers cannot forge a change on the offer, as they do not have all the copies. Regarding delivery, the standard procedure is for the salesperson who obtained the offer to make an appointment with the agent who obtained the listing, and to call on the sellers together and present the offer.

For the offer to become binding, the sellers must accept every- *Acceptance* thing in it. The rejection of even the smallest portion of the offer is a rejection of the entire offer. If the sellers wish to reject the offer but keep negotiations alive, the sellers can make a counteroffer. This is a written offer to sell to the buyer at a new price and with terms that are closer to the buyer's offer than the sellers' original asking price and terms. The agent prepares the counteroffer either by filling out a fresh purchase contract identical in all ways to the buyer's offer except for these changes, or by writing on the back of the offer (or on another sheet of paper) that the sellers offer to sell at the terms the buyer had offered except for the stated changes. The counteroffer is then dated and signed by the sellers, and a time limit is given to the buyer to accept. The sellers keep a copy, and the counteroffer is delivered to the buyer for his decision. If the counteroffer is acceptable to the buyer, he signs and dates it, and the contract is complete. Another commonly used but less desirable practice is to take the buyer's offer, cross out each item unacceptable to the seller, and write above or below it what the seller will accept. Each change is then initialed by the seller and buyer.

Returning to Figure 9.1, suppose that the sellers accept the offer *Notification* as presented to them. At [25] they indicate acceptance; at [26] they state that they employed the Lakeside Realty Company and agree on a commission of $5,400 for brokerage services, to be paid upon closing and recordation of the deed. Provisions are also included as to the amount of the commission if the sale is not completed. At [27] the sellers sign and date the contract and acknowledge receipt of a copy. The last step is to notify the buyer that his offer has been accepted, give him a copy of the completed agreement, and at [28] have him acknowledge receipt of it. If a party to a purchase contract dies after it has been signed, the deceased's heirs are, as a rule, required to fulfill the agreement. Thus, if a husband and wife sign a purchase contract and one of them dies, the sellers can look to the deceased's estate and the survivor to carry out the terms of the contract. Similarly, if a seller dies, the buyer is still entitled to receive the property as called for in the contract.

If the offer is rejected, it is good practice to have the sellers write the word *rejected* on the offer, followed by their signatures.

Federal Clauses In two instances the government requires that specific clauses be included in real estate sales contracts. First, an **amendatory language** clause must be included whenever a sales contract is signed by a purchaser prior to the receipt of an FHA Appraised Value or a VA Certificate of Reasonable Value on the property. The purpose is to assure that the purchaser may terminate the contract without loss when it appears that the agreed purchase price may be significantly above the appraised value. The specific clauses, which must be used verbatim, are available from FHA- and VA-approved lenders. Second, the Federal Trade Commission (FTC) requires that builders and sellers of new homes include **insulation disclosures** in all purchase contracts. Disclosures, which may be based on manufacturer claims, must cite the type, thickness, and R-value of the insulation installed in the home. The exact clause is provided by the builder or seller of the home based on model clauses provided by the National Association of Homebuilders as modified by local laws.

Preprinted Clauses The purchase contract in Figure 9.1 is designed to present and explain the basic elements of a purchase contract for a house. One popular preprinted purchase contract presently for sale to real estate agents consists of four legal-size pages that contain dozens of preprinted clauses. The buyer, seller, and agent select and fill in those clauses pertinent to their transaction. For example, if the home is a condominium, there are clauses that pertain to the condominium documents and maintenance reserves. If the home is in a flood zone, there is a clause for disclosing that fact to the buyer and the requirement of flood insurance by lenders. There are four different pest inspection and repair clauses from which the buyer and seller can choose. Smoke detector clauses and roof inspection clauses, as well as detailed contingency and default clauses are also included. There are clauses for personal property included in the sale and guarantees by the seller that electrical, heating, cooling, sewer, plumbing, built-in appliances, and so on, are all in normal working order at the closing. Additionally, there may be state-mandated clauses. For example, some states require specific, due-on-sale balloon payment and insulation disclosures. The benefit of preprinted clauses is that much of the language of the contract has already been written for the buyer, seller, and agent. But the buyer, seller, and agent must read all the clauses and choose those appropriate to the transaction.

Riders

A **rider** is any addition annexed to a document and made a part of the document by reference. A rider is usually written, typed, or printed on a separate piece of paper and stapled to the document. There will be a reference in the document that the rider is a part of the document and a statement in the rider that it is a part of the document. It is good practice to have the parties to the document place their initials on the rider. Riders are also known as **addenda** or **attachments.**

Negotiation

One of the most important principles of purchase contracts (and real estate contracts in general) is that nearly everything is negotiable and nearly everything has a price. In preparing or analyzing any contract, consider what the advantages and disadvantages of each condition are to each party to the contract. A solid contract results when buyers and sellers each feel that they have gained more than they have given up. The prime example is the sale price of the property itself. Sellers prefer the money over the property, while buyers prefer the property over the money. Each small negotiable item in the purchase contract has its price too. For example, a seller may agree to include the refrigerator for $200 more. Equally important in negotiating is the relative bargaining power of buyer and seller. A seller who is confident of having plenty of buyers at the asking price can elect to refuse offers for less money, and reject those with numerous conditions or insufficient earnest money. However, an owner who is anxious to sell and has received only one offer in several months may be quite willing to accept a lower price and numerous conditions.

THE BINDER

Throughout most of the United States, the real estate agent prepares the purchase contract as soon as the agent is about to (or has) put a deal together. Using preprinted forms available from real estate trade associations, title companies, and stationery stores, the agent fills in the purchase price, down payment, and other details of the transaction and has the buyer and seller sign it as soon as they reach agreement.

In parts of New York State, such as Nassau, Queens, and Suffolk counties, the practice is for the real estate agent to prepare a short-form contract called a **binder.** The purpose of a binder is to hold a deal together until a more formal purchase contract can be drawn by an attorney and signed by the buyer and seller. In the binder, the buyer and seller agree to the purchase price, the down payment, and how the balance will be financed. The brokerage commission (to whom and how much) is stated along with an agreement to meet again to draw up a more formal contract that will contain all the remaining details of the sale. The agent then arranges a meeting at the office of the seller's attorney. In attendance are the seller and his attorney, the buyer and his attorney, and the real estate agents responsible for bringing about the sale. Together they prepare a written contract which the buyer and seller sign. Note that when the seller's attorney writes the formal contract, the contract will favor the seller. This is because the seller's attorney is expected to protect the seller's best interests at all times. The purchaser, to protect his interests, should not rely on the seller's attorney for advice but should bring his own attorney.

What the Binder
Does Not Say

While it is easy to minimize the importance of a binder because it is replaced by another contract, it does, nonetheless, meet all the requirements of a legally binding contract. In the absence of another contract, it can be used to enforce completion of a sale by a buyer or seller. The major weakness of a binder is in what it *does not say.* For example, the binder probably makes no mention of a termite inspection, the type of deed the seller is expected to use, or the closing date. Unless the buyer and seller can agree on these matters at the formal contract meeting, a dilemma results. Certainly the buyer will wonder if refusal to meet all the seller's demands at the contract meeting will result in loss of the deposit money. If a stalemate develops, the courts may be asked to decide the termite question, deed type, closing date, and any other unresolved points. However, because this is costly and time consuming for all involved, give-and-take negotiation takes place at the contract meeting. If a completely unnegotiable impasse is reached, as a practical matter the binder is usually rescinded by the buyer and seller and the buyer's deposit returned.

If two or more parties want to express their mutual intention to buy, sell, lease, develop, or invest, and wish to do so without creating any firm legal obligation, they may use a **letter of intent.** Generally, such a letter contains an outline of the proposal and concludes with language to the effect that the letter is only an expression of mutual intent and that no liability or obligation is created by it. In other words, a letter of intent is neither a contract nor an agreement to enter into a contract. However, it is expected, and usually stipulated in the letter, that the parties signing the letter will proceed promptly and in good faith to conclude the deal proposed in the letter. The letter of intent is usually found in connection with commercial leases, real estate development, and construction projects, and with multimillion-dollar real estate sales.

LETTER OF INTENT

Historically in the United States, the sale of real estate was primarily a legal service. Lawyers matched buyers with sellers, wrote sales contracts, and prepared mortgages and deeds. When persons other than lawyers began to specialize in real estate brokerage, the question of who should write the sales contract became important. The lawyer was more qualified in matters of contract law, but the broker wanted something that could be signed the moment the buyer and seller were in agreement. For many years the solution was a compromise. The broker had the buyer and seller sign a binder, and they agreed to meet again in the presence of a lawyer to draw up and sign a more formal contract. The trend today, however, is for the real estate agent to prepare a complete purchase contract as soon as there is a meeting of the minds.

PRACTICING LAW

The preparation of contracts by real estate agents for their clients has not gone unnoticed by lawyers. The legal profession maintains that preparing contracts for clients is practicing law, and state laws restrict the practice of law to lawyers. This has been, and continues to be, a controversial issue between brokers and lawyers. Resolution of the matter has come in the form of **accords** between the real estate brokerage industry and the legal profession. In nearly all states courts have ruled that a real estate agent is permitted to prepare purchase, installment, and rental contracts provided the agent uses a preprinted form approved by a lawyer and provided the agent is limited to filling in only the blank spaces on the form. (Figure 9.1 illustrates this concept.) If the preprinted form requires extensive cross-outs, changes, and riders, the contract should be drafted by a lawyer. A real estate license is not a permit to practice law.

In the New York case of *Duncan and Hill Realty,* the state's highest court ruled that the broker was permitted to draft only "simple" contracts as part of brokerage operation. The broker must not hold himself out as an attorney, and cannot perform these services unless he is involved in the transaction. Brokers and their sales agents are permitted to insert into an approved, preprinted form only the basic provisions such as the purchase price, description of the property, and mortgage contingency. The real estate agent cannot insert into the contract any terms that require legal expertise. In the *Duncan and Hill* case, the broker had written in an acceleration clause and a default clause relating to a proposed mortgage and note that the seller was to take as part of the purchase price. The court ruled that this exceeded the broker's authority.

INSTALLMENT CONTRACTS

An installment contract (also known as a **land contract, conditional sales contract, contract for deed,** or **agreement of sale**) combines features from a sales contract, a deed, and a mortgage. An installment contract contains most of the provisions of the purchase contract described in Figure 9.1, plus wording familiar to the warranty deed described in Chapter 7, plus many of the provisions of the mortgage described in the next chapter.

The most important feature of an installment contract is that the seller does not deliver a deed to the buyer at the closing. Rather, the seller promises to deliver the deed at some future date. Meanwhile, the purchaser is given the right to occupy the property (the magic word is **possession**) and have, for all practical purposes, the rights, obligations, and privileges of ownership.

The widest use of the installment contract occurs when the buyer does not have the full purchase price in cash or is unable to borrow it from a lender. To sell under these conditions, the seller must accept a down payment plus monthly payments. To carry this out the seller can choose either to: (1) deliver a deed to the buyer at the closing and at the same moment take back from the buyer a promissory note and a mortgage secured by the property (a mortgage carryback), or (2) enter into an installment contract wherein the buyer makes the required payments to the seller before the seller delivers a deed to the buyer.

Vendor, Vendee

Historically, installment contracts were most commonly used to sell vacant land when the buyer put only a modest amount of money down and the seller agreed to receive the balance as installment payments. When all the installments were made, the seller delivered a deed to the purchaser. The terms of these contracts were usually weighted in favor of the seller. For example, if the buyer (called the **vendee**) failed to make all the payments on time, the seller (called the **vendor**) could rescind the contract, retain payments already made as rent, and retake possession of the land. Additionally, the seller might insert a clause in the installment contract prohibiting the buyer from recording it. The public records would continue to show the seller as owner and the seller could use the land as collateral for loans. That such a one-sided contract would even exist may seem surprising. But, if a buyer did not have all cash, or enough cash down to obtain financing from another source, the buyer was stuck with accepting what the seller offered, or not buying the property. Sellers took the position that if they were selling to buyers who were unwilling or unable to find their own sources of financing, then sellers wanted a quick and easy way of recovering the property if the payments were not made. By selling on an installment contract and not allowing it to be recorded, the seller could save the time and expense of regular foreclosure proceedings. The seller would simply notify the buyer in writing that the contract was in default, and thereby rescind it. Meanwhile, as far as the public records were concerned, title was still in the seller's name.

Public Criticism

Such strongly worded agreements received much public criticism, as did the possibility that even if the buyer made all the payments, the seller might not be capable of delivering good title. For example, the buyer could make all payments, yet find that the seller had encumbered the property with debt, had gone bankrupt, had become legally incapacitated, or had died.

Then, in the late 1970s, interest rates rose sharply. In order to sell their properties, sellers looked for ways of passing along the benefits of their fixed-rate, low-interest loans to buyers. The installment contract was rediscovered, and it moved from being used primarily to sell land to being used to sell houses and apartment buildings and even office buildings and industrial property. Basically, the seller kept the property and mortgage in the seller's name and made the mortgage payments from the buyer's monthly payments. This continued until the buyer found alternative financing, at which time the seller delivered the deed.

Protections With the increased popularity of installment contracts, a need was created for more sophisticated and more protective contracts. Simultaneously, courts and legislatures in various states were listening to consumer complaints and finding existing installment contract provisions too harsh. One by one, states began requiring that a buyer be given a specified period to cure any default before the seller could rescind. Some states began requiring that installment contracts be foreclosed like regular mortgages. And most states now require that installment contracts be recorded and/or prohibit a seller from enforcing nonrecording clauses.

Buyers have become much more sophisticated also. For example, it is common practice today to require the seller to place the deed (usually a warranty deed) in an escrow at the time the installment contract is made. This relieves a number of the aforementioned problems regarding the unwillingness or inability of the seller to prepare and deliver the deed later. Additionally, the astute buyer will require that a collection account be used to collect the buyer's payments and make the payments on the underlying mortgage. This is done using a neutral third party such as the escrow holder of the deed, a bank, or a trust company. The seller will probably insist that the buyer place one-twelfth of the annual property taxes and hazard insurance in the escrow account each month to pay for these items. The buyer will want to record the contract to establish the buyer's rights to the property. The buyer may also want to include provisions whereby the seller delivers a deed to the buyer and takes back a mortgage from the buyer once the buyer has paid, say, 30% or 40% of the purchase price.

If an installment contract is used for the purchase of real estate, it should be done with the help of legal counsel to make certain that it provides adequate safeguards for the buyer as well as the seller. In Chapter 19, the installment contract is discussed as a tool to finance the sale of improved property when other sources of financing are not available.

Between the moment that a buyer and seller sign a valid purchase contract and the moment the seller delivers a deed to the buyer, who holds title to the property? Similarly, under an installment contract, until the seller delivers a deed to the buyer, who holds title to the property? The answer, in both cases, is the seller. But this is only technically true because the buyer is entitled to receive a deed (and thereby title) once the buyer has completed the terms of the purchase or installment contract. During the period beginning with the buyer and seller signing the contract and ending with the seller delivering the deed, the buyer is said to hold **equitable title** to the property. The concept of equitable title stems from the fact that a buyer can enforce specific performance of the contract in a court of equity to get title. Meanwhile, the seller holds bare or naked title, i.e., title in name only and without full ownership rights.

EQUITABLE TITLE

The equitable title that a purchaser holds under a purchase or installment contract is transferable by subcontract, assignment, or deed. Equitable title can be sold, given away, or mortgaged, and it passes to the purchaser's heirs and devisees on the purchaser's death.

It is not unusual to see a property offered for sale wherein the vendee under an installment contract is offering those rights for sale. Barring any due-on-sale clause in the installment contract, this can be done. The buyer receives from the vendee an assignment of the contract and with it the vendee's equitable title. The buyer then takes possession and continues to make the payments called for by the contract. When the payments are completed, the deed and title transfer can be handled in one of two ways. One way is for the original seller to agree to deliver a deed to the new buyer. The other, and the most common way, is for the vendee to place a deed to the new buyer in escrow. When the last payment is made, the deed from the original seller to the vendee is recorded, and immediately after it, the deed from the vendee to the new buyer is recorded.

LEASE WITH OPTION TO BUY

An option is an agreement to keep an offer open for a fixed period of time. One of the most popular option contracts in real estate is the **lease with option to buy.** Often simply referred to as a **lease-option,** it allows the tenant to buy the property at preset price and terms during the option period. For a residential property, the lease is typically for 1 year, and the option to buy must be exercised during that time. Let's look more closely.

In a lease-option contract all the normal provisions of a lease are present, such as those shown in Figure 11.1. All the normal provisions of a purchase contract are present, such as those shown in Figure 9.1. In addition, there will be wording stating that the tenant has the option of exercising the purchase contract, provided the tenant notifies the landlord in writing of that intent during the option period. All terms of the purchase contract must be negotiated and in writing when the lease is signed. Both the tenant and the landlord must sign the lease. Only the landlord must sign the purchase contract and option agreement, although both parties often do so. If the tenant wants to buy during the option period, the tenant notifies the landlord in writing that the tenant wishes to exercise the purchase contract. Together they proceed to carry out the purchase contract as in a normal sale.

If the tenant does not exercise the option within the option period, the option expires and the purchase contract is null and void. If the lease also expires at the end of the option period, the tenant must either arrange with the landlord to continue renting or move out. Alternatively, they can negotiate a new purchase contract or a new lease-option contract.

Popularity

Lease-options are particularly popular in soft real estate markets in which a home seller is having difficulty finding a buyer. One solution is to lower the asking price and/or make the financing terms more attractive. However, the seller may wish to hold out in hopes that prices will rise within a year. In the meantime, the seller needs someone to occupy the property and provide some income.

The lease-option is attractive to a tenant because the tenant has a place to rent plus the option of buying any time during the option period for the price in the purchase contract. In other words, the tenant can wait a year and see if he or she likes the property and if values rise to or above the price in the purchase contract. If the tenant does not like the property and/or the property does not rise in value, the tenant is under no obligation to buy. Once the lease expires, the tenant is also under no obligation to continue renting.

To encourage a tenant to exercise the option to buy, the contract may allow the tenant to apply part or all of the rent paid to the purchase price. In fact, quite a bit of flexibility and negotiation can take place in creating a lease-option. For example, take a home that would rent for $750 per month and sell for $100,000 on the open market. Suppose the owner wants $110,000 and won't come down to the market price. Meanwhile, the home is vacant and there are mortgage payments to be made. The owner could offer a 1-year lease-option with a rental charge of $750 each month and an exercise price of $110,000. Within a year, $110,000 may look good to the tenant, especially if the market value of the property has risen significantly above $110,000. The tenant can exercise the option or, if not prohibited by the contract, sell it to someone who intends to exercise it. The owner receives $10,000 more for the property than he or she could have gotten last year, and the tenant has the benefit of any value increase above that.

Examples

Continuing the above example, what if the property rises to $105,000 in value? There is no economic incentive for the tenant to exercise the option at $110,000. The tenant can simply disregard the option and make an offer of $105,000 to the owner. The owner's choice is to sell at that price or continue renting the home, perhaps with another 1-year lease-option.

The owner can also charge the tenant extra for the privilege of having the option, but it must make economic sense to the tenant. Suppose in the foregoing example the purchase price is set equal to the current market value—that is, $100,000. This would be a valuable benefit to the tenant, and the owner could

Option Fee

charge an up-front cash fee for the option and/or charge above-market rent. The amounts would depend on the market's expectations regarding the value of this home a year from now. There is nothing special about a 1-year option period, although it is a very popular length of time. The owner and tenant can agree to a 3-month, 6-month, or 9-month option if it fits their needs, and the lease can run longer than the option period. Options for longer than 1 year are generally reserved for commercial properties. For example, a businessperson just starting out, or perhaps expanding, wants to buy a building but needs 1 or 2 years to see how successful the business will be and how much space will be needed.

Caveats

Be aware that lease-options may create income tax consequences that require professional tax counseling. Legal advice is also very helpful in preparing and reviewing the lease-option papers because the entire deal (lease, option, and purchase contract) must be watertight from the beginning. One cannot wait until the option is exercised to write the purchase contract or even a material part of it. If a real estate agent puts a lease-option together, the agent is entitled to a leasing commission at the time the lease is signed. If the option is exercised, the agent is due a sales commission on the purchase contract.

Evidence that the option to buy exists should be recorded, not only to establish the tenant's rights to purchase the property, but also to establish those rights back to the date the option was recorded. An option is an example of a unilateral contract. When it is exercised, it becomes bilateral. The lease portion of a lease-option is a bilateral contract. The party giving the option is called the **optionor** (owner in a lease-option). The party receiving the option is the **optionee** (tenant in a lease-option). Sometimes an option to buy is referred to as a **call.** You will see how an option can be used by a home builder to buy land in Chapter 19 and how options can be used to renew leases in Chapter 11.

RIGHT OF FIRST REFUSAL

Sometimes a tenant will agree to rent a property only if given an opportunity to purchase it before someone else does. In other words, the tenant is saying, "Mr. or Ms. Owner, if you get a valid offer from someone else to purchase this property, show it to me and give me an opportunity to match the offer." This is called a

right of first refusal. If someone presents the owner with a valid offer, the owner must show it to the tenant before accepting it. If the tenant decides not to match it, the owner is free to accept it.

A right of first refusal protects a tenant from having the property sold out from under him when, in fact, if the tenant knew about the offer, he would have been willing to match it. The owner usually does not care who buys, as long as the price and terms are the same. Therefore, an owner may agree to include a right of first refusal clause in a rental contract for little or no additional charge if the tenant requests it. The right of first refusal concept is not limited just to landlord-tenant situations, but those situations are as deep as we will go here.

Most real estate transactions involve the exchange of real estate for monetary consideration. However, among sophisticated real estate investors, exchanging real property for real property has become popular for two important reasons. First, real estate trades can be accomplished without large amounts of cash by trading a property you presently own for one you want. This sidesteps the intermediate step of converting real estate to cash and then converting cash back to real estate. Second, by using an exchange, you can dispose of one property and acquire another without paying income taxes on the profit in the first property at the time of the transaction. As a result, the phrase *tax-free exchange* is often used when talking about trading.

To illustrate, suppose that you own an apartment building as an investment. The value on your accounting books is $150,000, but its market value today is $250,000. If you sell for cash, you will have to pay income taxes on the difference between the value of the property on your accounting books and the amount you receive for it. If, instead of selling for cash, you find another building that you want and can arrange a trade, then for income tax purposes the new building acquires the accounting book value of the old and no income taxes are due at the time of the trade. Taxes will be due, however, if and when you finally sell rather than trade. The **tax-deferred exchange** rules apply to investment properties only. Owner-occupied dwellings are treated differently. The Internal Revenue Service permits a homeowner to sell and still postpone paying taxes on

EXCHANGE AGREEMENTS

the gain provided another home of equal or greater value is purchased within 24 months.

Trading Up

Real estate exchanges need not involve properties of equal value. For example, if you own debt free a small office building worth $100,000, you could trade it for a building worth $500,000 with $400,000 of mortgage debt against it. Alternatively, if the building you wanted was priced at $600,000 with $400,000 in debt against it, you could offer your building plus $100,000 in cash.

The vast majority of tax-deferred exchanges today consist of three transactions: the two conveyances and an escrow agreement with a **qualified intermediary (QI).** The qualified intermediary can be a title company, attorney, or in some cases, an independent company providing this service as tax advisors. The QI maintains control over the funds and the closing documents pursuant to the instructions contained in the escrow agreement. This allows the various parties to deposit documents and funds with the QI (often by mail) which makes it much more convenient. As a practical matter, the QI signs all documents relevant to the closing other than the conveyancing documents. The Internal Revenue Service rules allow the conveyancing documents to be executed by the parties to the transaction without involving the formality of the QI's execution. This prevents the QI from becoming "in the chain of title" which could further complicate the transaction.

Assume the party who wants to do the tax-deferred exchange is Seller 1, who signs a contract to convey real estate to Buyer 1. After executing a contract of sale, Seller 1 assigns his interest in the contract to the QI, then executes an **escrow agreement** with the QI that defines the QI's role. Seller 1 then locates the property he is interested in purchasing, and enters into a purchase contract to acquire that property; he then sends notice of designation of property to the qualified intermediary, then assigns his interest in the contract as purchaser to the qualified intermediary. In both transactions, the deed is drafted from Seller to Buyer (so the qualified intermediary owner never takes title to either tract). The qualified intermediary, who has escrowed the funds from transaction #1, then uses these proceeds to pay Seller 2 to complete transaction #2.

The key factor is that Seller 1 (taxpayer) has no control over the funds held by the qualified intermediary and cannot be deemed to be in receipt of those funds. In effect, the transaction results in Seller 1 conveying his property to the qualified intermediary and the qualified intermediary conveying the exchange property to the seller. Note Figure 9.2.

Although trading is a complicated business, it can also be very lucrative for real estate agents. Whereas an ordinary sale results in one brokerage commission, a two-party exchange results in two commissions, and a four-party exchange in four commissions.

The Internal Revenue Code allows nonsimultaneous exchanges to be tax deferred under certain circumstances. Such an exchange, commonly called a **delayed exchange,** occurs when property is exchanged for a right to receive property at a future date. It is a helpful technique when one party is willing to exchange out of a property but has not yet chosen a property to exchange into. Meanwhile the other parties to the exchange are ready and want to close. The delayed exchange allows the closing to take place by giving the party that has not chosen a property the right to designate a property and take title after the closing. The 1984 act specifically allows this, provided that: (1) the designated property is identified within 45 days of the original closing, (2) the title to the designated property is

Delayed Exchanges

Figure 9.2. Possible trading combinations.

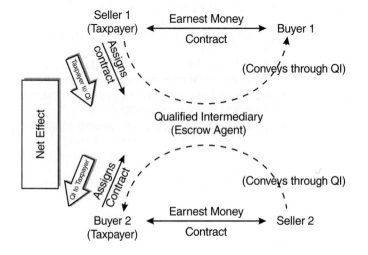

acquired within 180 days of the original closing, and (3) the designated property is received before the designating party's tax return is due. If these rules are not met the transaction will be treated as a sale for the designating party, not an exchange.

TYPICAL TRADE CONTRACT

Space does not permit a detailed review of a trade contract. However, very briefly, a typical trade contract identifies the traders involved and their respective properties; names the type of deed and quality of title that will be conveyed; names the real estate brokers involved and how much they are to be paid; discusses prorations, personal property, rights of tenants, and damage to the property; provides a receipt for the deposit that each trader makes; requires each trader to provide an abstract of title; and sets forth the consequences of defaulting on the contract. A single broker who represents more than one trader must disclose this to each trader being represented.

VOCABULARY REVIEW

*Match terms **a–s** with statements **1–19**.*

a. *As-is*
b. *Bill of sale*
c. *Binder*
d. *Closing date*
e. *Delayed exchange*
f. *Dry rot*
g. *Earnest money deposit*
h. *Equitable title*
i. *Installment contract*
j. *Lease-option*
k. *Letter of intent*
l. *Loan commitment letter*
m. *Optionee*
n. *Option fee*
o. *Purchase contract*
p. *Qualified intermediary (QI)*
q. *Right of first refusal*
r. *Time is of the essence*
s. *Vendee*

1. A written and signed agreement specifying the terms at which a buyer will purchase and an owner will sell.
2. A short-form purchase contract to hold a real estate transaction together until a more formal contract can be prepared and signed.
3. Money that accompanies an offer to purchase as evidence of good faith; also called the deposit.
4. Property offered for sale in its present condition with no guarantee or warranty of quality provided by the seller.
5. Rotted wood; usually the result of alternate soaking and drying over a long period of time.
6. The day on which the buyer pays the purchase money and the seller delivers title.
7. Written evidence of the sale of personal property.

8. A phrase meaning that all parties to a contract are expected to perform on time as a condition of the contract.

9. Also known as a conditional sales contract, land contract, contract for deed, or agreement of sale.

10. The buyer under a contract for deed.

11. The right to demand that title be conveyed upon payment of the purchase price.

12. Allows the tenant to buy the property at a preset price for a given period of time.

13. The right to match or better an offer before the property is sold to someone else.

14. Expresses a mutual intention to buy, sell, lease, develop, or invest without creating any firm legal obligation.

15. The party receiving an option.

16. An agreement by a lender to make a loan.

17. Money paid for the privilege of having an option.

18. A nonsimultaneous real estate trade.

19. A third-party escrow agent used in tax-deferred exchanges.

QUESTIONS AND PROBLEMS

1. Why is it necessary to include the extra step of preparing and signing a purchase contract when it would seem much easier if the buyer simply paid the seller the purchase price and the seller handed the buyer a deed?

2. Why is it preferable to prepare a purchase contract that contains all the terms and conditions of sale at the outset rather than to leave some items to be "ironed out" later?

3. What are the advantages and disadvantages of using preprinted real estate purchase contract forms?

4. Is it legal for a seller to accept an offer that is not accompanied by a deposit? Why or why not?

5. If a purchase contract for real property describes the land, is it also necessary to mention the fixtures? Why or why not?

6. How will the relative bargaining strengths and weaknesses of the buyer and seller affect the contract negotiation process?

7. Under an installment contract, what is the advantage to the seller of not having to deliver title to the buyer until all required payments are made?

8. What are the advantages of trading real estate rather than selling it? What do you consider the disadvantages to be?

9. What is a letter of intent?

ADDITIONAL READINGS

The Complete Book of Business Forms and Agreements, by **Cliff Roberson** (McGraw-Hill, 1994, 525 pages). Chapters 2 and 3 deal with real estate forms and agreements.

"Handling Offers and Counteroffers," by **G. E. Irby** (*Texas Realtor,* April 1990, p. 31).

Real Estate Contracts, by **Karl B. Holtzschue** (Practicing Law Institute 1985, 1988 supp., 319 pages). Discussion of closing of sales, contracts, and land contracts. Forms are also included.

Successful Real Estate Sales Contracts, by **Erik Jorgensen** (Axiom Press, 1983, 336 pages). Shows how to prepare contracts for the sale and exchange of homes, income property, and mobile homes. Contains numerous sample contracts.

10

The Principal-Broker Relationship – Agency

KEY • TERMS

Agent: the person empowered to act by and on behalf of the principal

Boycotting: two or more people conspiring to restrain competition

Commingling: the mixing of clients' or customers' funds with an agent's personal funds

Dual agency: representation of two or more principals in a transaction by the same agent

Middleman: a person who brings two or more parties together but does not represent either party

Ostensible authority: an agency relationship created by the conduct of the principal

Price fixing: two or more people conspiring to charge a fixed fee, having an anti-competitive effect

Principal: a person who authorizes another to act

Puffing: statements a reasonable person would recognize as nonfactual or extravagant

Third parties: persons who are not parties to a contract but who may be affected by it

AGENCY

When a property owner gives a real estate broker a listing authorizing the broker to find a buyer or a tenant and promising compensation if he does, an **agency relationship** is created. For an agency to exist, there must be a principal and an agent. The **principal** is the person who empowers another to act as his representative; the **agent** is the person who is empowered to act. When someone speaks about the laws of agency, he refers to those laws that govern the rights and duties of the principal, the agent, and the persons (called **third parties**) with whom they deal.

Agencies are divided into three categories: universal, general, and specific. A **universal agency** is very broad in scope, as the principal gives his agent the legal power to transact matters of all types for him. A **general agency** gives the agent the power to bind his principal in a particular trade or business. For example, the relationship between a real estate broker (principal) and his salesperson (agent) is considered a general agency. With a **special agency** the principal empowers his agent to perform only specific acts and no others. The special agent may not bind the principal by his acts. Applications of special agency include real estate listings, the topic we shall discuss next.

The principal in an agency relationship can be either a natural person or a legal person such as a corporation. Likewise, an agent can be either a natural person or a corporation such as a real estate brokerage company. The persons and firms with whom the principal and agent negotiate are called **third parties.** You will also hear these third parties referred to as the broker's **customers** and the principal referred to as the broker's **client.** Sometimes you will see the phrase "principals only" in real estate advertisements where property is offered for sale by its owner without the aid of a broker. This means the owner wants to be contacted by persons who want to buy and not by real estate agents who want to list the property.

Establishing the Agent's Authority

A written listing agreement outlines the agent's (broker's) authority to act on behalf of the principal (owner) and the principal's obligations to the agent. A written agreement is the preferred method of creating an agency because it provides a document evidencing the existence of the agency relationship.

Agency authority may also arise from custom in the industry, common usage, and conduct of the parties involved. For example, the right of an agent to post a "For Sale" sign on the listed property may not be expressly stated in the listing. However, if it is the custom in the industry to do so, and presuming there are no deed restrictions or city ordinances to the contrary, the agent has **implied authority** to post the sign. A similar situation exists with regard to showing a listed property to prospects. The seller of a home can expect to have it shown on weekends and evenings whereas a commercial property owner would expect showings only during business hours.

Ostensible authority is conferred when a principal gives a third party reason to believe that another person is his agent even though that person is unaware of the appointment. If the third party accepts this as true, the principal may well be bound by the acts of his agent. For example, you give your house key to a plumber with instructions that when the waste lines have been unstopped, the plumber is to lock the house and give the key to your next door neighbor. Even though you do not call and expressly appoint your neighbor as your agent to receive your key, once the plumber gives the key to your neighbor, your neighbor becomes your agent with regard to that key. Since you told the plumber to leave the key there, the plumber has every reason to believe that you appointed your neighbor as your agent to receive the key.

An **agency by ratification** is one established after the fact. For example, if an agent secures a contract on behalf of a principal and the principal subsequently ratifies or agrees to it, a court may hold that an agency was created at the time the initial negotiations started. An **agency by estoppel** can result when a principal fails to maintain due diligence over his agent and the agent exercises powers not granted to him. If this causes a third party to believe the agent has these powers, an agency by estoppel has been created. An **agency coupled with an interest** is said to exist when an agent holds an interest in the property he is representing, for example, if a broker lists a property and is part owner as well.

When a real estate broker accepts a listing, a **fiduciary relationship** is created. This requires that the agent exhibit trust and

Broker's Obligations to His Principal

honesty and exercise good business judgment when working on behalf of the principal. Specifically, the broker must faithfully perform the agency agreement, be loyal to the principal, exercise competence, and account for all funds handled by him in performing the agency. The broker also has certain obligations toward the third parties dealt with. Let us look at these requirements more closely.

Faithful Performance

Faithful performance (also referred to as **obedience**) means that the agent is to obey all legal instructions given by the principal, and to apply best efforts and diligence to carry out the objectives of the agency. For a real estate broker this means performance as promised in the listing contract. A broker who promises to make a "reasonable effort" or apply "diligence" in finding a buyer and then does nothing to promote the listing gives the owner legal grounds for terminating the listing. Faithful performance also means not departing from the principal's instructions. If the agent does so (except in extreme emergencies not foreseen by the principal), it is at the agent's own risk. If the principal thereby suffers a loss, the agent is responsible for that loss. For example, a broker accepts a personal note from a buyer as an earnest money deposit, but fails to tell the seller that the deposit is not in cash. If the seller accepts the offer and the note is later found to be worthless, the broker is liable for the amount of the note.

Another aspect of faithful performance is that the agent must personally perform the tasks delegated to him. This protects the principal who has selected an agent on the basis of trust and confidence from finding that the agent has delegated that responsibility to another person. However, a major question arises on this point in real estate brokerage, as a large part of the success in finding a buyer for a property results from the cooperative efforts of other brokers and their salespeople. Therefore, listing agreements usually include a statement that the listing broker is authorized to secure the cooperation of other brokers and pay them part of the commission from the sale.

A genuine concern arises over how much information a real estate broker is free to disclose to other real estate brokers or other industry members who rely on this information in determining statistical data, market values, and other pertinent real-estate-related information. For instance, can a real estate agent maintain a confidential relationship with the principal, yet disclose pertinent details of sales prices and financing terms related to the principal's business?

Probably no other area of agency is as fertile a ground for lawsuits as the requirement that, once an agency is created, the agent must be loyal to his principal. The law is clear in all states that in a listing agreement the broker (and the broker's sales staff) occupies a position of trust, confidence, and responsibility. As such, the agent is legally bound to keep the property owner fully informed as to all matters that might affect the sale of the listed property and to promote and protect the owner's interests.

Loyalty to Principal

Unfortunately, greed and expediency sometimes get in the way. As a result, numerous laws have been enacted for the purpose of protecting the principal and threatening the agent with court action for misplaced loyalty. For example, an out-of-town landowner who is not fully up to date on the value of his land visits a local broker and wants to list it for $30,000. The broker is much more knowledgeable of local land prices and is aware of a recent city council decision to extend roads and utilities to the area of this property. As a result, the broker knows the land is now worth $50,000. The broker remains silent on the matter, and the property is listed for sale at $30,000. At this price the broker can find a buyer before the day is over and have a commission on the sale. However, the opportunity for a quick $20,000 is too tempting to let pass. He buys the property (or to cover up, buys in the name of his wife or a friend) and shortly thereafter resells it for $50,000. Whether he sold the property to a buyer for $30,000 or bought it and resold it for $50,000, the broker did not exhibit loyalty to the principal. Laws and penalties for breach of loyalty are stiff: the broker can be sued for recovery of the price difference and the commission paid, his real estate license can be suspended or revoked, and he may be required to pay additional fines and money damages.

If a licensee intends to purchase a property listed for sale by his agency or through a cooperating broker, he is under both a moral and a legal obligation to make certain that the price paid is the fair market value, and that the seller knows who the buyer is and that the buyer is a licensee.

Loyalty to the principal also means that when seeking a buyer or negotiating a sale, the broker must continue to protect the owner's financial interests. Suppose that an owner lists his home at $82,000 but confides in the broker, "If I cannot get

Protecting the Owner's Interest

$82,000, anything over $79,000 will be fine." The broker shows the home to a prospect who says, "Eighty-two thousand is too much. What will the owner really take?" or "Will he take seventy-nine thousand?" Loyalty to the principal requires the broker to say that the owner will take $82,000, for that is the price in the listing agreement. If the buyer balks, the broker can suggest that the buyer submit an offer for the seller's consideration. State laws require that all offers be submitted to the owner, no matter what the offering price and terms. This prevents the agent from rejecting an offer that the owner might have accepted if he had known about it. If the seller really intends for the broker to quote $79,000 as an acceptable price, the listing price should be changed; then the broker can say, "The property was previously listed for $82,000, but is now priced at $79,000."

A broker's loyalty to the principal includes keeping the principal informed of changes in market conditions during the listing period. If, after a listing is taken, an adjacent landowner is successful in rezoning his land to a higher use and the listed property becomes more valuable, the broker's responsibility is to inform the seller. Similarly, if a buyer is looking at a property priced at $30,000 and tells the broker, "I'll offer $27,000 and come up if need be," it is the duty of the broker to report this to the owner. The owner can then decide if he wants to accept the $27,000 offer or try for more. If the broker does not keep the owner fully informed, he is not properly fulfilling his duties as the owner's agent.

Although the law is clear in requiring the broker to report to the owner all facts that may have a bearing on the property's ultimate sale, it is less clear about the broker-buyer relationship. This ambiguity sometimes places the broker in a difficult position if a prospective buyer is not fully aware of this and thinks instead that the broker is the buyer's own agent in the transaction. It is true that the broker owes the buyer honesty, integrity, and fair business dealings, but the broker must also make it clear to the buyer that he is the agent of the owner, and therefore loyal to the owner. Otherwise the broker becomes a dual agent, in which case the law requires that he make this known to everyone concerned.

Many licensees take fiduciary duty somewhat lightly, not understanding how consumers truly rely on them and trust their judgment. These principals feel truly cheated when they get less than complete loyalty from their real estate agent.

The duty of **reasonable care** implies competence and expertise on the part of the broker. It is the broker's responsibility to disclose all knowledge and material facts concerning a property to the principal. Also, the broker must not become a party to any fraud or misrepresentation likely to affect the sound judgment of the principal.

Reasonable Care

Although the broker has a duty to disclose all material facts of a transaction, legal interpretations are to be avoided. Giving legal interpretations of documents involved in a transaction can be construed as practicing law without a license, an act specifically prohibited by real estate licensing acts. Moreover, the broker can be held financially responsible for any wrong legal information given to a client.

The duty of reasonable care also requires an agent to take proper care of property entrusted to him by his principal. For example, if a broker is entrusted with a key to an owner's building to show it to prospects, it is the broker's responsibility to see that it is used for only that purpose and that the building is locked upon leaving. Similarly, if a broker receives a check as an earnest money deposit, he must promptly deposit it in a bank and not carry it around for several weeks.

The earnest money that accompanies an offer on a property does not belong to the broker, even though the broker possesses a check made out to him or her. New York law does not require a broker to maintain a separate escrow, or trust, account for each down payment; however, the holder of escrow funds must segregate the buyer's down payment in a special account and maintain records that properly and accurately allocate all funds in the account. A broker's placement of money belonging to a client or customer into his or her own personal account is called **commingling.** Although some states require brokers to deposit down payments in interest-bearing accounts, New York does not. Department of State regulations prohibit any broker from retaining any interest earned on deposit monies unless it is applied toward the broker's commission.

Accounting for Funds Received

A broker's fiduciary obligations are to the principal who has employed him. State laws nonetheless make certain demands on the broker in relation to the third parties the broker deals with

Broker's Obligations to Third Parties

on behalf of the principal. Foremost among these are honesty, integrity, and fair business dealing. This includes the proper care of deposit money and offers, as well as responsibility for written or verbal statements. Misrepresenting a property by omitting vital information is as wrong as giving false information. Disclosure of such misconduct usually results in a broker losing the right to a commission. Also possible are loss of the broker's real estate license and a lawsuit by any party to the transaction who suffered a financial loss because of the misrepresentation.

In guarding against misrepresentation, a broker must be careful not to make statements not known to be true. For example, a prospect looks at a house listed for sale and asks if it is connected to the city sewer system. The broker does not know the answer, but sensing it is important to making a sale, says yes. If the prospect relies on this statement, purchases the house, and finds out that there is no sewer connection, the broker may be at the center of litigation regarding sale cancellation, commission loss, money damages, and state license discipline. The answer should be, "I don't know, but I will find out for you."

Suppose the seller has told the broker that the house is connected to the city sewer system, and the broker, having no reason to doubt the statement, accepts it in good faith and gives that information to prospective buyers. If this statement is not true, the owner is at fault, owes the broker a commission, and both the owner *and* the broker may be subject to legal action for sale cancellation and money damages. When a broker must rely on information supplied by the seller, it is best to have it in writing and verify its accuracy. However, relying on the seller for information does not completely relieve the broker's responsibility to third parties. If a seller says his house is connected to the city sewer system and the broker knows that is impossible because there is no sewer line on that street, it is the broker's responsibility to correct the erroneous statement.

Disclosure to Third Parties

In addition to fair and honest business dealings, real estate licensees are required to disclose latent defects in the property and to disclose any interest in the real estate held by the licensee. Although the licensee owes a duty of confidence and loyalty to the principal, he cannot be a part of any fraud on the principal's behalf. If the principal should request that the licensee make any misrepresentations, the licensee should terminate the employment and refuse to engage in any such acts.

Agency Disclosure

In the past, buyers often assumed that real estate agents who showed them a property were working on their behalf. However, unless a real estate salesperson has specifically agreed to act as the buyer's agent, the salesperson was acting as an agent or subagent of the seller. All too often, buyers wrongly assume that the salesperson's loyalty is to the buyer, when, in fact, the salesperson's legal duty is one of undivided loyalty to the seller.

Because of this widespread misunderstanding, New York law provides that all buyers and sellers of residential real estate must now sign an **agency disclosure form** explaining the duties of each real estate agent involved in the transaction to each party to the transaction, so that everyone understands who is representing whom. (See Figure 10.1.) The law requires the licensee to present this form to a potential buyer or seller on the **"first substantive contact."** Practically speaking, a listing agent must present the disclosure form to the seller when they first meet to discuss a listing. Any agent or subagent of the seller must ask a buyer to sign an acknowledgment form when a buyer asks to see a house. An agent of the buyer must present the disclosure form to a client before the buyer's agency agreement is signed or to a seller at the time of their first substantive contact, usually when the buyer comes to see the seller's house. In the event that either buyer or seller refuse to sign the disclosure form, the licensee can sign an affidavit stating that he attempted to obtain the signature and was refused. Copies of all disclosure forms signed during the course of the sale must be provided to the clients who signed them and retained for 3 years by the real estate broker. The parties to a real estate contract must again sign an agency disclosure form when they enter into a contract unless the contract is prepared and executed by the attorneys for the parties.

DUAL AGENCY

A licensee may act as the agent of both the buyer and the seller, but only with the informed, written consent of both parties. In this situation, the licensee is said to be acting as a dual agent. Before agreeing to this arrangement, the buyer and seller must understand this situation's consequences, the most important of which is that each party surrenders the right to the undivided loyalty of the agent.

Figure 10.1.

DISCLOSURE REGARDING REAL ESTATE AGENCY RELATIONSHIPS

Before you enter into a discussion with a real estate agent regarding a real estate transaction, you should understand what type of agency relationship you wish to have with that agent.

New York State law requires real estate licensees who are acting as agents of buyers or sellers of property to advise the potential buyers or sellers with whom they work of the nature of their agency relationship and the rights and obligations it creates.

SELLER'S OR LANDLORD'S AGENT

If you are interested in selling or leasing real property, you can engage a real estate agent as a seller's agent. A seller's agent, including a listing agent under a listing agreement with the seller, acts solely on behalf of the seller. You can authorize a seller's or landlord's agent to do other things including hire subagents, broker's agents, or work with other agents such as buyer's agents on a cooperative basis. A subagent is one who has agreed to work with the seller's agent, often through a multiple listing service. A subagent may work in a different real estate office.

A seller's agent has, without limitation, the following fiduciary duties to the seller: reasonable care, undivided loyalty, confidentiality, full disclosure, obedience, and a duty to account.

The obligations of a seller's agent are also subject to any specific provisions set forth in an agreement between the agent and the seller.

In dealings with the buyer, a seller's agent should (a) exercise reasonable skill and care in performance of the agent's duties; (b) deal honestly, fairly, and in good faith; and (c) disclose all facts known to the agent materially affecting the value or desirability of property, except as otherwise provided by law.

BUYER'S OR TENANT'S AGENT

If you are interested in buying or leasing real property, you can engage a real estate agent as a buyer's or tenant's agent. A buyer's agent acts solely on behalf of the buyer. You can authorize a buyer's agent to do other things including hire subagents, broker's agents, or work with other agents such as seller's agents on a cooperative basis.

A buyer's agent has, without limitation, the following fiduciary duties to the buyer: reasonable care, undivided loyalty, confidentiality, full disclosure, obedience, and a duty to account.

The obligations of a buyer's agent are also subject to any specific provisions set forth in an agreement between the agent and the buyer.

In dealings with the seller, a buyer's agent should (a) exercise reasonable skill and care in performance of the agent's duties; (b) deal honestly, fairly, and in good faith; and (c) disclose all facts known to the agent materially affecting the buyer's ability and/or willingness to perform a contract to acquire seller's property that are not inconsistent with the agent's fiduciary duties to the buyer.

BROKER'S AGENTS

As part of your negotiations with a real estate agent, you may authorize your agent to engage other agents whether you are a buyer/tenant or seller/landlord. As a general rule, those agents owe fiduciary duties to your agent and to you. You are not vicariously liable for their conduct.

AGENT REPRESENTING BOTH SELLER AND BUYER

A real estate agent acting directly or through an associated licensee, can be the agent of both the seller/landlord and the buyer/tenant in a transaction, but only with the knowledge and informed consent, in writing, of both the seller/landlord and the buyer/tenant.

In such a dual agency situation, the agent will not be able to provide the full range of fiduciary duties to the buyer/tenant and seller/landlord.

The obligations of an agent are also subject to any specific provisions set forth in an agreement between the agent and the buyer/tenant and seller/landlord.

An agent acting as a dual agent must explain carefully to both the buyer/tenant and seller/landlord that the agent is acting for the other party as well. The agent should also explain the possible effects of dual representation including that by consenting to the dual agency relationship, the buyer/tenant and seller/landlord are giving up their right to undivided loyalty.

A BUYER/TENANT OR SELLER/LANDLORD SHOULD CAREFULLY CONSIDER THE POSSIBLE CONSEQUENCES OF A DUAL AGENCY RELATIONSHIP BEFORE AGREEING TO SUCH REPRESENTATION

GENERAL CONSIDERATIONS

You should carefully read all agreements to ensure that they adequately express your understanding of the transaction. A real estate agent is a person qualified to advise about real estate. If legal, tax, or other advice is desired consult a competent professional in that field.

Throughout the transaction you may receive more than one disclosure form. The law requires that each agent assisting in the transaction present you with this disclosure form. You should read its contents each time it is presented to you, considering the relationship between you and the real estate agent in your specific transaction.

Figure 10.1. (continued)

ACKNOWLEDGMENT OF PROSPECTIVE BUYER/TENANT

(1) I have received and read this disclosure notice.
(2) I understand that a seller's/landlord's agent, including a listing agent, is the agent of the seller/landlord exclusively, unless the seller/landlord and buyer/tenant otherwise agree.
(3) I understand that subagents, including subagents participating in a multiple listing service, are agents of the seller/landlord exclusively.
(4) I understand that I may engage my own agent to be my buyer's/tenant's broker.
(5) I understand that the agent presenting this form to me,

_____ of
(name of licensee)

_____ is
(name of firm)

(check applicable relationship)
____ an agent of the seller/landlord
____ my agent as a buyer's/tenant's agent

Dated:
Buyer/Tenant:

Dated:
Buyer/Tenant:

ACKNOWLEDGMENT OF PROSPECTIVE SELLER/LANDLORD

(1) I have received and read this disclosure notice.
(2) I understand that a seller's/landlord's agent, including a listing agent, is the agent of the seller/landlord exclusively, unless the seller/landlord and buyer/tenant otherwise agree.
(3) I understand that subagents, including subagents participating in a multiple listing service, are agents of the seller/landlord exclusively.
(4) I understand that a buyer's/tenant's agent is the agent of the buyer/tenant exclusively.
(5) I understand that the agent presenting this form to me,

_____ of
(name of licensee)

_____ is
(name of firm)

(check applicable relationship)
____ an agent of the seller's/landlord's agent
____ an agent of the buyer/tenant

Dated:
Seller/Landlord:

Dated:
Seller/Landlord:

ACKNOWLEDGMENT OF PROSPECTIVE BUYER/TENANT AND SELLER/LANDLORD TO DUAL AGENCY

(1) I have received and read this disclosure notice.
(2) I understand that a dual agent will be working for both the seller/landlord and buyer/tenant.
(3) I understand that I may engage my own agent as a seller's/landlord's agent or a buyer's/tenant's agent.
(4) I understand that I am giving up my right to the agent's undivided loyalty.
(5) I have carefully considered the possible consequences of a dual agency relationship.
(6) I understand that the agent presenting this form to me,

_____ of
(name of licensee)

_____ is
(name of firm)

a dual agent working for both the buyer/tenant and seller/landlord, acting as such with the consent of both the buyer/tenant and the seller/landlord and following full disclosure to the buyer/tenant and seller/landlord.

Dated:
Buyer/Tenant:

Dated:
Buyer/Tenant:

Dated:
Seller/Landlord:

Dated:
Seller/Landlord:

ACKNOWLEDGMENT OF THE PARTIES TO THE CONTRACT

(1) I have received, read, and understand the disclosure notice.
(2) I understand that _____ of
(name of licensee)

_____ is
(name of firm)

(check applicable relationship)
____ an agent of the seller/landlord
____ an agent of the buyer/tenant
____ a dual agent working for both buyer/tenant and seller/landlord, acting as such with the consent of both buyer/tenant and seller/landlord and following full disclosure to the buyer/tenant and seller/landlord.

I also understand that _____ of
(name of licensee)

_____ is
(name of firm)

(check applicable relationship)
____ an agent of the seller/landlord
____ an agent of the buyer/tenant
____ a dual agent working for both buyer/tenant and seller/landlord, acting as such with the consent of both buyer/tenant and seller/landlord and following full disclosure to the buyer/tenant and seller/landlord.

Dated:
Buyer/Tenant:

Dated:
Buyer/Tenant:

Dated:
Seller/Landlord:

Dated:
Seller/Landlord:

BUYER AGENCY

As stated in the foregoing, many agency relationships presume that the real estate broker represents the seller. In those situations where the broker represents the buyer, however, it is important to note that the same fiduciary duties (performance, accounting, reasonable care, and loyalty) presumably apply between the real estate broker and the buyer; the seller, in turn, becomes the third party. This creates a situation in which the seller is represented by the listing broker, but the buyer is represented by the buyer's broker. There are two areas of genuine concern: (1) the seller may take the cooperating broker into confidence because he or she thinks the cooperating broker represents the seller instead of the buyer; and (2) the listing broker may take the cooperating broker into confidence, relying on the presumption of subagency under the MLS system. In either case, this could result in a detrimental reliance. Therefore, the broker representing the buyer is required to disclose to the listing broker and seller immediately, if not sooner, that he or she represents the buyer in order to eliminate the potential for such a detrimental reliance. This disclosure must take place "at the first substantive contact" between the buyer's agent and the agent or subagent of the seller. This must be in the form of a written disclosure to the listing broker and seller. It would also be prudent to insert the buyer representation in the earnest money contract.

Disclosure of Material Facts

The agency disclosure form also highlights for consumers the agents' duties to disclose material facts relating to the sale. It tells a buyer that a seller's agent should disclose facts affecting the value or desirability of the property and tells the seller that the buyer's agent must be forthcoming about the buyer's ability and willingness to enter into a sales contract. Although the licensee owes a duty of confidence and loyalty to his principal, he cannot be a part of any fraud on the principal's behalf. If his principal should request that the licensee make any misrepresentations, the licensee should terminate his employment and refuse to engage in any such acts.

OWNER DISCLOSURE STATEMENT

Seller disclosure statements provide a detailed disclosure of house defects (or lack thereof) on a form often produced by a real estate trade association. The seller needs to fill out the forms, which are then presented to the buyer as a representation of the seller's statement of condition of the property. The seller is the most likely person to fill out the disclosure because the seller simply knows more about the property than anybody else. To date only three states (Maine, Texas, and California) have mandated seller disclosure statements. Twenty-four states recommend them but do not require them. Seven states require owner disclosures about health hazards, and 18 states are considering mandatory disclosures. The risks of using the form are nominal and the benefits are great.

In the last 10 years there has been extensive litigation involving the sales of real property based on misrepresentations and material omissions. When buyers sue, brokers often find themselves as defendants, because the seller is gone and the broker marketed the property. This creates an unfair burden on a broker who has neither knowledge of the defect nor the expertise to investigate the potential for defects.

For the seller's benefit, the seller disclosure form makes it necessary for the seller to reinvestigate the house. Very few of us have perfect homes. Many sellers simply overlook the defects (we all learn to live with them or forget about them, particularly when it's our house). This failure to disclose, however, results in misrepresentation on the part of the seller because of negligence or perhaps because the particular defect was innocently overlooked. In the worst case scenario, the seller may intentionally misrepresent, or intentionally fail to mention, a defect in order to induce the buyer to purchase. In all circumstances, the seller's disclosure form yields these benefits: (1) it informs the buyer as to which defects exist, (2) it provides a basis from which the buyer can conduct further investigation on the property, (3) it allows the buyer to make an informed decision as to whether or not to purchase, and (4) it may provide a more concrete basis for litigation if the buyer can determine that the seller filled out the disclosure statement incorrectly or failed to disclose a defect that the seller knew was material.

Similarly, brokers can find the disclosure statement beneficial because they now have written proof as to what disclosures were made to them (which should be compared with their listing agreement and the MLS disclosures) to assure consistency in marketing their product. In addition, knowing that there is a defect allows the broker to effectively market the property, disclosing the defects and therefore limiting liability for both the seller (they sometimes overlook potential liability in their eagerness to sell) and the broker.

Property Disclosure
Statements

The federal government, through the Department of Housing and Urban Development (HUD), has enacted legislation aimed at protecting purchasers of property in new subdivisions from misrepresentation, fraud, and deceit. The HUD requirements, administered by the Office of Interstate Land Sales Registration, apply primarily to subdivision lots located in one state and sold to residents of another state. The purpose of this law, which took effect in 1969 and was amended in 1979, is to require that developers give prospective purchasers extensive disclosures regarding the lots in the form of a **property report.**

The requirement that a property report be prepared according to HUD specifications was the response of Congress to the concern that all too often buyers were receiving inaccurate or inadequate information. For example, a color brochure might be handed to prospects picturing an artificial lake and boat marina within the subdivision, yet the developer has not obtained the necessary permits to build either and may never do so. A developer might imply that the lots being offered for sale are ready for building when in fact there is no sewer system and the soil cannot handle septic tanks. Prospects may not be told that many roads in the subdivision will not be built for several years, and that, when they are lot owners, they will face hefty paving assessments followed by annual maintenance fees because the county has no intention of maintaining the roads as public.

Property Report   In addition to addressing the aforementioned issues, the property report also discloses payment terms, what happens in the case of a default, any soil problems, distance to schools and stores, any additional costs to expect, availability of utilities, restrictive covenants, oil and mineral rights, etc. The property report must be given to each purchaser before a contract to purchase is signed. Failure to do so gives the purchaser the right to cancel any contract or agreement.

Not an Approval   The property report is *not* a government approval of the subdivision. It is strictly a disclosure of pertinent facts that the prospective purchaser is strongly encouraged to read before buying. A number of states have enacted their own disclosure laws. Typically these apply to developers of housing subdivisions, condominiums, cooperatives, and vacant lots. In these reports the developer is required to make a number of pertinent disclosures about the lot, structure, owners' association, neighborhood, financing terms, etc., and this must be given to the prospective purchaser before a purchase contract can be signed. Once signed, HUD and most states allow the buyer a "cooling-off" period of from 3 to 7 days during which the buyer can cancel the contract and receive all money back. Like the HUD property report, a state-required property report does not mean the state has approved or disapproved the subdivision. The property report is strictly a disclosure statement designed to help the prospective purchaser make an informed decision about buying.

Puffing refers to nonfactual or extravagant statements that a reasonable person would recognize as exaggeration. Thus, buyers may have no legal complaint against a broker who told them that a certain hillside lot had the most beautiful view in the world or that a listed property had the finest landscaping in the county. Usually reasonable buyers can see these things and make up their own mind. However, if a broker, in showing a rural property, says it has the world's purest well water, there had better be plenty of good water when the buyer moves in. If a consumer believes the broker and relies on the representation, the broker may have a potential liability. The line between puffing and misrepresentation is subjective. Avoid puffing.

Puffing

A broker's sales associates are general agents of the broker. A sales associate owes the broker the duties of competence, obedience, accounting, loyalty, and full disclosure. The broker's obligations to the sales associate are compensation, reimbursement, indemnification, and performance. In addition, the broker will authorize the extent to which the sales associate can bind the broker. For example, is the sales associate's signature by itself sufficient to bind the broker to a listing or must the broker also sign it? With regard to third parties, the sales associate owes them honesty, integrity, and fair business dealings. Because a sales associate is an agent of the broker and the broker is an agent of the principal, the sales associate is called a **subagent** of the principal.

Broker's Sales Staff

The principal also has certain obligations to the agent. Although these do not receive much statutory attention in most states, they

PRINCIPAL'S OBLIGATIONS

are important when the principal fails to live up to those obligations. The principal's primary obligation is **compensation.** Additionally, the agent is eligible for **reimbursement** for expenses not related to the sale itself. For example, if an agent had to pay a plumber to fix a broken pipe for the owner, the agent could expect reimbursement from the owner over and above the sales commission.

The other two obligations of the principal are indemnification and performance. Agents are entitled to **indemnification** upon suffering a loss through no fault of their own, such as when a misrepresentation by the principal to the agent was passed on in good faith to the buyer. The duty of **performance** means the principal is expected to do whatever can reasonably be done to accomplish the purpose of the agency, such as referring inquiries by prospective buyers to the broker.

ANTITRUST LAWS

Federal antitrust laws, particularly the Sherman Antitrust Act, have made a major impact on the real estate brokerage industry. The purpose of federal antitrust laws is to promote competition in an open marketplace. To some people not familiar with the real estate business, it could appear that all real estate brokers charge the same fee (*e.g.,* 6%). In fact and in practice, nothing is further from the truth. Real estate brokers establish their fees from a complex integration of market factors, and all real estate brokerage fees are a result of a negotiated agreement between the owner and the broker. In tougher markets a broker may charge a much higher fee (10% to 12% of the gross sales price). Very expensive property in a good market may be listed by a broker for an amount that is substantially less (2% to 5% of the gross sales price).

Price Fixing

Price fixing in any industry is so grossly anticompetitive and contrary to the free enterprise form of government, that price fixing is construed to be **per se** illegal. This means that the conduct of price fixing is, in itself, so illegal that no series of mitigating circumstances can correct it. Although a brokerage company can establish a policy on fees, they should be acutely aware that any hint, or any perceived hint, of price fixing among brokers can result in both civil and criminal penalties, i.e., if the court determines that a broker has engaged in price fixing with another broker or group of brokers, the licensee could serve time in the federal penitentiary in addition to paying a substantial fine. Consequently, brokers are well advised *never* to discuss their fees, under *any* circumstances, except with the owner of the property.

Another aspect of antitrust laws that has affected brokers has been boycotting of other brokers in the marketplace. This, too, is a violation of the Sherman Antitrust Act. In some circumstances, realtor trade associations have established rules for membership (e.g., unreasonably high fees) that have resulted in some brokers being unfairly excluded (e.g., those with part-time agents, "discount" brokers, etc.). Standards for membership are usually an attempt to upgrade the professionalism of the industry and maintain high standards. The difficulty encountered, however, is that when high-quality real estate brokers are excluded from competing with members of broker trade associations this results in an unfair market advantage for members. Antitrust cases involving boycotting have tended to recognize the procompetitive efforts of Boards of REALTORS®, MLS systems, and other similar trade associations, however. Therefore, Boards of REALTORS® and other trade associations can establish reasonable fees, residency requirements, and other pertinent requirements for membership. However no membership requirements can be established which may arbitrarily exclude licensed real estate brokers from participation.

Boycotting

Because of the trend in recent years to a more consumer-oriented and more litigious society, the possibility of a broker being sued has risen to the point that **errors and omission insurance (E&O)** has become very popular. The broker pays an annual fee to an insurance company that in turn will defend the broker and pay legal costs and judgments. Most E&O policies, as they are sometimes called, do not cover intentional acts of a broker to deceive, punitive damages, fraud, negligence, or misrepresentation when buying or selling for one's own account. Other than that, E&O offers quite broad coverage. This includes defending so-called nuisance cases in which the broker may not be at fault but must defend anyway. Moreover, E&O covers not only courtroom costs and judgments, but pretrial conferences and negotiations and out-of-court settlements. To-

ERRORS AND OMISSION INSURANCE

day E&O is simply a cost of the real estate business like rent, telephone, and automobile expenses.

VOCABULARY REVIEW

*Match terms **a–o** with statements **1–15**.*

a. *Buyer's broker*
b. *Commingling*
c. *Dual agency*
d. *Fiduciary relationship*
e. *Implied authority*
f. *Middleman*
g. *Principal*
h. *Property report*
i. *Price fixing*
j. *Boycotting*
k. *Sales associate*
l. *Special agency*
m. *Subagent*
n. *Third parties*
o. *Trust account*

1. A person who authorizes another to act.
2. Persons who are not parties to a contract but who may be affected by it.
3. An agency created for the performance of specific acts only.
4. A person who brings two or more parties together but does not assist in conducting negotiations.
5. One broker representing two or more parties in a transaction.
6. Mixing of clients' or customers' funds with an agent's personal funds.
7. Two or more listing brokers agreeing to charge a 7% commission.
8. A licensed salesperson or broker who works for a broker.
9. Agency authority arising from industry custom, common usage, and conduct of the parties involved.
10. A relationship that requires trust, honesty, and exercise of good business judgment.
11. A separate account for holding clients' and customers' money.
12. Refusing to work with another broker because of an arbitrary set of rules.
13. The agency relationship of a broker's sales associate to the seller.
14. A broker employed by and therefore loyal to the buyer.
15. Government-required information that must be given to purchasers in subdivisions.

QUESTIONS AND PROBLEMS

1. The laws of agency require that the agent be faithful and loyal to the principal. What does this mean to a real estate broker who has just taken a listing? What does it mean when a real estate broker represents the buyer?
2. What does broker cooperation refer to? How is it achieved?
3. When we speak of the laws of agency, to what are we referring?
4. What is an agency coupled with an interest?
5. What is the purpose of a property disclosure statement?
6. What is the purpose of errors and omissions insurance?

Agency Relationships in Real Estate, by **John W. Reilly** (Real Estate Education Company, 1987, 191 pages). Excellent treatment of the law of agency, written for real estate agents. Examines many fact situations and recommends good office procedure.

Real Estate Brokerage Management, 2nd Ed., by **Bruce Lindemann** (Prentice Hall, 1988, 320 pages). Focuses on practical application of management techniques and organizational form in the small to medium-sized residential firm.

Real Estate Ethics, 2nd Ed., by **William H. Pivar** (Real Estate Education Company, 1989, 160 pages). Discusses how to apply the REALTOR® Code of Ethics to a variety of fact situations.

ADDITIONAL READINGS

11

Real Estate Leases

KEY • TERMS

Assignment: the total transfer of the lessee's rights to another party

CPM, RPA: professional designations for property managers

Gross lease: lease in which tenant pays a fixed rent and the landlord pays all property expenses

Holdover tenant: one who stays beyond the term of the lease without the landlord's consent

Leasehold estate: a tenant's right to occupy a building or land

Lessee: the tenant

Lessor: the landlord

Net lease: lease in which tenant pays a base rent plus maintenance, property taxes, and insurance

Option clause: provision in a lease that gives the right at some future time to purchase or lease a property at a predetermined price

Quiet enjoyment: the right of possession and use of property without undue disturbance by others

Reversion: the right to retake possession at a future date

Sublessee: a lessee who rents from another lessee

Sublessor: a lessee who rents to another lessee

Sublet: to transfer only a portion of one's lease rights

Other chapters of this book discuss leases as estates in land (Chapter 5) and as a means of financing (Chapter 19). This chapter will look at leases from the standpoint of the tenant, the property owner, and the property manager. (During your lifetime you will be in one of these roles and perhaps all three.) Our discussion will begin with some important terminology. Then comes a sample lease document with explanation, plus information on locating, qualifying, and keeping tenants. The chapter concludes with information on job opportunities available in professional property management. Emphasis will be on residential property although a number of key points regarding commercial property leases will also be included.

A lease conveys to the **lessee** (tenant) the right to possess and use another's property for a period of time. During this time the **lessor** (the landlord or fee owner) possesses a **reversion** that entitles him or her to retake possession at the end of the lease period. Notice that a lease separates the right to use property from the property's ownership. The tenant gets the use of the property during the lease period and pays rent. The property owner is denied use of the property but receives rent in return. At the end of the lease the property owner gets the use of the property back but no more rent. The tenant no longer has the use of the property and no longer pays rent. This chapter describes how this very simple idea is carried out in practice.

THE LEASEHOLD ESTATE

A tenant's right to occupy land and/or buildings thereon is called a **leasehold estate.** The two most commonly found leasehold estates are the periodic estate and the estate for years. The periodic estate is one that continually renews itself for like periods of time until the tenant or landlord act to terminate it. A **month-to-month lease** is an example of this. An **estate for years** is a lease with a specific starting date and a specific ending date. It can be for any length of time, and it does not automatically renew itself. A lease for 1 year is an example. There are two other leasehold categories: estate at will and tenancy at sufferance. An **estate at will,** which is rarely found, can be terminated by either tenant or landlord at any time. For example, the owner of a rental house decides to sell it upon expiration of the current lease. The owner and tenant agree that the tenant will be able to continue to rent until the house is sold. A **tenancy at sufferance** occurs when a tenant stays beyond the legal tenancy without the consent of the landlord. The tenant is commonly called a **holdover tenant** and no advance notice is required for eviction. A holdover tenant differs from a trespasser only in that the original entry onto the property was legal.

CREATING A VALID LEASE

A lease is both a conveyance and a contract. As a conveyance it conveys rights of possession to the tenant in the form of a leasehold estate. As a contract it contains provisions for the payment of rent and any other obligations the landlord and tenant have to each other.

For a valid lease to exist, it must meet the usual requirements of a contract as described in Chapter 8. That is to say, the parties involved must be legally competent and there must be mutual agreement, lawful objective, and sufficient consideration. The main elements of a lease are: (1) the names of the lessee and lessor, (2) a description of the premises, (3) an agreement to convey (let) the premises by the lessor and to accept possession by the lessee, (4) provisions for the payment of rent, (5) the starting date and duration of the lease, and (6) signatures of the parties to the lease.

In most states, including New York, a lease for a term longer than 1 year must be in writing to be enforceable in court. A lease for 1 year or less or a month-to-month lease could be oral and still be valid, but as a matter of good business practice, any lease should be put in writing and signed. This gives all parties involved a written reminder of their obligations under the lease and reduces chances for dispute.

THE LEASE DOCUMENT

Figure 11.1 illustrates a lease document that contains provisions typically found in a residential lease. These provisions are presented in simplified language to help you more easily grasp the rights and responsibilities created by a lease.

Conveyance

The first paragraph is the conveyance portion of the lease. At [1] and [2] the lessor and lessee are identified. At [3] the lessor conveys to the lessee and the lessee accepts the property. A description of the property follows at [4] and the *term* of the conveyance at [5]. The property must be described so that there is no question as to the extent of the premises the lessee is

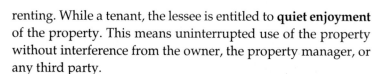

renting. While a tenant, the lessee is entitled to **quiet enjoyment** of the property. This means uninterrupted use of the property without interference from the owner, the property manager, or any third party.

If the lease illustrated here was a month-to-month lease, the wording at **[5]** would be changed to read, "commencing April 15, 19xx and continuing on a month-to-month basis until terminated by either the lessee or the lessor." A month-to-month rental is a very flexible arrangement. It allows the owner to recover possession of the property on 1-month notice and the tenant to leave on 1-month notice with no further obligation to the owner. In rental agreements for longer periods of time, each party gives up some flexibility to gain commitment from the other. Under a 1-year lease the owner commits the property to the tenant for a year. In return the tenant is committed to paying rent for a full year. In like manner, the owner has the tenant's commitment to pay rent for a year but loses the flexibility of being able to regain possession of the property until the year is over.

The balance of the lease document is concerned with contract aspects of the lease. At **[6]** the amount of rent that the lessee will pay for the use of the property is set forth. In an estate for years the usual practice is to state the total rent for the entire lease period. This is the total number of dollars the lessee is obligated to pay to the lessor. The lessee can vacate the premises before the lease period expires but is still liable for the full amount of the contract. The method of payment of the obligation is shown at **[7]**. Unless the contract calls for rent to be paid in advance, under common law it is not due until the end of the rental period. At **[8]** the lessor has taken a deposit in the form of the first monthly installment and acknowledges receipt of it. The lessor has also taken additional money as security against the possibility of uncollected rent or damage to the premises and for clean-up expenses. (The tenant is supposed to leave the premises clean.) The deposit is refunded, less legitimate charges, when the tenant leaves.

Items **[9]** through **[20]** summarize commonly found lease clauses. At **[9]** and **[10]** the lessor wants to maintain control over the use and occupancy of the premises. Without this, the land-

Contract

Figure 11.1.

LEASE

This lease agreement is entered into the __10th__ day of April , 19 _xx_ between[1]_John and Sally Landlord_ (hereinafter called the Lessor) and[2]_Gary and Barbara Tenant_ (hereinafter called the Lessee).[3] The Lessor hereby leases to the Lessee and the Lessee hereby leases from the Lessor the premises known as [4]__Apartment 24, 1234 Maple St., City, State__ for the term of[5]_one_ year beginning 12:00 noon on __April 15, 19xx__ and ending 12:00 noon on __April 15, 19xx__ unless sooner terminated as herein set forth.

The rent for the term of this lease is __$ 6,000.00__ [6] payable in equal monthly installments of __$ 500.00__[7]on the __15th__ day of each month beginning on __April 15, 19xx__. Receipt of the first monthly installment and __$ 500.00__ [8] as a security, damage, and clean-up deposit is hereby acknowledged. It is furthermore agreed that:

[9] The use of the premises shall be as a residential dwelling for the above named Lessee only.

[10] The Lessee may not assign this lease or sublet any portion of the premises without written permission from the Lessor.

[11] The Lessee agrees to abide by the house rules as posted. A current copy is attached to this lease.

[12]The Lessor shall furnish water, sewer, and heat as part of the rent. Electricity and telephone shall be paid for by the Lessee.

[13] The Lessor agrees to keep the premises structure maintained and in habitable condition.

[14] The Lessee agrees to maintain the interior of said premises and at the termination of this lease to return said premises to the Lessor in as good condition as it is now except for ordinary wear and tear.

[15]The Lessee shall not make any alterations or improvements to the premises without the Lessor's prior written consent. Any alterations or improvements become the property of the Lessor at the end of this lease.

Figure 11.1. (continued)

[16] *If the premises are not ready for occupancy on the date herein provided, the Lessee may cancel this agreement and the Lessor shall return in full all money paid by the Lessee.*

[17] *If the Lessee defaults on this lease agreement, the Lessor may give the Lessee three days notice of intention to terminate the lease. At the end of those three days the lease shall terminate and the Lessee shall vacate and surrender the premises to the Lessor.*

[18] *If the Lessee holds over after the expiration of this lease without the Lessor's consent, the tenancy shall be month to month at twice the monthly rate indicated herein.*

[19] *If the premises are destroyed or rendered uninhabitable by fire or other cause, this lease shall terminate as of the date of the casualty.*

[20] *The Lessor shall have access to the premises for the purpose of inspecting for damage, making repairs, and showing to prospective tenants or buyers.*

[21] John Landlord
Lessor

Sally Landlord
Lessor

[22] Gary Tenant
Lessee

Barbara Tenant
Lessee

lords might find the premises used for an entirely different purpose or by people they did not rent to. At **[11]** the tenant agrees to abide by the house rules. These normally cover such things as use of laundry and trash facilities, swimming pool rules, noise rules, and so on. Number **[12]** states the responsibility of the lessee and lessor with regard to the payment of utilities.

A strict legal interpretation of a lease as a conveyance means the tenant is responsible for upkeep and repairs unless the lessor promises in the lease contract to take care of these expenses. The paragraph at **[13]** is that promise. Consumerism has had a profound influence on this matter. Courts and legislatures now take the position that the landlord is obligated to keep a residential property repaired and habitable even though this is not specifically stated in the contract. (Commercial property still goes by the strict interpretation—that is, landlords must promise upkeep and repairs or tenants don't get them.)

Number [14] is the tenant's promise to maintain the interior of the dwelling. If the tenant damages the property, the tenant must repair or pay for it. Normal wear and tear are considered to be part of the rent. At paragraph [15] the landlords protect themselves against unauthorized alterations and improvements and then go on to point out that anything the tenant affixes to the building becomes realty. As realty, it remains a part of the building when the tenant leaves.

Paragraphs [16] through [19] deal with the rights of both parties if the premises are not ready for occupancy, if the lessee defaults after moving in, if the lessee holds over, or if the premises are destroyed. The lessor also retains the right (paragraph [20]) to enter the leased premises from time to time for business purposes.

Finally, at [21] and [22], the lessor and lessee sign. These signatures do not need to be notarized unless the lease is to be recorded. In that case only the lessor's signature is notarized. The purpose of recording is to give constructive notice that the lessee has an estate in the property. Normally, recording is done only when the lessee's rights are not apparent from inspection of the property or where the lease is to run for more than 3 years. From the property owner's standpoint, the lease is an encumbrance on the property. If the owner should subsequently sell the property or mortgage it, the lessee's tenancy remains undisturbed. The buyer or lender must accept the property subject to the lease.

If one of the lessors dies, the lease is still binding on the remaining lessor(s) and the estate of the deceased lessor. Similarly, if one of the lessees dies, the lease is still binding on the remaining lessee(s) and the estate of the deceased lessee. This practice is based on common law doctrine that applies to contracts in general (see Chapter 8, "Deceased Party"). The lessee and lessor can, however, agree to do otherwise. The lessee could ask the lessor to **waive** (give up) the right to hold the lessee's estate to the lease in the event of the lessee's death. For example, an elderly tenant about to sign a lease might want to add wording to the lease whereby the tenant's death would allow his estate to terminate the lease early.

LANDLORD-TENANT LAWS

Traditionally, courts have been strict interpreters of lease agreements. This philosophy still prevails for leases on commercial property. However, with regard to residential rental property, the trend today is for state legislatures to establish special landlord-tenant laws. The intent is to strike a reasonable balance between the responsibilities of landlords to tenants and vice versa. New York's Landlord and Tenant Laws can be found in Article 7 of the Real Property Law. Typically, these laws limit the amount of security deposit a landlord can require, tell the tenant how many days notice must be given before vacating a periodic tenancy, and require the landlord to deliver possession on the date agreed. The landlord must maintain the premises in a fit condition for living, and the tenant is to keep the unit clean and not damage it. The tenant is to obey the house rules, and the landlord must give advance notice before entering an apartment except in legitimate emergencies. Additionally, the laws set forth such things as the procedure for accounting for any deposit money not returned, the right of the tenant to make needed repairs and bill the landlord, the right of the landlord to file court actions for unpaid rent, and the proper procedure for evicting a tenant.

Several methods are used for setting rents. The most common is the **gross lease.** Under a gross lease, the tenant pays a fixed rent and the landlord pays all the operating expenses of the property. A tenant paying $450 per month on a month-to-month apartment lease or a person paying $12,000 per year for a 1-year house lease are both examples of fixed rents.

SETTING RENTS

A landlord will usually agree to a level rent for one year, but what happens if the tenant wants a longer lease term such as 2 years, 5 years, 10 years, 25 years, or 99 years? For these situations the following rent-setting methods are used in the real estate industry. The simplest approach is to have a **step-up** or **graduated rent.** For example, a 5-year office lease might call for monthly rents of 90 cents per square foot of floor space the first year, 95 cents the second year, $1.00 the third year, $1.05 the fourth year, and $1.10 the fifth. A residential tenant wishing a 2-year lease might find the landlord more receptive if the monthly rent were stepped up the second year.

Office and industrial leases of 5 or more years often include an **escalator** or **participation clause,** which allows the landlord to pass along to the tenant increases in such items as property taxes, utility charges, and maintenance. A variation is to have the tenant pay for all property taxes, insurance, repairs, utilities, and so on in addition to the base rent. This arrangement is called a **net lease** or a **triple net lease.** It is commonly used when an entire building is being leased and for long-term ground leases.

Another system for setting rents is the **percentage lease** wherein the owner receives a percentage of the tenant's gross receipts as rent. For example, a farmer who leases land may give the landowner 20% of the value of the crop when it is sold. The monthly rent for a small hardware store might be $600 plus 6% of gross sales above $10,000. A gasoline station may pay $1,000 plus 2¢ per gallon pumped. A supermarket may pay $7,500 plus 1½% of gross above $50,000 per month.

Still another way of setting rents on long-term leases is to create an **index lease** to index the rent to some economic indicator, such as an inflation index. If there is inflation, rents increase; if there is deflation, rents decrease. Arrangements such as step-ups, escalators, percentages, indexes, and net leases are all efforts by landlords to protect against rising costs of property operation and declining purchasing power, yet meet tenant's needs to have property committed to them for more than a year.

OPTION CLAUSES

Option clauses give the tenant the right at some future time to purchase or lease the property at a predetermined price. This gives a tenant flexibility. For example, suppose that a prospective tenant is starting a new business and is not certain how successful it will be. Therefore, in looking for space to rent, he will want a lease that allows an "out" if the new venture does not succeed, but will permit him to stay if the venture is successful. The solution is a lease with options. The landlord could offer a 1-year lease, plus an option to stay for 2 more years at a higher rent plus a second option for an additional 5 years at a still higher rent. If the venture is not successful, the tenant is obligated for only 1 year. But if successful, he has the option of staying 2 more years, and if still successful, for 5 years after that.

Another option possibility is to offer the tenant a lease that also contains an option to buy the property for a fixed period of time at a preset price. This is called a *lease with option to buy* and is discussed in Chapter 9.

Unless otherwise provided in the lease contract, a lessee may assign the lease or sublet. An **assignment** is the total transfer of the lessee's rights to another person. These parties are referred to as the **assignor** and the **assignee,** respectively. The assignee acquires all the right, title, and interest of the assignor, no more and no less. However, the assignor remains liable for the performance of the contract unless released in writing by the landlord.

To **sublet** means to transfer only a portion of the rights held under a lease. The **sublease** thereby created may be for a portion of the premises or part of the lease term. The party acquiring those rights is called the **sublessee.** The original lessee is the **sublessor** with respect to the sublessee. The sublessee pays rent to the lessee, who in turn remains liable to the landlord for rent on the entire premises.

ASSIGNMENT AND SUBLETTING

A **ground lease** is a lease of land alone. The lessor is the fee simple owner of the land and conveys to the lessee an estate for years typically lasting from 25 to 99 years. The lessee pays for and owns the improvements. Thus a ground lease separates the ownership of land from the ownership of buildings on that land. The lease rent, called the **ground rent,** is on a net lease basis. As a hedge against inflation, the rent is usually increased every 10 to 25 years, either by a graduated lease or by requiring a reappraisal of the land and then charging a new rent based on that valuation. Ground leases for residential properties can be found in Baltimore, Maryland; Orange County, California; and the state of Hawaii. Mostly, however, they are used for commercial and industrial properties such as office buildings, shopping centers, motels, and warehouses.

GROUND LEASE

A lease need not be restricted to the use of the earth's surface. In Chapter 4, it was shown that land extends from the center of the earth skyward. Consequently it is possible for one person to own the mineral rights, another the surface rights, and a third the air rights. The same possibilities exist with leases. A landowner can lease to an oil company the right to find and extract oil and gas below the surface and at the same time lease the surface rights to a farmer. In Chicago and New York City, railroads have leased surface and air rights above their downtown tracks for the purpose of constructing high-rise office buildings.

VERTICAL LEASE

CONTRACT RENT,
ECONOMIC RENT

The amount of rent that the tenant must pay the landlord for the use of the premises is called the **contract rent.** The rent that a property can command in the competitive open market is called the **economic rent.** When a lease contract is negotiated, the contract rent and economic rent are nearly always the same. However, as time passes, the market value of the right to use the premises may rise above the contract rent. When this occurs, the leasehold estate itself becomes valuable. That value is determined by the difference between the contract rent and the economic rent, and how long the lease has to run. An example would be a 5-year lease with 3 years left at a contract rent of $600 per month where the current rental value of the premises is now $800 per month. If the lease is assignable, the fact that it offers a $200-per-month savings for 3 years makes it valuable. Similarly, an oil lease obtained for $50 per acre before oil was discovered might be worth millions after its discovery. Conversely, when contract rent exceeds economic rent, the lease takes on a negative value.

LEASE TERMINATION

Most leases terminate because the term of the lease expires. The tenant has received the use of the premises and the landlord has received rent in return. However, a lease can be terminated if the landlord and the tenant mutually agree. The tenant surrenders the premises and the landlord releases him from the contract. This should, of course, be done in writing.

Eviction

If a tenant fails to live up to the terms of the lease agreement, the landlord has grounds for eviction. Usually this is for nonpayment of rent, but it could also be for violation of some other aspect of the agreement such as holding over past the term of the lease, bringing animals into a "no pets" apartment, occupancy by more than the number of persons specified in the agreement, or operating in an illegal manner on the premises. Called **actual eviction,** the process usually begins with the landlord having a notice served on the tenant requiring the tenant to comply with the lease agreement or move out. If the tenant neither complies nor vacates, the landlord takes the matter to court. If the landlord wins the case, either by a preponderance of evidence or because the tenant does not appear to contest the eviction, then the court will terminate the tenant's lease rights and authorize a marshall or sheriff to go on the premises and force the tenant out.

A lease agreement may also be terminated through **constructive eviction.** This occurs when the landlord does not keep the premises fit for occupancy and the tenant is forced to move. For example, the landlord may be continually failing to repair broken plumbing lines or a leaking roof. The tenant's legal remedies are to claim wrongful eviction, move out, stop paying rent, and sue the landlord for breach of contract, forcing the landlord either to make repairs or to terminate the lease, possibly with money damages.

A **retaliatory eviction** is one whereby a landlord evicts a tenant because of a complaint made by the tenant. For example, a tenant may have complained to public health officials or building and safety authorities about conditions on the premises that are in violation of health laws or building codes. The landlord may retaliate or threaten to retaliate with an eviction (or a rent increase or a decrease in services); however, this is illegal.

The government, under its right of **eminent domain,** can also terminate a lease, but must provide just compensation. An example of this would be construction of a new highway that requires the demolition of a building rented to tenants. Both the property owner and the tenants would be entitled to compensation.

Eminent Domain

A mortgage foreclosure can also bring about lease termination, depending on which contract has priority. If the mortgage was recorded before the lease was signed, then foreclosure of the mortgage also forecloses the lease. If the lease was recorded first, then the lease still stands. Because a lease can cloud a lender's title, wording is sometimes inserted in leases to make them subordinate to any future financing of the property. This is highly technical, but nonetheless a very significant matter in long-term shopping center, office building, and industrial leases.

For the most part, until 1970 the concept of residential **rent control** was reserved for wartime use in the United States. During World War I, six states and several major cities and,

RENT CONTROL

during World War II, the federal government imposed limits on how much rent an owner could charge for the use of real property. The purpose was twofold: (1) to discourage the construction of new housing so the resources could be channeled to war needs, and (2) to set ceilings so American households would not drive up prices by bidding against each other for available rental housing. With limits on rents, but no price controls on the cost of construction materials and labor, the construction of new housing was slowed without the need for a direct government order to stop building.

Within a few years after World War I and again after World War II, rent controls disappeared in nearly all parts of the country. The notable exception was New York City, where they have survived since the end of World War II and are still in use. However, beginning in the 1970s, a number of other cities enacted rent control laws. This time the major attraction was inflation protection.

Although it is true that since 1956 residential rents in the United States have not risen as rapidly as the general level of consumer prices, any relief from rent increases would nonetheless be welcomed by the 36% of American households who rent. The number of rental households in New York is closer to 50% because of the high proportion of renters in New York City. Most tenants recognize that newly constructed properties must command higher rents to meet higher construction, land, and interest costs. However, in existing buildings, they resent rent increases that have nothing to do with the original cost of the building or the cost of operating it. The argument of rent control supporters is that only increases in such things as property taxes, utilities, and maintenance should be passed on to tenants. The tenants' assumption in this argument is that rent alone is enough to attract dollars into housing investments. In reality, rents would have to be even higher if investors could not also look forward to price appreciation of their property.

Rent Control Experience   Experience to date strongly suggests that rent control creates more problems than it solves. In New York City and Washington, D.C., for example, it is generally agreed that controlled rents have taken existing dwelling units out of circulation. Despite relatively low vacancy rates, thousands of dwelling units are

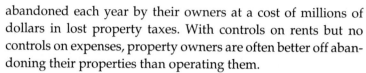

abandoned each year by their owners at a cost of millions of dollars in lost property taxes. With controls on rents but no controls on expenses, property owners are often better off abandoning their properties than operating them.

Another problem with controlled rents is that a vacating tenant may demand a substantial cash payment from a tenant who wants to move in. Although this is illegal, the vacating tenant may attempt to circumvent the law by requiring the incoming tenant to purchase his furniture for several times its actual worth. Sometimes this payment is called a "key fee," suggesting that the new tenant is purchasing the key. This places the actual cost of the controlled apartment much closer to the value of the unit on the open market, and the advantage of low, controlled rents is lost to the incoming tenant.

A side effect of rent control has been conversions of existing rental apartments to condominiums since there are no controls on sales prices of dwelling units. Some cities have responded by restricting conversions. Owners began to demolish buildings to build new condominiums; however, laws were then enacted to restrict demolition permits.

Other side effects of rent control in the United States are that lenders prefer not to lend on rent-controlled buildings. This is because lenders do not like to loan unless the investor is assured of reasonable returns. Developers find it hard to attract tenants to new rental units from rent-controlled buildings where they are enjoying below-market rents. Owner-occupied properties and noncontrolled properties are charged higher property taxes to make up for the falling values of controlled properties. Also there is a significant cost to the public to operate the government offices that administer the controls.

Rent Stabilization

Due to these problems, virtually all cities in New York abandoned rent control laws by the early 1970s. However, many adopted **rent stabilization** laws when vacancy decontrol laws resulted in quickly escalating rental costs. The Emergency Tenant Protection Act of 1974 authorized local governments facing housing shortages to impose new but more flexible controls. Rent stabilization laws require the state to establish a maximum base rent (MBR) for stabilized units. Once the MBR is established, the landlord must justify further increases based on improvements to the property or increased utility costs.

PROPERTY MANAGEMENT

As real estate becomes a more and more popular investment vehicle, more individuals are buying houses, apartment buildings, offices, and stores to rent out. Many choose to operate these themselves, thus entering the field of property management. Others hire professional managers, as do partnerships and corporations that own real estate. The balance of this chapter gives you a sampling of some of the things you can expect as a manager of residential property, as well as an overview of the employment opportunities in this important aspect of real estate.

Before Buying

Successful operation of rental property begins with building or selecting existing buildings that meet the needs of tenants. Although this sounds simple enough, in reality it requires considerable reading, legwork, and telephoning. There is no sense in building or buying one-bedroom apartment units when the local demand is for two-bedroom units. A wise investor will conduct an informal survey of existing rents and vacancy rates and gather information on the age, household status, and numbers of renters in the local rental market. Market rents are then compared with operating costs and the balance capitalized to determine how much to pay for the building. (This process is explained in Chapter 21 under "Income Approach.")

Advertising

The usual search pattern of a prospective residential tenant is to drive through neighborhoods of interest and to read newspaper classified ads. Thus, advertising money is most effectively spent on signs and arrows on and near the property plus newspaper advertising. Ads should tell enough about the property to motivate the prospect to call for an inspection. Signs should be well placed so prospects do not get lost trying to locate the property.

TENANT SELECTION

Just as a prospective tenant qualifies each house or apartment from the standpoint of suitability, the property manager must also qualify the tenant. If it appears that a prospect, once moved in, will not pay the rent, will be destructive to the premises, or will be obnoxious to the neighbors, the time to avoid the problem is before the tenant moves in.

A thorough application form, a personal interview with a seasoned manager, and a substantial security deposit are valuable screening tools. A thorough application form acts to discourage prospects who themselves feel only marginally qualified or who prefer not to divulge the information requested. It also provides a basis for checking the tenants' references. This includes talking with former landlords to ask why they left, checking with the local credit bureau to learn if they pay their bills on time, and, in some cities, checking with landlord's reference bureaus to find out if they left a previous apartment without paying rent.

The purpose of the interview is to determine whether or not the prospects have the income to support the rental and will be compatible with the other tenants. For example, if the project does not allow pets or disassembled automobiles on the premises, the manager will want to make certain the prospect understands this.

The requirement of a **security deposit** (against which the manager can deduct for unpaid rent or damage to the building) also serves as a screening device. If, for example, a prospect wants to rent a $400-per-month apartment but does not have the money for a $200 security deposit, it is doubtful that he will be able to pay $400 rent each month.

SECURITY DEPOSIT

Most states allow a damage deposit equal to one month's rent. In addition, many states also allow the landlord to collect the last month's rent in advance. A prospective tenant who, before moving in, can deposit the first and last month's rent plus a damage deposit not only provides an impressive financial picture but a solid cushion against future unpaid rent and damage.

Federal laws require owners and managers to disregard matters of race, color, religion, sex, national origin, disability, and familial status. State and local laws may extend this to age, marital status, presence of children, physical handicaps, sexual orientation, and welfare status. These laws cover not only the obvious discrimination of refusing to rent, but also discrimination in such matters as the size of the security deposit, choice of apartment unit, length of lease offered, and any number of more subtle discouragements. These laws are designed to give equal access to housing to anyone who can meet the financial requirements and is willing to abide by the lease contract and the house rules.

Rent Concessions

Two methods by which a building owner can attract tenants in an otherwise soft rental market are: (1) reduce the monthly rent, and (2) offer a rent concession. With a **rent concession,** the property owner keeps the rents at the same level, but offers a premium to entice a prospective tenant to move in. Often this is a free month's rent for prospects who will sign a 1-year lease. Alternatives are to offer the tenant a cash moving allowance or a free weekend vacation at a nearby resort. The philosophy behind using concessions rather than outright rent reductions is that when the rental market firms up, it is easier to stop offering concessions than it is to raise rents.

TENANT RETENTION

Tenant retention begins with finding tenants who will pay the rent and respect their contract agreements. Having once found good tenants, the next task is to keep them as long as possible. Besides the rent lost while the apartment is empty, the costs of apartment clean-up and finding a new tenant are high.

Statistically, about one-third of the units in a typical apartment project must be rerented each year. Certainly, many moves are as a result of job relocation or the need for larger or smaller quarters. But some moves occur because tenants find something they dislike about the way their apartments are managed. For example, if a building is poorly kept up or the manager gives the impression that he does not care about the tenants or the owner increases the rent with no apparent justification, people will move out. To retain tenants, the property owner and manager should think of them as permanent residents, even though turnover is expected. This begins with using a rental contract that an average tenant can read and understand. A complicated and legalistic contract may be seen by the tenant as the first step in a sparring match with management that will last as long as the tenant resides there. The tenant also expects the property to be clean and properly maintained and repairs to the unit made promptly.

Communications

Good communications between management and tenants is also crucial to tenant retention. If the swimming pool is closed or utilities shut off with no announcement or no apparent reason, tenants become disgusted and add it to their private lists of reasons for ultimately leaving. Tenants expect management to keep them informed through bulletin board announcements or notices placed under their doors. In many larger apartment projects, managers publish newsletters to keep tenants informed and provide a means by which tenants can communicate with one another. For example, one page can explain why rents must go up because of rising property taxes, maintenance, and utility costs, while another page announces the formation of a bowling league among project dwellers.

A very straightforward approach to improving tenant retention is to use leases. Once signed to a 1-year lease, a tenant is much less likely to leave after a few months than if on a month-to-month agreement. Similarly, leases for longer than 1 year will reduce tenant turnover even more, although residential tenants are often wary about committing themselves that far into the future. A tenant can also be encouraged to stay by offering a renewal lease at a slightly lower rate than that being offered to new tenants. Another inducement is to offer long-time tenants free carpet shampooing, drapery cleaning, and wall painting, all things normally done if the tenant leaves and the apartment must be rerented.

Leases

Ultimately, the success of a rental building depends on the ability of management to collect the rents due from tenants. In accomplishing this, it is generally agreed among property managers that a firm and consistent collection policy handled in a businesslike manner is the best approach. Monthly rent statements can be mailed to each tenant. More often, though, the tenant is told in the rental contract when the rent is due each month and is expected to pay it on time. Rents can also be collected door to door, but most managers prefer that rent checks be mailed or brought to their office when due. For security reasons some managers do not accept cash.

COLLECTING RENTS

When a tenant's rent is not received on time, the manager must decide what action to take. Is the lateness simply a matter of delayed mail or temporary but honest forgetfulness, or is the delay an early sign of a deeper problem, one that may cost the property owner lost rent and ultimately lead to eviction? The

Late Rents

accepted procedure is to wait 5 days before sending the tenant a reminder. This avoids generating a negative feeling when the problem was due to a minor delay, for it is a fact that the vast majority of tenants do pay their rent on time. However, if payment is not received by the tenth day after it was due, a second reminder goes out requesting that the tenant personally call on the manager. By meeting with the tenant, the manager may obtain an indication as to what the underlying problem is. If the tenant is suffering from a temporary financial setback, the manager can weigh the humanitarian side and the cost of rerenting the apartment against the possibility that payment will never be received.

Eviction Problems

When it is apparent that a delinquent tenant will never bring his rent up to date, it is time to ask the tenant to leave and for the manager to rerent the space. What happens if the tenant will neither leave nor pay the rent? Years ago it was not uncommon for an owner to enter a tenant's unit, remove all the tenant's belongings, and lock them up. The key to the apartment door was changed and the apartment rerented; if the delinquent tenant wanted his belongings back, he had to pay the back rent. Today's laws provide more protection for tenants, who may sue the landlord for removing personal belongings and locking them out. Meanwhile, a nonpaying tenant who is well versed in the law can remain for several rent-free weeks. This is possible because of the time required to go through the legal procedures of eviction. When the delinquent tenant finally leaves a month or two later, he may owe several hundred dollars in back rent. The legal cost of forcing payment may be more than what is owed.

Manager Remedies

More and more tenants are learning that if they are brash enough they can use the method just described to live rent-free and then move on. Others stop just short of the sheriff knocking on their door and leave on their own. The delinquent tenant hopes the manager or owner will not go to the trouble of pursuing the issue. Tenants are also learning to use the courts to pursue all sorts of real and fancied complaints against management, and managers are learning that judges often favor the tenant in these cases. What can owners and managers do about this? The best defense is careful tenant selection, substantial security deposits, good service, and a businesslike policy on rent collection. In other words, the old idea of filling up a building as fast as possible and later weeding out the problem tenants is no longer practical. Beyond that, the presence of a full-time manager means tenants are likely to take better care of the premises and are less likely to leave without paying the rent.

Managers can also make more effective use of the law by using the courts to obtain judgments against those who won't pay, those who move out without paying, and those who write bad checks for rent payments. Although a tenant may have left the area and it may not be worth the effort of locating him, the fact that a manager does take a firm stand serves as a deterrent to those planning the same tactics. For the nonpaying tenant, the judgment against him becomes part of his credit record and a warning to the next manager he approaches for an apartment.

On-site management is a term that refers to property management duties that are performed on the premises. Showing apartment units to prospective tenants, taking applications, conducting interviews, signing leases, maintaining good tenant relations, collecting rents, and handling vacancies and evictions are usually handled by a property manager at the rent site. The on-site manager, also called a **resident manager** or **superintendent,** is also responsible for the repair, maintenance, and security of the building and grounds. This includes ordering supplies as well as hiring tradespeople, gardeners, and a swimming pool maintenance firm. It involves walking through the entire premises at least once a day for security purposes and to make certain everything is working such as lights in the hallways, security doors, elevators, swimming pool pumps, and recreation equipment.

The resident manager is also responsible for keeping the premises clean and the trash collected and for supervising hired help. The resident manager is on call in the event of emergencies such as when a tenant or guest becomes boisterous, their heat or utilities shut down, or the fire alarm goes off. The resident manager also makes suggestions as to needed repairs

ON-SITE
MANAGEMENT

and improvements, needed changes in landlord-tenant policies, and ways to look after the building and its tenants better. The resident manager and management company are fiduciaries of the property owner as they hold a position of trust, responsibility, confidence, and fidelity toward the owner.

Management-Unit Ratios

A rule of thumb in apartment management is that one on-site manager can handle 50 or 60 units alone. With 60 to 100 units, the manager needs an assistant to help with management chores and to make it possible to have someone on the property at all times. In projects of over 100 units, a popular approach is to hire husband-wife teams, placing both on the payroll and adding assistants in proportion to project size. For example, a 150-unit apartment building would be managed by a husband-wife team and one assistant (usually a full-time custodian). A 200-unit building would have a husband-wife team plus two full-time assistants, and so on, adding an additional employee for each additional 50 to 60 apartment units. Larger projects also mean assistants can specialize. For example, in a 625-unit complex with a professional manager and nine assistants, two assistants might run the leasing office, two specialize in cleaning apartments when tenants leave, one acts as gardener, one as a repairman, one as a custodian, one as a rent collector and bookkeeper, and one as a recreational facilities director.

OFF-SITE MANAGEMENT

Off-site management consists of duties that can be accomplished without being on the premises. Examples of off-site management are accounting for rents collected, handling payrolls, and paying bills. All of these are well suited for computerized data processing, and property management programs are available. These programs not only computerize bookkeeping chores, but pinpoint late rental payments, ensure that lease renewals are mailed promptly, identify upcoming vacancies, and make any contract-required rent adjustments. These systems also keep track of every item that affects income and outgo, help manage cash flow so there is always enough money available to pay bills and the mortgage payment, and even type the checks. Moreover, available programs generate reports such as tenant directories, rent rolls, tenant ledgers, upcoming lease expirations, and unit vacancies. To further assist management, these programs generate operating statements for each property managed, construct budgets, make projections, and even analyze the financial health of the management firm.

Although a large part of off-site management is centered on accounting services, off-site managers have other responsibilities. For example, hazard and liability insurance must be purchased in the right coverages and for the best rates possible, resident managers must be hired and trained, bids for contracted services must be taken, and contracts awarded. Decisions regarding rent policies, rent levels, advertising, major repairs, and capital improvements are made off-site. The off-site manager may even be asked to recommend when to refinance or sell the property and buy another.

In reading this chapter, you may have become interested in a career in real property management. The most successful apartment managers seem to be those who have had previous experience in managing people and money and who are handy with tools. Those with prior military experience or experience as owners or managers of small businesses are eagerly sought after. Least successful as on-site property managers are those who see it as a quiet, peaceful retirement job, those who are unable to work with and understand people, those who cannot organize or make decisions, those without a few handyman skills, and those strictly looking for an 8-to-5, Monday-to-Friday job. Commercial and industrial property management positions tend to be filled by persons who have had prior property management experience and who have a good understanding of how business and industry make use of real estate.

A medium-to-large property management firm will have job opportunities for building service personnel, purchasing agents, bookkeepers, clerks, secretaries, office managers, field supervisors, and executive managers. In a small office, one person plus a secretary will be responsible for all the off-site duties.

JOB OPPORTUNITIES

Finding experienced and capable property managers is not an easy task. Formal education in property management is not widely available in the United States. Instead, most managers learn their profession almost entirely by experience. An individ-

Training Programs

ual property owner can place an advertisement in a newspaper and attract a manager from another project, but most professional management firms have found it necessary to develop their own internal training programs. With such a program a management firm can start a person with no previous property management experience as an assistant manager on a large project. If a person learns the job and enjoys the work, there could be a promotion to manager of a 50- or 60-unit building and an increase in salary. If this works well, there is a move to a larger complex with an assistant and another increase in salary. Each step brings more responsibility and more pay. This system provides a steady stream of qualified managers for the management firm. It is also a source of executive-level personnel for the off-site management office. In larger cities executive-level positions pay upwards of $100,000 per year.

The dominant professional organization in the property management field is the **Institute of Real Estate Management (IREM).** Established in 1933, the Institute is a division within the National Association of REALTORS®. Its primary purposes are to serve as an exchange medium for management ideas and to recognize specialists in the field. The Institute awards the designation **Certified Property Manager (CPM)** to members who successfully complete required educational courses and gain experience in property management. The Institute also offers an educational program for resident managers of apartment buildings. The designation **Accredited Resident Manager (ARM)** is awarded upon successful completion. Forty-five percent of all property to be managed in the United States is managed by IREM members and there are in excess of 10,000 CPMs.

Another management organization is the **Building Owners and Managers Institute (BOMI).** Incorporated in 1970, BOMI provides educational programs aimed primarily at the commercial property management industry. Seven courses are offered ranging from design, operation, and maintenance of buildings to accounting, insurance, law, investments, and administration. Successful completion of the seven courses leads to the designation of **Real Property Administrator (RPA).** BOMI also offers eight courses in heating, plumbing, refrigeration, air handling, electrical systems, control systems maintenance, energy management, and supervision as they apply to commercial buildings. Those who complete these courses receive the **Systems Maintenance Administrator (SMA)** designation.

Match terms **a–z** *with statements* **1–26.**

a. *Actual eviction*
b. *Assignment*
c. *Assignor*
d. *Constructive eviction*
e. *Contract rent*
f. *CPM, RPA*
g. *Gross lease*
h. *Ground rent*
i. *Holdover tenant*
j. *Landlord-tenant laws*
k. *Lessee*
l. *Lessor*
m. *Month-to-month lease*

n. *Net lease*
o. *On-site management*
p. *Option clause*
q. *Participation clause*
r. *Percentage lease*
s. *Quiet enjoyment*
t. *Rent concession*
u. *Rent control*
v. *Reversion*
w. *Security deposit*
x. *Step-up rent*
y. *Sublessee*
z. *Sublet*

1. The landlord.
2. The tenant.
3. Partial transfer of rights held under a lease.
4. Complete transfer of rights held under a lease.
5. One who holds a tenancy at sufferance.
6. Example of a periodic estate.
7. Entitles the landowner to retake possession at the end of the lease.
8. Rent charged for the use of land.
9. Specified rent increases at various points in time during the life of the lease.
10. A lease clause that allows the landlord to add to the tenant's rent any increases in property taxes, maintenance, and utilities during the life of the lease.
11. Gives a tenant the opportunity of renewing a lease at a predetermined rental without obligation to do so.
12. A lease under which the amount of rent paid is related to the income the lessee obtains from the use of the premises.
13. Describes leases wherein the tenant pays a fixed rent.
14. Entitles the tenant to uninterrupted use of the property without interference from the owner or third parties.
15. Statutes that set forth the responsibilities and rights of landlords and tenants.
16. A lease wherein a tenant pays a base rent plus maintenance, property taxes, and insurance.
17. The party acquiring possession under a sublet agreement.

18. The party who assigns his or her lease rights to another.
19. Nonpayment of rent would be grounds for this.
20. The amount of rent the tenant must pay the landlord as stated in the lease agreement.
21. An unfit premises would be grounds for this.
22. Government-imposed limits on how much a landlord can charge for space.
23. An advance deposit given by a tenant to a landlord against which the landlord can deduct for unpaid rent or damage.
24. A premium, such as a free month's rent, given to entice a prospective tenant to sign a lease.
25. A resident manager would be in this management category.
26. Professional designations for property managers.

QUESTIONS AND PROBLEMS

1. From the standpoint of the tenant, what are the advantages and disadvantages of a lease versus a month-to-month rental?
2. What remedies does a property manager in your state have when a tenant does not pay the rent and/or refuses to move out?
3. Does your state have a landlord-tenant code? What are its major provisions? If no specific code or act currently exists in your state, where does one look for laws pertaining to landlords and tenants?
4. What is the difference between contract rent and economic rent?
5. On what basis could a tenant claim constructive eviction? What would the tenant's purpose be in doing this?
6. Is an option to renew a lease to the advantage of the lessor or the lessee?
7. Is rent control currently in effect in your community? If so, what effects have these controls had on the sales of investment properties and on the construction of new rental buildings in your community?
8. If you were an apartment building manager interviewing prospective tenants, what questions would you ask?

ADDITIONAL READINGS

Commercial Real Estate Leases: Book 1, Preparation and Negotiation; Book 2, Forms, by **Mark A. Senn** (Wiley, 1990, 598 pages; 419 pages). Book 1 discusses negotiating leases of all different types of commercial property. Book 2 contains forms for office leases, shopping centers, and so on.

Property Management, 4th Ed., by **Robert Kyle** (Real Estate Education Company, 1991, 472 pages). Provides practical information on tenant relations, qualifying prospects, leasing procedures, fee setting, negotiating, and so on. Covers apartment buildings, cooperatives, condominiums, offices, stores, industrial and subsidized housing; includes the use of microcomputers and word processing.

Real Estate Brokerage Management, 3rd Ed., by **Bruce Lindeman** (Prentice Hall, 1994, 300 pages). Applies management techniques and organization for small to medium-sized businesses.

Successful Leasing and Selling of Retail Property, 3rd Ed., (Real Estate Education Company and Grubb & Ellis, 1989, 304 pages). Explains key ingredients the licensee needs to know about marketing retail property.

12

Condominiums, Cooperatives, PUDs, and Timeshares

KEY • TERMS

Bylaws: rules that govern how an owners' association will be run

CC&Rs: covenants, conditions, and restrictions by which a property owner agrees to abide

Common elements: those parts of a condominium that are owned by all the unit owners

Condominium: unit that provides individual ownership of a space of air plus undivided ownership of the common elements

Cooperative: land and building owned or leased by a corporation which, in turn, leases space to its shareholders

Limited common elements: common elements whose use is limited to certain owners

Planned unit development (PUD): individually owned lots and houses with community ownership of common areas

Proprietary lease: a lease issued by a cooperative corporation to its shareholders

Reserves: money set aside for expenses that do not occur every month

Resort timesharing: the exclusive use of a property for a specified number of days each year

The idea of combining community living with community ownership is not new. Two thousand years ago, the Roman Senate passed condominium laws that permitted Roman citizens to own individual dwelling units in multiunit buildings. This form of ownership resulted because land was scarce and expensive in Rome. After the fall of the Roman Empire, condominium ownership was used in the walled cities of the Middle Ages. Here it was primarily a defensive measure since residing outside the walls was dangerous because of roving bands of raiders. With the stabilization of governments after the Middle Ages the condominium concept became dormant. Then in the early twentieth century, in response to land scarcity in cities, the idea was revived in western Europe. From there the concept spread to several Latin American countries and, in 1951, to Puerto Rico. Puerto Rican laws and experience in turn became the basis for passage by Congress in 1961 of Section 234 of the National Housing Act. Designed as a legal model that condominium developers could follow in order to obtain FHA loan insurance, Section 234 also served as a model for state condominium laws now in effect across the United States.

In this chapter we'll begin with a discussion of condominiums, in particular an overview of their organization, operation, benefits, and drawbacks. Then we'll turn our attention to cooperatives, planned unit developments, and timesharing.

The first step in creating a **condominium** is for the state to pass laws that create the legal framework for condominium ownership. All states have passed them, and they are variously known as a state's horizontal property act, strata titles act, **condominium act,** or a similar name. New York's Condominium Act is Article 9B. of the Real Property Law. All follow the FHA model with each state's particular refinements. As the names suggest, these laws address the problem of subdividing the airspace over a given parcel of land. Prior to these acts, the legal framework that made it possible for people to own a cubicle of airspace plus an undivided interest in the shell of the building and the land under and around the building did not exist. Moreover, condominium acts had to be designed to be acceptable to lenders who would be asked to loan on condominiums, property tax authorities who would have to assess them, and income tax authorities

CONDOMINIUM

who would allow owners to deduct loan interest and property taxes. The lawmakers were successful, and today millions of people live in condominiums.

Physically, a condominium can take the shape of a 2-story garden apartment building, a 40-story tower with several living units on each floor, row houses, clustered houses, or even detached houses sharing a single parcel of land. Condominiums are not restricted to residential uses. In recent years, a number of developers across the nation have built office buildings and sold individual suites to doctors, dentists, and lawyers. The same idea has been applied to shopping centers and industrial space. A condominium does not have to be a new building: many existing apartment houses have been converted from rental status to condominium ownership with only a few physical changes to the building.

Separate and Common Elements

The distinguishing features of a condominium are its separate and common elements and its system of self-government. The separate elements, called **separate property,** are those areas in the condominium that are exclusively owned and used by the individual condominium owners. These are the individual dwelling units in the building. More precisely, the separate property is the airspace occupied by a unit. This is the space lying between the interior surfaces of the unit walls and between the floor and the ceiling. Everything else is a common element in which each unit owner holds an undivided interest. Thus the land and the shell of the building are **common elements** owned by all. Common elements include, for example, the manager's apartment, lobby, hallways, stairways, elevators, recreation areas, landscaping, and parking lot. Sometimes you will hear the term **limited common element.** This is a common element the use of which is restricted to a specific unit owner. Examples are assigned parking stalls and individual storage units.

Owners' Association

When a developer wants to create a condominium (either built from the ground up or the conversion of an existing building to condominium ownership), the developer prepares and records with the public recorder what is variously known as an enabling declaration, master deed, plan of condominium ownership, or **condominium subdivision.** This document, usually 50 to 150 pages long, converts a parcel of land held under a single deed into a number of individual separate property estates (the condominium units) and an estate composed of all the common elements. Survey maps are included to show the location of each condominium unit plus all the common elements.

The developer also creates a legal framework so that the unit owners can govern themselves. This is the condominium **owners' association** of which each unit purchaser automatically becomes a member. Although the association can be organized as a trust or unincorporated association, most often it is organized as a corporation in order to provide the legal protections normally afforded by a corporation to its owners. Additionally, it will be organized as not-for-profit, to avoid income taxes on money collected from members. The main purpose of the owners' association is to control, regulate, and maintain the common elements for the overall welfare and benefit of its members. The owners' association is a mini-government by and for the condominium owners.

The rules by which an owners' association operates are called its **bylaws**. They are prepared by the developer's attorney and recorded with the master deed. The bylaws provide the rules by which the association's board of directors is elected and set the standards by which the board must rule. The bylaws set forth how association dues (maintenance fees) will be established and collected, how contracts will be let for maintenance, management, and repair work, and how personnel will be hired.

Bylaws

Finally, the developer must file a list of regulations by which anyone purchasing a unit in the condominium must abide. These are known as **covenants, conditions, and restrictions (CC&Rs).** They tell a unit owner such things as not to store personal items on balconies or driveways, what color the exterior of the living room drapes should be, to what extent an owner can alter the exterior of the unit, and whether or not an owner can install a satellite television dish on the roof. Additional regulations may be embodied in a set of **house rules.** Typically, these govern such things as when the swimming pool and other recreation facilities will be open for use and when quiet hours will be observed in the building.

CC&Rs

Deed Each purchaser of a condominium unit receives a deed from the developer. The deed describes the location of the unit, both in terms of the unit number in the building and its surveyed airspace. The deed also describes the common elements and states the percentage interest in the common elements that the grantee is receiving. The deed is recorded on closing just like a deed to a house.

On selling, the owner has a new deed prepared that describes the unit and the common element interest and delivers it to the purchaser at closing. If the condominium is on leased land, the developer delivers a lease (or sublease) to the unit buyer. On resale, that lease is assigned to the buyer.

Voting Rules Once the units in the building have been sold and the association turned over to the unit owners, the unit owners can change the rules. Generally, the bylaws require a three-fourths vote and the CC&Rs require a two-thirds vote from the association members for a change. House rules can be changed with a simple majority or, in some cases, by the board of directors, without a vote of the association.

Board of Directors Condominium bylaws provide that a **board of directors** be elected by the association members. The board is authorized to administer the affairs of the condominium including purchasing of hazard and liability insurance for the common elements, arranging for maintenance and repair of common elements, enforcing CC&Rs and house rules, assessing and collecting a sufficient amount of monthly homeowner fees and special assessments, and listening to complaints and suggestions from unit owners as to how the condominium should be run.

Board members are usually elected at the annual meeting of the association, are unit owners, and serve for 1 year. Typically the board has 5 to 7 members on the board, and one will be elected as president, one as vice president, one as secretary, and one as treasurer. Meetings are held monthly unless added business requires more frequent meetings. Board meetings are usually open to all association members who can watch the proceedings and provide input. To help spread the work, the board appoints committees on which owners are asked to serve. Examples are landscaping, architectural, security, clubhouse, and social committees. Directors and committee members are usually not paid for their time.

Once a year the owners' association meets for an **annual meeting.** Besides the election of board members for the following year, this meeting provides an opportunity for association members to vote on major issues such as changes in the CC&Rs and bylaws, monthly maintenance fee increases, special assessments, and any other matters the board feels should be put to a general ownership vote rather than handled at a board meeting. Owners also receive an annual report of the fiscal health of the association and other information pertinent to their ownership.

Annual Meetings

Most condominium associations employ a condominium **management company** to advise the board and take care of day-to-day tasks. The management company is usually responsible for finding, hiring, and paying gardeners, trash haulers, janitors, repair personnel, and a pool maintenance firm. The management company collects maintenance fees and special assessments from unit owners, accounts for condominium expenses, handles the payroll, and pays for contracted services.

CONDOMINIUM MANAGEMENT

If the association chooses to hire an on-site manager, that person is usually responsible for enforcing the house rules, handling complaints or problems regarding maintenance, making daily security checks, and supervising the swimming pool and recreation areas. The extent of the manager's duties and responsibilities is set by the owners' association. The association should also retain the right to fire the resident manager and the management firm if their services are not satisfactory.

The costs of maintaining the common elements in a condominium are allocated among the unit owners in accordance with percentages set forth in the master deed. These are called **maintenance fees** or **association dues** and are collected monthly. Failure to pay creates a lien against the delinquent owner's unit. The amount collected is determined by the association's budget for the coming year, which is based on the board of director's estimate of the cost of month-to-month maintenance, insurance,

MAINTENANCE FEES

legal and management services, plus reserves for expenses that do not occur monthly.

Reserves   The importance of setting aside **reserves** each month is illustrated by the following example. Suppose it is estimated that the exterior of a 100-unit building will have to be painted every 7 years and that the cost is expected to be $25,200. To avoid a special painting assessment of $252 per unit, the association instead collects $3 per month from each unit owner for 84 months. If the reserves are kept in an interest-bearing savings account as they should be, less than $3 per month would need to be collected.

PROPERTY TAXES
AND INSURANCE   Since condominium law recognizes each condominium dwelling unit as a separate legal ownership, property taxes are assessed on each unit separately. Property taxes are based on the assessed value of the unit which is determined by its market value. As a rule, it is not necessary for the taxing authority to assess and tax the common elements separately because the market value of each unit reflects not only the value of the unit itself, but also the value of the fractional ownership in the common elements that accompanies the unit.

The association is responsible for purchasing hazard and liability insurance covering the common elements. Each dwelling unit owner is responsible for purchasing hazard and liability insurance for the interior of his or her dwelling.

Thus, if a visitor slips on a banana peel in the lobby or a hallway of the building, the association is responsible. If the accident occurs in an individual's unit, the unit owner is responsible. In a high-rise condominium, if the roof breaks during a heavy rainstorm and floods several apartments below, the association is responsible. If an apartment owner's dishwasher overflows and soaks the apartments below the apartment owner is responsible. If patio furniture is stolen from the swimming pool area, the association is responsible. If patio furniture (or any personal property for that matter) is stolen from an individual's unit, that is the unit owner's responsibility. Policies designed for associations and policies for condominium owners are readily available from insurance companies.

If a condominium unit is being rented, the owner needs to have landlord insurance, and tenants, for their own protection, need tenants' hazard and liability policies.

CONDOMINIUM FINANCING

Because each condominium unit can be separately owned, each can be separately financed. Thus, a condominium purchaser can choose whether or not to borrow against the unit. A purchaser who borrows can choose a large or small down payment and a long or short amortization period. If the buyer wants to repay early or refinance, those options are available. On resale, the buyer can elect to assume the loan, pay it off, or obtain new financing. In other words, while association bylaws, restrictions, and house rules may regulate the use of a unit, in no way does the association control how a unit may be financed.

Because each unit is a separate ownership, if a lender needs to foreclose against a delinquent borrower in the building, the remaining unit owners are not involved. They are neither responsible for the delinquent borrower's mortgage debt nor are they parties to the foreclosure.

Loan Terms

Loan terms offered condominium buyers are quite similar to those offered on houses. Typically, lenders make conventional, uninsured loans for up to 80% of value. With private mortgage insurance, this can be raised to 90% or 95%. On FHA-approved buildings, the FHA offers insurance terms similar to those for detached dwellings. Financing can also be in the form of an installment contract or a seller carryback.

Deposit Practices

If a project is not already completed and ready for occupancy when it is offered for sale, it is common for the developer to require a substantial deposit. The best practice is to place this in an escrow account payable to the developer on completion. Without this precaution, some developers use deposits to help pay the expenses of construction. Unfortunately, if the deposits are spent by a developer who goes bankrupt before the project is completed, the buyer receives neither a finished unit nor the return of the deposit. If the deposits are held in escrow, the buyers do not receive a unit but they do get their deposits back.

Condominium Conversions

During the late 1970s, the idea of condominium ownership became very popular in the United States. Builders constructed new condominiums at a rapid pace, but there were not enough to fill demand. Soon enterprising developers found that existing apartment buildings could be converted to condominiums and sold to the waiting public. Compared to new construction, a condominium conversion is often simpler, faster, and more profitable for the developer. The procedure involves finding an attractively built existing building that is well located and has good floor plans. The developer does a face-lift on the outside, adds more landscaping, paints the interior, and replaces carpets and appliances. The developer also files the necessary legal paperwork to convert the building and land into condominium units and common elements.

A potential problem area with condominium conversions, and one that a prospective buyer should be aware of, is that converted buildings are used buildings that were not intended as condominiums when built. As used buildings, there may be considerable deferred maintenance, and the building may have thermal insulation suitable to a time when energy costs were lower. If the building was originally built for rental purposes, sound-deadening insulation in the walls, floors, and ceilings may be inadequate. Fire protection between units may also be less than satisfactory. In contrast, newly built condominiums must meet current building code requirements regarding thermal and sound insulation, fire wall construction, and so forth.

It is worth noting that not all condominium conversions are carried out by developers. Enterprising tenants have successfully converted their own buildings and saved considerable sums of money. It is not uncommon for the value of a building to double when it is converted to a condominium. Tenants who are willing to hire the legal, architectural, and construction help they need can create valuable condominium homes for themselves in the same building where they were previously renters.

ADVANTAGES OF CONDOMINIUM LIVING

Compared to detached dwellings, condominium living offers a number of advantages and some disadvantages. On the advantage side, instead of 4 or 5 detached dwellings on an acre of land, a condominium builder can place 25 or even 100 living units. This spreads the cost of the site among more dwellings, and the builder does not have to construct the miles of streets, sewers, or utility lines that would be necessary to reach every house in a spread-out subdivision. Furthermore, the use of shared walls and foundations, in that one dwelling unit's ceiling is another's floor, and in that one roof can cover many vertically stacked units, can produce savings in construction materials and labor. In central city districts where a single square foot of vacant land can cost $100 or more, only a high-rise condominium can make housing units possible. In the suburbs, where land is cheaper, a condominium is often the difference between buying and renting for some people.

Another advantage is the lure of "carefree living," with such chores as lawn mowing, watering, weeding, snow removal, and building maintenance provided. For some people, it is the security often associated with clustered dwellings and nearby neighbors. Other advantages are extensive recreational and social facilities that are not economically feasible on a single-dwelling basis. It is common to find swimming pools, recreation halls, tennis and volleyball courts, gymnasiums, and even social directors at condominiums.

Lastly, we cannot overlook the psychological and financial advantages of ownership. Many large rental apartment projects produce the same economies of scale and amenities just described. Nonetheless, most Americans prefer to own rather than rent their dwellings. Part of the reason is the pride of owning something. Part comes from a desire for a savings program, the potential for capital appreciation, and income tax laws that favor owners over renters.

A major disadvantage of condominium living is the close proximity of one's neighbors and the extra level of government. In other words, buying into a condominium means buying into a group of people whose lifestyles may differ from yours and whose opinions as to how to run the association may also differ from yours. By way of contrast, if you buy a single-family detached house on a lot, you have (subject to zoning and legal restrictions) sole control over the use of it. You can choose to remodel or add on. You can choose what color to paint your house and garage, how many people and animals will live there, what type of landscaping to have, from whom to purchase property insurance, whether to rent it out or live in it, and so on. Your next-door neighbors have the same rights over their land. You cannot dictate to them what color to paint their houses,

DISADVANTAGES OF CONDOMINIUM LIVING

what kind of shrubs to grow, or whether to buy hazard insurance and from whom.

In a condominium, the owners have a considerable degree of control over each other in matters that affect the common good of the association. Moreover, certain decisions must be made as a group, such as what kinds of common-element hazard and liability insurance to carry, how much to carry, and from whom to purchase it. If there is an outdoor swimming pool, decisions must be made such as to what months it should be heated and how warm it should be kept. The group as a whole must decide on how the landscaping is to be maintained, who will do it, and how much should be spent. If there is to be security service, there must be another group decision as to how much, when, and who should be hired. If a large truck runs into a unit on the other end of the building, it's an association problem because each owner has an undivided interest in the whole building.

All matters affecting the condominium must be brought to the attention of the board of directors, often by way of a committee. All committee and board positions are filled by volunteers from the association. Thus, owning a condominium is not entirely carefree, and sometimes the board of directors will do things differently from what an individual owner would like. Another possibility is that there may be a lack of interested and talented people to serve as directors and on committees. Consequently, things that need to be done may be left undone, possibly posing a hazard to the association. Individual unit owners may be unaware of the management and maintenance requirements for a multimillion-dollar building and may have hired a management firm that knows (or does) even less.

BEFORE BUYING   If you are considering the purchase of a condominium unit, consider the preceding points with care. Also look closely at the association's finances. The association may not have adequate reserves for upcoming maintenance work such as painting the building and putting on a new roof. If so, existing owners and new buyers will be in for a rude surprise in the form of a special assessment. Check the budget to see if it covers everything adequately and ask about lawsuits against the association that might drain its finances.

Although articles of incorporation, CC&Rs, and bylaws make boring reading, if you offer to buy a condominium unit, you should make the offer contingent on your reading and approving them. These are the rules you agree to live by, and it's better to read them before committing to buy. You may find prohibitions against your pet cat or dog or against renting your unit while you are temporarily transferred overseas. (At the closing the seller must give you a current set of these documents along with the deed and keys to the unit. When you sell, you must give a current set to your buyer.)

Before buying, pay special attention to construction quality. Will ongoing maintenance be expensive? Is there deferred maintenance? Ask if the clubhouse and recreation facilities are owned by the association or by the developer who will continue to charge you for their use year after year. Is soundproofing between units adequate or will you hear your neighbor's piano, drums, and arguments? What is the owner-tenant mix? The most successful condominiums are predominantly owner occupied rather than renter occupied, because owners usually take more interest and care in their properties, and this in turn boosts resale values. The list of things to look for and ask about when buying into a condominium is too long to cover here, and bookstores have good books that will help you. But before moving on, the following two thoughts apply to any purchase of a condominium, cooperative, planned unit development, or timeshare. First, keep a balance between your heart and your head. It is easy to be enchanted to the point that no further investigation is made, perhaps knowing in advance it would sour the deal. Second, ask those who have already bought if they would buy again.

COOPERATIVE APARTMENTS

Now that you have just read about condominiums, take yourself back to the year 1900 in New York City. You've been renting an apartment unit in Manhattan for several years and would like to own it. Your neighbors in the building have expressed the same desire, but condominium legislation is more than half a century in the future. How would you and your neighbors accomplish this, given existing legal frameworks? Your answer is the corporate form of ownership, a form of multiperson ownership well established in America by that time. To carry out your collective desires, you form a not-for-profit corporation. Shares in the corporation are sold to the building's tenants and the money used as a down payment to buy the building. Title to the building is placed in the name of the corporation, and each shareholder receives from the corporation a lease to an apartment. Thus, the shareholders own the corporation, the corporation owns the building, and the corporation gives its shareholders leases to their apartments. Each month each shareholder makes a payment to the corporation to enable it to make the required monthly payment on the debt against the building and to pay for maintenance and repairs. Government of the building is handled by a board of directors that meets monthly and at an annual meeting of all the shareholders.

This form of residential ownership, which can be found in significant numbers in New York City, Miami, Chicago, San Francisco, and Honolulu, is called a **cooperative.** The individual shareholders are called **cooperators,** and the lease that the corporation gives to a shareholder is called a **proprietary lease.**

When a cooperator wishes to sell, the cooperator does not sell the apartment but rather the shares of stock that carry with it a proprietary lease on that apartment. Although for all practical purposes the transaction looks like a sale of real estate, from a legal standpoint it is a sale of corporate stock. As such, the listing and selling forms that are used for houses and condominiums are not suitable and special cooperative forms must be used.

Financing

Financing a cooperative is different from financing a house or condominium. When a cooperative apartment building is first organized, the entire property is in the name of the cooperative corporation, and there is one mortgage loan on all of it. To illustrate, suppose a 10-unit building will cost the cooperators $1,000,000 and all the units are considered equal in desirability. A lender will finance 70% of the purchase if the cooperators raise the remaining 30%. This requires the cooperators to sell 10 shares of stock, each share for $30,000 and good for one apartment unit in the building. The lender provides the remaining $700,000 to complete the purchase, and the corporation gives the lender a note for $700,000 secured by a mortgage against the building. Suppose the monthly payments on this loan are $7,000; each month each cooperator must contribute $700 toward the mortgage plus money to maintain and operate the building, pay the property taxes on it, and keep it insured.

What happens if one of the cooperators fails to make the monthly payment to the cooperative? For the cooperative to send the lender anything less than the required $7,000 per month puts the loan in default. This means the remaining cooperators must make up the difference. Meanwhile, they can seek voluntary reimbursement by the tardy cooperator, or, if that does not work, terminate him or her as a shareholder and resell the share to someone who will make the payments.

Default

What happens if a shareholder in good standing wants to sell the unit? Since the underlying mortgage is against the entire building, it is impossible to refinance a portion of the building. Only the whole building can be refinanced and that requires approval by the cooperators as a whole. Traditionally, this has forced the cooperator to sell the share for all cash or on an installment sale plan. This presents a handicap if the value of the share has increased substantially due to property value increase and reduction of the building's mortgage loan. As a solution, at least two states, New York and California, have enacted legislation allowing state-regulated lenders to make loans using cooperative stock as collateral.

Resale

A cooperative apartment is governed by its articles of incorporation, bylaws, CC&Rs, and house rules. The governing body is a board of directors elected by the cooperators. The board hires the services needed to maintain and operate the building just as in a condominium. Annual meetings are also held, just as in a condominium.

Government

Now that the condominium format is available, relatively few cooperatives are being organized. This is largely because the individual apartment unit in a condominium can be financed separately from the remainder of the building. Moreover, if one condominium unit owner fails to make loan payments, the remaining owners in the building are not responsible for that loan. The condominium unit owner also has the personal choice of whether to have no debt, a little debt, or a lot of debt against the unit. Unpaid property taxes are another potential difference. In a condominium each unit is taxed separately, and nonpayment brings a property tax foreclosure sale against only the delinquent unit, not the entire building.

Differences

Similarities

A similarity exists between condominiums and cooperatives with respect to the money collected each month for the general maintenance and upkeep of the building. In either case, nonpayment brings action against the tardy owner by the association, action that can result in foreclosure of that owner. Income tax rules effectively allow the same homeowner deductions on cooperatives as on condominiums and houses. However, a strict set of rules must be followed because technically a cooperator does not own real estate, but shares of stock.

New Legislation

Due to the financing difficulty and mutual liability potential associated with cooperatives, several states have enacted legislation that allows new cooperatives to be financed entirely by the sale of stock that in turn is pledged to a lender. This way the failure of one cooperator to make mortgage loan payments does not jeopardize the other cooperators. Also, a county assessor can assess each cooperator individually for property tax purposes if the board of directors so requests. This avoids joint liability. If you are considering the purchase of a cooperative, read the articles of incorporation, bylaws, CC&Rs, and house rules before buying. Some operate under old rules, some under new rules, some have rules you may be comfortable with, and some not.

Although the opening example in this section on cooperatives was one of tenants banding together to buy their building, cooperatives are also organized and sold by real estate developers. These can be existing buildings converted by developers to cooperative ownership and new buildings built by developers from the ground up. In either case, a prospective purchaser will find it worthwhile to reread earlier paragraphs in this chapter on deposit practices, conversions, advantages, and disadvantages before buying. Article 23A. of the General Business Law regulates syndication offerings in New York, including new condominiums or cooperatives as well as conversions of existing space.

PLANNED UNIT DEVELOPMENT

If you buy into a condominium, you get a dwelling unit as separate property plus an undivided interest in the land and other common elements. If you buy into a cooperative, you get stock in the corporation that owns the building and a lease on a particular apartment. If you buy into a **planned unit development (PUD),** you get a house and lot as separate property plus ownership in a community association that owns the common areas. Common areas may be as minimal as a few green spaces in open areas between houses or so extensive as to include parks, pools, clubhouse facilities, jogging trails, boat docks, horse trails, and a golf course.

Although you own your lot and house as separate property in a PUD, there will be CC&Rs to follow. The PUD developer establishes an initial set of CC&Rs, then turns them over to the association for enforcement. Thus, your lot and home are not quite all yours to do with as you please because your association can dictate what color you can paint the exterior of your home, what you can and cannot plant in your front yard, and how many people and pets can reside with you. As with condominiums and cooperatives, PUD CC&Rs are not meant to be burdensome for the sake of being burdensome, but rather to maintain the attractiveness and tranquility of the development, and in doing so to keep home values up.

The dwellings in a planned unit development typically take the form of detached houses and houses that share a common wall, such as row houses, townhouses, and cluster houses. Because each owner owns the land, vertical stacking of homes is limited to one owner and housing densities to 8 or 10 units per acre. Even though this is twice the density of a typical detached house subdivision, by careful planning a developer can give each owner the feeling of more spaciousness. One way is by taking advantage of uneven terrain. If a parcel contains some flat land, some hilly land, and some land covered with trees and a running stream, the dwellings can be clustered on the land best suited for building and thus preserve the stream, woods, and steep slopes in their natural state. With a standard subdivision layout the developer would have to remove the groves of trees, fill in the stream, and terrace the slopes, and would still be able to provide homes for only half the number of families.

Resort timesharing is a method of dividing up and selling a living unit at a vacation facility for specified lengths of time each year. The idea started in Europe in the 1960s when groups of individuals would jointly purchase ski resort lodgings and summer vacation villas with each owner taking a week or two of exclusive occupancy. Resort developers quickly recognized the market potential of the idea, and in 1969 the first resort timeshare

RESORT
TIMESHARING

opened in the United States. Since then hotels, motels, condominiums, townhouses, lodges, villas, recreational vehicle parks, campgrounds, houseboats, and even a cruise ship have been timeshared.

Right-to-Use Nearly all timeshares fall into one of two legal formats. The first is the **right-to-use** format. This gives the buyer a contractual right to occupy a living unit at a resort property for one week a year for a specific term of 20 to 40 years. The cost for the entire period is paid in advance. At the end of the contract term all of the buyer's possessory rights terminate unless the contract contains a renewal clause or a right to buy. The developer creates these contracts by either buying or leasing a resort property and then selling 50 one-week-a-year right-to-use contracts on each living unit. (The other two weeks of the year are reserved for maintenance.) Approximately 30% of the timeshare market is right-to-use.

Fee Simple The second format is **fee simple** ownership. Here, the timeshare purchaser obtains a fee ownership in the unit purchased. The purchaser owns the property for one week a year in perpetuity, and the sale is handled like a sale of real estate. There is a formal closing, a title policy, execution of a mortgage and note, and delivery of a recordable deed that conveys the timeshare interest. A developer offers fee timeshares by either building or buying a resort property and then selling 50 one-week-a-year fee simple slices in each unit, with the remaining two weeks for maintenance. Approximately 70% of the timeshare market is fee simple.

Costs The initial cost of a timeshare week at a resort in the United States is typically $6,000 to $10,000, depending on the quality and location of the resort, the time of year (low season or high season), and form of ownership (right-to-use is usually less expensive). Additionally, there is an annual maintenance fee of $140 to $500 per timeshare week. Buyers can purchase two or more timeshare weeks if they want a longer vacation. Some buyers purchase one week in the summer and one week in the winter.

Benefits The appeal of timesharing to developers is that a resort or condominium complex that can be bought and furnished for

$100,000 per unit can be resold in 50 timeshare slices at $6,000 each—that is, $300,000 a unit. The primary appeal of timesharing to consumers is having a resort to go to every year at a prepaid price. This is particularly appealing during inflationary times, although the annual maintenance fee can change. There may be certain tax benefits if the timeshare is financed and for property taxes paid on fee simple timeshares. The timeshare unit may also appreciate if it is in a popular and well-run resort.

Then again, some or all of these benefits may not materialize. First, the lump sum paid for a timeshare week does look cheaper than hotel bills year after year. However, the timeshare must be paid for in full in advance (or financed at interest), whereas the hotel is paid as it is used each year. Also, there is a timeshare maintenance fee of $20 to $40 per day that goes for clerk and maid service; linen laundry and replacement; structural maintenance and repairs; swimming pool service; hazard and liability insurance; reservations, collections, and accounting services; general management; and so on.

Second, going to the same resort for the same week every year for the next 40 years may become wearisome. Yet that is what a timeshare buyer is agreeing to do. And, if the week goes vacant, the maintenance fee must still be paid. To offset this, two large resort exchange services and several smaller ones exist, and some of the larger timeshare developers allow their buyers to exchange weeks among their various projects. There is a cost, however, to exchanging. There may be as many as three fees to pay: an initiation fee, an annual membership fee, and a fee when an exchange is made. These can amount to $100 or more for an exchange. Moreover, someone else with a timeshare week they don't want that you do want at the right time of the year must also be in the exchange bank. Satisfaction is usually achieved in exchanging by being flexible in accepting an exchange. Note, too, if you own an off-season week at one resort, you should not count on exchanging it for a peak-season vacation somewhere else. Exchange banks require members to accept periods of equal or lesser popularity.

Third, tax laws allowed deductions for interest expense on timeshares that are financed and for property taxes on fee simple timeshares. Timeshares have occasionally been touted as tax shelter vehicles; however, that theory has already met the ire of the Internal Revenue Service.

Fourth, although there have been several reported instances of timeshare appreciation, it is generally agreed in the timeshare industry and by consumer groups that the primary reason to purchase a resort timeshare is to obtain a vacation, not appreciation. In fact, a timeshare industry rule of thumb is that one-third of the retail price of a timeshare unit goes to marketing costs. This acts as a damper on timeshare resale prices and even suggests that a buyer may be able to purchase a timeshare on the resale market for less than the price from a developer.

Commitment

Against the comfort of knowing that, as a timeshare owner, one has a long-term commitment to use a resort, one also has a long-term commitment to its maintenance, repair, refurbishing, and management. This is similar to ownership in a condominium, except that ownership is split among as many as 50 owners for each unit. Will any owner have a large enough stake to want to take an active part in overseeing the management? Management usually falls to the developer who, having once sold out the project, may no longer have as much incentive to oversee things as carefully as during the sales period. The developer can turn the job over to a management firm, but who oversees that firm to make certain the timeshare owners get good service at a fair price?

State Regulation

Approximately 25 states have adopted timeshare regulations. Many of these follow the Model Timeshare Act designed by the National Association of Real Estate License Law Officials and the National Time-sharing Council and endorsed by the National Association of Realtors. Much timeshare legislation is in the form of consumer protection and disclosure (prospectus) requirements. Other legislation deals with how timeshares should be assessed for property taxation and what type of license a person employed to sell timeshares should hold, if any. Due to high-pressure sales techniques observed at some timeshare sales offices, a number of states have enacted mandatory cooling-off periods of 5 days during which a buyer can rescind the contract. Because of multimillion-dollar consumer losses due to uncompleted timeshare projects, sales of the same timeshare to more than one party, and money having been collected without ever issuing deeds, surety bonds and escrows are now required by some states. Meanwhile, any prospective timeshare purchaser or salesperson would do well to take plenty of time deciding, have all paperwork reviewed by an attorney before signing, and spend time talking to existing purchasers to ask if they would buy again.

Match terms **a–t** *with statements* **1–20.**

a. *Annual meeting*
b. *Board of directors*
c. *Bylaws*
d. *Covenants, Conditions, and Restrictions (CC&Rs)*
e. *Common elements*
f. *Condominium*
g. *Condominium act*
h. *Condominium subdivision*
i. *Cooperative*
j. *Cooperator*

k. *House rules*
l. *Maintenance fees*
m. *Management company*
n. *Owners' association*
o. *Proprietary lease*
p. *Planned unit development (PUD)*
q. *Reserves*
r. *Resort timesharing*
s. *Right-to-use*
t. *Separate property*

1. Individual ownership of a space of air plus undivided ownership of the common elements.
2. Ownership by a corporation which in turn leases space to its shareholders.
3. Roof, stairs, elevator, lobby, and so on, in a condominium.
4. An organization composed of unit owners in which membership is automatic on purchase of a unit.
5. Type of lease issued by a cooperative corporation to its shareholders.
6. A document that converts a parcel of land into a stratified subdivision; also called a master deed.
7. Rules that govern how the owners' association will be run.
8. A shareholder in a cooperative apartment.
9. Charges levied against unit owners to cover the costs of maintaining the common areas; also called association dues.
10. Form of community ownership in which the houses and lots are privately owned but title to common areas is held by an owners' association.
11. State legislation that creates the legal framework for condominium subdivisions.
12. That portion of a condominium that is the exclusive property of an individual unit owner.
13. Regulations by which a condominium owner must abide.
14. Rules for the use of the swimming pool and recreation facilities would be found here.
15. A governing body elected by association members.

16. A once-a-year business meeting of the entire association membership.
17. Advises the board of directors and takes care of day-to-day tasks.
18. The exclusive use of a property for a specified number of days each year.
19. A contractual right to occupy a living unit at a timeshare resort.
20. Money set aside from the budget for expenses that do not occur every month.

QUESTIONS AND PROBLEMS

1. Why are condominiums a popular alternative to single-family houses?
2. Who owns the land in a fee simple condominium project? In a cooperative?
3. What is the key difference between a proprietary lease in a cooperative and a landlord-tenant lease?
4. What is the purpose of the master deed in a condominium project?
5. To whom does the wall between two condominium units belong?
6. What are CC&Rs and what is their purpose?
7. What are maintenance fees? What happens if they are not paid?
8. If the owners' association carries hazard and liability insurance, why is it also advisable for each unit owner to purchase a hazard and liability policy?
9. Briefly explain the concept of right-to-use and fee simple timesharing.
10. Briefly explain how title to land in a PUD is held.

ADDITIONAL READINGS

Condominium Development Guide, by **Keith Romney** and **Brad Romney** (Warren, Gorham, & Lamont, 1990). Lengthy, legal, readable, practical, and detailed. This is the type of information one needs before developing a condominium. Contains procedures, analysis, and forms. Annual updates issued.

Income/Expense Analysis: Condos, Co-ops, PUDS (Institute for Real Estate Management, 1995). Updated annually.

"PUDS, Condos, and the Real Estate Salesperson: Selling Units in Planned Housing Requires Knowledge of Special Details," by **Audrey Parente** (*Real Estate Today*, May 1982, pp. 17–19).

Real Estate Broker's Guide to Resort Time Sharing, by **Richard Lynge** and **Keith Trowbridge** (Real Estate Education, 1984, 262 pages). Explains the field to anyone considering joining a timeshare sales program. Explains broker-developer relationship, resort quality, sales methods, commissions, and management procedures.

13

Title Closing and Escrow

KEY • TERMS

Closing meeting: a meeting at which the buyer pays for the property and receives a deed to it and all other matters pertaining to the sale are concluded

Escrow agent: the person placed in charge of an escrow

Escrow closing: the deposit of documents and funds with a neutral third party along with instructions as to how to conduct the closing

Prorating: the division of ongoing expenses and income items between the buyer and the seller

Real Estate Settlement Procedures Act (RESPA): a federal law that deals with procedures to be followed in certain types of real estate closings

Settlement statement: an accounting of funds to the buyer and the seller at the completion of a real estate transaction

Title closing: the process of completing a real estate transaction

Walk-through: a final inspection of the property just prior to settlement

Numerous details must be handled between the time a buyer and seller sign a sales contract and the day title is conveyed to the buyer. Title must be searched (Chapter 15), a decision made as to how to take title (Chapter 6), a deed prepared (Chapter 7), loan arrangements made (Chapters 16 through 20), property tax records checked (Chapter 22) and so forth. In this chapter we look at the final steps in the process, in particular, the buyer's walk-through, the closing meeting or escrow, prorations, and the settlement statement.

BUYERS'
WALK-THROUGH

To protect both the buyer and the seller, it is good practice for a buyer to make a **walk-through,** i.e., a final inspection of the property just prior to the settlement date. Quite possibly the buyer has not been on the parcel or inside the structure since the initial offer and acceptance. Now, several weeks later, the buyer wants to make certain that the premises have been vacated, that no damage has occurred, that the seller has left behind personal property agreed on, and that the seller has not removed and taken any real property. If the sales contract requires all mechanical items to be in normal working order, then the seller will want to test the heating and air conditioning systems, dishwasher, disposer, stove, garage door opener, and so on, and the refrigerator, washer, and dryer, if included. The buyer will also want to test all of the plumbing to be certain the hot water heater works, faucets and showers run, toilets flush, and sinks drain. A final inspection of the structure is made, including walls, roof, gutters, driveway, decks, patios, and so on, as well as the land and landscaping.

Note that a walk-through is not the time for the buyer to make the initial inspection of the property. That is done before the contract is signed, and if there are questions in the buyer's mind regarding the structural soundness of the property, a thorough inspection (possibly with the aid of a professional house inspector) should be conducted after signing the purchase contract, making the satisfactory inspection a condition to the buyer's obligation to purchase. The walk-through is for the purpose of giving the buyer the opportunity to make certain that agreements regarding the condition of the premises have been kept. If during the walk-through the buyer notes the walls were damaged when the seller moved out or the furnace does not function, the buyer (or the buyer's agent) notes these items and asks that funds be withheld at the closing to pay for repairs.

Title closing refers to the completion of a real estate transaction. This is when the buyer pays for the property and the seller delivers the deed. The day on which this occurs is called the **closing date.** Depending on where one resides in the United States, the title closing process is referred to as a **closing, settlement,** or **escrow.** All accomplish the same basic goal, but the method of reaching that goal can follow one of two paths.

TITLE CLOSING

In New York and other parts of the United States, particularly in the East, and to a certain extent in the mountain states, the Midwest, and the South, the title closing process is concluded at a meeting of all parties to the transaction or their representatives. Elsewhere, title closing is conducted by an escrow agent who is a neutral third party mutually selected by the buyer and seller to carry out the closing. With an escrow closing, there is no closing meeting; in fact, most of the closing process is conducted by mail. Let's look at the operation of each method.

When a meeting is used to close a real estate transaction, the seller meets in person with the buyer and delivers the deed. At the same time, the buyer pays the seller for the property. To ascertain that everything promised in the sales contract has been properly carried out, it is customary for the buyer and seller each to have an attorney present. The real estate agents who brought the buyer and seller together are also present, along with a representative of the firm that conducted the title search. If a new loan is being made or an existing one is being paid off at the closing, a representative of each lender may be present.

CLOSING
OR SETTLEMENT
MEETING

The first step after the buyer and seller sign a real estate sales contract is for their closing attorneys to contact each other. The custom in New York is for the seller's attorney to prepare the deed and deliver it to the buyer's attorney for review. Responsibility for obtaining the abstract of title varies from county to county. If a lender is involved, an attorney for the lender will want to inspect these documents so that any problems can be resolved before closing. If the buyer wants a property inspection report or a land survey, these should also be ordered before the closing date. When a new loan is involved, the closing is usually held at the office of the lender. Otherwise, it is held at the office of one of the attorneys.

Seller's Responsibilities at Closing

To assure a smooth closing, each person attending is responsible for bringing certain documents. The sellers and their attorney are responsible for preparing and bringing the deed together with the most recent property tax bill (and receipt if it has been paid). If required by the sales contract, they also bring the insurance policy for the property, the termite and wood-rot inspection report, deeds or documents showing the removal of unacceptable liens and encumbrances, a title insurance policy, a bill of sale for personal property, a survey map, a smoke alarm affidavit, and any needed offset statements or beneficiary statements. An **offset statement** is a statement by an owner or lienholder as to the balance due on an existing lien against the property. A **beneficiary statement** is a statement of the unpaid balance on a note secured by a trust deed. The loan payment booklet, keys to the property, garage door opener, and the like are also brought to the meeting. If the property is a condominium, cooperative, or planned unit development, the sellers bring to the closing such items as the articles of incorporation; bylaws; conditions, covenants, and restrictions (CC&Rs); annual budget; reserve fund status report; and management company's name. If the property produces income, existing leases, rent schedules, current expenditures, and letters advising the tenants of the new owner must also be furnished.

Buyer's Responsibilities at Closing

The buyers' responsibilities include having adequate settlement funds ready, having an attorney present if desired, and, if borrowing, obtaining the loan commitment and advising the lender of the meeting's time and place. The real estate agent is present and receives a commission check at that time and, as a matter of good business, makes certain that all goes well.

If a new loan is involved, the lender brings a check for the amount of the loan along with a note and mortgage for the borrower to sign. If an existing loan is to be paid off as part of the transaction, the lender is present to receive a check and release the mortgage held on the property. If a lender elects not to attend, the check and/or loan papers are given to the person in charge of the closing, along with instructions for their distribution and signing. A title insurance representative is also present to provide the latest status of title and the title insurance policy. If title insurance is not used, the sellers are responsible for bringing an abstract or asking the abstracter to be present.

The seller and the seller's attorney may be unaware of all the things expected of them at the closing meeting. Therefore, it is the duty of the agent who listed the property to make certain that they are prepared for the meeting. Similarly, it is the duty of the agent who found the buyer to make certain that the buyer and the buyer's attorney are prepared for the closing meeting. If the agent both lists and sells the property, the agent assists both the buyer and seller. If more than one agent is involved in the transaction, each should keep the other(s) fully informed so the transaction will go as well as possible. At all times buyers and sellers are to be kept informed as to the status of the closing. An agent should give them a preview of what will take place, explain each payment or receipt, and in general prepare the parties for informed participation at the closing meeting.

Agent's Duties

When everyone concerned has arrived at the meeting place, the closing begins. Those present record each other's names as witnesses to the meeting. The various documents called for by the sales contract are exchanged for inspection. The buyers and their attorney inspect the deed the sellers are offering, the title search and/or title policy, the mortgage papers, survey, leases, removals of encumbrances, and proration calculations. The lender also inspects the deed, survey, title search, and title policy. This continues until each party has a chance to inspect each document of interest.

The Transaction

A **settlement statement** (also called a closing statement) is given to the buyer and seller to summarize the financial aspects of their transaction. It is prepared by the person in charge of the closing, usually by one of the attorneys, either just prior to or at the meeting. It provides a clear picture of where the buyers' and sellers' money is going at the closing by identifying each party to whom money is being paid. (An example of a closing statement is given later in this chapter.)

If everyone involved in the closing has done his or her homework and comes prepared to the meeting, the closing usually goes smoothly. When everything is in order, the seller hands a completed deed to the buyer. Simultaneously, the buyer gives the seller a check that combines the down payment and net result of the prorations. The lender has the buyer sign the mortgage and note and hands checks to the seller and the existing lender, if one is involved. The seller writes a check to his real estate broker, attorney, and the abstracter. The buyer writes a check to his attorney. This continues until every document is signed and everyone is paid. At the end, everyone stands, shakes hands, and departs. The deed, new mortgage, and release of the old mortgage are recorded and the transaction is complete.

Dry Closing   Occasionally an unavoidable circumstance can cause delays in a closing. Perhaps an important document, known to be in the mail, has not arrived. Yet it will be difficult to reschedule the meeting. In such a situation, the parties concerned may agree to a **dry closing**. In a dry closing, all parties sign their documents and entrust them to the person in charge of the closing for safekeeping. No money is disbursed and the deed is not delivered until the missing paperwork arrives. When it does, the closing attorney completes the transaction and delivers the money and documents by mail or messenger.

ESCROW   The use of an **escrow** to close a real estate transaction involves a neutral third party called an **escrow agent,** escrow holder, or escrowee who acts as a trusted stakeholder for all the parties to the transaction. Instead of delivering a deed directly to the buyer at the closing meeting, the seller gives the deed to the escrow agent with instructions that it be delivered only after the buyer has completed all of the buyer's promises in the sales contract. Similarly, the buyer hands the escrow agent the money for the purchase price plus instructions that it be given to the seller only after fulfillment of the seller's promises. Let's look more closely at this arrangement.

A typical real estate escrow closing starts when a sales contract is signed by the buyer and seller. They select a neutral escrow agent to handle the closing. This may be the escrow department of a bank or savings and loan or other lending agency, an independent escrow company, an attorney, or the escrow department of a title insurance company. Sometimes real estate brokers offer escrow services. However, if the broker is earning a sales commission in the transaction, the broker cannot be classed as neutral and disinterested. Because escrow agents are entrusted with valuable documents and large sums of money, most states have licensing and bonding requirements that escrow agents must meet. Escrow closings are not often used in New York; the closing meeting is more common.

The Internal Revenue code now provides that the seller's proceeds from all sales of real estate must be reported to the Internal Revenue Service on their Form 1099. The responsibility for filing Form 1099 goes in the following order: the person responsible for the closing, the mortgage lender, the seller's broker, the buyer's broker, and any person designated by the U.S. Treasury. It is important to determine at the closing who needs to file the Form 1099. Since November 10, 1988, these forms must be filed at no charge to the taxpayer.

Reporting Requirements

When a real estate purchase contract is written, a closing date is also negotiated and placed in the contract. The choice of closing date will depend on when the buyer wants possession, when the seller wants to move out, and how long it will take to obtain a loan, title search, and termite report and otherwise fulfill the contract requirements. In a typical residential sale, this may take 30 to 60 days, with 45 days being a popular choice when new financing is involved.

DELAYS
AND FAILURE
TO CLOSE

Delays along the way are sometimes encountered and may cause a delay in the closing. This is usually not a problem as long as the buyer still intends to buy, the seller still intends to sell, and the delay is for a reasonable cause and a justifiable length of time. Many preprinted real estate purchase contracts include a statement that the broker may extend the time for performance including the closing date. Even if the contract contains a "time is of the essence" clause, unless there is supporting evidence in the contract that time really is of the essence, reasonable delays for reasonable causes are usually permitted by law.

Suppose the delay will be quite lengthy. For example, there may be a previously undisclosed title defect that will take months to clear or perhaps there are unusual problems in financing or there has been major damage to the premises. In such cases, relieving all parties from further obligations may be the wisest choice for all involved. If so, it is essential that the buyer and seller sign mutual release papers. These are necessary to rescind the purchase contract and cancel the escrow if one has been opened. The buyer's deposit is also returned. Without release papers the buyer still has a vaguely defined liability to buy and the seller can still be required to convey the property. A mutual release gives the buyer the freedom to choose another property and the seller the chance to fix the problem and remarket the property later.

A stickier problem occurs when one party wants out of the contract and attempts to use any delay in closing as grounds for contract termination. The buyer may have found a preferable property for less money and better terms. The seller may have received a higher offer since signing the purchase contract. Although the party wishing to cancel may threaten with a lawsuit, courts will rarely enforce cancellation of valuable contract rights because of reasonable delays that are not the fault of the other party. Moreover, courts will not go along with a reluctant buyer or seller who manufactures delays so as to delay the closing and then claim default and cancellation of the contract. If the reluctance continues and negotiations to end it fail, the performing party may choose to complete its requirements and then ask the courts to force the reluctant party to the closing table.

LOAN ESCROWS

Escrows can be used for purposes other than real estate sales transactions. For example, a homeowner who is refinancing his property could enter into a **loan escrow** with the lender. The conditions of the escrow would be that the homeowner deliver a properly executed note and mortgage to the escrow agent and that the lender deposit the loan money. Upon closing, the escrow agent delivers the documents to the lender and the money to the homeowner. Or, in reverse, an escrow could be used to pay off the balance of a loan. The conditions would be the borrower's deposit of the balance due and the lender's deposit of the mortgage release and note. Even the weekly office sports pool is an escrow—with the person holding the pool money acting as escrow agent for the participants.

PRORATING AT THE CLOSING

Ongoing expenses and income items must be **prorated** between the seller and buyer when property ownership changes hands.

Items subject to proration include property insurance premiums, property taxes, accrued interest on assumed loans, and rents and operating expenses if the property produces income. If heating is done by oil and the oil tank is partially filled when title transfers, that oil can be prorated, as can utility bills when service is not shut off between owners. Several sample prorations common to most closings will help clarify the process.

Hazard insurance policies for such things as fire, wind, storm, and flood damage are paid for in advance. At the beginning of each year of the policy's life, the premium for that year's coverage must be paid. When real estate is sold, the buyer may ask the seller to transfer the remaining coverage. The seller usually agrees if the buyer pays for the value of the remaining coverage on a prorated basis.

Hazard Insurance

The first step in prorating hazard insurance is to find out how often the premium is paid, how much it is, and what period of time it covers. Suppose that the seller has a 1-year policy that cost $180 and started on January 1 of the current year. If the property is sold and the closing date is July 1, the policy is half-used. Therefore, if the buyer wants the policy transferred, the buyer pays the seller $90 for the remaining 6 months of coverage.

Because closing dates do not always occur on neat, evenly divided portions of the year, nor do most items that need prorating, it is usually necessary to break the year into months and the months into days to make proration calculations. Suppose in the previous hazard insurance example that prorations are to be made on June 30 instead of July 1. This would give the buyer 6 months and 1 day of coverage. How much does the buyer owe the seller? The first step is to calculate the monthly and daily rates for the policy: $180 divided by 12 is $15 per month. Dividing the monthly rate of $15 by 30 days gives a daily rate of 50 cents. The second step is to add 6 months at $15 and 1 day at 50 cents. Thus, the buyer owes the seller $90.50 for the unused portion of the policy.

When a buyer agrees to assume an existing loan from the seller, an interest proration is necessary. For example, a sales contract calls for the buyer to assume a 9% mortgage loan with a principal balance of $80,505 at the time of closing. Loan payments are due

Loan Interest

the tenth of each month, and the sales contract calls for a July 3 closing date, with interest on the loan to be prorated through July 2. How much is to be prorated and to whom?

First, we must recognize that interest is normally paid in arrears. On a loan that is payable monthly, the borrower pays interest for the use of the loan at the end of each month he or she has had the loan. Thus, the July 10 monthly loan payment includes the interest due for the use of $80,505 from June 10 through July 9. However, the seller owned the property through July 2, and from June 10 through July 2 is 23 days. At the closing the seller must give the buyer enough money to pay for 23 days interest on the $80,505. If the annual interest rate is 9%, one month's interest is $80,505 times 9% divided by 12, which is $603.79. Divide this by 30 days to get a daily interest rate of $20.126. Multiply the daily rate by 23 to obtain the interest for 23 days, $462.90.

30-Day Month   In many parts of the country it is the custom when prorating interest, property taxes, water bills, and insurance to use a 30-day month because it simplifies proration calculations. Naturally, using a 30-day month produces some inaccuracy when dealing with months that do not have 30 days. If this inaccuracy is significant to the buyer and seller, they can agree to prorate either by using the exact number of days in the closing month or by dividing the year rate by 365 to find a daily rate. Some states avoid this question altogether by requiring that the exact number of days be used in prorating.

Rents   It is the custom throughout the country to prorate rents on the basis of the actual number of days in the month. Using the July 3 closing date again, if the property is currently rented for $450 per month, paid in advance on the first of each month, what would the proration be? If the seller has already collected the rent for the month of July, he is obligated to hand over to the buyer that portion of the rent earned between July 3 and July 31, inclusive, a period of 29 days. To determine how many dollars this is, divide $450 by the number of days in July. This gives $14.516 as the rent per day. Then multiply the daily rate by 29 days to get $420.96, the portion of the July rent that the seller must hand over to the buyer. If the renter has not paid the July rent by the July 3 closing date, no proration is made. If the buyer later collects the July rent, he must return 2 days' rent to the seller.

Prorated property taxes are common to nearly all real estate transactions. The amount of proration depends on when the property taxes are due, what portion has already been paid, and what period of time they cover. Property taxes are levied on an annual basis, but depending on the locality they may be due at the beginning, middle, or end of the tax year. In some cities in New York, property owners are permitted to pay in two or more installments.

Property Taxes

The property tax year is the calendar year in New York for town and county taxes. Suppose your annual taxes in the amount of $1,080 were paid on January 31, and the closing date is March 5. How is the proration made? In New York, it is customary to charge the buyer for the day of closing. This means the seller is liable for January 1 through March 4. The buyer is liable for March 5 through December 31. If we divide $1,080 by 12, we find that 1 month's taxes are $90. Dividing $90 by 30 gives a daily rate of $3. Since the taxes for the year have been paid in advance by the seller, the buyer owes the seller for the period March 5 through December 31. This is a total of 9 months and 27 days and amounts to $891.

In some districts, the school tax year runs from July 1 through the following June 30. School tax bills are sent out September 1 and are due on September 30. Suppose a closing takes place on August 5th. Since the current tax bill has not yet been received by the seller, it is customary to use the previous year's tax bill as a basis for calculations. The seller then pays the buyer for the period July 1 through August 4, a period of 1 month and 4 days. When the tax bill arrives in the mail, the buyer will pay for the whole year.

If the property being sold is a condominium unit or in a cooperative or a planned unit development, the monthly homeowners' association payment must be prorated. Suppose the monthly fee is $120 and is paid in advance on the first of the month. If the closing takes place on the 20th, then the buyer owes the sellers $40 for the unused portion of the month.

Homeowners' Association

Special assessments for such things as street improvements, water mains, and sewer lines are not usually prorated. As a rule, the selling price of the property reflects the added value of the improvements, and the seller pays any assessments in full before closing. This is not an ironclad rule; the buyer and seller in their sales contract can agree to do whatever they want about the assessment.

Proration Summary

Figure 13.1 summarizes the most common proration situations found in real estate closings. The figure also shows who is to be charged and who is to be credited and whether the proration is to be worked forward or backward from the closing date. As a rule, items that are paid in advance are prorated forward from the closing date—for example, prepaid fire insurance. Items that are paid in arrears, such as interest on an existing loan, are prorated backward from the closing date.

SAMPLE CLOSING

To illustrate the arithmetic involved, let us work through a residential closing situation. Note that this example is not particular to any region of the United States, but is rather a composite that shows you how the most commonly encountered residential closing items are handled.

Homer Leavitt has listed his home for sale with List-Rite Realty for $125,000, and the sales commission is to be 6% of the

Figure 13.1. Common prorations.

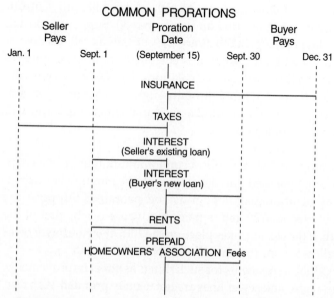

selling price. A salesperson from Quick-Sale Realty learns about the property through the multiple listing service and produces a buyer willing to pay $123,000 with $33,000 down. The offer is conditioned on the seller paying off the existing $48,000, 12% interest mortgage loan and the buyer obtaining a new loan for $90,000. Property taxes, school taxes, and heating oil in the home's oil tank are to be prorated as of the closing date. The buyer also asks the seller to pay for a termite inspection and repairs if necessary, a title search, an owner's title insurance policy, conveyance taxes, and one-half the closing fee. The seller accepts this offer on August 15, and they agree to close on September 15.

The property tax year for this home runs from January 1 through December 31. Mr. Leavitt has paid the taxes for the current year (through December 31). The hazard insurance policy (fire, windstorm, etc.) that the buyer wishes to assume was purchased by the seller for $240 and covers the period June 15 through the following June 14. The Safety Title Insurance Company will charge the buyer $525.00 for a combined title search, title examination, and owner's title policy package.

The buyer obtains a loan commitment from the Ajax National Bank for $90,000. To make this loan, the bank will charge a $900 loan origination fee, $100 for an appraisal, and $55 for a credit report on the buyer. The bank also requires a lender's title policy in the amount of $90,000 (added cost $90). The loan is to be repaid in equal monthly installments beginning October 1. The termite inspection by Dead-Bug Pest Company costs $100.00, and recording fees are $19 for the deed, $13.50 for the mortgage release and $37.00 for mortgage. The state levies a transfer tax on deeds of $2.00 per $500 of sales price. A mortgage tax is assessed on each transaction, which varies from one-half of 1% up to 1% of the mortgage amount, depending on the county. The seller is leaving $130 worth of heating oil for the buyer.

The buyer and seller have each hired an attorney to advise them on legal matters in connection with the sales contract and closing. They are to be paid $400.00 and $500.00, respectively, out of the settlement. List-Rite Realty and Quick-Sale Realty have advised the closing agent that they are splitting the $7,380 sales commission equally.

Finally, the $3,000 earnest money deposit that the buyer made with the offer is to be credited toward the down payment. Using this information, which is summarized in Table 13.1 for your convenience, let us see how a settlement statement is prepared.

SETTLEMENT
STATEMENT

Figure 13.2 is the HUD-1 Form, the most widely used residential settlement form in the United States, and it is filled out to reflect the transaction outlined in Table 13.1. Let us work through this sample transaction in order to see where each item is placed on the settlement statement. (You will notice that the buyer is referred to as the borrower in Figure 13.2. This is not important for the moment and will be explained later.)

Lines 101 and 401 of the settlement statement show the price the buyer is paying and the seller is receiving for the property. Line 103 is the total of the buyer's settlement charges from the reverse side of the form. (The reverse side will be covered in a moment.) Line 107 shows the property tax proration charge to the buyer and line 407 shows the same proration as a credit to the seller. Because the seller is required to pay the property taxes for a year in advance, the taxes are paid until January 1, 1997. However, since the buyer will occupy the house for 3 and a half months of the year, the buyer must give the seller $233.88 as part of the closing. The same principle applies to the school taxes which, in most communities in New York, cover the period of July 1 through June 30, although they are generally payable in September. On line 108 the buyer is charged $789.62 for the balance of the school tax year; on line 408, the seller is credited with this amount which he has already paid to the school district. The heating oil remaining in the heating system tank is charged to the buyer (line 109) and credited to the seller (line 409). The gross amount due from the buyer is tallied on line 120.

On line 201, the buyer is credited with the earnest money paid at the time the purchase contract was written. On the next line the buyer is credited with the new $90,000 loan.

Line 220 lists the total of the buyer's credits. Line 301 is the total amount due from the buyer for this transaction. The difference, on line 303, is the amount of cash needed from the buyer to close the transaction.

Table 13.1. Transaction Summary

	Amount	Comments
Sale Price	$123,000	
Down Payment	$ 33,000	
Deposit (Earnest Money)	$ 3,000	Credit to buyer's down payment.
Existing Loan	$ 48,000	Seller to pay off through settlement. Interest rate is 12%.
New Loan	$ 90,000	Monthly payments begin Nov. 1. Interest rate is 9.6%.
Loan Origination Fee	$ 900	Paid by buyer in connection with obtaining $90,000 loan.
Appraisal Fee	$ 100	
Credit Report	$ 55	
Lender's Title Policy	$ 525	Buyer pays Safety Title Co.
County Property Taxes	$ 1,000/yr	Paid one year in advance by buyer.
School Taxes	$ 800/yr	Paid one year in advance by buyer.
Hazard Insurance	$ 240/yr	12 month policy. Buyer pays.
Heating Oil	$ 130	Oil in tank. Transfer to buyer.
Pest Inspection	$ 120	Seller pays Dead-Bug Pest Co.
Property Tax Reserves	$ 1,680	12 months at $140 for lender.
Hazard Insurance Reserves	$ 80	4 months at $20 for lender.
Buyer's Attorney	$ 400	
Seller's Attorney	$ 500	
Closing Fee	$ 400	Ajax National Bank charge; buyer pays.
Conveyance Tax	$ 650	Seller pays.
Record Deed	$ 19	Buyer pays.
Record Mortgage Release	$ 13.50	Seller pays.
Record Mortgage	$ 37	Buyer pays.
Brokerage Commission	$ 7,380	Seller pays; to be split equally between List-Rite Realty and Quick-Sale Realty.
File Real Property Transfer Report	$ 25	Buyer pays.
File Transfer Gains Tax Affidavit	$ 5	Seller pays.

Settlement and Proration date is September 15. All prorations are to be based on a 30-day banker's month.

Seller's Side

On the seller's side of the settlement statement, line 420 shows the total dollars due the seller from the sales price and proration credits. Line 502 is the total of the seller's settlement costs from the reverse side of the form. On line 504 the seller is charged for the existing mortgage loan that is being paid off as part of

Figure 13.2.

A. SETTLEMENT STATEMENT

U.S. DEPARTMENT OF HOUSING
AND URBAN DEVELOPMENT

OMB NO. 2502-0265

B. TYPE OF LOAN			
1. [ ] FHA 2. [ ] FmHA 3. [X] Conv. Unis. 4. [ ] VA 5. [ ] Conv. Ins.	6. FILE NUMBER DELONE	7. LOAN NUMBER	8. MORTGAGE INS CASE NUMBER

C. NOTE: This form is furnished to give you a statement of actual settlement costs. Amounts paid to and by the settlement agent are shown. Items marked "[POC]" were paid outside the closing; they are shown here for informational purposes and are not included in the totals. 4.2 05-95 (4/DELONE)

D. NAME AND ADDRESS OF BORROWER	E. NAME AND ADDRESS OF SELLER	F. NAME AND ADDRESS OF LENDER
Heidi Delone 2424 Newpaige Lane City, State 00000	Homer Leavitt 1654 West 12th Street City, State 00000	Acme National Bank 1111 West 1st Street City, State 00000

G. PROPERTY LOCATION	H. SETTLEMENT AGENT 141777938	I. SETTLEMENT DATE
1654 West 12th Street City, NY 00000 Any County, New York	Honen & Wood, P.C. PLACE OF SETTLEMENT 126 State Street, 5th Floor City, State 00000	September 15, 1996

J. SUMMARY OF BORROWER'S TRANSACTION		K. SUMMARY OF SELLER'S TRANSACTION	
100. GROSS AMOUNT DUE FROM BORROWER		400. GROSS AMOUNT DUE TO SELLER	
101. Contract Sales Price	123,000.00	401. Contract Sales Price	123,000.00
102. Personal Property		402. Personal Property	
103. Settlement Charges to Borrower line 1400	4,036.89	403.	
104. Payoff Mortgage		404.	
105.		405.	
Adjustments for items paid by Seller in advance		Adjustments for items paid by Seller in advance	
106. Village Taxes to		406. Village Taxes to	
107. County taxes 09-16-96 to 01-01-97	233.88	407. County taxes 09-16-96 to 01-01-97	233.88
108. School Taxes 09-16-96 to 07-01-97	789.62	408. School Taxes 09-16-96 to 07-01-97	789.62
109. Fuel Oil Adjustment	130.00	409. Fuel Oil Adjustment	130.00
110.		410.	
111.		411.	
112.		412.	
120. GROSS AMOUNT DUE FROM BORROWER	128,190.39	420. GROSS AMOUNT DUE TO SELLER	124,153.50
200. AMOUNTS PAID BY OR IN BEHALF OF BORROWER		500. REDUCTIONS IN AMOUNT DUE TO SELLER	
201. Deposit or earnest money	3,000.00	501. Excess Deposit (see instructions)	
202. Principal Amount of New Loan(s)	90,000.00	502. Settlement Charges to Seller line 1400	8,510.50
203. Existing Loan(s) Taken Subject to		503. Existing Loans Taken Subject to	
204.		504. Payoff 1st Mtg to 1st National Bank	48,000.00
205.		505. Payoff of second mortgage loan	
206.		506. Deposit retained by seller	3,000.00
207.		507.	
208.		508.	
209.		509.	
Adjustments for items unpaid by Seller		Adjustments for items unpaid by Seller	
210. Village Taxes to		510. Village Taxes to	
211. County taxes to		511. County taxes to	
212. School Taxes to		512. School Taxes to	
213.		513.	
214.		514.	
215.		515.	
216.		516.	
217.		517.	
218.		518.	
219.		519.	
220. TOTAL PAID BY/FOR BORROWER	93,000.00	520. TOTAL REDUCTION AMOUNT DUE SELLER	59,510.50
300. CASH AT SETTLEMENT FROM/TO BORROWER		600. CASH AT SETTLEMENT TO/FROM SELLER	
301. Gross Amt Due from Borrower (line 120)	128,190.39	601. Gross Amount Due to Seller (line 420)	124,153.50
302. Less Amt Paid by/for Borrower (line 220)	(93,000.00)	602. Less Reductions Due Seller (line 520)	(59,510.50)
303. CASH [X] FROM [ ] TO BORROWER	35,190.39	603. CASH [X] TO [ ] FROM SELLER	64,643.00

The undersigned hereby acknowledge receipt of a completed copy of pages 1&2 of this statement & any attachments referred to herein.

BORROWER _____ Heidi Delone _____

BORROWER _____

SELLER _____ Homer Leavitt _____

SELLER _____

Figure 13.2. (continued)

SETTLEMENT STATEMENT PAGE 2

L. SETTLEMENT CHARGES	PAID FROM BORROWER'S FUNDS AT SETTLEMENT	PAID FROM SELLER'S FUNDS AT SETTLEMENT
700. Total Sales/Brokers Commissions Based on Price $ 123,000.00 @ 6.0000 % = 7,380.00		
Division of Commission (line 700) as follows:		
701. $ 3,690.00 to List-Rite Realty		
702. $ 3,690.00 to Quick Sale Realty		
703. Commission Paid at Settlement		7,380.00
704.		
800. ITEMS PAYABLE IN CONNECTION WITH LOAN		
801. Loan Origination Fee 1.0000 % to Acme National Bank	900.00	
802. Loan Discount % to		
803. Appraisal Fee to Acme National Bank	100.00	
804. Credit Report to Acme National Bank	55.00	
805. Flood Certification Fee to		
806. Title Exam Fee to		
807. Underwriting Fee to		
808.		
809.		
810.		
811.		
900. ITEMS REQUIRED BY LENDER TO BE PAID IN ADVANCE		
901. Interest from 09-15-96 to 10-01-96 @$ 18.493150/day(16 days 7.5000%)	295.89	
902. MIP TotIns. for LifeOfLoan for 360 months to US Department of HUD		
903. Hazard Insurance Premium for 1 years to Your Insurance Co. 240.00 [POC]		
904. to		
905.		
1000. RESERVES DEPOSITED WITH LENDER		
1001. Hazard Insurance 3.000 months @ $ 20.00 per month	60.00	
1002. Mortgage Insurance months @ $ per month		
1003. Village Taxes months @ $ per month		
1004. County taxes 10.999 months @ $ 66.67 per month	733.33	
1005. School Taxes 3.000 months @ $ 83.33 per month	250.03	
1006. months @ $ per month		
1007. months @ $ per month		
1008. Aggregate Adjustment	-413.36	
1100. TITLE CHARGES		
1101. Settlement or Closing Fee to Honen & Wood, P.C.	400.00	
1102. Abstract or Title Search to		
1103. Title Examination to		
1104. Title Insurance Binder to		
1105. Document Preparation to		
1106. Notary Fees to		
1107. Attorney's Fees to		
(includes above item numbers: 1101,1103,1105)		
1108. Title Insurance to Safety Title Insurance Company)	525.00	
(includes above item numbers:)		
1109. Lender's Coverage $ 90,000.00		
1110. Owner's Coverage $		
1111. Buyer's Attorney to Law Office	400.00	
1112. Seller's Attorney to Law Firm		500.00
1113.		
1200. GOVERNMENT RECORDING AND TRANSFER CHARGES		
1201. Recording Fees: Deed $ 19.00 ;Mortgage $ 37.00 ;Releases $ 13.50	56.00	13.50
1202. City/County Tax/Stamps: Deed $;Mortgage $		
1203. State Tax/Stamps: Deed $ 492.00 ;Mortgage $ 650.00	650.00	492.00
1204. Equalization & Assessment to Any County Clerk	25.00	
1205. Gains Tax Affidavit to Any County Clerk		5.00
1300. ADDITIONAL SETTLEMENT CHARGES		
1301. Survey to		
1302. Pest Inspection to Dead Bug Company		120.00
1303.		
1304.		
1305.		
1400. TOTAL SETTLEMENT CHARGES (Enter On Lines 103, Section J and 502, Section K)	4,036.89	8,510.50

By signing page 1 of this statement, the signatories acknowledge receipt of a completed copy of page 2 of this 2 page statement.

(4/DELONE)
Certified to be a true copy

Honen & Wood, P.C.
Settlement Agent

the closing. The $3000 deposit paid to the seller upon signing the contract is accounted for on line 506. Line 520 is a total of what must come out of the seller's funds at the closing. This is compared with the gross amount due the seller on line 601 and the difference (line 603) is the cash the seller will receive at the closing.

Settlement Charges　Continuing with Figure 13.2, the real estate commission is handled on lines 700, 701, and 702. Note that if the closing agent is to make a commission split, as shown here, the closing agent must have written instructions to do so from the real estate broker who is being paid by the seller. Otherwise, all the commission goes to the seller's broker, and the seller's broker pays the cooperating broker according to whatever agreement they have.

Lines 801, 803, and 804 indicate charges incurred by the buyer in connection with obtaining the new $90,000 loan. Line 901 shows the interest on the $90,000 loan calculated from the date of closing to the end of September. This brings the loan up to the first day of the next month and simplifies future bookkeeping for the monthly loan payments. At 7.5% the interest on $90,000 is $18.49 a day and the buyer is charged for 16 days.

As a condition for the loan the lender requires impound accounts for hazard insurance and property taxes. In order to have enough on hand to make the January property tax payment, the lender requires (line 1004) an immediate reserve of $733.33. Each month thereafter, one-twelfth of the estimated taxes for next year will be added to the buyer's monthly payment so as to have money in the impound account from which to pay taxes. The same concept applies to the school taxes and hazard insurance. On page 298 you will read about the Real Estate Settlement and Procedures Act which caps the amount of reserves a lender can demand from the borrower. Line 1008 represents a credit to the buyer in this transaction based on that cap (lines 1001 and 1005).

Line 1101 is the closing fee associated with this closing. Title insurance charges of $525 to the buyer for the lender's policy are itemized on line 1108. Line 1109 shows the coverage for each. The amounts paid from settlement funds to the attorneys of the buyer and seller are listed on lines 1111 and 1112. Note that the buyer and seller can choose to pay their attorneys outside of the closing. **Outside of the closing** or **outside of escrow** means a party to the closing has paid someone directly and not through the closing.

Government recording fees and conveyance taxes necessary to complete this transaction are itemized on lines 1201 and 1203 through 1205 and charged to the buyer and seller as shown. On line 1302 the settlement agent pays the pest inspection company on behalf of the seller. This is another item that is sometimes paid outside of the closing, that is, the seller can write a check directly to the termite company once the inspection has been made. On line 1400 the totals for both the buyer and seller are entered. The same totals are transferred to lines 103 and 502.

Note that Figure 13.2 shows both the buyer's side of the transaction and the seller's side. To preserve confidentiality, the seller may receive this settlement statement with lines 100 through 303 blacked out, and the buyer may receive this statement with lines 400 through 603 blacked out.

REAL ESTATE SETTLEMENT PROCEDURES ACT

In response to consumer complaints regarding real estate closing costs and procedures, Congress passed the **Real Estate Settlement Procedures Act (RESPA)** effective June 20, 1975, throughout the United States. The purpose of RESPA, which is administered by the U.S. Department of Housing and Urban Development (HUD), is to regulate and standardize real estate settlement practices when *federally related* first mortgage loans are made on one- to four-family residences, condominiums, and cooperatives. *Federally related* is defined to include FHA or VA or other government-backed or assisted loans, loans from lenders with federally insured deposits, loans that are to be purchased by FNMA, GNMA, FHLMC, or other federally controlled secondary mortgage market institutions, and loans made by lenders who make or invest more than $1 million per year in residential loans. As the bulk of all home loans now made fall into one of these categories, the impact of this law is far-reaching.

Restrictions

RESPA prohibits kickbacks and fees for services not performed during the closing process. For example, in some regions of the

United States prior to this act, it was common practice for attorneys and closing agents to channel title business to certain title companies in return for a fee. This increased settlement costs without adding services. Now there must be a justifiable service rendered for each closing fee charge. The act also prohibits the seller from requiring that the buyer purchase title insurance from a particular title company.

The Real Estate Settlement Procedures Act also contains restrictions on the amount of advance property tax and insurance payments a lender can collect and place in an impound or reserve account. The amount is limited to the property owner's share of taxes and insurance accrued prior to settlement, plus one-sixth of the estimated amount that will come due for these items in the 12-month period beginning at settlement. This requirement assures that the lender has an adequate but not excessive amount of money impounded when taxes and insurance payments fall due. If the amount in the reserve account is not sufficient to pay an item when it comes due, the lender must temporarily use its own funds to make up the difference. Then the lender bills the borrower or increases the monthly reserve payment. If there is a drop in the amount the lender must pay out, then the monthly reserve requirement can be reduced.

Considerable criticism and debate have raged over the topic of reserves. Traditionally, lenders have not paid interest to borrowers on money held as reserves, effectively creating an interest-free loan to themselves. This has tempted many lenders to require overly adequate reserves. RESPA sets a reasonable limit on reserve requirements and some states now require that interest be paid on reserves. Although not always required to do so, some lenders now voluntarily pay interest on reserves.

Benefits   Anyone applying for a RESPA-regulated loan will receive several benefits. First is a HUD information booklet explaining RESPA. Second is a good faith estimate of closing costs from the lender. Third, the lender will use the HUD Uniform Settlement Statement shown in Figure 13.2. Fourth, the borrower has the right to inspect the HUD Settlement Statement one business day before the day of closing.

The primary reason lenders are required to give loan applicants an estimate of closing costs promptly is to allow the loan applicant an opportunity to compare prices for the various services the transaction will require. Additionally, these estimates help the borrower estimate closing costs. Figure 13.3 illustrates a good faith estimate form.

Figure 13.3.

Good Faith Estimate of Closing Costs

The charges listed below are our Good Faith Estimate of some of the settlement charges you will need to pay at settlement of the loan for which you have applied. These charges will be paid to the title or escrow company that conducts the settlement. This form does not cover all items you will be required to pay in cash at settlement, for example, deposit in escrow for real estate taxes and insurance. You may wish to inquire as to the amounts of such other items. You may be required to pay other additional amounts at settlement. This is not a commitment to make a loan.

Services		Estimated Fees
801. Loan Origination Fee _____ % + $ _____		$
802. Loan Discount		$
803. Appraisal Fee		$
804. Credit Report		$
806. Mortgage Insurance Application Fee		$
807. Assumption Fee		$
808. Tax Service Fee		$
901. Interest		$
902. Mortgage Insurance Premium		$
1101. Settlement or Closing Fee		$
1106. Notary Fees		$
1109. Title Insurance, Lender's Coverage	List only those items borrower will pay	$
1109. Title Insurance, Owner's Coverage		$
1201. Recording Fees		$
1202. County Tax/Stamps		$
1203. City Tax/ Stamps		$
1302. Pest Inspection		$
1303. Building Inspection		$
↑		$
These numbers correspond to the HUD Settlement Statement	TOTAL	$

RESPA does not require the lender to disclose estimates of escrow impounds for property taxes and insurance, although the lender can voluntarily add these items to the form. A new RESPA regulation does, however, require servicers of loans to disclose their calculation of escrow estimates for taxes and insurance, and dictates how the lender must account for escrow deposits. Note also that RESPA allows lenders to make estimates in terms of ranges. For example, escrow fees may be stated as $150 to $175 to reflect the range of rates being charged by local escrow companies for that service.

A new regulation passed in 1996 now also requires that any affiliated business relationships between title companies, attorneys, real estate agents, and other service providers be disclosed along with the amount of fees to be charged so that the consumer can make a decision as to whether or not he wants to utilize those services. This prevents one service provider from requiring the use of other service providers, and passing along unreasonable fees to the consumer.

HUD Settlement Statement

The **HUD Settlement Statement (HUD-1)** used in Figure 13.2 is required of all federally related real estate lenders. Because it is actually a lender requirement, it uses the word *borrower* instead of buyer. However, if the loan is in connection with a sale, and most are, the buyer and the borrower are one and the same. The case where this is not true is when an owner is refinancing a property.

The HUD Settlement Statement has become so widely accepted that it is now used even when it is not required. Closing agents that handle high volumes of closings use computers with special HUD Settlement Statement programs to fill out these forms. The closing agent types the numbers onto a video screen and a tractor-fed printer with continuous-feed HUD forms takes care of the typing task.

With the huge refinancing boom in the early 1990s, the existing HUD-1 Statement didn't appear to have very good application since there was no buyer and seller, but only a borrower and a lender. HUD responded by promulgating a new closing statement called a HUD-1A Closing Statement, which is adapted primarily for refinancings. The existing HUD-1 Form can still be used if a HUD-1A Form is not available. The HUD-1A Form is shown in Figure 13.4.

[2] HUD-1A Settlement Statement

Settlement Statement
Optional Form for
Transactions without Sellers

**U.S. Department of Housing
and Urban Development**

OMB Approval No. 2502-0491

Name & Address of Borrower:

Name & Address of Lender:

Property Location: (if different from above)

Settlement Agent:

Place of Settlement:

Loan Number:

Settlement Date:

L. Settlement Charges		M. Disbursement to Others	
800. Items Payable in Connection with Loan			
801. Loan origination fee % to		1501.	
802. Loan discount % to		1502.	
803. Appraisal fee to		1503.	
804. Credit report to			
805. Inspection fee to		1504.	
806. Mortgage insurance application fee to			
807. Mortgage broker fee to		1505.	
808.			
809.		1506.	
810.			
811.			
900. Items Required by Lender to be Paid in Advance		1507.	
901. Interest from to @ $ per day			
902. Mortgage insurance premium for months to		1508.	
903. Hazard insurance premium for year(s) to		1509.	
904.		1510.	
1000. Reserves Deposited with Lender			
1001. Hazard insurance months @ $ per month		1511.	
1002. Mortgage insurance months @ $ per month			

Figure 13.4.

Figure 13.4. (continued)

1003. City property taxes	months @ $	per month	
1004. County property taxes	months @ $	per month	
1005. Annual assessments	months @ $	per month	
1006.	months @ $	per month	
1007.	months @ $	per month	
1008.	months @ $	per month	
1100. Title Charges			
1101. Settlement or closing fee to			
1102. Abstract or title search to			
1103. Title examination to			
1104. Title insurance binder to			
1105. Document preparation to			
1106. Notary fees to			
1107. Attorney's fees to			
(includes above item numbers	)		
1108. Title insurance to			
(includes above item numbers	)		
1109. Lender's coverage	$		
1110. Owner's coverage	$		
1111.			
1112.			
1113.			
1200. Government Recording and Transfer Charges			
1201. Recording fees:			
1202. City/county tax/stamps:			
1203. State tax/stamps:			
1204.			
1205.			
1300. Additional Settlement Charges			
1301. Survey to			
1302. Pest inspection to			
1303. Architectural/engineering services to			
1304. Building permit to			
1305.			
1306.			
1307.			
1400. Total Settlement Charges (enter on line 1602)			

1512.		
1513.		
1514.		
1515.		
1520. TOTAL DISBURSED (enter on line 1603)		
N. NET SETTLEMENT		
1600. Loan Amount		$
1601. Plus Cash/Check from Borrower		$
1602. Minus Total Settlement Charges (line 1400)		$
1603. Minus Total Disbursements to Others (line 1520)		$
1604. Equals Disbursements to Borrower (after expiration of any applicable rescission period required by law)		$

Borrower(s) Signature(s):

x

form HUD-1A (2/94)
ref. RESPA

Match terms **a–p** *with statements* **1–16.**

a. *Beneficiary statement*
b. *Closing date*
c. *Closing meeting*
d. *Deed delivery*
e. *Dry closing*
f. *Escrow agent*
g. *Escrow closing*
h. *Good faith estimate*

i. *HUD Settlement Statement
(HUD-1)*
j. *Loan escrow*
k. *Outside of the closing*
l. *Prorate*
m. *RESPA*
n. *Settlement statement*
o. *Title closing*
p. *Walk-through*

1. An accounting of funds to the buyer and seller at the completion of a real estate transaction.
2. Deposit of documents and funds with a neutral third party plus instructions as to how to conduct the closing.
3. The moment at which title passes from the seller to the buyer.
4. To divide the ongoing income and expenses of a property between the buyer and seller.
5. A federal law that deals with procedures to be followed in certain types of real estate closings.
6. The person or firm in charge of an escrow.
7. An escrow for the purpose of financing a property not in connection with a sale.
8. Refers to closing costs paid by the buyer or seller that did not go through the closing agent.
9. A list of anticipated closing costs given to the borrower by the lender as required by RESPA.
10. Federally related lenders are required to use this particular closing statement format.
11. The day on which the closing is finalized. Also called the settlement date.
12. The process of completing a real estate transaction.
13. A final inspection of the property just prior to the settlement date.
14. A meeting at which the buyer pays for the property and receives a deed for it; also called a settlement meeting.
15. Shows the unpaid balance on a loan and is provided by the lender.
16. A method to avoid rescheduling a closing meeting when a document, known to be on its way, has not yet arrived.

1. As a means of closing a real estate transaction, how does an escrow closing differ from a settlement meeting?
2. What are the duties of an escrow agent?
3. Is an escrow agent the agent of the buyer or the seller? Explain.
4. The buyer agrees to accept the seller's fire insurance policy as part of the purchase agreement. The policy costs $180, covers the

period January 16 through the following January 15 and the settlement date is March 12. How much does the buyer owe the seller (closest whole dollar)?

5. A buyer agrees to assume an existing 8% mortgage on which $45,000 is still owed; the last monthly payment was made on March 1 and the next payment is due April 1. Settlement date is March 12. Local custom is to use a 30-day month and charge the buyer interest beginning with the settlement day. Calculate the interest proration. To whom is it credited? To whom is it charged?

6. In a real estate closing, does the buyer or seller normally pay for the following items: conveyance tax, deed preparation, lender's title policy, loan appraisal fee, mortgage recording, and mortgage release?

7. Why is it important to have the buyer and seller sign mutual release papers if a transaction does not close?

ADDITIONAL READINGS

All about Escrow: Or How to Buy the Brooklyn Bridge and Have the Last Laugh, by **Sandy Gadow** (El Cerrito, 1989, 222 pages). Focuses on the closing of sales, closing of title, and escrows.

"The Bottom Line on Opening Escrow Accounts" (*Connecticut Realtor,* April 1994, pp. 10–11).

The Pocket Selling and Closing Guide For Real Estate Professionals, by **Ernie Blood** (Carmel, 1994, 232 pages).

"Title and Escrow General Information" (*Sacramento Realtor,* October 1994, p. 26) and "Common Difficulties with Escrow Closings" (*Sacramento Realtor,* October 1994, p. 27). Both articles offer short but easy-to-understand information on the closing of real estate.

14

Mortgage and Note

KEY • TERMS

Acceleration clause: provision in a note that allows the lender to demand immediate payment of entire loan if the borrower defaults

Deficiency judgment: a judgment against a borrower if the foreclosure sale does not bring enough to pay the balance owed

Equity of redemption: the right of a borrower to pay delinquent taxes and redeem a property at any time prior to a foreclosure sale

First mortgage: the mortgage loan with highest priority for repayment in the event of foreclosure

Foreclosure: the procedure by which a person's property can be taken and sold to satisfy an unpaid debt

Junior mortgage: any mortgage on a property that is subordinate to the first mortgage in priority

Mortgage: a document that makes a property security for the repayment of a debt

Mortgagee: the party receiving the mortgage; the lender

Mortgagor: the party who gives a mortgage; the borrower

Power of sale: allows a mortgagee to conduct a foreclosure sale without first going to court

Promissory note: a written promise to repay a debt

Subordination: voluntary acceptance of a lower mortgage priority than one would otherwise be entitled to

Two documents are involved in a mortgage loan: the first is the promissory note and the second is the mortgage. Although the use of mortgages is common in New York, in 16 states it is customary to use a deed of trust in preference to a mortgage. We begin by describing the promissory note and then discuss the mortgage document at length. This is followed by an explanation of foreclosure and brief descriptions of the deed of trust, equitable mortgage, security deed, and chattel mortgage.

PROMISSORY NOTE

The **promissory note** is a contract between a borrower and a lender. It establishes the amount of the debt, the terms of repayment, and the interest rate. A sample promissory note, usually referred to simply as a **note,** is shown in Figure 14.1. Some states use a **bond** to accomplish the same purpose as the promissory note. What is said here regarding promissory notes also applies to bonds.

To be valid as evidence of debt, a note must: (1) be in writing, (2) be between a borrower and lender both of whom have contractual capacity, (3) state the borrower's promise to pay a certain sum of money, (4) show the terms of payment, (5) be signed by the borrower, and (6) be voluntarily delivered by the borrower and accepted by the lender. If the note is secured by a mortgage or trust deed, it must say so. Otherwise, it is solely a personal obligation of the borrower. Although interest is not required to make the note valid, most loans do carry an interest charge; when they do, the rate of interest must be stated in the note. Finally, in some states it is necessary for the borrower's signature on the note to be acknowledged and/or witnessed.

Obligor, Obligee

Referring to Figure 14.1, number [1] identifies the document as a promissory note and [2] gives the location and date of the note's execution (signing). As with any contract, the location stated in the contract establishes the applicable state laws. For example, a note that says it was executed in Virginia will be governed by the laws of the state of Virginia. At [3] the borrower states that he has received something of value and in turn promises to pay the debt described in the note. Typically, the "value received" is a loan of money in the amount described in the note; it could, however, be services or goods or anything else of value.

Figure 14.1.

PROMISSORY NOTE SECURED BY MORTGAGE [1]

[2] <u>City, State</u>   <u>March 31, 19xx</u>

[3] *For value received, I promise to pay to* [4] <u>Pennywise Mortgage Company</u> , [5] *or order, at* <u>2242 National Blvd.,</u> <u>[City, State]</u> *, the sum of* [6] <u>Sixty thousand and no/100—</u> ————————— *dollars, with interest from* <u>March 31,</u> <u>19xx</u> *, on unpaid principal at the rate of* [7] <u>twelve</u> *percent per annum; principal and interest payable in installments of* [8] <u>six hundred seventeen and 40/100</u> ———————— *dollars on the* <u>first</u> *day of each month beginning* [9] <u>May 1, 19xx</u> *, and continuing until said principal and interest have been paid.*

[10] *This note may be prepaid in whole or in part at any time without penalty.*

[11] *There shall be a ten-day grace period for each monthly payment. A late charge of 2% will be added to each payment made after its grace period.*

[12] *Each payment shall be credited first on interest then due and the remainder on principal. Unpaid interest shall bear interest like the principal.*

[13] *Should default be made in payment of any installment when due, the entire principal plus accrued interest shall immediately become due at the option of the holder of the note.*

[14] *If legal action is necessary to collect this note, I promise to pay such sum as the court may fix.*

[15] *This note is secured by a mortgage bearing the same date as this note and made in favor of* <u>Pennywise Mortgage Company.</u>

[16] <u>Mort Gage</u>
Borrower

[17] [this space for witnesses and/or acknowledgment if required by state law]

The section of the note at [4] identifies to whom the obligation is owed, sometimes referred to as the **obligee,** and where the payments are to be sent. The words *or order* at [5] mean that the lender can direct the borrower (the **obligor**) to make payments to someone else if the lender sells the note.

The Principal

The **principal** or amount of the obligation, $60,000, is shown at [6]. The rate of interest on the debt and the date from which it will be charged is given at [7]. The amount of the periodic payment at [8] is calculated from the loan amortization tables discussed in Chapter 16. In this case, $617.40 each month for 30 years will return the lender's $60,000 plus interest at the rate of 12% per year on the unpaid portion of the principal. When payments will begin and when subsequent payments will be due are outlined at [9]. In this example, they are due on the first day of each month until the full $60,000 and interest have been paid. The clause at [10] is a **prepayment privilege** for the borrower. It allows the borrower to pay more than the required $617.40 per month and to pay the loan off early without penalty. Without this very important privilege, the note requires the borrower to pay $617.40 per month, no more and no less, until the $60,000 plus interest has been paid. On some note forms, the prepayment privilege is created by inserting the words *or more* after the word *dollars* where it appears between [8] and [9]. The note would then read "six hundred seventeen and 40/100 dollars or more . . . " The *or more* can be any amount from $617.41 up to and including the entire balance remaining.

Acceleration Clause

At [11] the lender gives the borrower a 10-day grace period to accommodate late payments. For payments made after that, the borrower agrees to pay a late charge of 2%. The clause at [12] states that, whenever a payment is made, the amount is applied first to the interest due on the loan, and then the remainder is applied to reducing the loan balance. Also, if interest is not paid, it too will earn interest at the same rate as the principal, in this example 12% per year. The provision at [13] allows the lender to demand immediate payment of the entire balance remaining on the note if the borrower misses any of the individual payments. This is called an **acceleration clause,** because it speeds up the remaining payments due on the note. Without this clause, the lender can only foreclose on the payments that have come due and have not been paid. In this example, that could take as long as 30 years. This clause also has a certain psychological value: Knowing that the lender has the option of calling the entire loan balance due upon default makes the borrower think twice about being late with the payments.

At **[14]** the borrower agrees to pay any collection costs incurred by the lender if the borrower falls behind in his payments. At **[15]** the promissory note is tied to the mortgage that secures it, making it a mortgage loan. Without this reference, it would be a personal loan. At **[16]** the borrower signs the note. A person who signs a note is sometimes referred to as a **maker** of the note. If two or more persons sign the note, it is common to include a statement in the note that the borrowers are "jointly and severally liable" for all provisions in the note. This means that the terms of the note and the obligations it creates are enforceable on the makers as a group and on each maker individually. If the borrower is married, lenders generally require both husband and wife to sign.

Signature

The mortgage is a separate agreement from the promissory note. Whereas the note is evidence of a debt and a promise to pay, the **mortgage** provides security (collateral) that the lender can sell if the note is not paid. The technical term for this is hypothecation. **Hypothecation** means the borrower retains the right to possess and use the property while it serves as collateral. In contrast, **pledging** means to give up possession of the property to the lender while it serves as collateral. An example of pledging is the loan made by a pawn shop. The shop holds the collateral until the loan is repaid. The sample mortgage in Figure 14.2 illustrates in simplified language the key provisions most commonly found in real estate mortgages used in the United States. Let us look at these provisions.

THE MORTGAGE INSTRUMENT

The mortgage begins at **[1]** with the date of its making and the names of the parties involved. In mortgage agreements, the person or party who hypothecates his property and gives the mortgage is the **mortgagor.** The person or party who receives the mortgage (the lender) is the **mortgagee.** For the reader's convenience, we shall refer to the mortgagor as the borrower and the mortgagee as the lender.

Figure 14.2.

MORTGAGE

[1] *THIS MORTGAGE is made this* <u>31st</u> *day of* <u>March,</u> <u>19xx</u> , *between* <u>Mort Gage</u> *hereinafter called the Mortgagor, and* <u>Pennywise Mortgage Company</u> *hereinafter called the Mortgagee.*

[2] *WHEREAS, the Mortgagor is indebted to the Mortgagee in the principal sum of* <u>sixty thousand and no/100</u> ——— —— *dollars, payable* <u>$617.40, including 12% interest per</u> <u>annum, on the first day of each month starting May 1, 19xx,</u> <u>and continuing until paid</u> , *as evidenced by the Mortgagor's note of the same date as this mortgage, hereinafter called the Note.*

[3] *TO SECURE the Mortgagee the repayment of the indebtedness evidenced by said Note, with interest thereon, the Mortgagor does hereby mortgage, grant, and convey to the Mortgagee the following described property in the County of* <u>Evans</u> *, State of New York;*

[4] *Lot 39, Block 17, Harrison's Subdivision, as shown on Page 19 of May Book 25, filed with the County Recorder of said County and State.*

[5] *FURTHERMORE, the Mortgagor fully warrants the title to said land and will defend the same against the lawful claims of all persons.*

[6] *IF THE MORTGAGOR, his heirs, legal representatives, or assigns pay unto the Mortgagee, his legal representatives or assigns, all sums due by said Note, then this mortgage and the estate created hereby SHALL CEASE AND BE NULL AND VOID.*

[7] *UNTIL SAID NOTE is fully paid:*

[8] *A. The Mortgagor agrees to pay all taxes on said land.*

[9] *B. The Mortgagor agrees not to remove or demolish buildings or other improvements on the mortgaged land without the approval of the lender.*

[10] *C. The Mortgagor agrees to carry adequate insurance to protect the lender in the event of damage or destruction of the mortgaged property.*

[11] *D. The Mortgagor agrees to keep the mortgaged property in good repair and not permit waste or deterioration.*

Figure 14.2. (continued)

IT IS FURTHER AGREED THAT:

[12] E.   *The Mortgagee shall have the right to inspect the mortgaged property as may be necessary for the security of the Note.*

[13] F. *If the Mortgagor does not abide by this mortgage or the accompanying Note, the Mortgagee may declare the entire unpaid balance on the Note immediately due and payable.*

[14] G. *If the Mortgagor sells or otherwise conveys title to the mortgaged property, the Mortgagee may declare the entire unpaid balance on the Note immediately due and payable.*

[15] H. *If all or part of the mortgaged property is taken by action of eminent domain, any sums of money received shall be applied to the Note.*

[16] *IN WITNESS WHEREOF, the Mortgagor has executed this mortgage.*

[17] [this space for witnesses   ___Mort Gage___   (SEAL)
and/or acknowledgment   Mortgagor
if required by state law]

At **[2]** the debt for which this mortgage provides security is identified. Only property named in the mortgage is security for that mortgage. At **[3]** the borrower conveys to the lender the property described at **[4]**. This is most often the property that the borrower purchased with the loan money, but this is not a requirement. The mortgaged property need only be something of sufficient value in the eyes of the lender; it could just as easily be some other real estate the borrower owns. At **[5]** the borrower states that the property is his and that he will defend its ownership. The lender will, of course, verify this with a title search before making the loan.

Provisions for the defeat of the mortgage are given at **[6]**. The key words here state that the "mortgage and the estate created hereby shall cease and be null and void" when the note is paid in full. This is the **defeasance clause.**

As you may have already noticed, the wording of **[3]**, **[4]**, and **[5]** is strikingly similar to that found in a warranty deed. In states taking the **title theory** position toward mortgages, the wording at [3] is interpreted to mean that the borrower is deeding his property to the lender. Sometimes you will see the words *Mortgage Deed* printed at the top of a mortgage for, in fact, a mortgage does technically deed the property to the lender, at least in title theory states. In **lien theory** states, such as New York, the wording at [3] gives only a lien right to the lender, and the borrower (mortgagor) retains title. In **intermediate theory** states, a mortgage is a lien unless the borrower defaults, at which time it conveys title to the lender. No matter which legal philosophy prevails, the borrower retains possession of the mortgaged property, and when the loan is repaid in full the mortgage is defeated as stated in the defeasance clause.

Covenants   After [7] there is a list of covenants (promises) that the borrower makes to the lender. They are the covenants of taxes, removal, insurance, and repair. These covenants protect the security for the loan.

In the **covenant to pay taxes** at [8], the borrower agrees to pay the taxes on the mortgaged property even though the title may be technically with the lender. This is important to the lender, because if the taxes are not paid they become a lien on the property that is superior to the lender's mortgage.

In the **covenant against removal** at [9], the borrower promises not to remove or demolish any buildings or improvements. To do so may reduce the value of the property as security for the lender.

The **covenant of insurance** at [10] requires the borrower to carry adequate insurance against damage or destruction of the mortgaged property. This protects the value of the collateral for the loan, for without insurance, if buildings or other improvements on the mortgaged property are damaged or destroyed, the value of the property might fall below the amount owed on the debt. With insurance, the buildings can be repaired or replaced, thus restoring the value of the collateral.

The **covenant of good repair** at [11], also referred to as the **covenant of preservation and maintenance,** requires the borrower to keep the mortgaged property in good condition. The clause at [12] gives the lender permission to inspect the property to make sure that it is being kept in good repair and has not been damaged or demolished.

If the borrower breaks any of the mortgage covenants or note agreements, the lender wants the right to terminate the loan. Thus, an **acceleration clause** is included at [13] to permit the lender to demand the balance be paid in full immediately. If the borrower cannot pay, foreclosure takes place and the property is sold.

When used in a mortgage, an **alienation clause** (also called a **due-on-sale clause**) gives the lender the right to call the entire loan balance due if the mortgaged property is sold or otherwise conveyed (alienated) by the borrower. An example is shown at [14]. The purpose of an alienation clause is twofold. If the mortgaged property is put up for sale and a buyer proposes to assume the existing loan, the lender can refuse to accept that buyer as a substitute borrower if the buyer's credit is not good. But, more importantly, lenders have been using it as an opportunity to eliminate old loans with low rates of interest. This issue, from both borrower and lender perspectives, is discussed in Chapter 18.

Alienation Clause

Number [15] is a **condemnation clause.** If all or part of the property is taken by action of eminent domain, any money so received is used to reduce the balance owing on the note.

Condemnation Clause

At [16] the mortgagor states that he has made this mortgage. Actually, the execution statement is more a formality than a requirement; the mortgagor's signature alone indicates his execution of the mortgage and agreement to its provisions. At [17] the mortgage is acknowledged and/or witnessed as required by state law for placement in the public records. Like deeds, mortgages must be recorded if they are to be effective against any subsequent purchaser, mortgagee, or lessee. The reason the mortgage is recorded, but not the promissory note, is that the mortgage deals with rights and interests in real property, whereas the note represents a personal obligation. Moreover, most people do not want the details of their promissory notes in the public records.

Most mortgage loans are paid in full either on or ahead of schedule. When the loan is paid, the standard practice is for the lender to return the promissory note to the borrower along with a document called a **satisfaction of mortgage** (or a **release of**

MORTGAGE SATISFACTION

mortgage). Issued by the lender, this document states that the promissory note or bond has been paid in full and the accompanying mortgage may be discharged from the public records. It is extremely important that this document be promptly recorded by the public recorder in the same county where the mortgage is recorded. Otherwise, the records will continue to indicate that the property is mortgaged. When a satisfaction or release is recorded, a recording office employee makes a note of its book and page location on the margin of the recorded mortgage. This is done to assist title searchers and is called a **marginal release.**

Partial Release

Occasionally, the situation arises where the borrower wants the lender to release a portion of the mortgaged property from the mortgage after part of the loan has been repaid. This is known as asking for a **partial release.** For example, a land developer purchases 40 acres of land for a total price of $500,000 and finances his purchase with $100,000 in cash plus a mortgage and note for $400,000 to the seller. In the mortgage agreement, he might ask that the seller release 10 acres free and clear of the mortgage encumbrance for each $100,000 paid against the loan. This would allow the subdivider to develop and sell those 10 acres without first paying the entire $400,000 remaining balance.

"SUBJECT TO"

If an existing mortgage on a property does not contain a due-on-sale clause, the seller can pass the benefits of that financing along to the buyer. (This can occur when the existing loan carries a lower rate of interest than is currently available on new loans.) One method of doing this is for the buyer to purchase the property **subject to** the existing loan. For example, in a purchase contract the buyer states that he is aware of the existence of the loan and the mortgage that secures it, but takes no personal liability for it. Although the buyer pays the remaining loan payments as they come due, the seller continues to be personally liable to the lender for the loan. As long as the buyer faithfully continues to make the loan payments, which he would normally do as long as the property is worth more than the debts against it, this arrangement presents no problem to the seller. However, if the buyer stops making payments before the loan is fully paid, even though it may be years later, in most states, the lender can require the seller to pay the balance due plus interest. This is true even though the seller thought he was free of the loan because he sold the property.

The seller is on safer ground if he requires the buyer to assume the loan (**assumption**). Under this arrangement, the buyer promises in writing to the seller that he will pay the loan, thus personally obligating himself to the seller. In the event of default on the loan, the lender will look to both the buyer and the seller because the seller's name is still on the original promissory note. The seller may have to make the payments, but can file suit against the buyer for the money.

ASSUMPTION

The safest arrangement for the seller is to ask the lender to **substitute** the buyer's liability for his. This releases the seller from the personal obligation created by his promissory note, and the lender can now require only the buyer to repay the loan. The lender will require the buyer to prove financial capability to repay by having the buyer fill out a loan application and by running a credit check on the buyer. The lender may also adjust the rate of interest on the loan to reflect current market interest rates. The seller is also on safe ground if the mortgage agreement or state law prohibits deficiency judgments, a topic that is explained later in this chapter.

NOVATION

A buyer who is to continue making payments on an existing loan will want to know exactly how much is still owing. A **certificate of reduction** is prepared by the lender to show how much of the loan remains to be paid. If a recorded mortgage states that it secures a loan for $35,000, but the borrower has reduced the amount owed to $25,000, the certificate of reduction will show that $25,000 remains to be paid. Roughly the mirror image of a certificate of reduction is the **estoppel certificate.** In it, the borrower is asked to verify the amount still owed and the rate of interest. The most common application of an estoppel certificate is when the holder of a loan sells the loan to another investor. The estoppel certificate avoids future confusion and litigation over misunderstandings as to how much is still owed on a loan. The word *estoppel* comes from Latin and means "to stop up."

ESTOPPEL

DEBT PRIORITIES   The same property can usually be used as collateral for more than one mortgage. This presents no problems to the lenders involved as long as the borrower makes the required payments on each note secured by the property. The difficulty arises when a default occurs on one or more of the loans, and the price the property brings at its foreclosure sale does not cover all the loans against it. As a result, a priority system is necessary. The debt with the highest priority is satisfied first from the foreclosure sale proceeds, then the next highest priority debt is satisfied, then the next, and so on until either the foreclosure sale proceeds are exhausted or all debts secured by the property are satisfied.

First Mortgage   In the vast majority of foreclosures, the sale proceeds are not sufficient to pay all the outstanding debt against the property; thus, it becomes extremely important that a lender know its priority position before making a loan. Unless there is a compelling reason otherwise, a lender will want to be in the most senior position possible. This is normally accomplished by being the first lender to record a mortgage against a property that is otherwise free and clear of mortgage debt; this lender is said to hold a **first mortgage** on the property. If the same property is later used to secure another note before the first is fully satisfied, the new mortgage is a **second mortgage,** and so on. The first mortgage is also known as the **senior mortgage.** Any mortgage with a lower priority is known as a **junior mortgage.** As time passes and higher priority mortgages are satisfied, the lower priority mortgages move up in priority. Thus, if a property is secured by a first and a second mortgage and the first is paid off, the second becomes a first mortgage. Note that nothing is stamped or written on a mortgage document to indicate if it is a first or second or third, etc. That can be determined only by searching the public records for mortgages recorded against the property that have not been released.

Subordination   Sometimes a lender voluntarily takes a lower-priority position than the lender would otherwise be entitled to by virtue of recording date. This is known as **subordination** and it allows a junior loan to move up in priority. For example, the holder of a first mortgage can volunteer to become a second mortgagee and allow the second mortgage to move into the first position.

Although it seems irrational that a lender would actually volunteer to lower its priority position, it is sometimes done by landowners to encourage developers to buy their land. For instance, a seller may finance the sale to a developer, but subordinate his first lien position to a bank that is financing the development loan. The seller is taking a risk, but sees an immediate increase in value in the property.

An interesting situation regarding priority occurs when chattels are bought on credit and then affixed to land that is already mortgaged. If the chattels are not paid for, can the chattel lienholder come onto the land and remove them? If there is default on the mortgage loan against the land, are the chattels sold as fixtures? The solution is for the chattel lienholder to record a **chattel mortgage** or a **financing statement.** This protects the lienholder even though the chattel becomes a fixture when it is affixed to land. A chattel mortgage is a mortgage secured by personal property. If the borrower defaults, the lender is permitted to take possession and sell the mortgaged goods. A more streamlined approach, and one used by most states today, is to file a financing statement as provided by the Uniform Commercial Code to establish lien priority regarding personal property.

Chattel Liens

Although relatively few mortgages are foreclosed, it is important to have a basic understanding of what happens when foreclosure takes place. First, knowledge of what causes **foreclosure** can help in avoiding it; and, second, if foreclosure does occur, one should know the rights of the parties involved. As you read the following material, keep in mind that to *foreclose* simply means to cut off. What the lender is saying is, "Mr. Borrower, you are not keeping your end of the bargain. We want you out so the property can be put into the hands of someone who will keep the agreements." (What is often unsaid is that the lender has commitments to its savers that must be met. Can you imagine going to your bank or savings and loan and asking for the interest on your savings account and hearing the teller say they don't have it because their borrowers have not been making payments?)

THE FORECLOSURE PROCESS

Although noncompliance with any part of the mortgage agreement by the borrower can result in the lender calling the entire

Delinquent Loan

balance immediately due, in most cases foreclosure occurs because the note is not being repaid on time. When a borrower runs behind in payments, the loan is said to be a **delinquent loan.** At this stage, rather than presume that foreclosure is automatically next, the borrower and lender usually meet and attempt to work out an alternative payment program. Contrary to early motion picture plots in which lenders seemed anxious to foreclose their mortgages, today's lender considers foreclosure to be the last resort. This is because the foreclosure process is time-consuming, expensive, and unprofitable. The lender would much rather have the borrower make regular payments. Consequently, if a borrower is behind in loan payments, the lender prefers to arrange a new, stretched-out payment schedule rather than immediately declare the acceleration clause in effect and move toward foreclosing the borrower's rights to the property.

If a borrower realizes that stretching out payments is not going to solve his financial problem, instead of presuming foreclosure to be inevitable, he can seek a buyer for the property who can make the payments. This, more than any other reason, is why relatively few real estate mortgages are foreclosed. The borrower, realizing the financial trouble, sells his property. It is only when the borrower cannot find a buyer and when the lender sees no further sense in stretching the payments that the acceleration clause is invoked and the path toward foreclosure is taken. In New York, the process is governed by the Real Property Actions and Proceedings Law **(RPAPL)**.

Foreclosure Routes   Basically there are two foreclosure routes: judicial and nonjudicial. **Judicial foreclosure** means taking the matter to a court of law in the form of a lawsuit that asks the judge to foreclose (cut off) the borrower. A **nonjudicial foreclosure** does not go to court and is not heard by a judge. It is conducted by the lender (or by a trustee) in accordance with provisions in the mortgage and in accordance with state law pertaining to nonjudicial foreclosures. Comparing the two, a judicial foreclosure is more costly and more time-consuming, but it does carry the approval of a court of law and it may give th e lender rights to collect the full amount of the loan if the property sells for less than the amount owed, as a deficiency judgment can be part of the same judicial proceeding. It is also the preferred method when the foreclosure case is complicated and involves many parties and interests. The nonjudicial route is usually faster, simpler, and cheaper, and it is preferred by lenders when the case is simple and straight-forward. Let us now look at foreclosure methods for standard mortgages.

JUDICIAL FORECLOSURE

The judicial foreclosure process begins with a title search. Next, the lender files a lawsuit naming as defendants the bor-rower and anyone who acquired a right or interest in the property after the lender recorded the mortgage. In the lawsuit, the lender identifies the debt and the mortgage securing it and states that it is in default. The lender then asks the court for a judgment directing that (1) the defendants' interests in the property be cut off in order to return the condition of title to what it was when the loan was made, (2) the property be sold at a public auction, and (3) the lender's claim be paid from the sale proceeds.

Surplus Money Action

A copy of the complaint along with a summons is delivered to the defendants. This officially notifies them of the pending legal action against their interests. A junior mortgage holder who has been named as a defendant has basically two choices. One choice is to allow the foreclosure to proceed and file a **surplus money action.** By doing this, the junior mortgage holder hopes that the property will sell at the foreclosure sale for enough money to pay all senior claims as well as its own claim against the bor-rower. The other choice is to halt the foreclosure process by making the delinquent payments on behalf of the borrower and then adding them to the amount the borrower owes the junior mortgage holder. To do this, the junior mortgage holder must use its own cash and decide whether this is a case of "good money chasing bad." In making this decision the junior mort-gage holder must consider whether or not it will have any better luck being paid than the holder of the senior mortgage did.

Notice of Lis Pendens

At the same time that the lawsuit to foreclose is filed with the court, a **notice of lis pendens** is filed with the county clerk's office where the property is located. This notice informs the public that a legal action is pending against the property. If the borrower attempts to sell the property at this time, the prospective buyer, on making a title search, will learn of the pending litigation. The buyer can still proceed to purchase the property but is now informed of the unsettled lawsuit.

Public Auction

The borrower, or any other defendant named in the lawsuit, may now reply to the suit by presenting his side of the issue to the court judge. If no reply is made, or if the issues raised by the reply are found in favor of the lender, the judge will order that the interests of the borrower and other defendants in the property be foreclosed and the property sold. The sale is usually a **public auction.** The objective is to obtain the best possible price for the property by inviting competitive bidding and conducting the sale in full view of the public. To announce the sale, the judge orders a notice to be posted on the courthouse door and advertised in local newspapers.

Equity of Redemption

The sale is conducted by the county sheriff or by a referee or master appointed by the judge. At the sale, which is held at either the property or at the courthouse, the lender and all parties interested in purchasing the property are present. If the borrower should suddenly locate sufficient funds to pay the judgment, the borrower can, up to the minute the property goes on sale, step forward and redeem the property. This privilege to redeem property anytime between the first sign of delinquency and the moment of foreclosure sale is the borrower's **equity of redemption.** If no redemption is made, the bidding begins. Anyone with adequate funds can bid. Typically, a cash deposit of 10% of the successful bid must be made at the sale, with the balance of the bid price due on closing, usually 30 days later.

While the lender and borrower hope that someone at the auction will bid more than the amount owed on the defaulted loan, the probability is not high. If the borrower was unable to find a buyer at a price equal to or higher than the loan balance, the best cash bid will probably be less than the balance owed. If this happens, the lender usually enters a bid of its own. The lender is in the unique position of being able to "bid the loan"— that is, the lender can bid up to the amount owed without having to pay cash. All other bidders must pay cash, as the purpose of the sale is to obtain cash to pay the defaulted loan. In the event the borrower bids at the sale and is successful in buying back the property, the junior liens against the property are not eliminated. Note however, that no matter who is the successful bidder, the foreclosure does not cut off property tax liens against the property. They remain.

If the property sells for more than the claims against it, including those of any junior mortgage holders, the borrower receives the excess. For example, if a property with $50,000 in claims against it sells for $55,000, the borrower will receive the $5,000 difference, less unpaid property taxes and expenses of the sale. However, if the highest bid is only $40,000, how is the $10,000 deficiency treated? The laws of the various states differ on this question. In New York, as in most states, the lender may pursue a **deficiency judgment** for the $10,000, and thereby proceed against the borrower's other unsecured assets. In other words, the borrower is still personally obligated to the lender for $10,000, and the lender is entitled to collect it. This may require the borrower to sell other assets.

Deficiency Judgment

To obtain a deficiency judgment in New York, the lender must request it within 90 days of the foreclosure sale. In calculating the amount of judgment allowed, New York courts use the higher of the property's sale price or its market value on the day of the sale as determined by the court. This is done to protect the debtor whose property sells for less than it is worth.

Several states have outlawed deficiency judgments in most foreclosure situations so that a lender cannot reach beyond the pledged property for debt satisfaction. In states that allow deficiency judgments, if a borrower is in a strong enough bargaining position, it is possible to add wording in the promissory note that the note is *without recourse*. This generally prohibits the lender from seeking a deficiency judgment. But this must be done before the note is signed.

The purchaser at the foreclosure sale receives either a **referee's deed in foreclosure** or a **sheriff's deed.** These are usually special warranty deeds that convey the title the borrower had at the time the foreclosed mortgage was originally made. The purchaser may take immediate possession, and the court will assist him in removing anyone in possession who was cut off in the foreclosure proceedings.

In states with **statutory redemption** laws, the foreclosed borrower has, depending on the state, from 1 month to 1 year or more after the foreclosure sale to pay in full the judgment and

Statutory Redemption

retake title. This leaves the high bidder at the foreclosure auction in the dilemma of not knowing if he will get the property for certain until the statutory redemption period has run out. Meanwhile, the high bidder receives a **certificate of sale** entitling him or her to a referee's or sheriff's deed if no redemption is made. Depending on the state, the purchaser may or may not get possession until then. If not, the foreclosed borrower may allow the property to deteriorate and lose value. Knowing this, bidders tend to offer less than what the property would be worth if title and possession could be delivered immediately after the foreclosure sale. In this respect, statutory redemption works against the borrower as well as the lender. This problem can be made less severe if the court appoints a **receiver** (manager) to take charge of the property during the redemption period. Judicial foreclosure with public auction is the predominant method in 21 states, and 9 of them allow a statutory redemption period.

STRICT FORECLOSURE

Strict foreclosure is a judicial foreclosure without a judicial sale and usually without a statutory redemption period. Basically, the lender files a lawsuit requesting that the borrower be given a period of time to exercise the equitable right of redemption or lose all rights to the property with title vesting irrevocably in the lender. Although this conjures up visions of a greedy lender foreclosing on a borrower who has nearly paid for the property and misses a payment or two, the court will give the borrower time to make up the back payments or sell the property on the open market. Much more likely is the situation in which the debt owed clearly exceeds the property's value. In this case, there is little to be gained by conducting a judicial sale. Strict foreclosure is the predominant method of foreclosure in two states (Connecticut and Vermont) and is occasionally used in others. Where the debt exceeds the property's value and the foreclosure prohibits a deficiency judgment, this method may be advantageous to the borrower.

POWER OF SALE

New York also permits a nonjudicial method of foreclosure by **power of sale,** also known as **sale by advertisement.** This clause, which must be placed in the mortgage before it is signed, gives the lender the power to conduct the foreclosure and sell the mortgaged property without taking the issue to court. The procedure begins when a lender files a **notice of default** with the county clerk's office. Next is a waiting period that is the borrower's equity of redemption. The property is then advertised at an auction held by the lender and open to the public. In New York, the precise procedures the lender must follow are set by Article 14 of the RPAPL.

A lender foreclosing under power of sale cannot award itself a deficiency judgment. If there is a deficiency as a result of the sale and the lender wants a deficiency judgment, the lender must go to court for it. Because power of sale foreclosures take place outside the jurisdiction of a courtroom, it is said that courts watch them with a jealous eye. If a borrower feels mistreated by power of sale proceedings, the borrower can appeal the issue to a court. Wise lenders know this and keep scrupulous records and follow foreclosure rules carefully. The wise junior mortgage holder will have already filed a **request for notice of default** with the county clerk's office when the junior mortgage was recorded. This document requires anyone holding a more senior lien to notify the junior mortgagee if a default notice has been filed. (Usually, the junior mortgagee is aware of the problem because if the borrower is not making payments to the holder of the first mortgage, the borrower probably is not making payments to any junior mortgage holders.)

Used as the predominant method of foreclosure in one state and to a lesser degree in three others, **entry and possession** is based on the lender giving notice to the borrower that the lender wants possession of the property. The borrower moves out and the lender takes possession, and this is witnessed and recorded in the public records. If the borrower does not peacefully agree to relinquish possession, the lender will have to use a judicial method of foreclosure.

ENTRY
AND POSSESSION

To avoid the hassle of foreclosure proceedings and possible deficiency judgment, a borrower may want to deed the mortgaged property to the lender voluntarily. In turn, the borrower should demand cancellation of the unpaid debt and a letter to that effect from the lender. This method relieves the lender of foreclosing and waiting out any required redemption periods, but it also presents the lender with a sensitive situation. With the borrower in financial distress and about to be foreclosed, it is

DEED IN LIEU
OF FORECLOSURE

quite easy for the lender to take advantage of the borrower. As a result, a court of law will usually side with a borrower who complains of any unfair dealings. Therefore, the lender must be prepared to prove conclusively that the borrower received a fair deal by deeding the property voluntarily to the lender in return for cancellation of the debt. If the property is worth more than the balance due on the debt, the lender must pay the borrower the difference in cash. A **deed in lieu of foreclosure** is a voluntary act by both borrower and lender and hence is sometimes called a "friendly foreclosure." Note also that a deed in lieu of foreclosure does not cut off the rights of junior mortgage holders. The lender, therefore, will have to make those payments or be foreclosed by the junior mortgage holder(s). Figure 14.3 summarizes through illustration the five methods of mortgage foreclosure just discussed.

INSTALLMENT CONTRACT FORECLOSURE

An installment contract (discussed in Chapter 9) is both a purchase contract and a debt instrument. In years past, if the buyer (vendee) stopped making the payments called for by the contract, the seller (vendor) simply rescinded the contract. The buyer gave up possession; the seller kept all the payments to date; and there was no deficiency judgment. (This is, in effect, a strict foreclosure without the protection of a court.)

State legislatures too often found installment contracts to be one-sided in favor of the seller, especially where the buyer had made a substantial number of payments and/or the property had appreciated in value. The need for added consumer protection became even more urgent with increased use of installment contracts in connection with house sales. As a result, many states have enacted legislation that requires installment contracts to be foreclosed like regular mortgages.

DEED OF TRUST

In some states, debts are often secured by trust deeds. Whereas a mortgage is a two-party arrangement with a borrower and a lender, the **trust deed,** also known as a **deed of trust,** is a three-party arrangement consisting of the borrower (the trustor), the lender (the beneficiary), and a neutral third party (a trustee). The key aspect of this system is that the borrower executes a deed to the trustee rather than to the lender. If the borrower pays the debt in full and on time, the lender instructs the trustee to reconvey title back to the borrower. If the borrower

Figure 14.3. Mortgage foreclosure simplified overview.

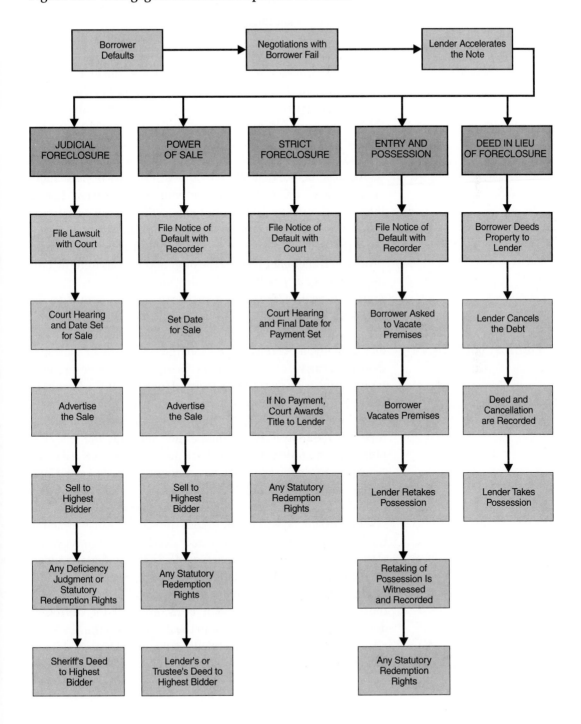

defaults on the loan, the lender instructs the trustee to sell the property to pay off the debt.

EQUITABLE MORTGAGE

An **equitable mortgage** is a written agreement that does not follow the form of a regular mortgage, but is considered by the courts to be one. For example, Black sells his land to Green, with Green paying part of the price in cash now and promising to pay the balance later. Normally, Black would ask Green to execute a regular mortgage as security for the balance due. However, instead of doing this, Black makes a note of the balance due him on the deed before handing it to Green. The laws of most states would regard this notation as an equitable mortgage. For all intents and purposes, it is a mortgage, although not specifically called one. Another example of an equitable mortgage can arise from the deposit money accompanying an offer to purchase property. If the seller refuses the offer and refuses to return the deposit, the courts will hold that the purchaser has an equitable mortgage against the seller's property in the amount of the deposit.

DEED AS SECURITY

Occasionally, a borrower gives a bargain and sale or warranty **deed as security** for a loan. On the face of it, the lender (grantee) would appear to own the property. However, if the borrower can prove that the deed was, in fact, security for a loan, the lender must foreclose like a regular mortgage if the borrower fails to repay. If the loan is repaid in full and on time, the lender is obligated to convey the land back to the borrower. Like the equitable mortgage, a deed used as security is treated according to its intent, not its label. New York automatically considers a deed used as security to be a lien, not a conveyance.

In one state, Georgia, the standard mortgage instrument is the **security deed.** This is a warranty deed with a reconveyance clause. The security deed transfers title to the lender and when all payments have been made on the accompanying note, the lender executes the reconveyance (or cancellation) clause on the reverse of the deed, and it is recorded. If the borrower defaults, a power of sale clause in the deed allows the lender to advertise and sell the property without going through judicial foreclosure.

Generally speaking, a lender will choose, and ask the borrower to sign, whatever security instrument provides the smoothest foreclosure in that state. To illustrate, some states require a statutory redemption period for a mortgage foreclosure but not for a deed of trust foreclosure. Some will allow power of sale for a deed of trust but not for a mortgage. All states allow the use of a deed of trust, but some require that it be foreclosed like a mortgage. More and more states require installment contracts to be foreclosed like mortgages. An analogy for the development of security instrument law is that of a plant growing up through a pile of rocks. Its path up may be twisted and curved, but it reaches its goal—the sunlight. Security instruments follow many paths, but always with one goal in mind—to get money to the borrower who uses it and then returns it to the lender.

CHOICE OF SECURITY INSTRUMENT

*Match terms **a–z** with statements **1–26**.*

VOCABULARY REVIEW

a. *Acceleration clause*
b. *Alienation clause*
c. *Assumption*
d. *Chattel mortgage*
e. *Covenant of insurance*
f. *Deed of trust*
g. *Defeasance clause*
h. *Deficiency judgment*
i. *Delinquent loan*
j. *Equitable mortgage*
k. *Equity of redemption*
l. *First mortgage*
m. *Foreclosure*
n. *Junior mortgage*
o. *Maker*
p. *Mortgage*
q. *Mortgagor*
r. *Partial release*
s. *Power of sale*
t. *Prepayment privilege*
u. *Promissory note*
v. *Public auction*
w. *Satisfaction of mortgage*
x. *Statutory redemption*
y. *Subject to*
z. *Subordination*

1. A document by which property secures the repayment of a debt.
2. A clause in a mortgage stating that the mortgage is defeated if the borrower repays the accompanying note on time.
3. The borrower's right, prior to the day of foreclosure, to repay the balance due on a delinquent loan.
4. A lawsuit filed by a lender that asks a court to set a time limit on how long a borrower has to redeem the property.
5. An agreement that is considered to be a mortgage in its intent even though it may not follow the usual mortgage wording.
6. A document wherein personal property is used as security for a promissory note.
7. The evidence of debt; contains amount owed, interest rate, repayment schedule, and a promise to repay.

8. One who gives a mortgage; the borrower.

9. A clause in a mortgage that allows the lender to call the loan due if the property changes ownership; also known as a due-on-sale clause.

10. A clause in a mortgage whereby the borrower agrees to keep mortgaged property adequately insured against destruction.

11. Discharge of a mortgage upon payment of the debt owed.

12. Release of a portion of a property from a mortgage.

13. The buyer personally obligates him- or herself to repay an existing mortgage loan as a condition of the sale.

14. The buyer of an already mortgaged property makes the payments but does not take personal responsibility for the loan.

15. Any mortgage lower in priority than a first mortgage.

16. Term used when the borrower is behind in loan payments.

17. A clause in a mortgage that gives the mortgagee the right to conduct a foreclosure sale without first going to court.

18. A judgment against a borrower if the sale of mortgaged property at foreclosure does not bring in enough to pay the balance owing.

19. The right of a borrower, after a foreclosure sale, to reclaim the property by repaying the defaulted loan.

20. Voluntary acceptance of a lower mortgage priority position than one would otherwise be entitled to.

21. A deed given to a trustee as security for a loan.

22. The mortgage loan with highest priority for repayment in the event of foreclosure.

23. A person who signs a promissory note.

24. Provision in a mortgage that allows the borrower to pay more than the required payment.

25. The usual procedure by which foreclosed properties are sold.

26. Mortgage provision that allows the lender to declare the loan due if the borrower defaults.

QUESTIONS AND PROBLEMS

1. Is a prepayment privilege to the advantage of the borrower or the lender?

2. What are the legal differences between lien theory and title theory?

3. How does strict foreclosure differ from foreclosure by sale? Which system does your state use?

4. A large apartment complex serves as security for a first, a second, and a third mortgage. Which of these is (are) considered junior mortgage(s)? Senior mortgage(s)?

5. Describe the procedure in your county that is used in foreclosing delinquent real estate loans.

6. What do the laws of your state allow real estate borrowers in the way of equitable and statutory redemption?

7. In a promissory note, who is the obligor? Who is the obligee?

8. Why does a mortgage lender insist on including mortgage covenants pertaining to insurance, property taxes, and removal?

9. What roles do a certificate of reduction and an estoppel certificate play in mortgage lending?

ADDITIONAL READINGS

"The Best Way to Finance Real Estate Investments," (*Financial Freedom Report Quarterly,* Winter 1994, pp. 65–67). This article offers different methods of financing real estate, including mortgages.

Encyclopedia of Mortgage and Real Estate Finance: Over 1,000 Terms Defined, Explained, and Illustrated, by **James Newell, Albert Santi**, and **Mitchell Chip** (Probus, 1991, 575 pages).

Essentials of Real Estate Finance, 7th Ed., by **David Sirota** (Real Estate Education Company, 1994, 337 pages). A clearly written introduction to the world of real estate finance.

Real Estate Finance, 7th Ed., by **John P. Wiedemer** (Prentice Hall, 1995, 320 pages). Focuses on the development of land; places primary emphasis on residential real estate.

Residential Mortgage Lending, 4th Ed., by **Marshall Dennis** and **Michael Robertson** (Prentice Hall, 1995, 352 pages). Written for students and professionals; includes mortgage lending techniques, procedures, law, history, and case studies of actual mortgage transactions.

15

Recordation, Abstracts, and Title Insurance

KEY • TERMS

Abstract of title: a summary of all recorded documents affecting title to a given parcel of land

Acknowledgment: a formal declaration by a person signing a document that he or she, in fact, did sign the document

Actual notice: knowledge gained from what one has actually seen, heard, read, or observed

Chain of title: the linkage of property ownership that connects the present owner to the original source of title

Constructive notice: notice given by the public records and by visible possession, coupled with the legal presumption that all persons are thereby notified

County clerk's office: a county government office wherein documents are entered in the public records

Marketable title: title that is free from reasonable doubt as to who is the owner

Quiet title suit: court-ordered hearings held to determine land ownership

Title insurance: an insurance policy against defects in title not listed in the title report or abstract

Torrens system: a state-sponsored method of registering land titles

In this chapter we shall focus on (1) the need for a method of determining real property ownership, (2) the process by which current and past ownership is determined from public records, (3) the availability of insurance against errors made in determining ownership, (4) the Torrens system of land title registration, and (5) the Uniform Marketable Title Act.

NEED FOR PUBLIC RECORDS

Until the enactment of the Statute of Frauds in England in 1677, determining who owned a parcel of land was primarily a matter of observing who was in physical possession. A landowner gave notice to the world of his claim to ownership by visibly occupying his land. When land changed hands, the old owner moved off the land and the new owner moved onto the land. After 1677 written deeds were required to show transfers of ownership. The problem then became one of finding the person holding the most current deed to the land. This was easy if the deedholder also occupied the land but more difficult if he did not. The solution was to create a government-sponsored public recording service where a person could record his deed. These records would then be open free of charge to anyone. In this fashion, an owner could post notice to all that he claimed ownership of a parcel of land.

Constructive Notice

There are two ways a person can give notice of a claim or right to land. One is by recording documents in the public records that give written notice to that effect. The other is by visibly occupying or otherwise visibly making use of the land. At the same time, the law holds interested parties responsible for examining the public records and looking at the land for this notice of right or claim. This is called **constructive notice.** Constructive notice (also sometimes referred to as **legal notice**) charges the public with the responsibility of looking in the public records and at the property itself to obtain knowledge of all who are claiming a right or interest. In other words, our legal system provides an avenue by which a person can give notice (recording and occupancy) and makes the presumption that anyone interested in the property has inspected the records *and* the property.

Inquiry Notice

A person interested in a property is also held by law to be responsible for making further inquiry of anyone giving visible or recorded notice. This is referred to as **inquiry notice** and is notice that the law presumes a reasonably diligent person would obtain by making further inquiry. For example, suppose you are considering the purchase of vacant acreage and, upon inspecting it, see a dirt road cutting across the land that is not mentioned in the public records. The law expects you to make further inquiry. The road may be a legal easement across the property. Another example is that any time you buy rental property, you are expected to make inquiry as to the rights of the occupants. They may hold substantial rights you would not know about without asking them.

Actual Notice   **Actual notice** is knowledge that one has actually gained based on what one has seen, heard, read, or observed. For example, if you read a deed from Jones to Smith, you have actual notice of the deed and Smith's claim to the property. If you go to the property and you see someone in possession, you have actual notice of that person's claim to be there.

Remember that anyone claiming an interest or right is expected to make it known either by recorded claim or visible use of the property. Anyone acquiring a right or interest is expected to look in the public records and go to the property to make a visual inspection for claims and inquire as to the extent of those claims.

Recording Acts   All states have passed **recording acts** to provide for the recording of every instrument (i.e., document) by which an estate, interest, or right in land is created, transferred, or encumbered. Within each state, each county has a **public recorder's office,** known variously as the County Recorder's Office, County Clerk's Office, Circuit Court Clerk's Office, County Registrar's Office, or Bureau of Conveyances. In New York, deeds and other instruments affecting title to real property are recorded in the County Clerk's Office where the property is located. The person in charge is called the recorder, clerk, or registrar. Located at the seat of county government, each public recorder's office will record documents submitted to it that pertain to real property in that county. Thus a deed to property in XYZ County is recorded with the public recorder in XYZ County. Similarly, anyone seeking information regarding ownership of land in XYZ County would go to the recorder's office in XYZ County. Some cities also maintain record rooms where deeds are recorded. The recording process itself involves photocopying the documents and filing them for future reference.

To encourage people to use public recording facilities, laws in each state decree that (1) a deed, mortgage, or other instrument affecting real estate is not effective as far as subsequent purchasers and lenders (without actual notice) are concerned if it is not recorded, and (2) prospective purchasers, mortgage lenders, and the public at large are presumed notified when a document is recorded. Figure 15.1 illustrates the concept of public recording.

The failure to record a deed does not affect the validity of the deed between the parties. However, an unrecorded deed is void against a subsequently recorded deed as long as the owner named in the recorded deed had no notice of the prior conveyance and the deed was taken in good faith for valuable consideration.

Unrecorded Interests

Although recording acts permit the recording of any estate, right, or interest in land, many lesser rights are rarely recorded. Month-to-month rentals and leases for a year or less fall into this category. Consequently, only an on-site inspection would reveal

Figure 15.1.

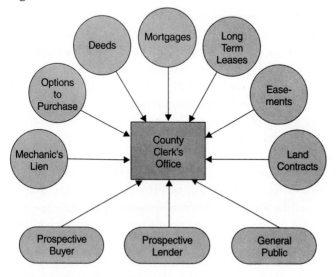

The County Clerk's Office serves as a central information station for changes in rights, estates, and interests in land.

their existence, or the existence of any developing adverse possession or prescriptive easement claim.

Summary

To summarize, if you are a prospective purchaser (or lessee or lender), you are presumed by law to have inspected both the land itself and the public records to determine the present rights and interests of others. If you receive a deed, mortgage, or other document relating to an estate, right, or interest in land, have it recorded *immediately* in the county in which the land is located. If you hold an unrecorded rental or lease, you should visibly occupy the property.

REQUIREMENTS
FOR RECORDING

A deed must be properly **acknowledged** and **proved** to be recorded in New York. The only person who can acknowledge a deed is the person who executed it, the grantor. Proof can only be made by a person who actually witnessed the execution of the deed and who at the same time placed on the deed his or her signature as the witness. The absence of proper acknowledgment or proof does not invalidate the deed by itself. The deed remains valid between the grantor and grantee. But it cannot be recorded and therefore would be void against subsequent purchasers who recorded a deed to the property.

Acknowledgment

An **acknowledgment** is a formal declaration by a person signing a document that he or she, in fact, did sign the document. Persons authorized to take acknowledgments include **notaries public,** recording office clerks, commissioners of deeds, judges of courts of record, justices of the peace, and certain others as authorized by state law. Commissioned military officers are authorized to take the acknowledgments of persons in the military; foreign ministers and consular agents can take acknowledgments abroad. If an acknowledgment is taken outside the state where the document will be recorded, either the recording county must already recognize the out-of-state official's authority or the out-of-state official must provide certification that he or she is qualified to take acknowledgments. The official seal or stamp of the notary on the acknowledgment normally fulfills this requirement.

An acknowledgment is illustrated in Figure 15.2. Notice the words; the person signing the document must personally appear before the notary and the notary must state that he or

Figure 15.2.

ACKNOWLEDGMENT FOR AN INDIVIDUAL

STATE OF _____

COUNTY OF _____   ss

On this _____ day of _____ , 19 ____ , before me, the undersigned, a Notary Public in and for said State, personally appeared [name of person executing document] known to me to be the person whose name is subscribed to the within instrument and acknowledged that he (she) executed the same [in some states, the words "by his (her) free act and deed" are added here]. Witness my hand and official seal.

[space for seal or
stamp of the notary   _____
public]   Signature of notary public

My commission expires _____
                          Date

she knows that person to be the person described in the document. If they are strangers, the notary will require proof of identity. The person acknowledging the document does so by voluntarily signing it in the presence of the notary. Note that it is the signer who does the acknowledging, not the notary. At the completion of the signing, a notation of the event is made in a permanent record book kept by the notary. This record is later given to the state government for safekeeping.

PUBLIC RECORDS ORGANIZATION

Each document brought to a public recorder's office for recordation is photocopied and then returned to its owner. The photocopy is placed in chronological order with photocopies of other documents. These are stamped with consecutive page numbers and bound into a book, often still referred to by its Latin name, **Liber**. These books are placed in chronological order on shelves that are open to the public for inspection. Before modern-day photocopying machines, public recorders' offices used large cameras with light-sensitive paper (from roughly 1920 to 1955). Before that, documents were copied by hand using typewriters (from roughly 1900 to 1920), and before that, copying was done in longhand. The current trend is toward entirely paperless systems wherein documents are recorded directly onto microfilm and then returned to their owners. Each document is assigned a book and page number or a reel and frame number. Microfilm readers are made available to anyone wanting to read the microfilms.

Filing incoming documents in chronological order is necessary to establish the chronological priority of documents; however, it does not provide an easy means for a person to locate all the documents relevant to a given parcel of land. Suppose that you are planning to purchase a parcel of land and want to make certain that the person selling it is the legally recognized owner. Without an index to guide you, you might have to inspect every document in every volume. Consequently, recording offices have developed systems of indexing. The two most commonly used are the grantor and grantee indexes, used by all states, and the tract index, used by nine states.

Tract Indexes

Of the two indexing systems, the **tract index** is the simplest to use. In it, one page is allocated to either a single parcel of land or to a group of parcels, called a *tract*. On that page you will find listed all the recorded deeds, mortgages, and other documents at the recorder's office that relate to that parcel. A few words describing each document are given, together with the book and page where a photocopy of the document can be found.

Grantor and Grantee Indexes

Grantor and grantee indexes are alphabetical indexes and are usually bound in book form. There are several variations in use in the United States, but the basic principle is the same. For each calendar year, the **grantor index** lists in alphabetical order all grantors named in the documents recorded that year. Next to each grantor's name is the name of the grantee named in the document, the book and page where a photocopy of the document can be found, and a few words describing the document. The **grantee index** is arranged by grantee names and gives the name of the grantor and the location and description of the document.

Example of Title Search

As an example of the application of the grantor and grantee indexes to a title search, suppose Robert T. Davis states that he is the owner of Lot 2, Block 2 in the Hilldale Tract in your county, and you would like to verify that statement in the public records. You begin by looking in the grantee index for his name, starting with this year's index and working backward in time. The purpose of this first step is to determine whether or not the property was ever granted to Davis. If it was, you will find his name in the grantee index and, next to his name, a book and page reference to a photocopy of his deed to that parcel.

The next step is to look through the grantor index for the period of time starting from the moment he received his deed up to the present. If he has granted the property to someone else, Davis's name will be noted in the grantor index with a reference to the book and page where you can see a copy of the deed. (Davis could have reduced your efforts by showing you the actual deed conveying the lot to him. However, you would still have to inspect the grantor index for all dates subsequent to his taking title to see if he has conveyed title to a new grantee. If you do not have the name of the property owner, you would first have to go to the property tax office.)

The Next Step

Suppose your search shows that on July 1, 1989, in Book 2324, page 335, a warranty deed from John S. Miller to Davis, for Lot 2, Block 2 of the Hilldale Tract was recorded. Furthermore, you find that no subsequent deed showing Davis as grantor of this land has been recorded. Based on this, it would appear that Davis is the fee owner. However, you must inquire further to determine if Miller was the legally recognized owner of the property when he conveyed it to Davis. In other words, on what basis did Miller claim his right of ownership and, subsequently, the right to convey that ownership to Davis? The answer is that Miller based his claim to ownership on the deed he received from the previous owner.

By looking for Miller's name in the 1989 grantee index and then working backward in time through the yearly indexes, you will eventually find his name and a reference to Lot 2, Block 2 in the Hilldale Tract. Next to Miller's name you will find the name of the grantor and a reference to the book and page where the deed was recorded.

Chain of Title

By looking for that name in the grantee index, you will locate the next previous deed. By continuing this process you can construct a chain of title. A **chain of title** shows the linkage of property ownership that connects the present owner to the original source of title. In most cases the chain starts with the original sale or grant of the land from the government to a private citizen. It is used to prove how title came to be **vested** in (i.e., possessed by) the current owner. Figure 15.3 illustrates the chain-of-title concept.

Sometimes, while tracing (running) a chain of title back through time, an apparent break or dead end will occur. This can happen because the grantor is an administrator, executor, sheriff, or judge, or because the owner died, or because a mortgage against the land was foreclosed. To regain the title sequence, one must search outside the recorder's office by checking probate court records in the case of a death, or by checking civil court actions in the case of a foreclosure. The chain must be complete from the original source of title to the present owner. If there is a missing link, the current "owner" does not have valid title to the property.

In addition to looking for grantors and grantees, a search must be made for any outstanding mortgages, judgments, actions pending, liens, and unpaid taxes that may affect the title. With regard to searching for mortgages, states again differ slightly. Some place mortgages in the general grantor and grantee indexes, listing the borrower (mortgagor) as the grantor and the lender (mortgagee) as the grantee. Other states, including New York, have separate index books for mortgagors and mortgagees. The process involves looking for the name of each owner in each annual **mortgagor index** published while that owner owned the land. If a mortgage is found, a further check will reveal whether or not it has been satisfied and released. If it has been released, the recorder's office will have noted on the margin of the recorded mortgage the book and page where the release is located. When one knows the lender's name, the mortgage location and its subsequent release can also be found by searching the **mortgagee index.**

Title may be clouded by judgments against recent owners, or there may be lawsuits pending that might later affect title. This information is found, respectively, on the **judgment rolls** and in the **lis pendens index** at the office of the county clerk. The term *lis pendens* is Latin for "pending lawsuits." A separate search is made for mechanic's liens against the property by

Figure 15.3. Chain of title.

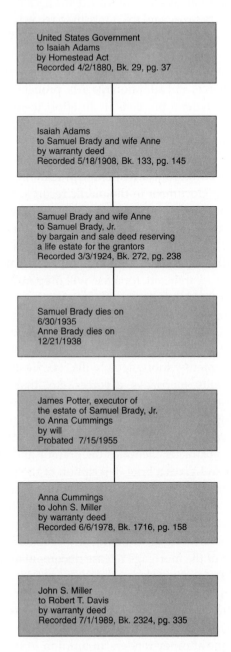

United States Government
to Isaiah Adams
by Homestead Act
Recorded 4/2/1880, Bk. 29, pg. 37

Isaiah Adams
to Samuel Brady and wife Anne
by warranty deed
Recorded 5/18/1908, Bk. 133, pg. 145

Samuel Brady and wife Anne
to Samuel Brady, Jr.
by bargain and sale deed reserving
a life estate for the grantors
Recorded 3/3/1924, Bk. 272, pg. 238

Samuel Brady dies on
6/30/1935
Anne Brady dies on
12/21/1938

James Potter, executor of
the estate of Samuel Brady, Jr.
to Anna Cummings
by will
Probated 7/15/1955

Anna Cummings
to John S. Miller
by warranty deed
Recorded 6/6/1978, Bk. 1716, pg. 158

John S. Miller
to Robert T. Davis
by warranty deed
Recorded 7/1/1989, Bk. 2324, pg. 335

workmen and material suppliers. This step includes both a
search of the public records and an on-site inspection of the land
for any recent construction activity or material deliveries. A visit

is made to the local tax assessor's office to check the tax rolls for unpaid property taxes, and to county map records to determine changes in deed restriction or subdivision plats. This does not exhaust all possible places that must be visited to do a thorough title search. A title searcher may also be found researching birth, marriage, divorce, and adoption records, probate records, military files, and federal tax liens in an effort to identify all the parties with an interest or potential interest in a given parcel of land and its improvements.

ABSTRACT OF TITLE

Although it is useful for the real estate practitioner to be able to find a name or document in the public records, full-scale title searching should be left to professionals. In a sparsely populated county, title searching is usually done on a part-time basis by an attorney. In more heavily populated counties, a full-time **abstracter** will search the records. These persons are experts in the field of title search and, for a fee, will prepare an abstract of title for a parcel of land.

An **abstract of title** is a complete historical summary of all recorded documents affecting the title of a property. It recites in chronological order all recorded grants and conveyances and recorded easements, mortgages, wills, tax liens, judgments, pending lawsuits, marriages, divorces, etc., that might affect title. The abstracter will summarize each document, note the book and page (or other source) where it was found and give the date it was recorded or entered. In the case of a deed, for example, the abstracter identifies the grantor and grantee and type of deed and gives a brief description of the property, any conditions or restrictions found in the deed, the date on the deed, the recording date, and the book and page. For a mortgage, the abstracter identifies the borrower and lender, gives a brief description of the mortgage contents, and if repaid, the book and page location of the mortgage release document and its date of recordation. The abstract also includes a list of the public records searched, and not searched, in preparing the abstract.

The abstract is next sent to an attorney. On the basis of the attorney's knowledge of law and the legal history presented in the abstract, the attorney renders an **opinion of title** as to who the fee owner is and names anyone else with a legitimate right or interest in the property. This opinion, when written, signed by the attorney, and attached to the abstract, is known in many states as a **certificate of title.** In some parts of the United States, this certified abstract is so valuable that it is brought up to date each time the property is sold and passed from seller to buyer.

Despite the diligent efforts of abstracters and attorneys to give as accurate a picture of land ownership as possible, there is no guarantee that the finished abstract, or its certification, is completely accurate. Persons preparing abstracts and opinions are liable for mistakes due to their own negligence, and they can be sued if that negligence results in a loss to a client. But what if a recorded deed in the title chain is a forgery? Or what if a married person represented himself on a deed as a single person, thus resulting in unextinguished dower rights? Or what if a deed was executed by a minor or an otherwise legally incompetent person? Or what if a deed contained an erroneous land description? Or what if a document was misfiled, or there were undisclosed heirs, or a missing will later came to light, or there was confusion because of similar names on documents? These situations can result in substantial losses to a property owner; yet the fault may not lie with the abstracter or attorney. Nor is the recorder's office responsible for verifying the contents of a deed, just that it shows an acceptable acknowledgment. The solution has been the organization of private companies to sell insurance against losses arising from title defects such as these as well as from errors in title examination.

"What Ifs"

Efforts to insure titles date back to the last century and were primarily organized by and for the benefit of attorneys who wanted protection from errors that they might make in the interpretation of abstracts. As time passed, **title insurance** became available to anyone wishing to purchase it. The basic principle of title insurance is similar to any form of insurance: many persons pay a small amount into an insurance pool that is then available if any one of them should suffer a loss. In some parts of the United States, it is customary to purchase the title insurance policy through the attorney who reads and certifies the abstract. Elsewhere it is the custom to purchase it from a title company that combines the search and policy in one fee.

TITLE INSURANCE

Title Report   When a title company receives a request for a title insurance policy, the first step is an examination of the public records. This is usually done by an abstracter or **title searcher** employed by the title company. A company attorney then reviews the findings and renders an opinion as to who the fee owner is and lists anyone else with a legitimate right or interest in the property such as a mortgage lender or easement holder. This information is typed up and becomes the **title report.** An example of a title report is illustrated in plain language in Figure 15.4. Sometimes called a **preliminary title report,** a title report does not commit the title company to insure the property nor is it an insurance policy. It does serve as the basis for a commitment to insure (also called a **binder**) and for the actual title insurance policy.

Notice how a title report differs from an abstract. Whereas an abstract is a chronologically arranged summary of all recorded events that have affected the title to a given parcel of land, a title report is more like a snapshot that shows the condition of title at a specific moment in time. A title report does not tell who the previous owners were; it only tells who the current owner is. A title report does not list all mortgage loans ever made against the land, but only those that have not been removed. The title report in Figure 15.4 states that a search of the public records shows Barbara Baker to be the fee owner of Lot 17, Block M, at the time the search was conducted.

In Part I, the report lists all recorded objections that could be found to Baker's fee estate, in this case, county property taxes, a mortgage, and two easements. In Part II, the title company states that there may be certain unrecorded matters that either could not be or were not researched in preparing the report. Note in particular that the title company does not make a visual inspection of the land nor does it make a boundary survey. The buyer is responsible for making the on-site inspection and for hiring a surveyor if uncertain as to the land's boundaries. It is also the buyer's responsibility to check the zoning of the land and any other governmental restrictions on the land.

Although an owner may purchase a title insurance policy on his property at any time, it is most often purchased when real estate is sold. In connection with a sale, the title report is used to verify that the seller is indeed the owner. Additionally, the title report alerts the buyer and seller as to what needs to be done to

Figure 15.4.

TITLE REPORT

The following is a report of the title to the land described in your application for a policy of title insurance.

LAND DESCRIPTION: *Lot 17, Block M, Atwater's Addition, Jefferson County, State of* ___New York___ .

DATE AND TIME OF SEARCH: *March 3, 19xx at 9:00 A.M.*

VESTEE: *Barbara Baker, a single woman*

ESTATE OR INTEREST: *Fee simple*

EXCEPTIONS:

PART I:

1. *A lien in favor of Jefferson County for property taxes, in the amount of $645.00, due on or before April 30, 19xx.*

2. *A mortgage in favor of the First National Bank in the amount of $30,000.00, recorded June 2, 1974, in Book 2975, Page 245 of the Official County Records.*

3. *An easement in favor of the Southern Telephone Company along the eastern five feet of said land for telephone poles and conduits. Recorded on June 15, 1946, in Book 1210, Page 113 of the Official County Records.*

4. *An easement in favor of Coastal States Gas and Electric Company along the north ten feet of said land for underground pipes. Recorded on June 16, 1946, in Book 1210, Page 137 of the Official County Records.*

PART II:

1. *Taxes or assessments not shown by the records of any taxing authority or by the public records.*

2. *Any facts, rights, interests, or claims that, although not shown by the public records, could be determined by inspection of the land and inquiry of persons in possession.*

3. *Discrepancies or conflicts in boundary lines or area or encroachments that would be shown by a survey, but which are not shown by the public records.*

4. *Easements, liens, or encumbrances not shown by the public records.*

5. *Zoning and governmental restrictions.*

6. *Unpatented mining claims and water rights or claims.*

bring title to the condition called for in the sales contract. For example, referring to Figure 15.4, the present owner (Barbara Baker) may have agreed to remove the existing mortgage so that the buyer can get a new and larger loan. Once this is done and the seller has delivered her deed to the buyer, the title company issues a title policy that deletes the old mortgage, adds the new mortgage, and shows the buyer as the owner. Note that title policies are often required by long-term lessees (10 years or more). They, too, want to know who has property rights superior to theirs.

Policy Premium

In some counties in New York, it is customary for the seller to pay the cost of both the title search and the insurance. In other counties, the seller pays for the search and the buyer for the insurance. In still others, the seller pays for the search and the buyer for the insurance. To find out the custom in a particular county, you can check with the County Clerk's Office. Customarily, when a property is sold, it is insured for an amount equal to the purchase price. This insurance remains effective as long as the buyer (owner) or his heirs have an interest in the property.

The insurance premium consists of a single payment. On the average-priced home, the combined charge for a title report and title insurance amounts to about of 1% of the amount of insurance purchased. Each time the property is sold, a new policy must be purchased. The old policy cannot be assigned to the new owner. Some title insurance companies offer reduced **reissue rates** if the previous owner's policy is available for updating.

Lender's Policy

Thus far our discussion of title insurance has centered on what is called an **owner's policy.** In addition, title insurance companies also offer what is called a **lender's policy.** This gives title protection to a lender who has taken real estate as collateral for a loan. There are three significant differences between an owner's title policy and a lender's title policy. First, the owner's policy is good for the full amount of coverage stated on the policy for as long as the insured or the insured's heirs have an interest in the property. In contrast, the lender's policy protects only for the amount owed on the mortgage loan. Thus, the coverage on a lender's policy declines and finally terminates when the loan is fully repaid. The second difference is that the lender's policy does not make exceptions for claims to ownership that could have been determined by physically inspecting the property. The third difference is that the lender's policy is assignable to subsequent holders of that same loan; an owner's policy is not.

The cost of a lender's policy (also known as a mortgagee's title policy or a loan policy) is similar to an owner's policy. Although the insurance company takes added risks by eliminating some exceptions found in the owner's policy, this is balanced by the fact that the liability decreases as the loan is repaid. When an owner's and a lender's policy are purchased at the same time, as in the case of a sale with new financing, the combined cost is only a few dollars more than the cost of the owner's policy alone. Note that the lender's policy covers only title problems. It does not insure that the loan will be repaid by the borrower.

The last item in a title policy is a statement as to how the company will handle claims. Although this "Conditions and Stipulations Section" is too lengthy to reproduce here, its key aspects can be summarized as follows. When an insured defect arises, the title insurance company reserves the right to either pay the loss or fight the claim in court. If it elects to fight, any legal costs the company incurs are in addition to the amount of coverage stated in the policy. If a loss is paid, the amount of coverage is reduced by that amount and any unused coverage is still in effect. If the company pays a loss, it acquires the right to collect from the party who caused the loss.

Claims for Losses

In comparing title insurance to other forms of insurance (e.g., life, fire, automobile), note that title insurance protects against something that has already happened but has not been discovered. A forged deed may result in a disagreement over ownership: The forgery is a fact of history, the insurance is in the event of its discovery. But in some cases the problem will never be discovered. For example, a married couple may be totally unaware of dower and curtesy rights and fail to extinguish them when they sell their property. If neither later claims them, when they die, the rights extinguish themselves, and the intervening property owners will have been unaffected.

Only a small part of the premiums collected by title insurance companies are used to pay claims. This is largely because title companies take great pains to maintain on their own premises complete photographic copies (often computer indexed) of the public records for each county in which they do business. These are called **title plants.** In many cases they are actually more complete and better organized than those available at the public recorder's office. The philosophy is that the better the quality of the title search, the fewer the claims that must be paid.

The Growth of Title Insurance

Four important factors have caused the title insurance business to mushroom. First, in a warranty deed the grantor makes several strongly worded covenants. As you will recall, the grantor covenants that he is the owner, that the grantee will not be disturbed in his possession, that there are no encumbrances except as stated in the deed, that the grantor will procure any necessary further assurance of title for the grantee, and that the grantor will bear the expense of defending the grantee's title and possession. Thus, signing a warranty deed places a great obligation on the grantor. By purchasing title insurance, the grantor can transfer that obligation to an insurance company.

Second, a grantee is also motivated to have title insurance. Even with a warranty deed, there is always the lingering question of whether or not the seller would be financially capable of making good on his covenants and warranties. They are useless if one cannot enforce them. Moreover, title insurance typically provides a grantee broader assurance than a warranty deed. For example, an outsider's claim must produce physical dispossession of the grantee before the covenant of quiet enjoyment is considered broken. Yet the same claim would be covered by title insurance before dispossession took place.

Third, the broad use of title insurance has made mortgage lending more attractive and borrowing a little easier and cheaper for real property owners. This is because title insurance has removed the risk of loss due to defective titles. As a result, lenders can charge a lower rate of interest. Secondary market purchasers of loans such as FNMA and FHLMC (Chapter 18) require title insurance on every loan they buy.

Marketable Title

Fourth, title insurance has made titles to land much more marketable. In nearly all real estate transactions, the seller agrees to deliver **marketable title** to the buyer. Marketable title is title that is free from reasonable doubt as to who the owner is. Even when the seller makes no mention of the quality of the title, courts ordinarily require that marketable title be conveyed. To illustrate, a seller orders an abstract prepared, and it is read by an attorney who certifies it as showing marketable title. The buyer's attorney feels that certain technical defects in the title chain contradict certification as marketable. He advises the buyer to refuse to complete the sale. The line between what is and what is not marketable title can be exceedingly thin, and differences of legal opinion are quite possible. One means of breaking the stalemate is to locate a title insurance company that will insure the title as being marketable. If the defect is not serious, the insurance company will accept the risk. If it is a serious risk, the company may either accept the risk and increase the insurance fee or recommend a quiet title suit.

When a title defect (also called a **cloud on the title** or a **title cloud**) must be removed, it is logical to remove it by using the path of least resistance. For example, if an abstract or title report shows unpaid property taxes, the buyer may require the seller to pay them in full before the deal is completed. A cloud on the title as a result of pending foreclosure proceedings can be halted by either bringing the loan payments up to date or negotiating with the lender for a new loan repayment schedule. Similarly, a distant relative with ownership rights might be willing, upon negotiation, to quitclaim them for a price.

Quiet Title Suit

Sometimes a stronger means is necessary to remove title defects. For example, the distant relative may refuse to negotiate or the lender may refuse to remove a mortgage lien, despite pleas from the borrower that it has been paid, or there is a missing link in a chain of title. The solution is a **quiet title suit** (also called a *quiet title action*). Forty-seven states including New York have enacted legislation that permits a property owner to ask the courts to hold hearings on the ownership of his land. At these hearings anyone claiming to have an interest or right to the land in question may present verbal or written evidence of that claim. A judge, acting on the evidence presented and the laws of his state, rules on the validity of each claim. The result is to recognize legally those with a genuine right or interest and to "quiet" those without a genuine interest.

Over a century ago, Sir Robert Torrens, a British administrator in Australia, devised an improved system of identifying land

THE TORRENS SYSTEM

ownership. He was impressed by the relative simplicity of the British system of sailing-ship registration. The government maintained an official ships' registry that listed on a single page a ship's name, its owner, and any liens or encumbrances against it. Torrens felt land titles might be registered in a similar manner. The system he designed, known as the **Torrens system** of land title registration, starts with a landowner's application for registration and the preparation of an abstract. This is followed by a quiet title suit at which all parties named in the abstract and anyone else claiming a right or interest to the land in question may attend and be heard.

Torrens Certificate of Title

Based on the outcome of the suit, a government-appointed **registrar of titles** prepares a **certificate of title.** This certificate names the legally recognized fee owner and lists any legally recognized exceptions to that ownership, such as mortgages, easements, long-term leases, or life estates. The registrar keeps the original certificate of title and issues a duplicate to the fee owner. (Although they sound similar, a Torrens certificate of title is not the same as an attorney's certificate of title. The former shows ownership and claims against that ownership as established by a court of law. The latter is strictly an opinion of the condition of title.)

New York title registration law is set forth in the Title Registration Act found in Article 12 of New York's Real Property Law. Registration proceedings under Article 12 are brought before the New York Supreme Court or to a justice sitting at special term in any of the counties within the judicial department where the property is located. Upon filing, the court refers the petition to an official examiner of title, who in the course of his title examination can call witnesses and examine them under oath. The court will then approve the examiner's report and issue a final order of judgment of registration unless it is determined that further information or evidence is necessary.

Once a title is registered, any subsequent liens or encumbrances against it must be entered on the registrar's copy of the certificate of title in order to give constructive notice. When a lien or encumbrance is removed, its notation on the certificate is canceled. In this manner, the entire concept of constructive notice for a given parcel of land is reduced to a single-page document open to public view at the registrar's office. This, Torrens argued, would make the whole process of title transfer much simpler and cheaper.

When registered land is conveyed, the grantor gives the grantee a deed. The grantee takes the deed to the registrar of titles, who transfers the title by canceling the grantor's certificate and issuing a new certificate in the name of the grantee. With a Torrens property, this is the point in time when title is conveyed, not when the deed is delivered by the grantor to the grantee. Any liens or other encumbrances not removed at the same time are carried over from the old to the new certificate. The deed and certificate are kept by the registrar; the grantee receives a duplicate of the certificate. If the conveyance is accompanied by a new mortgage, it is noted on the new certificate, and a copy of the mortgage is retained by the registrar. Except for the quiet title suit aspect, the concept of land title registration is quite similar to that used in the United States for registering ownership of motor vehicles.

Adoption

In the United States, the first state to have a land registration act was Illinois in 1895. Other states slowly followed, but often their laws were vague and cumbersome to the point of being useless. At one point, 20 states had land title registration acts, but since then 10 states have repealed their acts and only 10 remain. They are Hawaii, Massachusetts, Minnesota, New York, Colorado, Georgia, North Carolina, Ohio, Virginia, and Washington.

In all 10 states, Torrens coexists with the regular recording procedures described earlier in this chapter. Thus it is possible for a house on one side of a street to be Torrens registered and a house across the street to be recorded the regular way. Also, it may be customary to use Torrens in just certain areas of the state. In Minnesota, it's used in the Minneapolis area; in Massachusetts, the Boston area; and in New York, Suffolk County (eastern Long Island). In Hawaii, Torrens is used statewide, but primarily by large landowners and subdivision developers who want to clear up complex title problems. In the remaining 6 states, the public has made relatively little use of land title registration. This limited adoption of Torrens is because of, among other things, the promotion, widespread availability, and lower short-run cost of title insurance. (The quiet title suit can be costly.) Note, too, that although a state-run insurance fund is usually available to cover registration errors, some lenders feel this is not adequate protection and require title insurance.

Marketable Title Acts

At least 10 states have a **Marketable Title Act.** This is *not* a system of title registration. Rather, it is legislation aimed at making abstracts easier to prepare and less prone to error. This is done by cutting off claims to rights or interests in land that have been inactive for longer than the act's statutory period. In Connecticut, Michigan, Utah, Vermont, and Wisconsin, this is 40 years. Thus, in these states, a person who has an unbroken chain of title with no defects for at least 40 years is regarded by the law as having marketable title. Any defects more than 40 years old are outlawed. The result is to concentrate the title search process on the immediate past 40 years. Thus, abstracts can be produced with less effort and expense, and the chance for an error either by the abstracter or in the documents themselves is greatly reduced. This is particularly true in view of the fact that record-keeping procedures in the past were not as sophisticated as they are today.

The philosophy of a marketable title act is that a person has 40 years to come forward and make his claim known; if he does not, then he apparently does not consider it worth pursuing. As protection for a person actively pursuing a claim that is about to become more than 40 years old, the claim can be renewed for another 40 years by again recording notice of the claim in the public records. In certain situations, a title must be searched back more than 40 years (e.g., when there is a lease of more than 40-year duration or when no document affecting ownership has been recorded in over 40 years). In Nebraska, the statutory period is 22 years; in Florida, North Carolina, and Oklahoma, it is 30 years; in Indiana, 50 years.

Marketable title acts do not eliminate the need for legal notice, nor do they eliminate the role of adverse possession.

VOCABULARY REVIEW

Match terms **a–v** *with statements* **1–22.**

a. *Abstract of title*
b. *Acknowledgment*
c. *Actual notice*
d. *Chain of title*

e. *Constructive notice*
f. *Grantor-Grantee indexes*
g. *Inquiry notice*
h. *Lender's policy*

i. *Lis pendens index*
j. *Marketable title*
k. *Marketable Title Act*
l. *Notary public*
m. *Opinion of title*
n. *Owner's policy*
o. *County clerk's office*

p. *Quiet title suit*
q. *Title cloud*
r. *Title insurance*
s. *Title report*
t. *Title searcher*
u. *Torrens system*
v. *Vested*

1. Knowledge gained from what one has seen, heard, read, or observed.
2. Notice given by the public records or by visible possession coupled with the legal presumption that all persons are thereby notified.
3. A formal declaration, made in the presence of a notary public or other authorized individual, by a person affirming that he signed a document.
4. A person authorized to take acknowledgments.
5. A place where a person can enter documents affecting title to real estate.
6. A book at the public recorder's office that lists grantors alphabetically by name.
7. The linkage of ownership that connects the present owner to the original source of title.
8. A publicly available index whereby a person can learn of any pending lawsuits that may affect title.
9. A title defect.
10. A complete summary of all recorded documents affecting title to a given parcel of land.
11. Insurance to protect a property owner against monetary loss if his title is found to be imperfect.
12. A report made by a title insurance company showing current title condition.
13. A title policy written to protect a real estate lender.
14. Title that is free from reasonable doubt as to who the owner is.
15. Court-ordered hearings held to determine land ownership.
16. Laws that automatically cut off inactive claims to rights or interests in land.
17. A method of registering land titles that is similar to that of automobile ownership registration.
18. Claims to property rights the law presumes a reasonably diligent person would find through further investigation.
19. A statement as to the ownership of a property that is made by an attorney after reading the abstract.
20. An insurance policy against loss due to errors in title report preparation and inaccuracies in the public records.
21. A person trained and employed to examine the public records.
22. Possessed by; owned by.

QUESTIONS AND PROBLEMS

1. How much does your county clerk's office charge to record a deed? A mortgage? What requirements must a document meet before it will be accepted for recording?
2. Where is the county clerk's office for your community located?
3. Explain constructive notice.
4. What is the purpose of grantor and grantee indexes?
5. Why is it important that a title search be carried out in more places than just the county recorder's office?
6. What is the difference between a certificate of title issued by an attorney and a Torrens certificate of title?
7. How does a title report differ from an abstract?
8. What is the purpose of title insurance?
9. Thorsen sells his house to Williams. Williams moves in but for some reason does not record his deed. Thorsen discovers this and sells the house to an out-of-state investor who orders a title search, purchases an owner's title policy, and records his deed. Thorsen then disappears with the money he received from both sales. Who is the loser when this scheme is discovered: Williams, the out-of-state investor, or the title company? Why?
10. If you are located near the county clerk's office for your county, examine the records for a parcel of land (such as your home) and trace its ownership back through three owners.

ADDITIONAL READINGS

Real Estate Counseling, by **James Boykin** (Prentice Hall, 1984, 288 pages). Written for those who plan to offer real estate counseling services and for those who plan to use those services. Nineteen professional counselors offer advice on real estate analysis and decision making.

"Revolutionizing the Title Insurance," by **Maria Wood** (*Real Estate Forum,* Jan. 1994, pp. 38–40+). Sample title insurance policy forms.

"What's Covered in a Title Policy," by **Frederick Romanski** (*Real Estate Today,* July/Aug. 1983, p. 43). Also in the same issue, "What You Should Know About Title Insurance" and "Title Insurance: Buyer Security." These three articles explain the need for title insurance with eye-opening case histories of title problems.

16

Lending Practices

Whereas Chapter 14 dealt with the legal aspects of notes, mort-gages, and trust deeds, Chapters 16 and 17 deal with the money aspects of these instruments. We begin in this chapter with term loans, amortized loans, balloon loans, partially amortized loans, loan-to-value ratio, equity, and points. These topics are followed by the functions and importance of the FHA and VA, and private mortgage insurance. Chapter 17 discusses Truth in Lending and provides a helpful and informative description of the loan ap-plication and approval process you (or your buyer) will experi-ence when applying for a real estate loan. In Chapter 18, we look at sources and types of financing, including where to find mort-gage loan money, where mortgage lenders obtain their money, and various types of financing instruments such as the adjust-able rate mortgage, equity mortgage, wraparound mortgage, seller financing, and so forth. Note that from here on whatever is said about mortgages applies equally to trust deeds.

TERM LOANS

A loan that requires only interest payments until the last day of its life, at which time the full amount borrowed is due, is called a **term loan** (or straight loan). Until 1930, the term loan was the standard method of financing real estate in the United States. These loans were typically made for a period of 3 to 5 years. The borrower signed a note or bond agreeing: (1) to pay the lender interest on the loan every 6 months, and (2) to repay the entire amount of the loan upon **maturity;** that is, at the end of the life of the loan. As security, the borrower mortgaged the property to the lender.

Loan Renewal

In practice, most real estate term loans were not paid off when they matured. Instead, the borrower asked the lender, typically a bank, to renew the loan for another 3 to 5 years. The major flaw in this approach to lending was that the borrower might never own the property free and clear of debt. This left the borrower continuously at the mercy of the lender for renewals. As long as the lender was not pressed for funds, the borrower's renewal request was granted. However, if the lender was short of funds, no renewal was granted and the borrower was expected to pay in full.

The inability to renew term loans caused hardship to hun-dreds of thousands of property owners during the Great Depres-sion that began in 1930 and lasted most of the decade. Banks were unable to accommodate requests for loan renewals and at the same time satisfy unemployed depositors who needed to withdraw their savings to live. As a result, owners of homes, farms, office buildings, factories, and vacant land lost their property as foreclosures reached into the millions. The market was so glutted with properties being offered for sale to satisfy unpaid mortgage loans that real estate prices fell at a sickening pace.

In 1933, a congressionally legislated Home Owner's Loan Corporation (HOLC) was created to assist financially distressed homeowners by acquiring mortgages that were about to be foreclosed. The HOLC then offered monthly repayment plans tailored to fit the homeowner's budget that would repay the loan in full by its maturity date without the need for a balloon payment. The HOLC was terminated in 1951 after rescuing over a million mortgages in its 18-year life. However, the use of this stretched-out payment plan, known as an **amortized loan,** took hold in American real estate, and today it is the accepted method of loan repayment.

AMORTIZED LOANS

The amortized loan requires regular equal payments during the life of the loan, of sufficient size and number to pay all interest due on the loan and reduce the amount owed to zero by the loan's maturity date. Figure 16.1 illustrates the contrast between an amortized and a term loan. Figure 16.1A shows a 6-year, $1,000 term loan with interest of $90 due each year of its life. At the end of the sixth year, the entire **principal** (the amount owed) is due in one lump sum payment along with the final interest payment. In Figure 16.1B, the same $1,000 loan is fully amortized by making six equal annual payments of $222.92. From the borrower's standpoint, $222.92 once each year is easier to budget than $90 for 5 years and $1,090 in the sixth year.

Repayment Methods

Furthermore, the amortized loan shown in Figure 16.1 actually costs the borrower less than the term loan. The total payments made under the term loan are $90 + $90 + $90 + $90 + $90 + $1,090 = $1,540. Amortizing the same loan requires total payments of 6 × $222.92 = $1,337.52. The difference is due to the fact that under the amortized loan the borrower begins to pay back part of the $1,000 principal with the first payment. In the first year, $90 of the $222.92 payment goes to interest and the

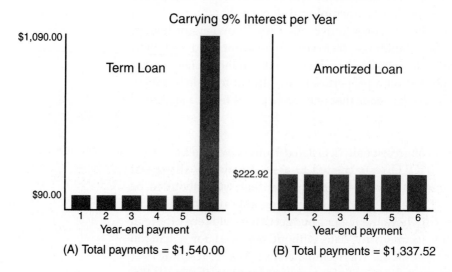

Figure 16.1. Repaying a 6-year $1,000 loan.

(A) Total payments = $1,540.00

(B) Total payments = $1,337.52

remaining $132.92 reduces the principal owed. Thus, the borrower starts the second year owing only $867.08. At 9% interest per year, the interest on $867.08 is $78.04; therefore, when the borrower makes the second payment of $222.92, only $78.04 goes to interest. The remaining $144.88 is applied to reduce the loan balance, and the borrower starts the third year owing $722.20. Figure 16.2 charts this repayment program. Notice that the balance owed drops faster as the loan becomes older, that is, as it matures.

Monthly Payments

As you have just seen, calculating the payments on a term loan is relatively simple compared with calculating amortized loan payments. The widespread use of computers has greatly simplified the calculations, however. To illustrate how the amortization works, though, we should note that **amortization tables** are published and used throughout the real estate industry. Table 16.1 shows the monthly payments per $1,000 of loan for interest rates from 5% to 15% for periods ranging from 5 to 40 years. (Amortization tables are also published for quarterly, semiannual, and annual payments.) When you use an amortization table, notice that there are five variables: (1) frequency of payment, (2) interest rate, (3) maturity, (4) amount of the loan, and (5) amount of the periodic payment. If you know any four of these, you can obtain the fifth variable from the tables. For example, suppose

Figure 16.2. Repaying a 6-year $1,000 amortized loan.

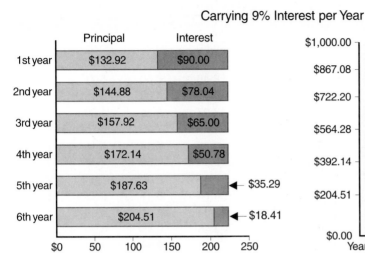

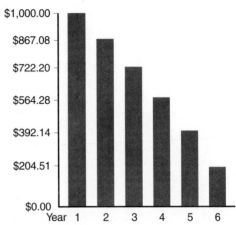

Carrying 9% Interest per Year

(A) Allocation of each annual
    payment to principal and interest

(B) Balance owed during each
    year of the loan

that you want to know the monthly payment necessary to amortize a $60,000 loan over 30 years at 10½% interest. The first step is to look in Table 16.1 for the 10½% line. Then locate the 30-year column. Where they cross, you will find the necessary monthly payment per $1,000: $9.15. Next, multiply $9.15 by 60 to get the monthly payment for a $60,000 loan: $549. If the loan is to be $67,500, then multiply $9.15 by 67.5 to get the monthly payment: $617.63.

Continuing the foregoing example, suppose we reduce the repayment period to 15 years. First look for the 10½% line, then go over to the 15-year column. The number there is $11.06. Next, multiply $11.06 by 60 to get the monthly payment for a $60,000 loan: $663.60. If the loan is to be $67,500, then multiply $11.06 by 67.5 to get the monthly payment: $746.55.

Amortization tables are also used to determine the amount of loan a borrower can support if you know how much the borrower has available to spend each month on loan payments. Suppose that a prospective home buyer can afford monthly principal and interest payments of $650 and lenders are making 30-year loans at 10%. How large a loan can this buyer afford? In

Loan Size

Table 16.1. Amortization Table Monthly Payment per $1,000 of Loan

Interest Rate per Year	Life of the Loan							
	5 years	10 years	15 years	20 years	25 years	30 years	35 years	40 years
5%	$18.88	$10.61	$ 7.91	$6.60	$5.85	$5.37	$5.05	$4.83
5½	19.11	10.86	8.18	6.88	6.15	5.68	5.38	5.16
6	19.34	11.11	8.44	7.17	6.45	6.00	5.71	5.51
6½	19.57	11.36	8.72	7.46	6.76	6.32	6.05	5.86
7	19.81	11.62	8.99	7.76	7.07	6.66	6.39	6.22
7½	20.04	11.88	9.28	8.06	7.39	7.00	6.75	6.59
8	20.28	12.14	9.56	8.37	7.72	7.34	7.11	6.96
8½	20.52	12.40	9.85	8.68	8.06	7.69	7.47	7.34
9	20.76	12.67	10.15	9.00	8.40	8.05	7.84	7.72
9½	21.01	12.94	10.45	9.33	8.74	8.41	8.22	8.11
10	21.25	13.22	10.75	9.66	9.09	8.78	8.60	8.50
10½	21.50	13.50	11.06	9.99	9.45	9.15	8.99	8.89
11	21.75	13.78	11.37	10.33	9.81	9.53	9.37	9.29
11½	22.00	14.06	11.69	10.67	10.17	9.91	9.77	9.69
12	22.25	14.35	12.01	11.02	10.54	10.29	10.16	10.09
12½	22.50	14.64	12.33	11.37	10.91	10.68	10.56	10.49
13	22.76	14.94	12.66	11.72	11.28	11.07	10.96	10.90
13½	23.01	15.23	12.99	12.08	11.66	11.46	11.36	11.31
14	23.27	15.53	13.32	12.44	12.04	11.85	11.76	11.72
14½	23.53	15.83	13.66	12.80	12.43	12.25	12.17	12.13
15	23.79	16.14	14.00	13.17	12.81	12.65	12.57	12.54

Table 16.1 find where the 10% line and the 30-year column meet. You will see 8.78 there. This means that every $8.78 of monthly payment will support $1,000 of loan. To find how many thousands of dollars $650 per month will support, just divide $650 by $8.78. The answer is 74.031 thousands or $74,031. By adding the buyer's down payment, you know what price property the buyer can afford to purchase. If interest rates are 7½%, the number from the table is 7.00 and the loan amount is $92,857. (You can begin to see why the level of interest rates is so important to real estate prices.)

As you have noticed, everything in Table 16.1 is on a monthly payment per thousand basis. With a full book of amortization tables rather than one page, it is possible to look up monthly payments for loans from $100 to $100,000, to determine loan maturities for each year from 1 to 40 years, and to calculate many more interest rates. Amortization books are available from most local bookstores.

An amortization table also shows the impact on the size of the monthly payment when the life of a loan is extended. For example, at 11% interest, a 10-year loan requires a monthly payment of $13.78 per thousand of loan. Increasing the life of the loan to 20 years drops the monthly payment to $10.33 per $1,000. Extending the loan payback to 30 years reduces the monthly payment to $9.53 per thousand. The smaller monthly payment is why 30 years is a popular loan term with borrowers. Note, however, that going beyond 30 years does not significantly reduce the monthly payment. Going from 30 to 35 years reduces the monthly payment by only 16¢ per thousand but adds 5 years of monthly payments. Extending the payback period from 35 to 40 years reduces the monthly payment by just 8¢ per $1,000 ($4 per month on a $50,000 loan) and adds another 60 months of payments at $464.50 per month. As a practical matter, amortized real estate loans are seldom made for more than 30 years.

Change in Maturity Date

The **budget mortgage** takes the amortized loan one step further. In addition to collecting the monthly principal and interest payment (often called $P + I$), the lender collects one-twelfth of the estimated cost of the annual property taxes and hazard insurance on the mortgaged property. The money for tax and insurance payments is placed in an **impound account** (also called an **escrow** or **reserve account**). When taxes and insurance payments are due, the lender pays them. Thus, the lender makes certain that the value of the mortgaged property will not be undermined by unpaid property taxes or by uninsured fire or weather damage. This form of mortgage also helps the borrower to budget for property taxes and insurance on a monthly basis. To illustrate, if insurance is $240 per year and property taxes are $1,800 per year, the lender collects an additional $20 and $150 each month along with the regular principal and interest payments. This combined principal, interest, taxes, and insurance payment is often referred to as a **PITI payment.**

BUDGET MORTGAGE

A **balloon loan** is any loan that has a final payment larger than any of the previous payments on the loan. The final payment is called a **balloon payment.** The term loan described at the begin-

BALLOON LOAN

ning of this chapter is a type of balloon loan. Partially amortized loans, discussed next, are another type of balloon loan. In tight money markets, the use of balloon loans increased considerably. Balloon loans with maturities as short as 3 to 5 years were commonplace. This arrangement gives the buyer (borrower) 3 to 5 years to find cheaper and longer-term financing elsewhere. If such financing does not materialize and the loan is not repaid on time, the lender has the right to foreclose. The alternative is for the lender and borrower to agree to an extension of the loan, usually at prevailing interest rates.

PARTIALLY AMORTIZED LOAN

When the repayment schedule of a loan calls for a series of amortized payments followed by a balloon payment at maturity, it is called a **partially amortized loan.** For example, a lender might agree to a 30-year amortization schedule with a provision that at the end of the tenth year all the remaining principal be paid in a single balloon payment. The advantage to the borrower is that for 10 years the monthly payments will be smaller than if the loan was completely amortized in 10 years. (You can verify this in Table 16.1.) However, the disadvantage is that the balloon payment due at the end of the tenth year might be the borrower's financial downfall. Just how large that balloon payment will be can be determined in advance by using a **loan balance table** (also called a **remaining balance table**). Presuming an interest rate of $11\frac{1}{2}\%$ and a 30-year loan, at the end of 10 years the loan balance table in Table 16.2 shows that for each $1,000 originally loaned, $929 would still be owed. If the original loan was for $100,000, at the end of 10 years $100 \times \$929 = \$92,900$ would be due as one payment. This qualifies it as a balloon loan.

As you can see from this example, when an amortized loan has a long maturity, relatively little of the debt is paid off during the initial years of the loan's life. Nearly all the early payments go for interest, so that little remains for principal reduction. For example, Table 16.2 shows that even after 16 years of payments on a 30-year, $11\frac{1}{2}\%$ loan, $82\frac{1}{2}\%$ of the loan is still unpaid. Not until this loan is about 6 years from maturity will half of it have been repaid.

EARLIER PAYOFF

During the late 1970s when inflation rates exceeded interest rates, the popular philosophy was to borrow as much as possible

Table 16.2. Balance Owing on a $1,000 Amortized Loan

Age of Loan (years)	9½% Annual Interest						Age of Loan (years)	11½% Annual Interest					
	Original Life (years)							Original Life (years)					
	10	15	20	25	30	35		10	15	20	25	30	35
2	$868	$934	$963	$978	$987	$992	2	$880	$944	$971	$984	$991	$995
4	708	853	918	952	971	983	4	729	873	935	965	981	989
6	515	756	864	921	953	971	6	539	784	889	940	967	982
8	282	639	799	883	930	957	8	300	672	831	909	950	972
10		497	720	837	902	940	10		531	759	870	929	960
12		326	625	781	869	920	12		354	667	821	902	945
14		119	510	714	828	896	14		132	553	759	868	926
16			371	633	780	866	16			409	682	825	903
18			203	535	721	830	18			228	585	772	873
20				416	650	787	20				462	704	836
22				273	564	735	22				308	620	789
24				100	460	671	24				115	513	729
26					335	595	26					380	655
28					183	503	28					211	561
30						391	30						444
32						256	32						296
34						94	34						110

for as long as possible. Then in the early 1980s inflation rates dropped below interest rates and the opposite philosophy became attractive to many borrowers. This was especially true for those who had borrowed (or were contemplating borrowing) at double-digit interest rates. Let us use as an example an $80,000 loan at 11½% interest. If the loan has a maturity of 30 years, from Table 16.1 we can determine the monthly payments to be $792.80. (Follow this example on your own.)

15-Year Loan

Suppose the maturity of the aforementioned loan is changed from 30 to 15 years. Looking at Table 16.1, the monthly payments would now be $935.20. This is $142.40 more per month, but the loan is fully paid in 15 years, not 30 years. The total amount of interest paid on the 15-year loan is (15 × 12 × $935.20) − $80,000 = $88,336. The total amount of interest paid on the 30-year loan is (30 × 12 × $792.80) − $80,000 = $205,408. Thus, for an extra $142.40 per month for 180 months (which amounts to $25,632) the borrower saves the difference between $205,408 and $88,336 (which is $117,072). Many borrowers consider this a very good return on their money. (It is, in fact, an 11½% compounded rate of return.) Lenders are more receptive to making fixed-rate loans for 15 years than for 30 years. This is because the lender is locked into the loan for 15 years, not 30 years. As a result, a lender is usually willing to offer a 15-year loan at a lower rate of interest than a 30-year loan. In view of these benefits to borrower and lender alike, the 15-year loan is becoming a popular home financing tool.

Biweekly Payments

A small but growing number of lenders offer a biweekly repayment plan. The loan is amortized as if it were going to last 30 years. But instead of paying once a month, the borrower makes one-half the monthly payment every two weeks. This may not sound like much of a difference but the results are eye-opening. Assume you borrow $100,000 at 13% interest, paying (see Table 16.1) $1,107 per month. You will retire the loan in 30 years at a cost of $298,520 in interest. If you decide to pay half of $1,107 every two weeks, the loan will be fully paid in just 18 years and will have cost you $160,023 in interest. This happens because biweekly compounding works in your favor and because you make 26 half-size payments a year, not 24.

Existing Loans

Borrowers with existing loans who want to celebrate with an early mortgage burning can simply add a few dollars each month to the required monthly payment. This can be particularly beneficial for people who borrowed at rates of 13%, 14%, and 15% or more. In effect, whatever extra amount is added to the monthly payment will "earn" interest at the loan's interest rate. Thus, if a loan has a 14% rate, early payments "earn" at 14%. If the borrower has no alternative places to invest that will yield 14%, then a few additional dollars each month will work miracles. For example, a 30-year, $100,000 loan at 14% interest requires monthly payments (see Table 16.1) of $1,185. Voluntarily adding an extra $19 per month reduces the maturity (payoff) date from 30 years to 25 years (see Table 16.1 again). If an extra $40 is added to the $19, the maturity date shrinks to 20 years. In other words, an extra $59 per month eliminates 10 years of payments.

You may be wondering why this has not been a popular idea with borrowers. There are two key reasons. First, there was a time in 1979 when inflation was 18% per year and 14% to borrow looked cheap by comparison. Second, when interest rates are around 6% and 7% (as they were in the 1960s and, more recently, in the 1990s), the mathematics of early payoff are not as impressive.

The relationship between the amount of money a lender is willing to loan and the lender's estimate of the market value of the property that will serve as security is called the **loan-to-value ratio** (often abbreviated **L/V** or **LTV ratio**). For example, a prospective home buyer wants to purchase a house priced at $80,000. A local lender appraises the house, finds it has a market value of $80,000, and agrees to make an 80% L/V loan. This means that the lender will loan up to 80% of the $80,000 and the buyer must provide at least 20% in cash. In dollars, the lender will loan up to $64,000 and the buyer must make a cash down payment of at least $16,000. If the lender appraises the home for more than $80,000 the loan will still be $64,000. If the appraisal is for less than $80,000 the loan will be 80% of the appraised value, and the buyer must pay the balance in cash. The rule is that price or value, whichever is lower, is applied to the L/V ratio. This rule exists to prevent the lender from overlending on a property just because the borrower overpaid for it.

LOAN-TO-VALUE RATIO

The difference between the market value of a property and the debt owed against it is called the owner's **equity.** On a newly purchased $80,000 home with a $16,000 cash down payment, the buyer's equity is $16,000. As the value of the property rises or falls and as the mortgage loan is paid down, the equity changes. For example, if the value of the home rises to $90,000 and the loan is paid down to $62,000, the owner's equity will be $28,000. If the owner completely repays the loan so that there is no debt against the home, the owner's equity is equal to the market value of the property.

EQUITY

Probably no single term in real estate finance causes as much confusion and consternation as the word *points*. In finance, the word **point** means 1% of the loan amount. Thus, on a $60,000 loan, one point is $600. On a $40,000 loan, three points is $1,200. On a $100,000 loan, eight points is $8,000.

The use of points in real estate mortgage finance can be split into two categories: (1) loan origination fees expressed in terms

LOAN POINTS

of points, and (2) the use of points to change the effective yield of a mortgage loan to a lender. Let us look at these two uses in more detail.

Origination Fee   When a borrower asks for a mortgage loan, the lender incurs a number of expenses, including such things as the time its loan officer spends interviewing the borrower, office overhead, the purchase and review of credit reports on the borrower, an on-site appraisal of the property to be mortgaged, title searches and review, legal and recording fees, and so on. For these, some lenders make an itemized billing, charging so many dollars for the appraisal, credit report, title search, and so on. The total becomes the **loan origination fee,** which the borrower pays to get the loan. Other lenders do not make an itemized bill, but instead simply state the origination fee in terms of a percentage of the loan amount, for example, one point. Thus, a lender quoting a loan origination fee of one point is saying that, for a $65,000 loan, its fee to originate the loan will be $650.

Discount Points   Points charged to raise the lender's monetary return on a loan are known as **discount points.** A simplified example illustrates their use and effect. If you are a lender and agree to make a term loan of $100 to a borrower for 1 year at 10% interest, you would normally expect to give the borrower $100 now (disregard loan origination fees for a moment) and, 1 year later, the borrower would give you $110. In percentage terms, the **effective yield** on your loan is 10% per annum (year) because you received $10 for your 1-year, $100 loan. Now suppose that instead of handing the borrower $100, you handed him $99 but still required him to repay $100 plus $10 in interest at the end of the year. This is a discount of one point ($1 in this case), and the borrower paid it out of the loan funds. The effect of this financial maneuver is to raise the effective yield (yield to maturity) to you without raising the interest rate itself. Therefore, if you loan out $99 and receive $110 at the end of the year, you effectively have a return of $11 for a $99 loan. This gives you an effective yield of $11 ÷ $99 or 11.1%, rather than 10%.

Calculating the effective yield on a discounted 20- or 30-year mortgage loan is more difficult because the amount owed drops over the life of the loan, and because the majority are paid in full ahead of schedule due to refinancing. Computers and calculators usually make these calculations; however, a useful rule of thumb states that on the typical home loan each point of discount raises the effective yield by $\frac{1}{8}$ of 1%. Thus, four discount points would raise the effective yield by approximately $\frac{1}{2}$ of 1% and eight points would raise it by 1%. Discount points are most often charged during periods of **tight money,** that is, when mortgage money is in short supply. During periods of **loose money**, when lenders have adequate funds to lend and are actively seeking borrowers, discount points disappear.

Real estate loans that are not insured by the FHA or guaranteed by the VA are termed **conventional loans.** Let's discuss the impact of the FHA and VA.

The Great Depression caused a major change in the attitude of the federal government toward home financing in the United States. In 1934, one year after the Home Owners Loan Corporation was established, Congress passed the National Housing Act. The Act's most far-reaching provision was to establish the Federal Housing Administration (FHA) for the purpose of encouraging new construction as a means of creating jobs. To accomplish this goal, the FHA offered to insure lenders against losses due to nonrepayment when they made loans on both new and existing homes. In turn, the lender had to grant 20-year fully amortized loans with loan-to-value ratios of 80% rather than the 3- to 5-year, 50% to 60% term loans common up to that time.

The FHA did its best to keep from becoming a burden to the American taxpayer. When a prospective borrower approached a lender for an FHA-secured home loan, the FHA reviewed the borrower's income, expenses, assets, and debts. The objective was to determine whether there was adequate room in the borrower's budget for the proposed loan payments. The FHA also sent inspectors to the property to make certain that it was of acceptable construction quality and to determine its fair market value. To offset losses that would still inevitably occur, the FHA charged the borrower an annual insurance fee of approximately $\frac{1}{2}$ of 1% of the balance owed on the loan. The FHA was immensely successful in its task. Not only did it create construction jobs, but it raised the level of housing quality in the nation and, in a pleasant surprise to taxpayers, actually returned annual profits to the U.S. Treasury. In response to its success, in 1946 Congress changed its status from temporary to permanent.

FHA INSURANCE PROGRAMS

Current FHA Coverage   The FHA has had a marked influence on lending policies in the real estate industry. Foremost among these is the widespread acceptance of the high loan-to-value, fully amortized loan. In the 1930s, lenders required FHA insurance before making 80% L/V loans. By the 1960s, lenders were readily making 80% L/V loans without FHA insurance. Meanwhile, the FHA insurance program was working so well that the FHA raised the portion it was willing to insure. In 1990, Congress established a new maximum loan-to-value ratio by passing the **Omnibus Budget Reconciliation Act** (OBRA). The OBRA calculation does not include closing costs, but the maximum L/V ratio is 98.75% for houses with a sales price of less than $50,000, and 97.75% for houses with a sales price in excess of $50,000. FHA now insures a lender for the lesser of: (1) the OBRA value, or (2) the "old rule," which is 97% of the appraised value up to an appraised value of $50,000. If the property's appraised value exceeds $50,000, FHA insures 97% of the first $25,000 plus 95% of the balance of its appraised value up to $125,000, and 90% of such value in excess of $125,000. Utilizing the new OBRA calculations, 100% of the good faith estimate of closing costs can be included in calculating the loan amount. To illustrate, on a $60,000 home the FHA would insure 97% of the first $25,000 and 95% of the remaining $35,000, for a total of $57,500, although new regulations require that seller-paid closing costs be deducted from the value of the property. In our example, this means a cash down payment of only $2,500 for the buyer. The borrower is not permitted to use a second mortgage to raise this $2,500. The FHA requires some down payment; otherwise, it would be too easy for the borrower to walk away from the debt and leave the FHA to pay the lender's insurance claim. Please be aware that the maximum amount the FHA will insure varies from city to city and is changed from time to time by the FHA. As of 1996, the maximum loan amount in high-cost areas was $155,250.

After December 15, 1989, private investors were banned from the FHA single-family program. In addition, no single-family loans originating on or after December 15, 1989 can be assumed by investors. Any loan made before December 15, 1989 may be assumed by an investor, but additional restrictions have to be met: (1) the balance due must be no more than 75% of the cost of the property; and (2) if the monthly mortgage payment exceeds the net rental income, the mortgage amount must be reduced so that its payment does not exceed the amount amortized by the net rental income.

Traditionally, FHA loans were popular because the 30-year fixed-rate loans could be assumed without any increase in interest. This is still true for loans that were originated prior to December 1, 1986. The assumption procedure can be one of two types, a simple assumption or a formal assumption. In the **simple assumption** procedure, the property is sold and the loan is assumed by the buyer without notification to the FHA or its agent. The seller remains fully liable to the FHA for full repayment. In the **formal assumption,** the property is not conveyed to a new buyer until the new buyer's creditworthiness has been approved by the FHA or its agent. When the creditworthy buyer assumes the loan, the seller may obtain a full release of liability from the FHA.

Assumability

If the FHA loan was originated between December 1, 1986, and December 15, 1989, the owner-occupant cannot sell the property with a loan assumption during the first 12 months after execution of the mortgage without creditworthiness approval for each person who assumes the loan. If the seller is an investor, the assumption cannot be made without prior approval during the first 24 months after execution of the mortgage. Failure to comply with either requirement results in an acceleration of the loan balance. After the 1- or 2-year loan period, the loan can be assumed without approval. If the assumption is a simple assumption, the seller remains fully liable for 5 years after the new mortgage is executed. If the loan is not in default after the 5 years, the seller is automatically released from liability.

If the loan was originated after December 15, 1989, the FHA requires the creditworthiness approval prior to the conveyance of title on all assumption loans. If the borrower assumes a mortgage loan, the lender cannot refuse to release the original borrower from liability on the loan.

The major disadvantage of an FHA loan is the relatively low loan limit. The FHA's mission is to serve buyers with limited funds who are looking for modestly priced housing. It is possible to get an FHA loan on a more expensive home, but the buyer must make such a large down payment that an FHA loan becomes impractical. You will, however, find existing FHA loans on more expensive homes in the resale market. This is because the loan was written 10 or 20 years ago and the value of the home has risen from modest to expensive since then. Nonetheless, these homes are often eagerly sought by buyers because the existing FHA loan is assumable and may carry an interest rate several percentage points below current market rates. Furthermore, a second mortgage can be used to finance the difference between the existing FHA loan and the buyer's down payment.

Mortgage Insurance

The FHA charges a one-time **Up Front Mortgage Insurance Premium (UFMIP)** that is paid when the loan is made. The amount of the UFMIP is 2.25% of the loan amount, although there are exceptions. For streamlined refinancing of loans originated before July 1, 1991, the premium remains at 3.8%. FHA mortgages with terms of 15 years or less charge 2%, with no annual premium if the loan-to-value ratio is less than 90%. The premium can be paid in cash or added to the amount borrowed. If borrowed, it can be over and above the FHA ceiling. Thus, if the ceiling is $90,000 and the loan requested is $90,000, the UFMIP will be $3,420 and the total amount financed will be $93,420. The $93,420 becomes the principal amount of the loan and an amortization table is used to find the monthly payment. If the loan is fully repaid within 7 years, the borrower is entitled to a refund of part of the UFMIP.

The FHA now also charges an annual premium amounting to ½ of 1% of the annual loan balance. One-twelfth of the annual premium is added to the monthly payment and must be included in the proposed monthly housing expense to qualify the borrower for the loan. The amount is calculated each year on the unpaid principal balance without UFMIP and excluding closing costs. Since 1994, if the down payment exceeds 10%, the term for premium payment is 11 years. If the down payment is 10% or less, the term of the premium is 30 years. Annual premiums are nonrefundable.

Floating Interest Rates

At one time, FHA set interest rate ceilings. Fixed-rate FHA loans are now negotiable and float with the market, and the seller also has a choice in how many points to contribute toward the borrower's loan. This can be none, some, or all the points, and the seller can even pay the borrower's MIP. Typical purchase contract language is, "The seller will pay X points and the buyer will pay not more than Y points and the agreed-on interest rate is $Z\%$." Thus, X is the contribution the seller will make, and the seller is protected from having to pay more. The buyer will pay any additional points, but not more than Y points. Beyond that, the buyer can cancel the purchase contract. That would happen if the market rates rose quickly while the rate at Z is fixed.

Thus far, we have been concentrating on the FHA's most popular program—mortgage insurance on single-family houses. The FHA's authority to offer this is found in **Section 203(b)** of Title II of the National Housing Act. These loans are commonly referred to as "Section 203(b)" loans. However, the FHA administers a number of other real estate mortgage insurance programs and several of the better-known ones are mentioned now.

Other FHA Programs

Under **Section 203(k),** the FHA insures mortgage loans made to finance home improvements. Under **Section 234,** the FHA insures loans on condominium units in a manner similar to Section 203(b). **Section 213** insures loans for cooperative housing projects. **Section 235** offers a single-family residence loan subsidy program.

Under **Section 245** the FHA will insure a graduated payment mortgage (GPM). This loan format allows the borrower to make smaller payments initially and to increase payment size gradually over time. The idea is to parallel the borrower's rising earning capacity. (GPMs receive more coverage in Chapter 19.) The FHA also insures adjustable rate mortgage loans with a program started in mid-1984. These are available to owner-occupants under Section 203(b) and 203(k) and carry an interest rate tied to 1-year U.S. Treasury securities. The rate can be adjusted up or down by not more than 1% annually or 5% over the life of the loan. Negative amortization—the addition of unpaid interest to the principal balance—is prohibited. (Adjustable loans receive more attention in Chapter 19.)

Before leaving the topic of the FHA, it is interesting to note that much of what we take for granted as standard loan practice today was the result of FHA innovation years ago. As already noted, standard real estate loan practice called for short-term renewable loans before 1934. Then the FHA boldly offered 20-year amortized loans. Once these were shown to be successful

Loan Qualification

investments for lenders, loans without FHA insurance were
made for 20 years. Later, when the FHA successfully went to 30
years, non–FHA-insured loans followed. The FHA also established loan application review techniques that have been widely
accepted and copied throughout the real estate industry. The
biggest step in this direction was to analyze a borrower's loan
application in terms of earning power.

HUD announced major revisions in its FHA single-family
underwriting guidelines in January 1995, giving lenders more
flexibility in considering an applicant's income and savings. The
new regulations provide that FHA may now participate in state
housing finance agencies and programs to use alternative qualifying methods, such as (1) the applicant's existing housing
payments, (2) tax benefits of home ownership, and (3) nonhousing
debt history. In addition, FHA now uses a 3-year test for income
stability instead of the previous 5-year test. Only debts extending 10 or more months are included into debt-to-income calculations and child care costs are no longer counted as a
recurring debt. FHA lenders can now also use a three-re-
pository merged credit report. HUD also gave FHA limited
approval for the use of automatic underwriting systems (discussed in Chapter 18).

Construction
Regulations

Since its inception, the FHA has imposed its own minimum
construction requirements. Often this was essential where
local building codes did not exist or were weaker than the
FHA wanted. Before issuing a loan, particularly on new construction, the FHA would impose minimum requirements as to
the quantity and quality of building materials to be used. Lot
size, street access, landscaping, siting, and general house design
also were required to fit within broad FHA guidelines. During
construction, an FHA inspector would come to the property
several times to check on whether or not work was being done
correctly.

The reason for such care in building standards was that the
FHA recognized that if a building is defective either from a
design or construction standpoint, the borrower is more likely to
default on the loan and create an insurance claim against the FHA.
Furthermore, the same defects will lower the price the property
will bring at its foreclosure sale, thus increasing losses to the FHA.
Because building codes are now becoming stricter and more

standardized in states, counties, and cities, the FHA anticipates eliminating its own minimum property standards. FHA has also softened its standards for property defects. The new FHA standards, which became effective January 1, 1995, advised underwriters to delete "conditions that have little or nothing to do with the safety and soundness of the property" from repair requirements stipulated by an appraiser.

As we leave our discussion of the FHA and go to the Department of Veteran Affairs, keep in mind that the FHA is not a lender. The FHA is an insurance agency. The loan itself is obtained from a savings and loan, bank, mortgage company, or similar lender. In addition to principal and interest payments, the lender collects an insurance premium from the borrower which is forwarded to the FHA. The FHA, in turn, guarantees repayment of the loan to the lender. This arrangement makes lenders much more willing to loan to buyers who are putting only 3% to 5% cash down. Thus, when you hear the phrase "FHA loan" in real estate circles, know that it is an FHA-*insured* loan, not a loan from the FHA.

In 1944, to show its appreciation to servicemen returning from World War II, Congress passed far-reaching legislation to aid veterans in education, hospitalization, employment training, and housing. In housing, the popularly named G.I. Bill of Rights empowered the Comptroller General of the United States to guarantee the repayment of a portion of first mortgage real estate loans made to veterans. For this guarantee, no fee would be charged to the veteran. Rather, the government itself would stand the losses. On March 15, 1989, the Veterans Administration was elevated to cabinet level and is now officially called the Department of Veteran Affairs, but still clings to its old initials, the VA.

DEPARTMENT OF VETERAN AFFAIRS

The original 1944 law provided that lenders would be guaranteed against losses up to 50% of the amount of the loan, but in no case more than $2,000. The objective was to make it possible for a veteran to buy a home with no cash down payment. Thus, on a house offered for sale at $5,000 (houses were much cheaper in 1944), this guarantee enabled a veteran to borrow the entire $5,000. From the lender's standpoint, having the top $2,000 of the loan guaranteed by the U.S. government offered the same

No Down Payment

asset protection as a $2,000 cash down payment. If the veteran defaulted and the property went into foreclosure, the lender had to net less than $3,000 before suffering a loss.

In 1945 Congress increased the guarantee amount to $4,000 and 60% of the loan and turned the entire operation over to the Veterans Administration (predecessor in interest to the VA). The VA was quick to honor claims, and the program rapidly became popular with lenders. Furthermore, the veterans turned out to be excellent credit risks, bettering, in fact, the good record of FHA-insured homeowners. The FHA recognizes this and gives higher insurance limits to FHA borrowers who have served in the Armed Forces.

To keep up with the increased cost of homes, the guarantee has been increased several times. Since February 1, 1988, the VA has used the sliding-scale system for calculating the applicable guarantee amounts. The guarantee increases with the amount of the loan using fixed dollar amounts and percentages of loan amounts. The current limits in effect since July, 1995 are shown in Table 16.3.

Table 16.3.

Loan Amount	Guarantee
Up to $45,000	50% of the Loan Amount
$45,001 to $56,250	$22,500
$56,251 to $144,000	40% of the Loan Amount
$144,001 and higher	25% of the Loan Amount

Some lenders will go higher if the borrower makes a down payment.

In the original G.I. Bill of 1944, eligibility was limited to World War II veterans. However, subsequent legislation has broadened eligibility to include any veteran who served for a period of at least 90 days in the armed forces of the United States or an ally between September 16, 1940 and July 25, 1947, or between June 27, 1950 and January 31, 1955. Any veteran of the United States who has served at least 181 days of continuous active duty from January 31, 1955 to the present is also eligible. If service was during the Vietnam conflict period (August 5, 1964, to May 7, 1975) or the Persian Gulf War, 90 days is sufficient to qualify. The veteran's discharge must be on conditions other than dishonorable, and the guarantee entitlement is good until used. If not remarried, the spouse of a veteran who died as a result of service can also obtain a housing guarantee. Active duty personnel can also qualify. Shorter active duty periods are allowed for service-connected disabilities.

To determine benefits, a veteran should make application to the Department of Veteran Affairs for a **certificate of eligibility,** which shows whether the veteran is qualified and the amount of guarantee available. This document is necessary to obtain a VA-guaranteed loan.

VA Certificates

The VA works diligently to protect veterans and reduce foreclosure losses. When a veteran applies for a VA guarantee, the property is appraised and the VA issues a **certificate of reasonable value.** Often abbreviated **CRV,** it reflects the estimated value of the property as determined by the VA staff appraiser. Similarly, the VA establishes income guidelines to make certain that the veteran can comfortably meet the proposed loan payments. Also, the veteran must agree to occupy the property. Pursuant to the newly enacted Safe Drinking Water Act, if the building was constructed after June 19, 1988, the CRV must now reflect a certification that any solders or fluxes used in construction did not contain more than 0.2% lead in any pipes, or that the pipe fittings used did not contain more than 8% lead.

The VA guarantees fixed-rate loans for as long as 30 years on homes, and no prepayment penalty is charged if the borrower wishes to pay sooner. Moreover, there is no due-on-sale clause that requires the loan to be repaid if the property is sold. The VA guarantees loans for the purchase of townhouses and condominiums, to build or improve a home, and to buy a mobile home as a residence. A veteran wishing to refinance an existing home or farm can obtain a VA-guaranteed loan provided there is existing debt that will be repaid. The VA also makes direct loans to veterans if there are no private lending institutions nearby.

Financial Liability

No matter what loan guarantee program is elected, the veteran should know that in the event of default and subsequent foreclosure he or she is required eventually to make good any losses suffered by the VA on the loan. (This is not the case with FHA-insured loans, in which the borrower pays for protection against foreclosure losses that may result from the loan.) Even if the veteran sells the property and the buyer assumes the VA loan, the veteran is still financially responsible if the buyer later defaults. To avoid this, the veteran must arrange with the VA to be released from liability. For VA loans underwritten after March 1, 1988, Congress created a new Guarantee and Indemnity Fund that allows a release from liability to the VA in the event of foreclosure provided that the following requirements are met:

1. The loan payments must be current.
2. The prospective purchasers must meet creditworthiness standards as required by the VA.
3. The prospective purchaser must assume full liability for repayment of the loan, including indemnity liability to the VA.

In the event borrowers are unable to make their mortgage payments, the VA offers an assistance procedure that may be helpful in declining markets. If the borrower can obtain a purchase offer that is insufficient to pay off the existing loan balance, a **compromise agreement** may allow the VA to pay the difference between the sales proceeds and the mortgage balance. To effect the compromise agreement, the borrower must be willing to find a purchaser who will pay fair market value of the house and the original borrower must agree to remain liable to the government for the amount that the VA pays to the noteholder.

A veteran is permitted a full new guarantee entitlement if complete repayment of a previous VA-guaranteed loan has been made. If a veteran has sold and let the buyer assume his VA loan, the balance of the entitlement is still available. For example, if a veteran has used $15,000 of his or her entitlement to date, the difference between $15,000 and the current VA guarantee amount is still available for use.

Funding Fee   From its inception until October 1, 1982, the VA made loan guarantees on behalf of veterans without a charge. Congress initially enacted a funding fee in 1982, increased it in 1991, and in 1993 established a funding fee with three categories of veterans, each with different fees depending on the veteran status and down payment. Note the new rates set out in Table 16.4. Funding fees for interest-rate-reduction refinancing loans were reduced to ½ of 1%. Funding fees on manufactured homes remain at 1% for all veterans and reservists. The fee still remains at ½ of 1% for assumptions by veterans or reservists. Funding fees can be added to the loan amount for calculating the loan-to-value ratio.

In 1992, Congress passed an historic change that eliminated the interest rate ceilings on VA loans. The new program allows an interest rate and discount points agreed on by the veteran and the lender. The program expired on December 31, 1995, but was reinstated on February 13, 1996. Discount points may not be financed on any loan except interest-rate-reduction refinancing loans (IRRRLs). IRRRLs closed after February 28, 1996 are limited to two discount points.

Interest Rates

On VA loans assumed prior to March 1, 1988, approval was not required prior to loan assumption. Therefore, sellers could sell their property on assumption without obtaining any approval from the VA, but sellers remained fully liable for repayment. As stated previously, they could be released from liability if the VA approved the creditworthiness of the new purchaser. After March 1, 1988, the VA required prior approval for transfer of the property. Federal law now requires that the mortgage or deed of trust and note for loans carry on the first page in type 2½ times larger than the regular type the following statement:

Assumption Requirements

THIS LOAN IS NOT ASSUMABLE WITHOUT THE PRIOR APPROVAL OF THE DEPARTMENT OF VETERANS ADMINISTRATION OR AUTHORIZED AGENT.

Table 16.4.

Down Payment	Veterans	National Guard & Reservists	Multiple Users
No down payment	2.00%	2.75%	3.00%
Down payment of at least 5%	1.50%	2.25%	1.50%
Down payment of 10% or more	1.25%	2.00%	1.25%

Because Congress frequently changes eligibility and benefits, a person contemplating a VA or FHA loan should make inquiry to the field offices of these two agencies and to mortgage lenders to ascertain the current status and details of the law, as well as the availability of loan money. Field offices also have information on foreclosed properties that are for sale. Additionally, one should query lenders as to the availability of state veteran benefits. A number of states offer special advantages, including mortgage loan assistance, to residents who have served in the armed forces.

Adjustable-Rate Mortgages

Since 1992, the VA has been allowed to issue its guarantee for an adjustable-rate mortgage. The approved plan is structured the same as the FHA ARM, underwritten at an interest rate 1% above the initial rate agreed on by the veteran and the lender. Increases in the interest rate are limited to an annual adjustment of 1%, and capped at 5% over the life of the loan. The index for calculating interest-rate adjustments is the weekly average yield on Treasury securities to a constant maturity of 1 year as reported by the Federal Reserve Board.

PRIVATE MORTGAGE INSURANCE

In 1957, the Mortgage Guaranty Insurance Corporation (MGIC) was formed in Milwaukee, Wisconsin as a privately owned business venture to insure home mortgage loans. Demand was slow but steady for the first 10 years and then grew rapidly until today when there are over a dozen private mortgage insurance companies. Like FHA insurance, the object of **private mortgage insurance (PMI)** is to insure lenders against foreclosure losses. But, unlike the FHA, PMI insures only the top 20% to 25% of a loan, not the whole loan. This allows a lender to make 90% and 95% L/V loans with about the same exposure to foreclosure losses as a 70% to 75% L/V loan. The borrower, meanwhile, can purchase a home with a cash down payment of either 10% or 5% rather than the 20% to 30% down required by lenders when mortgage insurance is not purchased. For this privilege the borrower pays a PMI fee of 1% or less when the loan is made plus an annual fee of a fraction of 1%. When the loan is partially repaid (for example, to a 70% L/V), the premiums and coverage can be terminated. PMI is also available on apartment buildings, offices, stores, warehouses, and leaseholds, but at higher rates than on homes.

Private mortgage insurers work to keep their losses to a minimum by first approving the lenders with whom they do business. Particular emphasis is placed on the lender's operating policy, appraisal procedure, and degree of government regulation. Once approved, a lender simply sends the borrower's loan application, credit report, and property appraisal to the insurer. Based on these documents, the insurer either agrees or refuses to issue a policy. Although the insurer relies on the appraisal prepared by the lender, the insurer sends, on a random basis, its own appraiser to verify the quality of the information being submitted. When an insured loan goes into default, the insurer has the option of either buying the property from the lender for the balance due or letting the lender foreclose and then paying the lender's losses up to the amount of the insurance. As a rule, insurers take the first option because it is more popular with lenders and it leaves the lender with immediate cash to relend. The insurer is then responsible for foreclosing.

Approval Procedure

The **Farmer's Home Administration (FmHA,** and termed **Farmer Mac),** is a federal agency under the U.S. Department of Agriculture. Like the FHA, it came into existence due to the financial crises of the 1930s. The FmHA offers programs to help purchase or operate farms. The FmHA will either guarantee a portion of a loan made by a private lender or it will make the loan itself. FmHA loans can also be used to help finance the purchase of homes in rural areas. Originally, Farmer Mac could provide only a 90% loan-to-value ratio. A new statute was enacted in 1996 to eliminate that ceiling. The new statute also allows Farmer Mac to offer intermediate and long-term fixed-rate loan products to lenders at more attractive rates, and authorizes Farmer Mac to act as a loan pooler for qualified loans. This allows the purchase of loans directly from originators and the issuance of guaranteed securities backed by the loans. Farmer Mac can now become a true secondary market delivering agricultural and rural housing for borrowers with the same benefits that Fannie Mae and Freddie Mac have effectively provided. Eligible loans are outside an incorporated area or metropolitan statistical area, and are limited to communities with populations of less than 2,500.

FARMER'S HOME ADMINISTRATION

VOCABULARY REVIEW

Match terms **a–l** *with statements* **1–12.**

a. *Amortized loan*
b. *Balloon payment*
c. *FmHA*
d. *Impound account*
e. *Loan balance table*
f. *Maturity*

g. *Partially amortized loan*
h. *PITI payment*
i. *Point*
j. *Principal*
k. *Section 203(b)*
l. *Term loan*

1. Balance owing on a loan.
2. A loan that requires the borrower to pay interest only until maturity, at which time the full amount of the loan must be repaid.
3. Refers to a monthly loan payment that includes principal, interest, property taxes, and property insurance.
4. An escrow or reserve account into which the lender places the borrower's monthly tax and insurance payments.
5. One-hundredth of the total amount; 1% of a loan.
6. A loan requiring periodic payments that include both interest and principal.
7. A payment that is larger than any of the previous payments.
8. The end of the life of a loan.
9. A loan with a series of amortized payments followed by a balloon payment at maturity.
10. Chart that shows the principal still owing during the life of a loan.
11. FHA's popular mortgage insurance program for houses.
12. A federal agency under the U.S. Department of Agriculture that will help purchase and operate farms and finance homes in rural areas.

QUESTIONS AND PROBLEMS

1. What is the major risk that the borrower takes when agreeing to a loan with a balloon payment?
2. Explain how an amortized loan works.
3. Using Table 16.1, calculate the monthly payment necessary to completely amortize a $65,000, 30-year loan at 11½% interest.
4. A prospective home buyer has a $10,000 down payment and can afford $800 per month for principal and interest payments. If 30-year, 11% amortized loans are available, what price home can the buyer afford?
5. Same problem as in number 4 except that the interest rate has dropped to 9%. What price home can the buyer afford now?
6. Using Table 16.2, calculate the balance still owed on a $90,000, 9½%, 30-year amortized loan that is 10 years old.
7. Explain the purpose and operation of the FHA 203(b) home mortgage insurance program.
8. What advantage does the Department of Veteran Affairs offer veterans who wish to purchase a home?
9. Explain points and their application to real estate lending.

"Learning Curve: Many Buyers Find Mortgage Lending Terminology Confusing, Even Frightening; Here's How You Take the Mystery out of Balloon Payments, Points, and PMI," by **Carylon Dopp** (*California Real Estate,* June 1991, pp. 40–41+).

Monthly Interest Amortization Tables (Contemporary Books, 1993, 283 pages). Tables cover interest rates from 5% to 28.75%, amounts from $50 to $160,000, and terms up to 40 years. Remaining balance and proration tables are also provided.

Residential Mortgage Lending, 4th Ed., by **Marshall W. Dennis** and **Michael Robertson** (Prentice Hall, 1995, 352 pages). Takes a practical approach for those presently involved in residential mortgage lending.

ADDITIONAL READINGS

17

The Loan and the
Consumer

KEY • TERMS

APR: the annual percentage rate as calculated under the federal Truth-in-Lending Act by combining the interest rate with other costs of the loan

Credit report: a report reflecting the credit-worthiness of a borrower by showing past credit history

Finance charge: the total amount the credit will cost over the life of the loan

Liquid asset: asset that is in cash or is readily convertible to cash

Redlining: a lender's refusal to make loans in certain neighborhoods

Regulation Z: federal regulations that implement the enforcement of the Truth-in-Lending Act

Truth-in-Lending Act: a federal law that requires certain disclosures when extending or advertising credit

The previous chapter discussed lending practices applied to the types of payment arrangements that can be made in retiring debt. Consumer protection was enabled through the Federal Consumer Credit Protection Act, and additional protections have been created through standardized loan procedures. This chapter will discuss the federal Truth-in-Lending Act and standard loan procedures that consumers need to use in order to make application for a loan.

TRUTH-IN-LENDING ACT

The **Federal Consumer Credit Protection Act,** popularly known as the **Truth-in-Lending Act,** went into effect in 1969. The act, implemented by Federal Reserve Board **Regulation Z,** requires that a borrower be clearly shown, before committing to a loan, how much he is paying for credit in both dollar terms and percentage terms. The borrower is also given the right to rescind (cancel) the transaction in certain instances. The act came into being because it was not uncommon to see loans advertised for rates lower than the borrower actually wound up paying. Once the act took effect, several weaknesses and ambiguities of the act and Regulation Z became apparent. Thus, the **Truth-in-Lending Simplification and Reform Act (TILSRA)** was passed by Congress and became effective October 1, 1982. Concurrently, the Federal Reserve Board issued a **Revised Regulation Z** (RRZ) which details rules and regulations for TILSRA. For purposes of discussion we refer to all of this as the Truth-in-Lending Act, or TIL.

Advertising

Whether you are a real estate agent or a property owner acting on your own behalf, TIL rules affect you when you advertise just about anything (including real estate) and include financing terms in the ad. If an advertisement contains any item from the TIL list of financing terms (called **trigger terms** and explained in the following), the ad must also include other required information. For example, an advertisement that reads: "Bargain! Bargain! Bargain! New 3-bedroom townhouses only $499 per month" may or may not be a bargain depending on other financing information missing from the ad.

Trigger Terms

Five specific disclosures must be included in any ad that contains even one of the following trigger terms: (1) the amount of down payment (for example, only 5% down, 10% down, $4,995 down, 95% financing); (2) the amount of any payment (for example, monthly payments only $499, buy for less than $650 a month, payments only 1% per month); (3) the number of payments (for example, only 36 monthly payments and you own it, all paid up in 10 annual payments); (4) the period of repayment (for example, 30-year financing, owner will carry for 5 years, 10-year second available); and (5) the dollar amount of any finance charge (finance this for only $999) or the statement that there is no charge for credit (pay no interest for 3 years).

If any of the aforementioned trigger terms is used, then the following five disclosures must appear in the ad: (1) the cash price or the amount of the loan; (2) the amount of down payment or a statement that none is required; (3) the number, amount, and frequency of repayments; (4) the annual percentage rate; and (5) the deferred payment price or total payments. Item 5 is not a requirement in the case of the sale of a dwelling or a loan secured by a first lien on the dwelling that is being purchased.

Annual Percentage Rate

The **annual percentage rate (APR)** combines the interest rate with the other costs of the loan into a single figure that shows the true annual cost of borrowing. This is one of the most helpful features of the law as it gives the prospective borrower a standardized yardstick by which to compare financing from different sources.

If the annual percentage rate being offered is subject to increase after the transaction takes place (such as with an adjustable rate mortgage), that fact must be stated, for example, "12% annual percentage rate subject to increase after settlement." If the loan has interest rate changes that follow a predetermined schedule, those terms must be stated, for example, "8% first year, 10% second year, 12% third year, 14% remainder of loan, 13.5% annual percentage rate."

If you wish to say something about financing and avoid triggering full disclosure, you may use general statements. The following would be acceptable: "assumable loan," "financing available," "owner will carry," "terms to fit your budget," "easy monthly payments," or "FHA and VA financing available."

Lending Disclosures

If you are in the business of making loans, the Truth-in-Lending Act requires you to make 18 disclosures to your borrower. Of these, the four that must be most prominently displayed on the papers the borrower signs are: (1) the amount financed, (2) the finance charge, (3) the annual percentage rate, and (4) the total payments.

The **amount financed** is the amount of credit provided to the borrower. The **finance charge** is the total dollar amount the credit will cost the borrower over the life of the loan. This includes such things as interest, borrower-paid discount points, loan fees, loan finder's fees, loan service fees, required life insurance, and mortgage guarantee premiums. On a long-term mortgage loan, the total finance charge can easily exceed the amount of money being borrowed. For example, the total amount of interest on an 11%, 30-year, $60,000 loan is just over $145,000.

The annual percentage rate was described earlier. The total payment is the amount in dollars the borrower will have paid after making all the payments as scheduled. In the aforementioned 11%, 30-year loan it would be the interest of $145,000 plus the principal of $60,000 for a total of $205,000.

The other 14 disclosures that a lender must make are as follows: (1) the identity of the lender; (2) the payment schedule; (3) prepayment penalties and rebates; (4) late payment charges; (5) any insurance required; (6) any filing fees; (7) any collateral required; (8) any required deposits; (9) whether or not the loan can be assumed; (10) the demand feature, if the note has one; (11) the total sales price of the item being purchased if the seller is also the creditor; (12) any adjustable rate features of the loan; (13) an itemization of the amount financed; and (14) a reference to any terms not shown on the disclosure statement but which are shown on the loan contract.

These disclosures must be delivered or mailed to the credit applicant within 3 business days after the creditor receives the applicant's written request for credit. The applicant must have this information before the transaction can take place—for example, before the closing.

Who Must Comply?

Any person or firm that regularly extends consumer credit subject to a finance charge (such as interest) or payable by written agreement in more than four installments must comply with the lending disclosures. This includes banks, savings and loans, credit unions, finance companies, and so on, as well as private individuals who extend credit more than five times a year.

Whoever is named on the note as the creditor must make the lending disclosures even if the note is to be resold. A key difference between the old and the new TIL acts is that the new TIL act does not include mortgage brokers or real estate agents as creditors just because they brokered a deal containing financing. This is because they do not appear as creditors on the note. But if a broker takes back a note for part of the commission on a deal, that is extension of credit and the lending disclosures must be made.

Exempt Transactions

Certain transactions are exempt from the lending disclosure requirement. The first exemption is for credit extended primarily for business, commercial, or agricultural purposes. This exemption includes dwelling units purchased for rental purposes (unless the property contains four or fewer units and the owner occupies one of them, in which case special rules apply).

The second exemption applies to credit over $25,000 secured by personal property unless the property is the principal residence of the borrower. For example, a mobile home that secures a loan over $25,000 qualifies under this exemption if it is used as a vacation home, but is not exempt if it is used as a principal residence.

Failure to Disclose

If the Federal Trade Commission (FTC) determines that an advertiser has broken the law, the FTC can order the advertiser to cease from further violations. Each violation of that order can result in a $10,000 civil penalty each day the violation continues.

Failure to disclose properly when credit is extended can result in a penalty of twice the amount of the finance charge with a minimum of $100 and a maximum of $1,000 plus court costs, attorney fees, and actual damages. In addition, the FTC can add a fine of up to $5,000 and/or 1 year imprisonment. If the required disclosures are not made or the borrower is not given the required 3 days to cancel (see the following), the borrower can cancel the transaction at any time within 3 years following the date of the transaction. In that event the creditor must return all money paid by the borrower, and the borrower returns the property to the creditor.

Right to Cancel

A borrower has a limited **right to rescission** (right to cancel) in a credit transaction. The borrower has 3 business days (counting Saturdays) to back out after signing the loan papers. This aspect of the law was inserted primarily to protect a homeowner from unscrupulous sellers of home improvements and appliances when the credit to purchase is secured by a lien on the home. Vacant lots for sale on credit to buyers who expect to use them for principal residences are also subject to cancellation privileges.

The right to rescind does not apply to credit used for the acquisition or initial construction of one's principal dwelling.

When a mortgage lender reviews a real estate loan application, the primary concern for both applicant and lender is to approve loan requests that show a high probability of being repaid in full and on time, and to disapprove requests that are likely to result in default and eventual foreclosure. How is this decision made? Loan analysis varies. However, the five major federal agencies have recently combined their requirements for credit reports. All loans intended for underwriting by Fannie Mae, Freddie Mac, HUD/FHA, VA, or Farmer's Home Administration must comply with the new standards. Figure 17.1 shows the new Uniform Residential Loan Application (a requirement for standardized loan application) and summarizes the key terms that a loan officer considers when making a decision regarding a loan request. Let's review these items and observe how they affect the acceptance of a loan by a lender.

LOAN APPLICATION AND APPROVAL

Note that in section [1] the borrower is requested to specify the type of mortgage and terms of the loan being sought. This greatly facilitates the lender's ability to determine the availability of the loan that the borrower may be seeking.

In section [2] the lender begins the loan analysis procedure by looking at the property and the proposed financing. Using the property address and legal description, an appraiser is assigned to prepare an appraisal of the property and a title search is ordered. These steps are taken to determine the fair market value of the property and the condition of title. In the event of default, the property is the collateral the lender must fall back on to recover the loan. If the loan request is in connection with a purchase rather than the refinancing of an existing property, the lender will know the purchase price. As a rule, loans are made on the basis of the appraised value or purchase price, whichever is lower. If the appraised value is lower than the purchase price, the usual procedure is to require the buyer to make a larger cash down payment. The lender does not want to overloan simply because the buyer overpaid for the property.

Figure 17.1.

BROKER: INV: MAC:

PRODUCER: PRODUCT CODE:

Uniform Residential Loan Application

This application is designed to be completed by the applicant(s) with the lender's assistance. Applicants should complete this form as "Borrower" or "Co-Borrower", as applicable. Co-Borrower information must also be provided (and the appropriate box checked) when ☐ the income or assets of a person other than the "Borrower" (including the Borrower's spouse) will be used as a basis for loan qualification or ☐ the income or assets of the Borrower's spouse will not be used as a basis for loan qualification, but his or her liabilities must be considered because the Borrower resides in a community property state, the security property is located in a community property state, or the Borrower is relying on other property located in a community property state as a basis for repayment of the loan.

I. TYPE OF MORTGAGE AND TERMS OF LOAN

[1]

Mortgage Applied for:	☐ VA ☐ FHA	☐ Conventional ☐ FmHA	☐ Other	Agency Case Number	Lender Case No.

Amount	Interest Rate	No. of Months	Amortization Type:	☐ Fixed Rate ☐ GPM	☐ Other (explain): ☐ ARM (type):
$	%				

II. PROPERTY INFORMATION AND PURPOSE OF LOAN

[2]

Subject Property Address (street, city, state, & zip code)	No. of Units

Legal Description of Subject Property (attach description if necessary)	Year Built

Purpose of Loan	☐ Purchase ☐ Refinance	☐ Construction ☐ Construction-Permanent	☐ Other (explain):	Property will be: ☐ Primary Residence ☐ Secondary Residence ☐ Investment

Complete this line if construction or construction-permanent loan.

Year Lot Acquired	Original Cost	Amount Existing Liens	(a) Present Value of Lot	(b) Cost of Improvements	Total (a + b)
	$	$	$	$	$

Complete this line if this is a refinance loan.

Year Acquired	Original Cost	Amount Existing Liens	Purpose of Refinance	Describe Improvements ☐ made ☐ to be made
	$	$		Cost: $

Title will be held in what Name(s)	Manner in which Title will be held	Estate will be held in: ☐ Fee Simple ☐ Leasehold (show expiration date)

Source of Down Payment, Settlement Charges and/or Subordinate Financing (explain)

III. BORROWER INFORMATION

Borrower	Co-Borrower

[3] Borrower's Name (include Jr. or Sr. if applicable)   **[4]** Co-Borrower's Name (include Jr. or Sr. if applicable)

Social Security Number	Home Phone (incl. area code)	Age	Yrs. School	Social Security Number	Home Phone (incl. area code)	Age	Yrs. School

☐ Married ☐ Separated ☐ Unmarried (include single, divorced, widowed)	Dependents (not listed by Co-Borrower) no. ages	☐ Married ☐ Separated ☐ Unmarried (include single, divorced, widowed)	Dependents (not listed by Borrower) no. ages

Present Address (street, city, state, zip code) ☐ Own ☐ Rent _____ No. Yrs.	Present Address (street, city, state, zip code) ☐ Own ☐ Rent _____ No. Yrs.

If residing at present address for less than two years, complete the following:

Former Address (street, city, state, zip code) ☐ Own ☐ Rent _____ No. Yrs.	Former Address (street, city, state, zip code) ☐ Own ☐ Rent _____ No. Yrs.

Former Address (street, city, state, zip code) ☐ Own ☐ Rent _____ No. Yrs.	Former Address (street, city, state, zip code) ☐ Own ☐ Rent _____ No. Yrs.

IV. EMPLOYMENT INFORMATION

Borrower	Co-Borrower

Name & Address of Employer ☐ Self Employed	Yrs. on this job	Name & Address of Employer ☐ Self Employed	Yrs. on this job
[5]	Yrs. employed in this line of work/profession	**[6]**	Yrs. employed in this line of work/profession

Position/Title/Type of Business	Business Phone (incl. area code)	Position/Title/Type of Business	Business Phone (incl. area code)

If employed in current position for less than two years or if currently employed in more than one position, complete the following:

Name & Address of Employer ☐ Self Employed	Dates (from - to)	Name & Address of Employer ☐ Self Employed	Dates (from - to)
	Monthly Income $		Monthly Income $

Position/Title/Type of Business	Business Phone (incl. area code)	Position/Title/Type of Business	Business Phone (incl. area code)

Name & Address of Employer ☐ Self Employed	Dates (from - to)	Name & Address of Employer ☐ Self Employed	Dates (from - to)
	Monthly Income $		Monthly Income $

Position/Title/Type of Business	Business Phone (incl. area code)	Position/Title/Type of Business	Business Phone (incl. area code)

Initials _____

Figure 17.1. (continued)

[7]

V. MONTHLY INCOME AND COMBINED HOUSING EXPENSE INFORMATION

Gross Monthly Income	Borrower	Co-Borrower	Total	Combined Monthly Housing Expense	Present	Proposed
Base Empl. Income*	$	$	$	Rent	$	
Overtime				First Mortgage (P&I)		$
Bonuses				Other Financing (P&I)		
Commissions				Hazard Insurance		
Dividends/Interest				Real Estate Taxes		
Net Rental Income				Mortgage Insurance		
OTHER (before completing, see the notice in "describe other income," below)				Homeowners Assn. Dues		
				Other:		
Total	$	$	$	Total	$	$

[8]   **[9]**

*Self Employed Borrower(s) may be required to provide additional documentation such as tax returns and financial statements.

Describe Other Income   Notice: Alimony, child support, or separate maintenance income need not be revealed if the Borrower (B) or Co-Borrower (C) does not choose to have it considered for repaying this loan.

B/C		Monthly Amount
		$

VI. ASSETS AND LIABILITIES

[10]

This Statement and any applicable supporting schedules may be completed jointly by both married and unmarried Co-Borrowers if their assets and liabilities are sufficiently joined so that the Statement can be meaningfully and fairly presented on a combined basis; otherwise separate Statements and Schedules are required. If the Co-Borrower section was completed about a spouse, this Statement and supporting schedules must be completed about that spouse also.

Completed ☐ Jointly ☐ Not Jointly

Description ASSETS	Cash or Market Value	Liabilities and Pledged Assets. List the creditor's name, address and account number for all outstanding debts, including automobile loans, revolving charge accounts, real estate loans, alimony, child support, stock pledges, etc. Use continuation sheet, if necessary. Indicate by (*) those liabilities which will be satisfied upon sale of real estate owned or upon refinancing of the subject property.		
Cash deposit toward purchase held by:	$	**Liabilities**	Monthly Payt. & Mos. Left to Pay	Unpaid Balance
		Name and address of Company	$ Payt./Mos.	$
List checking and savings accounts below				**[11]**
Name and address of Bank, S&L, or Credit Union				
		Acct. no.		
		Name and address of Company	$ Payt./Mos.	$
Acct. no.	$			
Name and address of Bank, S&L, or Credit Union				
		Acct. no.		
		Name and address of Company	$ Payt./Mos.	$
Acct. no.	$			
Name and address of Bank, S&L, or Credit Union				
		Acct. no.		
		Name and address of Company	$ Payt./Mos.	$
Acct. no.	$			
Name and address of Bank, S&L, or Credit Union				
		Acct. no.		
		Name and address of Company	$ Payt./Mos.	$
Acct. no.	$			
Stocks & bonds (Company name/number & description)	$			
		Acct. no.		
		Name and address of Company	$ Payt./Mos.	$
Life insurance net cash value	$			
Face amount: $				
Subtotal Liquid Assets	$			
Real estate owned (enter market value from schedule of real estate owned) **[12]**	$	Acct. no.		
Vested interest in retirement fund	$	Name and address of Company	$ Payt./Mos.	$
Net worth of business(es) owned (attach financial statement)	$			
Automobiles owned (make and year)	$			
		Acct. no.		
		Alimony/Child Support/Separate Maintenance Payments Owed to:	$	
Other Assets (itemize)	$	Job Related Expense (child care, union dues, etc.)	$	
		Total Monthly Payments	$	
Total Assets a.	$	**Net Worth (a minus b)** ► $	**Total Liabilities b.**	$

Figure 17.1. (continued)

VI. ASSETS AND LIABILITIES (cont.)

Schedule of Real Estate Owned (if additional properties are owned, use continuation sheet.)

Property Address (enter S if sold, PS if pending sale or R if rental being held for income) ▼	Type of Property	Present Market Value	Amount of Mortgages & Liens	Gross Rental Income	Mortgage Payments	Insurance, Maintenance, Taxes & Misc.	Net Rental Income
		$	$	$	$	$	$
Totals		$	$	$	$	$	$

List any additional names under which credit has previously been received and indicate appropriate creditor name(s) and account number(s):

[13]

Alternate Name	Creditor Name	Account Number

VII. DETAILS OF TRANSACTION		VIII. DECLARATIONS				
a. Purchase price	$		**Borrower**		**Co-Borrower**	
b. Alterations, improvements, repairs		If you answer "yes" to any questions a through i, please use continuation sheet for explanation.	Yes	No	Yes	No
c. Land (if acquired separately)		a. Are there any outstanding judgments against you?				
d. Refinance (incl. debts to be paid off)		b. Have you been declared bankrupt within the past 7 years?				
e. Estimated prepaid items		c. Have you had property foreclosed upon or given title or deed in lieu thereof in the last 7 years?				
f. Estimated closing costs		d. Are you a party to a lawsuit?				
g. PMI, MIP, Funding Fee		e. Have you directly or indirectly been obligated on any loan which resulted in foreclosure, transfer of title in lieu of foreclosure, or judgment? (This would include such loans as home mortgage loans, SBA loans, home improvement loans, educational loans, manufactured (mobile) home loans, any mortgage, financial obligation, bond, or loan guarantee. If "Yes," provide details, including date, name and address of Lender, FHA or VA case number, if any, and reasons for the action.)				
h. Discount (if Borrower will pay)						
i. Total costs (add items a through h)						
j. Subordinate financing		f. Are you presently delinquent or in default on any Federal debt or any other loan, mortgage, financial obligation, bond, or loan guarantee? If "Yes," give details as described in the preceding question.				
k. Borrower's closing costs paid by Seller						
l. Other Credits (explain)		g. Are you obligated to pay alimony, child support, or separate maintenance?				
		h. Is any part of the down payment borrowed?				
		i. Are you a co-maker or endorser on a note?				
m. Loan amount (exclude PMI, MIP, Funding Fee financed)		j. Are you a U.S. citizen?				
		k. 1.) Are you a permanent resident alien?				
n. PMI, MIP, Funding Fee financed		2.) Are you a permanent non-resident alien?				
o. Loan amount (add m & n)		l. Do you intend to occupy the property as your primary residence? If "Yes," complete question m below.				
p. Cash from/to Borrower (subtract j, k, l & o from i)		m. Have you had an ownership interest in a property in the last three years?				
		(1) What type of property did you own--principal residence (PR), second home (SH), or investment property (IP)?				
		(2) How did you hold title to the home--solely by yourself (S), jointly with your spouse (SP), or jointly with another person (O)?				

IX. ACKNOWLEDGEMENT AND AGREEMENT

The undersigned specifically acknowledge(s) and agree(s) that: (1) the loan requested by this application will be secured by a first mortgage or deed of trust on the property described herein; (2) the property will not be used for any illegal or prohibited purpose or use; (3) all statements made in this application are made for the purpose of obtaining the loan indicated herein; (4) occupation of the property will be as indicated above; (5) verification or reverification of any information contained in the application may be made at any time by the Lender, its agents, successors and assigns, either directly or through a credit reporting agency, from any source named in this application, and the original copy of this application will be retained by the Lender, even if the loan is not approved; (6) the Lender, its agent, successors and assigns will rely on the information contained in the application and I/we have a continuing obligation to amend and/or supplement the information provided in this application if any of the material facts which I/we have represented herein should change prior to closing; (7) in the event my/our payments on the loan indicated in this application become delinquent, the Lender, its agents, successors and assigns, may, in addition to all their other rights and remedies, report my/our name(s) and account information to a credit reporting agency; (8) ownership of the loan may be transferred to successor or assign of the Lender without notice to me and/or the administration of the loan account may be transferred to an agent, successor or assign of the Lender with prior notice to me; (9) the Lender, its agents, successors and assigns make no representations or warranties, express or implied, to the Borrower(s) regarding the property, the condition of the property, or the value of the property. **Certification:** I/We certify that the information provided in this application is true and correct as of the date set forth opposite my/our signature(s) on this application and acknowledge my/our understanding that any intentional or negligent misrepresentation(s) of the information contained in this application may result in civil liability and/or criminal penalties including, but not limited to, fine or imprisonment or both under the provisions of Title 18, United States Code, Section 1001, et seq. and liability for monetary damages to the Lender, its agents, successors and assigns, insurers and any other person who may suffer any loss due to reliance upon any misrepresentation which I/we have made on this application.

Borrower's Signature	Date	Co-Borrower's Signature	Date
X		X	

X. INFORMATION FOR GOVERNMENT MONITORING PURPOSES

The following information is requested by the Federal Government for certain types of loans related to a dwelling, in order to monitor the Lender's compliance with equal credit opportunity, fair housing and home mortgage disclosure laws. You are not required to furnish this information, but are encouraged to do so. The law provides that a Lender may neither discriminate on the basis of this information, nor on whether you choose to furnish it. However, if you choose not to furnish it, under Federal regulations this Lender is required to note race and sex on the basis of visual observation or surname. If you do not wish to furnish the above information, please check the box below. (Lender must review the above material to assure that the disclosures satisfy all requirements to which the Lender is subject under applicable state law for the particular type of loan applied for.)

BORROWER   I do not wish to furnish this information

Race/National Origin:
☐ American Indian or Alaskan Native ☐ Asian or Pacific Islander ☐ Black, not of Hispanic origin ☐ Hispanic ☐ White, not of Hispanic origin ☐ Other (specify)

Sex: ☐ Female ☐ Male

Co-Borrower   I do not wish to furnish this information

Race/National Origin:
☐ American Indian or Alaskan Native ☐ Asian or Pacific Islander ☐ Black, not of Hispanic origin ☐ Hispanic ☐ White, not of Hispanic origin ☐ Other (specify)

Sex: ☐ Female ☐ Male

To be Completed by Interviewer	Interviewer's Name (print or type)	Name and Address of Interviewer's Employer
This application was taken by:		
☐ face-to-face interview	Interviewer's Signature	Date
☐ by mail		
☐ by telephone	Interviewer's Phone Number (incl. area code)	

Figure 17.1. (continued)

Continuation Sheet/Residential Loan Application

Use this continuation sheet if you need more space to complete the Residential Loan Application. Mark **B** for Borrower or **C** for Co-Borrower.	Borrower:	Agency Case Number:
	Co-Borrower:	Lender Case Number:

I/We fully understand that it is a Federal crime punishable by fine or imprisonment, or both, to knowingly make any false statements concerning any of the above facts as applicable under the provisions of Title 18, United States Code, Section 1001, et seq.

Borrower's Signature:	Date	Co-Borrower's Signature:	Date
X		X	

Date received _____ by _____   Initials _____

Settlement Funds   Next, in section [2], the lender wants to know whether the borrower has adequate funds for settlement. Are these funds presently in a checking or savings account, or are they coming from the sale of the borrower's present property? In the latter case, the lender knows that the present loan is contingent on closing that escrow. If the down payment and settlement funds are to be borrowed, then the lender needs to be extra cautious as experience has shown that the less money a borrower personally puts into a purchase, the higher is the probability of default and foreclosure.

Purpose of Loan   The lender is also interested in the proposed use of the property. Lenders feel most comfortable when a loan is for the purchase or improvement of a property the loan applicant will actually occupy. This is because owner-occupants usually have pride of ownership in maintaining their property and even during bad economic conditions will continue to make the monthly payments. An owner-occupant also realizes that losing the home still means paying for shelter elsewhere. It is standard practice for lenders to ask loan applicants to sign a statement declaring whether they intend to occupy the property.

   If the loan applicant intends to purchase a dwelling to rent out as an investment, the lender will be more cautious because, during periods of high vacancy, the property may not generate enough income to meet the loan payments. At that point, a strapped-for-cash borrower is likely to default. Note too that lenders generally avoid loans secured by purely speculative real estate. If the value of the property drops below the amount owed, the borrower may see no further logic in making the loan payments.

   Finally, the lender assesses the borrower's attitude toward the proposed loan. A casual attitude, such as "I'm buying because real estate always goes up," or an applicant who does not appear to understand the obligation being undertaken would bring a low rating here. Much more welcome is the applicant who shows a mature attitude and understanding of the loan obligation and who exhibits a strong and logical desire for ownership.

Borrower Analysis   In sections [3] and [4] the lender begins an analysis of the borrower, and, if there is one, the co-borrower. At one time age, sex, and marital status played an important role in the lender's decision to lend or not to lend. Often the young and the old had trouble getting loans, as did women and persons who were single, divorced, or widowed. Today, the federal Equal Credit Opportunity Act prohibits discrimination based on age, sex, race, and marital status. Lenders are no longer permitted to discount income earned by women because a job is part-time or the woman is of childbearing age. If the applicant chooses to disclose it, alimony, separate maintenance, and child support must be counted in full. Young adults and single persons cannot be turned down because the lender feels they have not "put down roots." Seniors cannot be turned down as long as life expectancy exceeds the early risk period of the loan and collateral is adequate. In other words, the emphasis in borrower analysis is now focused on job stability, income adequacy, net worth, and credit rating.

Thus in sections [5] and [6] we see questions directed at how long the applicants have held their present jobs and the stability of the jobs themselves. An applicant who possesses marketable job skills and has been regularly employed with a stable employer is considered the ideal risk. Persons whose income can rise and fall erratically, such as commissioned salespersons, present greater risks. Persons whose skills (or lack of skills) or lack of job seniority result in frequent unemployment are more likely to have difficulty repaying a loan. In these sections the lender also inquires as to the number of dependents the applicant must support from his or her income. This information provides some insight as to how much will be left for monthly house payments.

In section [7] the lender looks at the amount and sources of the applicants' income. Quantity alone is not enough for loan approval since the income sources must be stable too. Thus a lender will look carefully at overtime, bonus, and commission income in order to estimate the levels at which these may be expected to continue. Interest, dividend, and rental income is considered in light of the stability of their sources also. Income from social security and retirement pensions is entered and added to the totals for the applicants. Alimony, child support, and separate maintenance payments received need not be revealed. However, such sums must be listed in order to be considered as a basis for repaying the loan.

Monthly Income

In section **[8]** the lender compares what the applicants have been paying for housing with what they will be paying if the loan is approved. Included in the proposed housing expense total are principal, interest, taxes, and insurance along with any assessments or homeowner association dues (such as in a condominium). Some lenders add the monthly cost of utilities to this list.

At **[9]** proposed monthly housing expense is compared with gross monthly income. A general rule of thumb is that monthly housing expense (PITI) should not exceed 25% to 30% of gross monthly income. A second guideline is that total fixed monthly expenses should not exceed 33% to 38% of income. This includes housing payments plus automobile payments, installment loan payments, alimony, child support, and investments with negative cash flows. These are general guidelines, but lenders recognize that food, health care, clothing, transportation, entertainment, and income taxes must also come from the applicants' income.

Assets and Liabilities

In section **[10]** the lender is interested in the applicants' sources of funds for closing and whether, once the loan is granted, the applicants have assets to fall back on in the event of an income decrease (a job layoff) or unexpected expenses (hospital bills). Of particular interest is the portion of those assets that are in cash or are readily convertible into cash in a few days. These are called **liquid assets.** If income drops, they are much more useful in meeting living expenses and loan payments than assets that may require months to sell and convert to cash—that is, assets that are **illiquid.**

Note in section **[10]** that two values are shown for life insurance. **Cash value** is the amount of money the policyholder would receive if the policy were surrendered to the insurance company or, alternatively, the amount the policyholder could borrow against the policy. **Face amount** is the amount that would be paid in the event of the insured's death. Lenders feel most comfortable if the face amount of the policy equals or exceeds the amount of the proposed loan. Obviously a borrower's death is not anticipated before the loan is repaid, but lenders recognize that its possibility increases the probability of default. The likelihood of foreclosure is lessened considerably if the survivors receive life insurance benefits.

In section [11] the lender is interested in the applicants' existing debts and liabilities for two reasons. First, each month these items compete against housing expenses for available monthly income. Thus high monthly payments in this section may lower the lender's estimate of what the applicants will be able to repay and, consequently, may influence the lender to reduce the size of the loan. The presence of monthly liabilities is not all negative: It can also show the lender that the applicants are capable of repaying their debts. Second, the applicants' total debts are subtracted from their total assets to obtain their **net worth,** reported at [12]. If the result is negative (more owed than owned) the loan request will probably be turned down as too risky. In contrast, a substantial net worth can often offset weaknesses elsewhere in the application, such as too little monthly income in relation to monthly housing expense or an income that can rise and fall erratically.

References

At number [13] lenders ask for credit references as an indicator of the future. Applicants with no previous credit experience will have more weight placed on income and employment history. Applicants with a history of collections, adverse judgments, foreclosure, or bankruptcy will have to convince the lender that this loan will be repaid on time. Additionally, the applicants may be considered poorer risks if they have guaranteed the repayment of someone else's debt by acting as a co-maker or endorser.

Redlining

In the past, it was not uncommon for lenders to refuse to make loans in certain neighborhoods regardless of the quality of the structure or the ability of the borrower to repay. This practice was known as **redlining,** and it effectively shut off mortgage loans in many older or so-called "bad risk" neighborhoods across the country. Today a lender cannot refuse to make a loan simply because of the age or location of a property; the neighborhood income level; or the racial, ethnic, or religious composition of the neighborhood.

A lender can refuse to lend on a structure intended for demolition; a property in a known geological hazard area; a single-family dwelling in an area devoted to industrial or commercial use; or a property that is in violation of zoning laws, deed covenants, conditions or restrictions, or significant health, safety, or building codes.

Loan-to-Value Ratios   The lender next looks at the amount of down payment the borrower proposes to make, the size of the loan being requested, and the amount of other financing the borrower plans to use. This information is then converted into loan-to-value ratios. As a rule, the larger the down payment is, the safer the loan is for the lender. On an uninsured loan, the ideal loan-to-value (L/V) ratio for a lender on owner-occupied residential property is 70% or less. This means the value of the property would have to fall more than 30% before the debt owed would exceed the property's value, thus encouraging the borrower to stop making loan payments.

Loan-to-value ratios from 70% through 80% are considered acceptable but do expose the lender to more risk. Lenders sometimes compensate by charging slightly higher interest rates. Loan-to-value ratios above 80% present even more risk of default to the lender, and the lender will either increase the interest rate charged on these loans or require insurance coverage from an outside insurer, such as the FHA or a private mortgage insurer.

Credit Report   As part of the loan application, the lender will order a **credit report** on the applicant(s). The applicant is asked to authorize this and to pay for the report. This provides the lender with an independent means of checking the applicant's credit history. A credit report that shows active use of credit with a good repayment record and no derogatory information is most desirable. The applicant will be asked by the lender to explain any negative information. Because it is possible for inaccurate or untrue information in a credit report to unfairly damage a person's credit reputation, Congress passed the **Fair Credit Reporting Act.** This act gives an individual the right to inspect his or her file at a credit bureau, correct any errors, and make explanatory statements to supplement the file.

As previously discussed, the five major federal agencies have recently combined their requirements for credit reports, and loans intended for underwriting by federal government agencies must comply with the new credit standards. Under these newly adopted rules, the name of the consumer reporting agency must be clearly identified, as well as who ordered the report and who is paying for it. The information must be obtained from at least two national repositories for each area in which the borrower resided in the past 2 years, and must be verified for the previous 2 years. An explanation must be provided if the information is unavailable, and all questions must be responded to, even if the answer must be "unable to verify." A history must be furnished and all missing information must be verified by the lender. The history must have been checked within 90 days of the credit report and the age of information that is not considered obsolete by the Fair Credit Reporting Act (7 years general credit date or 10 years for bankruptcy) must be indicated. If any credit information is incomplete or if undisclosed information is discovered, the lender must have a personal interview with the borrower. The lender is additionally required to warrant that the credit report complies with all of the new standards.

Match terms **a–f** *with statements* **1–6**.

VOCABULARY REVIEW

a. *Equity*
b. *Illiquid assets*
c. *Liquid assets*
d. *Redlining*
e. *Truth-in-Lending Act*
f. *Trigger term*

1. The market value of a property less the debt against it.
2. A federal law that requires certain disclosures when extending or advertising credit.
3. Assets that may require months to sell and convert to cash.
4. Credit information used in advertising that requires additional credit disclosures.
5. Refusal to make a real estate loan based solely on the location of the property.
6. Assets that are in cash or are readily convertible to cash in a few days.

QUESTIONS AND PROBLEMS

1. Why is the monthly income of a loan applicant more important to a lender than the sheer size of the applicant's assets?
2. What is the basic purpose of the Truth-in-Lending Act?
3. Will the annual percentage rate (APR) and interest rate reflected in the note be the same?
4. How does the Fair Credit Reporting Act help a borrower?
5. Why is a right of rescission important?

ADDITIONAL READINGS

"Truth in Lending Developments in 1990: The Changes Abate," by **Stanley Mabbitt, Robert Cook,** and **Timothy Meredith** (*Business Lawyer*, May 1991, pp. 1193–1221). Article discusses topics concerning consumer loans.

18

Sources of Financing

KEY • TERMS

Alienation clause: requires immediate repayment of the loan if ownership transfers; also called a due-on-sale clause

Automated underwriting systems: computerized systems for loan approval communication between a loan originator and the investor

Computerized loan origination: originating loans through the use of a networked computer system

Disintermediation: the result created when lenders are required to pay high rates of interest for deposits while receiving long-term income from low-interest-rate mortgage loans

Fannie Mae: a real estate industry nickname for the Federal National Mortgage Association

Freddie Mac: a real estate industry nickname for the Federal Home Loan Mortgage Corporation

Mortgage broker: one who brings together borrowers and lenders

Mortgage company: a firm that makes mortgage loans and then sells them to investors

Participation certificates: a certificate representing an undivided interest in a Freddie Mac pool

Primary market: the market in which lenders originate loans and make funds available to borrowers

Secondary mortgage market: a market in which mortgage loans can be sold to investors

Usury: charging an interest rate that is in excess of the legal rate

After reading this chapter, you will be able to (1) identify various mortgage lenders (the primary market), (2) describe where these lenders get much of their money (the secondary market), and (3) explain provisions of mortgage loan instruments that have an impact on the cost of funds. Many people feel that understanding the financing market is the most important of all real estate topics because, without financing, real estate profits and commissions would be difficult to achieve.

The **primary market** (also called the **primary mortgage market**) is where lenders originate loans—that is, where lenders make funds available to borrowers. The primary market is what the borrower sees as the source of mortgage loan money, the institution with which the borrower has direct and personal contact. It's the place where the loan application is taken, where the loan officer interviews the loan applicant, where the loan check comes from, and the place to which loan payments are sent by the borrower.

PRIMARY MARKET

These sources of funds can generally be divided into two markets: (1) those markets regulated by the federal government and (2) those markets that are not regulated by the government. The regulated lenders are commercial banks, savings and loan associations, and savings banks. The nonregulated lenders are commercial finance companies, investment bankers, life insurance companies, and finance companies. Nonregulated sources of funds are relatively new to the mortgage market and are not subject to the same restrictive regulations that are designed to protect the lender with deposits insured by the federal government. In today's markets, a purchaser is wise to contact both regulated and nonregulated lenders to make an adequate comparison of available loan money. Markets differ widely within states and even within certain urban areas. The regulated lenders are subject to examinations by federal regulators, pay risk-based premiums on their deposit insurance, and are restricted to certain loan-to-value ratios (discussed later).

Most borrowers assume that the loan they receive comes from depositors who visit the same bank or S&L to leave their excess funds. This is partly true. But this, by itself, is an inadequate source of loan funds in today's market. Thus, primary lenders often sell their loans in what is called the secondary market. Insurance companies, pension funds, and individual investors, as well as other primary lenders with excess deposits, buy these loans for cash. This makes more money available to a primary lender who, in turn, can loan these additional funds to borrowers. The secondary market is so huge that it rivals the entire U.S. corporate bond market in size of annual offerings. We return to the secondary market later in this chapter. Meanwhile, let's discuss the various lenders a borrower will encounter when looking for a real estate loan.

SAVINGS AND LOAN ASSOCIATIONS

Historically, the origin of **savings and loan associations** can be traced to early building societies in England and Germany and to the first American building society, the Oxford Provident Building Association, started in 1831 in Pennsylvania. These early building societies were cooperatives whose savers were also borrowers. As times progressed, savings and loan associations became a primary source of residential real estate loans. To encourage residential lending, the federally chartered savings and loans were required by federal regulation to hold at least 80% of their assets in residential loans. In addition, they were subjected to special tax laws that permitted a savings and loan association to defer payment of income taxes on profits, so long as those profits were held in surplus accounts and not distributed to the savings and loan association's owners. To qualify for the deferment, commercial loans were limited to no more than 18% of their assets. The remainder of the loans (82% or more) had to be in residential loans, which included apartment projects. During this same period, there were also limits on the interest rate that could be paid on savings accounts. This provided the savings and loan associations with a dependable source of funds at a fixed interest rate, which gave them the potential for making long-term loans at reasonable rates. For instance, if the passbook savings account was limited to $5\frac{1}{4}\%$ per annum, home loans in the vicinity of $7\frac{1}{2}\%$ to $8\frac{1}{2}\%$ would still allow for reasonable profit margins. Unfortunately, the nature of the finance markets began to change in the late 1970s when an inflationary economy caused interest rates to skyrocket. This created problems that were unforeseen by the savings and loan industry.

Disintermediation

In order to attract depositors, savings and loans offer, in addition to passbook accounts, **certificates of deposit (CDs)** at rates higher than passbook rates. These are necessary to compete with higher yields offered by U.S. Treasury bills, notes, and bonds and to prevent disintermediation. **Disintermediation** results when depositors take money out of their savings accounts and invest directly in government securities, corporate bonds, and money market funds. A major problem, and one that nearly brought the S&L industry to its knees in the late 1970s and early 1980s, was that S&Ls traditionally relied heavily on short-term deposits from savers and then loaned that money on long-term (often 30-year) loans to borrowers. When interest rates rose sharply in the 1970s, S&Ls either had to raise the interest paid to their depositors or watch depositors withdraw their savings and take the money elsewhere for higher returns. Meanwhile, the S&Ls were holding long-term, fixed-rate mortgage loans, and, with interest rates rising, borrowers were not anxious to repay those loans early.

Disintermediation was only the beginning of the problems. Loan demand at S&Ls was declining. In 1976, 57% of the residential mortgage loans were held by savings and loan institutions. By 1994, the percentage fell to 14%. There are many reasons for this flow of funds out of the savings and loan industry. One of the primary reasons, however, appears to be the deregulation of the lending industry. In March 1980, President Carter signed the Depository Institution's Deregulation and Monetary Control Act. It eliminated most of the S&Ls incentives to make residential mortgage loans and made other lending sources (such as banks) more competitive in those markets. While it raised the limits on insured deposits (up to $100,000 per depositor), it also loosened the restrictions on investments and loans that savings institutions could make. Many of the S&Ls began making higher-risk loans on undeveloped land, real estate development loans, and joint venture loans (often to themselves as developers!). Generally, the new law allowed S&Ls to use depositors' money to enter into higher-risk business ventures rather than stay with the low-risk residential loans that had been encouraged in the past. In addition, the proliferation of savings and loans during the 1980s resulted in many being managed by poorly trained administrators and officers. As in many other cases when a business enters a new, uncharted territory, many savings and loans were not prepared for the down cycles of real estate investment.

The Crisis of the 1980s

When the federal regulators enforced their reporting requirements, it created still another problem. If the savings and loan had invested and developed large quantities of real estate, it subjected itself to down cycles, as previously discussed. When reporting financial status to the federal government, however, the result was that a substantial asset base in real property (for instance, raw land cost of $8 million at acquisition) could be required to be "written down" to a smaller fair market value (for instance, $4 million), because the federal regulatory agencies require a realistic asset reporting value to reflect accurately the solvency of the savings and loan institution. When an institution's asset basis is depleted by 50%, it results in—an insolvent institution! Insolvent institutions are required by the federal government to be closed to protect depositors and maintain confidence in the system.

Restructuring the System

One comforting aspect of governmental regulation of lending institutions is that it provides a solvent recovery fund for the depositors in the event that a lending institution fails. For the savings and loan industry, it has traditionally been the Federal Savings and Loan Insurance Corporation. During the late 1970s and all of the 1980s, disintermediation, coupled with bad lending practices and the complications of deregulation, resulted in a substantial number of savings and loan institutions being declared insolvent. The FSLIC simply did not have enough funds to insure the deposits adequately. In short, the FSLIC was insolvent, and more urgent steps needed to be taken to resolve the issue.

In August 1989, President Bush signed into law a sweeping revision of the regulatory authorities governing savings and loans. This law is referred to as the **Financial Institutions Reform, Recovery, and Enforcement Act of 1989,** commonly called **FIRREA**. The law redefined or created seven new regulatory authorities and initiated a system of federally designated real property appraisers, discussed in greater detail in Chapter 21. Over the next several years, as many as two-thirds of the existing savings and loan associations may be closed or merged as a result of the new FIRREA legislation.

There is little doubt that in a few years, the savings and loan business as we knew it will cease to exist.

COMMERCIAL BANKS

The nation's 15,000 **commercial banks** store far more of the country's money than the S&Ls. However, only one bank dollar in six goes to real estate lending. Of the loans made by banks for real estate, the tendency is to emphasize short-term maturities and adjustable rate mortgages, since the bulk of a bank's deposit money comes from demand deposits (checking accounts) and a much smaller portion from savings and time deposits.

Oddly enough, the same factors that have plagued the S&Ls seem to have helped the commercial banks. During the Deregulation Acts of 1980 and 1982, banks began making more home loans, but they were short-term, with adjustable rates. These types of loans prevent the problem of disintermediation, as the loan rates can rise with the rates that are required by the source of funds. Commercial banks, too, have realized that first-lien residential loans are also very secure, low-risk loans. They have also determined maintaining all of a customer's loan accounts, including a home loan, in the bank's portfolio provides a market advantage. "One-stop banking" has become a very successful marketing tool. The merger of many banks into large multistate national banks has also created a larger source of funds to lend. To accommodate this higher demand and facilitate the organization of sources of funds for the bank's lending purposes, many banks have now organized their own mortgage departments to assist customers in making home loans, even through sources other than bank deposits.

MUTUAL SAVINGS BANKS

Important contributors to real estate credit in several states are the nation's 400 **mutual savings banks.** Started in Philadelphia in 1816 and in Boston in 1817, mutual savings banks are found primarily in the northeastern United States, where they compete aggressively for the savings dollar. The states of Massachusetts, New York, and Connecticut account for 75% of the nation's total. As the word *mutual* implies, the depositors are the owners, and the "interest" they receive is the result of the bank's success or failure in lending. Mutual savings banks offer accounts similar to those offered by S&Ls. To protect depositors, laws require mutual savings banks to place deposits in high-quality investments, including sound real estate mortgage loans.

LIFE INSURANCE COMPANIES

As a group, the nation's 2,200 **life insurance companies** have long been active investors in real estate as developers, owners, and long-term lenders. Although not federally regulated, life insurance companies are subject to state regulations. Their source of money is the premiums paid by policyholders. These premiums are invested and ultimately returned to the policy-holders. Because premiums are collected in regular amounts on regular dates and because policy payoffs can be calculated from actuarial tables, life insurers are in ideal positions to commit money to long-term investments. Life insurance companies channel their funds primarily into government and corporate bonds and real estate. The dollars allocated to real estate go to buy land and buildings, which are leased to users, and to make loans on commercial, industrial, and residential property. Generally, life insurers specialize in large-scale investments such as shopping centers, office and apartment buildings, and million-dollar blocks of home loans purchased in the **secondary mortgage market.**

Repayment terms on loans made by insurance companies for shopping centers, office buildings, and apartment complexes sometimes call for interest and a percentage of any profits from rentals over a certain level. These **participation loans,** which provide a "piece of the action" for the insurance company, also provide the insurance company with more inflation protection than a fixed rate of interest.

MORTGAGE COMPANIES

A **mortgage company** makes a mortgage loan and then sells it to a long-term investor. The process begins with locating borrowers, qualifying them, preparing the necessary loan papers, and, finally, making the loans. Once a loan is made, it is sold for cash on the secondary market. The mortgage company will usually continue to *service the loan*—that is, collect the monthly payments and handle such matters as insurance and property tax impounds, delinquencies, early payoffs, and mortgage releases.

Mortgage companies, also known as **mortgage bankers,** vary in size from one or two persons to several dozen. As a rule, they close loans in their own names and are locally oriented, finding and making loans within 25 or 50 miles of their offices. This gives them a feel for their market, greatly aids in identifying sound loans, and makes loan servicing much easier. For their efforts, mortgage bankers typically receive 1% to 3% of the amount of the loan when it is originated, and from $\frac{1}{4}$ to $\frac{1}{2}$ of

1% of the outstanding balance each year thereafter for servicing. Mortgage banking, as this business is called, is not limited to mortgage companies. Commercial banks, savings and loan associations, and mutual savings banks in active real estate areas often originate more real estate loans than they can hold themselves, and these are sold on the secondary market. Mortgage companies often do a large amount of their business in FHA and VA loans. As the shift in mortgage origination continues, it is important to note that the mortgage brokers' share (discussed next) of single-family conventional loans grew from 22% in 1980 to 58% in 1994. In New York, both mortgage bankers and mortgage brokers are licensed and regulated by the State Banking Department.

Mortgage brokers, in contrast to mortgage bankers, specialize in bringing together borrowers and lenders, just as real estate brokers bring together buyers and sellers. The mortgage broker does not lend money and usually does not service loans. The mortgage broker's fee is expressed in points and is usually paid by the borrower. Mortgage brokers are locally oriented, often small firms of from 1 to 10 persons. They seldom make loans in their own names as lender.

MORTGAGE BROKERS

The mortgage brokering businesses actually felt an explosion during the late 1980s and early 1990s. The secondary market (discussed later in this chapter) has made investors' funds more readily available, and virtually anyone with some expertise in loan qualifications can originate loans and sell to secondary market purchasers. As a result, the field has become crowded with new loan originators such as home builders, finance companies, commercial credit companies, insurance agents, attorneys, and real estate brokers. These have generally been considered nontraditional lenders, but they can originate mortgage loans with their own resources or, through various networks, have the loan funded directly through to the secondary market purchaser. These new loan originators have offered substantial competition to regulated lenders.

Whether or not a real estate broker may operate as a mortgage broker and collect a fee for placing a loan has been a "gray" area of the law. The concern expressed by some is that the fee retained by the broker (which is in addition to the real estate broker's fee) may be an undisclosed kickback, which violates the

Real Estate Settlement Procedures Act (see Chapter 13). Agency law also comes into play because a real estate broker may be representing the buyer on a loan while also representing the seller in the sale of the home. This may result in a duty for the listing broker to disclose everything the agent knows (including borrower financial information) to the principal (seller). Lenders also have some concern that the real estate agent may "fudge" mortgage qualification criteria to facilitate a lucrative sale. New changes in RESPA have now allowed the involvement of a broker in the mortgage process, provided proper disclosures are made to the borrower.

Computerized Loan Origination

The growth of computer networks has also enabled many independent loan processors to work under the guidance of large lending institutions and mortgage companies. Using a **Computerized Loan Origination (CLO),** real estate brokers, attorneys, insurance agents, or mortgage companies can arrange to have a computer link installed in their offices, connected to lenders' mainframe computers. By utilizing a series of questions, borrowers can obtain preliminary loan approval immediately from the loan originator with a firm acceptance or rejection from the lending institution within a few days, and the broker can even collect an additional fee (provided it is disclosed).

The CLO can put the real estate broker in a central role. It lets the agent serve as an information center and facilitator for a network of mortgage lenders, using the speed and convenience of the computer to transport information.

A full-featured CLO has three basic functions: (1) It provides information on current mortgage loan terms and loan types available on the market; (2) it conveys loan application information electronically; and (3) it monitors the loan approval process so that the agent can check on the progress of the loan application at any time. From the home buyer's perspective, the CLO provides the convenience of seeking home financing alternatives without calling and visiting a large number of local lenders, and in many cases it can increase the number of choices available. A broker should exercise caution, however, as conflicts, discussed previously, can exist.

SONYMA

The **State of New York Mortgage Agency (SONYMA)** helps to provide a valuable source of mortgage money for New York

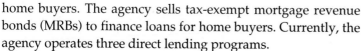

home buyers. The agency sells tax-exempt mortgage revenue bonds (MRBs) to finance loans for home buyers. Currently, the agency operates three direct lending programs.

The **Low Interest Rate Mortgage Program** provides below-market interest and low-down-payment loans to first-time home buyers with moderate incomes for one-to-four family homes or for coops, condominiums, and mobile homes. SONYMA loans are also available to buyers with somewhat higher incomes who purchase homes in SONYMA target areas. The income limits vary among regions of the state and according to family size.

The advantage of the **Conventional Rate Mortgage Program** is that it offers 100% financing (no down payment) on single-family homes and 98% financing on other properties for first-time home buyers, although there is a 2.5% origination fee. This program is available only to first-time home buyers with incomes ranging from a low of just under $60,000 for one-person households in many areas of the state to as high as $101,000 for a three-person household in some downstate areas.

First-time home buyers who are residents of rural areas in some New York counties have access to another **Mortgage Assistance Program** requiring only a 3% down payment with 5% interest. This program is limited to single-family homes.

For information on program availability, income and purchase price limits, and participating lenders, a prospective home buyer can call SONYMA.

ADDITIONAL NEW YORK PROGRAMS

New York provides a wide variety of other programs aimed at increasing the availability of affordable housing. While SONYMA is the principal source of direct loans to home buyers, the state's Housing Finance Agency provides below-market-rate loans to for-profit and nonprofit developers to build moderately priced housing. New York has more than 50 special programs targeted to people's special housing needs. Some programs are aimed at increasing homeownership while others focus on affordable rental housing; some target rehabilitation of existing housing while others encourage new construction; some are aimed at rural areas while others are directed at cities; some focus on the special needs of the elderly or the disabled. SONYMA and the State Division of Housing and Community Renewal are the best places to begin to look for information.

Lending institutions can also provide one-stop shopping for information about state as well as federal housing programs.

OTHER LENDERS

Pension funds and **trust funds** traditionally have channeled their money to high-grade government and corporate bonds and stocks. However, the trend now is to place more money into real estate loans. Already active buyers on the secondary market, pension and trust funds will likely become a still larger source of real estate financing in the future. In some localities, pension fund members can tap their own pension funds for home mortgages at very reasonable rates. The New York State Employee Pension Fund may invest in bonds backed by mortgage loans made on one-to-four family residences. Pension funds are an often overlooked source of primary market financing.

Finance companies that specialize in making business and consumer loans also provide limited financing for real estate. As a rule, finance companies seek second mortgages at interest rates 2% to 5% higher than the rates prevailing on first mortgages. First mortgages are also taken as collateral; however, the lenders already discussed usually charge lower interest rates for these loans and thus are more competitive.

Credit unions normally specialize in consumer loans. However, real estate loans are becoming more and more important as many of the country's 16,000 credit unions have branched out into first and second mortgage loans. Credit unions are an often overlooked but excellent source of home loan money.

Commercial finance companies also have entered the mortgage lending fields. These are private companies, such as General Electric Capital Mortgage Corporation, General Motors Acceptance Corporation, and Ford Motor Company, which are subject to neither banking restrictions nor deposit insurance regulations. They are becoming a more widely used source of finance money, particularly in affordable housing loans, discussed in the next chapter.

Individuals are sometimes a source of cash loans for real estate, with the bulk of these loans made between relatives or friends, often as investments with their IRAs or private pension plans that require a low-risk investment with attractive rates. Generally, loan maturities are shorter than those obtainable from the institutional lenders already described. In some cities, persons can be found who specialize in making or buying second and third mortgage loans of up to 10-year maturities. Individuals are beginning to invest substantial amounts of money in secondary mortgage market securities. Ironically, these investments are often made with money that would have otherwise been deposited in a savings and loan.

The **secondary market** (also called the **secondary mortgage market**) provides a way for a lender to sell a loan. It also permits investment in real estate loans without the need for loan origination and servicing facilities. Although not directly encountered by real estate buyers, sellers, and agents, the secondary market plays an important role in getting money from those who want to lend to those who want to borrow. In other words, think of the secondary market as a pipeline for loan money. Visualize that pipeline running via the Wall Street financial district in New York City, as Wall Street is now a major participant in residential mortgage lending. Figure 18.1 illustrates this pipeline and diagrams key differences between the traditional mortgage delivery system and the secondary market system.

SECONDARY MARKET

Notice in Figure 18.1 that, in the traditional system, the lender is a local institution gathering deposits from the community and then lending that money as real estate loans in the same community. Traditionally, each lender (S&L, mutual savings bank, commercial bank, credit union) was an independent unit that

Traditional Delivery System

Figure 18.1. Mortgage loan delivery systems.

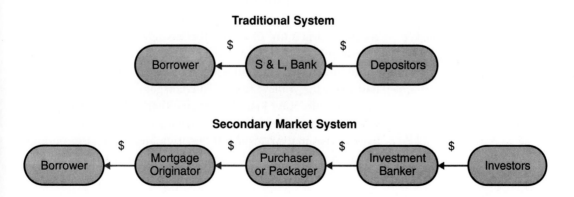

developed its own appraisal technique, loan application form, loan approval criteria, note and mortgage forms, servicing method, and foreclosure policy. Nonetheless, three major problems needed solving. The first occurred when an institution had an imbalance of depositors and borrowers. Rapidly growing areas of the United States often needed more loan money than their savers were capable of depositing. Stable regions had more depositors than loan opportunities. Thus it was common to see correspondent relationships between lenders, for example, a lender in Los Angeles would sell some of its mortgage loans to a savings bank in Brooklyn. This provided loans for borrowers and interest for savers. The system worked well, but required individual correspondent relationships.

The second problem occurs when depositors want to withdraw their money from their accounts and invest it in other sources. Lenders have to attract these depositors, raising their interest rates, which results in loan rates increasing. The third problem is timing. Lenders must borrow "short" (from their deposit relationships) and lend "long" (30-year mortgages). Savers, then, are encouraged to leave their money on deposit for longer periods of time.

The answer to these three problems is relatively simple: Find a market to sell your loans to investors who will pay cash for them and reimburse you, the primary lender. The result, then, is that there is an investor who is willing to hold the loan long-term for its guaranteed rate of return. The primary lender continues to make loans, gambling that he will find another investor in the secondary market to buy that loan for a long term. In effect, the primary lenders can make loans from the secondary market instead of from their deposits.

Secondary Market Delivery Systems

As shown in Figure 18.1, with the secondary market system the borrower obtains a loan from a mortgage originator. This includes mortgage companies, banks, CLOs, and thrifts that originate loans they intend to sell. The mortgage originator packages the loan with other loans and then either sells the package as a whole or keeps the package and sells securities that are backed by the loans in the package. If the originator is not large enough to package its own mortgages, it will sell the loans to someone who can.

There are now two sources for this secondary market. The first is private investors such as commercial banks, savings and loans, pension plans, trust funds, and other investors who are looking for low-risk, long-term returns on their investments. The second group of investors, relatively new in the investment business, is the investment "pools" or "poolers" who are looking for more security in their investments. This results in two primary investors in the secondary market: (1) the pure portfolio purchasers who are looking for the initial investments with an attractive return, and (2) the "poolers" who are looking for the longer term, more stable return.

A major stumbling block to a highly organized and efficient secondary market has been the uniqueness of both lenders and loans. Traditionally, each primary lender developed its own special loan forms and procedures. Moreover, each loan is a unique combination of real estate and borrower. No two are exactly alike. How do you package such diversity into an attractive package for investors? A large part of the answer has come through standardized loan application forms; standardized appraisal forms; standardized credit report forms; standardized closing statements; standardized loan approval criteria; and standardized promissory notes, mortgages, and trust deeds. Loan terms have been standardized into categories, for example, fixed-rate, 30-year loans; fixed-rate, 15-year loans; and various adjustable rate combinations. Additionally, nearly all loans must be insured. This can take the form of FHA or private mortgage insurance, or a VA guarantee on each loan in the package. Additionally, there will be some form of assurance of timely repayment of the mortgage package as a whole. The net result is a mortgage security that is attractive to investors who in the past have not been interested in investing in mortgages.

Standardized Loan Procedures

Let's now look at some of the key secondary market participants including the giants of the industry: the FNMA, GNMA, FHLMC, and Farmer Mac.

The **Federal National Mortgage Association (FNMA)** was organized by the federal government in 1938 to buy FHA mortgage loans from lenders. This made it possible for lenders to grant more loans to consumers. Ten years later it began purchas-

FNMA

ing VA loans. FNMA (fondly known in the real estate business and to itself as **"Fannie Mae"**) was successful in its mission.

In 1968 Congress divided the FNMA into two organizations: the Government National Mortgage Association (to be discussed in the next section) and the FNMA, as we know it today. As part of that division, the FNMA changed from a government agency to a private profit-making corporation, chartered by Congress but owned by its shareholders and managed independently of the government. Some 60 million shares of Fannie Mae stock are in existence, and it is one of the most actively traded issues on the New York Stock Exchange. Fannie Mae buys FHA and VA loans and, since 1972, conventional whole loans from lenders across the United States. Money to buy these loans comes from the sale of FNMA stock plus the sale of FNMA bonds and notes. FNMA bond and note holders look to Fannie Mae for timely payment of principal and interest on these bonds and notes, and Fannie Mae looks to its mortgagors for principal and interest payments on the loans it owns. Thus, Fannie Mae stands in the middle and, although it is very careful to match interest rates and maturities between the loans it buys and the bonds and notes it sells, it still takes the risk of the middleman. In this respect, it is like a giant thrift institution.

Commitments   Fannie Mae's method of operation is to sell commitments to lenders pledging to buy specified dollar amounts of mortgage loans within a fixed period of time and usually at a specified yield. Lenders are not obligated to sell loans to Fannie Mae if they can find better terms elsewhere. However, Fannie Mae must purchase all loans delivered to it under the terms of the commitments. Loans must be made using FNMA-approved forms and loan approval criteria. The largest loan Fannie Mae would buy in 1994 was $203,150 for a single-family unit. This limit is adjusted each year as housing prices change. Fannie Mae also buys loans on duplexes, triplexes, and fourplexes all at larger loan limits. Although the FNMA loan limit may seem inadequate for some houses and neighborhoods, the intention of Congress is that Fannie Mae cater to the mid-range of housing prices and leave the upper end of the market to others.

In addition to purchasing first mortgages, Fannie Mae also purchases second mortgages from lenders. FNMA forms and criteria must be followed and the loan-to-value ratio of the combined first and second mortgages cannot exceed 80% if owner-occupied and 70% if not owner-occupied. This is a very helpful program for a person who has watched the value of his or her home increase and wants to borrow against that increase without first having to repay the existing mortgage loan.

The demand for loans in the primary market could not match the demand that investors required in the secondary market, so Fannie Mae began purchasing large blocks of mortgage loans, and then assigned them to specified pools with an "agency guarantee" certificate which guaranteed long-term return to the pool investors. Fannie Mae guarantees to pass through to the certificate holders whatever principal, interest, and prepayments of principal are generated by the loans into the underlying pool of mortgage investors. Fannie Mae's pooling arrangements undertook the issuance of **mortgage-backed securities** (MBS). Utilizing this system of issuing securities that are backed by mortgages, the securities markets could then be used as a source for investment funds. In the fourth quarter of 1993, Fannie Mae held $146 billion dollars of loans in portfolio investments. At the same time, however, Fannie Mae had underwritten $473 billion in mortgage pools, totaling 20% of all residential loans. This is an incredible shift in loan procedures since 1982. This is also a strong indication that the government-guaranteed loan pools provide a much better procedure for making funds available in the secondary market. This, in turn, assures funds available for the primary market and long-term mortgage loans for individual home purchasers.

FNMA Pooling

Another innovation of Fannie Mae to help real estate is the **home seller program.** This is a secondary market for sellers who carry back mortgages. To qualify, the note and mortgage must be prepared by a FNMA-approved lender using standard FNMA loan qualification procedures. The note and mortgage may be kept by the home seller as an investment or sold to a FNMA-approved lender for possible resale to the FNMA.

Home Seller Program

In other developments, Fannie Mae has standardized the terms of adjustable rate mortgages it will purchase. This is a major step forward in reducing the proliferation of variety in these loans. Fannie Mae is also test marketing mortgage-backed securities in $1,000 increments to appeal to individuals, particularly for Individual Retirement Accounts. Additionally, Fannie Mae has started a collateralized mortgage obligation program and begun a mortgage pass-through program, both of which will be defined momentarily.

Revised Lending Practices

In 1992, as pressure increased from both Congress and HUD to become more socially responsible in lending practices, Congress passed legislation requiring stricter supervision of Fannie Mae by a HUD-appointed oversight committee. In March 1994, Fannie Mae announced a plan to provide one trillion dollars in financing over the rest of the decade to poor families, rural communities, and disabled people. Fannie Mae now cooperates with others in the purchase of 97% of conventional loans, working with local housing authorities, nonprofit associations, nonprofit housing groups, and private mortgage insurance, to spread the risk of some other loans.

GNMA

The **Government National Mortgage Association (GNMA,** popularly known to the industry and to itself as **"Ginnie Mae")** was created in 1968 when the FNMA was partitioned into two separate corporations. Ginnie Mae is a federal agency entirely within the Department of Housing and Urban Development (HUD). Although Ginnie Mae has some low-income housing functions, it is best known for its mortgage-backed securities (MBS) program. Previously discussed, the MBS program attracts additional sources of credit to FHA, VA, and FmHA mortgages. Ginnie Mae does this by guaranteeing timely repayment of privately issued securities backed by pools of these mortgages. Remember that the FNMA MBS program offers "agency guarantees" for their investors. GNMA offers a government guarantee of repayment, backed by the full faith and credit of the U.S. government.

Ginnie Mae Procedures

Ginnie Mae is limited to underwriting only HUD/FHA, VA, and certain Farmer's Home Administration loans. Ginnie Mae sets its own requirements for loans that can be accepted into their mortgage pool, then it subsequently approves loan poolers who are committed to comply with those requirements. Ginnie Mae examines the loans and the loan poolers before it can determine its ability to guarantee those loans into the loan pooler source of funds.

The result is that Ginnie Mae issues guarantee certificates, popularly known as "Ginnie Maes." By the fourth quarter of 1993, Ginnie Maes accounted for 13% of all residential loans. A Ginnie Mae certificate carries the equivalent of a U.S. government bond guarantee and pays the holder of those certificates, the loan pooler, an interest rate of 1% to $1\frac{1}{2}$% higher than that of a government bond.

The **Federal Home Loan Mortgage Corporation (FHLMC,** also known to the industry and to itself as **"Freddie Mac"** or the "Mortgage Corporation") was created by Congress in 1970. Its goal, like that of the FNMA and GNMA, is to increase the availability of financing for residential mortgages. Where FHLMC differs is that Freddie Mac deals primarily in conventional mortgages.

FHLMC

Freddie Mac was initially established to serve as a secondary market for S&L members of the Federal Home Loan Bank System. The ownership of Freddie Mac was originally held by more than 3,000 savings associations. In 1988, the shares were released and sold publicly by the savings associations. Unlike Ginnie Mae, which guarantees securities issued by others, Freddie Mac issues its own securities against its own mortgage pools. These securities are its participation certificates and collateralized mortgage obligations. By the third quarter of 1988, Freddie Mac held nearly $42 billion in its own loan portfolio, accounting for almost 16% of all outstanding loans in residential lending.

Participation certificates (PCs) allow a mortgage originator to deliver to Freddie Mac either whole mortgages or part interest in a pool of whole mortgages. In return, Freddie Mac gives the mortgage originator a PC representing an undivided interest in a pool of investment-quality conventional mortgages created from mortgages and mortgage interests purchased by Freddie Mac. Freddie Mac guarantees that the interest and principal on these PCs will be repaid in full and on time, even if the underlying mortgages are in default. (Freddie Mac reduces its losses by setting strict loan qualification criteria and requiring mortgage insurance on high loan-to-value loans.) The PCs can be kept as investments, sold for cash, or used as collateral for loans. PCs are popular investments for S&Ls, pension funds, and other institutional investors looking for high-yield investments. Indi-

Participation Certificates

viduals who can meet the $25,000 minimum also find PCs attractive. Freddie Mac also has a collateralized mortgage obligation program and plans to offer a trust for investments in mortgages. Both of these programs are designed to deal with the unpredictability of mortgage maturities caused by early repayment by dividing the cash flows from a mortgage pool into separate securities with separate maturities, which are then sold to investors.

As with Fannie Mae, Congress and HUD provide the oversight committee to Freddie Mac. New guidelines provided by HUD call for both Freddie Mac and Fannie Mae to purchase about 30% of their mortgages in inner-city areas and from lower-income home buyers. By the fourth quarter of 1993, Freddie Mac held a total of 15% of all the residential loans.

FARMER MAC

The newest agency created by Congress to underwrite loan pools is the Federal Agricultural Mortgage Corporation, known as Farmer Mac. The Agricultural Credit Act of 1987 established Farmer Mac as a separate agency within the Farm Credit System to establish the secondary market needed for farm real estate loans. Farmer Mac started actual operations in 1989.

Originally, Farmer Mac functioned similarly to Ginnie Mae in that it certified loan poolers rather than purchase loans. Farmer Mac guaranteed timely repayment of principal and interest in the loan pool, but did not guarantee any individual loans within that pool.

In 1996, Congress passed the **Farm Credit System Reform Act** allowing Farmer Mac to act as a pooler for qualified loans. Farmer Mac is now permitted to purchase loans directly from originators and to issue guaranteed securities backed by the loans. For the first time, Farmer Mac became a true secondary market.

Loan Qualification

To qualify for a pool, a loan must be collateralized by agricultural real estate located in the United States. The real estate can include a home, which can cost no more than $100,000, and must be located in a rural community with a population of 2,500 or less. The maximum loan is $2.5 million or the amount secured by no more than 1,000 acres, whichever is larger. The loan to value ratio must be less than 80%, and the borrower must be a

United States citizen engaged in agriculture and must demonstrate a capability to repay the loan.

The financial success of the three giants of the secondary mortgage market (FNMA, GNMA, and FHLMC) has brought private mortgage packagers into the marketplace. These are organizations such as MGIC Investment Corporation (a subsidiary of Mortgage Guaranty Investment Corporation); Residential Funding Corporation (a subsidiary of Norwest Mortgage Corp.); financial subsidiaries of such household-name companies as General Electric, Lockheed Aircraft, and Sears, Roebuck; and mortgage packaging subsidiaries of state realtor associations. These organizations both compete with the big three and specialize in markets not served by them. For example, Residential Funding Corp. will package mortgage loans as large as $500,000, well above the limits imposed by FNMA and FHLMC and limits on FHA and VA loans. All of these organizations will buy from loan originators who are not large enough to create their own pools.

PRIVATE CONDUITS

Before leaving the topic of the secondary market, it is important to note that, without electronic data transmission and computers, the programs just described would be severely handicapped. There are currently thousands of mortgage pools, each containing from $1 million to $500 million (and more) in mortgage loans. Each loan in a pool has its own monthly payment schedule, and each payment must be broken down into its principal and interest components and any property tax and insurance impounds. Computers do this work as well as issue receipts and late notices. The pool, in turn, will be owned by several dozen to a hundred or more investors, each with a different fractional interest in the pool. Once a month incoming mortgage payments are tallied, a small fee is deducted for the operation of the pool, and the balance is allotted among the investors—all by computer. A computer also prints and mails checks to investors and provides them with an accounting of the pool's asset level.

COMPUTERIZATION

The computer age has introduced a whole new system in underwriting procedures as they apply to the relationship between the loan originator and the investor (secondary market). In the "old days," underwriting guidelines would be published and circu-

AUTOMATED
UNDERWRITING
SYSTEMS

lated to the primary lenders weekly. As interest rates began to fluctuate wildly in the 1970s, the sheet was updated and circulated more often. In some real estate offices, one person was given the job of calling lenders daily for quotes on loan availability and interest rates.

The entire process is being overhauled by a computerized mortgage loan underwriting system with the introduction of Freddie Mac's loan prospector program, which was released for marketing in early 1985. At this time, the program is limited to Freddie Mac's approved sellers and servicers. This process is very streamlined. The regular uniform residential loan application is submitted to the lender and the lender then verifies the applicant's employment, income, and assets. This information is fed into the computer and is promptly analyzed by the computer program. If the borrower is accepted and if the loan-to-value ratio is greater than 80%, the application is then forwarded to a private mortgage insurer. Those that are not accepted are considered as "refer" or "caution." Those classified as "refer" are sent to the underwriting department with at least four reasons stating why the loan is referred. The "caution" category indicates that there are serious issues preventing the loan's purchase. The real estate can be appraised and a loan completely processed in as little as 2 hours if the lender requests an "expedited" appraisal. A nonexpedited appraisal can take less than 72 hours. Freddie Mac reports that about 60% of all applicants can be accepted in 4 minutes. It is anticipated that by using this streamlined program, the cost of processing the loan is cut in half.

FNMA now has its own software programs, called Desktop Originator (used by a broker or agent to submit information to a lender) and Desktop Underwriter (used by a lender to submit the application directly to FNMA). As with the Freddie Mac program, responses can be confirmed in seconds.

AVAILABILITY AND PRICE OF MORTGAGE MONEY

Thus far we have been concerned with the money pipelines between lenders and borrowers. Ultimately, though, money must have a source. These sources are savings generated by individuals and businesses as a result of their spending less than they earn (**real savings**) and of government-created money, called **fiat money** or "printing press money." This second source does not represent unconsumed labor and materials; instead it

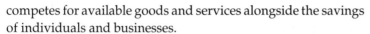

competes for available goods and services alongside the savings of individuals and businesses.

In the arena of money and capital, real estate borrowers must compete with the needs of government, business, and consumers. Governments, particularly the federal government, compete the hardest when they borrow to finance a deficit. Not to borrow would mean bankruptcy and the inability to pay government employees and provide government programs and services. Strong competition also comes from business and consumer credit sectors. In the face of such strong competition for loan funds, home buyers must either pay higher interest or be outbid.

One "solution" to this problem is for the federal government to create more money, thus making competition for funds easier and interest rates lower. Unfortunately, the net result is often too much money chasing too few goods, and prices are pulled upward by the demand caused by the newly created money. This is followed by rising interest rates as savers demand higher returns to compensate for losses in purchasing power. Many economists feel that the higher price levels and interest rates of the 1970s resulted from applying too much of this "solution" to the economy since 1965.

The alternative solution, from the standpoint of residential loans, is to increase real savings or decrease competing demands for available money. A number of plans and ideas have been put forth by civic, business, and political leaders. They include proposals to simplify income taxes and balance the federal budget, incentives to increase productive output, and incentives to save money in retirement accounts.

Usury

An old idea that has been tried, but is of dubious value for holding down interest rates, is legislation to impose interest rate ceilings. Known as **usury** laws and found in nearly all states, these laws were originally enacted to prohibit lenders from overcharging interest on loans to individuals. However, since the end of World War II, the ceilings in some states have failed to keep step with rising interest rates, with the result that borrowers are denied loans. Most states have raised usury limits in response to higher interest rates. But the rules and exceptions are so complex that a local attorney must be consulted. Additionally, the U.S. Congress passed legislation in 1980 that exempts from state usury limits most first-lien home loans made by institutional lenders. In the New York State Banking Law, the limit is currently set at 16%.

Price to the Borrower

Ultimately, the rate of interest the borrower must pay to obtain a loan is dependent on the cost of money to the lender, reserves for default, loan servicing costs, and available investment alternatives. For example, go to a savings institution and see what they are paying depositors on various accounts. To this add 2% for the cost of maintaining cash in the tills, office space, personnel, advertising, free gifts for depositors, deposit insurance, loan servicing, loan reserves for defaults, and a ¼% profit margin. This gives you an idea of how much borrowers must be charged.

Life insurance companies, pension funds, and trust funds do not have to "pay" for their money as do thrift institutions. Nonetheless, they do want to earn the highest possible yields, with safety, on the money in their custody. Thus, if a real estate buyer wants to borrow in order to buy a home, the buyer must compete successfully with the other investment opportunities available on the open market. To determine the rate for yourself, look at the yields on newly issued corporate bonds as shown in the financial section of your daily newspaper. Add ½ of 1% to this for the extra work in packaging and servicing mortgage loans and you will have the interest rate home borrowers must pay to attract lenders.

DUE-ON-SALE

From an investment risk standpoint, when a lender makes a loan with a fixed interest rate, the lender recognizes that during the life of the loan interest rates may rise or fall. When they rise, the lender remains locked into a lower rate. Most loans contain a **due-on-sale clause** (also called an **alienation clause** or a **call clause**). In the past, these were inserted by lenders so that if the borrower sold the property to someone considered uncreditworthy by the lender, the lender could call the loan balance due. When interest rates increase, though, lenders can use these clauses to increase the rate of interest on the loan when the property changes hands by threatening to accelerate the balance of the loan unless the new owner accepts a higher rate of interest.

PREPAYMENT

If loan rates drop it becomes worthwhile for a borrower to shop for a new loan and repay the existing one in full. To compensate, loan contracts sometimes call for a **prepayment penalty** in return for giving the borrower the right to repay the loan early. A typical prepayment penalty amounts to the equivalent of 6 months interest on the amount that is being paid early. However, the penalty varies from loan to loan and from state to state. Some loan contracts permit up to 20% of the unpaid balance to be paid in any one year without penalty. Other contracts make the penalty stiffest when the loan is young. In certain states, laws do not permit prepayment penalties on loans more than 5 years old. By federal law, prepayment penalties are not allowed on FHA and VA loans. In New York, no prepayment may be imposed for a residential mortgage loan that is 1 year old, and the right of prepayment must be stated in the loan contract. A prepayment penalty for a loan outstanding less than 1 year may be imposed only if the penalty was specified in the original contract.

Match terms **a–j** *with statements* **1–10.**

VOCABULARY REVIEW

a. *Automated underwriting systems*
b. *Computerized loan origination*
c. *Due-on-sale clause*
d. *Fannie Mae*
e. *Mortgage company*
f. *Mortgage-backed securities*
g. *Participation certificates*
h. *Prepayment penalty*
i. *Secondary mortgage market*
j. *Usury*

1. Securities issued, and backed by the mortgages securing the loans and the full faith of the federal government.
2. Requires immediate repayment of the loan if ownership transfers; also called an alienation clause.
3. A market where mortgage loans can be sold to investors.
4. A firm that makes mortgage loans and then sells them to investors.
5. A lending industry name for the Federal National Mortgage Association.
6. A certificate representing an undivided interest in a Freddie Mac pool.
7. Charging a rate of interest higher than that permitted by law.
8. Penalty charged for paying a loan off prior to maturity.
9. Computerized communication systems for loan approval between a loan originator and the investor.
10. Originating loans through the use of a networked computer system.

QUESTIONS AND PROBLEMS

1. What is the most significant difference between a mortgage broker and a mortgage banker?

2. In the secondary mortgage market, who provides the loan money?
3. What is meant by the term *loan servicing?*
4. By what financing methods do FNMA and GNMA provide money for real estate loans?
5. If a dollar is a dollar no matter where it comes from, what difference does it make if the source of a real estate loan was real savings or fiat money?
6. Why are the secondary market pooling arrangements successful?

ADDITIONAL READINGS

"Mortgage Paydown Options, Fixed-Rate vs. Adjustable-Rate Mortgages," by **William W. Welch, John Z. Zdanowicz,** and **Simon J. Pak** (*Real Estate Finance*, Winter 1993, pp. 25–31). Article discusses the options available for mortgages.

Real Estate Finance, 7th Ed., by **John Wiedemer** (Prentice Hall, 1995, 320 pages). Includes sources of long-term mortgage money, financing instruments, loan procedures, FNMA, FHLMC, GNMA, FHA, and VA; also includes loan analysis, carryback financing, and settlement procedures.

"What you need to know about mortgage brokers," by **Earl C. Gottschalk** (*Wall Street Journal,* April 9, 1993, p. C1.).

19

Types of Financing

KEY • TERMS

Adjustable rate mortgage (ARM): a mortgage on which the interest rate rises and falls with changes in prevailing interest rates

Asset integrated mortgage: a mortgage designed to create a savings from the down payment

Equity sharing: an arrangement whereby a party providing financing gets a portion of the ownership

Graduated payment mortgage: a mortgage with an interest rate and maturity that are fixed, but the monthly payment gradually rises, as the initial monthly payments are insufficient to fully amortize the loan

Negative amortization: accrual of interest on a loan balance so that, as loan payments are made, the loan balance rises

Option: a right, for a given period of time, to buy, sell, or lease property at specified price and terms

RAM: reverse-annuity mortgage

SAM: shared-appreciation mortgage

Seller financing: a note accepted by a seller instead of cash

Wraparound mortgage: a mortgage that encompasses any existing mortgages and is subordinate to them

New financing techniques have created an "alphabet soup" of mortgaging alternatives available to a borrower. With computerized loan origination, the expanded secondary market, and the availability of mortgage funds from nonregulated lending sources, a vast array of available mortgaging techniques and types of financing have been created. The documents (discussed in Chapter 14) and the sources of funds (discussed in Chapter 18) still remain the same, but the number of alternative types of financing continues to expand. In this chapter, types of financing are discussed, including adjustable rate mortgages, shared-appreciation mortgages, other generally accepted types of loans often encountered by a broker in real estate lending, and the newest concepts of the affordable housing programs.

ADJUSTABLE RATE MORTGAGES

As we have already seen, a major problem for savings institutions is that they are locked into long-term loans while being dependent on short-term savings deposits. As a result, savings institutions now prefer to make mortgage loans that allow the interest rate to rise and fall during the life of the loan. To make this arrangement more attractive to borrowers, these loans are offered at a lower rate of interest than a fixed-rate loan of similar maturity.

The first step toward mortgage loans with adjustable interest rates came in the late 1970s. The loan was called a **variable rate mortgage** and the interest rate could be adjusted up or down by the lender during the 30-year life of the loan to reflect the rise and fall in interest rates paid to savers by the lender.

Current Format

In 1981, the Federal Home Loan Bank Board (FHLBB) authorized savings institutions to make the type of adjustable mortgage loan you are most likely to encounter in today's loan marketplace. This loan format is called an **adjustable rate mortgage (ARM).** Other federal agencies followed, but used differing guidelines. By 1988, the federal government enacted new regulations that standardized the ARM requirements in all of the federal agencies. The main requirement is that the interest rate on these loans be tied to some publicly available index that is mutually acceptable to the lender and the borrower. Basically, the concept is the same as the variable rate mortgage: As interest rates rise and fall in the open market, the interest rate the lender is entitled to receive from the borrower rises and falls (Figure

19.1). The purpose is to match more closely what the savings institution receives from borrowers to what it must pay savers to attract funds.

The benefit of an ARM to a borrower is that ARMs carry an initial interest rate that is lower than the rate on a fixed-rate mortgage of similar maturity. This often makes the difference between being able to qualify for a desired home and not qualifying for it. Other advantages to the borrower are that if market interest rates fall, the borrower's monthly payments fall. (This happens without incurring prepayment penalties or new loan origination costs, which could be the case with a fixed-rate loan.) Most ARMs allow assumption by a new buyer at the terms in the ARM, and most allow total prepayment without penalty, particularly if there has been an upward adjustment in the interest rate.

For the borrower, the disadvantage of an ARM is that if interest rates rise, the borrower is going to pay more. During periods of rising interest rates, property values and wages presumably will also rise. But the possibility of progressively larger monthly payments for the family home is still not attractive. As a result, various compromises have been worked out between lenders and borrowers whereby rates can rise on loans, but not by too much. In view of the fact that about one-half of all mortgage loans being originated by thrifts, banks, and mortgage companies are now adjustable, let's take a closer look at what a borrower gets with this loan format.

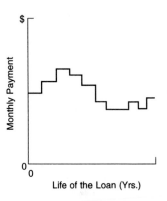

Figure 19.1. Adjustable rate mortgage.

Interest Rate

The interest rate on an ARM is tied to an **index rate.** As the index rate moves up or down, so do the borrower's payments when adjustment time arrives. Lenders and borrowers alike want a rate that genuinely reflects current market conditions for interest rates and that can be easily verified. By far the most popular index is the interest rate on 1-year U.S. Treasury securities. Next most popular is the cost of funds to thrift institutions as measured by the FHLBB. A few loans use 6-month Treasury bills as an index rate.

Margin

To the index rate is added the margin. The **margin** is for the lender's cost of doing business, risk of loss on the loan, and profit. Currently this runs from 2% to 3%, depending on the characteristics of the loan. The margin is a useful comparison device because if two lenders are offering the same loan terms and the same index, but one loan has a margin of 2% and the other 3%, then the one with the 2% margin will have lower loan payments. As a rule, the margin stays constant during the life of the loan. At each adjustment point in the loan's life, the lender takes the index rate and adds the margin. The total becomes the interest the borrower will pay until the next adjustment occurs.

Adjustment Period

The amount of time that elapses between adjustments is called the **adjustment period.** By far the most common adjustment period is 1 year. Less commonly used are 6-month, 3-year, and 5-year adjustment periods. When market rates are rising, the longer adjustment periods benefit the borrower. When market rates are falling, the shorter periods benefit the borrower because index decreases will show up sooner in their monthly payments.

Interest Rate Cap

Lenders are now required by federal law to disclose an **interest rate cap** or ceiling on how much the interest rate can increase for any one adjustment period during the life of the loan. If the cap is very low, say $\frac{1}{2}$% per year, the lender does not have much more flexibility than if holding a fixed-rate loan. Thus, there would be little reduction of initial rate on the loan compared with a fixed-rate loan. Compromises have prevailed, and the two most popular caps are 1% and 2% per year. In other words, the index rate may rise by 3%, but the cap limits the borrower's rate increase to 1% or 2%. Any unused difference may be added the next year, assuming the index rate has not fallen in the meantime. Since federal law now requires the ceiling, many lenders simply impose a very high ceiling (e.g., 18%) if they choose not to negotiate with the borrower.

Payment Cap

What if a loan's index rate rises so fast that the annual rate cap is reached each year and the lifetime cap is reached soon in the life of the loan? A borrower might be able to handle a modest increase in payments each year, but not big jumps in quick succession. To counteract this possibility, a **payment cap** sets a limit on how much the borrower's monthly payment can increase in any one year. A popular figure now in use is $7\frac{1}{2}$%. In other words, no matter how high a payment is called for by the index rate, the borrower's monthly payment can rise, at the most, $7\frac{1}{2}\%$ per year. For example, given an initial rate of 10% on a 30-year ARM for $100,000, the monthly payment of interest and principal is $878 (see Table 16.1). If the index rate calls for a 2% upward adjustment at the end of 1 year, the payment on the loan would be $1,029. This is an increase of $151 or 17.2%. A $7\frac{1}{2}\%$ payment cap would limit the increase to 107.5% × $878 = $943.85.

Negative Amortization

Although the $7\frac{1}{2}\%$ payment cap in the foregoing example protects the borrower against a monthly payment that rises too fast, it does not make the difference between what's called for ($1,029) and what's paid ($943.85) go away. The difference ($85.15) is added to the balance owed on the loan and earns interest just like the original amount borrowed. This is called **negative amortization:** instead of the loan balance dropping each month as loan payments are made, the balance owed rises. This can bring concern to the lender who can visualize the day the loan balance exceeds the value of the property. A popular arrangement is to set a limit of 125% of the original loan balance. At that point, either the lender accrues no more negative amortization or the loan is reamortized depending on the wording of the loan contract. *Reamortized* in this situation means the monthly payments will be adjusted upward by enough to stop the negative amortization.

Disclosures

In response to consumers' concern over adjustable rate mortgages, an amendment to Regulation Z became effective October 1, 1988. It requires creditors to provide consumers with more extensive information about the variable rate feature of ARMs. The amendments apply only to closed-end credit transactions secured by the consumer's principal dwelling. Transactions secured by the consumer's principal dwelling with a term of 1 year or less are exempt from the new disclosure. To comply with the amendment, lenders must provide consumers with a historical example that shows how actual changes in index values would have affected payments on a $10,000 loan, as well as provide a statement of initial and maximum interest rates. Lenders must also provide prospective borrowers with an educational brochure about ARMs called "The Consumer Handbook on Adjustable Rate and Mortgages" or a suitable substitute. All the information must be given to the consumer at the time the loan application form is provided or before a nonrefundable fee is paid, whichever is earlier. The maximum interest rate must be stated as a specified amount or stated in a manner in which the consumer may easily ascertain the maximum interest rate at the time of entering the obligation.

Choosing Wisely

When a lender makes an ARM loan, the lender must explain to the borrower, in writing, the *worst-case scenario*. In other words, the lender must explain what will happen to the borrower's payments if the index rises the maximum amount each period up to the lifetime interest cap. If there is a payment cap, that and any possibility of negative amortization must also be explained. If the borrower is uneasy with these possibilities, then a fixed-rate loan should be considered. Most lenders offer fixed-rate loans as well as adjustable rate loans. VA loans are fixed-rate loans, but FHA now provides an adjustable rate loan program.

"Teaser rate" adjustables have been offered from time to time by a few lenders and are best avoided. This type of loan is an ARM with an enticingly attractive, below-market initial rate. For example, the teaser rate may be offered at 2% below market. A borrower who cannot qualify at the market rate might be able to do so at the teaser rate. However, in a year the loan contract calls for a 2% jump followed by additional annual increases. This overwhelms the borrower who, unable to pay, allows foreclosure to take place.

GRADUATED PAYMENT MORTGAGE

The objective of a **graduated payment mortgage** is to help borrowers qualify for loans by basing repayment schedules on salary expectations. With this type of mortgage, the interest rate and maturity are fixed but the monthly payment gradually rises. For example, a 10%, $60,000, 30-year loan normally requires monthly payments of $527 for complete amortization. Under the graduated payment mortgage, payments could start out as low as $437 per month the first year, then gradually increase to $590 in the eleventh year and then remain at that level until the thirtieth year. Since the interest alone on this $60,000 loan is $500 per month, the amount owed on the loan actually increases during its early years. Only when the monthly payment exceeds the monthly interest does the balance owed on the loan decrease.

The FHA insures graduated payment mortgages under Section 245 and offers five repayment plans. This program is designed to appeal to first-time home buyers in the $15,000 to $25,000 income range because it enables them to tailor their installment payments to their expanding incomes, and thus buy a home sooner than under regular mortgage financing. An **adjustable graduated payment mortgage** combines variable interest with graduated payment features (Figure 19.2).

A variation of the graduated payment mortgage is the **growing equity mortgage.** This is a 30-year fixed-rate mortgage with monthly payments that are increased 3% to 7% each year. This loan is designed to parallel the borrower's income and fully repay itself in 12 to 15 years.

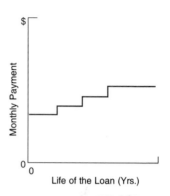

Figure 19.2. Graduated payment mortgage.

The basic concept of a **shared appreciation mortgage (SAM)** is that the borrower gives the lender a portion of the property's appreciation in return for a lower rate of interest (Figure 19.3). To illustrate, a lender who would otherwise charge 12% interest might agree to take 8% interest plus one-third of the appreciation of the property. The lender is accepting what amounts to a speculative investment in the property in return for a reduced interest rate. The borrower is able to buy and occupy a home that he or she might not otherwise be able to afford, but gives up part of any future price appreciation.

Despite the apparent advantages of the SAM, there are some major pitfalls. For example, at what point in the future is the gain recognized and the lender paid off? If the home is sold, the profits can be split in accordance with the agreement. However, what if the lender feels the home is being sold at too low a price? What if the home is not sold for cash? What if the borrower does not want to sell? One answer to the last situation is that the lender may set a time limit of 10 years on the loan. If the home has not been sold by that time, the home is appraised and the borrower pays the lender the lender's share of the appreciation. At a 10% appreciation rate, a $93,750 house would be worth $243,164 ten years later. If the lender was entitled to one-third of the $149,414 appreciation, the borrower would owe the lender $49,805 in appreciation plus the remaining $70,000 balance on the loan. Unless the borrower can pay cash, this would have to be refinanced at then current rates of interest. On the other hand, if the property experiences no appreciation in value, the borrower will have

SHARED-APPRECIATION MORTGAGE

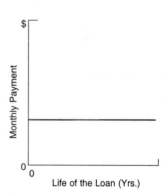

Figure 19.3. Shared-appreciation mortgage.

enjoyed a below-market-rate loan for 10 years and be responsible only for refinancing the remaining loan balance at that time.

EQUITY SHARING

Giving the party that provides the financing a "piece of the action in the deal" is not an innovation. Insurance companies financing shopping centers and office buildings have long used the idea of requiring part of the rental income and/or part of the profits plus interest on the loan itself. In other words, in return for providing financing, the lender wants to share in some of the benefits normally reserved for the equity holder, called **equity sharing**. The equity holder would agree to this either to get a lower rate of interest, such as in the aforementioned SAM, or to get financing when financing was scarce or where the equity holder was not big enough to handle the deal alone. For example, on a $5 million project, the lender might agree to make a loan of $4 million at a very attractive rate if it can buy a half-interest in the equity for $500,000.

Equity sharing is also found in residential financing. One variation is for an enterprising real estate person to find attractive income properties and sell a 50% equity interest to someone who wants to invest in real estate, but who has more money than time. The investor makes half of the down payment and signs for the loan. For this, the investor gets half of the income and profits and all of the tax deductions. The entrepreneur gets the other half of the income in return for the remaining down payment and the effort of finding and managing the property.

"Rich Uncle" Financing

A second variation of equity sharing is often called *"rich uncle" financing*. The investor may be a parent helping a son or daughter buy a home or a son or daughter buying a parent's present home while giving the parent(s) the right to occupy it. A third variation is for an investor to provide most of the down payment for a home buyer, collect rent from the home buyer, pay the mortgage payments and property taxes, and claim depreciation. Each party has a right to a portion of any appreciation and the right to buy out the other. The FHLMC now recognizes the importance of equity sharing and will buy mortgage loans on shared-equity properties. The FHLMC requires that the owner-occupant contribute at least 5% of the equity, that the owner-occupant and the owner-investor sign the mortgage and note, that both be individuals, and that there be no agreement requiring sale or buy-out within 7 years of the loan date. Equity sharing can provide attractive tax benefits; however, you must seek competent tax advice before involving yourself or someone else in such a plan.

Normally, we think of real estate mortgage loans as being secured solely by real estate. However, it is possible to include items classed as personal property in a real estate mortgage, thus creating a **package mortgage.** In residential loans, such items as the refrigerator, clothes washer, and dryer can be pledged along with the house and land in a single mortgage. The purpose is to raise the value of the collateral in order to raise the amount a lender is willing to loan. For the borrower, it offers the opportunity of financing major appliances at the same rate of interest as the real estate itself. This rate is usually lower than if the borrower finances the appliances separately. Once an item of personal property is included in a package mortgage, selling it without the prior consent of the lender is a violation of the mortgage.

PACKAGE MORTGAGE

A mortgage secured by two or more properties is called a **blanket mortgage.** Suppose you want to buy a house plus the vacant lot next door, financing the purchase with a single mortgage that covers both properties. The cost of preparing one mortgage instead of two is a savings. Also, by combining the house and lot, the lot can be financed on better terms than if it were financed separately, as lenders more readily loan on a house and land than on land alone. Note, however, that if the vacant lot is later sold separately from the house before the mortgage loan is fully repaid, it will be necessary to have it released from the blanket mortgage. This is usually accomplished by including in the original mortgage agreement a partial release clause that specifies how much of the loan must be repaid before the lot can be released.

BLANKET MORTGAGE

With a regular mortgage, the lender makes a lump-sum payment to the borrower, who, in turn, repays it through monthly payments to the lender. With a **reverse mortgage,** also known as a *reverse-annuity mortgage* or *RAM,* the lender has two alternatives: (1) payment to the homeowner in a lump sum (sometimes referred to as a "line of credit" RAM), or (2) monthly

REVERSE MORTGAGE

payments to the homeowner as an annuity for the reverse term of the loan. The reverse mortgage can be particularly valuable for an elderly homeowner who does not want to sell, but whose retirement income is not quite enough for comfortable living. The homeowner receives a monthly check, has full use of the property, and is not required to repay until he or she sells or dies. If the home is sold, money from the sale is taken to repay the loan. If the borrower dies first, the property is sold through the estate and the loan repaid. This seems like a great idea, but what if the borrower outlives the loan?

CONSTRUCTION LOAN

Under a **construction loan,** also called an **interim loan,** money is advanced as construction takes place. For example, a vacant lot owner arranges to borrow $60,000 to build a house. The lender does not advance all $60,000 at once because the value of the collateral is insufficient to warrant that amount until the house is finished. Instead, the lender will parcel out the loan as the building is being constructed, always holding a portion until the property is ready for occupancy or, in some cases, actually occupied. Some lenders specialize only in construction loans and do not want to wait 20 or 30 years to be repaid. In this case, the buyer will have to obtain a permanent long-term mortgage from another source for the purpose of repaying the construction loan. This is known as a *permanent commitment* or a **take-out loan,** since it takes the construction lender out of the financial picture when construction is completed and allows the lender to recycle its money into new construction projects.

BLENDED-RATE LOAN

Many real estate lenders still hold long-term loans that were made at interest rates below the current market. One way of raising the return on these loans is to offer borrowers who have them a **blended-rate loan.** Suppose you owe $50,000 on your home loan and the interest rate on it is 7%. Suppose further that the current rate on home loans is 12%. Your lender might offer to refinance your home for $70,000 at 9%, presuming the property will appraise high enough and you have the income to qualify. The $70,000 refinance offer would put $20,000 in your pocket (less loan fees), but would increase the interest you pay from 7% to 9% on the original $50,000. This makes the cost of the $20,000 14% per year. The arithmetic is as follows: you will now be paying 9% × $70,000 = $6,300 in interest. Before, you paid 7% × $50,000 = $3,500 in interest. The difference, $2,800, is what you pay to borrow the additional $20,000. This equates to $2,800 ÷ $20,000 = 14% interest. This is the figure you should use in comparing other sources of financing (such as a second mortgage) or deciding whether or not you even want to borrow.

A blended-rate loan can be very attractive in a situation in which you want to sell your home and you do not want to help finance the buyer. Suppose your home is worth $87,500 and you have the aforementioned $50,000, 7% loan. A buyer would normally expect to make a down payment of $17,500 and pay 12% interest on a new $70,000 loan. But, with a blended loan, your lender could offer the buyer the needed $70,000 financing at 9%, a far more attractive rate and one that requires less income in order to qualify. Blended loans are available on FHA, VA, and conventional loans held by the FNMA. Other lenders also offer them on fixed-rate assumable loans they hold.

Buy-downs are used to reduce the rate of interest a buyer must pay on a new mortgage loan. For example, suppose a builder has a tract of homes for sale and the current interest rate on home loans is 12%. Few buyers are willing to purchase at that interest rate. What the builder can do is to arrange with a lender to pay the lender discount points so that the lender can offer a loan to the buyer at a lower interest rate. This can be done for the life of the loan at the cost of about 8 discount points for every point of interest rate reduction, or, it can be done for a shorter period, such as the first 3 years of the loan's life (Figure 19.4). For example, the builder could offer 9% interest for the first 3 years of the loan. Not only is 9% more attractive than 12%, but more buyers can qualify for loans at 9% than at 12%. Although the buy-down is costly to the builder, it will help sell homes that might otherwise go unsold. Moreover, a buy-down will usually boost sales more than a price reduction of like amount. The builder offering the buy-down will usually take a price reduction equal to the discount points if the buyer will forego the buy-down. The disadvantage of a short-term buy-down is that market rates may not drop to allow refinancing and/or the buyer's income may not increase enough to accommodate the rising monthly payments.

BUY-DOWN MORTGAGE

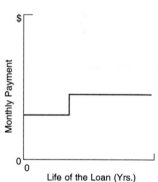

Figure 19.4. Buy-down mortgage.

EQUITY MORTGAGE

An **equity mortgage** is a loan arrangement wherein the lender agrees to extend a line of credit based on the amount of equity in a borrower's home. Since the Internal Revenue Code of 1986 limited interest deductions to home mortgages only, these loans have become one of the fastest growing areas of real estate lending. The maximum amount of the loan is generally 70% to 80% of the appraised value of the home minus any first mortgage or other liens against the property. The borrower need not take all the credit available, but rather can draw against the mortgage as needed. Some lenders specify a minimum amount per withdrawal. The borrower pays interest only on the amount actually borrowed, not the maximum available. The borrower then has several years to repay the amount borrowed. The interest rate is adjustable and tends to be 1 to 3 percentage points above the "prime rate" paid by large corporations.

The equity mortgage is typically a second mortgage that is used to tap the increase in equity resulting from rising home prices and first loan paydown. It's all done without having to refinance the first loan and uses the home as an asset against which the homeowner can borrow and repay as needed. Equity mortgages are very popular as a source of home improvement loans, money for college expenses, money to start a business, money for a major vacation, and money to buy more real estate.

AFFORDABLE HOUSING

An **affordable housing loan** is an umbrella term that covers many slightly different loans that target first-time home buyers and low- to moderate-income borrowers. Although there are no fixed standards for measurement, the generally accepted definition of a *low-income borrower* is a person or family with an income of not more than 80% of the median income for the local area. *Moderate income* is 115% of the median income for the area. *Median* means an equal number of people of incomes above or below the number. Funding for the programs is obtained through a commitment from an investor to buy the loans. Freddie Mac and Fannie Mae cooperate with local community, labor union, or trade associations by committing to buy a large block of mortgage loans provided they meet the agreed-on standards. Affordable housing loans can be privately insured through a mortgage guaranty insurance company or GE Capital Mortgage Insurance Corporation.

Underwriting standards for affordable housing loans are modified to recognize different forms of credit responsibility. Many
low- and moderate-income families do not have checking accounts. Recognizing the lack of payment records, most affordable housing programs accept timely payment of rent and utility
bills as credit criteria. Initial cash down payments can be reduced by allowing borrowing or acceptance of grants from
housing agencies or local communities, which sometimes offer
cash assistance. Studies indicate that lower-income families pay
a higher percentage of their income for housing than others, so
an affordable housing program allows a higher ratio of income
to be applied to housing (33% of gross income instead of 28%
found in similar loans; you may recall that the FHA housing
guideline is 29%).

Credit Criteria

One of the requirements to qualify for an affordable housing
loan is for the borrower to take a prepurchase home buyer
education course. Many of these first-time home buyers are
unaware of real estate brokers, title insurance, or appraisals.
These subjects, plus the care and maintenance of a home, are
included in the variety of courses now available through community colleges, banks, and mortgage companies. The four
major supporting entities of these programs are Fannie Mae,
Freddie Mac, MGIC, and GE Capital Mortgage Corporation. All
of these entities provide video tapes and course outlines that are
available for these educational purposes.

Consumer Education

Licensees should be aware that these programs are most
effective if presented to a group of applicants. If there is not a
program in your area, one could be started. An agent may want
to contact local lenders, as many are still not fully aware of the
opportunities available, and some tend to overlook the lower
income market for economic reasons. Participation in the program, however, greatly benefits their Community Reinvestment
Act rating. Effectively marketing these programs can be very
profitable and provide a great amount of personal satisfaction.

One of the most significant developments in mortgage lending
has been the introduction of a 3%-down-payment conventional loan. FIRREA and the Community Reinvestment Act
(discussed in Chapter 20) provided strong incentives for private
lenders to engage in affordable housing loans to help lower

97% Conventional Loan

middle-income homeowners. To encourage homeownership among lower- and middle-income people, General Electric Capital Mortgage Insurance Companies experimented with affordable housing loans, which it calls "community home buyer's program" loans. Results show that the rates of default among their borrowers prove to be as good or better than those of its regular loan portfolio. GE introduced a 97% conventional loan in February of 1994. Fannie Mae agreed to purchase 97% loans as long as the applicant met Fannie Mae guidelines, which include an income limit not to exceed 100% of the local area median income. Another conduit has been established by the investment banker Goldman Sachs to purchase these loans for buyers with up to 115% of area median income.

Asset Integrated Mortgage (AIM)

The **asset integrated mortgage (AIM)** is a new mortgage designed to create a savings from the down payment and is applicable primarily to borrowers expecting to make at least a 15 to 20% down payment. With this plan, the actual down payment would be about 5% while the rest of the cash is used to purchase a fixed annuity in the name of the borrower and held by the lender as additional collateral. This, in effect, makes a loan with a 95% loan-to-value ratio.

For instance, if a borrower purchased a $100,000 house and wants to make a $20,000 payment and finance $80,000 at $8\frac{1}{2}$% for 30 years, the monthly payment is $615.14. With an AIM, the borrower can make a down payment of $5,000 and deposit the $15,000 difference in a fixed annuity paying a market rate (e.g., 6.25% annually). This would increase the borrower's monthly payment to $730.47, but, over a period of time, the $15,000 fixed annuity accumulates at a compound interest which should offset the higher monthly payments. After 7 years, the cost of a regular mortgage with 20% paid down would amount to $71,660, while the asset integrated mortgage would show a net cost of only $58,120. Consider the example in Table 19.1.

SELLER FINANCING

When a seller is willing to accept part of the property's purchase price in the form of the buyer's promissory note accompanied by a mortgage or deed of trust, it is called **seller financing.** This allows the buyer to substitute a promissory note for cash, and the seller is said to be "taking back paper." Seller financing is

Table 19.1.

	Conventional Mortgage	Asset Integrated Mortgage
Cash down on house	$20,000	$5,000
Cash to annuity	-0-	$15,000
Loan amount	$80,000	$95,000
Monthly payments	$ 615	$ 730
Payments after 7 years	$51,660	$61,320
Initial cash down	$20,000	$20,000
Total cash outlay — 7 years	$71,660	$81,320
In 7 years the value of fixed annuity assuming a 6.25% rate annually	-0-	$23,200
Net amount paid after 7 years	$71,660	$58,120
Net after 25 years	$130,723	$113,274
Net after 30 years	$241,408	$184,632

popular for land sales (where lenders rarely loan), on property where an existing mortgage is being assumed by the buyer, and on property where the seller prefers to receive the money spread out over a period of time with interest instead of lump-sum cash. For example, a retired couple sells a rental home they own. The home is worth $120,000, and they owe $20,000. If they need only $60,000 in cash, they might be more than happy to take $60,000 down, let the buyer assume the existing mortgage, and accept the remaining $40,000 in monthly payments at current interest rates. Alternatively, the buyer and seller can agree to structure the $40,000 as an adjustable, graduated, partially amortized, or interest-only loan.

If the seller receives the sales price spread out over 2 or more years, income taxes are calculated using the installment reporting method discussed in Chapter 22. Being able to spread out the taxes on a gain may be an incentive to use seller financing. The seller should be aware, however, that the "paper" may not be convertible to cash without a long wait or without having to sell it at a substantial discount to an investor (although this can be remedied by a "balloon" provision). Additionally, the seller is responsible for servicing the loan and is subject to losses due to default and foreclosure.

Note that some real estate agents and lenders refer to a loan that is carried back by a seller as a **purchase money** loan. Others define a purchase money loan as any loan, carryback or institutional, that is used to finance the purchase of real property.

WRAPAROUND MORTGAGE

An alternative method of financing a real estate sale such as the one just reviewed is to use a **wraparound mortgage** or **wraparound deed of trust.** A *wraparound* encompasses existing mortgages and is subordinate (junior) to them. The existing mortgages stay on the property and the new mortgage wraps around them. Note Figure 19.5.

To illustrate, presume the existing $20,000 loan in the previous example carries an interest rate of 7% and that there are 10 years remaining on the loan. Presume further that current interest rates are 12%, and the current seller chooses to sell for $100,000. This is done by taking the buyer's $40,000 down payment and then creating a new junior mortgage (for $60,000) that includes not only the $20,000 owed on the existing first mortgage but also the $40,000 the buyer owes the seller. The seller continues to remain liable for payment of the first mortgage. If the interest rate on the wraparound is set at 10%, the buyer saves by not having to pay 12% as he would on an entirely new loan. The advantage to the seller is that she is earning 10%, not only on her $40,000 equity, but also on the $20,000 loan for which she is paying 7% interest. This gives the seller an actual yield of $11\frac{1}{2}\%$ on her $40,000. (The calculation is as follows. The seller receives 10% on $60,000, which amounts to $6,000. She pays 7% on $20,000, which is $1,400. The difference, $4,600, is divided by $40,000 to get the seller's actual yield of $11\frac{1}{2}\%$.) There is an additional point of concern. If the monthly payment on the underlying $20,000 debt includes taxes and insurance (PITI payment), the wraparound mortgage payment amount should also include taxes and insurance so that the monthly payment is sufficient to meet *all* of the underlying debt.

Wraparounds are not limited to seller financing. If the seller in the foregoing example did not want to finance the sale, a third-party lender could provide the needed $40,000 and take a

Figure 19.5.

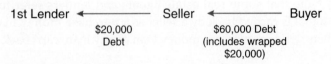

wraparound mortgage. The wraparound concept does not work when the underlying mortgage debt to be "wrapped" contains a due-on-sale clause. One other word of caution. If the seller defaults (and doesn't tell the buyer), the buyer may have an unwelcome surprise.

Another financing technique is **subordination.** For example, a person owns a $200,000 vacant lot suitable for building, and a builder wants to build an $800,000 building on the lot. The builder has only $100,000 cash and the largest construction loan available is $800,000. If the builder can convince the lot owner to take $100,000 in cash and $100,000 later, the buyer would have the $1 million total. However, the lender making the $800,000 loan will want to be the first mortgagee to protect its position in the event of foreclosure. The lot owner must be willing to take a subordinate position, in this case a second mortgage. If the project is successful, the lot owner will receive $100,000, plus interest, either in cash after the building is built and sold, or as monthly payments. If the project goes into foreclosure, the lot owner can be paid only if the $800,000 first mortgage claim is satisfied in full from the sale proceeds. As you can surmise here, the lot owner must be very careful that the money loaned by the lender actually goes into construction and that whatever is built is worth at least $800,000 in addition to the land.

SUBORDINATION

A **contract for deed,** also called an **installment contract** or **land contract,** enables the seller to finance a buyer by permitting him to make a down payment followed by monthly payments. However, title remains in the name of the seller. In addition to its wide use in financing land sales, it has also been a very effective financing tool in several states as a means of selling homes. For example, a homeowner owes $25,000 on his home and wants to sell it for $85,000. A buyer is found but does not have the $60,000 down payment necessary to assume the existing loan. The buyer does have $8,000, but for one reason or another cannot or chooses not to borrow from an institutional lender. If the seller is agreeable, the buyer can pay the seller $8,000 and enter into an installment contract with the seller for the remaining $77,000. The contract calls for monthly payments by the buyer to the seller that are large enough to allow the seller to meet the

CONTRACT
FOR DEED

payments on the $25,000 loan plus repay the $52,000 owed to the seller, with interest. Unless property taxes and insurance are billed to the buyer, the seller will also collect for these and pay them. When the final payment is made to the seller (or the property refinanced through an institutional lender), title is conveyed to the buyer. Meanwhile, the seller continues to hold title and is responsible for paying the mortgage. In addition to wrapping around a mortgage, an installment contract can also be used to wrap around another installment contract, provided it does not contain an enforceable due-on-sale clause. (Please see Chapter 9 for more about the contractual side of installment contracts.)

OPTION   When viewed as a financing tool, an **option** provides a method by which the need to finance the full price of a property immediately can be postponed. For example, a developer is offered 100 acres of land for a house subdivision but is not sure that the market will absorb that many houses. The solution is to buy 25 acres outright and take three 25-acre options at present prices on the remainder. If the houses on the first 25 acres sell promptly, the builder can exercise the options to buy the remaining land. If sales are not good, the builder can let the remaining options expire and avoid being stuck with unwanted acreage.

A popular variation on the option idea is the **lease with option to buy** combination. Under it, an owner leases to a tenant who, in addition to paying rent and using the property, also obtains the right to purchase it at a present price for a fixed period of time. Homes are often sold this way, particularly when the resale market is sluggish. (Please see Chapter 9 for more about a lease with option to buy.)

Options can provide speculative opportunities to persons with limited amounts of capital. If prices do not rise, the optionee loses only the cost of the option; if prices do rise, the optionee exercises the option and realizes a profit.

OVERLY CREATIVE   One seller-financing arrangement that deserves special attention
FINANCING?   because of its traps for the unwary is the **overencumbered property.** Institutional lenders are closely regulated regarding the amount of money they can loan against the appraised value of the property. Individuals are not regulated. The following illustrates the potential problem. Suppose a seller owns a house that

is realistically worth $100,000 and the mortgage balance is $10,000. A buyer offers to purchase the property, with the condition that he be allowed to obtain an $80,000 loan on the property from a lender. The $80,000 is used to pay off the existing $10,000 loan and to pay the broker's commission, loan fees, and closing costs. The remaining $62,000 is split $30,000 to the seller and $32,000 to the buyer. The buyer also gives the seller a note, secured by a second mortgage against the property, for $80,000. The seller may feel good about getting $30,000 in cash and an $80,000 mortgage, for this is more than the property is worth, or so it seems.

But the $80,000 second mortgage stands junior to the $80,000 first mortgage. That's $160,000 of debt against a $100,000 property. The buyer might be trying to resell the property for $160,000 or more, but the chances of this are slim. More likely the buyer will wind up walking away from the property. This leaves the seller the choice of taking over the payments on the first mortgage or losing the property completely to the holder of the first.

Although such a scheme sounds crazy when viewed from a distance, the reason it can be performed is that the seller wants more for the property than it's worth. Someone then offers a deal showing that price, and the seller looks the other way from the possible consequences. Real estate agents who participate in such transactions are likely to find their licenses suspended. State licensing authorities take the position that a real estate agent is a professional who should know enough not to take part in a deal that leaves the seller holding a junior lien on an overencumbered property. This, too, seems logical when viewed from a distance. But when sales are slow and commissions thin, it is sometimes easy to put commission income ahead of fiduciary responsibility. If in doubt about the propriety of a transaction, the Golden Rule of doing unto others as you would have them do unto you still applies. (Or, as some restate it: "What goes around, comes around.")

INVESTING IN MORTGAGES

Individuals can invest in mortgages in two ways. One is to invest in mortgage loan pools through certificates guaranteed by Ginnie Mae and Freddie Mac and available from stockbrokers. These yield about ½ of 1% below what FHA and VA borrowers are paying. In 1988, for example, this was approximately 10%, and the certificates are readily convertible to cash at current market prices on the open market if the investor does not want to hold them through maturity.

Individuals can also buy junior mortgages at yields above Ginnie Mae and Freddie Mac certificates. These junior mortgages are seconds, thirds, and fourths offered by mortgage brokers. They yield more because they are riskier as to repayment and much more difficult to convert to cash before maturity. "There is," as the wise old adage says, "no such thing as a free lunch." Thus, it is important to recognize that when an investment of any kind promises above-market returns, there is some kind of added risk attached. With junior mortgages, it is important to realize that when a borrower offers to pay a premium above the best loan rates available from banks and thrift institutions, it is because the borrower and/or the property does not qualify for the best rates.

Before buying a mortgage as an investment, one should have the title to the property searched. This is the only way to know for certain what priority the mortgage will have in the event of foreclosure. There have been cases where investors have purchased what they were told to be first and second mortgages only to find in foreclosure that they were actually holding third and fourth mortgages and the amount of debt exceeded the value of the property.

And how does one find the value of a property? By having it appraised by a professional appraiser who is independent of the party making or selling the mortgage investment. This value is compared to the existing and proposed debt against the property. The investor should also run a credit check on the borrower. The investor's final protection is, however, in making certain that the market value of the property is well in excess of the loans against it and that the property is well constructed, well located, and functional.

RENTAL   Even though tenants do not acquire fee ownership, **rentals** and **leases** are means of financing real estate. Whether the tenant is a bachelor receiving the use of a $30,000 apartment for which he pays $350 rent per month or a large corporation leasing a warehouse for 20 years, leasing is an ideal method of financing when the tenant does not want to buy, cannot raise the funds to buy, or prefers to invest available funds elsewhere. Similarly, **farm-**

ing leases provide for the use of land without the need to purchase it. Some farm leases call for fixed rental payment. Other leases require the farmer to pay the landowner a share of the value of the crop that is actually produced—say 25%—and the landowner shares with the farmer the risks of weather, crop output, and prices.

Under a **sale and leaseback** arrangement, an owner-occupant sells the property and then remains as a tenant. Thus, the buyer acquires an investment and the seller obtains capital for other purposes while retaining the use of the property. A variation is for the tenant to construct a building, sell it to a prearranged buyer, and immediately lease it back.

LAND LEASES

Although *leased land* arrangements are common throughout the United States for both commercial and industrial users and for farmers, anything other than fee ownership of residential land is unthinkable in many areas. Yet in some parts of the United States (for example, Baltimore, Maryland; Orange County, California; throughout Hawaii; and parts of Florida) homes built on leased land are commonplace. Typically, these leases are at least 55 years in length and, barring an agreement to the contrary, the improvements to the land become the property of the fee owner at the end of the lease. Rents may be fixed in advance for the life of the lease, renegotiated at present points during the life of the lease, or a combination of both.

To hedge against inflation, when fixed rents are used in a long-term lease, it is common practice to use **step-up rentals.** For example, under a 55-year house-lot lease, the rent may be set at $400 per year for the first 15 years, $600 per year for the next 10 years, $800 for the next 10 years, and so forth. An alternative is to renegotiate the rent at various points during the life of a lease so that the effects of land value changes are more closely equalized between the lessor and the lessee. For example, a 60-year lease may contain renegotiation points at the fifteenth, thirtieth, and forty-fifth years. At those points, the property would be reappraised and the lease rent adjusted to reflect any changes in the value of the property. Property taxes and any increases in property taxes are paid by the lessee.

FINANCING OVERVIEW

If people always paid cash for real estate, the last several chapters would not have been necessary. But 95% of the time they don't; so means have been devised to finance their purchases. This has been true since the beginning of recorded history and will continue into the future. The financing methods that evolve will depend on the problems to be solved. For example, long-term fixed-rate amortized loans were the solution to foreclosures in the 1930s, and they worked well as long as interest rates did not fluctuate greatly. Graduated payment loans were devised when housing prices rose faster than buyer's incomes. Adjustable rate loans were developed so that lenders could more closely align the interest they receive from borrowers with the interest they pay their savers. Extensive use of loan assumptions, wraparounds, and seller financing became necessary in the early 1980s because borrowers could not qualify for 16% and 18% loans and sellers were unwilling to drop prices.

With regard to the future, if mortgage money is expensive or in short supply, seller financing will play a large role. With the experience of rapidly fluctuating interest rates fresh in people's minds, loans with adjustable rates will continue to be widely offered. Fixed-rate loans will either have short maturities or carry a premium to compensate the lender for being locked into a fixed rate for a long period. When interest rates are low, borrowers with adjustable loans will benefit from lower monthly payments. If rates stay down long enough, fixed-rate loans will become more popular again.

VOCABULARY REVIEW

*Match terms **a–t** with statements **1–20**.*

a. *Adjustment period*
b. *Adjustable rate mortgage (ARM)*
c. *Blanket mortgage*
d. *Blended-rate loan*
e. *Buy-down mortgage*
f. *Carryback financing*
g. *Contract for deed*
h. *Equity mortgage*
i. *Equity sharing*
j. *Graduated payment mortgage*
k. *Interest rate cap*
l. *Negative amortization*
m. *Option*
n. *Overencumbered property*
o. *Package mortgage*
p. *Payment cap*
q. *Reverse mortgage*
r. *Sale and leaseback*
s. *Subordination*
t. *Wraparound mortgage*

1. The amount of time that elapses between interest rate changes on a loan.
2. A mortgage secured by two or more properties.

3. A mortgage secured by real and personal property.
4. To voluntarily give up a higher mortgage priority for a lower one.
5. A situation in which the loans against a property exceed the value of the property.
6. A financing arrangement whereby an owner-occupant sells the property and then remains as a tenant.
7. Results when monthly interest exceeds monthly payment and the difference is added to the principal.
8. A refinanced loan wherein the lender combines the interest rate of the existing loan with a current rate.
9. A mortgage wherein the lender extends a line of credit based on the amount of equity in a person's home.
10. A payment by the seller to the lender in order to reduce the interest rate for the buyer.
11. A loan wherein the lender makes monthly payments to the property owner who later repays in a lump sum.
12. The ceiling to which the interest rate on a loan can rise.
13. A limit on how much a borrower's payment can increase in any one year.
14. Acceptance by a seller of a note instead of cash.
15. An arrangement whereby a party providing financing gets a portion of the ownership.
16. A right, for a given period of time, to buy, sell, or lease property at preset price and terms.
17. A method of selling and financing property whereby the buyer obtains possession but the seller retains the title.
18. A mortgage loan on which the rate of interest can rise and fall with changes in prevailing interest rates.
19. A mortgage repayment plan that allows the borrower to make smaller monthly payments at first and larger ones later.
20. A debt instrument that encompasses existing mortgages and is subordinate to them.

QUESTIONS AND PROBLEMS

1. Regarding adjustable rate mortgage loans, what are the advantages and disadvantages to the borrower and lender?
2. What is an adjustable rate mortgage?
3. Explain why rentals and leases are considered forms of real estate financing.
4. What is the single most important precaution an investor can make before buying a junior mortgage?

ADDITIONAL READINGS

"The Consumer Handbook on Adjustable Rate and Mortgages." An educational brochure published by the federal government explaining ARM mortgages. It is available from most brokers who have an ARM loan program.

Handbook for Real Estate Market Analysis, by **J. Clapp** (Prentice Hall, 1987, 224 pages). Practical applications of real estate data collection and analysis.

Real Estate Finance, 7th Ed., by **John Wiedemer** (Prentice Hall, 1995, 320 pages). Includes sources of long-term mortgage money; financing instruments; loan procedures; FNMA, FHLMC, GNMA, FHA, and VA financing. Also includes loan analysis, carryback financing, and settlement procedures.

Real Estate Finance: A Practical Approach, by **Tom Morton** (Scott-Foresman, 1983, 407 pages). Includes information on creative financing, FHA, VA, FNMA, FHLMC loan guidelines, buyer qualification, and so on; includes glossary and appendices.

Residential Mortgage Lending, 3rd Ed., by **Marshall W. Dennis** (Prentice Hall, 1992, 416 pages). Explains residential mortgage lending, assuming no prior knowledge.

*   *   *

The following periodicals may also be of interest to you: *Freddie Mac Reports, Federal Reserve Bulletin, FHLBB News, Housing Finance, Housing Finance Review, National Savings and Loan League Journal, Real Estate Finance,* and *Real Estate Lenders Report.*

20

Fair Housing, ADA, Equal Credit, and Community Reinvestment

KEY • TERMS

Block busting: the illegal practice of inducing panic selling in a neighborhood for financial gain

Community Reinvestment Act: federal statute encouraging federally regulated lenders to increase their participation in low-income areas

Equal Credit Opportunity Act: federal law that provides for equal credit to borrowers

Familial status: one or more individuals under the age of 18 who are domiciled with a parent or other person having custody

Handicapped: having a physical or mental impairment that substantially limits one or more life activities, or having a record of such impairment

Human Rights Law: Article 15 of New York's Executive Law which enumerates unlawful discriminatory practices in New York

Jones v. **Mayer:** 1987 U.S. Supreme Court decision prohibiting without exception discrimination in housing based on race

Protected class: a class of people who by law are protected from discrimination

Steering: practice of directing home seekers to particular neighborhoods based on race, color, religion, sex, national origin, or handicapped or adults-only status

Tester: an individual or organization that responds to advertising and visits real estate offices to test for compliance with fair housing laws

It is almost impossible to explain fully the effects of federal legislation on real estate over the last 30 years. The scope and effect of the changes resulting from federal legislation is felt daily and has touched virtually every aspect of the real estate business. The federal government's emphasis on protection of individual rights was imposed because many states found this goal politically difficult to pursue and, in many cases, a long history of prejudice was an overwhelming obstacle.

FAIR HOUSING

Federal legislation has been liberally applied to virtually all areas of discrimination—race, color, creed, national origin, alienage, sex, marital status, age, familial status, and handicapped status. The theories supporting these federal laws are applied differently though, depending on the source of the law and enforcement of the applicable statute. Let's review these theories in greater detail.

CONSTITUTIONAL IMPACT ON OWNERSHIP OF REAL PROPERTY

The most fundamental rights in real property are obtained in the U.S. Constitution. These rights are so firmly established and so broadly affect real estate that they deserve discussion at the outset. The Declaration of Independence declared that all men are created equal and set the stage for an attitude of the government which we enjoy in the United States. With this forethought our founders wrote the United States Constitution which instilled in all citizens certain inalienable rights of which they can never be deprived. As far as real property ownership is concerned, the most significant of these rights are stated in the Fifth, Fourteenth, and Thirteenth Amendments to the Constitution.

The Fifth Amendment clearly states that no person shall "... be deprived of life, liberty, or property without due process of law, . . ." It was from this fundamental statement that we have developed the inherent right that nobody can have their property taken away without court proceedings. This concept has been expanded over the last 25 years or so to include the prohibition of certain types of discrimination, creating certain "protected classes" of people who may not be discriminated against.

To date, the types of discrimination that have been deemed "suspect" by the United States Supreme Court have included discrimination on the basis of race, color, religion, national origin, and alienage. This is logical in that a citizen of the United States cannot alter his race, color, national origin, or alienage, and is entitled to practice the religion of his choice. Therefore, very strict constitutional prohibitions have been established by the courts to eliminate this type of discrimination for any other citizen in the United States. It should be emphasized that there is no *constitutional* prohibition of discrimination on the basis of sex, age, or marital status.

One of the most significant areas of litigation has been based on racial discrimination. This has been applied to all federal activity through the Fifth Amendment, and to state and individual actions through enforcement of interpretation of the Thirteenth and Fourteenth Amendments to the Constitution.

The **Fourteenth Amendment** prohibits any state (as distinguished from the federal government) from depriving a person of life, liberty, or property without due process of law, and prohibits any state from denying any person within its jurisdiction the equal protection of the laws. The significant case in interpreting the Fourteenth Amendment as it applies to the states was *Shelley* v. *Kraemer.* In this Supreme Court case, some white property owners were attempting to enforce a deed restriction which required that all property owners must be Caucasian. The state courts granted the relief sought. The Supreme Court, however, reversed the case, stating that the action of state courts in imposing penalties deprived parties of other substantive rights without providing adequate notice. The opportunity to defend has long been regarded as a denial of due process of law as guaranteed by the Fourteenth Amendment. The court stated that equality and the enjoyment of property rights was regarded by the framers of the Fourteenth Amendment as an essential precondition to realization of other basic civil rights and liberties, which the Fourteenth Amendment was intended to guarantee. Therefore, it was concluded that the "equal protection" clause of the Fourteenth Amendment should prohibit the judicial enforcement by state courts of restrictive covenants based on race or color.

The **Thirteenth Amendment** to the United States Constitution prohibits slavery and involuntary servitude. This amendment formed the basis for the most significant landmark case on discrimination, *Jones* v. *Alfred H. Mayer Company.* That case basically held that any form of discrimination, even by individuals, creates a "badge of slavery," which, in turn, results in the violation of the Thirteenth Amendment. The Supreme Court stated that in enforcing the Civil Rights Act of 1866, Congress is empowered under the Thirteenth Amendment to secure to all citizens the right to buy whatever a white man can buy and the right to live wherever a white man can live. The court further stated, "If Congress cannot say that being a free man means at least this much, then the Thirteenth Amendment has a promise the Nation cannot keep." This case effectively prohibits discrimination of all types and is applicable to real estate transactions.

FAIR HOUSING LAWS

In addition to the constitutional issues, two major federal laws prohibit discrimination in housing. The first is the Civil Rights Act of 1866. It states that, "All citizens of the United States shall have the same right in every State and Territory, as is enjoyed by the white citizens thereof to inherit, purchase, lease, sell, hold, and convey real and personal property." In 1968, the Supreme Court affirmed that the 1866 act prohibits "all racial discrimination, private as well as public, in the sale of real property." The second is the **Fair Housing Law,** officially known as **Title VIII** of the Civil Rights Act of 1968, as amended. This law creates **protected classes** of people, making it illegal to discriminate on the basis of race, color, religion, sex, national origin, physical handicap, or familial status in connection with the sale or rental of housing and any vacant land offered for residential construction or use.

New Amendments

In 1988, the president signed a new amendment to the Civil Rights Act of 1968 which became effective on March 12, 1989. It expands the Civil Rights Act of 1968 to provide for housing for the handicapped as well as for people with children under the age of 18. The Civil Rights Act now provides protection for any form of discrimination based on race, color, religion, national origin, sex, *familial status,* or *handicapped status.* The new law's application may be very broad, and needs to be discussed in more detail.

Handicapped

The new amendment defines **handicapped** as:

1. having a physical or mental impairment that substantially limits one or more major life activities; or
2. having a record of having such an impairment; or
3. being regarded as having such an impairment.

The act apparently includes recovered mental patients as well as those who are presently suffering from a mental handicap.

The full extent of how the law barring discrimination against handicapped people will affect us is really not known. It is surely going to change our attitude about certain restrictions. It is assumed, for instance, that a blind person could live with a guide dog in a housing project that prohibits pets. The handicapped are also allowed to make reasonable modifications to existing units, as long as it is at the handicapped person's expense. The handicapped renter must also restore the unit to is original use upon termination of occupancy. The law also makes it unlawful for a landlord or owner to refuse to make reasonable accommodations, rules, policies, practices, or services when necessary to afford a handicapped person an equal opportunity to use and enjoy the dwelling. In addition, all new multifamily dwellings with four or more units must be constructed to allow access and use by handicapped persons. If the building has no elevators, only first floor units are covered by this provision. Doors and hallways in the buildings must be wide enough to accommodate wheelchairs. Light switches and other controls must be in convenient locations. Most rooms and spaces must be on an accessible route, and special accommodations such as grab bars in the bathrooms must be provided.

There are some exceptions under the handicapped person provision. The term *handicapped,* for instance, does not include current illegal use of or addiction to a controlled substance. Nor does handicapped status include any person whose tenancy imposes a direct threat to the health, safety, and property of others.

Since the statute was enacted, some cases have held that recovering drug addicts and alcoholics are handicapped, as are people infected with the HIV virus. Therefore, they cannot be discriminated against, and denial of housing as a result of these "handicaps" is a violation of the Fair Housing Act. This may result in unusual situations where recovering drug addicts (perhaps criminals) could be moving into a neighborhood and the neighbors are prohibited from discriminating against them or denying them housing (by enforcing deed restrictions or zoning ordinances) because it would have a discriminatory effect on the handicapped.

Familial Status   **Familial status** is defined as one or more individuals (who have not obtained the age of 18 years) being domiciled with a parent or another person having legal custody of such individual or individuals or the designee of such parent or other person having such custody, with the written permission of such parent or other person. These protections also apply to any person who is pregnant or is in the process of securing legal custody of any individual who has not obtained the age of 18 years.

The most significant effect of this amendment is that all homeowner association property, apartment projects, and condominiums now have to have facilities adapted for children and cannot discriminate against anyone on the basis of familial status when leasing, selling, or renting property.

There are specific exemptions to this portion of the act also. A building can qualify for an exemption if: (1) it provides housing under the state or federal program that the Secretary of Housing and Urban Development determines is specifically designed and operated to assist elderly persons; or (2) it provides housing intended for, and generally occupied only by, persons 62 years of age or older; or (3) it provides housing generally intended and operated for at least one person 55 years of age or older per unit and meets certain regulations which will be adopted by the Secretary of Housing and Urban Development.

The penalties for violation of the act are severe. The first violation of the act results in a fine of not more than $50,000, and for subsequent violations, a fine of not more than $100,000. The fines are in addition to other civil damages, potential injunctions, reasonable attorney's fees, and costs.

These new amendments to the Fair Housing Law have a significant impact for all licensees attempting to sell, list, lease, or rent real estate. It is now unlawful to refuse to sell or rent or to refuse to negotiate the sale or rental of any property based on familial status or handicapped status. Any printing and advertising material may not make any reference to a preference based on handicapped or familial status. As stated previously, the landlord cannot deny the right of a handicapped tenant to make any changes in the physical structure of the building provided that the tenant agrees to reinstate the building to its original form on leaving.

It is safe to say that many more situations and circumstances will occur that have not been specifically addressed by the statute. It is critically important that licensees recognize these two new prohibitions against discrimination and deem them just as serious violations of an individual's civil rights as are more traditional theories of race, color, religion, national origin, and sex.

Specifically, what do these two federal statutes prohibit, and what do they allow? The 1968 Fair Housing Law provides protection against the following acts if they discriminate against one or more of the **protected classes:**

1. Refusing to sell or rent to, deal or negotiate with any person;
2. Discriminating in the terms or conditions for buying or renting housing;
3. Discriminating by advertising that housing is available only to persons of a certain race, color, religion, sex, or national origin, those who are not handicapped, or adults only;
4. Denying that housing is available for inspection, sale, or rent when it really is available;
5. Denying or making different terms or conditions for home loans by commercial lenders;
6. Denying to anyone the use of or participation in any real estate services, such as brokers' organizations, multiple listing services, or other facilities related to the selling or renting of housing;
7. Steering or block busting.

Steering is the practice of directing home seekers to particular neighborhoods based on race, color, religion, sex, national origin, nonhandicapped status, or adult-only housing. Steering includes efforts to exclude minority members from one area of a city as well as to direct them to minority or changing areas. Examples include showing only certain neighborhoods, slanting property descriptions, and downgrading neighborhoods. Steering is often subtle, sometimes no more than a word, phrase, or facial expression. Nonetheless, steering accounts for the bulk of the complaints filed against real estate licensees under the Fair Housing Act.

Steering

Block busting is the illegal practice of inducing panic selling in a neighborhood for financial gain. Block busting typically starts

Block Busting

when one person induces another to sell a property cheaply by stating that an impending change in the racial or religious composition of the neighborhood will cause property values to fall, school quality to decline, and crime to increase. The first home thus acquired is sold (at a markup) to a minority member. This event is used to reinforce fears that the neighborhood is indeed changing. The process quickly snowballs as residents panic and sell at progressively lower prices. The homes are then resold at higher prices to incoming residents. Under New York law, when the Secretary of State believes that block busting is occurring in a community, he or she may issue a nonsolicitation order, which prohibits real estate agents from contacting residents in a designated area for the purpose of listing their property for sale. The Secretary of State may also issue a cease-and-desist order, designating an area in which homeowners who feel they are being harassed to sell can file a cease-and-desist notice with the Department of State. Both orders must carry an expiration date.

Note that block busting is not limited to fears over people moving into a neighborhood. In a Virginia case, a real estate firm attempted to gain listings in a certain neighborhood by playing on residents' fears regarding an upcoming expressway project.

Housing Covered by the 1968 Fair Housing Law

The 1968 Fair Housing Law applies to the following types of housing:

1. Single-family houses owned by private individuals when: (1) a real estate broker or other person in the business of selling or renting dwellings is used, and/or (2) discriminatory advertising is used;
2. Single-family houses not owned by private individuals;
3. Single-family houses owned by a private individual who owns more than three such houses or who, in any 2-year period, sells more than one in which the individual was not the most recent resident;
4. Multifamily dwellings of five or more units;
5. Multifamily dwellings containing four or fewer units, if the owner does not reside in one of the units.

Acts Not Prohibited by the 1968 Fair Housing Law

Not covered by the 1968 Fair Housing Law are the sale or rental of single-family houses owned by a private individual who owns three or fewer such single-family houses if: (1) a broker is not used, (2) discriminatory advertising is not used, and (3) no more than one house in which the owner was not the most recent resident is sold during any 2-year period. Not covered by the 1968 act are rentals of rooms or units in owner-occupied multi-dwellings for two to four families, if discriminatory advertising is not used. The act also does not cover the sale, rental, or occupancy of dwellings, which a religious organization owns or operates for other than a commercial purpose, to or by persons of the same religion, if membership in that religion is not restricted on account of race, color, or national origin. It also does not cover the rental or occupancy of lodgings that a private club owns or operates for its members for other than a commercial purpose. Housing for the elderly may also allow discrimination in not permitting children or young adult occupants in the development or building, provided that the housing is primarily intended for the elderly, has minimum age requirements (55 or 62), and meets certain HUD guidelines.

Note, however, that the listed acts *not* prohibited by the 1968 Fair Housing Law *are* prohibited by the 1866 Civil Rights Act when discrimination based on race occurs in connection with such acts.

There are three ways that adherence to the 1968 act can be enforced by someone who feels discriminated against. The first is to file a written complaint with the Department of Housing and Urban Development in Washington, D.C. The second is to file court action directly in a U.S. District Court or state or local court. The third is to file a complaint with the U.S. Attorney General. If a complaint is filed with HUD, HUD may investigate to see if the law has been broken; may attempt to resolve the problem by conference, conciliation, or persuasion; may refer the matter to a state or local fair housing authority; or may recommend that the complaint be filed in court. A person seeking enforcement of the 1866 act must file a suit in a federal court.

Fair Housing Enforcement

No matter which route is taken, the burden of proving illegal discrimination under the 1968 act is the responsibility of the person filing the complaint. If successful, the following remedies are available: (1) an injunction to stop the sale or rental of the property to someone else, making it available to the complainant; (2) money for actual damages caused by the discrimination; (3) punitive damages; and (4) court costs. There are also criminal penalties for those who coerce, intimidate, threaten, or interfere with a person's buying, renting, or selling of housing.

Agent's Duties

A real estate agent's duties are to uphold the 1968 Fair Housing Law and the 1866 Civil Rights Act. If a property owner asks an agent to discriminate, the agent must refuse to accept the listing. An agent is in violation of fair housing laws by giving minority buyers or sellers less than favorable treatment, by ignoring them, or by referring them to an agent of the same minority. Violation also occurs when an agent fails to use best efforts or does not submit an offer because of race, color, religion, sex, national origin, physical handicap, or occupancy by children.

Testers

From time to time a licensee may be approached by fair housing **testers.** These are individuals or organizations that respond to advertising and visit real estate offices to test for compliance with fair housing laws. The tester does not announce him- or herself as such or ask whether the office follows fair housing practices. Rather, the tester plays the role of a person looking for housing to buy or rent and observes whether or not fair housing laws are being followed. If not followed, the tester lodges a complaint with the appropriate fair housing agency.

New York Housing Law

New York State law prohibits discrimination on the same grounds as does federal law. The New York Human Rights Law found in Article 15 of the state's Executive Law prohibits discrimination in housing based on age and marital status. The state's Real Property Law also prohibits discrimination against families with children, pregnant women, or an adult who is in the process of seeking custody of a minor child. Unlike federal laws, the New York laws apply to commercial as well as residential real estate dealings. These laws do not apply to people who rent rooms in their own homes or to certain single-sex housing accommodations. Agents who sell, lease, or manage real estate, as well as the owners of the property, are bound by these antidiscrimination laws.

THE AMERICANS WITH DISABILITIES ACT

The **Americans with Disabilities Act (ADA)** was enacted on July 26, 1992, and deals primarily with commercial property. Generally stated, it provides access requirements and prohibits discrimination against people with disabilities in public accommodations, state and local government, transportation, telecommunications, and employment. Anyone who has had a physical or mental handicap, or who is "perceived" as having such, which interferes with a "major life activity" is covered by the Act.

The act specifically affects the real estate brokerage industry in that real estate licensees need to determine whether or not the product the licensee is selling, managing, or leasing is in compliance with the act. A licensee should always be cautioned, however, that the statute is very detailed, and there are a number of gray areas in the statute that still lack clear interpretation.

Scope

The antidiscrimination and the removal-of-barriers requirements of the ADA apply to "places of public accommodations." The accessibility requirements of the ADA with respect to new construction and alterations apply to public accommodations and "commercial facilities."

Places of public accommodations encompasses 12 categories of retail and service businesses, including places of lodging; food and drink establishments; places of exhibitionary entertainment; places of public gathering; sales and rental establishments; service establishments such as law firms, accounting firms, and banks; public transportation stations; places of public display or collection; places of recreation; educational facilities; social service center establishments; and exercise clubs. It is presumed that this definition includes brokerage offices, even if they are located in private homes.

Commercial facility is defined as a facility: (1) whose operations affect commerce; (2) that is intended for nonresidential use; and (3) that is not a facility expressly exempted from coverage under the Fair Housing Act of 1968.

The ADA broadly prohibits discriminating against those with disabilities by denying them the full and equal enjoyment of goods, services, facilities, privileges, advantages, and the accommodations of any place of public accommodation. Facilities need to be usable by those with disabilities.

All commercial facilities must also be accessible to the maximum extent feasible whenever alterations are being performed on the facility. Alteration is defined as any change that affects the usability of a facility. If the alterations are made to a lobby or work area of the public accommodation, a path of travel to the altered area and to the bathrooms, telephones, and drinking fountains serving that area must be made accessible to the extent that the added accessibility costs are not disproportionate to the overall cost of the original alteration. Disproportionate cost is defined for purposes of the act as cost that exceeds 20% of the original alteration. The cost of alteration means all costs and renovating in particular proportion to the facility in a 3-year period.

The act requires modifications to procedures so that disabled individuals are not excluded from regular programs. Places of public accommodations must make reasonable modifications to the policies and procedures in order to accommodate individuals with disabilities and not create restrictions that tend to screen out individuals with disabilities, such as requiring a person to produce a driver's license or not allowing more than one person in a clothes changing area when a disabled person needs the assistance of another. The act also requires auxiliary aids and services to ensure effective communication with individuals with hearing, vision, or speech impairments. These requirements would include interpreters, listening headsets, television closed caption decoders, telecommunication devices for the deaf, video tech displays, braille materials, and large print materials.

Several defenses and exclusions are available under the act, but most are extremely narrow in scope. In addition, there are few court precedents to help us with interpretation of the Americans with Disabilities Act. Problems in compliance will occur. For example, if a water fountain is placed low enough for someone in a wheelchair to use, what happens to the tall person who has difficulty in bending? Lowering a fire extinguisher for easier access to the person in the wheelchair also gives easier access to small children. Something that is "child proof" will also be inaccessible to someone with limited use of their hands.

Both the Department of Justice and private individuals may maintain a cause of action to enforce Title III against commercial building owners. The Department may seek monetary damages or injunctive relief, but private individuals are entitled only to seek injunctive relief under the statute. Apparently a tort claim may create a cause of action for monetary damages.

The **Equal Credit Opportunity Act** was originally passed to provide for equal credit for borrowers by making it unlawful to discriminate against an applicant for credit based on sex or marital status. In 1976, the act was amended to prohibit discrimination in any credit transaction based on race, color, religion, national origin, age (not including minors), receipt of income from a public assistance program, and the good faith exercise of rights under the Consumer Credit Protection Act.

EQUAL CREDIT OPPORTUNITY ACT

To effect this prohibition on discrimination, a creditor is prohibited from requiring certain information from the borrower:

Prohibited Requests

1. Information concerning a spouse or former spouse, except when that spouse will be contractually obligated for repayment or if the spouse resides in a community property state;
2. Information regarding the applicant's marital status unless the credit requested is for an individual's unsecured account, or unless the applicant resides in a community property state and the community property is to be relied on to repay the credit. Inquiries as to the applicant's marital status are limited, however, to categories of "married," "unmarried," and "separated." "Unmarried" includes single, divorced, and widowed persons and may be specified in the application.
3. Information concerning the source of an applicant's income without disclosing that information regarding alimony, child support, or separate maintenance is to be furnished only at the option of the applicant. The big exception to the rule is when the applicant expects to use any of those sources of income for repayment. If so, the lender may request this information.
4. Information regarding an applicant's birth control practices or any intentions concerning the bearing or rearing of children, although a lender still has the right to ask an applicant about the number and ages of any dependents or about dependent-related financial obligations.
5. Questions regarding race, color, religion, or national origin of the applicant.

There are minor exceptions when a real estate loan is involved. These exceptions are allowed in order to provide certain information that may be used by the federal government for the purposes of monitoring conformance with the Equal Credit Opportunity Act. When the information is requested, the lender is required to advise the applicants that the furnishing of the specific information is for purposes of monitoring the lender's compliance and is requested on a voluntary basis only. If the applicant does not wish to answer the questions, the lender simply notes the refusal on the application form. The refusal to give the information requested cannot be used in any way in considering whether or not credit is granted to the applicant. If the applicant agrees to provide the information on a voluntary basis, the following information can be furnished:

1. Race or national origin;
2. Sex, relating to gender only (not sexual preference);
3. Marital status (using the categories of married, unmarried, or separated).

When considering race and national origin only the following categories can be used: American Indian or Alaskan Native, Asian or Pacific Islander, Black, White, Hispanic, or "other."

Evaluating Credit Applications

As previously stated, the lender cannot use information obtained from an applicant that might be considered to be discriminatory. Each applicant has to be evaluated on the same basic information as any other individual person. Lenders can't refuse credit based on individual category, such as newlyweds, recent divorcees, and so on. The lender's rules must be applied uniformly to all applicants. The areas in which there can be no discrimination have already been discussed (sex, marital status, race, color, religion, national origin, age, public assistance) but some of these areas need to be discussed in greater detail.

Age

A lender is prohibited from taking an applicant's age into account in determining ability to repay. Neither can income from any public assistance program be taken into account. The only exception to this prohibition is minors, who lack contractual capacity and cannot enter into real estate transactions.

Children

As discussed in the previous sections on fair housing, the Equal Credit Opportunity Act has always provided that there can be no assumptions or statistics relating to the likelihood that a group of persons may bear children. In prior years, lenders required nonpregnancy affidavits and other indications that a young newly married couple would not endanger the income-producing capacity of the wife.

Income from part-time employment or retirement income cannot be discounted because of the basis of its source. However, the creditor may still consider the amount and probability of continuance of such income.

Part-Time Income

Alimony and child support and separate maintenance cannot be considered in evaluating a loan application unless the creditor determines that such payments are not likely to be made consistently. In such cases the lender has the right to determine whether or not the applicant has the ability to compel payment and the creditworthiness of the party who is obligated to make such payments.

Alimony and Child Support

The Equal Credit Opportunity Act requires a creditor to consider the separate record of the applicant. This prohibits the lender from tying the applicant's credit history to the past record of the spouse or former spouse.

Credit History

A creditor may consider an applicant's immigration status and whether or not he or she is a permanent resident of the United States.

Immigration Residency

If an applicant is denied credit the lender must give notice to the applicant and advise the rejected applicant of the federal agency that administers compliance with the Equal Credit Opportunity Act for that particular loan transaction. The statement of specific reasons must give the precise reason or reasons for the denial of credit. There are suggested guidelines for giving reasons for credit denial, including:

Credit Denial

1. unable to verify credit references;
2. temporary or irregular employment;
3. insufficient length of employment;
4. insufficient income;
5. excessive obligations;
6. inadequate collateral;
7. too short a period of residency;
8. delinquent credit obligation.

Failure to comply with the Equal Credit Opportunity Act or the accompanying federal regulations makes a creditor subject to a

Penalties

civil liability for damages limited to $10,000 in individual actions and the lesser of $500,000 or 1% of the creditor's net worth in class actions. The court may also award court costs and reasonable attorney's fees to an aggrieved applicant.

COMMUNITY REINVESTMENT ACT

The Housing and Community Redevelopment Act of 1977 took effect on November 6, 1978. The **Community Reinvestment Act (CRA)** expands the concept that regulated financial institutions must serve the needs of their communities. Whenever a financing institution regulated by the federal government applies for a charter, branch facility, office relocation, or acquisition of another financing institution, the record of the institution's help in meeting local credit needs must be one of the factors considered by the Federal Home Loan Bank Board.

The basic requirements of the Community Reinvestment Act for any institution applying for recognition are the following:

1. The institution must define its community by drawing a map that shows the areas served by the lender. This is essentially the area in which it does business and may overlap the area of another institution.
2. The institution must submit a list of types of credit it offers in that community. This list must also be made available to the public. The decision as to what types of loans an institution makes is still left to the institution, but the information must be made available to the public.
3. The lender must provide notice in its lobby that its performance is being evaluated by federal regulators. The notice must advise that a CRA statement and a File of Public Comments are available.

CRA Statement

The CRA Statement, which must be made available to the public as well as the federal regulators, contains both mandatory and optional information. The mandatory information consists of the following:

1. A map of the lender's definition of its community;
2. A list of credit services it offers;
3. A copy of the public notice; and
4. A File of Public Comments received in the past 2 years that relate to the CRA Statement.

The optional information that should be contained in the CRA Statement consists of:

1. A description of how current efforts help meet community needs and standards;
2. A periodic report of the institution's record in helping to meet community credit needs; and
3. A description of efforts made to ascertain credit needs of the community.

Part of the enforcement procedure of the Community Reinvestment Act calls for open hearings to be held on an application for a branch or any other internal expansions, should a protest be lodged against that expansion. Anyone may be asked to be placed on the list for notification of all pending applications. The federal regulating authority must determine whether or not a protest is "substantial" and could therefore justify a hearing within 10 days of the protest filing.

The Federal Home Loan Bank Board (FHLBB) has listed the following guidelines that various federal examiners look for when assessing CRA performances. Three major areas that require examination fall under Section 563e.7 of the Insurance of Accounts Regulations and are numbered (b), (h), and (j) of the Community Reinvestment Act.

FHLBB Guidelines

Subsection (b) concerns the extent of the institution's marketing and special credit-related programs to make members of the community aware of the credit services offered by the institution, such as public seminars, direct mailings or media campaigns, foreign language advertising, financial counseling, cooperative efforts with local governments or community groups seeking code compliance, and technical assistance for revitalization of their neighborhoods. Subsection (h) deals with the institution's participation including investments and local community development or redevelopment projects or programs. This includes HUD programs, economic development strategies, neighborhood reinvestment corporations, and neighborhood preservation projects.

Subsection (j) relates to the institution's participation in government insured, guaranteed, or subsidized loan programs for housing, small businesses, or small farms. This includes the lending institution's participation in government HUD programs, Veterans Administration programs, Department of Agriculture programs for rural housing loans guaranteed by the Farmer's Home Administration, or Small Business Administration loans. Other participation that can help to satisfy in both Subsections (h) and (j) involve community development block grants established by HUD. Housing finance agency development, rehabilitation, or home improvement programs for lower and moderate income residents are local development company loan programs.

Minorities   Most statutes and constitutions prohibit discrimination against **minorities.** Minorities are defined as any group, or any member of a group that can be identified either: (1) by race, color, religion, sex, or national origin; or (2) by any other characteristic on the basis of which discrimination is prohibited by federal, state, or local fair housing law. A *minority* group is not always a small group; the term refers to any group that can be distinguished in a particular situation from some other group on a basis of race, sex, national origin, or so forth. It has nothing to do with numbers or size of the group. Whenever whites are discriminated against, they too are a minority group.

It is very difficult to ascertain what impact the Community Reinvestment Act will have on lending institutions and practices of lenders generally. Many areas of the statute are vague, and it is difficult for the federal regulators to establish hard and fast rules because of the variety of different needs the lending institutions generally serve in different communities. As with a lot of other federal legislation, it may take some time before the full impact of this act is felt.

VOCABULARY REVIEW

Match terms **a–m** *with statements* **1–13.**

a. *American with Disabilities Act (ADA)*
b. *Block busting*
c. *Community Reinvestment Act (CRA)*
d. *Equal Credit Opportunity Act*
e. *Fair Housing Law*
f. *Familial status*
g. *Fourteenth Amendment*
h. *Handicapped*
i. *Minority*
j. *Steering*
k. *Tester*
l. *Thirteenth Amendment*
m. *Title VIII*

1. Applies federal prohibitions under the Bill of Rights to the state.
2. Federal fair housing law under the Civil Rights Act of 1968.
3. One or more individuals being domiciled with a parent or another person having legal custody of such individual.
4. Any group or member of a group that can be identified by race, color, religion, sex, or national origin.
5. The illegal practice of inducing panic selling in a neighborhood for financial gain.
6. The act of directing any group away from or to an integrated or minority neighborhood.
7. Having a physical or mental impairment that substantially limits one or more major life activities.
8. Law applying to single-family housing utilizing the services of a real estate broker.
9. The "badge of slavery" violates this constitutional amendment.
10. Federal statute requiring accessibility for commercial premises.
11. Federal statute prohibiting discrimination in lending practices.
12. Federal statute prohibiting discrimination in credit transactions.
13. An individual posing as a potential purchaser to determine whether or not discrimination exists in a real estate transaction.

QUESTIONS AND PROBLEMS

1. Can you refuse to sell a home to a person because he or she is a lawyer?
2. What is the difference between prohibitions under the United States Constitution and prohibitions under the civil rights statutes?
3. What has your local lender done to comply with the Community Reinvestment Act?
4. Why would the federal statutes designate brokerage services as a method of enforcing fair housing?
5. Can I discriminate against white Anglo-Saxon Protestants?
6. Have you ever been discriminated against? Please explain.
7. Can I direct a potential home purchaser to a neighborhood that I feel is "safer?" Please note that behavior is more important than feelings.

ADDITIONAL READINGS

"Community Reinvestment Offers Economic Alternative: Alternative Sources of Investment Capital Have Helped Stabilize Neighborhoods, Preserve Existing Jobs, and Create New Opportunities," by **Frank Altman** (*American City and County,* November 1992, pp. 58–60).

"Don't Discriminate: What Every Realtor Should Know about Fair Housing," by **Christine Olson** (*Texas Realtor,* March/April 1994, pp. 8–14). Article discusses brokers' liability and fairness to the handicapped.

Fair Housing Compliance: A Quick Reference for Real Estate Brokers and Agents, 3rd Ed. (National Association of REALTORS®, 47 pages). Gives a quick, easy-to-understand overview of fair housing.

Fair Housing, Fair Lending (Prentice Hall, 1992, 2 vols.). Provides information about laws and regulation, housing for the handicapped, age discrimination in lending, and current legislation.

21

Real Estate Appraisal

KEY • TERMS

Appraisal: an estimate of the value of something

Capitalize: to convert future income to current value

Comparables: properties that have sold recently that are similar to the subject property

Cost approach: land value plus current construction costs minus depreciation

Depreciation: loss in value due to deterioration and obsolescence

FIRREA: the Financial Institutions Reform, Recovery, and Enforcement Act of 1989

Gross rent multiplier (GRM): a number that is multiplied by a property's gross rents to produce an estimate of the property's worth

Highest and best use: that use of a parcel of land which will produce the greatest current value

Income approach: a method of valuing a property based on the monetary returns it can be expected to produce

Market approach: a method of valuing property based on recent sales of similar properties

Market value: the cash price that a willing buyer and a willing seller would agree on, given reasonable exposure of the property to the marketplace, full information as to the potential uses of the property, and no undue compulsion to act

Operating expenses: expenditures necessary to maintain the production of income

Scheduled gross, Projected gross: the estimated rent a fully occupied property can be expected to produce on an annual basis

State Board of Real Estate Appraisal: a board within the Department of State that oversees appraiser licensure and certification

USPAP: the Uniform Standards of Professional Appraisal Practice

PURPOSE AND USE OF APPRAISALS

An **appraisal** is a necessary part of most real estate transactions. Often the decision to buy, sell, or grant a loan on real estate hinges on a real estate appraiser's estimate of property value. Appraisals are also used to set prices on property listed for sale and to set premiums on fire insurance policies; they are used by government to acquire and manage public property and to establish property tax levels for taxpayers.

To *appraise* real estate means to estimate its value. Thus, an **informal appraisal** can be defined simply as an estimate of value. But a **formal appraisal** is more accurately defined as "an independently and impartially prepared written statement expressing an opinion of a defined value of an adequately described property as of a specific date, that is supported by the presentation and analysis of relevant market information."

THE REAL PROPERTY VALUATION PROCESS

The **valuation** process is the step-by-step procedure that appraisers use to conduct their work. The conventions for this process have been developed over a period of many years. However, this system has been refined and modified in recent years by the **Uniform Standards of Professional Appraisal Practice (USPAP).**

Following the guidelines of USPAP, the valuation process involves the following steps: (1) defining the appraisal problem; (2) conducting a preliminary analysis, formulating an appraisal plan, and collecting the data; (3) estimating the highest and best use of the land as if vacant, and the property as improved; (4) estimating land value; (5) estimating the improved property value through the appropriate value approaches; (6) reconciling the results to arrive at a defined value estimate; and (7) reporting the conclusion of value.

VALUE APPROACHES

The estimate can be made using any one of three approaches. The first approach involves locating similar properties that have sold recently and using them as benchmarks in estimating the value of the property being appraised. This is the **market approach,** also called the **market data approach** or **market comparison approach.** The second approach requires the appraiser to add together the cost of the individual components that make up the property being appraised. This is the **cost approach;** it starts with the cost of a similar parcel of vacant land and adds the cost of the lumber, concrete, plumbing, wiring, labor, and so on necessary to build a similar building. Depreciation is then subtracted. The third approach is to consider only the amount of net income that the property can reasonably be expected to produce for its owner plus any anticipated price increase or decrease. This is the **income approach.** For the person who owns or plans to own real estate, knowing how much a property is worth is a crucial part of the buying or selling decision. For the real estate agent, being able to estimate the value of a property is an essential part of taking a listing and conducting negotiations.

In this chapter you will see demonstrations of the market, cost, and income approaches and how they are used in determining market value. **Market value,** also called **fair market value,** is the most probable price that a property should bring in a competitive and open market under all conditions requisite to a fair sale, the buyer and seller each acting prudently, knowledgeably, and assuming the price is not affected by undue stimulus.

MARKET VALUE DEFINED

   This definition implies the consummation of a sale at a specified date, and the passing of title from seller to buyer under conditions whereby: (1) buyer and seller are typically motivated; (2) both parties are well informed or well advised, and each acting in what he or she considers his or her own best interest; (3) a reasonable time is allowed for exposure in the open market; (4) payment is made in terms of cash in U.S. dollars or in terms of financial arrangements comparable thereto; and (5) the price represents the normal consideration for the property sold, unaffected by special or creative financing or sales concessions granted by anyone associated with the sale. Market value is at the heart of nearly all real estate transactions.

Let's begin by demonstrating the application of the **market comparison approach** to a single-family residence. The residence to be appraised is called the **subject property** and is described as follows:

MARKET COMPARISON APPROACH

   The subject property is a one-story, wood-frame house of 1,520 square feet containing three bedrooms, two bathrooms, a living room, dining room, kitchen, and utility room. There is a two-car garage with concrete driveway to the street, a 300-square-foot concrete patio in the backyard, and an average amount of landscaping. The house is located on a 10,200-square-foot, level lot that measures 85 by 120 feet. The house is 12 years old, in good repair, and located in a well-maintained neighborhood of houses of similar construction and age.

Comparables

After becoming familiar with the physical features and amenities of the subject property, the next step in the market approach is to locate houses with similar physical features and amenities that have sold recently under market value conditions. These are known as **comparables** or "comps." The more similar they are to the subject property, the fewer and smaller the adjustments that must be made in the comparison process, and hence the less room for error. As a rule, it is best to use comparable sales no more than 6 months old. During periods of relatively stable prices, this can be extended to 1 year. However, during periods of rapidly changing prices even a sale 6 months old may be out of date.

Sales Records

To apply the market comparison approach, the following information must be collected for each comparable sale: date of sale, sales price, financing terms, location of the property, and a description of its physical characteristics and amenities. Recorded deeds at public records offices can provide dates and locations of recent sales. Although a deed seldom states the purchase price, nearly all states levy a deed transfer fee or conveyance tax, the amount of which is shown on the recorded deed. This tax can sometimes provide a clue as to the purchase price if the appraiser determines the amount of tax paid and divides it by the applicable tax rate.

Records of past sales can often be obtained from title and abstract companies. Property tax assessors keep records on changes in ownership as well as property values. Where these records are kept up to date and are available to the public, they can provide information on what has sold recently and for how much. Assessors also keep detailed records of improvements made to land. This can be quite helpful in making adjustments between the subject property and the comparables. For real estate salespeople, locally operated multiple listing services provide asking prices and descriptions of properties currently offered for sale by member brokers along with descriptions, sales prices, and dates for properties that have been sold. In some cities, commercially operated financial services publish information on local real estate transactions and sell it on a subscription basis.

To produce the most accurate appraisal possible, each sale used as a comparable should be inspected and the price and terms verified. An agent who specializes in a given neighborhood will have already visited the comparables when they were still for sale. The agent can verify price and terms with the selling broker or from multiple listing service sales records.

Verification

Three to five comparables usually provide enough basis for reliable comparison. To use more than five, the additional accuracy must be weighed against the extra effort involved. When the supply of comparable sales is more than adequate, one should choose the sales that require the fewest adjustments.

Number of Comparables

It is also important that the comparables selected represent current market conditions. Sales between relatives or close friends may result in an advantageous price to the buyer or seller, and sales prices that for some other reason appear to be out of line with the general market should not be used. Listings and offers to buy should not be used in place of actual sales. They do not represent a meeting of minds between a buyer and a seller. Listing prices indicate the upper limit of prices, whereas offers to buy indicate lower limits. Thus, if a property is listed for sale at $80,000 and offers have been made as high as $76,000, it is reasonable to presume the market price lies somewhere between $76,000 and $80,000.

Let us now work through the example shown in Table 21.1 to demonstrate the application of the market comparison approach to a house. We begin at lines 1 and 2 by entering the address and sale price of each comparable property. For convenience, we refer to these as comparables A, B, and C. On lines 3 through 10, we make time adjustments to the sale price of each comparable to make it equivalent to the subject property today. **Adjustments** are made for price changes since each comparable was sold, as well as for differences in physical features, amenities, and financial terms. The result indicates the market value of the subject property.

Adjustment Process

Table 21.1. Valuing a House by the Market Comparison Approach

Line	Item	Comparable Sale A		Comparable Sale B		Comparable Sale C	
1	Address	1702 Brookside Ave.		1912 Brookside Ave.		1501 18th Street	
2	Sale price	$91,800		$88,000		$89,000	
3	Time adjustment	sold 6 mos. ago, add 2%	+1,836	sold 3 mos. ago, add 1%	+918	just sold	0
4	House size	160 sq ft larger at $55 per sq ft	−8,800	20 sq ft smaller at $55/sq ft	+1,100	same size	0
5	Garage/carport	carport	+4,000	3-car garage	−2,000	2-car garage	0
6	Other	larger patio	−900	no patio	+1,800	built-in bookcases	−2,000
7	Age, upkeep, & overall quality of house	superior	−2,000	inferior	+1,200	equal	0
8	Landscaping	inferior	+1,000	equal	0	superior	−700
9	Lot size, features, & location	superior	−3,890	inferior	+900	equal	0
10	Terms & conditions of sale	equal	0	special financing	−1,500	equal	0
11	Total adjustments	−8,754		+2,418		−2,700	
12	ADJUSTED MARKET PRICE	$83,046		$90,418		$86,300	
13	Correlation process:						
	Comparable A $83,046 × 20% = $16,609						
	Comparable B $90,418 × 30% = $27,125						
	Comparable C $86,300 × 50% = $43,150						
14	INDICATED VALUE	$86,884					
	Round to	$86,900					

Time Adjustments

Returning to line 3 in Table 21.1, let us assume that house prices in the neighborhood where the subject property and comparables are located have risen 2% during the 6 months that have elapsed since comparable A was sold. If it were for sale today, comparable A would bring 2% or $1,836 more. Therefore, we must add $1,836 to bring it up to the present. Comparable B was sold 3 months ago, and to bring it up to the present we need to add 1% or $918 to its sales price. Comparable C was just sold and needs no time correction as its price reflects today's market.

When using the market comparison approach, all adjustments are made to the comparable properties, not to the subject property. This is because we cannot adjust the value of something for which we do not yet know the value.

House Size

Because house A is 160 square feet larger than the subject house, it is logical to expect that the subject property would sell for less money. Hence a deduction is made from the sales price of comparable A on line 4. The amount of this deduction could be based on the difference in floor area and the current cost of similar construction, minus an allowance for depreciation. It could also be determined by various market conditions, if comparable information is available. If we value the extra 160 square feet at $55 per square foot, we must subtract $8,800. For comparable B, the house is 20 square feet smaller than the subject house. At $55 per square foot, we add $1,100 to comparable B, as it is reasonable to expect that the subject property would sell for that much more because it is that much larger. Comparable C is the same-sized house as the subject property, so no adjustment is needed.

Garage and Patio Adjustments

Next, the parking facilities (line 5) are adjusted. We first look at the current cost of garage and carport construction and the condition of these structures. Assume that the value of a carport is $2,000; a one-car garage, $4,000; a two-car garage, $6,000; and a three-car garage, $8,000. Adjustments would be made as follows. The subject property has a two-car garage worth $6,000 and comparable A has a carport worth $2,000. Therefore, based on the difference in garage facilities, we can reasonably expect the subject property to command $4,000 more than comparable A. By adding $4,000 to comparable A, we effectively equalize this difference. Comparable B has a garage worth $2,000 more than the subject property's garage. Therefore, $2,000 must be subtracted from comparable B to equalize it with the subject property. For comparable C, no adjustment is required, as comparable C and the subject property have similar garage facilities.

At line 6, the subject property has a 300-square-foot patio in the backyard worth $1,800. Comparable A has a patio worth $2,700; therefore, $900 is deducted from comparable A's selling price. Comparable B has no patio. As it would have sold for

$1,800 more if it had one, a +$1,800 adjustment is required. The patio at comparable C is the same as the subject property's. However, comparable C has $2,000 worth of custom built-in living room bookcases that the subject property does not have. Therefore, $2,000 is subtracted from comparable C's sales price. Any other differences between the comparables and the subject property such as swimming pools, fireplaces, carpeting, drapes, roofing materials, and kitchen appliances would be adjusted in a similar manner.

Building Age,
Condition, and Quality

On line 7, we recognize differences in building age, wear and tear, construction quality, and design usefulness. Where the difference between the subject property and a comparable can be measured in terms of material and labor, the adjustment is the cost of that material and labor. For example, the $1,200 adjustment for comparable B reflects the cost of needed roof repair at the time B was sold. The adjustment of $2,000 for comparable A reflects the fact it has better-quality plumbing and electrical fixtures than the subject property. Differences that cannot be quantified in terms of labor and materials are usually dealt with as lump-sum judgments. Thus, one might allow $1,000 for each year of age difference between the subject and a comparable, or make a lump-sum adjustment of $2,000 for an inconvenient kitchen design.

Keep in mind that adjustments are made on the basis of what each comparable property was like on the day it was sold. Thus, if an extra bedroom was added or the house was painted after its sale date, these items are not included in the adjustment process.

Landscaping

Line 8 shows the landscaping at comparable A to be inferior to the subject property. A positive correction is necessary here to equalize it with the subject. The landscaping at comparable B is similar and requires no correction; that at comparable C is better and thus requires a negative adjustment. The dollar amount of each adjustment is based on the market value of lawn, bushes, trees, and the like.

Lot Features and
Location

Line 9 deals with any differences in lot size, slope, view, and neighborhood. In this example, all comparables are in the same neighborhood as the subject property, thus eliminating the need to judge, in dollar terms, the relative merit of one neighborhood over another. However, comparable A has a slightly larger lot and a better view than the subject property. Based on recent lot sales in the area, the difference is judged to be $890 for the larger lot and $3,000 for the better view. Comparable B has a slightly smaller lot judged to be worth $900 less, and comparable C is similar in all respects.

Line 10 in Table 21.1 accounts for differences in financing. As a rule, the more accommodating the terms of the sale to the buyer, the higher the sales price, and vice versa. We are looking for the highest cash price the subject property may reasonably be expected to bring, given adequate exposure to the marketplace and a knowledgeable buyer and seller not under undue pressure. If the comparables were sold under these conditions, no corrections would be needed in this category. However, if it can be determined that a comparable was sold under different conditions, an adjustment is necessary. For example, if the going rate of interest on home mortgages is 12% per year and the seller offers to finance the buyer at 9% interest, it is reasonable to expect that the seller can charge a higher selling price. Similarly, a seller who has a low-interest loan that can be assumed by the buyer can get a higher price. Favorable financing terms offered by the seller of comparable B enabled him or her to obtain an extra $1,500 in selling price. Therefore, we must subtract $1,500 from comparable B. Another situation that requires an adjustment on line 10 is if a comparable was sold on a rush basis. If a seller is in a hurry to sell, a lower selling price usually must be accepted than if the property can be given more time in the marketplace.

Terms and Conditions of Sale

Adjustments for each comparable are totaled and either added or subtracted from its sale price. The result is the **adjusted market price** shown at line 12. This is the dollar value of each comparable sale after it has gone through an adjustment process to make it the same as the subject property. If it were possible to evaluate precisely every adjustment, and if the buyers of comparables A, B, and C had paid exactly what their properties were worth at the time they purchased them, the three prices shown on line 12 would be the same. However, buyers are not that precise, particularly in purchasing a home where amenity value

Adjusted Market Price

influences price and varies considerably from one person to the next.

Reconciliation

While comparing the properties, it usually becomes apparent that some comparables are more like the subject property than others. The **reconciliation** process gives the appraiser the opportunity to assign more weight to the more similar comparables and less to the others. A mathematical weighting is one available technique. At line 13, comparable C is given a weight of 50% since it is more like the subject and required fewer adjustments. Moreover, this sameness is in areas where adjustments tend to be the hardest to estimate accurately: time, age, quality, location, view, and financial conditions. Of the remaining two comparables, comparable B is weighted slightly higher than comparable A because it is a more recent sale and required fewer adjustments overall.

In the correlation process, the adjusted market price of each comparable is multiplied by its weighting factor and totaled at line 14. The result is the **indicated value** of the subject property. It is customary to round off to the nearest $50 or $100 for properties under $10,000; to the nearest $250 or $500 for properties between $10,000 and $100,000; to the nearest $1,000 or $2,500 for properties between $100,000 and $250,000; and to the nearest $2,500 or $5,000 above that.

Unique Issues
Condominium,
Townhouse, and
Cooperative Appraisal

The process for estimating the market value of a condominium, townhouse, or cooperative living unit by the market approach is similar to the process for houses except that fewer steps are involved. For example, in a condominium complex with a large number of two-bedroom units of identical floor plan, data on a sufficient number of comparable sales may be available within the building. This would eliminate adjustments for differences in unit floor plan, neighborhood, lot size and features, age and upkeep of the building, and landscaping. The only corrections needed would be those that make one unit different from another. This would include the location of the individual unit within the building (end units and units with better views sell for more), the upkeep and interior decoration of the unit, a time adjustment, and an adjustment for terms and conditions of the sale.

When there are not enough comparable sales of the same floor plan within the same building and it is necessary to use different-sized units, an adjustment must be made for floor area. If the number of comparables is still inadequate and units in different condominium buildings must be used, adjustments will be necessary for neighborhood, lot features, management, up-keep, age, and overall condition of the building.

Subdivided lots zoned for commercial, industrial, or apartment buildings are usually appraised and sold on a square-foot basis. Thus, if apartment land is currently selling for $3.00 per square foot, a 100,000-square-foot parcel of comparable zoning and usefulness would be appraised at $300,000. Another method is to value on a front-foot basis. For example, if a lot has 70 feet of street frontage and if similar lots are selling for $300 per front foot, that lot would be appraised at $21,000. Storefront land is often sold this way. House lots can be valued either by the square foot, front foot, or lot method. The lot method is useful when one is comparing lots of similar size and zoning in the same neighborhood. For example, recent sales of 100-foot-by-100-foot house lots in the $18,000 to $20,000 range would establish the value of similar lots in the same neighborhood.

Rural land and large parcels that have not been subdivided are usually valued and sold by the acre. For example, how would you value 21 acres of vacant land when the only comparables available are 16-acre and 25-acre sales? The method is to establish a per-acre value from comparables and apply it to the subject land. Thus, if 16- and 25-acre parcels sold for $32,000 and $50,000 respectively, and are similar in all other respects to the 21-acre subject property, it would be reasonable to conclude that land is selling for $2,000 per acre. Therefore, the subject property is worth $42,000.

Market Approach to Vacant Land Valuation

A variation of the market comparison approach and one that is very popular with agents who list and sell residential property is the **competitive market analysis (CMA).** This method is based on the principle that value can be estimated, not only by looking at similar homes that have sold recently, but also by taking into account homes presently on the market plus homes that were listed for sale but did not sell. The CMA is a listing tool that a sales agent prepares in order to show a seller what the home is likely to sell for, and the CMA helps the agent decide whether or not to accept the listing.

Figure 21.1 shows a competitive market analysis form published by the National Association of Realtors®. The procedure

Competitive Market Analysis

Figure 21.1. Competitive market analysis.

Property Address _____ Date _____

For Sale Now: **[1]**	Bed-rms.	Baths	Den	Sq. Ft.	1st Loan	List Price	Days on Market	Terms			

Sold Past 12 Mos. **[2]**	Bed-rms.	Baths	Den	Sq. Ft.	1st Loan	List Price	Days on Market	Date Sold	Sale Price	Terms

Expired Past 12 Mos. **[3]**	Bed-rms.	Baths	Den	Sq. Ft.	1st Loan	List Price	Days on Market	Terms		

[4] F.H.A. – V.A. Appraisals

Address	Appraisal	Address	Appraisal

[5] Buyer Appeal   **[6]** Marketing Position

(Grade each item 0 to 20% on the basis of desirability or urgency)

Buyer Appeal	Marketing Position
1. Fine Location _____ %	1. Why Are They Selling _____ %
2. Exciting Extras _____ %	2. How Soon Must They Sell _____ %
3. Extra Special Financing _____ %	3. Will They Help Finance .... Yes ___ No ___ %
4. Exceptional Appeal _____ %	4. Will They List at Competitive Market Value .... Yes ___ No ___ %
5. Under Market Price _____ Yes ___ No ___ %	5. Will They Pay for Appraisal .... Yes ___ No ___ %
Rating Total _____ %	Rating Total _____ %

[7]
Assets _____

Drawbacks _____

Area Market Conditions _____

Recommended Terms _____

[8] Selling Costs

Brokerage	$
Loan Payoff	$
Prepayment Penalty	$
FHA – VA Points	$
Title and Escrow Fees: IRS Stamps Recons Recording	$
Termite Clearance	$
Misc. Payoffs: 2nd T.D., Pool, Patio, Water Softener, Fence, Improvement Bond.	$
	$
	$
Total	$

Top Competitive Market Value $ _____

[9]
Probable Final Sales Price $ _____

Total Selling Costs $ _____

Net Proceeds $ _____   Plus or Minus $ _____

The statements and figures presented herein, while not guaranteed, are secured from sources we believe authoritative

Prepared by _____

in preparing a CMA is to select homes that are comparable to the subject property. The greater the similarity is among the homes, the more accurate the appraisal will be and the more likely it is that the client will accept the agent's estimate of value and counsel. It is usually best to use only properties in the same neighborhood; this is easier for the seller to relate to and removes the need to compensate for neighborhood differences. The comparables should also be similar in size, age, and quality. Although a CMA does not require that individual adjustments be shown as in Table 21.1, it does depend on the agent's understanding of the process that takes place in that table. For this reason Table 21.1 and its explanation are important. A residential agent may not be called on to make a presentation as is done in Table 21.1; nonetheless, all those steps are considered and consolidated in the agent's mind before entering a probable final sales price on the CMA.

Homes for Sale   In section [1] of the CMA shown in Figure 21.1, similar homes presently offered for sale are listed. This information is usually taken directly from the agent's multiple listing service (MLS) book and, ideally, the agent will already have toured these properties and have firsthand knowledge of their condition. These are the homes the seller's property will compete against in the marketplace.

In section [2] the agent lists similar properties that have sold in the past several months. Ideally, the agent will have toured the properties when they were for sale. Sale prices are usually available through MLS sales records. Section [3] is for listing homes that were offered for sale but did not sell. In other words, buyers were unwilling to take these homes at the prices offered.

In section [4] recent FHA and VA appraisals of comparable homes can be included if it is felt that they will be useful in determining the price at which to list. Two words of caution are in order here. First, using someone else's opinion of value is risky. It is better to determine your own opinion based on actual facts. Second, FHA and VA appraisals often tend to lag behind the market. This means in a rising market they will be too low; in a declining market they will be too high.

Buyer Appeal   In section [5], buyer appeal, and in section [6], marketing position, the agent evaluates the subject property from the standpoint of whether or not it will sell if placed on the market. It is important to make the right decision to take or not to take a listing. Once the listing has been taken, the agent knows that valuable time and money must be committed to get a property sold. Factors that make a property more appealing to a buyer include good location, extra features, small down payment, low interest, meticulous maintenance, and a price below market. Similarly, a property is more saleable if the sellers are motivated to sell, want to sell soon, will help with financing, and will list at or below market. A busy agent wants to avoid spending time on overpriced listings, listings for which no financing is available, and listings whose sellers have no motivation to sell. Under the rating systems in sections [5] and [6], the closer the total is to zero, the less desirable the listing; the closer to 100%, the more desirable the listing.

Section [7] provides space to list the property's high and low points, current market conditions, and recommended terms of sale. Section [8] shows the seller how much to expect in selling costs. Section [9] shows the seller what to expect in the way of a sales price and the amount of cash that can be expected from the sale.

The emphasis in CMA is on a visual inspection of the data on the form in order to arrive at market value directly. No pencil and paper adjustments are made. Instead, adjustments are made in a generalized fashion in the minds of the agent and the seller. In addition to its application to single-family houses, CMA can be used on condominiums, cooperative apartments, townhouses, and vacant lots—provided sufficient comparables are available.

Gross Rent Multipliers

A popular market comparison method used when a property produces income is the **gross rent multiplier,** or **GRM.** The GRM is an economic comparison factor that relates the gross rent a property can produce to its purchase price. For apartment buildings and commercial and industrial properties, the GRM is computed by dividing the sales price of the property by its gross annual rent. For example, if an apartment building grosses $100,000 per year in rents and has just sold for $700,000, it is said to have a GRM of 7. The use of a GRM to value single-family houses is questionable since they are usually sold as owner-occupied residences rather than as income properties. Note that if you do work up a GRM for a house, it is customary to use the monthly (not yearly) rent.

Where comparable properties have been sold at fairly consistent gross rent multiples, the GRM technique presumes the subject property can be valued by multiplying its gross rent by that multiplier. To illustrate, suppose that apartment buildings were recently sold in your community as shown in Table 21.2. These sales indicate that the market is currently paying seven times gross. Therefore, to find the value of a similar apartment building grossing $24,000 per year, multiply by 7.00 to get an indicated value of $168,000.

The GRM method is popular because it is simple to apply. Having once established what multiplier the market is paying, one need only know the gross rents of a building to set a value. However, this simplicity is also the weakness of the GRM method because the GRM takes into account only the gross rent a property produces. Gross rent does not allow for variations in vacancies, uncollectible rents, property taxes, maintenance, management, insurance, utilities, or reserves for replacements.

Weakness of GRM   To illustrate the problem, suppose that two apartment buildings each gross $100,000 per year. However, the first has expenses amounting to $40,000 per year and the second, expenses of $50,000 per year. Using the same GRM, the buildings would be valued the same, yet the first produces $10,000 more in net income for its owner. The GRM also overlooks the expected economic life span of a property. For example, a building with an expected remaining life span of 30 years would be valued exactly the same as one expected to last 20 years, if both currently produce the same rents. One method of partially offsetting these errors is to use different GRMs under different circumstances. Thus, a property with low operating expenses and a long expected economic life span might call for

Table 21.2. Calculating Gross Rent Multipliers

Building	Sales Price		Gross Annual Rents		Gross Rent Multiplier
No. 1	$245,000	÷	$ 34,900	=	7.02
No. 2	$160,000	÷	$ 22,988	=	6.96
No. 3	$204,000	÷	$ 29,352	=	6.95
No. 4	$196,000	÷	$ 27,762	=	7.06
As a Group:	$805,000	÷	$115,002	=	7.00

a GRM of 7 or more, whereas a property with high operating expenses or a shorter expected life span would be valued using a GRM of 6 or 5 or even less.

COST APPROACH

There are times when the market approach is an inappropriate valuation tool. For example, the market approach is of limited usefulness in valuing a fire station, school building, courthouse, or highway bridge. These properties are rarely placed on the market and comparables are rarely found. Even with properties that are well suited to the market approach, there may be times when it is valuable to apply another valuation approach. For example, a real estate agent may find that comparables indicate a certain style and size of house is selling in a particular neighborhood for $150,000. Yet the astute agent discovers through the cost approach that the same house can be built from scratch, including land, for $125,000. The agent builds and sells ten of these and concludes that, yes, there really is money to be made in real estate. Let us take a closer look at the cost approach.

Table 21.3 demonstrates the **cost approach.** Step 1 is to estimate the value of the land on which the building is located. The land is valued as though vacant using the market comparison approach described earlier. In Step 2, the cost of constructing a similar building at today's costs is estimated. These costs include the current prices of building materials, construction wages, architect's fees, contractor's services, building permits, utility hookups, and so on, plus the cost of financing during the construction stage and the cost of construction equipment used at the project site. Step 3 is the calculation of the amount of money that represents the subject building's wear and tear, lack of usefulness, and obsolescence when compared with the new building of Step 2. In Step 4, depreciation is subtracted from

Table 21.3. Cost Approach to Value

Step 1:	Estimate land as vacant		$ 30,000
Step 2:	Estimate new construction cost of similar building	$120,000	
Step 3:	Less estimated depreciation	−12,000	
Step 4:	Indicated value of building		$108,000
Step 5:	Appraised property value by the cost approach		$138,000

today's construction cost to give the current value of the subject building on a used basis. Step 5 is to add this amount to the land value. Let us work through these steps.

In order to choose a method of estimating construction costs, one must decide whether cost will be approached on a reproduction or on a replacement basis. **Reproduction cost** is the cost at today's prices of constructing an *exact replica* of the subject improvements using the same or very similar materials. **Replacement cost** is the cost, at today's prices and using today's methods of construction, for an improvement having the same or *equivalent usefulness* as the subject property. Replacement cost is the more practical choice of the two as it eliminates nonessential or obsolete features and takes full advantage of current construction materials and techniques. It is the approach described here.

Estimating New Construction Costs

The most widely used approach for estimating construction costs is the **square-foot method.** It provides reasonably accurate estimates that are fast and simple to prepare.

Square-Foot Method

The square-foot method is based on finding a newly constructed building that is similar to the subject building in size, type of occupancy, design, materials, and construction quality. The cost of this building is converted to cost per square foot by dividing its current construction cost by the number of square feet in the building.

Cost information is also available from construction cost handbooks. Use of a **cost handbook** starts with selecting a handbook appropriate to the type of building being appraised. From photographs of houses included in the handbook along with brief descriptions of the buildings' features, the appraiser finds a house that most nearly fits the description of the subject house. Next to pictures of the house is the current cost per square foot to construct it. If the subject house has a better-quality roof, floor covering, or heating system; more or fewer built-in appliances or plumbing fixtures; or a garage, basement, porch, or swimming pool, the handbook provides costs for each of these. Figure 21.2 illustrates the calculations involved in the square-foot method.

Cost Handbooks

Estimating Depreciation   Having estimated the current cost of constructing the subject improvements, the next step in the cost approach is to estimate the loss in value due to depreciation since they were built. In making this estimate we look for three kinds of **depreciation:** physical deterioration, functional obsolescence, and economic obsolescence.

Physical deterioration results from wear and tear through use, such as wall-to-wall carpet that has been worn thin or a dishwasher, garbage disposal, or water heater that must be replaced. Physical deterioration also results from the action of nature in the form of sun, rain, heat, cold, and wind, and from damage due to plants and animal life such as tree roots breaking sidewalks and termites eating wood. Physical deterioration can also result from neglect (an overflowing bathtub) and from vandalism.

Functional obsolescence results from outmoded equipment (old-fashioned plumbing fixtures in the bathrooms and kitchen), faulty or outdated design (a single bathroom in a three- or four-bedroom house or an illogical room layout), inadequate structural facilities (inadequate wiring to handle today's household appliance loads), and overadequate structural facilities (high ceilings in a home).

Functional and physical obsolescence can be separated into curable and incurable components. **Curable depreciation** can be fixed at reasonable cost; for example, worn carpeting, a leaky roof, or outdated faucets in bathrooms. **Incurable depreciation** cannot be economically fixed and must simply be lived with; for example, an illogical room layout.

Economic obsolescence is the loss of value due to external forces or events. For example, a once-popular neighborhood becomes undesirable because of air or noise pollution or because surrounding property owners fail to maintain their properties. Or, a city that is dependent on a military base finds the base closed, and with the closure comes a big drop in demand for real estate. Or, the motel district in town loses customers because a new interstate highway has been built several miles away. An estimate of economic obsolescence is an important part of the cost approach to value.

Far more often, however, properties experience economic appreciation and not economic obsolescence. The appreciation can come from new industries moving into town, city growth

Figure 21.2. Square-foot method of cost estimating.

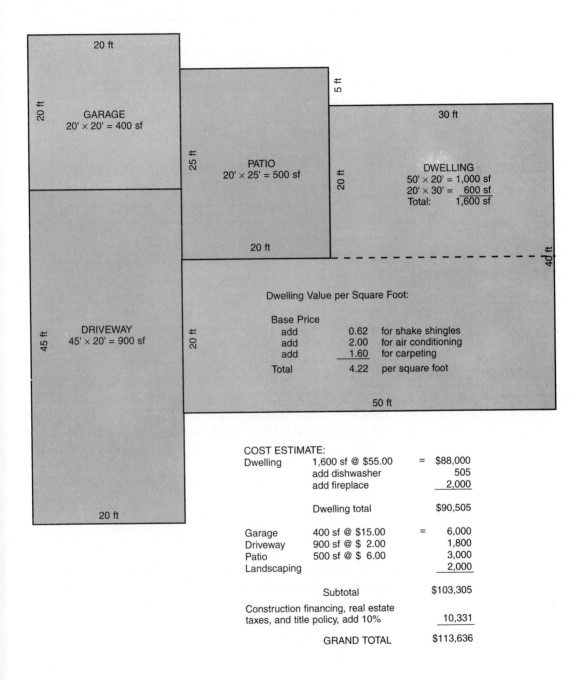

in a new direction, a shortage of land in beach or waterfront areas, and so on. Thus it is quite possible for the economic appreciation of a property to more than offset the depreciation it experiences. The result is a building that is physically and functionally depreciating and at the same time appreciating in value. Consequently, while the chronological age of a building is important to value, what is more important is the remaining economic life of the building and whether or not it is functionally adequate for use in the future. This is what real estate investors look for.

Final Steps in the Cost Approach

After calculating the current construction cost of the subject improvements and estimating the amount of depreciation, the next step is to subtract the amount of depreciation from the current construction cost to get the depreciated value of the improvements. This is added to the value of the land on which the subject improvements rest. The total is the value of the property by the cost approach.

INCOME APPROACH

The **income approach** considers the monetary returns a property can be expected to produce and converts that into a value the property should sell for if placed on the market today. This is called capitalizing the income stream. To **capitalize** means to convert future income to current value. To illustrate, suppose that an available apartment building is expected to return, after expenses, $18,000 per year. How much would you, as an investor, pay for the building? The answer depends on the return you require on each dollar you invest. Suppose you will accept a return of 9% per year. In that case you will pay $200,000 for this building. The calculation is as follows:

$$\frac{\text{Income}}{\text{Rate}} = \text{Value} \qquad \frac{\$18,000}{0.09} = \$200,000$$

This is the basic principle of capitalization. The appraisal work comes in estimating the net income a property will produce and looking at recent sales of similar properties to see what capitalization rates are currently acceptable to investors. Let us look at the techniques one would use in estimating a property's income. Pay close attention, because each $1 error in projected annual income or expenses can make a difference of from $8 to $15 in the market value of the property.

The best starting point is to look at the actual record of income and expenses for the subject property over the past 3 to 5 years. Although the future will not be an exact repetition of the past, the past record of a property is usually the best guide to future performance. These historical data are blended with the current operating experience of similar buildings in order to estimate what the future will bring. The result is a projected operating statement, such as the one shown in Table 21.4, which begins with the estimated rents that the property can be expected to produce on an annual basis. This is the **projected gross,** or **scheduled gross,** and represents expected rentals from the subject property on a fully occupied basis. From this, vacancy and collection losses are subtracted. These are based partly on the building's past experience and partly on the operating experience of similar buildings.

Income and Expense Forecasting

The next step is to itemize anticipated **operating expenses** for the subject property. These are expenses necessary to maintain the production of income. For an apartment building without recreational facilities or an elevator, the list in Table 21.4 is typical. Again, we must consider both the property's past operating expenses and what we expect those expenses to be in the future. For example, even though a property is currently being managed by its owner and no management fee is being paid, a typical management fee, say 5% of the gross rents, is included.

Operating Expenses

Not included as operating expenses are outlays for capital improvements, such as the construction of a new swimming pool, the expansion of parking facilities, and assessments for street improvements. Improvements are not classified as expenses because they increase the usefulness of the property, which increases the rent the property will generate and, therefore, the property's value.

Reserves for replacement are established for items that do not require an expenditure of cash each year. To illustrate, lobby furniture (and furniture in apartments rented as furnished) wears out a little each year, eventually requiring replacement. Suppose that these items cost $7,200 and are expected to last 6 years, at which time they must be replaced. An annual $1,200 reserve for replacement not only reflects wear and tear of the

Reserves

Table 21.4. Projected Annual Operating Statement (Also Called a Pro Forma Statement)

Scheduled gross annual income	$84,000	
Vacancy allowance and collection losses	4,200	
Effective gross income		$79,800
Operating expenses		
Property taxes	7,000	
Hazard and liability insurance	2,100	
Property management	4,200	
Janitorial services	1,500	
Gardener	1,200	
Utilities	3,940	
Trash pickup	850	
Repairs and maintenance	4,000	
Other	1,330	
Reserves for replacement		
Furniture & furnishings	1,200	
Stoves & refrigerators	600	
Furnace &/or air conditioning	700	
Plumbing & electrical	800	
Roof	750	
Exterior painting	900	
Total operating expenses		$31,070
Net operating income		$48,730
Operating expense ratio: $31,070 ÷ $79,800 = 38.9%		

furniture during the year, but also reminds us that to avoid having to meet the entire furniture and furnishings replacement cost out of one year's income, money should be set aside for this purpose each year. In a similar manner, reserves are established for other items that must be replaced or repaired more than once during the life of the building, but not yearly.

Net Operating Income The operating expense total is then subtracted from the effective gross income. The balance that remains is the **net operating income (NOI).** From the net operating income, the property owner receives both a return *on* and a return *of* investment. The return *on* investment is the interest received for investing money in the property. The return *of* investment is compensation for the fact that the building is wearing out.

Operating Expense Ratio

At this point, the **operating expense ratio** can be calculated. It is obtained by dividing the total operating expenses by the effective gross income. The resulting ratio provides a handy yardstick against which similar properties can be compared. If the operating expense ratio is out of step compared to similar properties, it signals the need for further investigation. A range of 25% to 45% is typical for apartment buildings. The Institute of Real Estate Management of the National Association of Realtors publishes books and articles that give typical operating ratios for various types of income properties across the United States. Local inquiry to appraisers and brokers who specialize in income properties also provides typical ratios for buildings in a community.

Capitalizing Income

The final step in the income approach is to capitalize the net operating income. In other words, what price should an investor offer to pay for a property that produces a given net income per year? The solution is: income ÷ rate = value. If the annual net operating income is $45,400 and if the investor intends to pay all cash, expects to receive a 10% return on his investment, and anticipates no change in the value of the property while he owns it, the solution is to divide $45,400 by 10%. However, most investors today borrow much of the purchase price and usually expect an increase in property value. Under these conditions, how much should the investor pay?

The best-known method for solving this type of investment question involves using the Ellwood Tables, published in 1959 by L. W. Ellwood, MAI. However, for the person who does not use these tables regularly, the arithmetic involved can prove confusing. As a result **mortgage-equity tables** are now available from bookstores. These allow the user to look up a single number, called an **overall rate,** and divide it into the net operating income to find a value for the property.

For example, suppose an investor who is interested in buying the aforementioned property can obtain an 11%, fully amortized, 25-year mortgage loan for 75% of the purchase price. He wants an 18% return on his equity in the property, plans to hold it 10 years, and expects it will increase 50% in value (after selling costs) during that time. How much should he offer to pay the seller? In Table 21.5, we look for an interest rate of 11% and for appreciation of 50%. This gives an overall rate of 0.10756 and the solution is:

$$\frac{\text{Income}}{\text{Overall rate}} = \text{Value} \qquad \frac{\$45{,}400}{0.10756} = \$422{,}090$$

Further exploration of the numbers in Table 21.5 shows that, as loan money becomes more costly, the overall rate rises, and as interest rates fall, so does the overall rate. If the investor can anticipate appreciation in value, the overall rate drops; if he can't, the overall rate climbs. You can experiment by dividing some of the other overall rates in this table into $45,400 to see how the value of this property changes under different circumstances.

Depreciation   The pro forma statement in Table 21.4 provides reserves for replacement of such items as the roof, furnace, air conditioning, plumbing, electrical system, exterior paint, and so forth. Nonetheless, as the building ages the style of the building becomes dated, the neighborhood changes, and the structure experiences physical deterioration. Allowance for this is usually accounted for in the selection of the capitalization rate. The lesser the degree of functional, economic, and physical obsolescence that is ex-

Table 21.5. Overall Rates—10-Year Holding Period, 25-Year Loan for 75% of the Purchase Price, 18% Investor Return

Appreciation, Depreciation	Loan Interest Rate			
	9%	10%	11%	12%
+100%	0.07251	0.07935	0.08631	0.09338
+ 50%	0.09376	0.10060	**0.10756**	0.11463
+ 25%	0.10439	0.11123	0.11819	0.12526
+ 15%	0.10864	0.11548	0.12244	0.12951
+ 10%	0.11077	0.11761	0.12457	0.13164
+ 5%	0.11289	0.11973	0.12669	0.13376
0	0.11502	0.12186	0.12882	0.13589
− 5%	0.11715	0.12399	0.13095	0.13802
− 10%	0.11927	0.12611	0.13307	0.14014
− 15%	0.12140	0.12824	0.13520	0.14227
− 25%	0.12565	0.13249	0.13945	0.14652
− 50%	0.13628	0.14312	0.15008	0.15715
− 100%	0.15753	0.16437	0.17133	0.17840

Source: *Financial Capitalization Rate Tables* (Boston: Financial Publishing). By permission.

pected to take place, the lower will be the acceptable "cap" rate, and vice versa.

In contrast to actual depreciation, the U.S. Treasury allows income property owners to deduct **fictional depreciation** as an expense when calculating income taxes. In late 1987, for example, the Treasury allowed the purchaser of an apartment building to completely depreciate the structure over a period of 27½ years, regardless of the age or condition of the structure. This figure may be an understatement of the remaining life of the structure, but it was chosen by Congress to create an incentive to invest in real estate, not as an accurate gauge of a property's life. Thus it is quite common to see depreciation claimed on buildings that are, in reality, appreciating because of rising income from rents and/or falling capitalization rates.

Fictional Depreciation

Whenever possible, all three appraisal methods discussed in this chapter should be used to provide an indication, as well as a cross-check, of a property's value. If the marketplace is acting rationally and is not restricted in any way, all three approaches will produce the same value. If one approach is out of line with the others, it may indicate an error in the appraiser's work or a problem in the market itself. It is not unusual to find individual sales that seem out of line with prevailing market prices. Similarly, sometimes buyers will temporarily bid the market price of a property above its replacement cost.

CHOICE OF APPROACHES

For certain types of real property, some approaches are more suitable than others. This is especially true for single-family residences. Here one must rely almost entirely on the market and cost approaches, as very few houses are sold on their ability to generate cash rent. Unless one can develop a measure of the "psychic income" in home ownership, relying heavily on rental value will lead to a property value below the market and cost approaches. Applying all three approaches to special-purpose buildings may also prove to be impractical. For example, in valuing a college or university campus or a state capitol building, the income and market approaches have only limited applicability.

When appraising a property that is bought for investment purposes, such as an apartment building, shopping center, office building, or warehouse, the income approach is the primary method of valuation. As a cross-check on the income approach, an apartment building should be compared with other apartment buildings on a price-per-apartment-unit basis or price-per-square-foot basis. Similarly, an office, store, or warehouse can be compared with other recent office, store, or warehouse sales on a price-per-square-foot basis. Additionally, the cost approach can be used to determine whether or not it would be cheaper to buy land and build than to buy an existing building.

RECONCILIATION OF APPROACHES

After applying the market, cost, and income approaches to the subject property, the appraiser must reconcile the differences found in the results. One method is to assign each approach a weighting factor based on a judgment of its relevance and reliability in the appraisal of this property. To demonstrate, the results of a 20-year-old, single-family house appraisal might be reconciled as follows:

Market approach	$180,000 × 75%	= $135,000
Cost approach	$200,000 × 20%	= $ 40,000
Income approach	$160,000 × 5%	= $ 8,000
Final indicated value		$183,000

What the appraiser is suggesting here is that recent sales of comparable properties have the most influence on current sales prices. Thus the market approach is given the most weight. The cost approach is given much less weight because it required a difficult judgment of accrued depreciation for the subject improvements. By weighting the income approach at only 5%, the appraiser is recognizing that houses in this neighborhood are mostly owner occupied, and rarely bought for rental purposes.

APPRAISER'S BEST ESTIMATE

It is important to realize that the appraised value is the appraiser's best *estimate* of the subject property's worth. Thus, no matter how painstakingly it is done, property valuation requires the appraiser to make many subjective judgments. For this reason it is not unusual for three highly qualified appraisers to look at the same property and produce three different appraised values. It is also important to recognize that an appraisal is made as of a specific date. It is not a certificate of value, good forever until used. If a property was valued at $115,000 on January 5th of this year, as more time elapses since January 5th, the appraised value becomes less accurate as an indication of the property's current worth.

An appraisal does not take into consideration the financial condition of the owner, the owner's health, sentimental attachment, or any other personal matter. An appraisal does not guarantee that the property will sell for the appraised market value. (The buyer and the seller determine the actual selling price.) Nor does buying at the appraised market value guarantee a future profit for the purchaser. (The real estate market can change.) An appraisal is not a guarantee that the roof will not leak, that there are no termites, or that everything in the building works. An appraisal is not an offer to buy, although a buyer can order one made so as to know how much to offer. An appraisal is not a loan commitment, although a lender can order one made so as to apply a loan-to-value ratio when making a loan.

APPRAISAL REGULATION
The Appraisal Foundation

Because of harsh economic times in many areas of the country, standards of appraisals have come under extremely close scrutiny by many lenders. For instance, two appraisers may appraise the same property for significantly different values while using the same data, both acting in good faith. It is hard to draw a distinction, however, between an error in judgment and a fraudulent appraisal. The more difficult question is: How can a lender, in reviewing an appraisal, distinguish between good and bad appraisals? At least part of the answer is being addressed by an organization called **The Appraisal Foundation.** It is a private organization whose purpose is to establish and approve (1) uniform appraisal standards, (2) appropriate criteria for the certification and recertification of qualified appraisers, and (3) appropriate systems for the certification and recertification of qualified appraisers.

To effect this result, The Appraisal Foundation has established two subcommittees: the Appraiser Qualifications Board and the Appraisal Standards Board. The first establishes criteria for appraisers. The second sets standards for the appraisal to be performed. The Foundation's aim is to disseminate such qualification criteria to various states, governmental entities, and others to assist them in establishing and maintaining an appropriate system for the certification and recertification of qualified appraisers.

Federal Regulation   Congress addressed the appraisal issue by enacting Title XI of the Financial Institutions Reform, Recovery, and Enforcement Act of 1989 (FIRREA). The act, for the first time in history, establishes standards that will have a far-reaching impact on the appraisal industry.

Congress also created the Appraisal Subcommittee of the Federal Financial Institution's Examination Council to establish standards. The Subcommittee looks exclusively to the Appraisal Foundation for establishing standards under FIRREA for both appraiser qualifications and appraisal standards, and has proven to be an excellent effort by leaders in the appraisal industry, coupled with the governmental enforcement powers, to establish standards that ultimately benefit lenders and the public in general.

Developing the Appraisal   FIRREA creates mandatory requirements for certain federally related real estate appraisals. These requirements are known as the **Uniform Standards of Professional Appraisal Practice,** commonly referred to as the **USPAP standards.**

In developing an appraisal, USPAP requires that the appraiser be aware of, understand, and correctly employ those recognized methods and techniques necessary to produce a credible appraisal. Specific requirements have been set for an appraiser's analysis, requiring consideration of current sales, options, or listings within certain time periods prior to the date of the appraisal. Specifically, this analysis of market data must consider all sales, options, or listings within 1 year for a one- to four-family residential property; and within 3 years for all other property types. The act further requires that the appraiser must consider and reconcile the quality and quantity of data available, and, within the approaches used, analyze the applicability or suitability of the approaches as pertaining to the subject parcel of real estate.

Departure Provisions   In 1994, significant changes were made to the USPAP. The uniform standards now provide for a departure provision that permits limited departures from the standards, which are classified as specific guidelines rather than binding requirements.

Before entering into an agreement to perform an appraisal that contains a departure, the following requirements must be met: (1) The appraiser must have determined that the appraisal or consulting process to be performed is not so limited that the resulting assignment would tend to mislead or confuse the client or the intended users of the report; (2) the appraiser must have advised the client that the assignment calls for something less than, or different from, the work required by the specific guidelines and that the report will clearly identify and explain the departure(s); and (3) the client must have agreed that the performance of a limited appraisal or consulting service would be appropriate.

The definition section of the USPAP defines "appraisal" as "the act or process of estimating value; an estimate of value," and then defines two types of appraisals:

1. A **complete appraisal,** which is defined as the act or process of estimating value without invoking the departure provision. A complete appraisal report may not depart from specific USPAP guidelines; and

2. A **limited appraisal,** defined as the act or process of estimating value performed under and resulting from invoking the departure provision.

In addition, the revised USPAP now define three optional levels of reporting.   *Reporting Options*

1. The **self-contained appraisal report,** which is the most detailed and encompassing of the report options. The length and descriptive detail in such a report should fully support (in a self-contained format) the conclusions of the appraiser.

2. The **summary report,** which is less detailed than a self-contained report. The information contained and the appraisal procedures that were followed may be summarized in this report rather than described in detail.

3. The **restrictive report** is the least detailed of the reporting options. Presentation of information is only minimal and is intended for use only by the client. This level of report must contain a prominent use restriction that limits the reliance on the report to the client and warns that the report cannot be properly understood without additional information from the work file of the appraiser.

Reporting Standards   USPAP also sets forth required standards for the appraisal report. Each self-contained appraisal report must: (1) identify and describe the real estate being appraised; (2) state the real property interest being appraised; (3) state the purpose and intended use of the appraisal; (4) define the value to be estimated; (5) state the effective date of the appraisal and the date of the report; (6) state the extent of the process of collecting, confirming, and reporting data; (7) state all assumptions and limiting conditions that affect the analyses, opinions, and conclusions; (8) describe the information considered, the appraisal procedures followed, and the reasoning that supports the analyses, opinions, and conclusions; (9) describe the appraiser's opinion of the highest and best use of the real estate, when such an opinion is necessary and appropriate; (10) explain and support the exclusion of any of the usual valuation approaches; (11) describe any additional information that may be appropriate to show compliance with, or clearly identify and explain permitted departures from the specific guidelines of Standard 1 (on developing an appraisal); (12) include a signed certification.

Each appraisal report must also: (1) clearly and accurately set forth the appraisal in a manner that will not be misleading; (2) contain sufficient information to enable person(s) who are expected to receive or rely on the report to understand it properly; and (3) clearly and accurately disclose any extraordinary assumption or limiting condition that directly affects the appraisal and indicate its impact on value.

USPAP requires that each written real property appraisal report include a signed certification similar in content to the following form:

I certify that, to the best of my knowledge and belief:

- The statements of fact contained in this report are true and correct.
- The reported analyses, opinions, and conclusions are limited only by the reported assumptions and limiting conditions, and are my personal, unbiased professional analyses, opinions, and conclusions.
- I have no (or only the specified) present or prospective interest in the property that is the subject of this report, and I have no (or only the specified) personal interest or bias with respect to the parties involved.

- My compensation is not contingent on the reporting of a predetermined value or direction in value that favors the cause of the client, the amount of the value estimate, the attainment of a stipulated result, or the occurrence of a subsequent event.
- My analyses, opinions, and conclusions were developed, and this report has been prepared, in conformity with the Uniform Standards of Professional Appraisal Practice.
- I have (or have not) made a personal inspection of the property that is the subject of this report. (If more than one person signs the report, this certification must clearly specify which individuals did and which individuals did not make a personal inspection of the appraised property).
- No one provided significant professional assistance to the person signing this report. (If there are exceptions, the name of each individual providing significant professional assistance must be stated.)

FORMATS OF APPRAISAL REPORTS

There are three traditional formats for written reports. The choice depends on the amount of detail required by the client, the intended use of the report, and the appraisal standards to be met. The format to be used also depends on the reporting option (self-contained, summary, or restricted). A brief description of reporting formats follows.

The Letter Report

The least formal letter report is usually only one to five pages long. It contains the conditions of the assignment, a summary of the nature and scope of the appraiser's investigation, and an opinion of value. Although brief, the letter report must describe the extent of the appraisal process performed and clearly state its detail. Whether reporting a complete or limited appraisal, the letter format is most suited to the restricted appraisal report. It is used most often when the client is familiar with the property and appraisal details are not needed.

The Form Report

The form report is an appraisal made on a preprinted form. A checklist is often used for describing and rating property characteristics. This makes the appraisal form a logical choice for the summary report option.

Institutions and government agencies use forms designed to suit their special needs. Standard forms are usually available for single-family residential, multifamily residential, commercial, and industrial properties. This is the most common type of report used for real estate loan appraisals.

The Narrative Report

The narrative appraisal is the longest and most formal of the appraisal reports. It is a step-by-step presentation of the facts used by the appraiser to arrive at a value. This report also contains a detailed discussion of the methods used to interpret the data presented. Narrative appraisal reports are used when the client needs to review each logical step taken by the appraiser. This is the preferred format for self-contained appraisal reports.

Review Appraisals

FIRREA also developed standards for reviewing appraisals and reporting their adequacy and appropriateness. In reviewing the appraisal, the appraiser must observe specific guidelines that identify the report being reviewed and the real property being appraised, the effective date of the report, and the date of the review. The review appraiser must also identify the scope of the review process to be conducted and form an opinion as to the adequacy and relevance of the data and propriety of any adjustments to the data. The opinion must also reflect the appropriateness of the appraisal and the methods and techniques used to develop the reasons for any disagreement with the appraiser.

Real Estate Analysis

An **analysis** is the act or process of providing information, recommendations, and/or conclusions on diversified problems in real estate other than estimating the value, and can include a number of different forms of analysis, such as cash flow analysis, feasibility analysis, investment analysis, or market analysis. This differs from an *appraisal*, which, under USPAP standards, is defined as the act or process of estimating value.

In developing the real estate analysis, the analyst must be aware of, understand, and correctly employ those recognized methods and techniques that are necessary to produce a credible analysis. The analyst must not commit a substantial error of omission or commission that significantly affects the analysis and must not render services in a careless or negligent manner which, when considering the results of the analysis, could be considered to be misleading. The analyst must also observe the following specific guidelines: (1) clearly identify the client's objective; (2) define the problem to be considered and the purpose and intended use of the analysis, consider the scope of the assignment, adequately identify the real estate under consideration, and describe any special limiting condition; (3) collect, verify, and reconcile such data as may be required to complete the assignment and withhold no pertinent information; (4) apply the appropriate tools and techniques of analysis to data collected; and (5) base all projections of the analysis on reasonably clear and appropriate evidence. Each type of analysis being utilized by the analyst has its own additional requirements and separate criteria.

In reporting the results of the real estate analysis, the analyst must communicate each analysis, opinion, and conclusion in a manner that is not misleading, and the report must contain sufficient information to enable the persons who receive it to understand it properly. The report must clearly and accurately disclose any extraordinary assumptions that would indicate an impact on the final conclusions or recommendation of the analysis.

The analysis report must contain a certification that is similar in content to that of the appraisal certification.

Appraiser Qualifications

To comply with new federal regulations established by the Appraisal Subcommittee, the Appraiser Qualifications Board of The Appraisal Foundation has established federal standards for certification and licensing of appraisers. Appraisers are now either licensed or certified as general or residential appraisers to be qualified to do appraisals for federally related institutions and regulated loans. The appraisers are certified or licensed by their representative state based on the examination, education, and experience requirements. Examinations are administered by a state board in accordance with The Appraisal Foundation guidelines. Applicants for general real estate appraiser certification must have successfully completed 165 classroom hours in courses approved by the state licensing board. Applicants for residential real estate appraiser certification must have successfully completed 120 classroom hours in courses approved by the board. In either category of certification, the course work submitted must have included a minimum of 15 hours of coverage of the Uniform Standards of Professional Appraisal Practice. Applicants for a real estate appraiser license must have successfully completed 75 classroom hours in classes approved by the board, including the 15 hours of coverage of Uniform Standards of Professional Appraisal Practice.

In addition to the educational requirements, an applicant for general real estate appraiser certification must provide evidence satisfactory to the state licensing board that the applicant possesses the equivalent of 2,000 hours of appraisal experience over a minimum of 2 calendar years. At least 1,000 hours of experience must be in nonresidential work. An applicant for a residential appraiser certification must provide evidence satisfactory to the board that the applicant possesses the equivalent of 2,000 hours of appraisal experience over a minimum of 2 calendar years. There is no requirement for nonresidential work.

New York Board of Real Estate Appraisal

In 1990, New York established its own state board of real estate appraisal, which adopted the USPAP standards, to oversee the licensing and certification of appraisers in New York. However, New York does not require that one who charges a fee to appraise real estate be licensed.

The state board, which is within the Department of State, issues three levels of licensure and certification, depending on experience and education. The board establishes requirements for appraisal reports. It also sets fees, develops and conducts examinations, prescribes continuing education requirements, and conducts disciplinary hearings against certificate or license holders who do not abide by its standards.

CHARACTERISTICS OF VALUE

Up to this point we have been concerned primarily with value based on evidence found in the marketplace and how to report it. Before concluding this chapter, we briefly touch on what creates value, the principles of real property valuation, and appraisal for purposes other than market value.

For a good or service to have value in the marketplace it must possess four characteristics: demand, utility, scarcity, and transferability. **Demand** is a need or desire coupled with the purchasing power to fill it, whereas **utility** is the ability of a good or service to fill that need. **Scarcity** means there must be a short supply relative to demand. Air, for example, has utility and is in demand, but it is not scarce. Finally, a good or service must be **transferable** to have value to anyone other than the person possessing it.

The **principle of anticipation** reflects the fact that what a person will pay for a property depends on the expected benefits from the property in the future. Thus, the buyer of a home anticipates receiving shelter plus the investment and psychic benefits of home ownership. The investor buys property in anticipation of future income.

The **principle of substitution** states that the maximum value of a property in the marketplace tends to be set by the cost of purchasing an equally desirable substitute property provided no costly delay is encountered in making the substitution. In other words, substitution sets an upper limit on price. Thus, if two similar houses are for sale, or two similar apartments are for rent, the lower-priced one will generally be purchased or rented first. In the same manner, the cost of buying land and constructing a new building sets a limit on the value of existing buildings.

PRINCIPLES OF VALUE

The **highest and best use** of a property is that use which will give the property its greatest current value. This means you must be alert to the possibility that the present use of a parcel of land may not be the one that makes the land the most valuable. Consider a 30-year-old house located at a busy intersection in a shopping area. To place a value on that property based on its continued use as a residence would be misleading if the property would be worth more with the house removed and shopping or commercial facilities built on the land instead.

Highest and Best Use

The **principle of competition** recognizes that where substantial profits are being made, competition is encouraged. For example, if apartment rents increase to the point where owners of existing apartment buildings are making substantial profits, builders and investors are encouraged to build more apartment buildings.

Applied to real estate, the **principle of supply and demand** refers to the ability of people to pay for land coupled with the relative scarcity of land. This means that, on the demand side, attention must be given to such matters as population growth, personal income, and preferences of people. On the supply side, you must look at the available supply of land and its relative

Supply and Demand

scarcity. When the supply of land is limited and demand is great, the result is rising land prices. Conversely, where land is abundant and there are relatively few buyers, supply and demand are in balance at only a few cents per square foot.

The **principle of change** reminds us that real property uses are always in a state of change. Although change may be imperceptible on a day-to-day basis, it can easily be seen over longer periods of time. Because the present value of a property is related to its future uses, the more potential changes can be identified, the more accurate the estimate of its present worth will be.

Diminishing Marginal Returns

The **principle of diminishing marginal returns,** also called the **principle of contribution,** refers to the relationship between added cost and the value it returns. It tells us that we should invest dollars whenever they will return to us more than $1 of value and we should stop when each dollar invested returns less than $1 in value.

The **principle of conformity** holds that maximum value is realized when there is a reasonable degree of homogeneity in a neighborhood. This is the basis for zoning laws across the country; certain tracts in a community are zoned for single-family houses, others for apartment buildings, stores, and industry. Within a tract there should also be a reasonable amount of homogeneity. For example, a $200,000 house would be out of place in a neighborhood of $90,000 houses.

MULTIPLE MEANINGS OF THE WORD VALUE

When we hear the word *value,* we tend to think of market value. However, at any given moment in time, a single property can have other values too. This is because value or worth is very much affected by the purpose for which the valuation was performed. For example, **assessed value** is the value given a property by the county tax assessor for purposes of property taxation. **Estate tax value** is the value that federal and state taxation authorities establish for a deceased person's property; it is used to calculate the amount of estate taxes that must be paid. **Insurance value** is concerned with the cost of replacing damaged property. It differs from market value in two major respects: (1) the value of the land is not included, because only the structures are presumed destructible; and (2) the amount of coverage is based on the replacement cost of the structures.

Loan value is the value set on a property for the purpose of making a loan.

When two or more adjoining parcels are combined into one large parcel it is called **assemblage.** The increased value of the large parcel over and above the sum of the smaller parcels is called **plottage value.** For example, local zoning laws may permit a six-unit apartment building on a single 10,000-square-foot lot. However, if two of these lots can be combined, zoning laws could permit as many as 15 units. This makes the lots more valuable if sold together.

Plottage Value

Rental value is the value of a property expressed in terms of the right to its use for a specific period of time. The fee simple interest in a house may have a market value of $80,000, whereas the market value of one month's occupancy might be $600.

Rental Value

Replacement value is value as measured by the current cost of building a structure of equivalent utility. **Salvage value** is what a structure is worth if it has to be removed and taken elsewhere, either in whole or dismantled for parts. Because salvage operations require much labor the salvage value of most buildings is very low.

Replacement Value

    This list of values is not exhaustive, but it points out that the word *value* has many meanings. When reading an appraisal report, always read the first paragraph to see why the appraisal was prepared. Before preparing an appraisal, make certain you know its purpose and then state it at the beginning of your report.

Whenever supply and demand are unbalanced because of excess supply, a **buyer's market** exists. This means buyers can negotiate prices and terms more to their liking, and sellers who want to sell must accept them. When the imbalance occurs because demand exceeds supply it is a **seller's market;** sellers are able to negotiate prices and terms more to their liking as buyers compete for the available merchandise.

BUYER'S AND SELLER'S MARKETS

    A **broad market** means that many buyers and sellers are in the market at the same time. This makes it relatively easy to establish the price of a property and for a seller to find a buyer quickly, and vice versa. A *thin market* is said to exist when there are only a few buyers and a few sellers in the market at the same time. It is often difficult to appraise a property in a thin market because there are so few sales to use as comparables.

PROFESSIONAL
APPRAISAL
SOCIETIES

During the 1930s, two well-known professional appraisal societies were organized: The **American Institute of Real Estate Appraisers (AIREA)** and the **Society of Real Estate Appraisers.** Although a person offering services as a real estate appraiser didn't need to be associated with either of these groups, there were advantages to membership. Both organizations developed designation systems to recognize appraisal education, experience, and competence. The Society and AIREA were unified in 1991, renamed the Appraisal Institute, and are now considered to provide the most highly respected designations in the industry. Within the Appraisal Institute, the highest-level designation is the MAI (Member of the Appraisal Institute). To become an MAI requires a 4-year college degree or equivalent education, various Appraisal Institute courses, examinations, an income property demonstration appraisal, and at least 4,500 hours (with a maximum of 1,500 hours allowed in a 12-month period) of appraisal experience. There are about 6,000 MAIs in the United States. Also available is the SRA designation (Senior Residential Appraiser) for residential appraisers that requires a 4-year college degree or acceptable alternative, appraisal course work, a passing appraisal examination score, a residential demonstration appraisal, and 3,000 hours of experience in residential real estate, with a maximum of 1,500 hours allowed in any 12-month period.

In addition to the Appraisal Institute, there are several other professional appraisal organizations in the United States, including the National Association of Independent Fee Appraisers, the Farm Managers and Rural Appraisers, the National Society of Real Estate Appraisers, and the American Society of Appraisers. All exist to promote and maintain high standards of appraisal services and all offer a variety of appraisal education and designation programs.

VOCABULARY
REVIEW

*Match terms **a–z** with statements **1–26**.*

a. *Adjustments*
b. *Appraisal*
c. *Buyer's market*
d. *Capitalize*

e. *Comparables*	o. *Market approach*
f. *Competitive market analysis (CMA)*	p. *Market value*
	q. *Net operating income (NOI)*
g. *Cost approach*	r. *Operating expenses*
h. *Curable depreciation*	s. *Physical deterioration*
i. *Depreciation*	t. *Principle of substitution*
j. *Functional obsolescence*	u. *Replacement cost*
k. *Gross rent multiplier (GRM)*	v. *Reproduction cost*
	w. *Scheduled gross income*
l. *Highest and best use*	x. *Square-foot method*
m. *Income approach*	y. *Subject property*
n. *Incurable depreciation*	z. *The Appraisal Foundation*

1. Properties similar to the subject property that have sold recently.
2. Cost, at today's prices and using today's methods of construction, to build an improvement having the same usefulness as the subject property.
3. Cost at today's prices of constructing an exact replica of the subject improvements using the same or similar methods.
4. A method of valuing property based on the prices of recent sales of similar properties.
5. Land value plus current construction costs less depreciation.
6. The property that is being appraised.
7. Corrections made to comparable properties to account for differences between them and the subject property.
8. A property valuation and listing technique that looks at properties currently for sale, recent sales, and properties that did not sell, and which does not make specific dollar adjustments for differences.
9. Depreciation resulting from wear and tear of the improvements.
10. Depreciation resulting from improvements that are inadequate, overly adequate, or improperly designed for today's needs.
11. The estimated rent a fully occupied property can be expected to produce on an annual basis.
12. To convert future income to current value.
13. Gross income less operating expenses, vacancies, and collection losses.
14. Expenditures necessary to maintain the production of income.
15. Acts as an upper limit on prices; the lower priced of two similar properties will usually sell first.
16. An estimate of the value of something.
17. A method of valuing property based on the monetary return it is expected to produce.
18. A number that is multiplied by a property's gross rents to produce an estimate of its worth.
19. A method for estimating construction costs that is based on the cost per square foot to build a structure.
20. Depreciation that can be fixed at reasonable cost.

21. Depreciation that cannot be fixed at reasonable cost.
22. Organization whose purpose is to establish appraisal standards.
23. A market in which there are few buyers and many sellers.
24. That use of a parcel of land that will produce the greatest current value for the parcel.
25. Loss in value due to deterioration and obsolescence.
26. The cash price that a willing buyer and a willing seller would agree on, given reasonable exposure of the property to the marketplace, full information as to the potential uses of the property, and no undue compulsion to act.

QUESTIONS AND PROBLEMS

1. When making a market comparison appraisal, how many comparable properties should be used?
2. How useful are asking prices and offers to buy when making a market comparison appraisal?
3. In the market approach, are the adjustments made to the subject property or to the comparables? Why?
4. Why is it important when valuing vacant land that comparable properties have similar zoning, neighborhoods, size, and usefulness?
5. Explain the use of gross rent multipliers in valuing real properties. What are the strengths and the weaknesses of this method?
6. What are the five steps used in valuing an improved property by the cost approach?
7. Briefly explain the concept of the income approach to valuing real property.
8. Explain how the competitive market analysis method differs from the standard market approach method. Which method is better? And for what?
9. What precaution does the principle of diminishing marginal returns suggest to a real estate owner?
10. With regard to appraising a single-family house, what type of appraisal format would most likely be requested by a lender? A prospective buyer? An executor of an estate? A highway department?
11. Why was The Appraisal Foundation formed? What should its impact be on the appraisal industry?

ADDITIONAL READINGS

The Art of Real Estate Appraisal: Dollars and Cents Answers to Your Questions, by **William J. Ventolo** and **Martha R. Williams** (Dearborn Financial Publishing, 1992, 190 pages). Provides a good overview of appraising single-family home and residential construction; also provides good techniques based on sales comparison.

Basic Real Estate Appraisal, 3rd Ed., by **Richard M. Betts** and **Silas J. Ely** (Prentice Hall, 1994, 496 pages). Provides a practical guide to real estate appraisal for students, real estate professionals, and consumers. This text continuously references and explains the Uniform Standards of Professional Appraisal Practice and their impact on the appraisal process.

The Dictionary of Real Estate Appraisal, 3rd Ed., (Appraisal Institute, 1994, 527 pages). Provides explanations and definitions for all real estate appraisal terminology.

The Language of Real Estate Appraisal, by **Jeffrey D. Fisher** and **Robert S. Martin** (Real Estate Education, 1991, 264 pages). New dictionary that includes terms and definitions commonly used in the industry.

22

Taxes and Assessments

KEY• TERMS

Adjusted sales price: the sales price of a property less commissions, fix-up, and closing costs

Ad valorem taxes: taxes charged according to the value of a property

Assessed value: a value placed on a property for the purpose of taxation

Assessment appeal board: local governmental body that hears and rules on property owner complaints of overassessment

Basis: the price paid for property; used in calculating income taxes

Documentary tax: a fee or tax on deeds and other documents payable at the time of recordation

Installment sale: sale of real estate in which the proceeds of the sale are deferred beyond the year of sale

Mill rate: property tax rate that is expressed in tenths of a cent per dollar of assessed valuation

Tax certificate: a document issued at a tax sale that entitles the purchaser to a deed at a later date if the property is not redeemed

Tax lien: a charge or hold by the government against property to insure the payment of taxes

The largest single source of income for local government programs and services in America is the property tax. Schools (from kindergarten through 2-year colleges), fire and police departments, local welfare programs, public libraries, street maintenance, parks, and public hospital facilities are mainly supported by property taxes. Some state governments also obtain a portion of their revenues from this source.

PROPERTY TAXES

Property taxes are **ad valorem** taxes. This means that they are levied according to the value of one's property; the more valuable the property is, the higher the tax will be, and vice versa. The underlying theory of ad valorem taxation is that those owning the more valuable properties are wealthier and hence able to pay more taxes.

How does a local government determine the amount of tax to collect each year from each property owner? Step 1 is local budget preparation and appropriation. Step 2 is the appraisal of all taxable property within the taxation district. Step 3 is to allocate the amount to be collected among the taxable properties in the district. Let's look more closely at this process.

Each taxing body prepares its *budget* for the coming year. Taxing bodies include counties, cities, boroughs, towns and villages, and, in some states, school boards, sanitation districts, and county road departments. Each budget, along with a list of sources from which the money will be derived, is enacted into law. This is the **appropriation process.** Then estimated sales taxes, state and federal revenue sharing, business licenses, and city income taxes are subtracted from the budget. The balance must come from property taxes.

Budget and Appropriation

Next, the valuation of the taxable property within each taxing body's district must be determined. A county or state assessor's office **appraises** each taxable parcel of land and the improvements thereon. Appraisal procedures vary from state to state. In New York State, the appraised value is the estimated fair market cash value of the property. This is the cash price one would expect a buyer and a seller to agree on in a normal open-market transaction.

Appraisal and Assessment

The appraised value is converted into an assessed value on which taxes are based. In some states, the **assessed value** is set equal to the appraised value; in others, it is a percentage of the appraised value. Mathematically, the percentage selected makes no difference as long as each property in a taxing district is treated equally. Consider two houses with appraised values of $60,000 and $120,000, respectively. Whether the assessed values are set equal to appraised values or at a percentage of appraised values, the second house will still bear twice the property tax burden of the first.

Tax Rate Calculation   The assessed values of all properties subject to property taxation are added together in order to calculate the tax rate. To explain this process, suppose that a building lies within the taxation districts of the Westside School District, the city of Rostin, and the county of Pearl River. The school district's budget for the coming year requires $800,000 from property taxes, and the assessed value of taxable property within the district is $20 million. By dividing $800,000 by $20 million, we see that the school district must collect a tax of 4 cents for every dollar of assessed valuation. This levy can be expressed three ways: (1) as a mill rate, (2) as dollars per hundred, or (3) as dollars per thousand. All three rating methods are found in the United States. Dollars per thousand or per hundred are used in New York State.

As a **mill rate,** this tax rate is expressed as mills per dollar of assessed valuation. Since 1 mill equals one-tenth of a cent, a 4-cent tax rate is the same as 40 mills. Expressed as *dollars per hundred,* the same rate would be $4 per hundred of assessed valuation. As *dollars per thousand,* it would be $40 per thousand.

The city of Rostin also calculates its tax rate by dividing its property tax requirements by the assessed value of the property within its boundaries. Suppose that its needs are $300,000 and the city limits enclose property totaling $10 million in assessed valuation. (In this example, the city covers a smaller geographical area than the school district.) Thus the city must collect 3 cents for each dollar of assessed valuation in order to balance its budget.

The county government's budget requires $2 million from property taxes and the county contains $200 million in assessed valuation. This makes the county tax rate 1 cent per dollar of assessed valuation. Table 22.1 shows the school district, city, and

Table 22.1. Expressing Property Tax Rates

	Mill Rate	Dollars per Hundred	Dollars per Thousand
School district	40 mills	$4.00	$40.00
City	30	3.00	30.00
County	10	1.00	10.00
Total	80 mills	$8.00	$80.00

county tax rates expressed as mills, dollars per hundred, and dollars per thousand.

Applying the Rate

The final step is to apply the tax rate to each property. For example, to determine the tax on a home with an assessed value of $20,000 using a dollars per hundred rate, divide the $20,000 assessed valuation by $100 and multiply by $8. The result is $1,600. To insure collection, a lien for this amount is placed against the property. It is removed when the tax is paid. Property tax liens are superior to other types of liens. A mortgage foreclosure does not clear property tax liens; they still must be paid.

To avoid duplicate tax bill mailings, it is a common practice for all taxing bodies in a given county to have the county collect for them at the same time that the county collects on its own behalf. As a general rule, the property tax year for municipalities in New York runs from January 1 through December 31. The tax year for most school districts runs from July 1 through June 30, with taxes usually payable on September 1.

Because of the monumental volume of numbers and calculations necessary to budget, appropriate, appraise, assess, and calculate property taxes, computers are widely used in property tax offices. Computers also prepare property tax bills, account for property tax receipts, and mail computer-generated notices to those who have not paid.

UNPAID PROPERTY TAXES

If you own real estate and fail to pay the property taxes, you will lose the property. In New York, a law that became effective in January, 1995 establishes a uniform statewide system of procedures for foreclosing on delinquent properties.

The timetable for the rest of the foreclosure process is determined by the lien date, which is usually the first day of the fiscal year. Ten months after the lien date, the enforcing officer of each tax district records a list of delinquent tax liens in the county clerk's office. The list identifies the owners and location of each delinquent parcel and the amount of the lien against the property. If the property taxes are still unpaid 2 years after the lien date, the tax lien will be foreclosed by a **proceeding in rem.** The property will be sold and the proceeds of the sale will be given to the holder of the lien. A proceeding in rem is a proceeding against the property only and does not involve any recovery against the owner of the property if the proceeds of the sale are not sufficient to cover the amount of the lien. Three months before the foreclosure sale, the enforcement officer must file another petition in the county clerk's office listing the delinquent properties. Before the tax sale, regular notices about the impending sale must be published in the newspaper and notice must be given to the owners of record explaining the consequences of their nonpayment of taxes. The owner may redeem the property at any time before the sale by paying the delinquent taxes and other charges incurred by the local government. Under the new law, the costs can be substantial since they include interest, penalties, mailing, and publication costs, and the costs of title searches and legal services incurred in the foreclosure process. If the taxes are not paid by the time of the sale, the owner loses all right and interest in the property. The local government may allow the delinquent owner to pay the charges in installments if it chooses. The new provisions apply to any tax lien on or after January 1, 1995.

As always, there are some exceptions. Local governments can choose to extend the time for foreclosure from 2 years to 3 or 4 years for residential properties. Also, cities, counties, and towns that adopted a local law regarding delinquent tax collections earlier than 1993 or were authorized to collect delinquent taxes by a special provision in their charter or administrative code by January 1, 1994 are not required to adopt the new procedures. As of this writing, 11 counties, 24 cities, 1 town, and approximately 100 villages have chosen to opt out of the new system. The tax enforcement officer of a taxing unit (usually the county treasurer or the commissioner of finance) or the Office of Real Property Services can provide information about whether a local government has chosen to maintain a different scheme.

In other states, the sale is held soon after the delinquency occurs and the redemption period follows. At the sale, a **tax**

certificate or **certificate of sale** in the amount of the unpaid taxes is sold. The purchaser is entitled to a deed to the property provided the delinquent taxpayer, or anyone holding a lien on the property, does not step forward and redeem it during the following redemption period. If the property is redeemed, the purchaser receives all money back plus interest. The reason that a lienholder (such as a mortgage lender) is allowed to redeem a property is that if the property taxes are not paid, the lienholder's creditor rights in the property are cut off due to the superiority of the tax lien.

The right of government to divorce a property owner from land for nonpayment of property taxes is well established by law. However, if the sale procedure is not properly followed, the purchaser may later find the property's title successfully challenged in court. Thus, it behooves the purchaser to obtain a title search and title insurance and, if necessary, to conduct a quiet title suit.

By law, assessment procedures must be uniformly applied to all properties within a taxing jurisdiction. To this end, the assessed values of all lands and buildings are made available for public inspection. These are the **assessment rolls.** They permit property owners to compare the assessed valuations on their properties with assessed valuations on similar properties. If owners feel overassessed, they can then file an appeal before an **assessment appeal board.** In New York, each local government has a Board of Assessment Review which hears taxpayer grievances after the tentative assessment roll is filed and before it is finalized. The board must notify each taxpayer of its final determination of value. A taxpayer who is not satisfied with the board's determination may bring suit either in Small Claims Court or the Supreme Court within 30 days of the board's final determination. Note that the appeal process deals only with the methods of assessment and taxation, not with the tax rate or the amount of tax.

ASSESSMENT APPEAL

In New York, assessment rolls are normally prepared by cities and towns. Two counties, Nassau and Tompkins, have opted instead for a countywide assessment system. Villages may choose to impose their own assessments but these are used for village purposes only. Counties, except for Nassau and Tomp-

EQUALIZATION RATES

kins, and school districts use the assessment rolls prepared by cities and towns to determine the tax levy on each property.

Although all local governments are required to assess property at its market value, many communities have not yet complied and still impose "fractional" assessments. These fractional assessments typically value all properties at a uniform percentage of their full or market value. Whenever a taxing district crosses local government lines, an **equalization rate** must be applied to relate the assessed values on a local assessment roll to a common standard of full value which is estimated by the state. School districts, for example, often cross town lines. The use of equalization rates places the local assessment roll of each town on an equal footing for the purpose of calculating school taxes. The state equalization rate is prepared by the **Office of Real Property Services** based on information submitted by local assessors. Counties and school districts may develop their own equalization rates or use the state rate for taxing districts that include more than one assessing unit.

PROPERTY TAX EXEMPTIONS

More than half the land in many cities and counties is exempt from real property taxation. This is because governments and their agencies do not tax themselves or each other. Thus, government-owned offices of all types, public roads and parks, schools, military bases, and government-owned utilities are exempt from property taxes. Also exempted are most properties owned by religious and charitable organizations (so long as they are used for religious or charitable purposes), hospitals, and cemeteries. In rural areas of many states, large tracts of land are owned by federal and state governments, and these too are exempt from taxation.

Property tax exemptions are used to attract industries. For example, a local government agency buys industrial land and buildings and leases them to industries at a price lower than would be possible if they were privately owned and hence taxed. Alternatively, outright property tax reductions can be granted for a certain length of time to newly established or relocating firms. The rationale is that the cost to the public is outweighed by the economic boost that the new industry brings to the community. A number of states grant assessment reductions to homeowners. This increases the tax burden for households that rent and for commercial properties.

New York grants the traditional exemptions for municipal property school districts, religious and nonprofit organizations, historic properties, and fraternal and veterans' organizations. It also allows local governments to offer property tax exemptions to homeowners over 65 years old on a sliding scale from 20% to a maximum of 45% of assessed value depending on the household income.

Property taxes on similarly priced homes within a city or county can vary widely when prices change faster than the assessor's office can reappraise. As a result, a home worth $90,000 in one neighborhood may receive a tax bill of $1,800 per year, while a $90,000 home in another neighborhood will be billed $2,400. When the assessor's office conducts a reappraisal, taxes in the first neighborhood will suddenly rise 33%, undoubtedly provoking complaints from property owners who were unaware that previously they were underassessed. In times of slow-changing real estate prices, reappraisals were made only once every 10 years. Today, assessors are developing computerized appraisal systems that can make adjustments annually.

PROPERTY TAX VARIATIONS

As an aid to keeping current on property value changes, state law requires purchasers to advise the assessor's office of the price and terms of their purchases by filing a Real Property Transfer Report. This form is usually available in the county clerk's office and must be filed before the new deed will be accepted for recording. This information, coupled with building permit records and on-site visits by assessor's office employees, provides the data necessary to update assessments regularly.

The amount of property taxes a property owner may expect to pay varies from one city to the next and from one state to the next. Why is this? The answer is found by looking at the level of services offered, other sources of revenue, taxable property, and government efficiency. Generally, cities with low property taxes offer fewer services to their residents. This may be by choice, such as offering smaller welfare payments, lower school expenditures per student, no subsidized public transportation, fewer parks and libraries, or because the city does not include the cost of some services in the property tax. For example, sewer fees may be added to the water bill and trash may be hauled by private firms. Lower rates can also be due to location. Wage rates are lower in some regions of the country, and a city not subject to ice and snow will have lower street maintenance expenses. Finally, a city may have other sources of revenue, such as oil royalties from wells on city property.

Property tax levels are also influenced by the ability of local tax districts to obtain federal funds and state revenues (especially for schools), and to share in collections from sales taxes, license fees, liquor and tobacco taxes, and fines.

The amount and type of taxable property in a community greatly affects local tax rates. Taxable property must bear the burden created by tax-exempt property, whereas privately owned vacant land, stores, factories, and high-priced homes generally produce more taxes than they consume in local government services and help to keep rates lower. Finally, one must look at the efficiency of the city. Has it managed its affairs in prior years so that the current budget is not burdened with large interest payments on debts caused by deficits in previous years? Is the city or county itself laid out in a compact and efficient manner, or does its sheer size make administration expensive? How many employees are required to perform a given service?

Tax Limitation Measures

Unhappy with rising property taxes, particularly when real estate prices were skyrocketing in the 1970s, voters in a number of states went to the polls and voted to limit property tax increases. In some states limits have been placed on the amount of taxes that can be collected. In other states limits have been placed on how much government can spend. The cooling off in real estate price increases that began in 1980 has taken much of the urgency out of capping property tax increases. As a result, fewer such measures have been seen on ballots, and when they do appear, they do not pass as easily as they once did.

SPECIAL
ASSESSMENTS

Often the need arises to make local municipal improvements that will benefit property owners within a limited area, such as the paving of a street, the installation of street lights, curbs, storm drains, and sanitary sewer lines, or the construction of irrigation and drainage ditches. Such improvements can be provided through **special assessments** on property.

The theory underlying special assessments is that the improvements must benefit the land against which the cost will be charged, and the value of the benefits must exceed the cost. The area receiving the benefit of an improvement is the **improvement district** or **assessment district,** and the property within that district bears the cost of the improvement. This is different from a **public improvement.** A public improvement, such as reconstruction of the city's sewage plant, benefits the general public and is financed through the general (ad valorem) property tax. A local improvement, such as extending a sewer line into a street of homes presently using septic tanks or cesspools, does not benefit the public at large and should properly be charged only to those who directly benefit. Similarly, when streets are widened, owners of homes lining a 20-foot-wide street in a strictly residential neighborhood would be expected to bear the cost of widening it to 30 or 40 feet and to donate the needed land from their front yards. But a street widening from two lanes to four to accommodate traffic not generated by the homes on the street is a different situation because the widening benefits the public at large. In this case, the street widening is funded from public monies and the homeowners are paid for any land taken from them.

Forming an Improvement District

An improvement district can be formed by the action of a group of concerned citizens who want and are willing to pay for an improvement. Property owners desiring the improvement take their proposal to the local board of assessors or similar public body in charge of levying assessments. A public notice showing the proposed improvements, the extent of the improvement district, and the anticipated costs is prepared by the board. This notice is mailed to landowners in the proposed improvement district, posted conspicuously in the district, and published in a local newspaper. The notice also contains the date and place of public hearings on the matter at which property owners within the proposed district are invited to voice their comments and objections.

Confirmation

If the hearings result in a decision to proceed, then under the authority granted by state laws regarding special improvements, a local government ordinance is passed that describes the project and its costs and the improvement district boundaries. An assessment roll is also prepared that shows the cost to each parcel in the district. Hearings are held regarding the assessment roll. When everything is in order, the roll is **confirmed** (approved). Then the contract to construct the improvements is awarded and work is started.

The proposal to create an improvement district can also come from a city council, board of trustees, or board of supervisors. When this happens, notices are distributed and hearings are held to listen to objections from affected parties. Objections are ruled on by a court of law and, if the objections are found to have merit, the assessment plans must be revised or dropped. Once approved, assessment rolls are prepared, more hearings are held, the roll is confirmed, and the contract is awarded.

Bond Issues   On completion of the improvement, each landowner receives a bill for his portion of the cost. If the cost to a landowner is less than $100, the landowner either pays the amount in full to the contractor directly or to a designated public official who, in turn, pays the contractor. If the assessment is larger, the landowner can immediately pay it in full or let it **go to bond.** If he lets it go to bond, local government officials prepare a bond issue that totals all the unpaid assessments in the improvement district. These bonds are either given to the contractor as payment for his work or sold to the public through a securities dealer, and the proceeds are used to pay the contractor. The collateral for the bonds is the land in the district on which assessments have not been paid.

The bonds spread the cost of the improvements over a period of 5 to 10 years and are payable in equal annual (or semiannual) installments plus accumulated interest. Thus, a $2,000 sewer and street-widening assessment on a 10-year bond would be charged to a property owner at the rate of $200 per year (or $100 each 6 months) plus interest. As the bond is gradually retired, the amount of interest added to the regular principal payment declines.

Like property taxes, special assessments are a lien against the property. Consequently, if a property owner fails to pay the assessment, the assessed property can be sold in the same manner as when property taxes are delinquent.

Apportionment   Special assessments are apportioned according to benefits received rather than by the value of the land and buildings being assessed. In fact, the presence of buildings in an improvement district is not usually considered in preparing the assessment roll; the theory is that the land receives all the benefit of the improvement. Several illustrations can best explain how assessments are apportioned. In a residential neighborhood, the assessment for installation of storm drains, curbs, and gutters is made on a **front-foot basis.** Property owners are charged for each foot of their lots that abuts the street being improved.

In the case of a sanitary sewer line assessment, the charge per lot can be based either on front footage or on a simple count of the lots in the district. In the latter case, if there are 100 lots on the new sewer line, each would pay 1% of the cost. In the case of a park or playground, lots nearest the new facility are deemed to benefit more and thus are assessed more than lots located farther away. This form of allocation is very subjective, and usually results in spirited objections at public hearings from those who do not feel they will use the facility in proportion to the assessment that their lots will bear.

We now turn to the income taxes that are due if one sells a personal residence for more than was paid. Income taxes are levied by the federal government, by 44 states (the exceptions are Florida, Nevada, South Dakota, Texas, Washington, and Wyoming), and by 48 cities, including New York City, Baltimore, Pittsburgh, Philadelphia, Cincinnati, Cleveland, and Detroit. The discussion here centers on the federal income tax and includes key provisions of the **Internal Revenue Code of 1986,** also known as the **Tax Reform Act of 1986,** as it applies to owner-occupied residences. State and city income tax laws generally follow the pattern of federal tax laws.

INCOME TAXES ON THE SALE OF ONE'S RESIDENCE

The first step in determining the amount of taxable gain on the sale of an owner-occupied residence is to calculate the home's **basis.** This is the price originally paid for the home plus any fees paid for closing services and legal counsel, and any fee or commission paid to help find the property. If the home was built rather than purchased, the basis is the cost of the land plus the cost of construction, such as the cost of materials and construction labor, architect's fees, building permit fees, planning and zoning commission approval costs, utility connection charges, and legal fees. The value of labor contributed by the homeowner

Calculating a Home's Basis

and free labor from friends and relatives cannot be added. If the home was received as compensation, a gift, an inheritance, or in a trade, or if a portion of the home was depreciated for business purposes, special rules apply that will not be covered here, and the seller should consult the Internal Revenue Service (IRS).

Assessments for local improvements and any improvements made by the seller are added to the original cost of the home. An improvement is a permanent betterment that materially adds to the value of a home, prolongs its life, or changes its use. For example, finishing an unfinished basement or upper floor, building a swimming pool, adding a bedroom or bathroom, installing new plumbing or wiring, installing a new roof, erecting a new fence, and paving a new driveway are considered to be improvements and are added to the home's basis. Maintenance and repairs are not added as they merely maintain the property in ordinary operating condition. Fixing gutters, mending leaks in plumbing, replacing broken windowpanes, and painting the inside or outside of the home are considered maintenance and repair items. However, repairs made as part of an extensive remodeling or restoration job may be added to the basis.

Calculating the Amount Realized The next step in determining taxable gain is to calculate the **amount realized** from the sale. This is the selling price of the home less selling expenses. Selling expenses include brokerage commissions, advertising, legal fees, title services, escrow or closing fees, and mortgage points paid by the seller. If the sale includes furnishings, the value of those furnishings is deducted from the selling price and reported separately as personal property. If the seller takes back a note and mortgage which are

Table 22.2. Calculation of Gain

Buy home for $90,000; closing costs are $500	Basis is	$90,500
Add landscaping and fencing for $3,500	Basis is	$94,000
Add bedroom and bathroom for $15,000	Basis is	$109,000
Sell home for $125,000; sales commissions and closing costs are $8,000	Amount realized	$117,000
Calculation of gain:	Amount realized	$117,000
	Less basis	−109,000
	Equals gain	$ 8,000

immediately sold at a discount, the discounted value of the note is used, not its face amount.

The **gain on the sale** is the difference between the amount realized and the basis. Table 22.2 illustrates this with an example. Unless the seller qualifies for tax postponement or tax exclusion as discussed next, this is the amount to be reported as gain on the seller's annual income tax forms. To increase compliance with this rule, effective January 1, 1987, reporting of real estate transactions on IRS Form 1099 is required of persons in the following order: (1) the person responsible for the closing, (2) the mortgage lender, (3) the seller's broker, (4) the buyer's broker, and (5) any person designated by the IRS.

Calculating Gain on the Sale

The income tax law of the United States provides that if a seller purchases another home, the gain on the sale of the first home is automatically postponed if the seller meets two conditions. The first condition is that another home must be purchased and occupied within the time period beginning 24 months before the closing date of the old home and ending 24 months after the closing date. A seller who decides to build has the same 48 months to finish and occupy the new home. These time limits must be strictly observed or the deferment is lost.

Income Tax Postponement

The second condition is that the next home must cost as much as or more than the adjusted sales price of the previous home. The **adjusted sales price** is the selling price of the old home less selling expenses and fix-up expenses. Fix-up expenses are for fix-up and repair work performed on the home to make it more saleable. For fix-up and repair work to be deductible, the work must be performed during the 90-day period ending on the day the contract to sell is signed, and it must be paid for within another 30 days. Table 22.3 illustrates the method for calculating adjusted sales price.

If the new home costs less than the adjusted sales price of the old, there will be a taxable gain. For example, if the old home had a basis of $150,000 and an adjusted sales price of $225,000, and the new home cost $215,000, then there would be a taxable gain of $10,000 and a postponed gain of $65,000. The basis of the new home is $215,000 minus the postponed gain of $65,000— that is, $150,000.

Table 22.3. Adjusted Sales Price

Selling price of old home	$250,000
Less selling expenses	− 18,000
Less fix-up costs	− 7,000
Equals adjusted sales price	$225,000

      Postponement of gain is continued from one home to the next as long as the cost of each subsequent home exceeds the adjusted sales price of the previous home, and as long as the owner maintains residency at least 24 months between sales. (A shorter turnover period is usually allowed for work-related moves.) The basis of the first home is simply carried forward and included in the basis of the second home, which in turn is carried forward to the third home, and so on. Note that it is not the amount of cash one puts into a home, or the size of the mortgage that counts, but the sales price. Thus it is possible to move from a home with a small mortgage to a slightly more expensive home with a large mortgage and finish the transaction with cash in the pocket and postponed taxes. Additionally, the law does not restrict the type of home one may own and occupy. Thus the seller of a single-family residence can buy another house, or a condominium, or a cooperative (or vice versa) and still qualify for postponement. Table 22.4 illustrates a progression of tax-deferred residence replacements.

LIFETIME EXCLUSION   The postponement of taxes on gains as one moves from one home to the next works well as long as consistently more expensive homes are purchased. However, there may come a time in the homeowner's life when a smaller and presumably less ex-

Table 22.4. Tax-Deferred Residence Replacement

1. Cost and improvements for first home	$ 50,000
2. Adjusted sales price of first home	80,000
3. Gain on sale of first home	30,000
4. Cost of second home	105,000
5. Basis in second home (line 4 minus line 3)	75,000
6. Adjusted sales price of second home	130,000
7. Gain on sale of second house (line 6 minus line 5)	55,000
8. Cost of third home	160,000
9. Basis in third home (line 8 minus line 7)	105,000

pensive home is needed. To soften the tax burden that such a move usually causes, Congress has enacted legislation that allows a once-in-a-lifetime election to avoid tax on up to $125,000 of gain on the sale of one's residence. To qualify for this, one must be 55 years of age or older on the date of sale and have owned and occupied the residence for at least 3 of the 5 years preceding the sale. Any profit over $125,000 is taxable, but may be postponed if another residence is purchased in accordance with the rules previously described. For example, a person owning a $225,000 home with a basis of $50,000 could sell and move to a $100,000 home with no taxable gain. A person owning a $175,000 home with a $50,000 basis could sell, rent an apartment rather than buy again, and have no taxable gain. By combining postponement with this $125,000 exclusion it is quite possible to eliminate the taxable gain from a lifetime of homeownership.

Prior to January 1, 1987, any gain that could not be deferred was categorized as either a short-term or a long-term gain. Short-term meant a holding period of 6 months or less, and long-term meant a holding period of more than 6 months. Tax treatment excluded 60% of long-term gains from one's income, thus lowering the income taxes due on the gain. As of January 1, 1987, the 60% exclusion was repealed and both long-term and short-term gain are now 100% taxable at ordinary income tax rates. Although ordinary rates were reduced in 1987 and 1988, they were increased in 1993; the net effect is still a higher tax on gains. One aspect of the old rules appears to have remained: A loss on the sale of a personal residence cannot be used as a deduction against other income.

TAXABLE GAIN

When a gain cannot be postponed or excluded, a popular method of deferring income taxes is to use the **installment method** of reporting the gain. This can be applied to homeowner gains that do not qualify for postponement or exclusion.

INSTALLMENT METHOD

Suppose that your property, which is free and clear of debt, is sold for $100,000. The real estate commission and closing costs are $7,500 and your basis is $40,000. As a result, the gain on this sale is $52,500. If you sell for all cash, you are required to pay all the income taxes due on that gain in the year of sale, a situation that may force you into a higher tax bracket. A solution is to sell to the buyer on terms rather than to send him or her to a lender to obtain a loan.

For example, if the buyer pays you $20,000 down and gives you a promissory note calling for a principal payment of $5,000, plus interest this year, and a principal payment of $25,000 plus interest in each of the next 3 years, your gain is calculated and reported as follows. Of each dollar of sales price received, 52.5 cents is reported as gain. Thus, $10,500 is reported this year and in each of the next 3 years. The interest you earn on the promissory note is reported and taxed separately as interest income.

If there is a $30,000 mortgage on the property that the buyer agrees to assume, the $100,000 sales price is reduced by $30,000 to $70,000 for tax-calculating purposes. The portion of each dollar paid to you by the buyer that must be reported as gain is $52,500 divided by $70,000, or 75%. If the down payment is $20,000 followed by $10,000 per year for 5 years, you would report 75% of $20,000, or $15,000 this year and $7,500 in each of the next 5 years. The gain is taxed at the income tax rates in effect at the time the installment is received.

If you sell by the installment method, that is, you sell property at a gain in one taxable year and receive one or more payments in later taxable years, the installment method of reporting is automatically applied. If this is not suitable, you can elect to pay all the taxes in the year of sale. The installment method is only available to those who are not "dealers" in real property. All dealers in real property are required to pay all the taxes in the year of sale.

PROPERTY TAX AND INTEREST DEDUCTIONS

The Internal Revenue Code of 1986 retains the deductibility of state and local real estate taxes. A homeowner can deduct real property taxes and personal property taxes from other income when calculating income taxes. This applies to single-family residences, condominiums, and cooperatives. The deduction does not extend to special assessment taxes for improvement districts.

The Internal Revenue Code of 1986 also retains the deductibility of interest, subject to two limitations that will be discussed separately. However, the basic rule is that interest paid to finance the purchase of a home is deductible against a homeowner's other income. Also deductible are interest paid on improvement district bonds, loan prepayment penalties, and the deduction of points on new loans that are clearly distinguishable as interest and not service fees for making the loan. Loan points paid by a seller to help a buyer obtain an FHA or VA loan are not deductible as interest (it is not the seller's debt), but can be deducted from the home's selling price in computing a gain or loss on the sale. FHA mortgage insurance premiums are not deductible nor are those paid to private mortgage insurers.

The Internal Revenue Code limits the interest deduction to the taxpayer's principal residence plus one other residence.

INTEREST DEDUCTION LIMITATIONS

All of the interest is deductible on a loan to purchase a first or second home, although the aggregate amount of acquisition indebtedness may not exceed $1 million. However, if a home is refinanced and the amount borrowed exceeds the home's basis (original cost plus improvements, etc.), the interest on the excess amount is not deductible. The aggregate amount of home equity indebtedness may not exceed $100,000. Thus, a homeowner will not only want to keep records of his or her home's basis for sale purposes but also as information for refinancing. Also, if refinancing above basis is for medical or educational purposes, then careful records of those expenses must be kept in order to justify the deduction.

From an individual taxpayer's standpoint, the ability to deduct property taxes and mortgage interest on one's residence becomes more valuable in higher tax brackets. As viewed from a national standpoint, the deductibility of interest and property taxes encourages widespread ownership of the country's land and buildings.

Because tax rules for real estate are continually changing, only the major rules have been reported and discussed here. As a real estate owner or agent you need a source of more frequent and more detailed information such as the annual income tax guide published by the Internal Revenue Service (free) or the privately published guides available in most bookstores. Additionally, you may wish to subscribe to a tax newsletter for up-to-the-minute tax information.

IMPACT ON REAL ESTATE

Please be aware that tax law changes have an impact on real estate values. In the past, tax laws have been very generous to real estate—particularly deductions for depreciation and interest as well as credits for the rehabilitation of old buildings. Many otherwise uneconomic real estate projects have become economically feasible because of tax laws. Changes in tax laws to reduce the incentive to buy real estate have had a dramatic effect on real estate investors and, predictably, on the sales prices of parcels of real estate.

AGENT'S LIABILITY FOR TAX ADVICE

The real estate industry's desire for professional recognition, coupled with the results of several key court cases, strongly suggests that a real estate agent be reasonably knowledgeable about taxes. This does not mean the agent must have knowledge of tax laws at the level of an accountant or tax attorney, nor does it mean that an agent can plead ignorance of tax laws. Rather it means that a real estate agent is now liable for tax advice (or lack of it) if the advice is material to the transaction. Giving such advice is now common in the brokerage business. An agent should have enough general knowledge of real estate tax laws to be able to answer basic questions accurately and to warn clients and recommend tax counsel if the questions posed by the transaction are beyond the agent's knowledge. Note that the obligation to inform exists even when a client fails to ask about tax consequences. This obligation is stated to avoid situations in which, after the deed is recorded, the client says, "Gee, I didn't know I'd have to pay all these taxes, my agent should have warned me," and then sues the agent. Lastly, if the agent tries to fill the role of accountant or tax attorney for the client, then the agent will be held liable to the standards of an accountant or tax attorney.

To summarize, an agent must be aware of tax laws that affect the properties the agent is handling. An agent has a responsibility to alert clients to potential tax consequences, liabilities, and advantages whether they ask for it or not. Lastly, an agent is responsible for the quality and accuracy of tax information given out by the agent.

CONVEYANCE TAXES

Before 1968, the federal government required the purchase and placement of federal **documentary tax** stamps on deeds. The rate was 55 cents for each $500 or fraction thereof computed on the "new money" in the transaction. Thus, if a person bought a home for $75,000 and either paid cash or arranged for a new mortgage, the tax was based on the full $75,000. If the buyer assumed or took title subject to an existing $50,000 loan, then the tax was based on $25,000. Examples of federal documentary tax stamps, which look much like postage stamps, can still be seen on deeds recorded prior to 1968.

Effective January 1, 1968, the federal deed tax program ended, and many states took the opportunity to begin charging a deed tax or **conveyance tax** of their own. New York State adopted fee schedules that are substantially the same as the federal government previously charged. In New York, there are as many as three different taxes that may have to be paid in order to record a mortgage. The first is a general mortgage tax of $0.50 per $100 of debt. The second is a tax of $0.25 per $100 of debt and is applied to mortgages recorded in counties where there is a subsidized public transportation authority. It does not apply to the first $10,000 of debt on one- and two-family dwellings. The third tax is also $0.25 per $100 of debt and is used to fund the New York Mortgage Agency Insurance program. This tax applies only to one- to six-family dwellings. The first two taxes just discussed are paid by the borrower. The third one mentioned is paid by the lender. Taxes on deeds and mortgages are paid to the county clerk and are in addition to the charge for recording the deed or mortgage document.

Match terms **a–p** *with statements* **1–16.**

VOCABULARY REVIEW

a. *Adjusted sales price*	**i.** *Improvement district*
b. *Ad valorem tax*	**j.** *Installment method*
c. *Appropriation process*	**k.** *Long-term capital gain*
d. *Assessed value*	**l.** *Mill rate*
e. *Assessment appeal board*	**m.** *Public improvement*
f. *Assessment roll*	**n.** *Special assessments*
g. *Conveyance tax*	**o.** *Tax certificate*
h. *Front-foot basis*	**p.** *Tax deed*

1. A tax rate expressed in tenths of a cent per dollar of assessed valuation.
2. According to value.
3. A document issued at a tax sale that entitles the purchaser to a deed at a later date if the property is not redeemed.
4. The enactment of a taxing body's budget and sources of money into law.
5. A book that contains the assessed value of each property in the county or taxing district.

6. A document conveying title to property purchased at a tax sale.
7. A value placed on a property for the purpose of taxation.
8. Assessments levied to provide publicly built improvements that will primarily benefit property owners within a small geographical area.
9. A charge or levy based directly on the measured distance that a parcel of land abuts a street.
10. Sales price of a property less fix-up costs, sales commissions, closing, and other selling costs.
11. A preferential income tax treatment on the sale of an appreciated asset before 1987.
12. Sale of an appreciated property structured to spread out the payment of income taxes on the gain.
13. Body that hears complaints from property owners regarding their assessments.
14. A state or local tax charged on deeds at the time of recording.
15. The geographical area that will be assessed for a local improvement.
16. An improvement that benefits the public at large and is therefore financed by general property taxes.

QUESTIONS AND PROBLEMS

1. Explain the process for calculating the property tax rate for a taxation district.
2. The Southside School District contains property totaling $120 million in assessed valuation. If the district's budget is $960,000, what will the mill rate be?
3. Continuing with Problem 2, if a home situated in the Southside School District carries an assessed valuation of $40,000, how much will the homeowner be required to pay to support the district this year?
4. The Lakeview Mosquito Abatement District levies an annual tax of $0.05 per $100 of assessed valuation to pay for a mosquito control program. How much does that amount to for a property in the district with an assessed valuation of $10,000?
5. In your county, if a property owner wishes to appeal an assessment, what procedure must be followed?
6. If the property taxes on your home were to rise 90% in 1 year, where would you go to protest the increase: to the assessment appeal board, to the city council, or to the county government? Explain.
7. How does the amount of tax-exempt real estate in a community affect nonexempt property owners?
8. What methods and techniques are used by your local assessor's office to keep up to date with the changing real estate prices?
9. The Smiths bought a house in 1963 for $21,000, including closing costs. Five years later they made improvements costing $2,000 and 5 years after that they made more improvements that cost $5,000. Today they sell the house; the sales price is $68,000, and commissions and closing costs total $5,000. For income tax purposes, what is their gain?
10. Continuing with Problem 9, a month after selling, the Smiths purchase a two-bedroom condominium for $58,000, including closing costs.

What is their taxable gain now? (Assume that the Smiths are less than 55 years of age.)

11. What is the conveyance tax rate in your state? What would the conveyance tax be on a $100,000 home?

ADDITIONAL READINGS

Real Estate Investment and Taxation, 4th Ed., by **Stephen D. Messner** (Prentice Hall, 1991, 546 pages). Analyzes and compares the relative benefits of real estate investment opportunities.

"Reducing Property Tax Liabilities," (*Mortgage and Real Estate Executive Report,* May 15, 1994, pp. 7–8). Article points out circumstances that could allow you to reduce your property taxes.

"Taking on the Tax Assessor: When the Market Value of Your Property Changes, So Should Your Assessed Value," by **Marsha Bertrand** (*Financial Freedom Report Quarterly,* Winter 1994, pp. 98–100).

Tax Information on Selling Your Home (Internal Revenue Service, 1995, Publication 523). This publication is free and is offered annually from the IRS.

23

Basic Principles of Construction

KEY • TERMS

Bearing beam: a continuous built-up wooden girder (usually three 2×10s nailed together)

Bottom and top plates: the horizontal structural members of the wall system

Floor joists: horizontal beams running from one wall to another to support the floor

Footing: usually a poured concrete base which distributes the weight of the structure uniformly over a wide solid base

Footing drains: continuous perforated pipe at the level of the footing to divert water away from the structure

Foundation wall: a concrete block or poured concrete wall that distributes the weight of the structure uniformly to the footings

Header (or lintel): a horizontal beam across door and window openings that extends between two studs and is supported on each side by one or more jacks

Lally columns: columns that support the bearing beam spaced approximately every 6 feet. A lally column is a concrete-filled steel post

National Electric Code (NFPA 70): the code providing minimum electrical requirements for a home in most communities in New York State

Reinforcing rods: continuous steel rods embedded in the concrete footing

Ridge beam: a wooden member running the full length of the roof into which the roof rafters are nailed

R-value: a term that describes a material's resistance to the transfer of heat, a higher R-value indicating a greater insulating value

Sill plate: usually a pressure-treated 2×6 fastened to the foundation wall by anchors embedded in the concrete

Sill sealer: a styrofoam blanket laid on top of the foundation wall

Stud: a vertical structural member of the wall system to which the sheathing and exterior siding are attached

Subfloor: a working platform that provides a base for additional floor finishes

A working knowledge of construction basics is important to anyone who wishes to make a career in real estate. This chapter will familiarize you with the terminology of basic construction. To accomplish this, we will walk through the procedure for building a new house from the ground up.

Construction in New York State is governed by the **New York State Uniform Fire Prevention and Building Code,** which went into effect in 1984. The Uniform State Code is designed to ensure the safety of all residential and commercial construction in New York State. All new construction or substantial improvements to buildings after that time must comply with the State code. Enforcement authority rests with the cities, villages, or towns that chose to accept it. They may, however, opt out, and the authority then shifts to the next level of government. The city, then, may opt out to the county, which may opt out to the state.

RESIDENTIAL AND COMMERCIAL

The first step in constructing a house is to obtain a building permit from the appropriate authority. The permit approval process can be painless, or agonizingly slow, depending on how many agencies have jurisdiction over your project. Building permits are usually issued by a city or town building inspector, although in some communities the county or state might issue the permit.

Before issuing the permit, the building department will usually require you to submit an application with a plot plan and two sets of construction drawings. The plot plan shows the proposed location of structures to be built on the lot, and the building inspector will review it to ensure that they meet the zoning and planning requirements of the community. The two sets of plans are necessary so that the building inspector can review them for code compliance. He will make comments and/or changes and return one copy to you with your building permit. The retained copy remains on permanent file with the building department.

The construction drawings show the detail for each of the major structural and mechanical systems: foundation, framing, plumbing, heating, ventilation, and air conditioning (HVAC), and electrical. When the inspector is satisfied that your plans comply with the code, he will issue a building permit that must be displayed on the site during construction.

Because a building permit is a property right, which cannot be withdrawn without due process, the inspector must take care in reviewing your plans. He may request any clarifying information to ensure compliance with the code and may even require you to submit drawings stamped by a civil engineer. If, in reviewing the plans, the inspector misses a code violation, the approval does not allow you to violate the code. As the building progresses, if he finds on further review or during his periodic inspections that there is a code violation, you must correct it.

Schedule of Inspections

The building department determines the inspection schedule. Typically, it includes an inspection of the excavation, footings, foundation before backfilling, framing, insulation, plumbing, electric, and a final inspection. The plumbing inspection usually includes an inspection of all HVAC systems. Sometimes a framing inspection is required before and after the installation of mechanical and drainage systems. If there are no problems with the inspections, or the problems are corrected the building inspector issues a certificate of occupancy (CO).

SITE DEVELOPMENT
AND FOUNDATION

Excavation is more than merely digging a hole for the foundation. It is the beginning of the overall construction. The excavation should also take into account the final grading, landscaping, and drainage systems.

Once the excavation is completed, the site is ready to pour **footings.** The purpose of the footing is to distribute the weight of the structure uniformly over a wide solid base. Although there are provisions in the code for several types of footings, typically the footing consists of poured concrete and is generally twice the width of the foundation wall. Although not always required, most building inspectors will not permit footings to be poured without **reinforcing rods.** Reinforcing rods are continuous steel rods embedded in the concrete footing. **Footing drains** are usually required and are occasionally placed just after the footings are poured. These are continuous perforated pipe at the level of the footing to divert water away from the structure.

Once the footings are poured and pass inspection, the next step is pouring the **foundation walls** (Figure 23.1). The foundation wall distributes the weight of the structure uniformly to the footings. While the code provides for several types of foundation walls, most contractors, building inspectors, and homeown-

Figure 23.1. Foundation dampproofing and waterproofing.

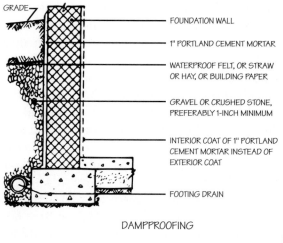

GRADE

FOUNDATION WALL

1" PORTLAND CEMENT MORTAR

WATERPROOF FELT, OR STRAW
OR HAY, OR BUILDING PAPER

GRAVEL OR CRUSHED STONE,
PREFERABLY 1-INCH MINIMUM

INTERIOR COAT OF 1" PORTLAND
CEMENT MORTAR INSTEAD OF
EXTERIOR COAT

FOOTING DRAIN

DAMPPROOFING

Footing drains of clay tile, asbestos cement, bituminized fiber, or concrete, 4 inches to 6 inches in diameter, are to be installed wherever water may accumulate against cellar or basement walls and floors, or flow into cellars or basements, or create hydrostatic pressure. Drains are to be laid with open joints protected at the top with building paper. Drains are then to be covered with not less than 12 inches of gravel or other porous material, preferably 1-inch minimum size. Drains are to be connected to tight joint pipe or tile leading to a dry well or sewer or other outlet.

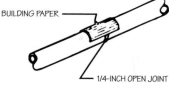

BUILDING PAPER

1/4-INCH OPEN JOINT

Leveling bed is to be of concrete and may be of lightweight aggregate.

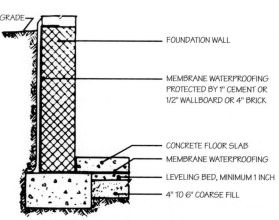

GRADE

FOUNDATION WALL

MEMBRANE WATERPROOFING
PROTECTED BY 1" CEMENT OR
1/2" WALLBOARD OR 4" BRICK

CONCRETE FLOOR SLAB
MEMBRANE WATERPROOFING
LEVELING BED, MINIMUM 1 INCH
4" TO 6" COARSE FILL

WATERPROOFING

ers prefer poured concrete. The foundation will generally be eight or ten inches thick and up to 7 feet 6 inches high. The foundation is treated with a sealer up to grade level to keep dampness out. Once the drain tiles are in place and the sealer is applied, the foundation is ready for inspection. The foundation must be approved before the site can be backfilled.

The next step is installing the first floor deck. Many builders delay backfilling until the deck is complete because damage to the foundation wall is less likely to occur after the deck is on.

*FIRST FLOOR DECK
AND WALLS*

Construction of the deck begins by applying a **sill sealer,** which is a styrofoam blanket laid on top of the foundation wall. Next comes the installation of the **sill plate,** usually a pressure-treated 2×6 fastened to the foundation wall by anchors embedded in the concrete (Figure 23.2). After the sill plate is in place, the **bearing beam** is put in place. This is a continuous built-up wooden girder (usually three 2×10s nailed together). The bearing beam is supported by **lally columns,** sufficiently spaced (typically every 6 feet) to carry the anticipated floor load and adequately supported (normally a 2 ft×2 ft×1 ft concrete base poured at the same time as the footings). A lally column is a concrete-filled steel post. (See Figure 23.3.)

After the bearing beam is in place, the next step is laying out the **floor joists** (most commonly a 2×10). A joist is a horizontal beam running from one wall to another to support the floor. The size and spacing of the floor joists are determined by the design requirements; they are usually spaced 16 inches on center (OC), or 16 inches apart, measured from the center of one board to the center of another.

After the floor joists are in place, work begins on the **subfloor** (usually ¾-inch plyscore or wafer board). The subfloor acts as a working platform and provides a base for additional floor finishes. With the installation of the subfloor, the deck is complete (Figure 23.2).

Wall System   The **wall system** consists of a bottom plate, a double top plate, and studs. The purpose of this system is to distribute the roof

Figure 23.2. Floor framing.

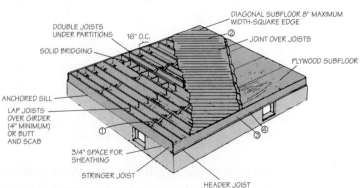

DIAGONAL SUBFLOOR 8" MAXIMUM WIDTH-SQUARE EDGE

DOUBLE JOISTS UNDER PARTITIONS

16" O.C.

JOINT OVER JOISTS

SOLID BRIDGING

PLYWOOD SUBFLOOR

ANCHORED SILL

LAP JOISTS OVER GIRDER (4" MINIMUM) OR BUTT AND SCAB

3/4" SPACE FOR SHEATHING

STRINGER JOIST

HEADER JOIST

Figure 23.3. Continuous built-up girders, three or more supports.

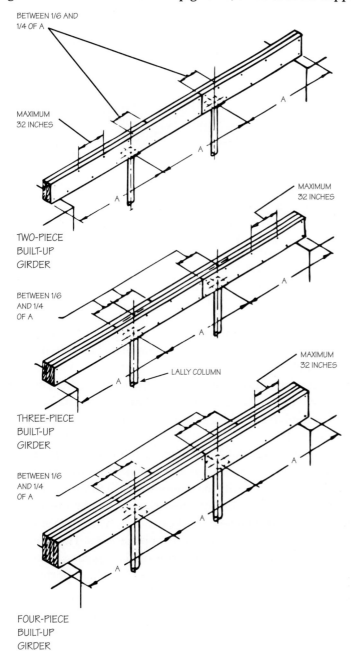

BETWEEN 1/6 AND 1/4 OF A

MAXIMUM 32 INCHES

TWO-PIECE
BUILT-UP
GIRDER

BETWEEN 1/6
AND 1/4
OF A

MAXIMUM
32 INCHES

LALLY COLUMN

THREE-PIECE
BUILT-UP
GIRDER

BETWEEN 1/6
AND 1/4
OF A

MAXIMUM
32 INCHES

FOUR-PIECE
BUILT-UP
GIRDER

Assembly Requirements—When girders made up of joists nailed together side by side are continuous over three or more supports, joints in joists are to be located between one sixth and one quarter the span length from an intermediate support. No two adjoining joists, nor more than one third the total number, are to be jointed on the same side of the support.

Nailing—Two-piece girders are to be nailed from one side with 10-penny nails, two near each end of each piece, others staggered with a distance of 16 inches between nails in a horizontal line; or girders are to be nailed from each side with 10-penny nails, two near each end of each joist, others staggered with a distance of 32 inches between nails in a horizontal line.

Three-piece girders are to be nailed with 20-penny nails on each side with two near each end of each piece, including intermediate joints, and with the others staggered with a distance of not more than 32 inches between nails in a horizontal line.

Four-piece girders are to be assembled as shown, and nailed with 20-penny nails as specified for the three-piece girder.

Anchoring—Girders are to be securely anchored to masonry piers, nailed to wood posts, or bolted to steel columns.

loads of the structure uniformly to the deck. Walls are usually erected in sections. The **stud** is the vertical structural member of

Figure 23.4. Combined slab and foundation (thickened edge slab).

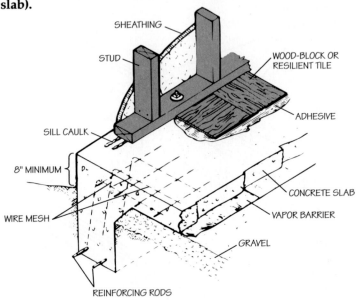

this system to which the sheathing and exterior siding are attached. Studs are nailed to the **bottom plate** (also often called a sole plate) and the **top plate** and then raised into position. Generally the outside walls are constructed first, then the inside walls. All the walls are temporarily braced in position. The top plate is doubled in such a way as to tie all the members together (Figure 23.4).

Window and door openings in the exterior and interior bearing walls require headers and **supporting studs** (commonly called jacks) to ensure the uniform distribution of the loads above to the supporting systems below. A **header** (also called a lintel) is a horizontal beam that extends between two studs and is supported on each side by one or more jacks. The number of jacks is determined by the width of the opening. Normally, openings greater than 6 feet require double supporting jacks (Figure 23.5).

Exterior Sheathing   After the first floor wall system is complete, the exterior **sheathing** is applied (Figure 23.6). The sheathing, which may be either plywood or structural insulating board, ties the wall system together and provides a base for the exterior siding.

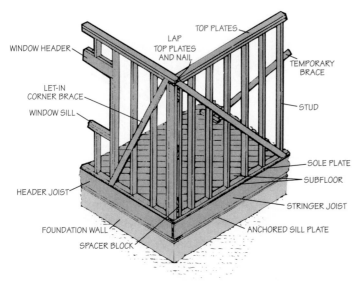

Wall framing used with platform construction.

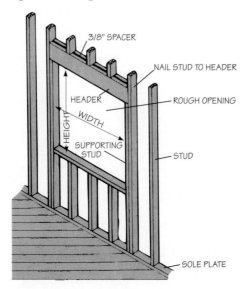

Figure 23.5. Headers for windows and door openings.

After the exterior sheathing is in place, a builder will start work on the second floor deck, repeating the construction of the first floor deck (Figure 23.7). In a one-story home he would be ready to begin work on the roof system. Roof systems are traditionally composed of ceiling joists, rafters, a ridge, and collars.

ROOF SYSTEM

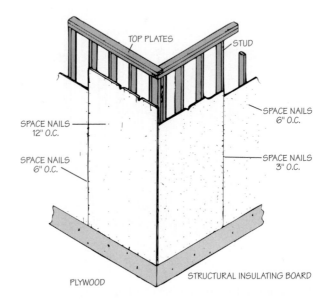

Vertical application of plywood or structural insulating board sheating.

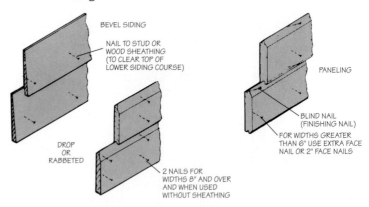

Figure 23.6. Exterior siding.

The construction of the roof system usually begins with the laying out of the ceiling joists. Like the floor joists, they are generally 16-inch OC and go wall to wall. The next step is the placement of the **ridge beam.** This is a wooden member that runs the full length of the roof into which the **roof rafters** are nailed. After the ridge is in place, the roof rafters are set in place, secured on the top to the ridge beam and on the bottom to the

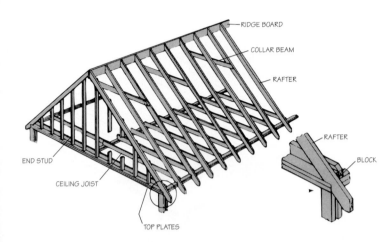

Ceiling and roof framing

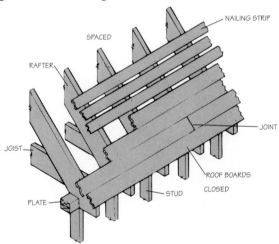

Figure 23.7. Installation of board roof sheathing, showing both closed and spaced types.

ceiling joists. This completes the "triangle" which prevents the roof load from pushing the walls out. **Collars** tie the rafter on one side of the building to the rafter on the other side and are generally spaced about every 4 feet. Collars prevent roof sagging by distributing the load more uniformly in the system. After the roof rafters are in place, the roof sheathing is applied, normally $\frac{1}{2}$- or $\frac{5}{8}$-inch plyscore. The sheathing supplies a deck for the roof shingles (Figure 23.8).

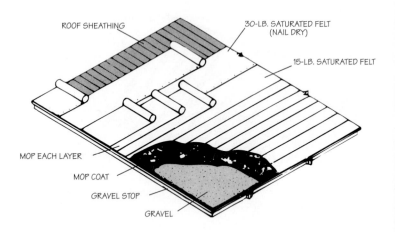

Built-up roof.

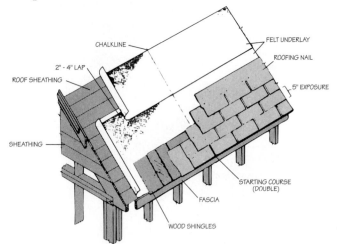

Figure 23.8. Application of asphalt shingles.

*ENERGY
CONSERVATION
CODE*

The energy crisis of the seventies raised the consciousness of people across the country about the importance of our dependence on foreign oil and our need to reduce energy consumption. In 1978 New York passed the State Energy Conservation Construction Code which called for the development of standards for all new construction. The new code applies to all new public and private buildings and to major renovations. The code became effective in 1979 and the estimated energy saving in a single-family home was 31%, 60% in an office building, when compared to a structure of conventional design.

The code requires that the **building envelope** meet a minimum energy efficiency level. The building envelope is all of the parts of the building that separate the indoor space from the outside space, typically the floors, walls, windows, doors, and roof. Most new homes in New York are designed to comply with Part 5 of the State Energy Code. Part 5 establishes specific **R-value** requirements for each part of the building envelope. An R-value describes a material's resistance to the transfer of heat: the higher the R-value, the greater its resistance (the greater its insulating value). The easiest way to comply with the insulation requirements for one- and two-family homes is by adhering to the acceptable standards enumerated in Part 5. The R-values proscribed in Part 5 vary for different areas of the state. Any builder who deviates from the standard as set forth in Part 5 must provide evidence to the building department that the alternative design also meets the minimum insulation standards. This usually requires more complicated and costly calculations and often the certification of an architect or engineer. Consequently, builders rarely venture outside of the requirements of Part 5.

The typical single-family house will meet Part 5 of the Energy Code in the following manner. The builder will keep the glazing area (window exposure) below 17% of the gross wall area. He will either use styrofoam insulation on the outside of his foundation wall or he will stud out the basement area and insulate between the studs or finally, he could insulate the floor joists underneath the first floor deck. Any of these will meet Part 5 of the Code for the basement area.

Moving to the exterior walls on the first floor, he has the option of 2×4 construction with insulation board for sheathing and fiberglass between the studs or 2×6 construction with regular plyscore sheathing and 6-inch insulation between the studs. The top floor ceiling joists require insulation with R-values between R-30 and R-38 depending on where in New York the home is being built. Part 5 also specifies insulation that is needed around skylights and fireplaces.

To maintain the effectiveness of insulation and to allow the escape of unwanted moisture and pollutants within a structure, good ventilation is essential. The greatest percentage of moisture in a house is eliminated simply by installing a ridge vent (a continuous opening along the roof ridge) or gable end vents. In addition, the code requires that any areas without natural ventilation such as laundry rooms or bathrooms have mechanical ventilation.

There are a number of excellent insulating products. The most common in new residential construction are fiberglass, cellulose, and styrofoam. UFFI (urea formaldehyde foam insulation) is no longer used because of problems with the release of formaldehyde gasses. The problems were generally limited to a short period following the application of the insulation, so that a buyer who finds UFFI insulation in a home today need not worry that it poses a hazard.

PLUMBING   After the framing is completed and inspected, the mechanical systems, i.e., plumbing, heating, and electric can be roughed in. While all three installations may occur together, the logical sequence is to install the sewage disposal system first. Two types are most prevalent: (1) an on-site system usually designed by an engineer and specific to the site, or (2) a municipal system. The sewage disposal system in a house must accomplish the removal of waste products and at the same time prevent odors from the municipal system or the septic system from entering the house. Efficient removal of sewage is accomplished through proper pipe sizing and sloping. Venting and trapping prevents sewer gas from entering the living space. Most sewage disposal pipe is PVC or plastic piping. While some municipalities may still require some cast iron for drains, there are fewer and fewer. Local building departments will provide information about local regulations.

After the sewage system, it is customary to install the water system. Water is supplied to most homes through either a municipal water system or some type of on-site well. The quality of the water is determined by New York State's Health Department regulations. Water distribution throughout the property is governed by New York State's Building Code. Since localities may impose more stringent regulations, you must check with the building department for any local variations. The distribution system within the home must deliver potable water to all fixtures with sufficient pressure. This requires the proper choice of materials and size of piping. Lead pipe and lead solders on copper pipe are no longer used because they were found to contaminate the drinking water. In new homes, at the present time, most builders choose copper pipe. Plastic pipe is beginning to become more common. Brass and galvanized pipe is no longer in use.

HEATING SYSTEMS

The primary determining factor in the choice of a heating system for most homes is the cost of the available energy source. Generally speaking, if natural gas is available, it is usually the least expensive source, followed by oil and finally electricity. Any of these energy sources can supply the various types of heating units found in single-family dwellings. The most common types are hot water/baseboard supplied through a boiler, warm air supplied by either a furnace or a heat pump, and resistance electric baseboard heat. There seems to be a present preference for hot water baseboard heat supplied by a boiler. The next in order of preference is warm air supplied by a furnace.

Hot water baseboard heat is the most expensive of the heating systems to install. It consists of a boiler, that heats a quantity of water, with one or more circulators to distribute the heated water to the baseboard registers and back to the boiler for reheating. It can be thermostatically controlled from one or more zones depending on the quality and sophistication of the installation. If air conditioning is desired, a separate system with the necessary duct work will have to be installed.

Warm Air

Warm air heating systems are somewhat less expensive to install than hot water systems. It consists of a furnace which heats air for circulation through duct work to registers which discharge the heated air into rooms and a cold air return duct to return air to the furnace for reheating. This system has the advantage of allowing for relatively inexpensive central air conditioning.

Central Air Conditioning

Central air conditioning is usually an accessory feature of a home's warm air heating system. There are three major components in an air conditioning system: a compressor, a condenser, and an evaporator. The process of cooling a home begins when a liquid refrigerant is introduced into a coil and allowed to evaporate. As the refrigerant evaporates, it absorbs heat from the room air moving through the evaporator coil. The heated gas then returns to a compressor, which compresses the gas back into a liquid. The liquid is discharged into another coil (a condenser), which surrenders the heat removed from the conditioned space to the outside. There are two common types of condensers: air cooled and water-cooled. Water-cooled systems were predominant before water metering was common. Today, most systems are air-cooled. An air conditioner is a heat transfer unit and consequently is rated in British thermal units (BTUs) or, in the case of larger units, tonnage. Air conditioning units are identical in many respects to refrigeration units with similar life expectancies, approximately 11 years, although many last years longer.

Heat Pumps   A heat pump is merely a central air conditioner operating in reverse. Some systems, through a series of valves, merely change the direction of the liquid flow for winter heating purposes. In this case, the outside condenser now becomes the evaporator, which absorbs heat from the outside and transfers it to the interior.

Electric   The electrical requirements for a home in most communities in New York State are governed by the National Electric Code (NFPA 70). A community may adopt more stringent standards if it chooses.

It is the custom in most, but not all, communities to require an outside agency to do the electrical inspections in their community. The two most commonly used agencies are the New York Board of Fire Underwriters or the Middle Department Inspection Agency Incorporated.

Components of   The three most commonly used electrical terms are **volts, watts,**
Electricity   and **amps** (ampere). Watts equals volts times amps ($W = V \times A$). An *amp* is a measure of electrical current (flow). A *volt* is a measure of electrical potential (force). A *watt* is a measure of electrical power (work). An often used analogy for explaining these terms is the flow of water through a garden hose. The ampere is analogous to the amount (gallons per minute) of water flowing through the hose. The volt is analogous to the pressure (pounds per square inch) in the hose. The watt is analogous to the amount of work a person is required to do to carry the water delivered through the hose up a flight of stairs.

Size of Electric Service   Electrical systems for buildings are rated in amps and are sized to the expected electrical needs of the building. Service of 150 to 200 amps is now the norm throughout most of New York. Almost every new house is powered beyond any reasonable expected electrical demand. Because demand for new appliances and the energy to run them was expected to increase rapidly from the early 1950s on, service requirements were increased. What was not anticipated at the time, however, was the improved energy efficiency of these appliances.

The easiest way to determine the size of the electrical service is to read it directly from the service box, which is usually located in the basement. It is printed on the main breaker on the main fuse. Circuit breakers and fuses serve the same purpose, namely protecting the circuit against over current. The size of a fuse or a circuit breaker is determined by the gauge of the wire in the circuit; for example, a 10-gauge wire normally requires a 30-amp fuse or breaker, a 12-gauge wire normally requires a 20-amp fuse or breaker, a 14-gauge wire normally requires a 15-amp fuse, and so on. The perceived advantage of the circuit breaker over a fuse is that a circuit breaker can be reset. In the case of a 220-amp circuit, when the breaker trips, it will disconnect the two hot legs in the circuit. The disadvantage in using a circuit breaker is that the manufacturer normally guarantees only that it will perform according to the specifications once. No one changes a breaker until it can no longer be reset. Unlike a tripped breaker, a blown fuse must be thrown away and replaced. On the other hand, the disadvantage of the fuse is its easy replacement and the result that a homeowner often puts in the wrong size replacement fuse. In the case of a 220-amp circuit, if there's a problem with one leg, only the fuse on that leg will blow. This can permit current to flow from the other leg which will leave the appliance charged and can damage some motors that must have both legs functioning to work properly.

Electric service may run from a utility company's pole to a home either above or below the ground. If the service is above ground, a **service head** (commonly called a weather head) is attached to the home. If the service is below ground, the service head is attached to the utility pole. In either case, the homeowner's responsibility for maintaining the system begins at the service head.

There are two commonly used types of wiring found in residential houses. **BX cable** is a flexible metal tube (greenfield tube) surrounding two electrical conductors (normally a black wire and a white wire). The purpose of the metal tube surrounding

Electrical Wire

the conductors is to protect them from physical damage and to supply a ground for the electrical circuit. Most commonly found in new homes today is a product called **romex** cable. This also contains black and white conductors, but instead of the protective metal cover, there is a plastic cover. An additional uninsulated wire is contained in this sheath to provide the ground necessary for the circuit.

Because the Uniform Building Code applies to new construction and substantial additions, many variations on these standards will be found in older homes. These older dwellings must comply only with the code that was in effect at the time they were constructed.

VOCABULARY REVIEW

Match terms a–h with 1–8.

a. *Bearing beam*
b. *Building codes*
c. *Building envelope*
d. *Building permit*
e. *Certificate of occupancy*
f. *Footings*
g. *Header*
h. *Ridge beam*

1. A wooden beam that supports the roof rafters.
2. Those parts of the building that separate the indoor and outdoor spaces.
3. A horizontal beam (also called a lintel) extending between two studs supported by one or more jacks.
4. A document issued by a building department stating that a structure meets local zoning and building code requirements and is ready for use.
5. A poured concrete base for the foundation walls.
6. Local and state laws that set minimum construction standards
7. A continuous girder supported by columns on which the floor joists rest.
8. A document issued by a local building department once the inspector is satisfied a builder's plans comply with the code.

QUESTIONS AND PROBLEMS

1. Explain the difference between a performance code and a specification code.
2. Give examples of each type of code.
3. Why might a local building department want to impose some regulations more stringent than those in the New York State Building Code?
4. Does the building code in your community vary from the state code?
5. List the major structural components and mechanical systems of a residential building.
6. Discuss the advantages and disadvantages of some of the commonly used heating systems.

24

Land-Use Control

KEY • TERMS

Building codes: local and state laws that set minimum construction standards

Certificate of occupancy: a government-issued document that states a structure meets local zoning and building code requirements and is ready for use

Downzoning: rezoning of land from a higher-density use to a lower-density use

Environmental impact statement (EIS): a report that contains information regarding the effect of a proposed project on the environment of an area

Land-use control: a broad term that describes any legal restriction that controls how a parcel of land may be used

Master plan: a comprehensive guide for the physical growth of a community

Nonconforming use: an improvement that is inconsistent with current zoning regulations

Restrictive covenants: clauses placed in deeds and leases to control how future owners and lessees may or may not use the property

Variance: allows an individual landowner to vary from zoning requirements

Zoning laws: public regulations that control the specific use of land

Land-use control is a broad term that describes any legal restriction that controls how a parcel of land may be used. Land-use controls can be divided into two broad categories: public controls and private controls. Examples of public controls are zoning, building codes, subdivision regulations, and master plans. Private controls come in the form of deed restrictions.

For further discussion, it should be noted that all methods of land-use control are coming under some level of scrutiny. The United States Supreme Court has recently held that land cannot be regulated such that it is rendered totally valueless, and has also held that any such regulation of one's private land must bear some "rough proportionality" to the benefit that the regulation gives to the public. A number of recent cases have prohibited the enforcement of certain zoning ordinances or deed restrictions because they result in discrimination under the Federal Fair Housing Act (recall previous discussions on handicapped and familial status in Chapter 20), so the following discussion on land-use control must be tempered with the knowledge that these methods of land-use control are not absolute.

ZONING Rudimentary forms of zoning can be traced back as far as medieval times when regulations prohibited certain activities from taking place within the town wall. In colonial America, cities and towns regulated the location of foul-smelling industries such as tallow rendering and leather tanning. In the late 1880s, Boston limited the heights of buildings, as did Baltimore, Indianapolis, and Washington, D.C. Between 1909 and 1915, Los Angeles adopted a complex series of land-use laws. However, credit for the first truly comprehensive and systematic zoning law goes to New York City in 1916. Three years in the making, it went beyond anything up to that time and set a basic pattern that has been followed and refined by American cities, towns, and counties ever since.

Zoning laws divide land into zones (districts) and, within each zone, regulate the purpose for which buildings may be constructed, the height and bulk of the buildings, the area of the lot that they may occupy, and the number of persons that they can accommodate. Through zoning, a community can protect existing land users from encroachment by undesirable uses and ensure that future land uses in the community will be compatible with one another. Zoning can also control development so that each parcel of land will be adequately serviced by streets, sanitary and storm sewers, schools, parks, and utilities.

The authority to control land use is derived from the basic police power of each state to protect the public health, safety, morals, and general welfare of its citizens. Through an enabling act passed by the state legislature, the authority to control land use is also given to individual towns, cities, and counties. These local government units then pass zoning ordinances that establish the boundaries of the various land-use zones and determine the type of development permitted in each of them. By going to your local zoning office, you can learn how a parcel of land is zoned. By then consulting the zoning ordinance, you can see the permitted uses for the parcel.

For convenience, zones are identified by code abbreviations such as R (residential), C (commercial), I or M (industrial-manufacturing), and A (agriculture). Within general categories are subcategories; for example, single-family residences, two-family residences, low-rise apartments, and high-rise apartments. Similarly, there will usually be several subcategories of commercial ranging from small stores to shopping centers and several subcategories of manufacturing ranging from light, smoke-free to heavy industry.

Zoning Symbols

Additionally, overlay zoning categories such as RPD (residential planned development) and PUD (planned unit development) can be utilized. These are designed to permit a mixture of land uses within a given parcel. For example, a 640-acre parcel may contain open spaces plus clusters of houses, townhouses, and apartments, and perhaps a neighborhood shopping center. Another combination zone is RO (residential-office) that allows apartment buildings alongside or on top of office buildings.

Note that there is no uniformity to zoning classifications in the United States. A city may use *A* to designate apartments while the county uses *A* to designate agriculture. Similarly, one city may use *I* for industrial and another city use *I* for institutional (hospitals and universities, for example).

In New York, when the zoning ordinance describes a permitted use for land within a zone, owners are said to be entitled to use their land in that way **"as of right."** As long as they comply with the requirements of the ordinance by allowing for the proper setbacks and square footage requirements, for example, decisions to issue building permits are not discretionary.

Land-Use Restrictions   Besides telling landowners the uses to which they may put their land, the zoning ordinance imposes additional rules. For example, land zoned for low-density apartments may require 1,500 square feet of land per living unit, a minimum of 600 square feet of living space per unit for one bedroom, 800 square feet for two bedrooms, and 1,000 square feet for three bedrooms. The zoning ordinance may also contain a setback requirement that states that a building must be placed at least 25 feet back from the street, 10 feet from the sides of the lot, and 15 feet from the rear lot line. The ordinance may also limit the building's height to 2½ stories and require two parking spaces for each dwelling unit. As can be seen, zoning encourages uniformity.

Enforcement   Zoning laws are enforced by virtue of the fact that in order to build a person must obtain a building permit from city or county government. Before a permit is issued, the proposed structure must conform with government-imposed structural standards and comply with the zoning on the land. A landowner who builds without a permit can be forced to tear down the building.

Nonconforming Use   When an existing structure does not conform with a new zoning law, it is "grandfathered in" as a **nonconforming use.** Thus, the owner can continue to use the structure even though it does not conform to the new zoning. However, the owner is not permitted to enlarge or remodel the structure, or to extend its life. When the structure is ultimately demolished, any new use of the land must be in accordance with the zoning law. If you are driving through a residential neighborhood and see an old store or service station that looks very much out of place, it is probably a nonconforming use structure that was allowed to stay because it was built before the current zoning on the property went into effect.

Amendment   Once a zoning ordinance has been passed, it can be changed by **amendment.** Thus, land previously zoned for agriculture may be changed to residential. Land along a city street that has become a major thoroughfare may change from residential to commercial. An amendment can be initiated by a property owner in the area to be rezoned or by local government. Either way, notice of the proposed change must be given to all property owners in and around the affected area, and a public hearing must be held so that property owners and the public at large may voice their opinions on the matter.

In New York, a property owner who wants to deviate from existing zoning regulations must apply for a zoning variance. The initial application is made to the administrative official charged with zoning enforcement.

Variance

New York recognizes two principle types of variances. A property owner may request an **area variance** if a building cannot be placed on the lot without violating the dimensional requirements of the zoning ordinance, for example, if the lot is not deep enough to allow a home to be built that meets the setback requirements. An area variance is often granted, as the request is usually for a relatively inconsequential relaxation of the rules.

A **use variance** is one that seeks to change the use permitted for land, for example, from residential to commercial. This type of variance is more controversial than an area variance. It is far more often denied unless owners can prove that hardship conditions not of their making would result from disapproval.

An owner who is denied either type of variance may request a hearing before the **zoning board of appeals** (ZBA). A ZBA exists at each level of government. The ZBA must hold a hearing on the variance to provide an opportunity for members of the community to voice any concerns they might have about the impact of a proposed variance.

In New York, the traditional tests for granting variances developed by the courts have been spelled out in the General City, Town, and Village Laws. These recently adopted statues spell out in the law, or codify, a balancing test developed by New York courts over the years.

New York Variance Statutes

In the case of an area variance, the law directs the zoning board of appeals to weigh the interests of the individual property owner against those of the community by considering five specific questions.

1. Would the proposed variance have an undesirable impact on the neighboring properties and the neighborhood?
2. Could the problem be solved in some other way?
3. How substantial is the proposed variance?
4. Will the variance adversely affect the environment?
5. Is the problem self-created?

The ZBA may still grant an area variance even if the problem is self-created. The new statutes replace the traditional terms for granting an area variance, which required the owner to show that the zoning limitations caused "practical difficulty" and/or "economic injury" before requesting a variance.

For a use variance, the unnecessary hardship test is spelled out in the revised statutes. The owner must demonstrate that: (1) the permitted use denies the owner all economic use or benefit from the property; (2) the hardship is unique to that property in the zone; (3) granting the variance would not alter the essential character of the neighborhood; and (4) the hardship is not self-created.

In the case of a use variance, if the hardship is self-created, a variance will probably be denied. The unnecessary hardship test is a difficult one to meet and owners who buy property in residential neighborhoods should not expect to succeed in applying for such a variance.

In approving either type of variance, the ZBA must grant the minimum variance needed to allow property owners to make use of their land and may impose reasonable conditions and restrictions to minimize the impact of the variance on the neighborhood.

Decisions of the zoning board of appeals may be appealed further in New York State Supreme Court by way of an Article 78 proceeding, so-called because it is found in Article 78 of New York's Civil Practice Law and Rules. This section of law applies whenever a citizen of New York institutes an action against a public body or officer of the state or any local government.

Conditional-Use Permit

The conditional-use permit is another mechanism that allows a builder to depart from the applicable zoning regulations within a district. A conditional-use permit, also known as a special use or special exception permit, is usually quite restrictive, and if the conditions of the permit are violated, the permit is no longer valid. For example, a neighborhood grocery store operating under a conditional-use permit can only be a neighborhood grocery store. The structure cannot be used as an auto parts store. The various zoning ordinances in New York typically list the conditional uses that may be permitted in each district, describe how to apply for them, and enumerate the criteria for granting them. However, unlike permits as of right, the granting of conditional-use permits is discretionary on the part of the local authority.

Spot zoning refers to the rezoning of a small area of land in an existing neighborhood. For example, a neighborhood convenience center (grocery, laundry, barbershop) might be allowed in a residential neighborhood provided it serves a useful purpose for neighborhood residents and is not a nuisance.

Spot Zoning

Downzoning means that land previously zoned for higher-density uses (or more active uses) is rezoned for lower-density uses (or less active uses). Examples are downzoning from high-rise commercial to low-rise commercial, apartment zoning to single-family, and single-family to agriculture. Although a landowner's property value may fall as a result of downzoning, no compensation is made to the landowner because land is not "taken"(discussed later) as with eminent domain.

Downzoning

A **buffer zone** is a strip of land that separates one land use from another. Thus, between a large shopping center and a neighborhood of single-family homes, there may be a row of garden apartments. Alternatively, between an industrial park and a residential subdivision, a developer may leave a strip of land in grass and trees rather than build homes immediately adjacent to the industrial buildings. Note that *buffer zone* is a generic term and not necessarily a zoning law category.

Buffer Zone

Cluster zoning is an alternative arrangement in which houses are allowed to be built more closely together than in a traditional residential zone in exchange for larger open spaces for recreational use. However, the total number of dwellings in a cluster zone cannot be greater than the number that would be permitted in a traditional residential zone.

Cluster Zoning

Incentive Zoning

New York's City, Town, and Village Laws have recently been revised specifically to provide for incentive zoning. Incentive zoning is used by a local government for the purpose of advancing its "specific physical, cultural, and social policies in accordance with the ... comprehensive plan." Examples of benefits that a local government may confer are additional parks, special housing, or social or cultural facilities.

Legality, Value

A zoning law can be changed or struck down if it can be proved in court that it is unclear, discriminatory, unreasonable, not for the protection of the public health, safety, and general welfare, or not applied to all property in a similar manner. A topical, but difficult, legal issue involves "taking." When property is zoned so that it destroys or severely limits its use, it becomes condemnation, not zoning, because the property has been effectively "taken."

Zoning alone does not create land value. For example, zoning a hundred square miles of lonely desert or mountain land for stores and offices would not appreciably change its value. Value is created by the number of people who want to use a particular parcel of land for a specific purpose. To the extent that zoning channels that demand to certain parcels of land and away from others, zoning does have a powerful impact on property value.

SUBDIVISION REGULATIONS

Before a building lot can be sold, a subdivider must comply with government regulations concerning street construction, curbs, sidewalks, street lighting, fire hydrants, storm and sanitary sewers, grading and compacting of soil, water and utility lines, minimum lot size, and so on. In addition, the subdivider may be required either to set aside land for schools and parks or to provide money so that land for that purpose may be purchased nearby. These are often referred to as **mapping requirements** and, until the subdivider has complied with all state and local regulations, the subdivision will not be approved. Without approval the plan cannot be recorded which, in turn, means that the lots cannot be sold to the public. A subdivider who tries to sell lots without approval can be stopped by a government court order and, in some states, fined. Moreover, permits to build will be refused to lot owners and anyone who bought from the subdivider is entitled to a refund.

In New York, a subdivision must first be approved by the local planning board before a **plat,** or subdivision map can be filed in the county clerk's office. State law requires the filing of this map before any subdivided land can be sold. Typically, the local legislative body authorizes the planning board to review and approve subdivision plans. The state statutes set forth the specific infrastructure details that must be included in the plans including provision for streets, parks, sidewalks, drainage, and the like. Statutes also require that the developer post a bond as an assurance that the promised improvements will be made. Until the subdivider has complied with all state (and, if any, local) requirements, the subdivision will not be approved or recorded. A subdivider who tries to sell lots without approval faces stiff penalties.

Article 9-A of the Real Property Law is designed to protect New York residents from fraudulent sales practices whether the land is located in New York or in another state. Before any subdivided land may be sold or leased the subdivider is required to prepare an offering statement that describes the background of the individual(s) involved in the venture, information about the financial condition of the developers, and a detailed project description. Article 9-A allows a lessee or purchaser of subdivided lands who is not represented by an attorney to rescind the lease or purchase offer within 10 days after acceptance by the subdivider and requires the subdivider to refund any deposit within 10 days of the notice of cancellation.

Anyone who is convicted of offering subdivided land for sale or lease in New York before an offering statement is filed with the Secretary of State is guilty of a felony. Anyone who is responsible for misrepresentation in the offering or in the selling of subdivided lands is guilty of a misdemeanor. If real estate brokers or sales agents are involved in such a misrepresentation, the Department of State may revoke their licenses. Anyone who implies that the state has recommended or endorsed the lease or purchase of the subdivided lands is guilty of a misdemeanor and is subject to a fine of up to $1,000 and/or imprisonment up to 1 year. The Department may seek court action to ban any developer who is found guilty of fraudulent sales practices from doing any future business in the state relating to the sale of land.

These protections are similar to those included in the Interstate Land Sales Full Disclosure Act mentioned in Chapter 10 to protect consumers from fraudulent sales. As with violations of the state law, violations of the federal law carry stiff penalties including fines of up to $5,000 and imprisonment for up to 5 years.

BUILDING CODES

Recognizing the need to protect public health and safety against slipshod construction practices, state and local governments have enacted **building codes.** These establish minimum acceptable material and construction standards for such things as structural load and stress, windows and ventilation, size and location of rooms, fire protection, exits, electrical installation, plumbing, heating, lighting, and so forth.

Before a building permit is granted, the design of a proposed structure must meet the building code requirements. During construction, local building department inspectors visit the construction site to make certain that the codes are being observed. Finally, when the building is completed, a **certificate of occupancy** is issued to the building owner to show that the structure meets the code. Without this certificate, the building cannot be legally occupied.

Traditionally, the establishment of building codes has been given by states to individual counties, cities, and towns. The result has been a lack of uniformity from one local government to the next, often adding unnecessary construction costs and occasionally leaving gaps in consumer protection. The trend today is toward statewide building codes that overcome these weaknesses and at the same time improve the uniformity of mortgage collateral for the secondary mortgage market. New York adopted a Uniform Building and Fire Prevention Code, which became effective in 1984. This code is discussed further in Chapter 23, "Basic Principles of Construction."

DEED RESTRICTIONS

Although property owners tend to think of land-use controls as being strictly a product of government, it is possible to achieve land-use control through private means. In fact, Houston, Texas operates without zoning and relies almost entirely on private land-use controls to achieve a similar effect.

Private land-use controls take the form of **deed** and **lease restrictions.** In the United States it has long been recognized that the ownership of land includes the right to sell or lease it on whatever legally acceptable conditions the owner wishes, including the right to dictate to the buyer or lessee how the land shall or shall not be used. For example, a developer can sell the lots in a subdivision subject to a restriction written into each deed that the land cannot be used for anything but a single-family residence containing at least 1,200 square feet of living area. The legal theory is that if buyers or lessees agree to the restrictions, they are bound by them. If the restrictions are not obeyed, any lot owner in the subdivision can obtain a court order to enforce compliance. The only limit to the number of restrictions that owners may place on their land is economic. If the deed carries too many restrictions, the landowner may find that no one wants the land.

Deed restrictions, also known as **restrictive covenants,** can be used to dictate such matters as the purpose of the structure to be built, architectural requirements, setbacks, size of the structure, and aesthetics. In neighborhoods with view lots, restrictive covenants are often used to limit the height to which trees may be permitted to grow. Deed restrictions cannot be used to discriminate on the basis of race, color, religion, sex, or national origin; if they do, they are unenforceable by the courts.

PLANNING AHEAD FOR DEVELOPMENT

When a community first adopts a zoning ordinance, the usual procedure is to recognize existing land uses by zoning according to what already exists. Thus, a neighborhood that is already developed with houses is zoned for houses. Undeveloped land may be zoned for agriculture or simply left unzoned. As a community expands, undeveloped land is zoned for urban uses and a pattern develops that typically follows the availability of new roads, the aggressiveness of developers, and the willingness of landowners to sell. All too often this results in a hodgepodge of land-use districts, all conforming internally because of tightly enforced zoning, but with little or no relationship among them. This happens because they were created over a period of years without the aid of a long-range land use plan that took a comprehensive view of the entire growth pattern of the city. Because uncoordinated land use can have a negative impact on both the quality of life and the economic vitality of a community, more attention is now being directed toward land-use master plans to guide the development of towns and cities, districts, coastlines, and even whole states.

Master Plan

To prepare a **master plan** (or **general plan** or **comprehensive plan**), a city or regional planning commission is usually created. The first step is a physical and economic survey of the area to be planned. The physical survey involves mapping existing roads, utility lines, developed land, and undeveloped land. The economic survey looks at the present and anticipated economic base of the region, its population, and its retail trade facilities. Together the two surveys provide the information on which a master plan is built. The key is to view the region as a unified entity that provides its residents with jobs and housing as well as social, recreational, and cultural opportunities. In doing so, the master plan uses existing patterns of transportation and land use and directs future growth so as to achieve balanced development. For example, if agriculture is important to the area's economy, special attention is given to retaining the best soils for farming. Waterfront property may also receive special planning protection. Similarly, if houses in an older residential area of town are being converted to rooming houses and apartments, that transition can be encouraged by planning apartment usage for the area. In doing this, the master plan guides those who must make day-to-day decisions regarding zoning changes and gives individual property owners a long-range idea of what their properties may be used for in the future.

Although New York has no statewide master plan, state law does provide for planning at the county and regional level and authorizes intermunicipal cooperation in planning and zoning. The Adirondack and Catskill Park regulations are frequently cited as models for effective planning on a broad regional scale. Although the laws encourage planning boards to consider the region of which they are a part in the planning process, most planning activity occurs within traditional city, town, and village boundaries.

The planning board is distinct from a zoning commission. The zoning commission is the body that is convened to develop the original zoning ordinance and official map. Once the ordinance is adopted, the zoning commission no longer continues to function. However, members of the zoning commission may and often do serve on the planning board.

The appointment, composition, function, and duties of the planning board are spelled out in the City, Town, and Village Laws. Under these laws, the planning boards have broad advisory powers and may also be given specific responsibility to consider applications for variances, special-use permits, and subdivision approval and to review site plans.

State statutes authorize city, town, and village planning boards to adopt a **comprehensive master plan** to serve as a blueprint for growth within the boundaries of the locality. The comprehensive plan takes into account the existing physical and economic characteristics of a community and identifies objectives for future growth that attempt to achieve balanced development. New York statutes provide specific direction to the planning boards to consider historic and cultural resources, coastal and natural resources, and sensitive environmental areas in the planning process. The State's Town Law also requires that the planning board must appoint an additional member who derives at least 50% of his or her income from farming if 20% of the town's land is devoted to agricultural use. It is important to note, however, that this plan is an advisory document and is not binding, unlike the official map that was adopted along with the zoning ordinance. The official map is placed on file in the county clerk's office. Once it is adopted by the local legislative body, it conclusively establishes the location of streets, highway systems, drainage systems, and parks in the community.

Planning and zoning districts and regulations may be amended if, as often happens, growth in an area dictates that a change in use would be beneficial to the community.

Planning for Waterfront Development

In 1972, the federal government adopted the **Coastal Zone Management Act** which declared a national policy of restoration and preservation of coastal areas. The act encouraged states to adopt management programs, and in 1981 New York adopted the **Waterfront Revitalization and Coastal Resources Act** (WRCRA). The WRCRA outlines a planning framework for communities on inland waterways. The statute sets forth a list of planning objectives that call for the balancing of economic, ecological, and recreational considerations in making waterfront improvements. Local governments may apply to the Secretary of State for funding of local government waterfront revitalization programs by submitting plans for development that are consistent with the objectives listed in the statute.

Long-Run Continuity

To assure long-run continuity, a master plan should look at least 15 years into the future and preferably 25 years or more. It must also include provisions for flexibility in the event that the city or region does not develop as expected, such as when population grows faster or slower than anticipated. Most importantly, the plan must provide for a balance between the economic and social functions of the community. For example, to emphasize culture and recreation at the expense of adequate housing and the area's economic base will result in the slow decay of the community because people must leave to find housing and jobs. Meetings of the local planning board and zoning board of appeals are subject to New York's Open Meetings Law which requires that every meeting of a public body be open to the public and held in an accessible building unless an executive session is convened. There are few exceptions to the open meetings law.

Actions of these boards are also subject to the **State Environmental Quality Review Act (SEQRA).** Under SEQRA, planning and zoning boards must require an **environmental impact statement** (EIS) on any proposed action that may have a significant effect on the environment. If a board determines that a request for a variance or any proposed zoning change will have a significant effect on the environment, it will require the owner to prepare an EIS which must provide detailed information about how the proposed change will affect such things as population density, automobile traffic, noise, air quality, water and sewage facilities, drainage, energy consumption, and the like. The information in the EIS allows a neutral decision maker and members of the community to judge the environmental benefits and costs of the project. With this information at hand, better decisions regarding land use can be made. The information that must be included in an EIS is set forth in Environmental Conservation Law (§ 8-0109).

ENVIRONMENTAL
IMPACT
STATEMENTS

The purpose of an **environmental impact statement (EIS),** also called an **environmental impact report (EIR),** is to gather into one document enough information about the effect of a proposed project on the total environment so that a neutral decision maker can judge the environmental benefits and costs of the project. For example, a city zoning commission considering a zone change can request an EIS that will show the expected impact of the change on such things as population density, automobile traffic, noise, air quality, water and sewage facilities, drainage, energy consumption, school enrollments, employment, public health and safety, recreation facilities, wildlife, and vegetation. The idea is that with this information at hand, better decisions regarding land uses can be made. When problems can be anticipated in advance, it is easier to make modifications or explore alternatives.

At the city and county level, where the EIS requirement has the greatest effect on private development, the EIS usually accompanies the development application that is submitted to the planning or zoning commission. Where applicable, copies are also sent to affected school districts, water and sanitation districts, and highway and flood control departments. The EIS is then made available for public inspection as part of the hearing process on the development application. This gives concerned civic groups and the public at large an opportunity to voice their opinions regarding the anticipated benefits and costs of the proposed development. If the proposed development is partially or wholly funded by state or federal funds, then state or federal hearings are also held.

PRECAUTIONS

Because zoning can greatly influence the value of a property, it is absolutely essential that when you purchase real estate you be aware of the zoning for the parcel. You need to know what the zoning will allow and what it won't; whether the parcel is operating under a restrictive or temporary permit; and what the zoning and planning departments might allow on the property in the future. Where there is any uncertainty or where a zone change or variance will be necessary in order to use the property the way you want to, a conservative approach is to make the offer to buy contingent on obtaining planning and zoning approval before going to settlement.

If you are a real estate agent, you must stay abreast of zoning and planning and building matters regarding the properties you list and sell. A particularly sensitive issue that occurs regularly is a property listed for sale that does not meet zoning and/or building code requirements. For example, suppose the current (or previous) owner of a house has converted the garage to a den or bedroom without obtaining building permits and without providing space for parking elsewhere on the parcel.

Legally, this makes the property unmarketable. If you, as agent, sell this property without telling the buyer about the lack of permits, you've given the buyer grounds to sue you for misrepresentation and the seller for rescission. When faced with a situation like this, you should ask the seller to obtain the necessary permits. If the seller refuses and the buyer still wants to buy, make the problem very clear to the buyer and have the buyer sign a statement indicating acceptance of title under these conditions. You can also refuse to accept the listing if it looks as though it will create more trouble than it's worth.

Professionals

The point here is that the public has a right to expect real estate agents to be professionals in their field. Thus the agent is expected to be fully aware of the permitted uses for a property and whether or not current uses comply. This is necessary to properly value the property for listing and to provide accurate information to prospective buyers. Even if the seller in the foregoing example was unaware of the zoning and building violations, it is the agent's responsibility to recognize the problem and inform the seller. An agent cannot take the position that if the seller didn't mention it, then the agent needn't worry about it, and if the buyer later complains, it's the seller's problem, not the agent's. Recent court decisions clearly indicate that the agent has a responsibility to inform the seller of a problem so that the seller cannot later complain to the agent, "You should have told me about that when I listed the property with you and certainly before I accepted the buyer's offer."

WINDFALLS
AND WIPE-OUTS

Planning and zoning tend to provide **windfall gains** for the owners of land that has been authorized for development, while landowners who are prohibited from developing their land suffer financial **wipe-outs.** This has been a major stumbling block to the orderly utilization of land in America. It is only natural that landowners want their land to be zoned for a use that will make it more valuable; however, not all land can be zoned for housing, stores, and offices. Some land must be reserved for agriculture and open spaces. If local and state governments embark on bold land planning programs, how will these financial inequities be resolved?

The past and current position of government and the courts is that if land-use restrictions are for the health, safety, and general welfare of the community at large, then under the rules of police power individual landowners are not compensated for any resulting loss in value. Only when there is an actual physical taking of land are owners entitled to compensation under the rules of eminent domain. In today's environmentally conscious society, this often results in pitting landowners who want to develop their land against those who want to prevent development. For example, a government planning agency in one state stretched the limits of police power to deny an urban landowner a permit to build on his property, and told him he should grow flowers for the public's enjoyment. Many decisions like this could ultimately undermine planning efforts. Yet government planning agencies do not have the money to buy all the land that they would like to see remain undeveloped.

In 1993, the United States Supreme Court decided the case of *Lucas* v. *South Carolina Coastal Council* in which it declared that the State's regulatory policy was so extreme that it amounted to a regulatory "taking" of Lucas' beachfront property. Lucas was a developer who purchased two expensive oceanfront lots intending to construct luxury homes. After he bought the land, a change in the law prohibited any building on the land because it was an environmentally-sensitive barrier reef and his permit was denied. The Supreme Court ruled that this was taking by regulation because it deprived Lucas of any economically viable use of his land. Decisions like *Lucas* involving regulatory takings can make some planning choices prohibitively expensive for governments.

The solution may come from some radical new thinking about land and the rights to use it. The new planning idea is to eliminate windfalls and wipe-outs by creating **transferable development rights (TDRs).** Previously, the right to develop a parcel of land could not be separated from the land itself. Now planners are exploring the idea of separating the two so that development rights can be transferred to land where greater density will not be objectionable. For example, suppose that within a given planning district there is an area of high-quality farmland that planners feel should be retained for agriculture and not be paved over with streets and covered with buildings. Also in the district is an area deemed more suitable for urban uses and hence an area where government will concentrate on constructing streets,

TRANSFERABLE DEVELOPMENT RIGHTS

schools, parks, waterlines, and other public facilities. To direct growth to the urban area, it is planned and zoned for urban uses. Meanwhile, areas designated for agriculture are forced to remain as farmland. Ordinarily, this would result in windfall gains for the owner of the urban land and a loss in land value for the owner of the farmland.

With the TDR concept in effect, owners of farmland are allowed to sell development rights to the owners of urban land. By purchasing development rights, urban landowners are permitted to develop their land more intensely than otherwise would be permissible. This compensates farmers for the prohibition against developing their land. For the TDR concept to work, there must be a comprehensive regional master plan.

TDRs could be traded on the open market like stocks and bonds. Alternatively, a government agency could pay cash for the value of rights lost. This would be financed by selling those rights to owners in districts to be developed.

Where Used   To date, Chicago and New York City have made use of TDRs for the purpose of protecting historical buildings not owned by the government. Owners who agree not to tear down their buildings are given TDRs that can be sold to other nearby landowners. TDRs are also being used to protect open spaces, farm land, and environmentally sensitive land in parts of Pennsylvania, Virginia, Florida, Vermont, New Jersey, Maryland, and Puerto Rico. In a number of states the TDR concept is still being tested in court cases. It appears that much of the legal debate centers on the concept of separating the right to develop land from the land itself. The idea is new and has few legal precedents. But, for that matter, the concept of zoning faced the same problems when it was new.

VOCABULARY REVIEW

*Match terms **a–n** with statements **1–14**.*

a. *Amendment*
b. *Buffer zone*
c. *Building codes*
d. *Certificate of occupancy*
e. *Downzoning*
f. *EIS or EIR*
g. *Land-use control*
h. *Mapping requirement*
i. *Master plan*
j. *Nonconforming use*
k. *Restrictive covenants*
l. *Spot zoning*
m. *Variance*
n. *Zoning laws*

1. A broad term used to describe any legal restriction (such as zoning) that controls how a parcel of land may be used.
2. Public regulations that control the specific use of land.
3. An improvement that is inconsistent with current zoning regulations.
4. A comprehensive guide for a community's physical growth.
5. Clauses placed in deeds and leases to control how future owners and lessees may or may not use the property.
6. A government-issued document stating that a structure meets zoning and building code requirements and is ready for use.
7. A report that contains information regarding the effect of a proposed project on the environment.
8. Method used to change a zoning ordinance.
9. Permit that allows an individual landowner to vary from a zoning ordinance without changing the ordinance.
10. The rezoning of a small area of land in an existing neighborhood.
11. Local and state laws that set minimum construction standards.
12. A strip of land that separates one land use from another.
13. Rezoning of land from a higher-density use to a lower-density use.
14. State and local regulations pertaining to subdivisions that a subdivider must meet before selling lots.

QUESTIONS AND PROBLEMS

1. For land-use control to be successful, why is it necessary to consider the rights of individual property owners as well as the public as a whole?
2. Explain how a city obtains its power to control land use through zoning.
3. What is the purpose of a variance?
4. In your community, what are the letter/number designations for the following: high-rise apartments, low-rise apartments, single-family houses, stores, duplexes, industrial sites?
5. What is the difference between master planning and zoning?
6. What is the purpose of an environmental impact statement?
7. How would the use of transferable development rights reduce windfalls and wipe-outs for land owners?
8. Does any city or county in your state currently use transferable development rights? What have been the results?

ADDITIONAL READINGS

Ethical Land Use: Principles of Policy and Planning, by **Timothy Beatley** (John Hopkins University Press, 1994, 302 pages).

"Reflections on the Use of Land: The Book That Put the Concept of Growth Management on the Map," by **Phyllis Myers** (*Planning,* November 1993, pp. 8–11). Easy-to-understand article that discusses land use and control.

Zoning and Land-Use Controls, by **Patrick Rohan** (Matthew Bender, updated annually). This is a 10-volume set of books on zoning law that covers almost every aspect of zoning and land-use controls.

25

Environmental Issues

KEY • TERMS

Asbestos: a fire-retardant material found in many home building products, especially insulation and floor and ceiling tiles, which can cause serious lung disease

Biological pollutants: usually moisture-related problems including dust mites, molds, bacteria, and pollen

CFCs: chlorofluorocarbons; a chemical compound found in refrigerants that depletes the earth's ozone layer

CPSC: Consumer Product Safety Commission; the federal agency that is a source of information on consumer safety issues

Chlordane: a chemical used in pesticides, especially those used to treat termite infestation, that may pose a cancer risk after long-term exposure

EMFs: electromagnetic fields; a force field that emanates from power lines and many common household appliances

Radon: a cancer-causing radioactive gas that can seep into a home from below the ground

UFFI: urea-formaldehyde foam insulation; an insulating material no longer in use due to the release of formaldehyde fumes after its application

USTs: underground storage tanks; regulated by Article 10 of New York's Environmental Conservation Law

The number of environmental laws that have affected real estate development has expanded tremendously in recent years. In 1982, Congress passed a **Comprehensive Environmental Response, Compensation, and Liability Act** (commonly referred to as **CERCLA**). CERCLA imposed on any person who, at the time of disposal of any hazardous substance, owned or operated the facility at which such hazardous substance was disposed of, and any person who arranged for disposal, or any persons who have accepted hazardous substances for transport to disposal or treatment sites, joint and several liability for damages resulting from that disposal. Subsequent legislation involved changes in the Clean Water Act, which provides for a prohibition against storm water discharges. Similar federal statutes have been passed affecting asbestos, radon gas, lead poisoning, wetland areas, endangered species, and underground storage tanks. New York, like many states, has adopted its own regulatory programs, often imposing more stringent standards than the federal government. As a result of these new laws, purchasers are being required to exercise a level of "due diligence" in investigating sites prior to acquisition. A licensee should also be particularly aware that pertinent questions concerning environmental hazards may be directed to the broker and the broker may be under a "should-have-known" duty of care to report problems relating to these environmental hazards.

One result of these federal laws has been for prospective purchasers to undertake **environmental assessments** before acquiring property. Many banks are routinely requiring such assessments in sales of commercial property. Their principal purpose is to protect purchasers and their creditors from liability for the cost of environmental clean-ups. Prescribed by common practice rather than by law, environmental assessments typically involve three phases. Phase I includes an on-site visual inspection of the property, interviews with owners and area residents as to the use and possession of the property, and review of historical aerial photographs and public records to determine past use and possession of the property. A Phase II assessment typically involves sampling of the soil and water for the presence of hazardous substances. A Phase III assessment involves further sampling, establishing limits of the contamination, and developing a plan for remedial action and clean-up.

Chlorofluorocarbons

Another new set of environmental regulations deals with the handling of **chlorofluorocarbons (CFCs).** CFCs are contained in refrigerants commonly found in the home in air conditioning and refrigeration systems. Because the chlorine atoms in CFCs deplete the earth's protective ozone layer and contribute to global warming, the US and 23 other countries have agreed to regulate and control their use. As a result of this agreement, known as the Montreal Protocol, Congress banned CFCs as propellants in aerosol cans in the US in 1978. In 1990, Congress amended the law to require the containment of any CFC removed from any container or system, and prohibited the venting of CFCs into the atmosphere. The agreement calls for a ban on all CFC production by the year 2000. CFCs are no longer produced in the United States.

Homeowners need to know that, as of November 1994, any technician who installs, services, or disposes of any appliance containing these refrigerants must be certified. Homeowners who own the equipment are not exempt from this law and are subject to its penalties. Violations of the act are punishable by fines of up to $25,000 per violation per day.

Underground Storage Tanks

Concern for pollution of the state's water resources by unreported or undetected spills from underground storage tanks led to the enactment of Article 10 of the state's Environmental Conservation Law in 1963. This law requires owners and operators of facilities that store bulk quantities of petroleum in aboveground or underground tanks to take daily measurements from their storage containers so that leaks can be promptly detected and fixed. Operators of these facilities are required to keep daily records that must be available for inspection. Regulations developed pursuant to this law spell out procedures to be followed when leaks are detected. They also set standards for the construction and installation of new or substantially modified storage tanks.

Electromagnetic Fields

Electromagnetic fields (EMFs), which emanate from electric power lines, have so far escaped regulation. Computers, microwave ovens, electric blankets, cellular phones, and many other common household appliances also emit EMFs. Although EMFs are feared to present a hazard in the form of increased cancers—especially childhood cancers—studies have not been conclusive.

Because the exposure is so prevalent, regulation is not likely to occur unless and until an indisputable connection to ill health effects is documented. Nevertheless, the studies to date have yielded enough data to fan the fires of suspicion, and these fears have had a discernible effect on real estate sales where properties are close to power lines. Although studies to date have been inconclusive, they have raised serious concern. This controversy will continue to simmer until clearer answers are found.

Many products used in the home have been linked to health concerns, including serious cancer risks. Although some indoor air problems have relatively simple solutions, others require the hiring of contractors with special training.

INDOOR AIR CONTAMINANTS

Asbestos is a mineral fiber that was heavily used in home insulation, floor and ceiling tiles, and roofing materials because of its fire-resistant properties. Although it is rarely used today, asbestos remains in many homes, schools, and industrial and commercial buildings. Undisturbed asbestos has no ill health effects, but normal maintenance and repair work can cause the fibers to break down. When microscopic-sized fibers enter the lungs they can cause scarring that may lead to breathing problems or cancerous growth. Potential health effects of exposure to asbestos include: **asbestosis,** a disease caused by scarring of the lungs; **lung cancer,** especially if long-term exposure is aggravated by cigarette use or exposure; **mesothelioma,** a rare form of cancer that affects the lining of the lung or abdomen; and possibly other types of cancer. All three health effects may not be apparent until many years after the harm has been done. It is important to note, however, that the risk of developing any of these problems is small unless there is long-term exposure. Although public and commercial building owners have substantial asbestos removal programs underway, a homeowner who finds asbestos tiles or insulation need not be concerned if the asbestos material is undisturbed or undamaged. Sealing off the area where asbestos is found may be preferred to removal. A state-certified laboratory can test for asbestos levels in the home and, if testing indicates a problem, the State Department of Labor will provide information about licensed asbestos removal contractors in your area.

Asbestos

The Consumer Product Safety Commission maintains a hotline to answer questions about asbestos in products in a home, and to provide advice about testing and removal or repair (1 (800) 638-CPSC).

Lead Contamination   Lead-based paint is the major source of lead poisoning in the home, especially if it is cracking and chipping. It is a particular danger to children who ingest it. Congress banned lead-based paint in 1978. New laws have been passed at both the federal and state levels that attempt to deal with existing contamination.

At the federal level, the Residential Lead-Based Paint Hazard Reduction Act of 1992 requires sellers of housing built before 1978 to disclose all known information on lead-based paint. Regulations that detail a homeowner's responsibility under this new law have finally been adopted. They include giving a purchaser 10 days to conduct a lead-based paint inspection or risk assessment requiring landlords to disclose all known information on lead-based hazards in the dwelling. Sellers and/or landlords are now required to give special disclosures to prospective buyers and/or tenants, and real estate agents are given the burden of assuring compliance. They impose civil and criminal penalties for sellers, landlords, and agents who fail to comply with the regulations. The Environmental Protection Agency (EPA) and the Department of Housing and Urban Development (HUD) finalized these regulations in 1996.

New York has also passed the Lead Poisoning Prevention Act of 1992 (New York State Public Health Law Title X), and Department of Health regulations promulgated pursuant to the new law went into effect in January, 1995. The regulations establish a program of screening for children under the age of 6 for the presence of lead. As a result of finding elevated levels of lead in the blood of children, the Department of Health can require an environmental investigation of their home and may require remedial action to contain or remove the source of the problem at the cost of the homeowner.

High levels of lead contamination can cause coma, convulsions, and death, whereas low levels of contamination may cause damage to the nervous system, interfere with growth, and cause behavior problems in children. Although stomach aches, irritability, fatigue, vomiting, and constipation are among the possible signs of lead contamination, a child may have no symptoms at all. Adults, especially pregnant women, can also suffer harmful effects from lead contamination. Lead-contaminated water pipes, soil, and dust; lead-based insecticides; and industry emissions can also cause lead poisoning in children and adults.

Although testing laboratories approved by the State Department of Health can analyze a paint chip to determine its lead content, only a blood test can detect lead poisoning in people. As with asbestos, containment of the hazard may be the preferred and less expensive remedy for a house where contamination is found. Health authorities may recommend removal and replacement of lead paint only when it is in poor repair.

Radon is a naturally occurring radioactive gas that cannot be seen or smelled. According to the Surgeon General, it is the second leading cause of lung cancer leading to death. Smokers who are also exposed to radon in their homes are at even greater risk of developing lung cancer. Buyers now often ask whether a home has been tested for radon. Passive testing kits are available from hardware stores, usually for under $20, and from the New York State Health Department at cost (as little as $4). Active testing kits, that require power to operate, cost a bit more and provide a more reliable result. Several technologies are available, but the two general types are short-term and long-term tests. A short-term test takes from 2 to 90 days, depending on the type of technology used. These are appropriate if you need to get the results relatively quickly for the purpose of selling a home. A long-term test, which lasts for more than 90 days, is more reliable since radon levels in your home can vary throughout the year.

Radon

Outdoor radon levels average 0.4 pCi/L (picocuries per liter of water). Indoor levels average 1.3 pCi/L. If testing shows that the level in a particular home is higher than 4 pCi/L, the EPA recommends that you take remedial action. The EPA estimates that the cost of remediation will range from $500 to $2,500 depending on the construction of the home.

Remediation includes procedures from sealing cracks and openings in the foundation, to preventing radon from entering the home by either a **sub-slab depressurization** or **soil suction** method, to a system that uses fans and pipes to direct the gas away from the house. Radon can be removed by an active or passive system. A passive system relies on air currents to draw the gas away from the house while an active system uses a fan to draw radon from below the house and direct it away. In houses with a full basement, sub-slab depressurization is accomplished by applying suction to drain tiles or to the hollow area of the blocks in a house with a block wall foundation and using a sump pump to remove the gas. In houses with a crawl space, radon levels may be lowered by actively or passively ventilating the crawl space, but water pipes in the crawl space need to be insulated if this method is used. Another method used in houses with a crawl space is a soil suction technique known as **submembrane depressurization.** This simply means covering the earth floor with a heavy plastic sheet and drawing the radon from under the sheet with a vent pipe and fan. A **heat recovery ventilator** installed in the basement is also effective for radon ventilation.

Both the state and federal governments certify contractors to fix radon problems. Certified federal contractors carry identification. A list of qualified contractors in your area can be obtained from the New York State Radon Office in the State Health Department at (518) 458-6451.

Polychlorinated
Biphenyls

Polychlorinated biphenyls (PCBs) are toxic chemicals that were banned in 1976. Most New Yorkers have heard about PCBs in connection with industrial pollution. However, PCBs were also used in the sealed component parts of some electric appliances found in the home. Although relatively few homes may be affected, submersible pumps containing PCBs still exist in private drinking wells. There is some risk that the chemicals can leak into the drinking water supply. PCB leakage may be detected by an oily smell in the drinking water. If you suspect a problem and confirm that there is an older pump operating a private well, you can call the manufacturer or have your well tested. State and county health departments can provide a list of laboratories that can test for PCBs. If testing confirms PCB contamination, the pump should be replaced and the well water treated until it is safe.

Urea-Formaldehyde
Foam Insulation

Real estate multiple listings often indicate whether a house contains **urea-formaldehyde foam insulation (UFFI).** Problems were found in the early 1970s as a result of formaldehyde fumes being released form UFFI after it was applied. Because of these problems, UFFI is no longer used and is not likely to pose any danger to a home buyer today. The release of fumes is usually a problem only when a product containing formaldehyde is new, and release virtually stops after a short period of time. Formaldehyde gas can also be found in plywood, furniture, and drapes and is irritating to the eyes, mucous membranes, and the respiratory tract. Long-term exposure has led to cancer in laboratory animals, but most homeowners' exposure is likely to be short-term. When this problem is detected in a home, good ventilation to allow the gas to escape, a dehumidifier, and air conditioning may help to reduce levels of the gas. There are state-certified labs that test for formaldehyde. A list of these can be obtained from the State Health Department in Albany or one of its regional offices.

Chlordane is a chemical that was widely used in pesticides, especially for termite control, beginning in 1947. Its use was restricted at the state and federal levels in the 1970s, and was finally banned in New York in 1987. Because the chemical may take more than 20 years to break down, chlordane may still be a concern for homeowners today. Chlordane may be more prevalent where the pesticide application was improper, causing fumes to circulate through the home heating system. Short-term exposure can cause acute poisoning with toxic effects on the central nervous system; however, most homeowners are not likely to be exposed to high enough levels of chlordane to suffer these violent symptoms. According to the EPA, long-term exposure to low levels of chlordane may increase the risk of cancer. If you suspect its presence, state-certified labs can test for chlordane. Removing the primary source of the contamination and ensuring good ventilation is recommended. Because of the persistence of this chemical, however, eliminating it entirely is expensive and difficult.

Biological pollutants is a term that covers a range of problems commonly found in homes, including dust mites, molds, bacteria, and pollen. Biological pollutants require nutrients and moisture to prosper. Some people are especially sensitive to these pollutants and the most common problem in homes is an allergic reaction. A homeowner who suffers symptoms should survey the house for areas of moisture buildup and

Chlordane

Biological Pollutants

eliminate them. Such areas are typically found in basements, attics, and bathrooms, or any area without proper ventilation or vapor barriers. Dehumidifiers and air conditioners can also help reduce pollutants from the air. Cleaning the filters on heating and cooling systems and cleaning appliances can help eliminate environments for pollutants. Dust mites live in bedding and carpeting and can be eliminated only by warm water washing.

Carbon Monoxide

Carbon monoxide is a colorless, odorless gas that can cause nausea, vomiting, and even unconsciousness or death if there is prolonged exposure in an unventilated area. The greatest hazards in the home come from faulty furnaces, hot water heaters, gas dryers, or other appliances that are not properly vented. Commercial detectors can be purchased, but they are relatively expensive. The best protection against excessive carbon monoxide in the home is proper installation and ventilation of appliances.

RESIDENTIAL DRINKING WATER SUPPLY

Unlike the relatively recent developments previously discussed, drinking water quality has been a traditional concern in residential real estate sales, especially, of course, in rural areas. The New York State Uniform Fire Prevention and Building Code requires that all residences must be supplied with potable water. Potable water is that which conforms to the chemical and bacteriologic standards of the State Sanitary Code. The code is a set of regulations developed by the Department of Health pursuant to the state's Public Health Law. It specifies the maximum level of specific contaminants allowed in the water supply.

Where a municipal system is available, homeowners are assured that routine testing of the public water supply is conducted. Where a public water supply is not available, homeowners must find a private water supply. Most drill wells of their own, although developers or other commercial suppliers of water may be available in some areas. The sanitary code also prescribes performance standards for rural well and septic systems. These standards must be met before the local authority can issue a certificate of occupancy for a home. Banks also normally require wells to meet water quality and quantity (or yield) tests before approving a residential mortgage. Local governments may impose more stringent performance standards, require specific construction standards, and impose regulations about the location of the well and septic system on a property.

When a new well is constructed it must be disinfected with chlorine bleach. After sitting for 12 to 24 hours, the bleach is pumped out and the well is tested for contaminants, by either a state or commercial laboratory. The disinfection process must be repeated until sampling produces potable water.

Rural homeowners who rely on wells must take responsibility for monitoring their own water supply. A well that may have produced water of excellent quality at first may later be affected by contaminants seeping in. Contamination is often obvious from foul odors or discoloration of the well water. The source of the seepage must be located and sealed off and the well disinfected before it is safe to drink the water.

Many problems can arise with well water, including contamination from bacteria or minerals, excessive alkalinity, calcium hardness, or turbidity. A homeowner who suspects a problem should get a sample tested immediately. Some county health departments and many commercial laboratories approved by the state health department will help to test well water and recommend remedial treatment.

Septic Systems

As previously mentioned, local governments may set more stringent standards than those in the State Sanitary Code. Today, most local health departments file as-built drawings that specify the septic system design they will approve (Figure 25.1). The design of the system in these drawings will take into account regulations that local health departments have adopted to accommodate any special conditions in the area, such as the prevalence of heavy clay soil or the protection of an underground aquifer.

The purpose of the septic system is to break down sewage coming from the residence. Generally there are three steps in the process. The first is the collection of all effluent from the house via the main drain into a septic tank (the size is usually determined by the number of bedrooms in the home) where the solids settle out and are eventually broken down by bacterial action. The liquids overflow the septic tank into a distribution box that circulates the effluent to the laterals, a series of perforated pipes buried in the ground. The liquid is then absorbed into the leach

Figure 25.1. Private water supply and sewage disposal layout.

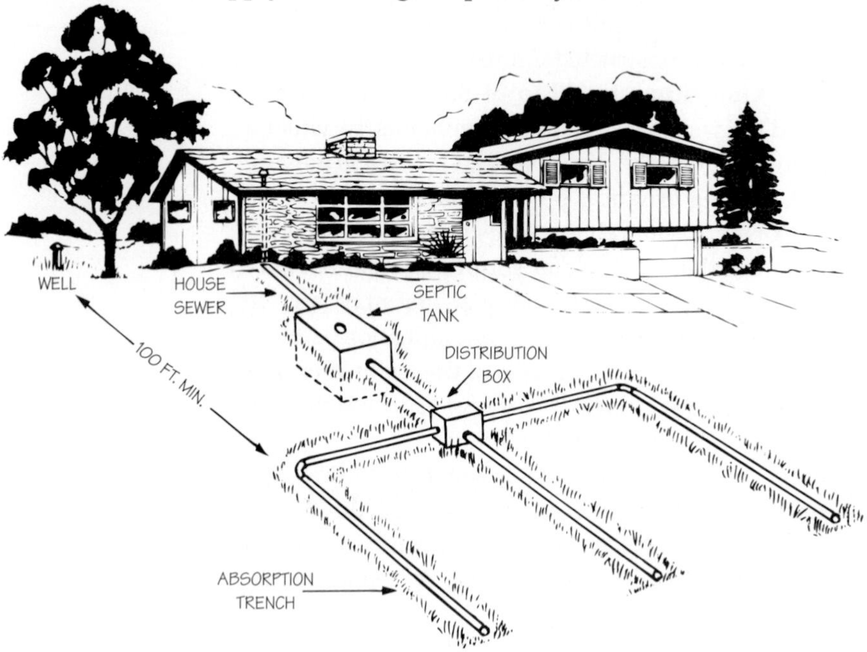

field where it escapes through the process of transpiration to the atmosphere.

Environmental regulation continues to be a rapidly expanding field affecting the real estate industry. Real estate professionals must keep on top of these issues for their own benefit as well as for the benefit of their clients.

VOCABULARY REVIEW

Match terms **a–r** *with statements* **1–18**.

a. *As-built drawings*
b. *Asbestos*
c. *CERCLA*
d. *CPSC*
e. *Carbon monoxide*
f. *Chlordane*
g. *Chlorofluorocarbons*
h. *Due diligence*
i. *Electromagnetic fields*

j. *Environmental assessment*
k. *Lead*
l. *Montreal Protocol*
m. *PCBs*
n. *Radon*
o. *State Sanitary Code*
p. *UFFI*
q. *Underground storage tanks*
r. *Uniform Fire Prevention and Building Code*

1. A federal statute that imposes penalties on those who illegally dispose of hazardous waste.

2. A pesticide used to control termites.
3. Bulk petroleum storage vehicles regulated by the state's Environmental Conservation Law.
4. A treaty signed by 23 countries agreeing to ban the use of CFCs by the year 2000.
5. A colorless, odorless gas that can cause death without proper ventilation.
6. A type of home insulation that sometimes released formaldehyde gas after application.
7. The New York State code that regulates residential construction.
8. The New York State code that regulates water quality.
9. The standard of care purchasers must use to determine whether hazardous waste exists on a site before it is purchased.
10. Emissions from power lines and many other sources, that are suspected of increasing the risk of cancer.
11. A fire-resistant mineral fiber used in insulation, which can cause serious lung disease.
12. A federal regulatory agency that provides consumers with product information.
13. A contaminant formerly found in paint, water pipes, and elsewhere, that poses a serious risk of illness, especially for children and pregnant women.
14. A prepurchase investigation to protect purchasers from liability for former environmental contamination.
15. A radioactive, underground gas that seeps into homes.
16. A toxic chemical contaminant usually associated with industrial pollution, but also found in some water well pumps and other household appliances.
17. A term used to describe preapproved drawings for septic systems.
18. A chemical compound used as a refrigerant, which depletes the ozone layer.

QUESTIONS AND PROBLEMS

1. Describe the major provisions of recent federal legislation designed to mitigate the hazards of lead paint.
2. Discuss the notion of due diligence as it relates to CERCLA.
3. What are some additional requirements of the new lead regulations in New York?
4. Where can homeowners be advised to turn to find out more about possible environmental hazards in their homes or in homes they are interested in purchasing?

26

Real Estate and the Economy

KEY • TERMS

Base industry: an industry that produces goods or services for export from the region

Cost-push inflation: higher prices due to increased costs of labor and supplies

Demand-pull inflation: higher prices due to buyers bidding against each other

Economic base: the ability of a region to export goods and services to other regions and receive money in return

Federal Reserve Board: the governing board of the nation's central bank

Monetization of the debt: the creation of money by the Federal Reserve to purchase Treasury securities

Real: inflation-adjusted

Real-cost inflation: higher prices due to greater effort needed to produce the same product today versus several years ago

Service industry: an industry that produces goods and services to sell to local residents

Earlier chapters of this book described real estate from the standpoints of what it is, how you convey it, how you finance it, how it is taxed, how you rent it, how you value it, how you insure it, and how you broker it. In this chapter we will look at the very important role of regional and national economics in giving value to real estate. In particular, this chapter will discuss the need for an economic base to support real estate values, short-run changes in housing demand when a new industry moves into town or an old one closes, long-run effects on housing demand caused by population and income changes, and the impact of federal tax, fiscal, and monetary policies. The chapter will conclude with a look at inflation, a review of the 1975–1995 period for real estate, the importance of watching the Federal Reserve, and an outlook for the future.

ECONOMIC BASE

In order to survive, a city (or town or region) must export goods and services so that its residents may purchase goods and services not produced locally. To illustrate, Hollywood produces films for theaters and television stations across the country. Income from these films permits residents in Hollywood to purchase things not produced in Hollywood such as cars and trucks made in Detroit. The money Detroit receives is used to buy farm products. A farming region produces farm products in order to generate income with which to buy farm machinery, gasoline, fertilizer, clothing, and vacations. In turn, the economy of a resort area is kept alive with the money spent there by vacationers, and on and on.

The ability of a city or region to produce a commodity or service that can bring in money from outside its area is called its **economic base.** Industries that produce goods and services for export are called **base, export,** or **primary industries.** Thus, film making is a base industry for Hollywood, automobile manufacturing is a base industry for Detroit, and agriculture is a base industry in the Midwest. Producers of goods and services that are not exported are called **service, filler,** or **secondary industries.** This category includes local school systems, supermarkets, doctors, dentists, drugstores, and real estate agencies.

Effect on Property Values

Because land is immovable, the existence of base industries is *absolutely essential* to maintaining local real estate values. Unless a region or city exports, it will die economically, and the value of local real estate will fall. An extreme example of this can be found in the abandoned mining towns of yesteryear. Before the discovery of mineral riches, land was often worth but a few dollars an acre for grazing purposes. With the discovery of minerals and subsequent mine development, land that was suitable for town sites zoomed in value. A new and far richer economic base industry than grazing brought wealth and people into the area, and grazing land was suddenly in demand for homesites, stores, and offices. Years later, when the mines played out and mineral wealth could no longer be exported from the area, outside money ceased to flow into the town. Miners were laid off and moved to other towns where jobs could be found. Without the miners' money, service industries folded and their employees left. The demand for real estate dropped and real estate prices fell, often all the way back to their value for grazing purposes.

Vulnerability   The extent to which regions and cities are vulnerable to changes in economic base depends on how many different kinds of base industries are present and the ability of those industries to export their products consistently. Thus, a city that relies on a single base industry is much more vulnerable than a city with a diversified group of base industries. For example, a city or town that has grown up around a military base will suffer if that base is cut back in size or closed down. In the neighbor cities of Seattle and Tacoma, Washington, real estate prices have been directly influenced by the rise and fall of airplane orders at the area's largest employer, Boeing Aircraft. The economy of Detroit has been hurt by the change in consumer buying preferences to foreign-made cars. The steel-making region that spans Indiana, Ohio, Pennsylvania, and West Virginia has been adversely impacted by steel mill shutdowns due to better prices on steel from abroad. Towns that rely heavily on the lumber industry have seen their economies and real estate prices hurt by the drop in demand for lumber following the end of the last housing boom. The economies of farm communities and the prices of farm land are tied to the rise and fall of farm product prices.

Sometimes these events galvanize concerned citizens, property owners, and business people into action. Seattle and Tacoma have been busy attracting industries other than aircraft manufacturing so as to smooth out the ups and downs of the aircraft business. Oregon repealed its unitary tax on business firms and is actively courting electronics companies. Some steel mills have been bought by employees determined to keep them open and competitive with foreigners.

Just how important is a base industry job to a local economy? As a rule, for each additional person employed in a base industry, another two persons will be employed in local service industries. Thus, if an electronics firm moves into a community and creates 100 new base industry jobs, opportunities will be created for another 200 persons in jobs such as retail store clerks, restaurant services, gas station operators, gardeners, bankers, doctors, dentists, lawyers, police, firefighters, school teachers, and members of local government—to name only a few.

If you understand what is happening in local base industries, you can calculate the need for land and housing. For example, the 100 base industry jobs created by the electronics firm result in 200 service jobs, for a total of 300 new job opportunities in the community. If every three jobs require two households (more than one person working in some families) and each household averages 2.9 persons, then 300 jobs will provide income for 200 households containing a total of 580 persons. The ultimate effect of the 300 new jobs on local employment and housing demand will depend on what portion of the jobs can be filled from within the community and the extent of vacant housing. If the community is already operating at full employment and has no vacant housing to speak of, the addition of 100 base jobs will result in a demand for land, building materials, and labor necessary to provide 200 new housing units. From the standpoint of local government, 580 more people must be supplied with schools, parks, streets, libraries, water, sewage treatment, and police and fire protection.

There is no way to accurately anticipate housing market cycles, whether good or bad. However, the cycles never seem to last too long. But because it takes time to develop raw land into homes, offices, and stores, the supply of developed real estate cannot immediately respond to sudden changes in demand. As a result, price changes for developed real property can be rapid and dramatic over short periods of time.

Employment Multiplier

SHORT-RUN DEMAND FOR HOUSING

Increase in Demand   To illustrate, suppose that in a given community there are presently 5,000 single-family houses and their average value is $82,000. A new industry moves into the community and increases the demand for houses by 100. Local builders, recognizing the new demand, set to work adding 100 houses to the available housing stock. However, it will take time to acquire land, file subdivision maps, acquire building permits, grade the land, and construct the houses. The entire process typically takes 10 to 36 months. Meanwhile the available supply of houses remains fixed. The result will be an increase in house prices as the newly arriving employees bid against each other for a place to live in the existing housing stock. The result is diagrammed in Figure 26.1. Demand Curve 1 represents the demand for houses at various prices before the new employees arrive. Supply and demand are in balance at $82,000 per house, as shown at A.

Next, the new industry moves in. The new employees added to the housing market produce Demand Curve 2. Prices rise owing to competition for the existing houses. This increase literally rations the existing stock of 5,000 houses among 5,100 households. Prices rise until enough existing owners decide to

Figure 26.1. Short-run supply-demand picture.

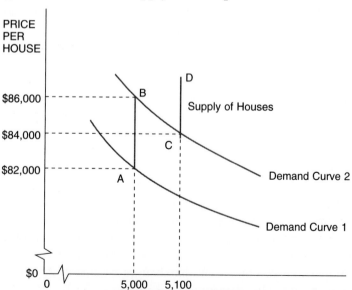

NUMBER OF HOUSES

sell and enough new buyers are priced out of the market. Once again, supply and demand are in balance, with 5,000 houses occupied by 5,000 families. This is point B, $86,000.

At last, the 100 new houses that were started in response to the new demand are completed and are on the market. At what price must these be offered in order to sell them all? It would appear that $86,000 is the answer, as that is what houses are now selling for. However, the supply-demand relationship in Figure 26.1 shows that only 5,000 houses are in demand at $86,000, not 5,100 houses. To find out at what price the additional 100 houses will be absorbed by the market, we must travel along Demand Curve 2 to 5,100 houses. At point C, the market will absorb 5,100 houses if they are priced at $84,000 each. Thus, a temporary glut of homes causes prices to be reduced slightly. This price softening applies to the builders of the 100 new houses and to the owners of the other 5,000 homes if they wish to sell during this temporary oversupply situation.

Increase in Supply

Aware of the oversupply of houses on the market, builders will react by halting building activity until those units are sold and demand starts pushing prices upward again to D, at which time the process repeats itself. Over a period of years, the supply pattern for houses takes on a stair-step appearance as temporary shortages and temporary excesses alternate.

Just as a short-run increase in demand can cause a quick run-up in prices, a short-run decrease in demand has the opposite effect because supply cannot be decreased as fast as demand falls. This situation is diagrammed in Figure 26.2 with supply and demand in balance at 5,100 houses at $84,000 each. Suppose there is an overnight cutback of jobs and, as a result, 100 homeowners decide to sell and move out of the community. This would cause demand to shift downward from Demand Curve 2 to Demand Curve 1. To sell 100 houses, it is necessary for prices to fall from $84,000 (point C) to $80,000 (point E). Without an increase in the economic base of the community, only a reduction in the supply of existing houses through demolition, disasters, and conversions to other uses will push prices back up along Demand Curve 1. If supply falls to 5,000 houses, prices will go to $82,000 (point F).

Decrease in Demand

Effect of Inflation   The presence of inflation will cushion the drop in dollar values when demand shifts to Demand Curve 1 in Figure 26.2. Similarly, the drop in prices from B to C in Figure 26.1 will be milder in the presence of moderate inflation. In the presence of high inflation, prices may not drop, but actually rise. However, if you strip away the masking effect of inflation, Figures 26.1 and 26.2 accurately portray what actually happens when demand suddenly changes and supply cannot react fast enough. Although we have been talking in terms of houses, the same concept applies to vacant lots, apartment buildings, townhouses, condominiums, office buildings, factories, hotels and motels, store space, and so forth.

LONG-RUN DEMAND FOR HOUSING   Future demand for housing in the United States can be seen by looking at the population in terms of age distribution and the ability of people to obtain income at various age levels. As shown in Figure 26.3, during the first 10 years of life, a person earns no income and is dependent on others, usually parents, for sustenance. During junior high school, high school, and college (if any) a person has part-time jobs but is usually still dependent on others for financial support.

Figure 26.2. Short-run drop in demand.

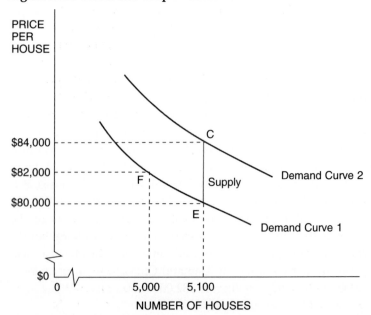

Figure 26.3. Lifetime income curve.

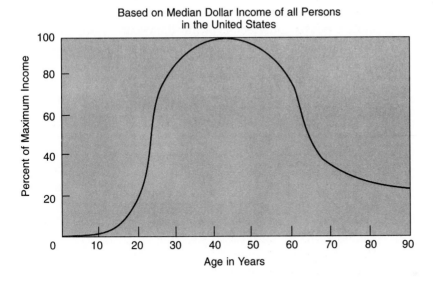

Based on Median Dollar Income of all Persons
in the United States

On leaving school and entering the labor market on a full-time basis, a person's income rises quickly, reflecting increased productive capacity in society. As skills increase, income continues to rise rapidly. In another decade the rise stops increasing as rapidly, although it still advances. Then, somewhere between the ages of 40 and 60, depending on a person's skills and the usefulness of those skills in society, the person's health and/or the desire to slow down, the peak earning year occurs. For those with 4 years of college or the equivalent, this occurs around age 55. For the nation as a whole, it occurs in the mid-forties. The peak earning year is followed at first by mild decreases in income and then by more rapid decreases as retirement occurs.

Buying Pattern

With this earning pattern in mind, you can see the progression of housing demand. When a person is young and setting up a household for the first time, income is low and so are accumulated assets. Thus, housing that requires no equity investment at a minimum cost is needed; that is, an inexpensive rental with no frills. During the next decade, income increases and the household can increase the quality of its rental unit. At the same time, savings accumulate, which, coupled with the ability to make loan payments, enable the household to meet the down payment and loan requirements for a modest housing purchase. As the family grows and income increases, it can move to larger, more expensive quarters. Typically this occurs between the ages of 35 and 45. Another upward move in house size and price usually occurs between 45 and 55 when the family reaches its maximum income.

As the children move out and income peaks and then begins to recede, the household begins to consider a smaller and less expensive dwelling unit. The need for less expensive housing becomes even more compelling on retirement and a further reduction in income. Retirement income typically is not sufficient to support the large home bought during the peak earning years. However, the household has an equity that it can now consolidate into a smaller residence that is fully or nearly fully paid for.

AGE DISTRIBUTION

With the foregoing pattern in mind, let us now turn our attention to Figure 26.4 where the population of the United States is graphed according to its age distribution. The lines labeled 1970, 1980, and 1990 are based on the U.S. census; the 2000 line represents government-prepared population projections based on the fact that persons on the 1980 line will be 10 and 20 years older, respectively, minus losses due to deaths and additions due to immigration.

There are two peaks in the 1980 age distribution line. The smaller of the two, identified as [1], represents persons aged 50 to 60 years in 1980. These persons were born during the decade of the 1920s, a period of economic prosperity in most parts of the United States. Moving to the left, the dip at [2] represents children born during the economic depression that spanned the 1930s. By 1980, they were 40 to 50 years old. Moving again to the left, a substantial upward rise is encountered at [3]. This is the famed World War II and postwar "baby boom." It started in 1940 and lasted until 1960. In 1960, the number of births per year began to decline and continued to decline in each subsequent year through 1978. This is shown at [4].

Housing Demand

Of particular interest is the huge wave of demand from the 1940–1960 baby boom that is working its way across Figure 26.4. How does this translate into housing demand? Beginning in the early 1960s, the United States experienced a growing

Figure 26.4. Age distribution of the U.S. population for the years 1970, 1980, 1990, and 2000.

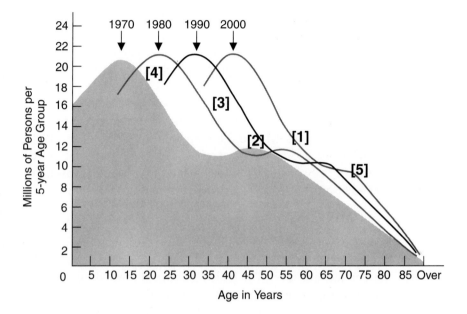

demand for inexpensive rentals by persons under 25 years of age. By 1985, that demand peaked as all children born from 1940 to 1960 became 25 years or older. Between 1965 and 1975, the number of persons in the United States aged 25 through 34 increased by 9 million and resulted in the formation of 5 million households. Each household required a housing unit suitable to its income characteristics. Between 1975 and 1985, this age group grew by another 9 million persons and created an additional 5 million households, each of which required a place to live.

In addition to producing new households, the 1940–1960 children are climbing the income ladder and have more money to spend on housing. And, as they get older, they want to own, not rent. Government statistics show that 60% of all heads of households aged 35 through 44 are homeowners, and among those 45 through 54 years old, 75% are owners. (The percentages are even higher if there are children present.) Buying of more expensive homes will continue until the year 2015, at which time persons born in 1960 will reach the age of 55. Because personal income

More Homeowners

patterns decline after that age, a retrenchment into more modest housing will then be observed.

After 1985, the baby boomers have made fewer new purchases, except for moving up to bigger housing. Demand for housing by those in the peak new-home purchasing years has slowed somewhat as that population is now smaller in number than the baby boomers.

Over 65 Although the dominant factor in housing demand in the next several decades will be the maturing members of the 1940–1960 baby boom, we must not overlook the present steady growth in households over the age of 65 years. Households aged 65 and above have grown in numbers and, as may be seen at [5], did so until 1995. At that time there began a 10-year pause in growth because persons born during the decade of the 1930s reached the age of 65. Following that, the over-65 group will again grow in numbers as those born between 1940 and 1960 reach this age level. The housing demand created by these age groups may primarily be the result of their investments, pensions, social security income, public welfare, and assets accumulated earlier in life such as the family home, but the newer emerging health-conscious older population may remain a much larger percentage of the labor force than may have been anticipated. The largest part of the growth in the elderly population is projected to occur between the years 2010 and 2050.

Another Wave When the children born after 1960 reach the age at which they want to have a residence of their own (usually 18 to 25 years of age), they will find large amounts of housing available as the persons born between 1940 and 1960 climb the lifetime income curve and upgrade their housing. Unless some of the housing being abandoned by the 1940–1960 group can be used to accommodate households over the age of 65, this situation will probably cause a slowdown in new housing construction. The United States has already experienced a virtual halt in new elementary school construction because of the drop in births after 1960. This came after a 15-year-long frantic effort to build schoolrooms.

In 1978, the drop in births that began in 1960 began to reverse itself. Now the baby-boom children are having children of their own. This will make a third wave in the age distribution of the U.S. population and, with it, a new wave of housing demand when those children form households.

Thus far we have talked about the requirement of an economic base to support local land values and the effect on housing demand of population age groups and income levels. Now let us look at the influence on real estate caused by the federal government's tax rules, laws, deficits, and monetary policies.

GOVERNMENTAL IMPACT

Real estate has long been favored with special income tax treatment. For years, tax laws have allowed homeowners to deduct property taxes and mortgage loan interest when calculating state and federal taxes. To illustrate, for a person in a 28% tax bracket, an 8% interest rate costs, after taxes, only 5.76%. Similarly, property taxes of $1,500 per year cost, after taxes, only $1,080.

Tax Laws

Owners of improved investment property can deduct costs of operating and maintaining the property plus depreciation on the improvements. For most investment properties owned between 1940 and 1980, depreciation expense was more of an accounting entry than a market reality. This was the result of rising real estate prices coupled with tax rules that allowed improvements to be depreciated over accounting lives shorter than their useful lives. Moreover, pre-1987 tax rules allowed depreciation to be accelerated, i.e., taken sooner rather than later. Since depreciation is deductible at tax time and not repaid until years later when the property is sold, tax policies allowing short accounting lives and accelerated depreciation made real estate a very attractive investment.

In the fall of 1986, a tax bill was passed by Congress and signed by the president that made drastic changes in the income tax treatment of real estate. (Details of this tax bill are in Chapter 22.) This law repealed the long-term capital gain exclusion, repealed accelerated depreciation on real estate, extended minimum depreciation periods from 19 years to 27½ years for residential and to 31½ years for commercial, and placed tight limits on real estate losses that could be deducted from other income. Each of these made real estate less attractive from a tax standpoint. And, since tax treatment is one of the deciding factors in buying investment real estate, these tax changes greatly influence what

1986 Tax Bill

people can and will pay for a property. Most of the 1986 tax law changes fell on real estate investors, with relatively few on homeowners. Of note in the 1986 tax bill is a tax credit allowed for the rehabilitation of old and historic structures. The intent of Congress is to induce people to renovate rather than tear down older structures. Also, a tax credit is available for those who will own and operate low-income rental housing.

Lending Regulations   A new trend developed in the 1980s. Poor lending practices caused many traditional lending sources to close, leaving their shareholders, depositors, and investors with nothing. Federal regulators were often blamed for not overseeing banks and savings and loans associations carefully enough so that the public interest would be protected. The result was a new wave of federal regulation of lending institutions. Credit may now be cheaper, but the lending standards are much tougher. Lenders may now require more collateral or more equity for a loan than in the past.

FISCAL POLICY   Few home buyers can afford to pay all cash for a place to live; most must borrow. As a result, the housing industry is very sensitive to the price and availability of loan money. Not only does this affect contractors and construction workers, but also appliance and furniture manufacturers, lumber mills, cement factories, real estate appraisers, and real estate agents. Anyone connected with the manufacture, sale, or resale of housing is directly affected by the price and availability of mortgage loan money to home buyers.

If federal, state, or local governments cannot balance their budgets, they too must borrow. When they do, they compete with home buyers and businesses for available savings in the capital markets. Of these, government gets its needs filled first at whatever the interest cost. This is because if a government did not borrow it would not have enough to pay its bills and would be bankrupt. This leaves home buyers and businesses to compete for what is left over. For the most part, state and local governments have learned to live within their budgets. But the federal government has not. Defense spending and social spending in excess of income have produced federal deficits nearly every year since 1940. These were not terribly worrisome at first, but by the 1970s financing the federal deficit was taking progressively larger and larger chunks of money out of the capital markets. By the middle of the 1980s, annual federal deficits were $200 billion and absorbing that much of the country's, and indeed the world's, capital. This borrowing continued to increase through the mid-1990s. What is left is available to businesses and home buyers, but at high interest rates. In view of this, it is generally agreed among economists that if the federal government will learn to live within its means, interest rates will come down for everyone. Some administrations have attempted budget cuts, but Congress must approve them. As long as Congress perceives that there is voter support for federally supported projects, they are unwilling to cut back on spending. The deficit, then, continued because of the lack of past congressional efforts to the contrary. Beginning in the mid-1990s, both Congress and the president finally began real efforts to cut the government deficit. The 1994 elections that marked the mid-term of the Clinton presidency saw both houses of Congress change from Democratic to Republican control. Many observers attributed the change to widespread voter support for downsizing government. Time will tell whether the new Congress can translate that support into meaningful spending reductions.

The **Federal Reserve Board,** by its monetary policy effected through the Federal Reserve Banks, has the ability to create and destroy money. This is done by any of the following mechanisms: (1) open-market purchases and sales of Treasury securities, (2) changes in the discount rate charged to banks, and (3) changes in the reserve requirements of banks. We omit a detailed explanation of each of these and go directly to the point: the Federal Reserve can create money. This is useful because in an economy that grows 3% a year, a 3% increase in the money supply is necessary to keep prices from falling. At the same time, however, there is the temptation to print more money than needed for economic growth because this new money can be used to buy back Treasury securities that were created to fund the federal deficit. The short-term result of such purchases is to drop interest rates, which benefits the government, business, and housing. Unfortunately, the longer-run effect (beyond 2 years) is more inflation as there is now more money in circula-

MONETARY POLICY

tion without a corresponding increase in goods and services to buy.

When inflation is apparent, savers become wise and respond by buying equity assets such as real estate to hedge against further inflation and by raising the rate of interest they will accept to compensate for inflation. Thus, any benefits of creating extra money by the Federal Reserve are lost over the long term.

SECONDARY MORTGAGE MARKET

A very important influence on real estate activity and prices in the United States has been the secondary mortgage market. Before the 1970s, home loan money came mostly from savings and loans, mutual savings banks, commercial banks, and life insurance companies. This was a relatively limited source of money that tended to keep a lid on real estate prices. With the advent of the Federal National Mortgage Association, the Government National Mortgage Association, the Federal Home Loan Mortgage Corporation, and other secondary mortgage market operators, previously untapped sources of loan money were now available to real estate borrowers. Individuals and pension funds that had avoided making mortgage loans because of the work involved could now invest with ease and a guarantee of safety. Additionally, a secondary market provides a place to sell a mortgage that a lender does not want to hold until maturity. Much of the money raised in the secondary market has been used (and will continue to be used) to fund the 1940–1960 baby-boom children as they buy housing. However a lot of that money also helped fuel real estate speculation and inflation in the late 1970s through the mid-1980s. The secondary market now is producing some drag on prices because of substantial foreclosure losses in the late 1980s and early 1990s, the insolvency of the FSLIC, and glutted portfolios of real estate owned (REOs) by lenders in both the primary and secondary markets.

TYPES OF INFLATION

In nearly all years since World War II, prices of consumer commodities and real estate have risen. Although inflation is currently not as pressing an issue as it was in the 1970s and 1980s, there are four concepts with which you should be familiar: cost-push inflation, demand-pull inflation, monetary inflation, and real-cost inflation.

The increasing cost of inputs necessary to manufacture a product or offer a service results in what is called **cost-push inflation.** To illustrate, an automobile manufacturer increases the price of cars because labor and materials cost more. Similarly, a builder of new homes will include in the home price any increases in the prices of lumber, bricks, concrete, metal, construction labor, construction loans, and government permits.

Cost-Push Inflation

When buyers bid against each other to buy something that has been offered for sale, **demand-pull inflation** results. For example, three buyers for a choice lot may bid $75,000, $76,000 and $77,000, respectively. Demand-pull inflation is basically the result of too much money chasing too few goods. This type of inflation usually has little to do with the actual cost of producing the particular goods or services being sought. Instead, it reflects what buyers feel they would have to pay elsewhere for the same thing.

Demand-Pull Inflation

Monetary inflation results from the creation of excessive amounts of money by government. The classic example of this was in Germany during the first 5 years after World War I. In an effort to provide money to solve all the war-torn country's problems at once, the German government created and spent money on a grand scale. However, there was no parallel increase in goods and services to be purchased with that money. The result was demand-pull inflation as millions of people with pockets and, later, wheelbarrows stuffed with newly printed currency, fought to buy everything from bread and vegetables to real estate. Within a few years, prices rose on the order of 1 million percent before the printing presses were finally shut down.

Monetary Inflation

To a lesser degree, monetary inflation is used today by many countries. Allowing the money supply to grow faster than the available supply of goods and services causes a temporary economic stimulus by placing more money in people's hands. But the ultimate result is a reduction in the purchasing power of that money.

Real-cost inflation is inflation caused by the increased effort necessary to produce the same quantity of a good or service. For example, much easy-to-develop land has already been built

Real-Cost Inflation

on, forcing developers to utilize land that requires more effort to bulldoze into usable lots. Another example is water service to new lots. Local water districts that once could supply the town's population from a few wells or a nearby lake or river must now travel many miles to find water. The additional cost of the water system and pumping charges must be added to the user's water bill.

1975–1990 PERIOD

The period from 1975 to 1990 has been one of the most dramatic in American economic history. In many areas, real estate prices doubled and tripled between 1975 and 1990. Inflation zoomed upward, interest rates reached record highs, and real estate was the favored investment. Then, in the early 1990s, inflation fell dramatically, real estate prices stalled, and interest rates retreated. What the country witnessed was a combination of the issues discussed thus far in this chapter at work in the marketplace. Let's take a closer look at what happened then and what may happen in the future.

In 1975, members of the leading edge of the 1940–1960 baby boom were adults in the market ready for their first housing purchases. Simultaneously, the Equal Credit Opportunity Act made it easier to qualify for loans, and the secondary mortgage market was opening previously untapped sources of loan money. Added to this was the lack of new housing for sale because of a drop in housing starts in connection with a recession in 1974–1975.

As federal spending and money growth policies designed to end the recession took hold, interest rates fell, people regained jobs, and the mood of the country turned bullish. People began buying homes again and, against a backdrop of limited supply, quickly pulled prices upward. Rising prices usually dampen demand. But several other factors were involved that made buying real estate, and in particular buying homes, very attractive.

Low Real Interest

The first factor was the low **real** (i.e., inflation-adjusted) cost of interest. Although interest rates for homes ranged from 8% to 10% between 1975 and 1978, inflation and home prices were rising faster. Thus, it made sense to borrow and buy real estate; in fact, the more the better. Since it was possible to buy with as little as 10% down, buyers were realizing enormous returns on their investments. Persons who received $60,000 for houses bought earlier for $40,000 were now making down payments on $80,000 houses. These sellers were taking their money into $110,000 houses while those sellers were buying $150,000 houses and so on.

As already noted, tax laws allow the deduction of interest. During the 1970s, wage increases of 10% per year and more were common. This pushed wage earners into higher tax brackets and made interest deductions even more valuable. Meanwhile, increases from appreciation were not taxable until the property sold and then received preferential long-term capital gains treatment. Thus, despite higher interest and higher home prices, as long as prices continued to rise substantially real estate seemed to be an assured ticket to quick wealth.

Tax Benefits

The boom came to a turning point in late 1979. Politically, high inflation (at one point reaching a rate of 18% per year) became a national political issue. Federal Reserve policy changed from one of generous monetary growth to one of restrained monetary growth. Lenders made higher-risk real estate loans (at high interest rates) and sometimes invested in real estate, in an effort to keep pace with inflation.

Reversal

    Tighter regulations by the federal government for high risk loans resulted in fewer loans, regulated appraisals, and tighter credit standards. More importantly, fewer loans were being renewed because of the tighter lending requirements imposed by the new federal regulations. The existing loans had to be written down, and many lenders became insolvent. The initial effect was most severe in the southwestern states where the real property values had dropped, which then affected the loan-to-value ratios. By 1992, the Southwest was recovering, but the Northeast and southern California were beginning to have similar difficulties. The nation is now experiencing relatively low interest rates. This is partly because the tighter credit standards imposed on lenders to lower risk and increase stability have resulted in availability of money, and partly because of the loss of government jobs and business downsizing as the government reduces its size. Overall, this results in fewer people who can qualify for loans.

Looking Ahead   Expectations about inflation (or the lack of it) and interest rates lag behind the actual changes. At the midpoint of the 1980 decade, much of the home buying public was unsure what to make of things. House prices, on average, essentially remained stable for the first half of the decade while interest rates were slow to drop. Many investors were left with high-priced properties that could not be sold except at below-market interest rates or below acquisition prices. More generous depreciation schedules offered by the 1981 tax act did help real estate's attractiveness, but investors and speculators remained unimpressed with housing and turned to office buildings, with depreciation being the carrot. However, even this carrot produced a problem as millions of square feet of office space built between 1981 and 1985 remained vacant at the end of the decade while someone was making the interest payments. The Tax Reform Act of 1986 made these investments even more unattractive into the late 1980s. There are now fewer investors in the market, and many commercial properties are now selling for less than original construction cost. As the real estate market moves into the latter half of the 1990s, supply will still outpace demand in most commercial markets. Prices will be more dependent on quality, desirability, and cash flow, rather than on federal economic indicators. In short, real estate as a commodity has to compete more evenly with other investment alternatives. Although interest rates have risen somewhat in the mid-1990s, the increases to date have been relatively modest and have had only a marginal impact on the industry.

Owner-Occupants   No longer a speculator's market, the housing market is returning to an owner-occupant market. Owner-occupants receive the benefits of occupancy and the psychological value of owning their home. As such, they are less demanding of appreciation potential compared with investors who, sensing an unrewarding investment, will avoid it or sell out of it and go elsewhere with their capital. Thus, it appears that for the foreseeable future, success in new construction will go to those who appeal best to the owner-occupant's needs, tastes, and pocketbook. The 1990s have brought falling interest rates, and more creditworthy owner-occupants are able to qualify for loans and buy homes. This, along with the availability of money due to the rapid growth of money supplies for residential loans in the secondary market (not generally available for commercial loans) has especially helped the residential resale market and those owners who need to refinance existing loans. The issue, again, appears to be risk. The secondary market relies on low-risk, qualified home buyers, utilizing standard loan documentation. There is still less money available for the higher-risk, tougher credit, commercial markets. Those lenders that survived the loose lending practices of the early 1980s learned from their mistakes and now have much more conservative loan criteria.

If you plan to develop or invest in real estate, it is very helpful to watch Federal Reserve statistics so as to better anticipate changes in interest rates. Although the marketplace is the ultimate decider of interest rates, the actions of the Federal Reserve Board can and do provide a powerful push on rates. For example, even though mortgage rates were already rising by 1978 as lenders tried to stay ahead of inflation, Federal Reserve action in 1979 and 1980 to slow money supply growth helped interest rates go higher. By 1989, the Federal Reserve Board was carefully increasing the money supply in order to reduce interest rates and thus keep the U.S. economy from falling into another recession.

WATCHING THE FED

To understand the Federal Reserve Board, you need to know that the Board has four objectives for the American economy: (1) high employment, (2) stable prices, (3) steady growth in the nation's productive capacity, and (4) a stable foreign exchange value for the dollar. During a recession, employment and economic growth are of primary importance, and the Federal Reserve Board adds extra money to the banking system as it did to pull out of the 1974–1975 recession. In the late 1970s, stable prices and a stable dollar were the prime concerns. This required a slowdown in the growth of the money supply, which the Federal Reserve Board effected. By the end of 1984, inflation was down to 4% and the dollar was very strong. In 1985, the Federal Reserve was gingerly touching the money accelerator to buoy a banking industry beleaguered by high interest rates, to ward off recession, and to take the edge off what many considered to be an overly strong dollar. The early 1990s saw the Fed drop the cost of money to member banks to a 20-year low, but lending regulations have stemmed the potential inflation by requiring tighter credit standards. In the mid-1990s, the Fed began slightly adjusting interest rates again in an effort to control inflation.

MONETARY BASE   Week-to-week changes in the results of Federal Reserve monetary policy can be found each Friday in the *Wall Street Journal* under "Federal Reserve Data." Of these, the most important is the **monetary base** figure. This shows the legal reserves of banks at the Federal Reserve plus cash in the hands of the public. If this grows faster than the real (i.e., inflation-adjusted) rate of growth of the country's gross domestic product (GDP), one can assume that the nation's money supply will soon be expanding at a greater rate than real gross domestic product. This will cause interest rates to fall and economic growth to be stimulated. Two years down the road it may turn to inflation, depending on how the Fed deals with credit standards.

THE OUTLOOK   As this material is being written, there are two likely economic scenarios pending and in both the federal deficit plays a leading role. The first scenario is that Congress will not balance its budget. This means the Federal Reserve Board must decide whether or not to expand the money supply in order to buy back the deficit—that is, **monetize the debt.** Failure to expand the money supply will allow interest rates to rise dramatically and cause a recession worse than the 1985–1986 recession, which itself was the worst since the 1930s. Yet creating money in excess of increases in goods and services will cause inflation and high interest costs, just as it did in the 1975–1979 period. To date, the Fed has managed to control the supply to maintain low inflation but has had difficulty dealing with the prospect of a recession.

The second scenario is that Congress will bring about a meaningful reduction in the size of the federal deficit. This would reduce the need of the U.S. Treasury to compete with businesses and home buyers for available loan funds. With less competition, interest rates will fall. This will attract more loan funds as lenders become confident that rates won't soon be rising. Lower rates will reduce the federal deficit still further as interest paid on existing government debt gradually drops. The cost of this attractive scenario is overall fiscal belt tightening:

recipients of government spending programs would have to receive less. Alternatively, Congress could continue to raise taxes to pay for its spending (as it did in 1993), or it could apply a combination of the two.

There is a very close parallel between the federal government's money problems and the money problems of a free-spending married couple who discovered credit cards. At first, the couple found that a credit card could help them buy a few things that their monthly paychecks would not have covered. But instead of repaying the credit card balance, more items were purchased until the limit on the card was reached. Flush with the pleasures of living beyond their monthly paychecks, another credit card was obtained. Purchases were made with it until it, too, reached its maximum. Now the first two credit card companies were demanding monthly payments, so a third credit card, this one with cash borrowing privileges, was obtained. This card was used to make payments on the previous two cards and buy still more on credit. Soon all three credit card companies wanted monthly repayments so the couple took out a loan at the bank, mortgaging the appreciation in their house to do so. The buying continued and soon another loan was taken out with a finance company to make payments on the existing loans and buy more things. Then one day, there were simply no more places to borrow, yet the payments on all those loans kept coming due. The couple was advised by a credit counselor that they had two choices: declare bankruptcy or adopt an austerity budget and start repaying the loans. If you were in their shoes, which would you choose? If you were in the U.S. Congress, which would you choose for the country? Or, would you look for one more lender to keep the deficits going a little while longer?

A Parallel

There is no lack of household formation potential in the United States. Additionally, there is a large stock of existing housing in the country plus the capacity to build 2 million new housing units every year. The main question will continue to be who gets what—that is, how housing will be distributed. Because real estate is so sensitive to the price and availability of loanable funds, the answer will depend heavily on competition from the government.

VOCABULARY REVIEW

Match terms **a–j** *with statements* **1–10.**

a. *Base industry*
b. *Cost-push inflation*
c. *Demand-pull inflation*
d. *Economic base*
e. *Federal Reserve Board*

f. *Monetary inflation*
g. *Monetize the debt*
h. *Real*
i. *Real-cost inflation*
j. *Service industry*

1. An industry that produces goods or services for export from the region.
2. An industry that produces goods or services to sell to local residents.
3. The ability of a region to export goods and services to other regions.
4. Higher prices due to buyers bidding against each other.
5. Higher prices due to greater effort needed to produce the same product today.
6. Higher prices due to increased costs of labor and supplies.
7. Results from increasing the money supply faster than increases in goods and services to buy.
8. Governing board of the nation's central bank.
9. Inflation-adjusted.
10. The creation of money by the Federal Reserve to purchase Treasury securities.

QUESTIONS AND PROBLEMS

1. List and rank in order of importance the base industries that support your community. How stable are they? Are any new ones coming? Are any existing ones leaving?
2. What would be the effect of a new industry creating 500 new jobs in your community? Is there sufficient vacant housing available? What would be the effect of a loss of 500 jobs?
3. Does the population age distribution of your community differ from that of the United States as a whole? How would this affect demand for housing in your area?
4. What was the effect of the Reagan years on inflation? What are the good points? The bad points?
5. What was the intent of government in passing the Equal Credit Opportunity Act?
6. Identify three specific examples of cost-push inflation that you have personally observed or read about during the past 12 months.
7. Have the Clinton years resulted in a marked change from the Bush years? Why or why not?
8. What are the economic goals of the Federal Reserve Board?
9. What are the advantage and the disadvantage of monetizing the federal debt?
10. If money supply grows slower than real gross national product, would the result be rising prices or falling prices?

Essentials of Real Estate Economics, 4th Ed., by **Dennis J. McKenzie** and **Richard M. Betts** (Prentice Hall, 1996, 470 pages). An excellent, easy-to-read study of economics as it applies to real estate.

"Growth and Change: The Economy and Real Estate" (*Urban Land,* March 1991, pp. 4–15). Includes statistics on economic conditions and how they affect the real estate market.

Real Estate in the U. S. Economy: Impacts on GNP, Income, and Employment (National Association of REALTORS®, 1988, 72 pages).

"Real Estate Values and the Economy: Impacts of Falling Property Values," by **David Wyss** (*Real Estate Perspectives—Quarterly Report,* July 1992, pp. 2–3).

ADDITIONAL READINGS

APPENDIX A

New York State Licensing Law

§ 440. Definitions.

1. Whenever used in this article "real estate broker" means any person, firm or corporation, who, for another and for a fee, commission or other valuable consideration, lists for sale, sells, at auction or otherwise, exchanges, buys or rents, or offers or attempts to negotiate a sale, at auction or otherwise, exchange, purchase or rental of an estate or interest in real estate, or collects or offers or attempts to collect rent for the use of real estate, or negotiates or offers or attempts to negotiate, a loan secured or to be secured by a mortgage, other than a residential mortgage loan, as defined in section five hundred ninety of the banking law, or other incumbrance upon or transfer of real estate, or is engaged in the business of a tenant relocator, or who, notwithstanding any other provision of law, performs any of the above stated functions with respect to the resale of condominium property originally sold pursuant to the provisions of the general business law governing real estate syndication offerings. In the sale of lots pursuant to the provisions of article nine-a of this chapter, the term "real estate broker" shall also include any person, partnership, association or corporation employed by or on behalf of the owner or owners of lots or other parcels of real estate, at a stated salary, or upon a commission, or upon a salary and commission, or otherwise, to sell such real estate, or any parts thereof, in lots or other parcels, and who shall sell or exchange, or offer or attempt or agree to negotiate the sale or exchange, of any such lot or parcel of real estate. For purposes of this subdivision the term, "interest in real estate" shall include the sale of a business wherein the value of the real estate transferred as part of the business is not merely incidental to the transaction, and shall not include the assignment of a lease, and further, the transaction itself is not otherwise subject to regulation under state or federal laws governing the sale of securities. In connection with the sale of a business the term "real estate broker" shall not include a person, firm or corporation registered pursuant to the provisions of article twenty-three-A of the general business law or federal securities laws.

2. **"Associate real estate broker"** means a licensed real estate broker who shall by choice elect to work under the name and supervision of another individual broker or another broker who is licensed under a partnership, trade name or corporation. Such individual shall retain his or her license as a real estate broker as provided for in this article; provided, however, that the practice of real estate sales and brokerage by such individual as an associate broker shall be governed exclusively by the provisions of this article as they pertain to real estate salespersons. Nothing contained herein shall preclude an individual who elects to be licensed as an associate broker from also retaining a separate

real estate broker's license under an individual, partnership, trade name or corporation.

3. **"Real estate salesperson"** means a person associated with a licensed real estate broker to list for sale, sell or offer for sale, at auction or otherwise, to buy or offer to buy or to negotiate the purchase or sale or exchange of real estate, or to negotiate a loan on real estate other than a mortgage loan as defined in section five hundred ninety of the banking law, or to lease or rent or offer to lease, rent or place for rent any real estate, or collects or offers or attempts to collect rent for the use of real estate for or in behalf of such real estate broker, or who, notwithstanding any other provision of law, performs any of the above stated functions with respect to the resale of a condominium property originally sold pursuant to the provisions of the general business law governing real estate syndication offerings.

4. **"Tenant relocator"** means any person, firm, corporation, partnership, or any legal entity whatsoever, which, for another and for a fee, commission or other valuable consideration, supervises, organizes, arranges, coordinates, handles or is otherwise in charge of or responsible for the relocation of commercial or residential tenants from buildings or structures that are to be demolished, rehabilitated, remodeled or otherwise structurally altered.

5. **"Association, associated; or associated with"** whenever used in this article shall be deemed to make reference to a salesperson's relationship with his or her broker. Nothing in this article shall be deemed or construed to be indicative or determinative of the legal relationship of a salesperson to a broker nor shall any provision of this article be deemed or construed to alter or otherwise affect the legal responsibility of a real estate broker to third parties for the acts of anyone associated with such broker pursuant to this article.

§ 440-a. License required for real estate brokers and salespersons.

No person, co-partnership or corporation shall engage in or follow the business or occupation of, or hold himself or itself out or act temporarily or otherwise as a real estate broker or real estate salesperson in this state without first procuring a license therefor as provided in this article. No person shall be entitled to a license as a real estate broker under this article, either as an individual or as a member of a co-partnership, or as an officer of a corporation, unless he or she is nineteen years of age or over, a citizen of the United States or an alien lawfully admitted for permanent residence in the United States. No person shall be entitled to a license as a real estate salesperson under this article unless he or she is over the age of eighteen years. No person shall be entitled to a license as a real estate broker or real estate salesperson under this article who has been convicted in this state or elsewhere of a felony, and who has not subsequent to such conviction received executive pardon therefor or a certificate of good conduct from the parole board, to remove the disability under this section because of such conviction. No person shall be entitled to a license as a real estate broker or real estate salesman under this article who does not meet the requirements of section 3-503 of the general obligations law.

Notwithstanding the above, tenant associations, and not-for-profit corporations authorized in writing by the commissioner of the department of the city of New York charged with enforcement of the housing maintenance code of such city to manage residential property owned by such city or appointed by a court of competent jurisdiction to manage residential property owned by such city shall be exempt from the licensing provisions of this section with respect to the properties so managed.

§ 440-b. Licenses in Putnam county.

On and after the first day of July, nineteen hundred thirty four, no person, copartnership or corporation shall engage in or follow the business or occupation of, or hold himself or itself out temporarily or otherwise as a real estate broker or real estate salesperson in the county of Putnam, without first procuring a license therefor as provided in this article, except that such license in such county shall be granted and issued, without the written examination provided in this article, to a person, copartnership or corporation who was engaged in business as a real estate broker or real estate salesperson in such county prior to the first day of January, nineteen hundred thirty-four.

§ 441 . Application for license.

1. Form. (a) Any person, copartnership or corporation desiring to act as a real estate broker or any person desiring to act as a real estate salesperson on or after the first day of October, nineteen hundred and twenty-two, shall file with the department of state at its office in Albany an application for the kind of license desired, in such form and detail as the department shall prescribe, and conforming to the requirements of section 3-503 of the general obligations law, setting forth the following, if the application be for a broker's license:

(i) The name and residence address of the applicant, and if an individual the name under which he intends to conduct business.

(ii) If the applicant be a copartnership the name and residence address of each member thereof and the name under which the business is to be conducted; or, if the applicant be a corporation, the name of the corporation and the name and residence address of each of its officers.

(iii) The place or places, including the city, town or village, with the street and number, where the business is to be conducted.

(iv) The business or occupation theretofore engaged in by the applicant, or, if a copartnership, by each member thereof, or, if a corporation, by each officer thereof, for a period of two years, immediately preceding the date of such application, setting forth the place or places where such business or occupation was engaged in and the name or names of employers, if any.

(v) The form, information and statement required by section 3-503 of the general obligations law.

(b) Such further information as the department may reasonably require shall be furnished by the applicant including sufficient proof of having taken and passed a written examination and answered such questions as may be prepared by the department to enable it to determine the trustworthiness of the applicant if an individual, or of each member of a copartnership or each officer of a corporation for whom a license as a broker is asked, and his or their competency to transact the business of real estate broker in such a manner as to safeguard the interests of the public. In determining competency, the department shall require proof that the person being tested to qualify to apply for a broker's license has a fair knowledge of the English language, a fair understanding of the general purposes and general legal effect of deeds, mortgages, land contracts of sale, and leases, a general and fair understanding of the obligations between principal and agent, as well as of the provisions of this act. The applicant must also furnish proof that he has attended for at least ninety hours and has successfully completed a real estate course or courses approved by the secretary of state as to method and content and supervision which approval may be withdrawn if in the opinion of the secretary of state said course or courses are not being conducted properly as to method, content and supervision, and that either the applicant has actively participated in the general real estate brokerage business as a licensed real estate salesperson under the supervision of a licensed real estate broker for a period of not less than one year or has had the equivalent experience in general real estate business for a period of at least two years, the nature of which experience shall be established by affidavit duly sworn to under oath and/or other and further proof required by the department of state.

(c) In the event the applicant shall be a licensed salesperson under this article and shall have submitted acceptable proof pursuant to the provisions of either paragraph (d) of subdivision one-A of this section or paragraph (a) of subdivision three of this section of having attended and successfully completed forty-five hours of an approved real estate course or courses within four years of the date of the application, the department may accept and credit same against the ninety hours required hereunder.

1-A. (a) **Every application** for a real estate salesperson's license shall set forth:

(i) The name and residence address of the applicant.

(ii) The name and principal business address of the broker with whom he is to be associated.

(iii) The business or occupation engaged in for the two years immediately preceding the date of the application, setting forth the place or places where such business or occupation was engaged in, and the name or names of employers if any.

(iv) The length of time he has been engaged in the real estate business.

(v) The form, information and statement required by section 3-503 of the general obligations law.

(b) Each applicant for a salesperson's license shall provide such further information as the department may reasonably require, appearing at such time and place as may be designated by the department, to take a written examination and answer such questions as may be prepared by the department to enable it to determine the trustworthiness of the applicant and the applicant's competence to transact the business of real estate salesperson in such a manner as to safeguard the interests of the public, including the applicant's working knowledge of the basic concepts of law pertaining to contracts, real property, agency and this article which govern conduct of such business, mastery of basic skills needed to perform the applicant's duties, working knowledge of the ethical obligations of a real estate salesperson, and knowledge of the provisions of the general obligations law pertaining to performance of the applicant's duties.

(c) Each application for either a broker's or salesperson's license under this article shall be subscribed by the applicant; or if made by a copartnership it shall be subscribed by a member thereof, or if made by a corporation it shall be subscribed by an officer thereof and shall conform to the requirements of section 3-503 of the general obligations law. Each application shall contain an affirmation by the person so subscribing that the statements therein are true under the penalties of perjury. An application for a license shall be accompanied by the appropriate license fee, as hereinafter prescribed in this article.

(d) Anything to the contrary herein notwithstanding, on and after the effective date of this paragraph, no salesperson's license or conditional license shall be issued by the department unless the application therefor has been accompanied by proof that prior to such application the applicant has attended at least forty-five hours and successfully completed a real estate course or courses approved by the secretary of state as to method and content and supervision, which approval may be withdrawn if in the opinion of the secretary of state said course or courses are not properly conducted as to method, content and supervision.

2. Renewals. Any license granted under the provision hereof may be renewed by the department upon application therefor by the holder thereof, in such form as the department may prescribe and conforming to the requirements of section 3-503 of the general obligations law, and payment of the fee for such license. In case of application for renewal of license, the department may dispense with the requirement of such statements as it deems unnecessary in view of those contained in the original application for license but may not dispense with the requirements of section 3-503 of the general obligations law. A renewal period within the meaning of this act is considered as being a period of two years from the date of expiration of a previously issued license. The department shall require any applicant, who does not apply for renewal of license within such period, to qualify by passing the written examination as provided herein, and may require any licensee who has not yet passed the written examination, and who cannot reasonably prove to the satisfaction of the department, that he can meet the competency requirements, to pass the written examination before a renewal of license shall be granted; provided, however, that a person who failed or was unable to renew his license by reason of his induction or enlistment in the armed forces of the United States shall not be required to take or pass such examination.

3. (a) No renewal license shall be issued any licensee under this article for any license period commencing November first, nineteen hundred ninety-five unless such licensee shall have within the two year period immediately preceding such renewal attended at least twenty-two and one-half hours and successfully completed a continuing education real estate course or courses approved by the secretary of state as to method, content and supervision, which approval may be withdrawn if in the opinion of the secretary of state such course or courses are not being conducted properly as to method, content and supervision. The licensee

shall provide an affidavit, in a form acceptable to the department of state, establishing the nature of the continuing education acquired and shall provide such further proof as required by the department of state. The provisions of this paragraph shall not apply to any licensed real estate broker who is engaged full time in the real estate business and who has been licensed under this article for at least fifteen consecutive years immediately preceding such renewal.

(b) Notwithstanding the provisions of section four hundred one of the state administrative procedure act, except as provided in this paragraph, no license issued under this article shall continue in effect beyond the period for which it is issued if the proof of attendance required hereunder is not submitted and accepted prior to such expiration date. The department in its discretion may however issue a temporary renewal license for such period of time it deems appropriate to permit the submission of the required proof of attendance when the failure to submit such proof is not due to the fault of the licensee.

(c) The secretary of state, no later than November first, nineteen hundred seventy-nine, shall promulgate rules establishing the method, content and supervision requirements of the continuing education real estate course or courses provided for in this section. In establishing the requirements for the continuing education course or courses, the secretary of state shall permit alternatives with respect to content and method of presentation in consideration of the type of brokerage practiced and the availability of the sources of such course or courses in different areas of the state. Each course shall, however, be presented in an appropriate class room setting, have an established curriculum composed primarily of real estate practice and professional responsibility and ethics and properly prepared written materials of the subject matter which shall be distributed as part of the course. It shall be taught by a qualified faculty with attorneys presenting legal subjects. Credit shall be awarded on the basis of one hour for each sixty minutes of actual attendance and records shall be maintained of attendance at each session which shall be transmitted to the department at the conclusion of the course.

(d) The state real estate board, created pursuant to section four hundred forty-two-i of this article, shall not have the power to promulgate any rule, regulation or guidance requiring continuing education for real estate brokers or salespeople except those requirements set forth in subdivisions two and three of section four hundred forty-two-k of this article.

4. The fees provided for by this section shall not be refundable.

§ 441-a. License and pocket card.

1. The department of state, if satisfied of the competency and trustworthiness of the applicant, shall issue and deliver to him a license in such form and manner as the department shall prescribe, but which must set forth the name and principal business address of the licensee, and, in the case of a real estate salesperson, the name and business address of the broker with whom the salesperson is associated.

2. Terms. A license issued or reissued under the provisions of this article shall entitle the person, copartnership or corporation to act as a real estate broker, or, if the application is for a real estate salesperson's license, to act as a real estate salesperson in this state up to and including the thirty-first day of October of the year in which the license by its terms expires.[*]

3. Place of business; business sign required. Except as otherwise provided in this article, each licensed real estate broker shall have and maintain a definite place of business within this state, and shall conspicuously post on the outside of the building in which said office is conducted a sign of a sufficient size to be readable from the sidewalk indicating the name and the business of the applicant as a licensed real estate broker, unless said office shall be located in an office, apartment or hotel building, in which event the name and the words "licensed real estate broker" shall be posted in the space provided for posting of names of occupants of the building, other than the mail box. Where the applicant for a real estate broker's license maintains more than one place of business, the broker shall apply for and the department shall

issue a supplemental license for each branch office so maintained upon payment to the department of state for each supplemental license so issued the same fee prescribed in this supplemental license so issued the same fee prescribed in this article for a license to act as a real estate broker. Such fee shall accompany such application and shall be non-refundable. For purposes of this subdivision, the principal residence of a real estate broker or salesperson shall not be deemed a place of business solely because such broker or salesperson shall have included the residence telephone number in his business cards.

4. Display of license. The license of a real estate broker shall be conspicuously displayed in his principal place of business at all times. Licenses issued for branch offices shall be conspicuously displayed therein. The display of a real estate broker's license, the term whereof has expired, by any person, partnership or corporation not duly licensed as a real estate broker for the current license term is prohibited.

5. Change of address. Notice in writing in the manner and form prescribed by the department shall be given the department at its offices in Albany by a licensed real estate broker on his own behalf and on behalf of each salesperson associated with him of any change in his or its principal business address. The filing fee of ten dollars for each licensee named therein shall accompany such notice. Such change by a licensee without such notification shall operate to suspend his license until such suspension shall be vacated by the department.

6. Pocket card. The department shall prepare, issue and deliver to each licensee a pocket card in such form and manner as the department shall prescribe, but which shall contain the name and business address of the licensee, and, in the case of a real estate salesperson, the name and business address of the broker with whom he or she is associated and shall certify that the person whose name appears thereon is a licensed real estate broker or salesperson, as may be. Such cards must be shown on demand. In the case of loss, destruction or damage, the secretary of state may, upon sub-

---

[*]This provision is superceded pursuant to subsequent enactment of subdivision "7" herein.

mission of satisfactory proof, issue a duplicate pocket card upon payment of a fee of ten dollars.

7. License term. From and after the date when this subdivision shall take effect, the term for which a license shall be issued or reissued under this article shall be a period of two years.

8. Death of broker. A license issued to a real estate broker who was, at the time of his death, the sole proprietor of a brokerage office may be used after the death of such licensee by his duly appointed administrator or executor in the name of the estate pursuant to authorization granted by the surrogate under the provisions of the surrogate's court procedure act for a period of not more than one hundred twenty days from the date of death of such licensee in order to complete any unfinished realty transactions in the process of negotiation by the broker or his salespersons existing prior to his decease. There shall be endorsed upon the face of the license, after the name of the decedent, the words "deceased", the date of death and the name of the administrator or executor under whose authority the license is being used. The period of one hundred twenty days may be extended upon application to the secretary of state, for good cause shown, for an additional period not to exceed one hundred twenty days. A license expiring during such period or extension shall be automatically renewed and continued in effect during such period or extension. No fee shall be charged for any such license or renewal thereof.

9. Except for changes made on a renewal application, the fee for changing an address on a license shall be ten dollars.

10. Except for changes made on a renewal application, the fee for changing a name or for changing the status of real estate broker's license shall be one hundred fifty dollars. The fee for changing a salesperson's name shall be fifty dollars.

11. If a real estate salesperson shall leave the service of a real estate broker, the real estate broker shall file a termination of association notice on such form as secretary may designate. The fee for terminating the record of association shall be ten dollars. The salesperson's license may be endorsed to a new sponsoring broker upon the establishment of a new record of association filed with the department of state. The fee for filing a record of association shall be ten dollars.

§ 441-b. License fees.

1. The fee for a license issued or reissued under the provisions of this article entitling a person, copartnership or corporation to act as a real estate broker shall be one hundred fifty dollars. The fee for a license issued or reissued under the provisions of this article entitling a person to act as a real estate salesperson shall be fifty dollars. Notwithstanding the provisions of subdivision seven of section four hundred forty-one-a of this article, after January first, nineteen hundred eighty-six, the secretary of state shall assign staggered expiration dates for outstanding licenses that have been previously renewed on October thirty-first of each year from the assigned date unless renewed. If the assigned date results in a term that exceeds twenty-four months, the applicant shall pay an additional prorated adjustment together with the regular renewal fee. The secretary of state shall assign dates to existing licenses in a manner which shall result in a term of not less than two years.

1-A. The fee for a person to take an examination offered by the secretary of state pursuant to this article shall be fifteen dollars. Fees collected for written examinations shall be paid into the licensing examination services account pursuant to section ninety-seven-aa of the state finance law.

2. Corporations and copartnerships. If the licensee be a corporation, the license issued to it shall entitle the president thereof or such other officer as shall be designated by such corporation, to act as a real estate broker. For each other officer who shall desire to act as a real estate broker in behalf of such corporation an additional license expiring on the same date as the license of the corporation shall be applied for and issued, as hereinbefore provided, the fee for which shall be the same as the fee required by this section for the license to the corporation. No license as a real estate salesperson shall be issued to any officer of a corporation nor to a member of a copartnership licensed as a real estate broker. If the licensee be a copartnership the license issued to it shall entitle one member thereof to act as a real estate broker, and for each other member of the firm who desires to act as a real estate broker an additional license expiring on the same date as the license of the copartnership shall be applied for and issued, as hereinbefore provided, the fee for which shall be the same as the fee required by this section for the license to the copartnership. In case a person licensed individually as a real estate broker thereafter becomes an officer of a corporation or a member of a copartnership an application shall be made in behalf of such corporation or copartnership for a broker's license for him as its representative for the remainder of the then current license term, provided that the license and pocket card previously issued to the licensee in his individual capacity shall have been returned to the department whereupon the department shall cause a properly signed endorsement to be made without charge on the face of such license and pocket card as to such change of license status and return the license and pocket card to the licensee.

3. Disposition of fees. The department of state shall on the first day of each month make a verified return to the department of taxation and finance of all fees received by it under this article during the preceding calendar month, stating from what city or county received and by whom and when paid. The department shall on or before the tenth day of each month pay into the state treasury all monies to its credit on account of fees under this article, at the close of business on the last day of the preceding month.

§ 441-c. Revocation and suspension of licenses.

1. Powers of department. (a) The department of state may revoke the license of a real estate broker or salesperson or suspend the same, for such period as the department may deem proper, or in lieu thereof may impose a fine not exceeding one thousand dollars payable to the department of state, or a reprimand upon conviction of the licensee of a violation of any provision of this article, or for a material misstatement in the application for such license, or if such licensee has been guilty of fraud or fraudulent practices, or for dishonest or misleading advertising, or has demonstrated untrustworthiness or incompetency to act as a real estate broker or salesperson, as the case may be. In the case of a real estate broker engaged in the business of a tenant relocator, untrustworthiness or incom-

petency shall include engaging in any course of conduct including, but not limited to, the interruption or discontinuance of essential building service, that interferes with or disturbs the peace, comfort, repose and quiet enjoyment of a tenant.

(b)(i) The provisions of this paragraph shall apply in all cases of licensed broker or licensed salesman arrears in payment of child support or combined child and spousal support referred to the department by a court pursuant to the requirements of section two hundred forty-four-c of the domestic relations law or pursuant to section four hundred fifty-eight-b of the family court act.

(ii) Upon receipt of an order from the court pursuant to one of the foregoing provisions of law, the department, if it finds such person to be so licensed, shall within thirty days of receipt of such order from the court, provide notice to the licensee of, and initiate, a hearing which shall be held by it at least twenty days and no more than thirty days after the sending of such notice to the licensee. The hearing shall be held solely for the purpose of determining whether there exists as of the date of the hearing proof that full payment of all arrears of support established by the order of the court to be due from the licensee have been paid. Proof of such payment shall be a certified check showing full payment of established arrears or a notice issued by the court or the support collection unit, where the order is payable to the support collection unit designated by the appropriate social services district. Such notice shall state the full payment of all arrears of support established by the order of the court to be due have been paid. The licensee shall be given full opportunity to present such proof of payment from the court or support collection unit at the hearing in person or by counsel. The only issue to be determined by the department as a result of the hearing is whether the arrears have been paid. No evidence with respect to the appropriateness of the court order or ability of the respondent party in arrears to comply with such order shall be received or considered by the department.

(iii) Notwithstanding any inconsistent provision of this article or of any other provision of law to the contrary, the license of a real estate broker or salesman shall be suspended if at the hearing, provided for by subparagraph two of this paragraph, the licensee fails to present proof of payment as required by such subdivision. Such suspension shall not be lifted unless the court or the support collection unit, where the court order is payable to the support collection unit designated by the appropriate social services district, issues notice to the department that full payment of all arrears of support established by the order of the court to be due have been paid.

(iv) The department shall inform the court of all actions taken hereunder as required by law

(v) This paragraph applies to support obligations paid pursuant to any order of child support or child and spousal support issued under provisions of article three-A or section two hundred thirty-six or two hundred forty of the domestic relations law, or article four, five or five-A of the family court act.

(vi) Notwithstanding any inconsistent provision of this article or of any other provision of law to the contrary, the provisions of this paragraph shall apply to the exclusion of any other requirements of this article and to the exclusion of any other requirement of law to the contrary.

2. Determination of department. In the event that the department shall revoke or suspend any such license, or impose any fine or reprimand on the holder thereof, its determination shall be in writing and officially signed. The original of such determination, when so signed, shall be filed in the office of the department and copies thereof shall be served personally or by registered mail upon the broker or salesperson and addressed to the principal place of business of such broker or salesperson, and to the complainant. All brokers' and salesperson's licenses and pocket cards shall be returned to the department of state within five days after the receipt of notice of a revocation or suspension, or in lieu thereof, the broker or salesperson whose license has been revoked or suspended shall make and file an affidavit in form prescribed by the department of state, showing that the failure to return such license and pocket card is due either to loss or destruction thereof.

3. The display of a real estate broker's license after the revocation or suspension thereof is prohibited.

4. Whenever the license of a real estate broker or real estate salesperson is revoked by the department, such real estate broker or real estate salesperson shall be ineligible to be relicensed either as a real estate broker or real estate salesperson until after the expiration of a period of one year from the date of such revocation.

§ 441-d. Salesperson's license suspended by revocation or suspension of employer's license.

The revocation or suspension of a broker's license shall operate to suspend the license of each real estate salesperson associated with such broker, pending a change of association of the salesperson or the expiration of the period of suspension of the broker's license. Such suspension of the salesperson's license shall be deemed to be a discontinuance of association with the broker being suspended.

§ 441-e. Denial of license; complaints; notice of hearing.

1. Denial of license. The department of state shall, before making a final determination to deny an application for a license, notify the applicant in writing of the reasons for such proposed denial and shall afford the applicant an opportunity to be heard in person or by counsel prior to denial of the application. Such notification shall be served personally or by certified mail or in any manner authorized by the civil practice law and rules. If the applicant is a salesperson or has applied to become a salesperson, the department shall also notify the broker with whom such salesperson is associated, or with whom such salesperson or applicant is about to become associated, of such proposed denial. If a hearing is requested, such hearing shall be held at such time and place as the department shall prescribe. If the applicant fails to make a written request for a hearing within thirty days after receipt of such notification, then the notification of denial shall become the final determination of the department. The department, acting by such officer or person in the department as the secretary of state may designate, shall have the power to subpoena and bring before the officer or person so designated any person in this state, and administer an oath to and take testimony of any person or cause his deposition to be taken. A subpoena issued under this section shall be regulated by the civil practice law and rules. If, after such hearing, the application is denied, written notice of such denial shall be served upon the applicant personally or by certified mail or in any manner authorized by the civil practice law and rules, and if the applicant is a salesperson, or has applied to become a salesperson, the department shall notify the broker with whom such applicant is associated.

2. Revocation, suspension, reprimands, fines. The department of state shall, before revoking or suspending any license or imposing any fine or reprimand on the holder thereof, and at least ten days prior to the date set for the hearing, notify in writing the holder of such license of any charges made and shall afford such licensee an opportunity to be heard in person or by counsel in reference thereto. Such written notice may be served by delivery of same personally to the licensee, or by mailing same by certified mail to the last known business address of such licensee, or by any method authorized by the civil practice law and rules. If said licensee be a salesperson, the department shall also notify the broker with whom he is associated of the charges by mailing notice by certified mail to the broker's last known business address. The hearing on such charges shall be at such time and place as the department shall prescribe.

3. Power to suspend a license. The department, acting by such officer or person in the department as the secretary of state may designate, shall have the power to suspend a license pending a hearing and to subpoena and bring before the officer or person so designated any person in this state, and administer an oath to and take testimony of any person or cause his deposition to be taken. A subpoena issued under this section shall be regulated by the civil practice law and rules.

§ 441-f. Judicial review.

The action of the department of state in granting or refusing to grant or to renew a license under this article or in revoking or suspending such a license or imposing any fine or reprimand on the holder thereof or refusing to revoke or suspend such a license or impose any fine or reprimand shall be subject to review by a proceeding brought under and pursuant to article seventy-eight of the civil practice law and rules at the instance of the applicant for such license, the holder of a license so revoked, suspended, fined or reprimanded or the person aggrieved.

§ 442. Splitting commissions.

No real estate broker shall pay any part of a fee, commission or other compensation received by the broker to any person for any service, help or aid rendered in any place in which this article is applicable, by such person to the broker in buying, selling, exchanging, leasing, renting or negotiating a loan upon any real estate including the resale of a condominium unless such a person be a duly licensed real estate salesperson regularly associated with such broker or a duly licensed real estate broker or a person regularly engaged in the real estate brokerage business in a state outside of New York.

Furthermore, notwithstanding any other provision of law, it shall be permissible for a broker properly registered pursuant to the provisions of article twenty-three-A of the general business law who earns a commission on the original sale of a cooperative or homeowners association interest in real estate, including condominium units to pay any part of a fee, commission or other compensation received for bringing about such sale to a person whose principal business is not the sale or offering of cooperatives or homeowners association interests in real property, including condominium units in this state but who is either: (i) a real estate salesperson duly licensed under this article who is regularly associated with such broker; (ii) a broker duly licensed under this article; or a person regularly engaged in the real estate brokerage business in a state outside of New York.

Except when permitted pursuant to the foregoing provisions of this section no real estate broker shall pay or agree to pay any part of a fee, commission, or other compensation received by the broker, or due, or to become due to the broker to any person, firm or corporation who or which is or is to be a party to the transaction in which such fee, commission or other compensation shall be or become due to the broker.

§ 442-a. Compensation of salespersons; restrictions.

No real estate salesperson in any place in which this article is applicable shall receive or demand compensation of any kind from any person, other than a duly licensed real estate broker with whom he is associated, for any service rendered or work done by such salesperson in the appraising, buying, selling, exchanging, leasing, renting or negotiating of a loan upon any real estate.

§ 442-b. Discontinuance or change of salesperson's association; report.

When the association of any real estate salesperson shall have been terminated for any reason whatsoever, his broker shall forthwith notify the department of state thereof in such manner as the department shall prescribe. Where change of such salesperson's association is the basis for such termination, the salesperson's successor broker shall forthwith notify the department of such change in such manner as the department shall prescribe, such notice to be accompanied by a fee of ten dollars. No real estate salesperson shall perform any act within any of the prohibitions of this article from and after the termination for any cause of his association until he thereafter shall have become associated with a licensed real estate broker.

§ 442-c. Violations by salespersons; broker's responsibility.

No violation of a provision of this article by a real estate salesperson or employee of a real estate broker shall be deemed to be cause for the revocation or suspension of the license of the broker, unless it shall appear that the broker had actual knowledge of such violation or retains the benefits, profits or proceeds of a transaction wrongfully negotiated by his salesperson or employee after notice of the salesperson's or employee's misconduct. A broker shall be guilty of a misdemeanor for having any salesperson associated with his firm who has not secured the required license authorizing such employment.

§ 442-d. Actions for commissions; license prerequisite.

No person, copartnership or corporation shall bring or maintain an action in any court of this state for the recovery of compensation for services rendered, in any place in which this article is applicable, in the buying, selling, exchanging, leasing, renting or negotiating a loan upon any real estate without alleging and proving that such person was a duly licensed real estate broker or real estate salesperson on the date when the alleged cause of action arose.

§ 442-e Violations.

1. Misdemeanors; triable in court of special sessions. Any person who violates any provision of this article shall be guilty of a misdemeanor. The commission of a single act prohibited by this article shall constitute a violation hereof. All courts of special sessions, within their respective territorial jurisdictions, are hereby empowered to hear, try and determine such crimes, without indictment, and to impose the punishments prescribed by law therefor.

2. Attorney general to prosecute. Criminal actions for violations of this article shall be prosecuted by the attorney general, or his deputy, in the name of the people of the state, and in any such prosecution the attorney general, or his deputy, shall exercise all the powers and perform all the duties which the district attorney would otherwise be authorized to exercise or to perform therein. The attorney general shall, upon a conviction for a violation of any provision of this article, and within ten days thereafter, make and file with the department of state a detailed report showing the date of such conviction, the name of the person convicted and the exact nature of the charge.

3. Penalty recoverable by person aggrieved. In case the offender shall have received any sum of money as commission, compensation or profit by or in consequence of his violation of any provision of this article, he shall also be liable to a penalty of not less than the amount of the sum of money received by him as such commission, compensation or profit and not more than four times the sum so received by him, as may be determined by the court, which penalty may be sued for and recovered by any person aggrieved and for his use and benefit, in any court of competent jurisdiction.

4. In any prosecution under this article, any person, firm or corporation who, for another, performs or offers to perform or attempts or offers to attempt, the performance of any one of the acts set forth in section four hundred forty of this article, shall be presumed to do so for a fee, commission or other valuable consideration, but such presumption shall not arise out of a single transaction, except upon proof of repeated and successive acts, offers or attempts of a like nature.

5. The secretary of state shall have the power to enforce the provisions of this article and upon complaint of any person, or on his own initiative, to investigate any violation thereof or to investigate the business, business practices and business methods of any person, firm or corporation applying for or holding a license as a real estate broker or salesperson, if in the opinion of the secretary of state such investigation is warranted. Each such applicant or licensee shall be obliged, on request of the secretary of state, to supply such information as may be required concerning his or its business, business practices or business methods, or proposed business practices or methods.

6. For the purpose of enforcing the provisions of this article and in making investigations relating to any violation thereof, and for the purpose of investigating the character, competency and integrity of the applicants or licensees hereunder, and for the purpose of investigating the business, business practices and business methods of any applicant or licensee, or of the officers or agents thereof, the department of state, acting by such officer or person in the department as the secretary of state may designate, shall have the power to subpoena and bring before the officer or person so designated any person in this state and require the production of any books or papers which he deems relevant to the inquiry and administer an oath to and take testimony of any person or cause his deposition to be taken with the same fees and mileage and in the same manner as prescribed by law for civil cases in a court of record, except that any applicant or licensee or officer or agent thereof shall not be entitled to such fees and/or mileage. Any person, duly subpoenaed, who fails to obey such subpoena without reasonable cause or without such cause refuses to be examined or to answer any legal or pertinent question as to the character or qualification of such applicant or licensee or such applicant's or licensee's business, business practices and methods or such violations, shall be guilty of a misdemeanor.

7. In any criminal proceeding before any court or grand jury, or upon any investigation before the department of state for a violation of any of the provisions of this section, the court or grand jury or the secretary of state, his deputy or other officer conducting the investigation, may confer immunity, in accordance with the provisions of section 50.20 or 190.40 of the criminal procedure law.

§ 442-f. Saving clause.

The provisions of this article shall not apply to receivers, referees, administrators, executors, guardians or other persons appointed by or acting under the judgment or order of any court; or public officers while performing their official duties, or attorneys at law.

§ 442-g. Nonresident licensees.

1. A nonresident of this state may become a real estate broker or a real estate salesperson by conforming to all of the provisions of this article, except that a nonresident broker regularly engaged in the real estate business as a vocation who is licensed and maintains a definite place of business in another state, which offers the same privileges to the licensed brokers of this state, shall not be required to maintain a place of business within this state. Anything to the contrary herein notwithstanding, if any state prohibits or restricts the right of a resident of this state to become a licensed nonresident real estate broker or salesperson, then the issuance of such a license to an applicant resident in such state shall be similarly restricted. The department of state shall recognize the license issued to a real estate broker or salesperson by another state as satisfactorily qualifying him for license as broker or salesperson, as the case may be, under this section; provided that the laws of the state of which he is a resident require that applicants for licenses as real estate brokers and salespersons shall establish their competency by written examinations but permit licenses to be issued to residents of the State of New York duly licensed under this article, without examination. If the applicant is a resident of a state which has not such requirement then the applicant must meet the examination requirement as provided herein and the department of state shall issue a license to such nonresident broker or salesperson upon payment of the license fee and the filing by the applicant with the department of a certified copy of the applicant's license issued by such other state.

2. Every nonresident applicant shall file with his application or renewal application an irrevocable consent on a form prescribed by the department of state submitting himself to the jurisdiction of the courts of this state and designating the secretary of state of the state of New York as his agent upon whom may be served any summons, subpoena or other process against him in any action or special proceeding. Such process may issue in any court in this state having jurisdiction of the subject matter, and the process shall set forth that the action or special proceeding is within the jurisdiction of the court.

3. Service of such process upon the secretary of state shall be made by personally delivering to and leaving with him or his deputy or with any person authorized by the secretary of state to receive such service, at the office of the department of state in the city of Albany, duplicate copies of such process together with a fee of five dollars if the action is solely for the recovery of a sum of money not in excess of two hundred dollars and the process is so endorsed, and a fee of ten dollars in any other action or proceeding, which fee shall be a taxable disbursement. If such process is served upon behalf of a county, city, town or village, or other political subdivision of the state, the fee to be paid to the secretary of state shall be five dollars, irrespective of the amount involved or the nature of the action on account of which such service of process is made. If the cost of registered mail for transmitting a copy of the process shall exceed two dollars, an additional fee equal to such excess shall be paid at the time of service of such process. Proof of service shall be by affidavit of compliance with this subdivision filed by or on behalf of the plaintiff together with the process, within ten days after such service, with the clerk of the court in which the action or special proceeding is pending. Service made as provided in this section shall be complete ten days after such papers are filed with the clerk of the court

and shall have the same force and validity as if served on him personally with the state and within the territorial jurisdiction of the court from which the process issues.

4. The secretary of state shall promptly send one of such copies by registered mail, return receipt requested, to the nonresident broker or nonresident salesperson at the post office address of his main office as set forth in the last application filed by him.

5. Nothing in this section shall affect the right to serve process in any other manner permitted by law.

§ 442-h. Rules of the secretary of state.

1. The secretary of state, and not the state real estate board established under section four hundred forty-two-i of this article, shall adopt such rules and regulations as the secretary of state may determine are necessary for the administration and enforcement of this section.

2. (a) If, after a public hearing and a reasonable investigation, the secretary of state determines that the owners of residential real property within a defined geographic area are subject to intense and repeated solicitations by real estate brokers and salespersons to place their property for sale with such real estate brokers or salespersons, and that such solicitations have caused owners to reasonably believe that property values may decrease because persons of different race, ethnic, social, or religious backgrounds are moving or are about to move into the neighborhood or geographic area, the secretary of state may adopt a rule, to be known as a nonsolicitation order, directing all real estate brokers and salespersons to refrain from soliciting residential real estate listings within the subject area. Each area subject to such an order shall be bounded or otherwise specifically defined in the order. The nonsolicitation order shall be subject to such terms and conditions as the secretary of state may determine are, on balance, in the best interest of the public, including but not limited to the affected owners and licensees. A nonsolicitation order may prohibit any or all types of solicitation directed towards particular homeowners, including but not limited to letters, postcards, telephone calls, door-to-door calls and handbills. Every nonsolicitation order shall contain a provision setting forth the day, month and year that the order shall become effective, as well as the day, month and year that the order shall expire. A nonsolicitation order shall not be effective for more than five years. However, a nonsolicitation order and the boundaries of the area where it applies may be re-adopted or amended from time to time in accordance with the procedures set forth herein.

(b) No real estate broker shall establish a new principal office or branch office within any geographic area which is the subject of a nonsolicitation order without prior approval from the secretary of state. The secretary of state may deny any application for the establishment or relocation of a principal office or branch office if approval of the application would cause the total number of principal and branch offices within the subject area to exceed the total number of principal and branch offices that were licensed within the area on the date the nonsolicitation order became effective.

3. (a) If the secretary of state determines that some owners of residential real property within a defined geographic area are subject to intense and repeated solicitation by real estate brokers and salespersons to place their property for sale with such real estate brokers or salesperson, the secretary of state may adopt a rule establishing a cease and desist zone, which zone shall be bounded or otherwise specifically defined in the rule. After the secretary of state has established a cease and desist zone, the owners of residential real property located within the zone may file an owner's statement with the secretary of state expressing their wish not to be solicited by real estate brokers or salespersons. The form and content of the statement shall be prescribed by the secretary of state. After a cease and desist zone has been established by the secretary of state, no real estate broker or salesperson shall solicit a listing from any owner who has filed a statement with the secretary of state if such owner's name appears on the current cease and desist list prepared by the secretary of state. The prohibition on solicitation shall apply to direct forms of solicitation such as the use of the telephone, the mail, personal contact and other forms of direct solicitation as may be specified by the secretary of state.

(b) The secretary of state shall compile a cease and desist list for each zone established pursuant to paragraph (a) of this subdivision. In addition to such other information as the secretary of state may deem appropriate, each cease and desist list shall contain the name of each owner who has filed an owner's statement with the secretary, as well as the address of the property within the zone to which the owner's statement applies. The secretary of state shall print a list for each zone. Each list shall be revised and reprinted at least annually on or before December thirty-first and shall be made available to the public and to real estate brokers at a reasonable price to be set by the secretary of state and approved by the director of the division of the budget. Additions or deletions shall be made to each list only at the time the list is reprinted, and the secretary of state shall not issue amendments or addenda to any printed list.

(c) No rule establishing a cease and desist zone shall be effective for longer than five years. However, the secretary of state may re-adopt the rule to continue the cease and desist zone for additional periods not to exceed five years each. Whenever a rule establishing a cease and desist zone shall have expired or shall have been repealed, all owner's statements filed with the secretary of state pursuant to that rule shall also expire. However, an owner may file a new statement with the secretary of state if a new rule is adopted establishing a cease and desist zone containing the owner's property. Once the boundaries of a cease and desist zone have been established by rule of the secretary of state, the boundaries may not be changed except by repeal of the existing rule and adoption of a new rule establishing the new boundaries.

§ 442-i. State real estate board.

1. There is hereby established within the department of state a state real estate board which shall consist of the secretary of state, the executive director of the consumer protection board, and thirteen additional members. At least five of these members shall be "real estate brokers", each of whom, at the time of appointment, shall be licensed and qualified as a real estate broker under the laws of New York state and shall have been engaged in the real estate business in this state for a period of not less than ten years prior to appointment. The remaining members shall be "public members" who shall not be real estate licensees.

2. The thirteen members shall be appointed as follows: seven members shall be appointed by the governor, three of whom shall be real estate brokers and four of whom shall be public members; two members shall be appointed by the temporary president of the senate, one of whom shall be a real estate broker and one of who shall be a public member; two members shall be appointed by the speaker of the assembly, one of whom shall be a real estate broker and one of whom shall be a public member; one member shall be appointed by the minority leader of the senate, who shall be either a real estate broker or a public member; and one member shall be appointed by the minority leader of the assembly, who shall be either a real estate broker or a public member.

3. Each appointed member shall serve for a term of two years; at any point during such term the appointed member may be removed by the person who appointed such member. In the event that any of said members shall die or resign during the term of office, the successor shall be appointed in the same way and with the same qualifications as set forth above. A member may be reappointed for successive terms but no member shall serve more than ten years in his or her lifetime.

4. A majority of members currently serving on the board shall be required in order to pass any resolution or to approve any matter before the board. The secretary of state shall be chairperson of the board. The vice-chairperson and a secretary shall be elected from among the members. A board member who fails to attend three consecutive meetings shall forfeit the seat unless the secretary of state, upon written request from the member, finds that the member should have been excused from a meeting because of illness or death of a family member.

5. Each member of the board shall receive no compensation other than reimbursement for actual and necessary expenses.

6. The board shall meet no fewer than three times per year and at the call of the secretary of state or a majority of the board. In addition to regularly scheduled meetings of the board, there shall be at least one public hearing each year in New York city, one public hearing each year in Buffalo, and one public hearing each year in Albany. At least fifteen days prior to the holding of any of these public hearings pursuant to this subdivision, the board shall give public notice of the hearing in a newspaper of general circulation in each area where the public meeting is to be held. The purpose of these hearings shall be to solicit from members of the public, suggestions, comments, and observations about real estate practice in New York state.

§ 442-j. Effect of invalid provision.

Should the courts of this state declare any provision of this article unconstitutional, or unauthorized, or in conflict with any other section or provision of this article, then such decision shall affect only the section or provision so declared to be unconstitutional or unauthorized and shall not affect any other section or part of this article.

§ 442-k. Powers and duties of the state real estate board.

1. The state real estate board shall have the power to promulgate rules or regulations affecting brokers and sales persons in order to administer and effectuate the purposes of this article, except that matters pertaining to commingling money of a principal, rendering accounts for a client, managing property for a client, broker's purchase of property listed with him or her, inducing breach of contract of sale or lease, and records of transactions to be maintained are reserved for the exclusive regulatory authority of the secretary of state. The secretary of state, and not the state real estate board, shall promulgate rules and regulations to administer or implement the provisions of sections four hundred forty-one and four hundred forty-two-h of this article. In addition, the secretary of state shall have exclusive regulatory authority to promulgate rules regarding the duties and responsibilities of real estate brokers and salespersons with regard to the handling of clients' funds.

2. Authority to examine applicants. The board is empowered to prescribe the content for the courses of study for the examination and education of persons licensed under this article. The board shall advise the secretary of state on policies governing the administration of the examinations.

3. Approval of schools. The board shall establish the rules and regulations governing the approval by the secretary of state of schools to offer or conduct courses required either for licensure under this article or for the satisfaction of the continuing education requirements contained in paragraph (a) of subdivision three of section four hundred forty-one of this article.

4. Study of laws and regulations. The board shall study the operation of laws and regulations with respect to the rights, responsibilities and liabilities of real estate licensees arising out of the transfer of interests in real property and shall make recommendation on pending or proposed legislation affecting the same, with the exception of legislation affecting section four hundred forty-two-h of this article.

5. Enforcement programs and activities. The board shall advise and assist the secretary of state in carrying out the provisions and purposes of this article and make recommendations concerning the programs and activities of the department in connection with the enforcement of this article.

6. Administration and enforcement. The department of state shall have the power and its duty shall be to administer and enforce the laws and regulations of the state relating to those activities involving real estate for which licensing is required under this article and to instruct and require its agents to bring prosecutions for unauthorized and unlawful practice.

7. Reports to legislative committees. The board shall submit annually a report to the judiciary committee of the state assembly and the judiciary committee of the state senate, containing a description of the types of complaints received, status of cases, and the length of time from the initial complaint to any final disposition.

§ 443. Disclosure regarding real estate agency relationship; form[*]

1. Definitions. As used in this section, the following terms shall have the following meanings:

a. "Agent" means a person who is licensed as a real estate broker or real estate sales associate under section 440-a of this article and is acting in a fiduciary capacity.

b. "Buyer" means a transferee or lessee in a residential real property transaction and includes a person who executes an offer to purchase or to lease residential real property from a seller through an agent, or who has engaged the services of an agent with the object of entering into a residential real property transaction as a transferee or lessee.

c. "Buyer's agent" means an agent who contracts to locate residential real property for a buyer or who finds a buyer for a property and presents an offer to purchase to the seller or seller's agent and negotiates on behalf of the buyer.

d. "Listing agent" means a person who has entered into a listing agreement to act as an agent of the seller for compensation.

e. "Listing agreement" means a contract between an owner or owners of residential real property and an agent, by which the agent has been authorized to sell or lease the residential real property or to find or obtain a buyer or lessee therefor.

f. "Residential real property" means real property improved by a one-to-four family dwelling used or occupied, or intended to be used or occupied, wholly or partly, as the home or residence of one or more persons, but shall not refer to (i) unimproved real property upon which such dwellings are to be constructed or (ii) condominium or cooperative apartments in a building containing more than four units.

g. "Seller" means the transferor or lessor in a residential real property transaction, and includes an owner who lists residential real property for sale or lease with an agent, whether or not a transfer or lease results, or who receives an offer to purchase or lease residential real property.

h. "Seller's agent" means a listing agent who acts alone, or an agent who acts in cooperation with a listing agent, acts as a seller's subagent or acts as a broker's agent to find or obtain a buyer for residential real property.

2. This section shall apply only to transactions involving residential real property.

3. a. A listing agent shall provide the disclosure form set forth in subdivision four of this section to

---

[*] To obtain a disclosure form for distribution, please contact the Division of Licensing Services.

a seller prior to entering into a listing agreement with the seller and shall obtain a signed acknowledgement from the seller, except as provided in paragraph f of this subdivision.

b. A seller's agent shall provide the disclosure form set forth in subdivision four of this section to a buyer or buyer's agent at the time of the first substantive contact with the buyer and shall obtain a signed acknowledgment from the buyer, except as provided in paragraph f of this subdivision.

c. A buyer's agent shall provide the disclosure form to the buyer prior to entering into an agreement to act as the buyer's agent and shall obtain a signed acknowledgment from the buyer, except as provided in paragraph f of this subdivision. A buyer's agent shall provide the form to the seller or seller's agent at the time of the first substantive contact with the seller and shall obtain a signed acknowledgment from the seller or the seller's listing agent, except as provided in paragraph f of this subdivision.

d. The parties to a contract of purchase and sale shall sign the acknowledgment of the parties to the contract. If attorneys for the buyer and seller arrange for the preparation and execution of a contract, the real estate licensees are not responsible for obtaining the acknowledgment of the parties as required by this paragraph.

e. The agent shall provide to the buyer or seller copy of the signed acknowledgment and shall maintain a copy of the signed acknowledgment for not less than three years.

f. If the seller or buyer refuses to sign an acknowledgment of receipt pursuant to this subdivision, the agent shall set forth under oath or affirmation a written declaration of the facts of the refusal and shall maintain a copy of the declaration for not less than three years

4. The following shall be the disclosure form:

DISCLOSURE REGARDING REAL ESTATE AGENCY RELATIONSHIPS

Before you enter into a discussion with a real estate agent regarding a real estate transaction, you should understand what type of agency relationship you wish to have with that agent.

New York State law requires real estate licensees who are acting as agents of buyers or sellers of property to advise the potential buyers or sellers with whom they work of the nature of their agency relationship and the rights and obligations it creates.

SELLER'S OR LANDLORD'S AGENT

If you are interested in selling or leasing real property, you can engage a real estate agent as a seller's agent. A seller's agent, including a listing agent under a listing agreement with the seller, acts solely on behalf of the seller. You can authorize a seller's or landlord's agent to do other things including hire subagents, broker's agents or work with other agents such as buyer's agents on a cooperative basis. A subagent is one who has agreed to work with the seller's agent, often through a multiple listing service. A subagent may work in a different real estate office.

A seller's agent has, without limitation, the following fiduciary duties to the seller: reasonable care, undivided loyalty, confidentiality, full disclosure, obedience and a duty to account.

The obligations of a seller's agent are also subject to any specific provisions set forth in an agreement between the agent and the seller.

In dealings with the buyer, a seller's agent should (a) exercise reasonable skill and care in performance of the agent's duties; (b) deal honestly, fairly and in good faith; and (c) disclose all facts known to the agent materially affecting the value or desirability of property, except as otherwise provided by law.

BUYER'S OR TENANT'S AGENT

If you are interested in buying or leasing real property, you can engage a real estate agent as a buyer's or tenant's agent. A buyer's agent acts solely on behalf of the buyer. You can authorize a buyer's agent to do other things including hire subagents, broker's agents or work with other agents such as seller's agents on a cooperative basis.

A buyer's agent has, without limitation, the following fiduciary duties to the buyer: reasonable care, undivided loyalty, confidentiality, full disclosure, obedience and a duty to account.

The obligations of a buyer's agent are also subject to any specific provisions set forth in an agreement between the agent and the buyer.

In dealings with the seller, a buyer's agent should (a) exercise reasonable skill and care in performance of the agent's duties; (b) deal honestly, fairly and in good faith; and (c) disclose all facts known to the agent materially affecting the buyer's ability and/or willingness to perform a contract to acquire seller's property that are not inconsistent with the agent's fiduciary duties to the buyer.

BROKER'S AGENTS

As part of your negotiations with a real estate agent, you may authorize your agent to engage other agents whether you are a buyer/tenant or seller/landlord. As a general rule, those agents owe fiduciary duties to your agent and to you. You are not vicariously liable for their conduct.

AGENT REPRESENTING BOTH SELLER AND BUYER

A real estate agent acting directly or through an associated licensee, can be the agent of both the seller/landlord and the buyer/tenant in a transaction, but only with the knowledge and informed consent, in writing, of both the seller/landlord and the buyer/tenant.

In such a dual agency situation, the agent will not be able to provide the full range of fiduciary duties to the buyer/tenant and seller/landlord.

The obligations of an agent are also subject to any specific provisions set forth in an agreement between the agent and the buyer/tenant and seller/landlord.

An agent acting as a dual agent must explain carefully to both the buyer/tenant and seller/landlord that the agent is acting for the other party as well. The agent should also explain the possible effects of dual representation, including that by consenting to the dual agency relationship the buyer/tenant and seller/landlord are giving up their right to undivided loyalty.

A BUYER/TENANT OR SELLER/LANDLORD SHOULD CAREFULLY CONSIDER THE POSSIBLE CONSEQUENCES OF A DUAL AGENCY RELATIONSHIP BEFORE AGREEING TO SUCH REPRESENTATION.

GENERAL CONSIDERATIONS

You should carefully read all agreements to ensure that they adequately express your understanding of the transaction. A real estate agent is a person qualified to advise about real estate. If legal, tax or other advice is desired, consult a competent professional in that field.

Throughout the transaction you may receive more than one disclosure form. The law requires each agent assisting in the transaction to present you with this disclosure form. You should read its contents each time it is presented to you, considering the relationship between you and the real estate agent in your specific transaction.

Acknowledgment of Prospective Buyer/Tenant

(1) I have received and read this disclosure notice.

(2) I understand that a seller's/landlord's agent, including a listing agent, is the agent of the seller/landlord exclusively, unless the seller/landlord and buyer/tenant otherwise agree.

(3) I understand that subagents, including subagents participating in a multiple listing service, are agents of the seller/landlord exclusively.

(4) I understand that I may engage my own agent to be my buyer's/tenant's broker.

(5) I understand that the agent presenting this form to me,

_____ of
(name of licensee)

_____ is
(name of firm)

(check applicable relationship)

___ an agent of the seller/landlord

___ my agent as a buyer's/tenant's agent

Dated: _____

Buyer/tenant: _____

Dated: _____

Buyer/tenant: _____

Acknowledgment of Prospective Seller/Landlord

(1) I have received and read this disclosure notice.

(2) I understand that a seller's/landlord's agent, including a listing agent, is the agent of the seller/landlord exclusively, unless the seller/landlord and buyer/tenant otherwise agree.

(3) I understand that subagents, including subagents participating in a multiple listing service, are agents of the seller/landlord exclusively.

(4) I understand that a buyer's/tenant's agent is the agent of the buyer/tenant exclusively.

(5) I understand that the agent presenting this form to me,

_____ of
(name of licensee)
_____ is
(name of firm)

(check applicable relationship)

___ my agent as a seller's/landlord's agent

___ an agent of the buyer/tenant

Dated: _____

Seller/landlord: _____

Dated: _____

Seller/landlord: _____

Acknowledgment of Prospective Buyer/Tenant and Seller/Landlord to Dual Agency

(1) I have received and read this disclosure notice.

(2) I understand that a dual agent will be working for both the seller/landlord and buyer/tenant.

(3) I understand that I may engage my own agent as a seller's/landlord's agent or a buyer's/tenant's agent.

(4) I understand that I am giving up my right to the agent's undivided loyalty.

(5) I have carefully considered the possible consequences of a dual agency relationship.

(6) I understand that the agent presenting this form to me,

_____ of
(name of licensee)
_____ is
(name of firm)

___ a dual agent working for both the buyer/tenant and seller/landlord, acting as such with the consent of both the buyer/tenant and seller/landlord and following full disclosure to the buyer/tenant and seller/landlord.

Dated: _____   Dated: _____

Buyer/tenant: _____ Seller/landlord: _____

Dated: _____   Dated: _____

Buyer/tenant: _____ Seller/landlord: _____

Acknowledgment of the Parties to the Contract

(1) I have received, read and understand this disclosure notice.

(2) I understand that _____ of
(name of real estate licensee)

_____ is
(name of firm)

(check applicable relationship)

___ an agent of the seller/landlord

___ an agent of the buyer/tenant

___ a dual agent working for both the buyer/tenant and seller/landlord, acting as such with the consent of both buyer/tenant and seller/landlord and following full disclosure to the buyer/tenant and seller/landlord.

I also understand that _____ of
(name of real estate licensee)

_____ is
(name of firm)

(check applicable relationship)

___ an agent of the seller/landlord

___ an agent of the buyer/tenant

___ a dual agent working for both the buyer/tenant and seller/landlord, acting as such with the consent of both buyer/tenant and seller/landlord and following full disclosure to the buyer/tenant and seller/landlord.

Dated: _____   Dated: _____

Buyer/tenant: _____   Seller/landlord: _____

Dated: _____   Dated: _____

Buyer/tenant: _____   Seller/landlord: _____

5. This section shall not apply to a real estate licensee who works with a buyer or a seller in accordance with terms agreed to by the licensee and buyer or seller and in a capacity other than as an agent, as such term is defined in paragraph a of subdivision one of this section.

6. Nothing in this section shall be construed to limit or alter the application of the common law of agency with respect to residential real estate transactions.

§ 443-a. Disclosure obligations.

1. Notwithstanding any other provision of law, it is not a material defect or fact relating to property offered for sale or lease, including residential property regardless of the number of units contained therein, that:

(a) an owner or occupant of the property is, or was at any time suspected to be, infected with human immunodeficiency virus or diagnosed with acquired immune deficiency syndrome or any other disease which has been determined by medical evidence to be highly unlikely to be transmitted through occupancy of a dwelling place; or

(b) the property is, or is suspected to have been, the site of a homicide, suicide or other death by accidental or natural causes, or any crime punishable as a felony.

2. (a) No cause of action shall arise against an owner or occupant of real property, or the agent of such owner or occupant, or the agent of a seller or buyer of real property, for failure to disclose in any real estate transaction a fact or suspicion contained in subdivision one of this section.

(b) Failure to disclose a fact contained in subdivision one of this section to a transferee shall not be grounds for a disciplinary action against a real estate agent or broker licensed pursuant to this article.

(c) As used in this section, the terms "agent", "buyer" and "seller" shall have the same meanings as such terms are defined in section four hundred forty-three of this article.

3. Notwithstanding the fact that this information is not a material defect or fact, if such information is important to the decision of the buyer to purchase or lease the property, the buyer may, when negotiating or making a bona fide offer, submit a written inquiry for such information. The buyer or the agent of the buyer shall provide the written request to the seller's agent or to the seller if there is no seller's agent. The seller may choose whether or not to respond to the inquiry. The seller's agent, with the consent of the seller and subject to applicable laws regarding privacy, shall report any response and information to the buyer's agent or to the buyer if there is no buyer's agent. If there is no seller's agent, the seller shall inform the buyer's agent, or the buyer if there is no buyer's agent, whether or not the seller chooses to provide a response.

4. This section shall preempt any local law inconsistent with the provisions of this section.

RELATED STATUTES AND LAWS
REAL PROPERTY LAW

§ 242 Disclosure prior to the sale of real property.

1.(a) Any person, firm, company, partnership or corporation offering to sell real property to which no utility electric service is provided shall provide written notice to the prospective purchaser or to the prospective purchaser's agent, clearly indicating this fact. Such notice shall be provided prior to accepting a purchase offer.

(b) Any prospective or actual purchaser who has suffered a loss due to a violation of this section is entitled to recover any actual damages incurred from the person offering to sell said real property.

(c) The provisions of this subdivision shall not apply in instances where the real property being sold lies within the applicable free footage allowance or service lateral specified by the public service commission in rule, regulation or public utility tariff.

2. Disclosure prior to the sale of real property to which utility surcharge payments attach. (a) Any person, firm, company, partnership or corporation offering to sell real property against which an electric or gas utility surcharge is assessed for the purpose of defraying the costs associated with an electric or gas line extension, or for the purpose of defraying the costs associated with related facilities, shall provide written notice to the prospective purchaser or the prospective purchaser's agent, stating as follows: "This property is subject to an electric and/or gas utility surcharge". In addition, such notice shall also state, the type and purpose of the surcharge, the amount of the surcharge and whether such surcharge is payable on a monthly, yearly or other basis. Such notice shall be provided by the seller prior to accepting a purchase offer.

(b) Any prospective or actual purchaser who has suffered a loss due to a violation of this subdivision is entitled to recover any actual damages incurred from the person offering to sell or selling said real property.

§ 333-c Lands in agricultural districts; disclosure.

Prior to the sale, purchase, or exchange of real property located partially or wholly within an agricultural district established pursuant to the provisions of article twenty-five-AA of the agriculture and markets law, the prospective grantor shall deliver to the prospective grantee a notice which states the following:

"It is the policy of this state and this community to conserve, protect and encourage the development and improvement of agricultural land for the production of food, and other products, and also for its natural and ecological value. This notice is to inform prospective residents that the property they are about to acquire lies partially or wholly within an agricultural district and that farming activities occur within the district. Such farming activities may include, but not be limited to, activities that cause noise, dust and odors."

Failure of the seller to provide such information to the buyer shall not prevent the recording officer from filing such deed.

UNITED STATES CODE

42 USCA § 3604. It shall be unlawful ...

To make, print, or publish, or cause to be made, printed, or published any notice, statement or advertisement, with respect to the sale or rental of a dwelling that indicates any preference, limitation, or discrimination based on race, color, religion, sex, handicap, familial status, or national origin, or an intention to make any such preference, limitation, or discrimination.

APPENDIX B

New York Licensing Regulations

§ 175.1. Commingling money of principal.

A real estate broker shall not commingle the money or other property of his principal with his own and shall at all times maintain a separate, special bank account to be used exclusively for the deposit of said monies and which deposit shall be made as promptly as practicable. Said monies shall not be placed in any depository, fund or investment other than a federally insured bank account. Accrued interest, if any, shall not be retained by, or for the benefit of, the broker except to the extent that it is applied to, and deducted from, earned commission, with the consent of all parties.

§ 175.2. Rendering account for client.

A real estate broker shall, within a reasonable time, render an account to this client and remit to him, any monies collected for his client, and unexpended for his account.

§ 175.3. Managing property for client.

(a) **When acting** as an agent in the management of property a real estate broker shall not accept any commission, rebate or profit on expenditures made for his client without his full knowledge and consent.

(b) **A person, firm** or corporation licensed or acting as a real estate broker, and having on deposit or otherwise in custody or control any money furnished as security by a tenant of real property, shall treat, handle and dispose of such money (including any required interest thereon) in compliance with the requirements of section 7-103 of the General Obligations Law. Failure to so comply, including failure to pay, apply or credit any required interest, shall constitute grounds for disciplinary or other appropriate action by the Secretary of State.

§ 175.4. Broker's purchase of property listed with him.

A real estate broker shall not directly or indirectly buy for himself property listed with him, nor shall he acquire any interest therein without first making his true position clearly known to the listing owner.

§ 175.5. Disclosure of interest to client.

Before a real estate broker buys property for a client in the ownership of which the broker has an interest, he shall disclose his interest to all parties to the transaction.

§ 175.6. Broker's sale of property in which he owns an interest.

Before a real estate broker sells property in which he owns an interest, he shall make such interest known to the purchaser.

§ 175.7. Compensation

A real estate broker shall make it clear for which party he is acting and he shall not receive compensation from more than one party except with the full knowledge and consent of all parties.

§ 175.8. Negotiating with party to exclusive listing contract.

No real estate broker shall negotiate the sale, exchange or lease of any property directly with an owner or lessor if he knows that such owner, or lessor, has an existing written contract granting exclusive authority in connection with such property with another broker.

§ 175.9. Inducing breach of contract of sale or lease.

No real estate broker shall induce any party to a contract of sale or lease to break such contract for the purpose of substituting in lieu thereof a new contract with another principal.

§ 175.10. Broker's offering property for sale must be authorized.

A real estate broker shall never offer a property for sale or lease without the authorization of the owner.

§ 175.11. Sign on property.

No sign shall ever be placed on any property by a real estate broker without the consent of the owner.

§ 175.12. Delivering duplicate original of instrument.

A real estate broker shall immediately deliver a duplicate original of any instrument to any party or parties executing the same, where such instrument has been prepared by such broker or under his supervision and where such instrument relates to the employment of the broker or to any matters pertaining to the consummation of a lease, or the purchase, sale or exchange of real property or any other type of real estate transaction in which he may participate as a broker.

§ 175.13. Accepting services of another broker's salesperson or employee.

A real estate broker shall not accept the services of any salesperson or employee in the organization of another real estate broker without the knowledge of the broker and no real estate broker should give or permit to be given or directly offer to give anything of value for the purpose of influencing or rewarding the actions of any salesperson or employee of another real estate broker in relation to the business of such broker or the client of such broker without the knowledge of such broker.

§ 175.14. Terrnination of salesperson's association with broker.

A real estate salesperson shall, upon termination of his association with a real estate broker, forthwith turn over to such broker any and all listing information obtained during his association whether such information was originally given to him by the broker or copied from the records of such broker or acquired by the salesperson during his association.

§ 175.15. Automatic continuation of exclusive listing contract.

No real estate broker shall be a party to an exclusive listing contract which shall contain an automatic continuation of the period of such listing beyond the fixed termination date set forth therein.

§ 175.16. Temporary salesperson's permit.

A temporary real estate salesperson's permit issued on or before April 20, 1960, pursuant to the provisions of paragraph 1-A of section 441 of the Real Property Law and having an expiration date subsequent to April 21, 1960, shall continue in full force and effect until the expiration date set forth in such permit.

§ 175.17. Prohibitions in relation to solicitation.

(a) No broker or salesperson shall induce or attempt to induce an owner to sell or lease any residential property or to list same for sale or lease by making any representations regarding the entry or prospective entry into the neighborhood of a person or persons of a particular race, color, religion or national origin.

(b) (1) No licensed real estate broker or salesperson shall solicit the sale, lease or the listing for sale or lease of residential property after such licensee has received written notice from an owner thereof that such owner or owners do not desire to sell, lease or list such property.

(2) Notice provided under the provisions of this subdivision to a real estate broker shall constitute notice to all associate brokers and salespersons who are employed by the real estate broker.

(c) (1) No licensed real estate broker or salesperson shall solicit the sale, lease or the listing for sale or lease of residential property from an owner of residential property located in a designed cease-and-desist zone if such owner has filed a cease-and-desist notice with the Department of State indicating that such owner or owners do not desire to sell, lease or list their residential property and do not desire to be solicited to sell, lease or list their residential property.

(2) The following geographic areas are designated as cease-and-desist zones, and, unless sooner redesignated, the designation for the following cease-and-desist zones shall expire on the following dates:

Zone	Expiration Date
County of Bronx	October 25, 1999

Within the County of Bronx as follows:

All that area of land in the County of Bronx, City of New York, otherwise known as Community Districts 9, 10, 11 and 12, and bounded and described as follows: Beginning at a point at the intersection of Bronx County and Westchester County boundary and Long Island Sound; thence southerly along Long Island Sound while including City Island to East River; thence westerly and northwesterly along East River to Bronx River; thence northwesterly and northerly along Bronx River to Sheridan Expressway; thence northeasterly along Sheridan Expressway to Cross Bronx Expressway; thence southeasterly and easterly along Cross Bronx Expressway to Bronx River Parkway; thence northerly and northeasterly along Bronx River Parkway to East 233rd Street; thence westerly along East 233rd Street to Van Cortlandt Park East; thence northerly along Van Cortlandt Park East to the boundary of Westchester County and Bronx County; thence easterly along the boundary of Westchester County and Bronx County to Long Island Sound and the point of beginning.

Zone	Expiration Date
County of Nassau	October 25, 1999

Within the County of Nassau as follows:

All that area of land in the County of Nassau, otherwise known as Elmont and North Valley Stream, and bounded and described as follows: Beginning at a point at the intersection of Hempstead Turnpike and the Nassau-Queens boundary, thence easterly along Hempstead Turnpike to Plainfield Avenue; thence northerly along Plainfield Avenue to Chelsea Street; thence easterly along Chelsea Street to the intersection of Chelsea Street and Makofske Avenue; thence northeasterly along the boundary of the Village of South Floral Park to a point between Webster Street and Clay Street; thence easterly along the boundary of the Village of Floral Park to a point between Landau Avenue and Crest Avenue; thence northerly along the boundary of the Village of Floral Park to Monroe Street; thence easterly along Monroe Street to Covert Avenue; thence northerly along Covert Avenue to Tulip Avenue; thence southeasterly along Tulip Avenue to Barrymore Boulevard; thence southerly along Barrymore Boulevard to Hempstead Turnpike; thence westerly along Hempstead Turnpike to Lucille Avenue; thence southerly along Lucille Avenue to Gavrin Boulevard; thence easterly along Gavrin Boulevard to Franklin Avenue; thence southerly along Franklin

Avenue to the boundary of the Village of Valley Stream; thence westerly along the Village of Valley Stream to the Nassau-Queens boundary; thence northerly along the Nassau-Queens boundary to Hempstead Turnpike and the point of beginning.

All that area of land in the County of Nassau, otherwise known as Freeport, bounded and described as follows: Beginning at a point at the intersection of Pleasant Avenue and North Main Street, thence southerly along North Main Street to Holloway Street; thence easterly along Holloway Street to Ellison Avenue; thence southerly along Ellison Avenue to Woodside Avenue; thence easterly along Woodside Avenue to Babylon Turnpike; thence southeasterly along Babylon Turnpike to Meadowbrook Parkway; thence southerly along Meadowbrook Parkway to the point at which Meadowbrook Parkway and the Merrick River are the closest; thence southerly along the Merrick River to Freeport Creek; thence southerly along the western boundary of South Cow Meadow to the point at which the western boundary of South Cow Meadow intersects the boundary of Cow Meadow Preserve; thence westerly along the boundary of Cow Meadow Preserve to Hudson Bay; thence southerly along Hudson Bay to The Narrows; thence westerly along The Narrows to Long Creek; thence northwesterly along Long Creek to Freeport Bay; thence northwesterly along the shoreline of Freeport Bay to Millburn Creek; thence northerly along Millburn Creek to Millburn Pond; thence northerly from Millburn Pond to the intersection of Millburn Lane and Seaman Avenue while including Mayfair Court, Mayflower Court and Meadowbrook Court; thence northerly from the intersection of Willowbrook Lane and Seaman Avenue to the intersection of West Forest Avenue and Brookside Avenue while including Delaware Circle and Moore Circle; thence northerly along Brookside Avenue to a point directly west of the intersection of Pleasant Avenue and Main Street; thence directly easterly to the intersection of Pleasant Avenue and Main Street and the point of beginning.

Zone	Expiration Date
County of Queens	October 25, 1999

(3) The names and addresses of owners who have filed a cease-and-desist notice with the Department of State shall be compiled according to the street address for each cease-and-desist zone. Following the first compilation of a list, the list shall be revised and updated annually on or before December 31st. Individual lists shall be identified by geographic area and year.

(4) A copy of each cease-and-desist list shall be available for inspection at the following offices of the Department of State:

Department of State
Division of Licensing Services
*162 Washington Ave.
Albany, New York 12231-0001
(*to be amended:
Current Address
84 Holland Avenue
Albany, New York 12208-3490)

Department of State
Division of Licensing Services
State Office Building Annex
164 Hawley Street
Binghamton, New York 13901-4053

Department of State
Division of Licensing Services
65 Court Street
Buffalo, New York 14202-3471

Department of State
Division of Licensing Services
Hughes State Office Building
Syracuse, New York 13202-1428

Department of State
Division of Licensing Services
State Office Building
Veterans Memorial Highway
Hauppauge, New York 11788-5501

**Department of State
Division of Licensing Services
114 Old Country Road
Mineola, New York 11501-4459
(** This office has been closed.)

Department of State
Division of Licensing Services
270 Broadway
New York, New York 10007-2372

(5) The cost of each list compiled pursuant to this subdivision shall be $10 and shall be available upon written request to the following address:

Department of State
Division of Licensing Services
270 Broadway
New York, New York 10007-2372

(6) The original cease-and-desist notice shall be filed with the Department of State's Division of Licensing Services at 270 Broadway, New York, New York 10007-2372, and shall be available for public inspection and copying upon written request and appointment.

(7) For the purposes of the Real Property Law, section 411-c, it shall not be a demonstration of untrustworthiness or incompetence for a licensee to solicit an owner who had filed a cease-and-desist notice with the Department of State if the owner's name and address do not appear on the current cease-and-desist list compiled by the Department of State pursuant to paragraph (c)(3) of this section.

(d) (1) For the purposes of this section, solicitation shall mean an attempt to purchase or rent or an attempt to obtain a listing of property for sale, for rent or for purchase. Solicitation shall include but not be limited to use of the telephone, mails, delivery services, personal contact or otherwise causing any solicitation, oral or written, direct or by agent:

    (i) to be delivered or presented to the owner or anyone else at the owner's home address;

    (ii) to be left for the owner or anyone else at the owner's home address; or

    (iii) to be placed on any vehicle, structure or object located on the owner's premises.

(2) Solicitation shall not include classified advertising in regularly printed periodicals that are not primarily real estate related; advertisements placed in public view if they are not otherwise in violation of this section; or radio and television advertisements.

(e) For the purposes of this section, residential property shall mean one-, two- or three-family houses, including a cooperative apartment or condominium.

§ 175.18. Use of trade or corporate name.

No licensed real estate broker or applicant applying for a real estate broker's license, may use a trade or corporate name which, in the opinion of the Department of State, is so similar to the trade name or corporate name of any licensed real estate broker that confusion to the public will result therefrom.

§ 175.19. Net listing agreements.

(a) The term net listing as used herein shall mean an agency or other agreement whereby a prospective seller of real property or an interest therein, lists such property or interest for sale with a licensed real estate broker authorizing the sale thereof at a specified net amount to be paid to the seller and authorizing the broker to retain as commission, compensation, or otherwise, the difference between the price at which the property or interest is sold and the specified net amount to be received by the seller.

(b) No real estate broker shall make or enter into a "net listing" contract for the sale of real property or any interest therein.

§ 175.20. Branch offices.

(a) Every branch office shall be owned, maintained and operated only by the licensed broker to whom the license for such office is issued. A branch office shall not be conducted, maintained and operated under an arrangement whereby a licensed salesperson or employee of the broker shall pay, or be responsible for, any expense or obligation created or incurred in its conduct, maintenance or operation, or under any other arrangement, the purpose, intent or effect of which shall permit a licensed salesperson or employee to carry on the business of real estate broker for his own benefit, directly, or indirectly, in whole or in part.

(b) Every branch office shall be under the direct supervision of the broker to whom the license is issued, or a representative broker of a corporation or partnership holding such license. A salesperson

licensed as such for a period of not less than two years and who has successfully completed a course of study in real estate approved by the Secretary of State, may be permitted to operate such a branch office only under the direct supervision of the broker provided the names of such salesperson and supervising broker shall have been filed and recorded in the division of licenses of the Department of State.

(c) Supervision of such a licensed salesperson shall in addition to the requirements of section 175.21(a) of this Part, include guidance, oversight, management, orientation, instruction and supervision in the management and operation of the branch office and the business of real estate broker conducted therein.

(d) No broker shall relocate his principal office or any branch office without prior approval of the department.

§ 175.21. Supervision of salesperson by broker.

(a) The supervision of a real estate salesperson by a licensed real estate broker, required by subdivision 1(d) of section 441 of the Real Property Law, shall consist of regular, frequent and consistent personal guidance, instruction, oversight and superintendence by the real estate broker with respect to the general real estate brokerage business conducted by the broker, and all matters relating thereto.

(b) The broker and salesperson shall keep written records of all real estate listings obtained by the salesperson, and of all sales and other transactions effected by, and with the aid and assistance of, the salesperson, during the period of his association, which records shall be sufficient to clearly identify the transactions and shall indicate the dates thereof. Such records must be submitted by the salesperson to the Department of State with his application for a broker's license.

(c) Participation in the general real estate brokerage business as a licensed real estate salesperson shall consist of active service under the supervision of a licensed real estate broker for at least 35 hours per week for 50 weeks in each year required for qualification under the law.

§ 175.22. Ownership of voting stock by salespersons prohibited.

No licensed real estate salesperson may own, either singly or jointly, directly or indirectly, any voting shares of stock in any licensed real estate brokerage corporation with which he is associated.

§ 175.23. Records of transactions to be maintained.

(a) Each licensed broker shall keep and maintain for a period of three years, records of each transaction effected through his office concerning the sale or mortgage of one-to-four family dwellings. Such records shall contain the names and addresses of the seller, the buyer, mortgagee, if any, the purchase price and resale price, if any, amount of deposit paid on contract, amount of commission paid to broker or gross profit realized by the broker if purchased by him for resale, expenses of procuring the mortgage loan, if any, the net commission or net profit realized by the broker showing the disposition of all payments made by the broker. In lieu thereof each broker shall keep and maintain, in connection with each such transaction a copy of (1) contract of sale, (2) commission agreement, (3) closing statement, (4) statement showing disposition of proceeds of mortgage loan.

(b) Each licensed broker engaged in the business of soliciting and granting mortgage loans to purchasers of one-to-four family dwellings shall keep and maintain for a period of three years, a record of the name of the applicant, the amount of the mortgage loan, the closing statement with the disposition of the mortgage proceeds, a copy of the verification of employment and financial status of the applicant, a copy of the inspection and compliance report with the Baker Law requirements of FHA with the name of the inspector. Such records shall be available to the Department of State at all times upon request.

§ 175.24. Exclusive listings–residential property.

(a) Residential property as used in this section shall not include condominiums or cooperatives but shall be limited to one-, two- or three-family dwellings.

(b) In all commission agreements obtained by a broker which provide for an exclusive listing of residential property, the broker shall have attached to the listing or printed on the listing and signed or initialed by the homeowner or the homeowner's agent the following explanation in type size of not less than six points:

"EXPLANATION:
An "exclusive right to sell" listing means that if you, the owner of the property, find a buyer for your house, or if another broker finds a buyer, you must pay the agreed commission to the present broker.

An "exclusive agency" listing means that if you, the owner of the property find a buyer, you will not have to pay a commission to the broker. However, if another broker finds a buyer, you will owe a commission to both the selling broker and your present broker."

(c) If an exclusive listing of residential property is obtained by a broker who is a member of a multiple listing service,

(1) he shall give to the homeowner a list of the names and addresses of all member brokers; and

(2) the listing agreement shall provide that the homeowner shall have the option of having all negotiated offers to purchase the listed residential property submitted either through the listing broker or submitted through the selling broker.

§ 175.25. Advertising.

(a) All advertisements placed by a broker must indicate that the advertiser is a broker or give the name of the broker and his telephone number.

(b) All advertisements placed by a broker which state that property is in the vicinity of a geographical area or territorial subdivision must include as part of such advertisement the name of the geographical area or territorial subdivision in which such property is actually located.

§ 175.26. Posting of business signs.

For purposes of compliance with subdivision 3 of section 441-a of Article 12 of the Real Property Law, in an apartment building where the posting of signs is not permitted in the lobby pursuant to the rules and regulations of the building, said sign must be posted on the corridor wall next to the entrance door of the dwelling unit or on the entrance door of the dwelling unit or on the entrance door of the dwelling unit in which the business is conducted.

§ 175.27. Disclaimer.

Nothing in this Part is intended to be, or should be construed as, an indication that a salesperson is either an independent contractor or employee of a broker.

PART 176
APPROVAL OF REAL ESTATE COURSES

Section

§ 176.1. Approved entities.

Real estate courses and offerings may be given by any college or university accredited by the Commissioner of Education of the State of New York or by a regional accrediting agency accepted by said Commissioner of Education; public and private vocational schools; real estate boards; and real estate-related professional societies and organizations. No real estate course of study seeking approval may be affiliated with or controlled by any real estate broker, salesperson, firm, or company or franchise, or controlled by a subsidiary of any real estate broker or franchise.

§ 176.2. Request for approval of courses of study.

Applications for approval to conduct courses of study to satisfy the requirements for licensed real estate salesperson and broker shall be made sixty days before the proposed course is to be conducted. The application shall be prescribed by the Department to include the following:

(a) name and business address of the proposed school which will present the course;

(b) if applicant is a partnership, the names and home addresses of all the partners of the entity;

(c) if applicant is a corporation, the names and home addresses of persons who own five percent or more of the stock of the entity;

(d) the name, home and business address and telephone number of the education coordinator that will be responsible for administering the regulations contained in this part;

(e) locations where classes will be conducted;

(f) title of each course to be conducted;

(g) final examination to be presented for each course, including the answer key;

(h) all times included on each test form must be consistent with content specifications indicated for each course. Weighing of significant content areas should fall within the weight ranges indicated. All reference sources used to support each correct answer must be included. Linkage to each answer must be indicated with a footnote showing page number, subject matter, etc.;

(i) description of materials that will be distributed;

(j) the books that will be used for the outline and the final exams; and

(k) detailed outline for local concerns when applying for broker course approval.

§ 176.3. Subjects for study–real estate salesperson.

The following are the required subjects to be included in the course of study in real estate for licensure as a real estate salesperson, and the required number of hours to be devoted to each such subject:

Salesperson's Course

Subject Matter	Hours
License Law and Regulations	4
Law of Agency	13
*Real Estate Instruments and Estates and Interests	*10
Real Estate Financing	5
Land Use Regulations	2
Introduction to Construction	3
Valuation	2
Human Rights and Fair Housing	4
Environmental Issues	2
Instruction	45 Hours
Final Examination	3 Hours
	48 Hours

*Includes contracts, leases, and deeds.

All approved courses must use this course syllabus in conducting their program.

§ 176.4. Subjects for study–real estate broker.

The education qualifications for real estate broker's license requires the completion of:

(a) an approved real estate salesperson's course; and

(b) an approved real estate broker's course.

Before enrolling a student into an approved broker's course, the education coordinator must be provided with evidence of a signed statement from the student indicating that he/she has successfully completed the salesperson's course. Proof of the student's completion of the prerequisite course must be kept on file by the education coordinator. The following are the required subjects to be included in the course of study in real estate for licensure as a real estate broker and the required number of hours to be devoted to each subject:

Broker's Course

Subject Matter	Hours
Real Estate Broker's responsibility to manage, administer, and supervise an office in compliance with License Laws	5
Real Estate Broker's responsibility to supervise compliance with the Law of Agency	8

Real Estate Financing	5
Investment Properties	5
Property Management	5
Conveyance of Real Property (Voluntary & Involuntary Alienation)	2
Construction II	3
Subdivision and Development	3
Taxes and Assessments	2
Title Closing and Costs	2
Appraisal Principles	2
*Local Concerns	*3
Instruction	45 Hours
Final Examination	3 Hours
	48 Hours

*Includes non-solicitation orders, cease and desist regulations, land use for agriculture and forestry, environmental issues, or other topics subject to approval.

All approved courses must use this course syllabus in conducting their program.

§ Sec. 176.5. Computation of instruction time.

To meet the minimum statutory requirement, attendance shall be computed on the basis of an hour equaling 50 minutes. For every 50 minutes of instruction there shall be an additional 10 minute break. The time of the breaks shall be left to the discretion of the individual education coordinator. Breaks shall not be considered optional, nor are they to be used to release the class earlier than scheduled.

§ Sec. 176.6. Attendance and examinations.

(a) To satisfactorily complete any course offered for study, a person must physically attend 36 hours of class instruction, exclusive of sessions devoted to review and/or examination.

(b) Students that fail to attend the required scheduled class hours may, at the discretion of the approved entity, make up the missed subject matter during subsequent classes presented by the approved entity.

(c) Final examinations may not be taken by any student that has not satisfied the attendance requirement.

(d) A make up examination may be presented to students at the discretion of the approved entity.

Make up examinations must be submitted for approval to the Department in accordance with guidelines noted in Section 176.2 (g) and (h) of this part.

(e) **Final examinations** shall be written and presented within a reasonable time frame after the completion of the course work.

§ 176.7. Certificate of successful completion.

A certificate of successful completion of a course of study in real estate approved by the department shall be issued to a person who completes same when he or she shall have attended the required aggregate number of hours of such course of study, provided such student shall have also received a passing mark in the examinations for all subjects given. The certificate may contain a certification of the course of study or for a subject course or courses as applicable.

§ 176.8. Facilities.

Each course shall be presented in such premises and in such facilities as shall be necessary to properly present the course. No course shall be presented in any real estate broker's office or the office of any association of real estate brokers except as otherwise may be permitted under this Part.

§ 176.9. Retention of examination papers.

All persons and organizations conducting approved courses of study shall retain examination papers for persons attending for a period of five years after the completion thereof, and such papers shall at all times during such period be available for inspection by duly authorized representatives of the department.

§ 176.10. Change in approved course of study.

There shall be no change or alteration in any approved course of study of any subject or in any instruction staff without prior written notice to and approval by the department.

§ 176.11. Faculty.

(a) **Each instructor,** as certified by the Department of State, for an approved real estate course of study, shall submit a resume to the department and meet the following criteria, and shall achieve at least 100 points based on the following scale which include real estate brokerage/specialty experience, instructional experience and academic achievement.

(b) **In order to** receive approval as an instructor, an individual must achieve one hundred points in the system employed below:

1. Section One

A maximum of 50 points can be claimed in this section.

(a) Licensed as a real estate broker or salesperson
Each year of experience = 10 points

or

(b) Work experience in a specialized field directly related to real estate
Each year of experience = 10 points

or

(c) Attorney, admitted to New York State Bar
Each year of experience = 10 points

2. Section Two

A maximum of 50 points can be claimed in this section.
Experience as an instructor = 10 points for each year

3. Section Three

A maximum of 30 points can be claimed in this section. Formal academic achievement in a specialized subject matter directly related to real estate (five points for each 30 hour course successfully completed)

4. Section Four

Fifty points can be claimed in this section.
Formal training in the techniques of organizing and presenting instructional material

5. Section Five

Only one selection may be made in this section. The holder of one of the following:

AAS Degree	10 points
B.A. or B.S. Degree	20 points
M.A. or L.L.D. Degree	30 points
B.A., B.S. or M.A. with a	
Major in Real Estate	50 points
	Total

(c) All points claimed are subject to verification within two years of application.

(d) Any applicant who fails to provide evidence of claimed points may be subjected to disciplinary action.

§ 176.12. Examinations.

All examinations required for course credit given shall be written, given within a reasonable time after the completion of the course work, and no examination may be used unless it is approved by the department. The failure of the final examination shall be final and constitute failure of the course.

§ 176.13. Advertising.

No advertising pertaining to an approved course may be circulated or distributed unless it is first approved by the department.

§ 176.14. Auditing.

A duly authorized designee of the department may audit any course offered, and may verify attendance and inspect the records of attendance of the course at any time during its presentation or thereafter.

§ 176.15. College degree major in real estate.

Evidence satisfactory to the department of the successful completion of a course of study at any accredited college or university in the United States of America, approved by the Commissioner of Education of the State of New York or by a regional accrediting agency accepted by said Commissioner of Education, which has a program leading to a recognized collegiate degree, which includes therein a major in real estate, may be deemed acceptable for the educational credit under sections 176.3 and 176.4 of this Part, provided attendance at such real estate course is not less than 90 hours in the case of an applicant for licensure as a real estate broker, and 45 hours in the case of an applicant for licensure as a real estate salesperson, and the applicant presents evidence of the issuance of a bachelor's degree and that he has passed the required course in real estate.

§ 176.16. Suspensions and denials of course approval.

Within 30 days after the receipt of the application for approval of an offering, the department shall inform the entity as to whether the offering has been approved, denied, or whether additional information is needed to determine the acceptability of the offering. The department may deny, suspend, or revoke the approval of a real estate course or a real estate instructor, if it is determined that they are not in compliance with the law and rules, or if the offering does not adequately reflect and present current real estate knowledge as a basis for a level of real estate practice. If disciplinary action is taken, a written order of suspension, revocation or denial of approval will be issued. Anyone who objects to such denial, suspension or revocation shall have the opportunity to be heard by the Secretary of State or his designee.

§ 176.17. Open to public.

All courses approved pursuant to this Part shall be open to all members of the public regardless of the membership of the prospective student in any real estate board, or real estate related professional society or organization.

§ 176.18. Credit for courses taken under former rules.

(a) Notwithstanding the repeal of the former Part 176 of this Title, an approved school may continue to provide the course of study authorized under the provisions of such Part to and including the completion of the 1979 summer session of such school, if any, subject to the provisions for crediting such course set forth in subdivisions (b) and (c) of this section.

(b) Any person who has successfully completed or completes a real estate course of 45 credit hours in an approved school under the provisions of the former Part 176 superseded by this Part, on or after June 1, 1978, shall, for a period of three years subsequent to the completion of such course be entitled to be credited for such 45 hours in relation to an application for licensure as a real estate salesperson or broker, made on or after November 1, 1979; provided, however, in the case of a broker's license, the applicant shall also have completed a course of study of 45 hours at an approved school whose curriculum shall have been specifically approved by the department for this purpose.

(c) The repeal of the former Part 176, and the adoption of this Part, shall not affect the right of an applicant for a real estate broker's license who otherwise qualifies to obtain such a license upon application filed prior to November 1, 1979 based upon the completion of a course of study in an approved school in accordance with the provisions of such former Part.

§ 176.19. Schedule of sessions.

Each school or entity conducting an approved course of study in real estate shall, at least 15 days prior to the first class session of each course, file a schedule of the dates, hours and subject matter of the sessions to be held in such course.

§ Sec. 176.20. Certificate of completion.

Evidence of successful completion of the course must be furnished to students in certificate form. The certificate must indicate the following: name of the entity; Real Estate Salesperson's Course, 45 hours, or Real Estate Broker's Course, 45 hours; code number of the entity; a statement that the student, who shall be named, has satisfactorily completed a course of study in real estate subjects approved by the Secretary of State in accordance with the provisions of chapter 868 of the Laws of 1977, and that his or her attendance record was satisfactory and in conformity with the law, and that such course was completed on a stated date. The certificate must be signed by the owner or course coordinator and dated, and must have affixed thereto the official seal of the school or entity.

§ 176.21. Fees.

Each school or entity shall pay an annual registration fee of $300 for each 12 months or part thereof, and an additional registration fee of $150 for each 12 months or part thereof for each location in excess of one where courses are to be given, said period to run from each September 1 to the subsequent August 31. For each teacher employed to teach the Real Estate Broker's or Real Estate Salesperson's course, each school or entity shall pay a one-time registration fee of $25. Fees shall be payable on submission of the application or applications, and are nonrefundable.

PART 177
CONTINUING EDUCATION

Section

177.1.   General requirement.
177.2.   Approved entities.
177.3.   Request for approval of course of study.
177.4.   Successful completion of course.
177.5.   Credit for teaching.
177.6.   Extension of time to complete courses.
177.7.   Computation of instruction time.
177.8.   Attendance.
177.9.   Examinations.
177.10. Advertising.
177.11. Auditing.
177.12. Retention of examination papers.
177.13. Change in approved course of study.
177.14. Suspensions and denials of course
          approval.
177.15. Open to public.
177.16. Facilities.
177.17. Faculty.
177.18. Continuing education credit.
177.19. Fees.

§ 177.1. General requirement.

(a) Renewals. No renewal license shall be issued to any real estate broker or salesperson for any license period commencing on or after 11/1/95 unless such licensee shall provide evidence of completion of 22½ hours of approved continuing education within the two year period immediately preceding such renewal, or upon the first such renewal, an otherwise previously valid 45 hours of continuing education for the l991–1995 continuing education cycle. However, such continuing education requirement shall not apply to any licensed real estate broker who is engaged full time in the real estate business and who has been licensed for at least fifteen consecutive years immediately preceding such renewal.

(b) Course approval. No offering of a course of study in the real estate field for the purpose of compliance with the continuing education requirements of subdivision 3 of section 441 of the Real Property Law shall be acceptable for credit unless such course of study shall have been approved by the department under the provisions of this Part.

§ 177.2. Approved entities.

Continuing education real estate courses and offerings may be given by any college or university accredited by the Commissioner of Education of the State of New York or by a regional accrediting agency approved by said Commissioner of Education; public or private vocational schools; real estate boards; and real estate-related professional societies and organizations. No real estate course of study seeking approval may be affiliated with or controlled by a real estate broker, salesperson, firm or company or real estate franchise, or controlled by a subsidiary of any real estate broker or real estate franchise. The following types of instruction shall not be acceptable as meeting continuing education requirements:

(a) general training or education to prepare a student for passing a real estate broker's or salesperson's examination which is not part of an approved course under Part 176 of this Title;

(b) offerings in mechanical office and business skills, such as typing, speed reading, memory improvement, report writing, personal motivation, salespersonship and sales psychology; and

(c) sales promotion meetings.

§ 177.3. Request for approval of course of study.

Requests for approval of courses of study in the real estate field to be given to satisfy the requirements for continuing education under the provisions of this Part shall be made 60 days before the proposed course is to be given, and on a form prescribed by the department which shall include the following:

(a) name, address and telephone number of the applicant;

(b) if applicant is a partnership, the names of the partners in the entity; if a corporation, the names of any persons who own five percent or more of the stock of the entity;

(c) title of each course to be offered;

(d) date and location of each course offered;

(e) duration and time of each course offered;

(f) procedure for taking attendance;

(g) a detailed outline of the subject matter of each course or seminar containing at least 22½ hours of instruction, or of each course module containing at least 3 hours of instruction, together with the time sequence of each segment thereof, the faculty for each segment, and teaching techniques used in each segment;

(h) description of materials to be distributed to the participants;

(i) if applicable, copies of examinations for each course, including the answers to all questions; and

(j) the names and qualifications of teachers, instructors or presenters for each segment, including a statement indicating whether the real estate broker's or salesperson's license of any of such teachers, instructors or presenters has ever been revoked, suspended or surrendered.

§ 177.4. Successful completion of course.

Any subject course for continuing education shall be accepted for credit on the basis of attendance only. The entity must submit to the department the names and license registration numbers of all individuals who successfully complete the approved course.

§ 177.5. Credit for teaching.

A licensee who shall teach an approved real estate course pursuant to Part 176 of this Subchapter or an approved subject offered for continuing education shall be credited with two hours for each hour of actual teaching performed. Records of such teaching shall be maintained by the person or organization presenting the course and certified on forms prescribed by the department. The records of such teaching shall be deemed records of attendance for all purposes of these rules.

§ 177.6. Extension of time to complete courses.

The department may grant an extension to any licensee who evidences bona fide hardship precluding completion of the continuing education requirements prior to the time the renewal application is to be filed. A licensee seeking such an extension shall file the appropriate renewal application, together with the evidence demonstrating such hardship, together with a written request for such extension. Any renewal license granted, based upon such an application, shall be conditional for the period the department shall grant the licensee to complete the required continuing education courses. The department, for such further good cause shown, may grant a further extension as shall be appropriate under the circumstances.

§ 177.7. Computation of instruction time.

To meet the minimum statutory requirement, attendance shall be computed on the basis of an hour equaling 60 minutes. The instruction periods may be shorter or longer than 60 minutes; in such case, appropriate time periods shall be added to obtain the total course time.

§ 177.8. Attendance.

The person or organization conducting the course shall certify to the department the name of each licensed person who successfully completed the course of study and his or her license registration number, and shall maintain its attendance records and a copy of such report for five years and, in addition, shall maintain the following record concerning the course:

(a) **the approval** number issued by the department for the course;

(b) **the offering,** title and description of the course;

(c) **the dates** and hours the course was given; and

(d) **the names** of the persons who took the course and whether they passed or failed.

§ 177.9. Examinations.

If applicable, all examinations required for course credit given shall be written and given within a reasonable time after the completion of the course work. No examination may be used unless it is approved by the department.

§ 177.10. Advertising.

No advertising pertaining to an approved course may be circulated or distributed unless it is first approved by the department.

§ 177.11. Auditing.

A duly authorized designee of the department may audit any course offered and may verify attendance and inspect the records of attendance of the course at any time during its presentation or thereafter.

§ 177.12. Retention of examination papers.

All persons and organizations conducting approved continuing education courses of study shall retain examination papers for persons attending for a period of five years after the completion thereof, and such papers shall at all times during such period be available for inspection by duly authorized representatives of the department.

§ 177.13. Change in approved course of study.

There shall be no change or alteration in any approved course of study of any subject or in any instruction staff without prior written notice to, and approval by, the department.

§ 177.14. Suspensions and denials of course approval.

Within 30 days after the receipt of the application for approval of an offering, the department shall inform the entity as to whether the offering has been approved, denied, or whether additional information is needed to determine the acceptability of the offering. The department may deny, suspend or revoke the approval of a real estate course or a real estate instructor, if it is determined that they are not in compliance with the law and rules or if the offering does not adequately reflect and present current real estate knowledge as a basis for a level of real estate practice. If disciplinary action is taken, a written order of suspension, revocation, or denial of approval will be issued. Anyone who objects to such denial, suspension or revocation shall have the opportunity to be heard by the Secretary of State or his designee.

§ 177.15. Open to public.

All courses approved pursuant to this Part shall be open to all members of the public regardless of the membership of the prospective student in any real estate board, or real estate-related professional society or organization.

§ 177.16. Facilities.

Each course shall be presented in such premises and in such facilities as shall be necessary to properly present the course. No course shall be presented in any real estate broker's office or the office of any association of real estate brokers, except as otherwise may be permitted under these rules.

§ 177.17. Faculty.

A person intending to present an approved course shall first be qualified pursuant to § 176.11 of this Title.

§ 177.18. Continuing education credit.

(a) A licensee who has received credit for qualifying courses pursuant to Part 176 of this Subchapter, and has used said qualifying courses to secure a real estate broker's or salesperson's license during a period of time as defined in section 441(3)(a) of the Real Property Law, shall receive continuing education credit for such courses for such period.

(b) No continuing education course will be considered for continuing education credit more than once within the two year cycle of renewal.

§ 177.19. Registration period.

Each registration or renewal period for approved programs or courses shall be for 12 months or a part thereof, said period to commence on January 1 or date thereafter and to continue until December 31.

PART 178
NONSOLICITATION ORDERS

§ 178.1. Definition of nonsolicitation order.

A nonsolicitation order is a directive to all real estate brokers and real estate salespersons. The nonsolicitation order directs that all brokers and salespersons must refrain from soliciting listings for the sale of residential property within a designated geographic area. A nonsolicitation order prohibits any and all types of solicitation directed at or toward homeowners in the designated geographic area. The types of solicitation that are prohibited include but are not limited to letters, postcards, telephone calls, door-to-door calls, handbills, and postings in public areas. In addition, a nonsolicitation order may contain such other terms or conditions as the Secretary of State may determine are, on balance, in the best interest of the public, which shall include but not be limited to the affected owners and licensees.

§ 178.2. [Reserved]

§ 178.3. Residential property.

For the purposes of this Part, the term residence or residential property shall include any of the following:

(a) a one-family residence;

(b) a two-family residence;

(c) a three-family residence;

(d) a residential cooperative apartment; and

(e) a residential condominium unit.

§ 178.4. Boundary streets.

For the purposes of this Part, a nonsolicitation area shall include all properties abutting the boundary streets named in the description of the nonsolicitation area. The intent being that the nonsolicitation area shall include properties on both sides of the boundary streets.

§ 178.5. Prohibited forms of solicitation.

(a) Within a nonsolicitation area, no real estate broker or real estate salesperson shall engage in any form of solicitation where the purpose of such solicitation is directly or indirectly, to obtain a listing of residential property for sale and where such solicitation is directed at or toward a homeowner or occupant of residential property within a designated nonsolicitation area.

(b) The following are examples of the types of solicitation that are prohibited:

(1) letters;

(2) postcards;

(3) handbills or leaflets or fliers;

(4) direct advertising delivered by mail or other service;

(5) telephone calls;

(6) door-to-door calls; and

(7) postings in public places.

(c) The following is not prohibited by a nonsolicitation order. Advertisements that are published in newspapers of general circulation:

(1) if such newspaper has a general readership throughout the metropolitan New York City area or throughout a substantial portion of the metropolitan New York City area;

(2) if such newspaper is published not less than once per week; and

(3) if such newspaper is sold by subscription or by individual copy and is not distributed free of charge.

PART 179
DETERMINATION OF
REAL ESTATE EXPERIENCE

Section

179.1. Qualifying experience.

179.2. Point system.

179.3. Experience point schedule.

§ 179.1. Qualifying experience.

An applicant for licensure as a real estate broker must possess one year of full-time experience as a licensed real estate salesperson under the supervision of a licensed real estate broker or the equivalent full-time experience in general real estate business for a period of at least two years.

§ 179.2. Point system.

(a) An applicant will receive credit for such experience according to the point system set forth in section 179.3 of this Part.

(b) 1750 points shall equate to a year of full-time experience.

(c) Upon request by the department, either prior to or after licensure, an applicant shall provide documentation or other proof to substantiate any or all of the experience claimed by the applicant. Failure to promptly provide the requested documentation or proof shall be grounds to deny the application, or if the applicant has been licensed, shall be grounds to suspend or revoke such license. Any false claim of experience shall be grounds to deny the application, or if the applicant has been licensed, shall be grounds to suspend or revoke such license.

§ 179.3. Experience point schedule.

(a) Experience points shall be credited an applicant in accordance with the following schedule:

Real Estate Broker Point System for Licensed Salesperson Activity Only

Category	Point Value
RESIDENTIAL SALES:	
1. Single Family, condo, co-op unit, multi-family (2 to 8 unit), farm (with residence, under 100 acres)	250
2. Exclusive listings	10
3. Open listings	1
4. Binders effected	25
5. Co-op unit transaction approved by seller and buyer that fails to win Board of Directors approval	100
RESIDENTIAL RENTALS:	
6. Rentals or subleases effected	25
7. Exclusive Listings	5
8. Open Listings	1
9. Property Management	
- Lease renewal	2
- Rent collections per tenant/ per year	1
COMMERCIAL SALES:	
10. Taxpayer	400
11. Office Building	400
12. Apartment Building (9 units or more)	400
13 . Shopping Center	400
14. Factory/Industrial warehouse	400
15. Hotel/Motel	400
16. Transient garage/parking lot	400

17. Multi-unit commercial
    condominium   400
18. Urban commercial development
    site   400
19. Alternative sale type transaction   400
20. Single-tenant commercial condo   250
21. Listings   10

COMMERCIAL LEASING:

22. New Lease-aggregate rental $1
    to $200,000   150
23. New Lease-aggregate rental
    $200,000 to $1 million   250
24. New Lease-aggregate rental
    over $1 million   400
25. Renewal-aggregate rental
    $1 to $200,000   75
26. Renewal-aggregate rental
    $200,000 to $1 million   125
27. Renewal-aggregate rental
    over $1 million   200
28. Listings   10

COMMERCIAL FINANCING: (includes residential properties of more than four units):

29. $1 to $500,000   200
30. $500,000 to $5,000,000   300
31. Over $5,000,000   400

MISCELLANEOUS:

32. Sale vacant lots, land
    (under 100 acres)   50
33. Sale vacant land
    (more than 100 acres)   150
34. Other must be fully explained   —

TOTAL POINTS NEEDED: 1750

(b) An applicant shall have the burden of establishing to the satisfaction of the department that the applicant actually performed the work associated with the real estate transaction claimed as experience credit.

APPENDIX C

Real Estate Math Review

Percent (%) means part per hundred. For example, 25% means 25 parts per hundred; 10% means 10 parts per hundred. Percentages are related to common and decimal fractions as follows:

5%	=	0.05	=	$\frac{1}{20}$
10%	=	0.10	=	$\frac{1}{10}$
25%	=	0.25	=	$\frac{1}{4}$
75%	=	0.75	=	$\frac{3}{4}$
99%	=	0.99	=	$\frac{99}{100}$

A percentage greater than 100% is greater than 1. For example:

110%	=	1.10	=	$1\frac{1}{10}$
150%	=	1.50	=	$1\frac{1}{2}$
200%	=	2.00	=	2
1,000%	=	10.0	=	10

To change a decimal fraction to a percentage, move the decimal point two places to the right and add the % sign. For example:

0.001	=	0.1%
0.01	=	1%
0.06	=	6%
0.35	=	35%
0.356	=	35.6%
1.15	=	115%

A percentage can be changed to a common fraction by writing it as hundredths and then reducing it to its lowest common denominator. For example:

20%	=	$\frac{20}{100}$	=	$\frac{1}{5}$
90%	=	$\frac{90}{100}$	=	$\frac{9}{10}$
225%	=	$\frac{225}{100}$	=	$2\frac{1}{4}$

ADDING
AND SUBTRACTING
DECIMALS

To add decimals, place the decimal points directly over one another. Then place the decimal point for the solutions in the same column and add. For example:

$$
\begin{array}{r}
6.25 \\
1.10 \\
\underline{10.277} \\
17.627
\end{array}
$$

If you are working with percentages, there is no need to convert to decimal fractions; just line up the decimal points and add. For example:

$$
\begin{array}{r}
68.8\% \\
6.0\% \\
\underline{25.2\%} \\
100.0\%
\end{array}
$$

When subtracting the same methods apply. For example:

$$
\begin{array}{rr}
1.00 & 100\% \\
\underline{-0.80} & \underline{-80\%} \\
0.20 & 20\%
\end{array}
$$

When there is a mixture of decimal fractions and percentages, first convert them all either to percentage or to decimal fractions.

MULTIPLYING
AND DIVIDING
DECIMALS

Multiplying decimals is like multiplying whole numbers except that the decimal point must be correctly placed. This is done by counting the total number of places to the right of the decimal point in the numbers to be multiplied. Then round off the same number of places in the answer. The following examples illustrate this:

$$
\begin{array}{cccccc}
0.6 & 0.2 & 1.01 & 6 & 6 & 0.03 \\
\underline{\times\ 0.3} & \underline{\times\ 0.2} & \underline{\times\ 2} & \underline{\times\ 0.1} & \underline{\times\ 0.11} & \underline{\times\ 0.02} \\
0.18 & 0.04 & 2.02 & 0.6 & 0.66 & 0.0006
\end{array}
$$

When dividing, the process starts with properly placing the decimal point. A normal division then follows. When a decimal number is divided by a whole number, place the decimal point in the answer directly above the decimal point in the problem. For example:

$$
\begin{array}{cc}
\underline{1.03} & \underline{0.033} \\
3)3.09 & 3)0.099
\end{array}
$$

To divide by a decimal number, you must first change the divisor to a whole number. Then you must make a corresponding change in the dividend. This is done by simply moving both decimal points the same number of places to the right. For example, to divide 0.06 by 0.02, move the decimal point of each to the right two places.

$0.02 \overline{)0.06}$ becomes $2 \overline{)6}$

$0.5 \overline{)3}$ becomes $5 \overline{)30}$

$0.05 \overline{)30}$ becomes $5 \overline{)3,000}$

When multiplying or dividing with percentages, first convert them to decimal form. Thus 6% of 200 is

$$\begin{array}{r} 200 \\ \times\quad 0.06 \\ \hline 12.00 \end{array}$$

A simple way to solve rate problems is to think of
 the word **is** as = (an equal sign).
 the word **of** as × (a multiplication sign).
 the word **per** as ÷ (a division sign).

for example:
 "7% of $50,000 is $3,500"
translates:
 "7% × $50,000 = $3,500"

Another formula for solving rate problems is: The Whole times the Percentage Rate equals a Part, or, $W \times R = P$
 What do you do if they give you the whole and the part and ask for the rate? Just use the simple circle formula:

 Insert the values that you are given in the circle. The position of the numbers will tell you whether to multiply or divide.
 For example, you start with $4,000 (the Whole) and you end up with some percent of that number, like $360 (the Part). When you put $4,000 in for W, and $360 for P, you will notice that $360 is on top of $4,000, which means $360 is being divided by $4,000.

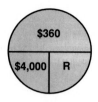

$$\frac{360}{4000} = 0.09 \text{ so } 360 \text{ is } 9\% \text{ of } 4,000.$$

Problem 1

Beverly Broker sells a house for $60,000. Her share of the commission is to be 2.5% of the sales price. How much does she earn?

Her commission is 2.5% of $60,000
Her commission = 0.025 × $60,000
Her commission = $1,500

Problem 2

Sam Salesman works in an office which will pay him 70% of the commission on each home he lists and sells. With a 6% commission, how much would he earn on a $50,000 sale?

His commission is 70% of 6% of $50,000
His commission = 0.70 × 0.06 × $50,000
His commission = $2,100

Problem 3

Newt Newcomer wants to earn $21,000 during his first 12 months as a salesman. He feels he can average 3% on each sale. How much property must he sell?

3% of sales is $21,000
0.03 × sales = $21,000
        sales = $21,000 ÷ 0.03
        sales = $700,000

Note: An equation will remain an equation as long as you make the same change on both sides of the equal sign. If you add the same number to both sides, it is still an equation. If you subtract the same amount from each side, it is still equal. If you multiply both sides by the same thing, it remains equal. If you divide both sides by the same thing, it remains equal.

Problem 4

An apartment building nets the owners $12,000 per year on their investment of $100,000. What percent return are they receiving on their investment?

$12,000 is ____% of $100,000

$12,000 = ____% × $100,000

$$\frac{\$12,000}{\$100,000} = 12\%$$

Problem 5

Smith wants to sell his property and have $47,000 after paying a 6% brokerage commission on the sales price. What price must Smith get?

$47,000 is 94% of selling price

$47,000 = 0.94 × selling price

$$\frac{\$47,000}{0.94} = \text{selling price}$$

$50,000 = selling price

Problem 6

Miller sold his home for $75,000, paid off an existing loan of $35,000 and paid closing costs of $500. The brokerage commission was 6% of the sales price. How much money did Miller receive?

amount =	$75,000
less	$4,500 (0.6 × 75,000)
less	$35,000 (pay off)
less	$500 (closing costs)
yields	$35,000 to receive

Problem 7

The assessed valuation of the Kelly home is $100,000. If the property tax rate is $6.00 per $100 of assessed valuation, what is the tax?

The tax is $\dfrac{\$6.00}{\$100}$ of $100,000

$$\text{tax} = \frac{\$6.00}{\$100} \times \$100,000$$

tax = $6,000

Problem 8
Property in Clark County is assessed at 75% of market value. What should the assessed valuation of a $40,000 property be?

Assessed valuation is 75% of market value
Assessed valuation = 0.75 × $40,000
Assessed valuation = $30,000

Problem 9
An insurance company charges $0.24 per $100 of coverage for a one-year fire insurance policy. How much would a $40,000 policy cost?

Cost is $\frac{\$0.24}{\$100}$ of $40,000

Cost = $\frac{\$0.24}{\$100}$ × $40,000

Cost = $96

AREA MEASUREMENT

The measurement of the distance from one point to another is called linear measurement. Usually this is along a straight line, but it can also be along a curved line. Distance is measured in inches, feet, yards, and miles. Less commonly used are chains (66 feet) and rods (16 and a half feet). Surface areas are measured in square feet, square yards, acres (43,560 square feet) and square miles. In the metric system, the standard unit of linear measurement is the meter (39.37 inches). Land area is measured in square meters and hectares. A hectare contains 10,000 square meters or 2.471 acres.

To determine the area of a square or rectangle, multiply its length times its width. The formula is:

Area = Length × Width
A = L × W

Problem 10
A parcel of land measures 660 feet by 330 feet. How many square feet is this?

Area = 660 feet × 330 feet
Area = 217,800 square feet

How many acres does this parcel contain?

Acres = 217,800 ÷ 43,560
Acres = 5

If a buyer offers $42,500 for this parcel, how much is the offering per acre?

$42,500 ÷ 5 = $8,500

To determine the area of a right triangle, multiply one-half of the base times the height:

A = ½ × B × H
A = ½ × 25 × 50
A = 625 square feet

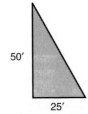

A = ½ × B × H
A = ½ × 40 × 20
A = 400 square feet

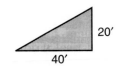

To determine the area of a circle, multiply 3.14 (π) times the square of the radius:

$A = \pi \times r^2$
$A = 3.14 \times 40^2$
A = 3.14 × 1,600
A = 5,024 sq ft

> **Note:** Where the diameter of a circle is given, divide by two to get the radius.

To determine the area of composite figures, separate them into their various components. Thus:

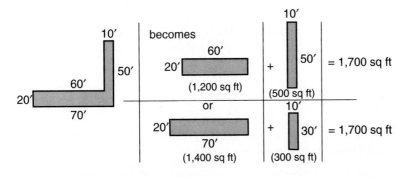

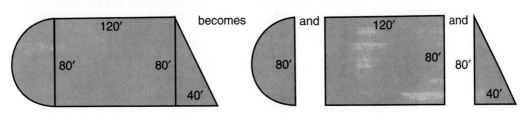

VOLUME MEASUREMENT

Volume is measured in cubic units. The formula is:
Volume = Length × Width × Height
$$V = L \times W \times H$$

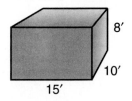

For example, what is the volume of a room that is 10 ft by 15 ft with an 8 ft ceiling?

$V = 10' \times 15' \times 8'$

$V = 1,200$ cu ft

Caution: When solving area and volume problems, **make certain that all the units are the same.** For example, if a parcel of land is one-half mile long and 200 ft wide, convert one measurement so that both are expressed in the same unit; thus the answer will be either in square feet or in square miles. There is no such area measurement as a mile-foot. If a building is 100 yards long by 100 feet wide by 16'6" high, convert to 300 ft by 100 ft by 16.5 before multiplying.

RATIOS
AND PROPORTIONS

If the label on a five-gallon can of paint says it will cover 2,000 square feet, how many gallons are necessary to cover 3,600 sq ft?

A problem like this can be solved two ways:
One way is to find out what area one gallon will cover. In this case 2,000 sq ft ÷ 5 gallons = 400 sq ft per gallon. Then divide 400 sq ft/gal into 3,600 sq ft and the result is 9 gallons.
The other method is to set up a proportion:

$$\frac{5 \text{ gal}}{2,000 \text{ sq ft}} = \frac{Y \text{ gal}}{3,600 \text{ sq ft}}$$

This reads, "5 gallons is to 2,000 sq ft as 'Y' gallons is to 3,600 sq ft." To solve for "Y," multiply both sides of the proportion by 3,600 sq ft. Thus:

$$\frac{5 \text{ gal} \times 3,600 \text{ sq ft}}{2,000 \text{ sq ft}} = Y \text{ gal}$$

Divide 2,000 sq ft into 3,600 sq ft and multiply the result by 5 gallons to get the answer.

FRONT-FOOT
CALCULATIONS

When land is sold on a front-foot basis, the price is the number of feet fronting on the street times the price per front foot.

Price = front footage × rate per front foot

Thus a 50 ft × 150 ft lot priced at $1,000 per front foot would sell for $50,000. Note that in giving the dimensions of a lot, the first dimension given is the street frontage. The second dimension is the depth of the lot.

APPENDIX D
Interest Tables

Compound Sum of Single Dollar

Year	2%	4%	6%	8%	10%	12%	14%	16%	18%	20%	22%	25%	30%	40%
1	1.020	1.040	1.060	1.080	1.100	1.120	1.140	1.160	1.180	1.200	1.220	1.250	1.300	1.400
2	1.040	1.082	1.124	1.166	1.210	1.254	1.300	1.346	1.392	1.440	1.488	1.563	1.690	1.960
3	1.061	1.125	1.191	1.260	1.331	1.405	1.482	1.561	1.643	1.728	1.816	1.953	2.197	2.744
4	1.082	1.170	1.262	1.360	1.464	1.574	1.689	1.811	1.939	2.074	2.215	2.441	2.856	3.842
5	1.104	1.217	1.338	1.469	1.611	1.762	1.925	2.100	2.288	2.488	2.703	3.052	3.713	5.378
6	1.126	1.265	1.419	1.587	1.772	1.974	2.195	2.436	2.700	2.986	3.297	3.851	4.827	7.530
7	1.149	1.316	1.504	1.714	1.949	2.211	2.502	2.826	3.185	3.583	4.023	4.768	6.275	10.541
8	1.172	1.369	1.594	1.851	2.144	2.476	2.853	3.278	3.759	4.300	4.908	5.960	8.157	14.758
9	1.195	1.423	1.689	1.999	2.358	2.773	3.252	3.803	4.435	5.160	5.987	7.451	10.604	20.661
10	1.219	1.480	1.791	2.159	2.594	3.106	3.707	4.411	5.234	6.192	7.305	9.313	13.786	28.925
11	1.243	1.539	1.898	2.332	2.853	3.479	4.226	5.117	6.176	7.430	8.912	11.642	17.921	40.496
12	1.268	1.601	2.012	2.518	3.138	3.896	4.818	5.936	7.288	8.916	10.872	14.552	23.298	56.694
13	1.294	1.665	2.133	2.720	3.452	4.363	5.492	6.886	8.599	10.699	13.264	18.190	30.287	79.371
14	1.319	1.732	2.261	2.937	3.797	4.887	6.261	7.988	10.147	12.839	16.182	22.737	39.373	
15	1.346	1.801	2.397	3.172	4.177	5.474	7.138	9.266	11.974	15.407	19.742	28.422	51.185	
16	1.373	1.873	2.540	3.426	4.595	6.130	8.137	10.748	14.129	18.488	24.085	35.527	66.541	
17	1.400	1.948	2.693	3.700	5.054	6.866	9.276	12.468	16.672	22.186	29.384	44.409	86.503	
18	1.428	2.026	2.854	3.996	5.560	7.690	10.575	14.462	19.673	26.623	35.849	55.511		
19	1.457	2.107	3.026	4.316	6.116	8.613	12.056	16.776	23.214	31.948	43.735	69.389		
20	1.486	2.191	3.207	4.661	6.727	9.646	13.743	19.461	27.393	38.337	53.357	86.736		
21	1.516	2.279	3.400	5.034	7.400	10.804	15.667	22.574	32.323	46.005	65.096			
22	1.546	2.370	3.603	5.437	8.140	12.100	17.861	26.186	38.142	55.206	79.417			
23	1.577	2.465	3.820	5.871	8.954	13.552	20.361	30.376	45.007	66.247	96.888			
24	1.608	2.563	4.049	6.341	9.850	15.179	23.212	35.236	53.108	79.497				
25	1.641	2.666	4.292	6.848	10.835	17.000	26.462	40.874	62.668	95.396				

Source: John J. Hampton, *Handbook for Financial Decision Makers,*
Reston Publishing Company, Reston, Virginia, 1979.

Compound Sum of Annuity of $1

Year	2%	4%	6%	8%	10%	12%	14%	16%	18%	20%	22%	25%	30%	40%
1	1.000	1.000	1.000	1.000	1.000	1.000	1.000	1.000	1.000	1.000	1.000	1.000	1.000	1.000
2	2.020	2.040	2.060	2.080	2.100	2.120	2.140	2.160	2.180	2.200	2.220	2.250	2.300	2.400
3	3.060	3.122	3.184	3.246	3.310	3.374	3.440	3.506	3.572	3.640	3.708	3.813	3.990	4.360
4	4.121	4.246	4.375	4.506	4.641	4.779	4.921	5.066	5.215	5.368	5.524	5.766	6.187	7.104
5	5.204	5.416	5.637	5.867	6.105	6.353	6.610	6.877	7.154	7.442	7.740	8.207	9.043	10.846
6	6.308	6.633	6.975	7.336	7.716	8.115	8.535	8.977	9.442	9.930	10.442	11.259	12.756	16.324
7	7.434	7.898	8.394	8.923	9.487	10.089	10.730	11.414	12.141	12.916	13.740	15.073	17.583	23.853
8	8.583	9.214	9.897	10.637	11.436	12.300	13.233	14.240	15.327	16.499	17.762	19.842	23.858	34.395
9	9.754	10.583	11.491	12.488	13.579	14.776	16.085	17.518	19.086	20.799	22.670	25.802	32.015	49.153
10	10.949	12.006	13.181	14.487	15.937	17.549	19.337	21.321	23.521	25.959	28.657	33.253	42.619	69.814
11	12.168	13.486	14.971	16.645	18.531	20.655	23.044	25.733	28.755	32.150	35.962	42.566	56.405	98.739
12	13.412	15.026	16.870	18.977	21.384	24.133	27.271	30.850	34.931	39.580	44.873	54.208	74.326	
13	14.680	16.627	18.882	21.495	24.522	28.029	32.088	36.786	42.218	48.496	55.745	68.760	97.624	
14	15.973	18.292	21.015	24.215	27.975	32.393	37.581	43.672	50.818	59.196	69.009	86.949		
15	17.293	20.024	23.276	27.152	31.772	37.280	43.842	51.659	60.965	72.035	85.191			
16	18.639	21.824	25.672	30.324	35.949	42.753	50.980	60.925	72.938	87.442				
17	20.011	23.697	28.212	33.750	40.544	48.884	59.117	71.673	87.067					
18	21.412	25.645	30.905	37.450	45.599	55.750	68.393	84.141						
19	22.840	27.671	33.759	41.446	51.158	63.440	78.968	98.603						
20	24.297	29.778	36.785	45.762	57.274	72.052	91.024							
21	25.783	31.969	39.992	50.423	64.002	81.699								
22	27.298	34.248	43.392	55.457	71.402	92.502								
23	28.844	36.618	46.995	60.893	79.542									
24	30.421	39.083	50.815	66.765	88.496									
25	32.029	41.646	54.864	73.106	98.346									

Source: John J. Hampton, *Handbook for Financial Decision Makers*,
Reston Publishing Company, Reston, Virginia, 1979.

APPENDIX E
Present Value Tables

Present Value of Single Dollar

Year	2%	4%	6%	8%	10%	12%	14%	16%	18%	20%	22%	24%	25%	30%	40%
1	0.980	0.962	0.943	0.926	0.909	0.893	0.877	0.862	0.847	0.833	0.820	0.806	0.800	0.769	0.714
2	0.961	0.925	0.890	0.857	0.826	0.797	0.769	0.743	0.718	0.694	0.672	0.650	0.640	0.592	0.510
3	0.942	0.889	0.840	0.794	0.751	0.712	0.675	0.641	0.609	0.579	0.551	0.524	0.512	0.455	0.364
4	0.924	0.855	0.792	0.735	0.683	0.636	0.592	0.552	0.516	0.482	0.451	0.423	0.410	0.350	0.260
5	0.906	0.822	0.747	0.681	0.621	0.567	0.519	0.476	0.437	0.402	0.370	0.341	0.328	0.269	0.186
6	0.888	0.790	0.705	0.630	0.564	0.507	0.456	0.410	0.370	0.335	0.303	0.275	0.262	0.207	0.133
7	0.871	0.760	0.665	0.583	0.513	0.452	0.400	0.354	0.314	0.279	0.249	0.222	0.210	0.159	0.095
8	0.853	0.731	0.627	0.540	0.467	0.404	0.351	0.305	0.266	0.233	0.204	0.179	0.168	0.123	0.068
9	0.837	0.703	0.592	0.500	0.424	0.361	0.308	0.263	0.225	0.194	0.167	0.144	0.134	0.094	0.048
10	0.820	0.676	0.558	0.463	0.386	0.322	0.270	0.227	0.191	0.162	0.137	0.116	0.107	0.073	0.035
11	0.804	0.650	0.527	0.429	0.350	0.287	0.237	0.195	0.162	0.135	0.112	0.094	0.086	0.056	0.025
12	0.788	0.625	0.497	0.397	0.319	0.257	0.208	0.168	0.137	0.112	0.092	0.076	0.069	0.043	0.018
13	0.773	0.601	0.469	0.368	0.290	0.229	0.182	0.145	0.116	0.093	0.075	0.061	0.055	0.033	0.013
14	0.758	0.577	0.442	0.340	0.263	0.205	0.160	0.125	0.099	0.078	0.062	0.049	0.044	0.025	0.009
15	0.743	0.555	0.417	0.315	0.239	0.183	0.140	0.108	0.084	0.065	0.051	0.040	0.035	0.020	0.006
16	0.728	0.534	0.394	0.292	0.218	0.163	0.123	0.093	0.071	0.054	0.042	0.032	0.028	0.015	0.005
17	0.714	0.513	0.371	0.270	0.198	0.146	0.108	0.080	0.060	0.045	0.034	0.026	0.023	0.012	0.003
18	0.700	0.494	0.350	0.250	0.180	0.130	0.095	0.069	0.051	0.038	0.028	0.021	0.018	0.009	0.002
19	0.686	0.475	0.331	0.232	0.164	0.116	0.083	0.060	0.043	0.031	0.023	0.017	0.014	0.007	0.002
20	0.673	0.456	0.312	0.215	0.149	0.104	0.073	0.051	0.037	0.026	0.019	0.014	0.012	0.005	0.001
25	0.610	0.375	0.233	0.146	0.092	0.059	0.038	0.024	0.016	0.010	0.007	0.005	0.004	0.001	
30	0.552	0.308	0.174	0.099	0.057	0.033	0.020	0.012	0.007	0.004	0.003	0.002	0.001		
40	0.453	0.208	0.097	0.046	0.022	0.011	0.005	0.003	0.001	0.001					
50	0.372	0.141	0.054	0.021	0.009	0.003	0.001	0.001							

Present Value of Annuity of $1

Year	2%	4%	6%	8%	10%	12%	14%	16%	18%	20%	22%	24%	25%	30%	40%
1	0.980	0.962	0.943	0.926	0.909	0.893	0.877	0.862	0.847	0.833	0.820	0.806	0.800	0.769	0.714
2	1.942	1.886	1.833	1.783	1.736	1.690	1.647	1.605	1.566	1.528	1.492	1.457	1.440	1.361	1.224
3	2.884	2.775	2.673	2.577	2.487	2.402	2.322	2.246	2.174	2.106	2.042	1.981	1.952	1.816	1.589
4	3.808	3.630	3.645	3.312	3.170	3.037	2.914	2.798	2.690	2.589	2.494	2.404	2.362	2.166	1.849
5	4.713	4.452	4.212	3.993	3.791	3.605	3.433	3.274	3.127	2.991	2.864	2.745	2.689	2.436	2.035
6	5.601	5.242	4.917	4.623	4.355	4.111	3.889	3.685	3.498	3.326	3.167	3.020	2.951	2.643	2.168
7	6.472	6.002	5.582	5.206	4.868	4.564	4.288	4.039	3.812	3.605	3.416	3.242	3.161	2.802	2.263
8	7.325	6.733	6.210	5.747	5.335	4.968	4.639	4.344	4.078	3.837	3.619	3.421	3.329	2.925	2.331
9	8.162	7.435	6.802	6.247	5.759	5.328	4.946	4.607	4.303	4.031	3.786	3.566	3.463	3.019	2.379
10	8.983	8.111	7.360	6.710	6.145	5.650	5.216	4.833	4.494	4.192	3.923	3.682	3.571	3.092	2.414
11	9.787	8.760	7.887	7.139	6.495	5.937	5.453	5.029	4.656	4.327	4.035	3.776	3.656	3.147	2.438
12	10.58	9.385	8.384	7.536	6.814	6.194	5.660	5.197	4.793	4.439	4.127	3.851	3.725	3.190	2.456
13	11.34	9.986	8.853	7.904	7.103	6.424	5.842	5.342	4.910	4.533	4.203	3.912	3.780	3.223	2.468
14	12.11	10.56	9.295	8.244	7.367	6.628	6.002	5.468	5.008	4.611	4.265	3.962	3.824	3.249	2.477
15	12.85	11.12	9.712	8.559	7.606	6.811	6.142	5.575	5.092	4.675	4.315	4.001	3.859	3.268	2.484
16	13.58	11.65	10.11	8.851	7.824	6.974	6.265	5.669	5.162	4.730	4.357	4.033	3.887	3.283	2.489
17	14.29	12.17	10.48	9.122	8.022	7.120	6.373	5.749	5.222	4.775	4.391	4.059	3.910	3.295	2.492
18	14.99	12.66	10.83	9.372	8.201	7.250	6.467	5.818	5.273	4.812	4.419	4.080	3.928	3.304	2.494
19	15.68	13.13	11.16	9.604	8.365	7.366	6.550	5.877	5.316	4.844	4.442	4.097	3.942	3.311	2.496
20	16.35	13.59	11.47	9.818	8.514	7.469	6.623	5.929	5.353	4.870	4.460	4.110	3.954	3.316	2.497
25	19.52	15.62	12.78	10.68	9.077	7.843	6.873	6.097	5.467	4.948	4.514	4.147	3.985	3.329	2.499
30	22.40	17.29	13.77	11.26	9.427	8.055	7.003	6.177	5.517	4.979	4.534	4.160	3.995	3.332	2.500
40	27.36	19.79	15.05	11.93	9.779	8.244	7.105	6.234	5.548	4.997	4.544	4.166	3.999	3.333	2.500
50	31.42	21.48	15.76	12.23	9.915	8.304	7.133	6.246	5.554	4.999	4.545	4.167	4.000	3.333	2.500

APPENDIX F

Measurement Conversion Table

Mile =
- 5,280 feet
- 1,760 yards
- 320 rods
- 80 chains
- **= 1.609 kilometers**

Square mile =
- 640 acres
- **= 2.590 sq kilometers**

Acre =
- 43,560 sq ft
- 4,840 sq yds
- 160 sq rods
- **= 4,047 sq meters**

Rod =
- 16.5 feet
- **= 5.029 meters**

Chain =
- 66 feet
- 4 rods
- 100 links
- **= 20.117 meters**

Meter =
- 39.37 inches
- **= 1,000 millimeters**
- 3.281 feet
- **= 100 centimeters**
- 1.094 yards
- **= 10 decimeters**

Kilometer =
- 0.6214 miles
- 3,281 feet
- 1,094 yards
- **= 1,000 meters**

Square meter =
- 10,765 sq ft
- 1.196 sq yds
- **= 10,000 sq centimeters**

Hectare =
- 2.47 acres
- 107,600 sq ft
- 11,960 sq yds
- **= 10,000 sq meters**

Square kilometer =
- 0.3861 sq miles
- 247 acres
- **= 1,000,000 sq meters**

Kilogram =
- 2.205 pounds
- **= 1,000 grams**

Liter =
- 1.052 quarts
- 0.263 quarts
- **= 1,000 milliliters**

Metric ton =
- 2,205 pounds
- 1.102 tons
- **= 1,000 kilograms**

APPENDIX G

Answers to Chapter Questions and Problems

CHAPTER 2   **Licensing Laws and Professional Affiliation**

VOCABULARY REVIEW

a. 6	**e.** 5	**i.** 1	**m.** 11	**q.** 19	**u.** 16
b. 21	**f.** 18	**j.** 14	**n.** 2	**r.** 9	**v.** 21
c. 13	**g.** 23	**k.** 15	**o.** 22	**s.** 8	**w.** 7
d. 17	**h.** 12	**l.** 4	**p.** 3	**t.** 10	

QUESTIONS AND PROBLEMS

1. In deciding on a compensation schedule for his salespersons, a broker must consider office overhead, employee retention, and the emphasis he wishes to place on listing versus selling.

2. Generally speaking, a real estate license is required when a person, who for compensation or the promise of compensation, lists or offers to list, sells or offers to sell, buys or offers to buy, negotiates or offers to negotiate, either directly or indirectly, for the purpose of bringing about a sale, purchase, option to purchase, exchange, auction, lease or rental of real estate. New York also requires that real estate appraisers, property managers, mortgage bankers, rent collectors, and tenant relocators hold real estate licenses.

3. Early license laws were primarily aimed at protecting the public by qualifying license applicants based on their honesty, truthfulness and good reputation. Real estate examinations and education requirements were added later.

4. New York writes its own questions. The frequency of exams varies in different parts of the state. Check with the division of licensing services.

5. New York requires sales agents and brokers to take 22½ hours of continuing education classes in each two-year renewal period.

6. The Secretary of State is Alexander G. Treadwell.

7. Licenses can be suspended for any violation of Article 12-A, and the department may impose a fine of up to $1,000 (see Appendix A, § 441-c).

8. The purpose of a bond requirement or a recovery fund is to have funds available that can be drawn upon in the event that a court judgment against a licensee, resulting from a license-related wrongdoing, is uncollectible.

9. The purpose of the National Association of Realtors is to promote the general welfare of the real estate industry by encouraging fair dealing among Realtors and the public, supporting legislation to protect property rights, offering education for members, and in general doing whatever is necessary to build the dignity, stability, and professionalization of the industry.

10. An employment contract will cover such matters as compensation, training, hours of work, company identification, fees and dues, expenses, use of automobile, fringe benefits, independent contractor status, termination of employment, and general office policies and procedures.

11. You would want to consider location, compensation, broker's reputation, working hours, broker support, training opportunities, advertising policy, expense reimbursement, and fringe benefits.

The Principal-Broker Relationship—Employment   CHAPTER 3

VOCABULARY REVIEW

a.	8	**d.**	2	**g.**	5
b.	4	**e.**	9	**h.**	1
c.	3	**f.**	6	**i.**	7

QUESTIONS AND PROBLEMS

1. An exclusive right to sell listing protects the broker by entitling him to a commission no matter who sells the property. The exclusive agency listing puts the broker in competition with the owner by allowing the owner to find a buyer and owe no commission. The open listing adds other brokers to the competition as any number of brokers can have the listing simultaneously and the owner can still sell it himself and pay no commission.

2. Ready, willing, and able buyer means a buyer who is ready to buy at the seller's price and terms and who has the financial capacity to do so.

3. Listings are usually terminated with the completion of the agency objective, namely finding a buyer or a tenant. Lacking a buyer, termination usually results when the listing period expires. A listing can also be terminated if the broker fails to perform as agreed in the listing or if the broker and principal mutually agree to terminate.

4. The broker employed by the seller focuses on making the sale, marketing. The broker employed by the buyer focuses on obtaining the product to suit the buyer's needs and potential uses.

CHAPTER 4   **Nature and Description of Real Estate**

VOCABULARY REVIEW

a.	17	**f.**	15	**j.**	1	**n.**	8	**r.**	6
b.	19	**g.**	21	**k.**	22	**o.**	12	**s.**	5
c.	11	**h.**	10	**l.**	13	**p.**	7	**t.**	14
d.	4	**i.**	9	**m.**	16	**q.**	18	**u.**	2
e.	20							**v.**	3

QUESTIONS AND PROBLEMS

1. Requires local answer.
2.

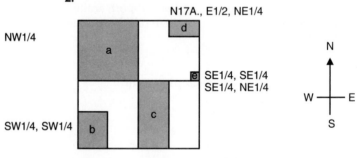

3. (a) 160 acres   (c) 80 acres   (e) 2½ acres
   (b) 40 acres   (d) 17 acres
4. (a) NE¼   (d) W½ of the SE¼ of the NW¼
   (b) E½ of the SE¼   (e) NE¼ of the SE¼ of the NW¼
   (c) SW¼ of the NW¼

5.

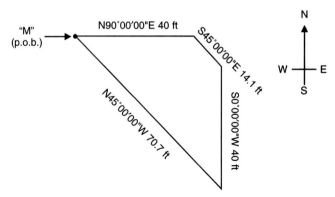

6. No. In the general public interest, laws have been passed that give aircraft the right to pass over land provided they fly above certain altitudes.
7. The key to a door, although highly portable, is adapted to the door and as such is real property.
8. Requires individualized answer. However, as a general rule, anything that is permanently attached is real property and anything that is not attached is personal property.
9. Requires local answer.
10. Unless corrections are made (and they usually are) survey inaccuracies would result.

Rights and Interests in Land   CHAPTER 5

VOCABULARY REVIEW

a. 8	**e.** 13	**i.** 6	**m.** 21	**q.** 22	**u.** 24
b. 4	**f.** 20	**j.** 11	**n.** 10	**r.** 18	**v.** 17
c. 14	**g.** 7	**k.** 9	**o.** 12	**s.** 23	**w.** 15
d. 19	**h.** 5	**l.** 1	**p.** 2	**t.** 3	**x.** 16

QUESTIONS AND PROBLEMS
1. For a freehold estate to exist, there must be actual possession of the land (that is, ownership) and the estate must be of unpredictable duration. Leasehold estates do not involve ownership of the land and are of determinate length. Freehold estate cases are tried under real property laws. Leasehold cases are tried under personal property laws.
2. An easement is created when a landowner fronting on a public byway deeds or leases a landlocked portion of his land to another person. This would be an easement by necessity. A second method is by prolonged use and is called an easement by prescription.

3. New York requires all assets jointly acquired during marriage to be divided equitably in a divorce.
4. England, Spain, and France.
5. The holder of an easement coexists side by side with the landowner; that is, both have a shared use of the land in question. The holder of a lease obtains exclusive right of occupancy and the landowner is excluded during the term of the lease.
6. An encumbrance is any impediment to clear title. Examples are lien, lease, easement, deed restriction, and encroachment.
7. Requires local answer. (Answers will likely center around zoning, building codes, general land planning, rent control, property taxation, eminent domain, and escheat.)
8. New York has an automatic exemption of $10,000.

CHAPTER 6   **Forms of Ownership**

VOCABULARY REVIEW

a.	8	**e.**	5	**i.**	14	**m.**	9	**q.** 7
b.	1	**f.**	12	**j.**	4	**n.**	3	
c.	16	**g.**	11	**k.**	13	**o.**	2	
d.	10	**h.**	17	**l.**	15	**p.**	6	

QUESTIONS AND PROBLEMS
1. The key advantage of sole ownership is flexibility–the owner can make all decisions without approval of co-owners. The key disadvantages are responsibility and the high entry cost.
2. Undivided interest means that each co-owner has a right to use the entire property.
3. The four unities are
   Time: each must acquire ownership at the same moment.
   Title: all must acquire their interests from the same source.
   Interest: each owns an undivided whole of the property.
   Possession: all have the right to use the whole property.
4. Right of survivorship means that upon the death of a joint tenant, his interest in the property is extinguished and the remaining joint tenants are automatically left as the owners.
5. Tenancy by the entirety.
6. Yes.
7. The three women would be considered to be tenants in common with each owning an undivided one-third interest.

8. No assumption can safely be made based on name only. Inquiry must be made into whether the land in question was separate or community property.

9. The key differences are in the financial liability of the limited partners, the limited management role of the limited partners, and the fact that limited partners are not found in a general partnership.

10. REITs offer investors single taxation, built-in management, small minimum investment, and liquidity.

Transferring Title

CHAPTER 7

VOCABULARY REVIEW

a. 21	**g.** 14	**l.** 20	**q.** 3	**v.** 10
b. 15	**h.** 16	**m.** 1	**r.** 12	**w.** 25
c. 22	**i.** 5	**n.** 17	**s.** 11	**x.** 2
d. 18	**j.** 23	**o.** 24	**t.** 19	**y.** 8
e. 9	**k.** 6	**p.** 4	**u.** 13	**z.** 26
f. 7				

QUESTIONS AND PROBLEMS

1. Yes. The fact that a document is a deed depends on the wording it contains, not what it is labeled or not labeled.

2. Title passes upon delivery of the deed by the grantor to the grantee and its willing acceptance by the grantee.

3. The full covenant and warranty deed offers the grantee protection in the form of the grantor's assurances that he is the owner and possessor, that the grantee will not be disturbed after taking possession by someone else claiming ownership, that the title is not encumbered except as stated in the deed, and that the grantor will procure and deliver to the grantee any subsequent documents necessary to make good the title being conveyed.

4. Warranty deed. It provides the grantee with the maximum title protection available from a deed.

5. The hazards of preparing one's own deeds are that any errors made will cause confusion and may make the deed legally invalid. Preprinted deeds may not be suitable for the state where the land is located or for the grantor's purpose. An improperly prepared deed, once recorded, creates errors in the public records.

6. Dower right, curtesy right, community property right, mortgage right of redemption, tax lien, judgment lien, mechanic's lien, undivided interest held by another, inheritance rights, and easements are all examples of title clouds.

7. When a person dies without leaving a will, state law directs how that person's assets are to be distributed.

8. An executor is named by the deceased in the will to carry out its terms. In the absence of a will, the court appoints an administrator to settle the deceased's estate.
9. Holographic wills are legal in New York. Formal wills require two witnesses.
10. No. Occupancy on a rental basis is not hostile to the property owner but, rather, is by permission.
11. Requires local answer.

CHAPTER 8   **Contract Law**

VOCABULARY REVIEW

a. 12	**e.** 23	**i.** 10	**m.** 16	**q.** 26	**u.** 15	**y.** 6
b. 20	**f.** 1	**j.** 25	**n.** 5	**r.** 7	**v.** 4	**z.** 19
c. 14	**g.** 8	**k.** 11	**o.** 13	**s.** 18	**w.** 17	
d. 4	**h.** 22	**l.** 3	**p.** 21	**t.** 9	**x.** 2	

QUESTIONS AND PROBLEMS

1. An expressed contract is the result of a written or oral agreement. An implied contract is one that is apparent from the actions of the parties involved. (Examples will vary with personal experiences.)
2. A legally valid contract requires: (a) legally competent parties, (b) mutual agreement, (c) lawful objective, (d) sufficient consideration or cause, and (e) a writing when required by law.
3. A void contract has no legal effect on any party to the contract and may be ignored at the pleasure of any party to it. A voidable contract is a contract that is able to be voided by one of its parties.
4. Examples of legal incompetents include: minors, insane persons, drunks, and felons. (Exceptions are possible in the latter two.)
5. An offer can be terminated by the passage of time and by withdrawal prior to its acceptance. Passage of time can be in the form of a fixed termination date for the offer or, lacking that, a reasonable amount of time to accept as fixed by a court of law.
6. Mistake as applied to contract law arises from ambiguity in negotiations and mistake of material fact.
7. Consideration is one of the legal requirements of a binding contract. The concept of one party doing something and receiving nothing in return is foreign to contract law. Examples are money, goods, services, and forbearance.
8. The parties to a legally unenforceable contract can still voluntarily carry out its terms. However, compliance could not be enforced by a court of law.

9. Alternatives include: mutual rescission, assignment, novation, partial performance, money damages, unilateral rescission, specific performance suit, or liquidated damages.
10. His primary concern would be whether money damages would suitably restore his position or whether actual performance is necessary.

Real Estate Sales Contracts   CHAPTER 9

VOCABULARY REVIEW

a. 4	**e.** 18	**i.** 9	**m.** 15	**q.** 13
b. 7	**f.** 5	**j.** 12	**n.** 17	**r.** 8
c. 2	**g.** 3	**k.** 14	**o.** 1	**s.** 10
d. 6	**h.** 11	**l.** 16	**p.** 19	

QUESTIONS AND PROBLEMS
1. The purchase contract provides time to ascertain that the seller is capable of conveying title, time to arrange financing, and time to carry out the various terms and conditions of the contract.
2. Anything left to be "ironed out" later is an area for potential disagreement and possibly a lost deal. Moreover, the basic contract requirement of a meeting of the minds may be missing.
3. The advantages are convenience (the bulk of the contract is already written) and time (it is faster to fill out a form than construct a contract from scratch). The disadvantages are that a preprinted contract may not adequately fit a given transaction and the blank spaces still leave room for errors.
4. A seller can accept an offer with or without a deposit. (An exception is that some court-ordered sales require a specified deposit.)
5. Most fixtures are considered by law to be a part of the land and therefore do not need separate mention. However, mention is made of any fixture that might be open to a difference of opinion.
6. If a seller is not under pressure to sell quickly and/or there are plenty of buyers in the marketplace, he can hold out for price and terms to his liking. If a buyer is aware of other buyers competing for the same property, he will act quickly and meet (or offer close to) the seller's price and terms. If the seller is in a rush to sell or is afraid that there are few buyers for his property in the market, he will negotiate terms more to the buyer's liking rather than risk not making the sale. If the buyer is aware of this, he can hold out for price and terms to his liking.

7. The advantages to the seller of holding title in an installment contract sale are that the seller still holds title in the event of the buyer's default and may be able to pledge the property as collateral for a loan.

8. The key advantages of trading are the tax-free exchange possibility and the need for little or no cash to complete the transaction. The disadvantages are in finding suitable trade property for all parties involved and in the fact that there are more transaction details in a trade (compared to a cash sale) that can go awry and ruin the trade.

9. A letter of intent is a mutual expression of interest to carry out some business objective. No firm, legal obligation is created.

CHAPTER 10   **The Principal-Broker Relationship—Agency**

VOCABULARY REVIEW

a. 14	**e.** 9	**i.** 7	**m.** 13
b. 6	**f.** 4	**j.** 12	**n.** 2
c. 5	**g.** 1	**k.** 8	**o.** 11
d. 10	**h.** 15	**l.** 3	

QUESTIONS AND PROBLEMS

1. **Faithful:** the broker must perform as promised in the listing contract and not depart from the principal's instructions.
Loyal: the broker owes his allegiance to the principal and as such works for the benefit of the principal. This means promoting and protecting the principal's best interests and keeping him informed of all matters that might affect the sale of the listed property.

2. Broker cooperation refers to the sharing of a single commission fee among the various brokers who brought about a sale. It is achieved by an agreement between the listing broker and the cooperating brokers.

3. The laws of agency refer to the legal responsibilities of a broker to his principal and vice versa.

4. An agency coupled with an interest exists when the agent holds an interest in the property he is representing.

5. The purpose of a property disclosure statement is to require that sellers of subdivisions provide prospective purchasers with information regarding the property they are being asked to buy.

6. Errors and omissions insurance is designed to defend and pay certain legal costs and judgments arising from business negligence suits.

Real Estate Leases   CHAPTER 11

VOCABULARY REVIEW

a. 19	**e.** 20	**i.** 5	**m.** 6	**q.** 10	**u.** 22	**y.** 17
b. 4	**f.** 26	**j.** 15	**n.** 16	**r.** 12	**v.** 7	**z.** 3
c. 18	**g.** 13	**k.** 2	**o.** 25	**s.** 14	**w.** 23	
d. 21	**h.** 8	**l.** 1	**p.** 11	**t.** 24	**x.** 9	

QUESTIONS AND PROBLEMS

1. A lease assures a tenant space at the rent stated in the lease. But it also requires the tenant to pay for the total time leased. A month-to-month arrangement commits a tenant to one month at a time; however, it also commits the landlord for only one month at a time.
2. The landlord or manager must bring a special proceeding to eject the tenant.
3. New York's Real Property has many tenant protections, including an implied warranty of habitability.
4. Contract rent is the amount of rent the tenant must pay the landlord. Economic rent is market value rent.
5. The tenant's basis would be that the premises are unfit to occupy as intended in the lease. The tenant's purpose is to either get the problem fixed or terminate the lease.
6. An option to renew is to the advantage of the lessee.
7. Requires local answer.
8. Questions asked will center on the prospective tenant's ability to pay the rent each month and willingness to abide by the lease contract. Names and addresses of the prospect's current employer and previous landlord would be requested and checked to verify information supplied by the tenant. A credit check would also be run.

Condominiums, Cooperatives, PUDs, and Timeshares   CHAPTER 12

VOCABULARY REVIEW

a. 16	**e.** 3	**i.** 2	**m.** 17	**q.** 20
b. 15	**f.** 1	**j.** 8	**n.** 4	**r.** 18
c. 7	**g.** 11	**k.** 14	**o.** 5	**s.** 19
d. 13	**h.** 6	**l.** 9	**p.** 10	**t.** 12

QUESTIONS AND PROBLEMS

1. Condominiums are often cheaper to buy than a single-family house, are often better located, may offer better security and maintenance, and can be individually financed.
2. Each condominium unit owner holds an undivided interest in the land in a fee simple condominium project. The corporation owns the land in a cooperative.

3. A proprietary lease is a lease issued by a corporation to its stockholders. The lease "rent" is actually the stockholder's share of the cost of operating the building and repaying the debt against it. In a residential lease, the tenant pays for use of the premises, is not responsible for operating expenses nor debt repayment, and does not have an ownership interest in the premises.

4. The master deed converts a given parcel of land into a condominium subdivision.

5. The wall between two condominium apartments belongs to the condominium owners as a group.

6. CC&Rs are the covenants, conditions, and restrictions by which a property owner agrees to abide. They are established for the harmony and well-being of the owners as a group.

7. Maintenance fees (association dues) pay for common operating costs and are spread among the unit owners. Failure to pay creates a lien against the delinquent owner's unit.

8. The owners' association hazard and liability policy covers only the common elements. To be protected against property loss and accident liability within a dwelling unit, the owner must have his own hazard and liability policy.

9. Right-to-use is a contractual right whereas fee simple is ownership of real estate.

10. In a PUD each owner holds title to the land occupied by his unit and is a member of an owners' association which holds title to the common areas.

CHAPTER 13   **Title Closing and Escrow**

VOCABULARY REVIEW

a. 15	**e.** 16	**i.** 10	**m.** 5
b. 11	**f.** 6	**j.** 7	**n.** 1
c. 14	**g.** 2	**k.** 8	**o.** 12
d. 3	**h.** 9	**l.** 4	**p.** 13

QUESTIONS AND PROBLEMS

1. The key difference is that an escrow holder is a common agent of the parties to the transaction. This eliminates the need for each party to attend the closing and personally represent himself.

2. Escrow agent duties include preparation of escrow instructions, holding buyer's earnest money, ordering a title search, obtaining title insurance, making prorations, loan payoffs, loan disbursement, deed and mortgage delivery, and handling papers and paperwork relative to the transaction.

3. The escrow agent is an agent of the buyer with respect to the buyer's role in the transaction and an agent of the seller with respect to the seller's role. The same holds true for the lender, title company, and so on. The escrow agent's duty is to treat all parties fairly and not to serve one party to the exclusion of the other.

4. $180 divided by 12 equals $15 per month or 50¢ per day. Using standard 30-day months and presuming the buyer is the owner commencing with the settlement date, there are one month and 26 days used, and 10 months and 4 days remaining. For this remaining coverage, the buyer pays the seller 10 times $15 plus 4 times $0.50 equals $152.00.

5. Daily rate equals $45,000 times 8% divided by 360 equals $10. The buyer is credited 11 days times $10 equals $110. The seller is debited the same amount.

6.

Buyer:	Seller:
lender's title policy	conveyance tax
loan appraisal fee	deed preparation
mortgage recording	mortgage release

7. Without release papers, the buyer still has a vaguely defined liability to buy and the seller can still be required to sell.

Mortgage and Note   CHAPTER 14

VOCABULARY REVIEW

a. 26	e. 10	i. 16	m. 4	q. 8	u. 7	y. 14
b. 9	f. 21	j. 5	n. 15	r. 12	v. 25	z. 20
c. 13	g. 2	k. 3	o. 23	s. 17	w. 11	
d. 6	h. 18	l. 22	p. 1	t. 24	x. 19	

QUESTIONS AND PROBLEMS

1. A prepayment privilege is to the advantage of the borrower. Without it the debt cannot be repaid ahead of schedule.

2. Lien theory sees a mortgage as creating only a lien against a property whereas title theory sees a mortgage as conveying title to the lender subject to defeat by the borrower.

3. Strict foreclosure gives title to the lender, whereas foreclosure by sale requires that the foreclosed property be sold at public auction and the proceeds used to repay the lender. (Part two requires local answer.)

4. The first mortgage is the senior mortgage while the second and third mortgages are classed as junior mortgages.

5. The mortgagee must get court approval to force the sale of the property. The property is sold at public auction to the highest bidder after all interested parties have been notified.

6. The owner may redeem the property at any time before the sale.
7. The obligor is the party making the obligation; that is, the borrower. The obligee is the party to whom the obligation is owed; that is, the lender.
8. The lender includes mortgage covenants pertaining to insurance, property taxes, and removal in order to protect the value of the collateral for the loan.
9. A certificate of reduction is prepared by the lender and shows how much remains to be paid on the loan. An estoppel certificate provides for a borrower's verification of the amount still owed and the rate of interest.

CHAPTER 15   **Recordation, Abstracts, and Title Insurance**

VOCABULARY REVIEW

a.	10	**e.**	2	**i.**	8	**m.**	19	**q.**	9	**u.**	17
b.	3	**f.**	6	**j.**	14	**n.**	11	**r.**	20	**v.**	22
c.	1	**g.**	18	**k.**	16	**o.**	5	**s.**	12		
d.	7	**h.**	13	**l.**	4	**p.**	15	**t.**	21		

QUESTIONS AND PROBLEMS
1. Requires local answer; documents must be acknowledged, certified, or proved as required by the real property law.
2. Requires local answer.
3. By visibly occupying a parcel of land or by recording a document in the public records, a person gives constructive notice that he is claiming a right or interest in that parcel of land.
4. The grantor and grantee indexes are used to locate documents filed in the county clerk's office.
5. Although the bulk of the information necessary to conduct a title search can be found in the county clerk's office, it may also be necessary to inspect documents not kept there, for example, marriage records, judgment lien files, probate records, and the U.S. Tax Court.
6. A certificate of title issued by an attorney is his opinion of ownership, whereas a Torrens certificate of title shows ownership as determined by a court of law.
7. A title report shows the condition of title at a specific moment in time. An abstract provides a complete historical summary of all recorded documents affecting title. From this, an attorney renders an opinion as to the current condition of title.
8. The purpose of title insurance is to protect owners and lenders from monetary loss caused by errors in title report preparation and inaccuracies in the public records.

9. Although Williams did not record his deed, his occupancy of the house constitutes legal notice. The out-of-state investor, who probably felt safe because he bought a title insurance policy, apparently did not read the fine print, which, in most owner's policies, does not insure against facts, rights, interests, or claims that could be ascertained by an on-site inspection or by making inquiry of persons in possession. The out-of-state investor is the loser unless he can recover his money from Thorsen.

10. Requires local answer.

Lending Practices

VOCABULARY REVIEW

a.	6	**e.**	10	**i.**	5
b.	7	**f.**	8	**j.**	1
c.	12	**g.**	9	**k.**	11
d.	4	**h.**	3	**l.**	2

QUESTIONS AND PROBLEMS

1. The major risk is that when the balloon payment is due, the borrower will not have the cash to pay it, and will not be able to find a lender to refinance it.
2. An amortized loan requires equal, periodic payments of principal and interest such that the loan balance owing will be zero at maturity. During the life of the loan, payments are first applied to interest owing and then to principal. As the balance owed is reduced, less of each monthly payment is taken for interest and more applied to principal reduction until finally the loan is repaid.
3. $65 \times \$9.91 = \$644.15$ per month
4. $\$800 \div \$9.53 \times \$1,000 + \$10,000 = \$93,945$
5. $\$800 \div \$8.05 \times \$1,000 + \$10,000 = \$109,379$
6. $\$902 \times 90 = \$81,180$
7. The purpose of Section 203b insurance is to qualify buyers of modest-priced homes for low down-payment loans. This is done by insuring lenders against loan default and charging borrowers an insurance premium for this.
8. The VA offers a qualified veteran the opportunity of purchasing a home with no cash down payment.
9. A point is 1 percent. It is a method of expressing loan origination fees and discounts in connection with lending. Discount points are used to increase the effective rate of interest (yield) to the lender without changing the quoted interest rate.

CHAPTER 16

CHAPTER 17   **The Loan and the Consumer**

VOCABULARY REVIEW

a.	1	**c.**	6	**e.**	2
b.	3	**d.**	5	**f.**	4

QUESTIONS AND PROBLEMS

1. As a rule, it is from the borrower's monthly income that monthly loan payments will be made. The assets, although substantial in size, may not be available for monthly payments.
2. The basic purpose of the Truth-in-Lending Act is to show the borrower how much he will be paying for credit in percentage terms and in total dollars.
3. No. The annual percentage rate calculation normally includes the interest rate in the note, therefore, the APR will typically be higher; it would more reflect a percentage rate higher than the interest rate.
4. The Fair Credit Reporting Act controls accuracy and fairness for consumers in the granting of credit.
5. The right of rescission allows a borrower to back out of a transaction for three business days after executing the loan document. It is intended to eliminate loan sharking and high pressure tactics in obtaining loans from consumers.

CHAPTER 18   **Sources of Financing**

VOCABULARY REVIEW

a.	9	**d.**	5	**g.**	6	**j.**	7
b.	10	**e.**	4	**h.**	8		
c.	2	**f.**	1	**i.**	3		

QUESTIONS AND PROBLEMS

1. A mortgage broker brings borrowers and lenders together. A mortgage banker makes loans and then resells them.
2. The main source is investors who buy mortgage-backed securities.
3. Loan servicing refers to the care and upkeep of a loan once it is made. This includes payment collection and accounting, handling defaults, borrower questions, loan payoff processing, and mortgage releasing.
4. FNMA buys, by auction, mortgage loans. These purchases are financed by the sale of FNMA stock and bonds as well as the sale of these loans to investors. GNMA guarantees timely repayment of privately-issued securities backed by pools of federally-insured mortgages.

5. A loan dollar that is the result of real savings won't cause inflation. That is because the borrower is using goods and services the saver has foregone. But a fiat money dollar does not represent available goods and services; instead it competes with real savings dollars and pushes prices up.

6. There is a large volume of investors who are willing to invest in the low-risk (mortgage-backed) notes, which makes more money available for home loans. It is a benefit for both the home mortgage borrower and the investor.

Types of Financing CHAPTER 19

VOCABULARY REVIEW

a. 1	**e.** 10	**i.** 15	**m.** 16	**q.** 11
b. 18	**f.** 14	**j.** 19	**n.** 5	**r.** 6
c. 2	**g.** 17	**k.** 12	**o.** 3	**s.** 4
d. 8	**h.** 9	**l.** 7	**p.** 13	**t.** 20

QUESTIONS AND PROBLEMS

1. Adjustable rate loans share the risk of changing interest rates between the borrower and the lender. The lender feels more comfortable knowing the interest rate charged will change with the cost of money to the lender.

2. An adjustable rate mortgage is a loan on which the interest rate can be adjusted up or down as current interest rates change.

3. Rentals and leases are considered financing forms as they allow a person the use of something without having to first pay the full purchase price.

4. Above all, the investor should make certain that the realistic market value of the property is well in excess of the loans against it.

Fair Housing, ADA, Equal Credit, and Community Reinvestment CHAPTER 20

VOCABULARY REVIEW

a. 10	**c.** 11	**e.** 8	**g.** 1	**i.** 4	**k.** 13	**m.** 2
b. 5	**d.** 12	**f.** 3	**h.** 7	**j.** 6	**l.** 9	

QUESTIONS AND PROBLEMS

1. Yes, lawyers are not a protected class of individuals, so long as this is the only reason you are not selling to him. Remember that if that lawyer is a minority, he may have a discrimination suit on other grounds.

2. The United States Constitution deals primarily with fundamental rights; race, color, creed, national origin, and alienage. The statutes have expanded the coverage to sex and marital status, age, and handicapped discrimination theories.
3. Requires local answer but should include posting of CRA disclosures and advertising in local community publications.
4. Brokerage services are regulated and monitored by every individual state through their various licensing laws. Brokers also have the most significant effect in marketing and sales of real estate throughout the country, therefore the regulation of fair housing through brokers reaches more people faster and is easier to monitor in specific controls on every individual.
5. No, constitutional protections extend to white, Anglo-Saxon persons as they do to any other class, based on race, color, creed, national origin, or alienage.
6. Requires individual answer.
7. No, even if a real estate agent thinks that a neighborhood is safer, it may be perceived by the consumer that they are being "steered" for any number of other different reasons. It is best to always let the purchaser decide which neighborhoods they want to choose to avoid complications of steering and discrimination allegations.

CHAPTER 21 **Real Estate Appraisal**

VOCABULARY REVIEW

a. 7	**e.** 1	**i.** 25	**m.** 17	**q.** 13	**u.** 2	**y.** 6
b. 16	**f.** 8	**j.** 10	**n.** 21	**r.** 14	**v.** 3	**z.** 22
c. 23	**g.** 5	**k.** 18	**o.** 4	**s.** 9	**w.** 11	
d. 12	**h.** 20	**l.** 24	**p.** 26	**t.** 15	**x.** 19	

QUESTIONS AND PROBLEMS
1. Enough comparables should be used to reasonably estimate market value but not so many as to involve more time and expense than is gained in added information. For a single-family house, three to five good comparables are usually adequate.
2. Asking prices are useful in that they set an upper limit on value. Offering prices are useful in that they set a lower limit on value.
3. Adjustments are made to the comparable properties. This is because it is impossible to adjust the value of something for which one does not yet know the value.
4. Using comparables that are not similar to the subject property with respect to zoning, neighborhood characteristics, size, or usefulness, requires adjustments that are likely to be very inaccurate or impossible to make.

5. Gross rent times gross rent multiplier equals indicated property value. The strength of this approach is in its simplicity. Its weakness is also in its simplicity as it overlooks anything other than gross rents.

6. The five steps are (1) estimate land value as though vacant, (2) estimate new construction cost of a similar building, (3) subtract estimated depreciation from construction cost to obtain, (4) the indicated value of the structure, and (5) add this to the land value.

7. The income approach values a property based on its expected monetary returns in light of current rates of return being demanded by investors.

8. In the standard market comparison approach, a specific dollar adjustment is made for each item of difference between the comparables and the subject property. With competitive market analysis, adjustments are made in a generalized fashion in the minds of the agent and the seller. The CMA approach is usually preferred for listing homes for sale because there is less room for disagreement. The standard market approach is preferred for appraisal reports as it shows exactly how the appraiser valued the adjustments.

9. The principle of diminishing marginal returns warns against investing more than the capitalized value of the anticipated net returns.

10. All, under the new regulations, would require a formal appraisal report, although the departure provisions could be invoked.

11. The Appraisal Foundation was formed to establish regulations for the appraisal industry. It will raise standards for the appraisal industry.

Taxes and Assessments

CHAPTER 22

VOCABULARY REVIEW

a. 10	e. 13	i. 15	m. 16
b. 2	f. 5	j. 12	n. 8
c. 4	g. 14	k. 11	o. 3
d. 7	h. 9	l. 1	p. 6

QUESTIONS AND PROBLEMS

1. Sources of funds other than property taxes are subtracted from the district budget. The remainder is then divided by the total assessed valuation of property in the district to obtain the tax rate.

2. $960,000 divided by $120,000,000 equals 8 mills

3. $40,000 times $0.008 equals $320

4. $10,000 times $0.05 divided by $100 equals $5
5. Requires local answer.
6. Requires local interpretation. However, the point is that the assessor does not set the tax rate. The assessor only applies it. If the complaint is in regard to assessment procedures, the assessment appeal process is taken. If it is in regard to the tax rate, then city, county, school board, or state budget makers are responsible.
7. The greater the amount of tax-exempt property in a taxation district, the less taxable property is available to bear the burden of taxation.
8. Requires local answer.
9. $68,000 − $5,000 − ($21,000 + $2,000 + $5,000) = $35,000
10. $68,000 − $5,000 − $58,000 = $5,000

CHAPTER 23   **Basic Principles of Construction**

VOCABULARY REVIEW

a. 7   d. 8   g. 3
b. 6   e. 4   h. 1
c. 2   f. 5

QUESTIONS AND PROBLEMS

1. A performance code requires a structure or its component parts to perform up to a certain standard; a specification code requires that specific materials be used or that the structure be constructed in a specific manner. For example, a performance code might require that a roof be constructed to withstand a particular snow load, while a specification code might require that snow slides be installed and that the roof have a particular pitch or incline.
2. The New York State Building Code is a performance code. The New York Fire Underwriters Association's code is based on specifications.
3. A local building department might choose to impose restrictions tailored to particular geographic or physical conditions prevalent in an area. For example, waterfront communities might require that barriers to beach erosion be constructed; energy codes might be more stringent in communities in the colder regions of the state.
4. Requires local answer.
5. The major structural systems are the foundation and framing systems; the major mechanical systems include the plumbing, electric, heating, ventilation, and air conditioning systems. Builders often use the shorthand "HVAC" to describe the last three of these.

6. Baseboard/hot water is popular because it is easy to install and unobtrusive. It also introduces moisture to the rooms. Forced warm air is favored because it is usually less expensive to install and has the advantage of being readily adaptable to the installation of central air conditioning. Some homeowners think a hot air system makes the air too dry. Electric baseboard heat is the least expensive to install but, in most areas of the state, the most expensive to operate.

Land-Use Control   CHAPTER 24

VOCABULARY REVIEW

| a. | 8 | c. | 11 | e. | 13 | g. | 1 | i. | 4 | k. | 5 | m. | 9 |
| b. | 12 | d. | 6 | f. | 7 | h. | 14 | j. | 3 | l. | 10 | n. | 2 |

QUESTIONS AND PROBLEMS

1. The individual property owner does not consider his property to be a community resource. Thus, any substantial progress in land planning and control in the future must also consider the right of the individual to develop his land.
2. The authority of government to control land use is derived from the state's right of police power. Through enabling acts, this authority is passed on to the counties, cities, and towns in the state.
3. A variance allows an individual landowner to deviate from strict compliance with zoning requirements for his land. A variance must be consistent with the character of the neighborhood and general objectives of zoning as they apply to that neighborhood.
4. Requires local answer.
5. A master plan takes a broad look at the entire land-use picture in a community, county, or region. The object is to view the area as a unified entity that provides its residents with jobs and housing as well as social, recreational, and cultural activities. In contrast, zoning laws tell a landowner specifically how a parcel of land may be used, and what type and size structures may be placed on it.
6. The purpose of an EIS is to gather information about the effect of a proposed project on the environment so that the anticipated environmental costs and benefits of the project may be considered along with the economic and humanitarian aspects.
7. Transferable development rights would equalize financial windfalls and wipe-outs by requiring those whose land is approved for urban uses to purchase development

rights from those whose land is prohibited from development.
8. Requires local answer.

CHAPTER 25   **Environmental Issues**

VOCABULARY REVIEW

a. 17	**e.** 5	**i.** 10	**m.** 16	**q.** 3
b. 11	**f.** 2	**j.** 14	**n.** 15	**r.** 7
c. 1	**g.** 18	**k.** 13	**o.** 8	
d. 12	**h.** 9	**l.** 4	**p.** 6	

QUESTIONS AND PROBLEMS
1. Due diligence means that prospective buyers have an obligation to ask reasonable questions and investigate indications of possible contamination. For example, standing water with obvious discoloration should raise a reasonable person's suspicions.
2. A new federal law requires sellers, lessors, *and their agents,* to disclose any information they know about lead-based paint in homes they are attempting to sell or lease. The law requires the seller/lessor only to provide notice and an opportunity for the buyer/lessor to inspect. It does not require the owner to remediate. It applies only to residences built before 1978 when lead-based paint was banned.
3. The New York statute requires preschool children to have blood tests for lead contamination, and the Health Department may require homeowners to remediate a problem found in their residence if a child's lead levels are found to be elevated.
4. The New York State Health Department's Center for Environmental Health is the best place to start. They can be helpful with most of your questions or direct you to the proper place. Their toll free number is 1-800-458-1188.

CHAPTER 26   **Real Estate and the Economy**

VOCABULARY REVIEW

a. 1	**c.** 4	**e.** 8	**g.** 10	**i.** 5
b. 6	**d.** 3	**f.** 7	**h.** 9	**j.** 2

QUESTIONS AND PROBLEMS
1. Requires local answer.
2. Requires local answer.
3. Requires local answer.

4. The Reagan years slowed inflation and they lowered interest rates, making housing more affordable. They also resulted in a loss of jobs as the economy was restructured.
5. The purpose of the Equal Credit Opportunity Act is to require lenders to make credit available without regard to sex or marital status.
6. Requires individual answer.
7. Clinton has attempted to avoid supply-side economics, but the effect has not produced a marked change.
8. The economic goals of the Federal Reserve Board are high employment, stable prices, steady growth, and a stable foreign exchange value for the dollar.
9. The advantage is that in the short-run interest rates can be pushed down which gives the economy a boost. The disadvantage is that inflation will result.
10. Rising prices.

APPENDIX H

Sample New York Real Estate Forms[1]

---

[1]The forms in this appendix are reprinted with the permission of Capital Region Multiple Listing Service, Inc., 838 Western Avenue, Albany, NY 12203.

CAPITAL REGION MULTIPLE LISTING SERVICE, INC. 266410
5/25/95

THIS IS A LEGALLY BINDING CONTRACT. IF NOT FULLY UNDERSTOOD
WE RECOMMEND CONSULTING AN ATTORNEY BEFORE SIGNING.

EXCLUSIVE RIGHT TO SELL LISTING AGREEMENT

Property Type

1F

Property Address _____

1. Grant of Exclusive Right to Sell
In consideration of _____ (hereinafter
referred to as BROKER) submitting the above-described property to the Capital Region Multiple Listing Service (hereinafter referred to as CRMLS) under
its Multiple Listing Rules and Regulations and in further consideration of said BROKER undertaking to find a purchaser for said property, the undersigned
OWNER (the word OWNER refers to each and all parties who have an ownership interest in the property) hereby grants to said BROKER, the sole and
exclusive right to sell the property for $ _____ , from _____ , 19 ____ until and including
_____ , 19 _____ . The OWNER hereby authorizes the BROKER to submit this listing to the CRMLS and make an offer of
subagency to all participants in the CRMLS and any other cooperating agent authorized under the law to receive a commission and with whom the listing
BROKER deems it appropriate to cooperate in the SELLER's best interest.

2. Owner's Authorization and Obligation
The OWNER understands that in order to facilitate and expedite the sale of said property, the OWNER hereby authorizes the BROKER to make and
use photographs of said property, grants the BROKER exclusive "FOR SALE" sign privilege on said property, consents that said property may be shown
at any reasonable hour, and agrees to refer any and all inquires concerning said property to BROKER.
It is agreed that this property is listed in full compliance with local, state and federal fair housing laws against discrimination on the basis of race,
color, religion, sex, national origin; handicap, age, marital status, or children.

3. Marketing Activity
The OWNER grants to the BROKER full discretion to determine the appropriate marketing approach for the property. BROKER will undertake to provide a ready, willing and able purchaser and in order to do so will engage in marketing activity which may include advertising, showing of listed premises
and/or the conduct of open houses.

4. Subsequent Offers
Upon the OWNER's acceptance of a purchase offer that does not stipulate the property is to remain on the market: (Owner's initial "A" or "B")
A. _____ the BROKER shall hold any subsequent offers as backups, which shall be conveyed to the OWNER only in the event the previously-
accepted contract is deemed cancelled, null and void.
B. _____ the BROKER shall convey any subsequent offers to the OWNER, with the understanding that the OWNER should consult an attorney
regarding any subsequent offers because a binding contract for the property may already exist and brokerage commission claims may
be involved.

5. CRMLS Not Agent
The OWNER understands and agrees that CRMLS is not the OWNER's agent and that none of the terms of this agreement shall make it the
OWNER's agent.

6. Purchaser's Mortgage (If Applicable)
The OWNER agrees to accept a purchase offer contingent for a reasonable period of time, on the Purchaser's ability to finance the purchase price
by any of the prevailing methods of mortgage financing. Any other type of mortgage loan or financing must be approved by the OWNER.

7. Disclosure of Terms of Purchase
A. Terms of purchase will be disclosed upon closing to the members of CRMLS.
B. The OWNER further agrees that upon acceptance of a purchase offer, the terms of the purchase may be disclosed (Owner's initials:
_____ yes; or _____ no).

8. Presentation of Purchase Offer
The OWNER authorizes the_____ (listing/selling) BROKER to submit purchase offers to the OWNER.

9. Possession of Key to Property
The OWNER understands that providing the BROKER with the key to the property does not in any way make the BROKER the custodian of said
property or responsible therefor.

10. Rental of Property
Should the OWNER desire to rent the property during the period of this agreement, the BROKER is hereby granted the sole and exclusive right to
rent the property, exclusive "FOR RENT" sign privilege and the OWNER agrees to pay the BROKER a rental commission of _____
for the first year of the lease which is due and will be paid (check one) ☐ upon the execution of the lease, or ☐ upon the date of occupancy. The commission for each and any subsequent year of the lease, or renewal thereof, is due and payable at the commencement of each year of the lease period.

11. Brokerage Fee: Amount, When Due and Payable
If, during the period of this agreement, or any extension thereof, a transfer, sale of exchange of the property is made, effected or agreed upon with
anyone, the OWNER agrees to pay the BROKER a commission of _____ % of the sale or exchange price, or $ _____ , whichever is greater.
Broker acknowledges that they will pay a fee of _____ % of the sale or exchange price, or $ _____ to any CRMLS participant acting in the
capacity of subagent. BROKER further acknowledges that they will pay a fee of _____ % of the sale or exchange price, or $ _____
to any other cooperating agent authorized under the law to receive a commission. Further, this commission will be due and payable if:
(a) prior to the expiration date of this agreement, a purchaser for the property is procured by a licensed agent or any participant in CRMLS at
a sales price and terms acceptable to the OWNER; or
(b) after the expiration date of this agreement and during the _____ months thereafter, **without the services of a licensed agent,** a
purchaser buys the property who was (i) shown the property by a licensed agent or participant in CRMLS and/or (ii) made aware of the
property by a participant in CRMLS or the OWNER during the term of the listing; or
(c) during the period of this agreement, the OWNER himself sells or agrees to sell the property.

12. Application of Deposit
The OWNER authorizes the LISTING BROKER to hold any and all deposits made as part of the purchase price in an escrow account until closing
or cancellation of the purchase contract with written consent of all parties to the contract. In the event of a claim of default by the seller or the purchaser,
the deposits will be held by the broker in an escrow account pending final resolution or the written mutual consent of the parties. OWNER further agrees
that the BROKER shall apply and pay any deposits or other money received as part of the purchase price toward the brokerage fee which is due under
this agreement.

13. Inspection Contingencies
The Owner agrees to accept a purchase offer contingent, for a reasonable period of time, on the Purchaser's ability to obtain inspections regarding
unknown circumstances which could affect the habitability of the property.

14. Termination
I understand that I may revoke the Listing Broker's authority to be my agent at any time, but that if I do so, the Listing Broker nevertheless shall retain
its contract rights, which may include but are not limited to recovery of its commission, advertising expenses, and/or other damages incurred by reason of
my early termination of this listing.

15. Entire Agreement
The OWNER has read and understands this agreement and the property data section and does hereby acknowledge receipt of a copy thereof. This
agreement shall be binding on the parties hereto.

---

16. THE UNDERSIGNED DOES HEREBY CERTIFY THAT THE FOLLOWING EXPLANATIONS ARE UNDERSTOOD
An "EXCLUSIVE RIGHT TO SELL" listing means that if you, the OWNER of a property find a buyer for your house, or if another broker
finds a buyer, you must pay the agreed commission to the present BROKER.
An "EXCLUSIVE AGENCY" listing means that if you, the OWNER of the property, find a buyer, you will not have to pay a commission to the
BROKER. However, if another BROKER finds a buyer, you will owe a commission to both the selling BROKER and your present BROKER.
I have been given a Roster of the Capital Region MLS, Inc.

Owner's Initials _____

ACCEPTED BY:

_____   _____
Broker   Owner

675

CAPITAL REGION MULTIPLE LISTING SERVICE, INC.

STANDARD FORM
CONTRACT FOR PURCHASE AND SALE OF REAL ESTATE

REALTOR®

EQUAL HOUSING OPPORTUNITY

THIS IS A LEGALLY-BINDING CONTRACT. IF NOT FULLY UNDERSTOOD, WE RECOMMEND
ALL PARTIES TO THE CONTRACT CONSULT AN ATTORNEY BEFORE SIGNING.

1. **IDENTIFICATION OF PARTIES TO THE CONTRACT**
    A. **SELLER**—The Seller is _____
    residing at _____
    (the word "Seller" refers to each and all parties who have an ownership interest in the property).
    B. **PURCHASER**—The Purchaser is _____
    residing at _____
    (the word "Purchaser" refers to each and all of those who sign below as Purchaser).

2. **PROPERTY TO BE SOLD**
    The property and improvements which the Seller is agreeing to sell and which the Purchaser is agreeing to purchase is known as
    _____
    located in the city, village or town of _____ in _____ County,
    State of New York. This property includes all the Seller's rights and privileges, if any, to all land, water, streets and roads annexed
    to, and on all sides of the property. The lot size of the property is approximately _____ .

3. **ITEMS INCLUDED IN SALE**

Heating and Lighting Fixtures	Storm Windows and Screens	Television Aerials
Built-in Kitchen Appliances	Storm and Screen Doors	Smoke Detectors
Built-in Bathroom and Kitchen Cabinets	Water Softeners (if owned by Seller)	Alarm Systems
Drapery Rods and Curtain Rods	Plumbing Fixtures	Shrubbery, Trees, Plants, and
Shades and Blinds	Pumps	Fencing in the Ground
Wall-to-Wall Carpeting as placed	Awnings	Fireplace insert, doors and/or screen

    The items listed above, if now in or on said premises are represented to be owned by the Seller, free from all liens and encum-
    brances, and are included in the sale "as is," on the date of this offer, together with the following items: _____
    _____
    _____

4. **ITEMS EXCLUDED FROM SALE**
    The following items are excluded from the sale: _____
    _____
    _____

5. **PURCHASE PRICE**
    The purchase price is _____ DOLLARS ($ _____)
    The Purchaser shall pay the purchase price as follows:
    a. $ _____ deposit with this contract.
    b. $ _____ additional deposit on _____
    c. $ _____ in cash or certified check at closing
    d. $ _____ _____
    e. $ _____ _____

6. **MORTGAGE CONTINGENCY**
    This Agreement is contingent upon Purchaser obtaining approval of a ☐ conventional, ☐ FHA or ☐ VA (if FHA or VA, see attached
    required addendum) or _____ mortgage loan of $ _____ for a term of not more than _____ years
    at an initial ☐ fixed or ☐ adjustable nominal interest rate not to exceed _____ percent. Purchaser agrees to use diligent
    efforts to obtain said approval and shall apply for the mortgage loan within _____ business days after the Seller has
    accepted this contract. Purchaser agrees to apply for such a mortgage loan to two lending institutions, if necessary. This con-
    tingency shall be deemed waived unless Purchaser shall notify _____ (_____
    Office) in writing as called for in paragraph 22 no later than_____of Purchaser's inability to
    obtain said approval. If the Purchaser so notifies, then this agreement shall be deemed cancelled, null and void, and all deposits
    made hereunder shall be returned to the Purchaser.

7. **MORTGAGE EXPENSE AND RECORDING FEES**
    The mortgage recording tax imposed on the mortgagor, mortgage and deed recording fees, expenses of drawing papers and any
    other expenses to be incurred in connection with procuring a mortgage, shall be paid by the Purchaser.

8. **OTHER TERMS** (if any)_____
    _____
    _____

9. **TITLE AND SURVEY**
    A ☐ 40-year abstract of title, tax search and any continuations thereof, or a ☐ fee title insurance policy, shall be obtained at the
    expense of ☐ Purchaser or ☐ Seller. (If both boxes are checked, the option of whether an Abstract of Title or fee policy is provided
    shall be that of the party paying for same.) The Seller shall cooperate in providing any available survey, abstract of title or title in-
    surance policy information, without cost to Purchaser. The Purchaser shall pay the cost of updating any such survey or the cost
    of a new survey.

10. **CONDITIONS OF PREMISES**
    The buildings on the premises are sold "as is" without warranty as to condition, and the Purchaser agrees to take title to the build-
    ings "as is" and in their present condition subject to reasonable use, wear, tear and natural deterioration between the date hereof
    and the closing of title: except that in the case of any destruction within the meaning of the provisions of Section 5–1311 of the
    General Obligations Law of the State of New York entitled "Uniform Vendor and Purchaser Risk Act," said section shall apply to
    this contract.
    A. This Agreement is contingent upon a determination by a Certified Exterminator that the premises are free from infestation
    or damage by wood-destroying organisms; this determination to be made at Purchaser's expense and to be completed by
    _____ and, if premises are not free from infestation or damage, then Purchaser
    shall have the option, by written notice to be given within five (5) days after date in this paragraph, to cancel this contract.
    B. This Agreement is contingent upon a written determination, at Purchaser's expense, by a New York State registered architect
    or licensed engineer, by a third party who is _____ , or other qualified person,
    that the premises are free from any substantial structural, mechanical, electrical, plumbing, roof covering, water or sewer defects.
    The term substantial to refer to any individual defect which will reasonably cost over $1,000.00 to correct. This contingency shall
    be deemed waived unless the Purchaser shall notify_____no later than
    _____ , as called for in paragraph 22, of such substantial defect(s), and furthermore supplies
    a written copy of the inspection report. If the Purchaser so notifies, then this Agreement shall be deemed cancelled, null and void

676

and all deposits made hereunder shall be returned to Purchaser or, at Purchaser's option, said cancellation may be deferred for a period of ten (10) days in order to provide the parties an opportunity to otherwise agree in writing.

The following buildings or items on the premises are excluded from this inspection: _____
_____

11. **CONDITIONS AFFECTING TITLE**

The Seller shall convey and the Purchaser shall accept the property subject to all covenants, conditions, restrictions and easements of record and zoning and environmental protection laws so long as the property is not in violation thereof and any of the foregoing does not prevent the intended use of the property for the purpose of _____ ;
also subject to any existing tenancies, any unpaid installments of street or other improvement assessments payable after the date of the transfer of title to the property, and any state of facts which an inspection and/or accurate survey may show, provided that nothing in this paragraph renders the title to the property unmarketable.

12. **DEED**

The property shall be transferred from Seller to Purchaser by means of a Warranty Deed, with Lien Covenant, or _____
_____ deed, furnished by the Seller. The deed and real property transfer gains tax affidavit will be properly prepared and signed so that it will be accepted for recording by the County Clerk in the County in which the property is located. If the Seller is transferring the property as an executor, administrator, trustee, committee or conservator, the deed usual to such cases shall be accepted.

13. **NEW YORK STATE TRANSFER TAX AND MORTGAGE SATISFACTION**

The Seller agrees to pay the New York State Real Property Transfer Tax as set by law and further agrees to pay the expenses of procuring and recording satisfactions of any existing mortgages.

14. **TAX AND OTHER ADJUSTMENTS**

The following, if any, shall be apportioned so that the Purchaser and Seller are assuming the expenses of the property and income from the property as of the date of transfer of title:
a. rents and security deposits. Seller shall assign to Purchaser all written leases and security deposits affecting the premises.
b. taxes, sewer, water rents, and condominium as homeowner association fees.
c. municipal assessment yearly installments except as set forth in item 11.
d. fuel, based upon fair market value at time of closing as confirmed by a certification provided by Seller's supplier.

15. **RIGHT OF INSPECTION AND ACCESS**

Purchaser and/or a representative shall be given access to the property for any tests or inspections required by the terms of this contract upon reasonable notice to the Seller or a representative. Purchaser and/or a representative shall be given the right of inspection of the property, at a reasonable hour, within 48 hours prior to transfer of title.

16. **TRANSFER OF TITLE/POSSESSION**

The transfer of title to the property from Seller to Purchaser will take place at the office of the lender's attorney if the Purchaser obtains a mortgage loan from a lending institution. Otherwise, the closing will be at the office of the attorney for the Seller. The closing will be on or before _____. Possession shall be granted upon transfer of title unless otherwise mutually agreed upon in writing signed by the parties.

17. **DEPOSITS**

It is agreed that any deposits by the Purchaser are to be deposited with the Listing Broker at _____
_____ as part of the purchase price.

If the Seller does not accept the Purchaser's offer, all deposits shall be returned to Purchaser.

If the offer is accepted by the Seller, all deposits will be held in escrow by the Listing Broker until the contingencies and terms have been met. The Purchaser will receive credit on the total amount of the deposit toward the purchase price. Broker shall then apply the total deposit to the brokerage fee. Any excess of deposit over and above the fee earned will go to the Seller.

If the contingencies and terms contained herein cannot be resolved, or in the event of default by the Seller or the Purchaser, the deposits will be held by the Broker pending a resolution of the disposition of the deposits.

18. **TIME PERIOD OF OFFER**

Purchaser and Seller understand and agree that, unless earlier withdrawn, this offer is good until _____ a.m. _____ p.m., _____ , 19 _____ , and if not accepted by the Seller prior to that time, then this offer becomes null and void.

19. **REAL ESTATE BROKER**

The Purchaser and Seller agree that _____
and _____ brought about the sale, and Seller agrees to pay the Brokers' commission to_____ as agreed to in the listing agreement.

20. **ATTORNEYS APPROVAL CLAUSE**

This agreement is contingent upon Purchaser and Seller obtaining approval of this Agreement by their attorney as to all matters, without limitation. This contingency shall be deemed waived unless Purchaser's or Seller's attorney on behalf of their client notifies _____ in writing, as called for in paragraph 22, of their disapproval of the Agreement no later than _____. If Purchaser's or Seller's attorney so notifies, then this Agreement shall be deemed cancelled, null and void, and all deposits shall be returned to the Purchaser.

21. **ADDENDA**

The following attached addenda are part of this Agreement:

a. _____ b. _____ c. _____
d. _____ e. _____ f. _____
g. _____ h. _____ i. _____

22. **NOTICES**

All notices contemplated by this agreement shall be in writing, delivered by (a) certified or registered mail, return receipt requested, postmarked no later than the required date; (b) by telecopier/facsimile transmitted by such date; or (c) by personal delivery by such date.

23. **ENTIRE AGREEMENT**

This contract contains all agreements of the parties hereto. There are no promises, agreements, terms, conditions, warranties, representations or statements other than contained herein. This Agreement shall apply to and bind the heirs, legal representatives, successors and assigns of the respective parties. It may not be changed orally.

Dated: _____ Time: _____ Dated: _____ Time: _____

_____ _____
Purchaser   Seller

_____ _____
Purchaser   Seller

_____ _____
Selling Broker   Listing Broker

New York State Department of Taxation and Finance

Combined Real Property Transfer Gains Tax Affidavit Real Estate Transfer Tax Return Credit Line Mortgage Certificate

For department use only

See instructions (TP-584-I) before completing this form. Please print or type.

Schedule A - Information Relating to Conveyance

(Transferor/grantor)	Name *(if individual; last, first, middle initial)*		Social security number
☐ Individual ☐ Corporation ☐ Partnership ☐ Other	Mailing address	ZIP code	Federal employer identification number
(Transferee/grantee)	Name *(if individual; last, first, middle initial)*		Social security number
☐ Individual ☐ Corporation ☐ Partnership ☐ Other	Mailing address	ZIP code	Federal employer identification number

Location and description of property conveyed

Tax map designation			Address	City/Village	Town	County
Section	Block	Lot				

Type of property conveyed *(check applicable box)*

1 ☐ 1 - 3 family house
2 ☐ Residential cooperative
3 ☐ Residential condominium
4 ☐ Vacant land
5 ☐ Commercial/Industrial
6 ☐ Apartment building
7 ☐ Office building
8 ☐ Other _____

Date of conveyance

month	day	year

Percentage of real property conveyed which is residential real property _____ %
(see instructions)

Condition of conveyance *(check all that apply)*

a. __ Conveyance of fee interest

b. __ Acquisition of a controlling interest (state percentage acquired _____ %)

c. __ Transfer of a controlling interest (state percentage transferred _____ %)

d. __ Conveyance to cooperative housing corporation

e. __ Conveyance pursuant to or in lieu of foreclosure or enforcement of security interest *(attach Form TP-584.1, Schedule E)*

f. __ Conveyance which consists of a mere change of identity or form of ownership or organization *(attach Form TP-584.1, Schedule F)*

g. __ Conveyance for which credit for tax previously paid will be claimed *(attach Form TP-584.1, Schedule G)*

h. __ Conveyance of cooperative apartment(s)

i. __ Syndication

j. __ Conveyance of air rights or development rights

k. __ Contract assignment

l. __ Option assignment or surrender

m. __ Leasehold assignment or surrender

n. __ Leasehold grant

o. __ Conveyance of an easement

p. __ Conveyance for which exemption from transfer tax is claimed (complete Schedule C, Part III)

q. __ Conveyance of property partly within and partly without the state

r. __ Other *(describe)* _____

Schedule B - Real Property Transfer Gains Tax Affidavit (Article 31-B of the Tax Law)

☐ Check this box if a *Tentative Assessment and Return* is being filed with respect to your current transfer, and proceed to Schedule C without completing the following affidavit. Also, enter the assessment number shown on the *Tentative Assessment:* _____.

I (we) certify that: *(check appropriate box)*

1 ☐ The transfer of real property consists of the execution of a contract to sell real property without the use or occupancy of such property or the granting of an option to purchase real property without the use or occupancy of such property.

2 ☐ The transfer is a transfer of real property where the consideration is less than $500,000, and the transfer is neither (A) pursuant to a cooperative or condominium plan, nor (B) a partial or successive transfer (i.e., a transfer that is one of a series of transfers of contiguous or adjacent interests in real property e.g., subdivided parcels).

3 ☐ The transfer is a transfer of real property by tenants in common, joint tenants or tenants by the entirety where the aggregate consideration is less than $500,000. (All such transferors must sign this form.)

4 ☐ The conveyance is not a transfer of real property within the meaning of section 1440.7 of Article 31-B of the Tax Law. (Attach documents supporting such claim, and sign on back as required.)

5 ☐ The transfer of real property consists of premises wholly occupied and used by the transferor **exclusively** as his residence, including a cooperative apartment or condominium occupied by the transferor exclusively as a residence. **(This exemption may only be claimed and attested to by a transferor that is an individual, estate or trust.)**

6 ☐ Transferor is the state of New York, or any of its agencies, instrumentalities, political subdivisions, or public corporations, including a public corporation created pursuant to an agreement or compact with another state or Canada.

7 ☐ Transferor is the United Nations or any other international organization of which the United States is a member, the United States of America or any of its agencies or instrumentalities.

Schedule C - Real Estate Transfer Tax Return (Article 31 of the Tax Law)

Part I - Computation of Tax Due

1	Enter amount of consideration for conveyance *(if you are claiming a total exemption from tax, enter consideration and proceed to Part III)*	1	
2	Continuing lien deduction *(see instructions if property is taken subject to mortgage or lien)*	2	( )
3	Taxable consideration *(subtract line 2 from line 1)*	3	
4	Tax due: $2 for each $500, or fractional part thereof, of consideration on line 3	4	
5	Amount of credit claimed *(see instructions and attach Form TP-584.1, Schedule G)*	5	( )
6	Total tax due* *(subtract line 5 from line 4)*	6	

Part II - Computation of Additional Tax Due on the Conveyance of Residential Real Property for $1 Million or More

1	Enter amount of consideration for conveyance (from Part I, line 1)	1	
2	Taxable consideration *(multiply line 1 by the percentage of the premises which is residential real property; see instructions)*	2	
3	Total additional transfer tax due* *(1% of line 2)*	3	

*Please make check(s) payable to the county clerk where the recording is to take place or if the recording is to take place in New York City, make check(s) payable to the **NYC Department of Finance.** If no recording is required, send your check(s) made payable to the **Department of Taxation and Finance,** directly to the NYS Tax Department, TTTB-Transfer Tax, P O Box 5045, Albany NY 12205-5045.

For recording officer's use	Amount received ▶	Part I $	Date received	Transaction number
		Part II $		

Schedule C - (continued)

Part III - Explanation of Exemption Claimed in Part I, line 1 *(check any boxes that apply)*

The conveyance of real property is exempt from the real estate transfer tax for the following reason:

a. Conveyance is to the United Nations, the United States of America, the state of New York or any of their instrumentalities, agencies or political subdivisions (or any public corporation, including a public corporation created pursuant to agreement or compact with another state or Canada)..a ☐

b. Conveyance is to secure a debt or other obligation...b ☐

c. Conveyance is without additional consideration to confirm, correct, modify or supplement a prior conveyance............c ☐

d. Conveyance of real property is without consideration and not in connection with a sale, including conveyances conveying realty as bona fide gifts..d ☐

e. Conveyance is given in connection with a tax sale..e ☐

f. Conveyance is a mere change of identity or form of ownership or organization where there is no change in beneficial ownership. (This exemption cannot be claimed for a conveyance to a cooperative housing corporation of real property comprising the cooperative dwelling or dwellings.)..f ☐

g. Conveyance consists of deed of partition...g ☐

h. Conveyance is given pursuant to the federal bankruptcy act..h ☐

i. Conveyance consists of the execution of a contract to sell real property without the use or occupancy of such property or the granting of an option to purchase real property without the use or occupancy of such property...........................i ☐

j. Conveyance of an option or contract to purchase real property with the use or occupancy of such property where the consideration is less than $200,000 and such property was used solely by the grantor as his personal residence and consists of a 1-, 2-, or 3-family house, a residential individual condominium unit, or the sale of stock in a cooperative housing corporation in connection with the grant or transfer of a proprietary leasehold covering an individual residential cooperative unit...j ☐

k. Conveyance is not a conveyance within the meaning of section 1401(e) of Article 31 of the Tax Law *(attach documents supporting such claim)*..k ☐

l. Other *(attach explanation)*...l ☐

Schedule D - Credit Line Mortgage Certificate (Article 11 of the Tax Law)

Complete the following only if the interest being transferred is a fee simple interest.

I (we) certify that: *(check appropriate box)*

1 ☐ The real property being sold or transferred is not principally improved nor will it be improved by a one- to six-family owner-occupied residence or dwelling.

2 ☐ The real property being sold or transferred is not subject to an outstanding credit line mortgage.

3 ☐ The real property being sold or transferred is subject to an outstanding credit line mortgage. However, an exemption from the tax is claimed for the following reason.

    ☐ The transfer of real property is a transfer of a fee simple interest to a person or persons who held a fee simple interest in the real property (whether as a joint tenant, a tenant in common or otherwise) immediately prior to the transfer.

    ☐ The transfer of real property is (A) to a person or persons related by blood, marriage or adoption to the original obligor or to one or more of the original obligors or (B) to a person or entity where a majority of the beneficial interest in such real property after the transfer is held by the transferor or such related person or persons.

    ☐ The transfer of real property is a transfer to a trustee in bankruptcy, a receiver, assignee or other officer of a court.

    ☐ Other (attach detailed explanation).

4 ☐ The real property being transferred is presently subject to an outstanding credit line mortgage. However, no tax is due for the following reason:

    ☐ A certificate of discharge of the credit line mortgage is being offered at the time of recording the deed.

    ☐ A check has been drawn payable for transmission to the credit line mortgagee or his agent for the balance due, and a satisfaction of such mortgage will be recorded as soon as it is available.

5 ☐ The real property being transferred is subject to an outstanding credit line mortgage on record at _____ (insert liber and page or reel or other identification of the mortgage). The maximum principal amount expressed in the mortgage is _____ . No exemption from tax is claimed and the tax of _____ is being paid herewith. *(Make check payable to county clerk where deed will be recorded or, if the recording is to take place in New York City, make check payable to the NYC Department of Finance.)*

Signature and Affirmation (both the transferor(s)/grantor(s) and transferee(s)/grantee(s) must sign).

The undersigned, being duly sworn, depose and say under penalty of perjury that the above return, including any affidavit, certification, schedule or attachment, has been examined by the undersigned, and is, to the best of his/her knowledge, true and complete and made in good faith pursuant to Articles 11, 31 and 31-B of the New York State Tax Law.

_____	_____	_____	_____
Transferor/grantor	Title	Transferee/grantee	Title

Subscribed to and sworn before me   Subscribed to and sworn before me

this _____ day of _____ , 19 _____.   this _____ day of _____ , 19 _____.

State of _____   State of _____

County of _____   County of _____

Reminder: Did you complete all of the required information in Schedules A and B? Were you required to complete Schedules C and D? If you checked e, f and g in Schedule A, did you complete TP-584.1? Have you attached your check(s) made payable to the county clerk or city register where recording will take place or, if the recording is in New York City, to the *NYC Department of Finance*? If no recording is required, send your check(s), made payable to the *Department of Taxation and Finance*, directly to the NYS Tax Department, TTTB-Transfer Tax, P O Box 5045, Albany NY 12205-0545.

679

C1. SWIS Code

C2. Date Deed Recorded |___/___/___|
Month   Day   Year

C3. Book |_____| **C4. Page** |_____|

REAL PROPERTY TRANSFER REPORT

STATE OF NEW YORK

STATE BOARD OF REAL PROPERTY SERVICES

RP - 5217

RP-5217 Rev 7/95

PROPERTY INFORMATION

1. Property Location
STREET NUMBER   STREET NAME

CITY OR TOWN   VILLAGE   ZIP CODE

2. Buyer Name
LAST NAME / COMPANY   FIRST NAME

LAST NAME / COMPANY   FIRST NAME

3. Tax Billing Address Indicate where future Tax Bills are to be sent if other than buyer address (at bottom of form)
LAST NAME / COMPANY   FIRST NAME

STREET NUMBER AND STREET NAME   CITY OR TOWN   STATE   ZIP CODE

4. Indicate the number of Assessment Roll parcels transferred on the deed |_____| # of Parcels **OR** |___| Part of a Parcel

(Only if Part of a Parcel) Check as they apply:

4A. Planning Board with Subdivision Authority Exists |___|

4B. Subdivision Approval was Required for Transfer |___|

4C. Parcel Approved for Subdivision with Map Provided |___|

5. Deed Property Size |_____| X |_____| **OR** |_____|
FRONT FEET   DEPTH   ACRES

6. Seller Name
LAST NAME / COMPANY   FIRST NAME

LAST NAME / COMPANY   FIRST NAME

7. Check the box below which most accurately describes the use of the property at the time of sale:

Check the boxes below as they apply:

8. Ownership Type is Condominium |___|

9. New Construction on Vacant Land |___|

10A. Property Located within an Agricultural District |___|

10B. Buyer received a disclosure notice indicating that the property is in an Agricultural District |___|

A	___	One Family Residential	E	___	Agricultural	I	___	Community Service
B	___	2 or 3 Family Residential	F	___	Commercial	J	___	Industrial
C	___	Residential Vacant Land	G	___	Apartment	K	___	Public Service
D	___	Non-Residential Vacant Land	H	___	Entertainment / Amusement	L	___	Forest

---

SALE INFORMATION

11. Sale Contract Date |___/___/___|
Month   Day   Year

12. Date of Sale / Transfer |___/___/___|
Month   Day   Year

13. Full Sale Price |_____, ___, ___ 0, 0|

(Full Sale Price is the total amount paid for the property including personal property. This payment may be in the form of cash, other property or goods, or the assumption of mortgages or other obligations.) *Please round to the nearest whole dollar amount.*

14. Indicate the value of personal property included in the sale |_____, ___, ___ 0, 0|

15. Check one or more of these conditions as applicable to transfer:

A	___	Sale Between Relatives or Former Relatives
B	___	Sale Between Related Companies or Partners in Business
C	___	One of the Buyers is also a Seller
D	___	Buyer or Seller is Government Agency or Lending Institution
E	___	Deed Type not Warranty or Bargain and Sale (Specify Below)
F	___	Sale of Fractional or Less than Fee Interest (Specify Below)
G	___	Significant Change in Property Between Taxable Status and Sale Dates
H	___	Sale of Business is Included in Sale Price
I	___	Other Unusual Factors Affecting Sale Price (Specify Below)
J	___	None

ASSESSMENT INFORMATION - Data should reflect the latest Final Assessment Roll and Tax Bill

16. Year of Assessment Roll from which information taken |____|

17. Total Assessed Value (of all parcels in transfer) |_____|

18. Property Class |____|-|___| **19. School District Name** |_____|

20. Tax Map Identifier(s) / Roll Identifier(s) (If more than four, attach sheet with additional identifier(s))

CERTIFICATION

I certify that all of the items of information entered on this form are true and correct (to the best of my knowledge and belief) and I understand that the making of any willful false statement of material fact herein will subject me to the provisions of the penal law relative to the making and filing of false instruments.

BUYER

BUYER SIGNATURE   DATE

STREET NUMBER   STREET NAME (AFTER SALE)

CITY OR TOWN   STATE   ZIP CODE

SELLER

SELLER SIGNATURE   DATE

BUYER'S ATTORNEY

LAST NAME   FIRST NAME

AREA CODE   TELEPHONE NUMBER

NEW YORK STATE COPY

Index and Glossary

Estate at will: a leasehold estate that can be terminated by a lessor or lessee at any time 109, 233

Estate for years: any lease with a specific starting time and a specific ending time 108, 233

Estate in severalty: owned by one person, sole ownership 119

Estate tax value 500

Estoppel certificate: a document in which a borrower verifies the amount still owed and the interest rate 315

Eviction 242, 250

Exchanging real estate 207; delayed exchange 209; *illustrated* 209

Exclusive agency listing: a listing wherein the owner reserves the right to sell the property himself, but agrees to list with no other broker during the listing period 49

Exclusive authority to purchase 52

Exclusive authority to sell (same as exclusive right to sell) 49

Exclusive right to sell: a listing that gives the broker the right to collect a commission no matter who sells the property during the listing period 45, 49

Execute: the process of completing, performing, or carrying out something 175

Executed: means that performance has taken place 175

Executor: a person named in a will to carry out its instructions (masculine) 153; executrix (feminine) 154

Executor's deed: a deed used to convey the real property of a deceased person 154

Executory: in the process of being completed 175

Expressed contract: a contract made orally or in writing 165

F

Face amount: the dollar amount of insurance coverage 392

Fair Credit Reporting Act 394

Fair housing laws 448; block busting 451; Civil Rights Act 448; discrimination complaints 451; discrimination penalties 450; enforcement 453; exemptions 450; familial status and 450; handi-capped and 446; leases 247; steering 451; Supreme Court 446

Fair market value. *See* Market value

Faithful performance: a requirement that an agent obey all legal instructions given to him by his principal 216

Familial status: one or more individuals (who have not obtained the age of 18 years) being domiciled with a parent or another person having legal custody of such individual or individuals or the designee of such parent or other person having such custody, with the written permission of such parent or other person 450

Fannie Mae: a real estate industry nickname for the Federal National Mortgage Association 410

Farm brokerage 7

Farm Credit System 414

Farmer Mac: a real estate industry nickname for Federal Agricultural Mortgage Corporation 414

Farmer's Home Administration (FmHA) 377

Farming leases 440

Federal Agricultural Mortgage Corporation (Farmer Mac) 414

Federal clauses: refers to government-required clauses in real estate contracts 196

Federal Consumer Credit Protection Act (Truth-in-Lending Act) 381

Federal Home Loan Mortgage Corporation (FHLMC): provides a secondary mortgage market facility for savings and loan associations 413

Federal Housing Administration 365; insurance limits 366; programs 369, 370

Federal National Mortgage Association (FNMA): provides a secondary market for real estate loans 409; pooling by 411

Federal Reserve Board: governing board of the nation's central bank 589, 595

Federal Savings and Loan Insurance Corporation (FSLIC) 400

Fee simple: the largest, most complete bundle of rights one can hold in land, land ownership 95, 274; fee simple timesharing 274

Fee simple determinable estate: a fee estate limited by the happening of a certain event 104

Fee simple subject to condition subsequent: the grantor has the right to terminate the fee estate 104

Fee simple upon condition precedent: title does not take effect until a condition is performed 104

Feudal system: all land ownership rests in the name of the king 91

Fiat money: money created by the government, printing press money 416

Fictional depreciation: depreciation deductions as allowed by tax law 489

Fictitious business name: a name other than the owner's that is used to operate a business 22

Fiduciary: a person in a position of trust, responsibility, and confidence for another such as a broker for his client 215

Fiduciary relationship 215

Finance charge 383

Finance companies as lenders 406

Financial Institutions Reform, Recovery, and Enforcement Act of 1989 (FIRREA) 400

Financial liability: the amount of money one can lose, one's risk exposure; investing 129; VA 373

Financing: lending practices 353, 379; mortgage and note 305; sources 396; types 421

Financing alternatives: carryback 435; contract for deed 437; creative 432; lease-option 204; rentals and leases 440; subordination 437; wraparound mortgage 436

Financing statement: a recorded document designed to protect the rights of a chattel lienholder 317

Finding a broker to work for 28

FIRREA 400

First mortgage: the mortgage loan with highest priority for repayment in event of foreclosure 316

First refusal. *See* Right of first refusal

First substantive contact 221

Fiscal policy: government policy to balance or not balance budgets 588